STUDENT SERVICES

A Handbook
for the Profession

Ursula Delworth
Gary R. Hanson
and Associates

STUDENT SERVICES

A Handbook
for the Profession

 Jossey-Bass Publishers
San Francisco • Washington • London • 1980

STUDENT SERVICES
A Handbook for the Profession
by Ursula Delworth, Gary R. Hanson, and Associates

Copyright © 1980 by: Jossey-Bass Inc., Publishers
433 California Street
San Francisco, California 94104
&
Jossey-Bass Limited
28 Banner Street
London EC1Y 8QE

Library of Congress Cataloging in Publication Data

Main entry under title:
Student services.

   Includes bibliographic references and indexes.
   1. Personnel service in education—Handbooks,
manuals, etc. I. Delworth, Ursula. II. Hanson,
Gary R.
LB1027.5.S852   371.4   80-8008
ISBN 0-87589-476-3

Manufactured in the United States of America

JACKET DESIGN BY WILLI BAUM

FIRST EDITION

Code 8035

The Jossey-Bass
Series in Higher Education

Preface

This book is for people who help students enter, enjoy, endure, and exit from college. In the time between entrance and exit, those of us who work with students hope the services we provide will help students to grow and to develop their potential. The ends are clear but the means of achieving them are not.

For too long, our helping profession has struggled to survive with a shaky philosophical foundation, insufficient conceptual models, and little supporting research to evaluate the impact our services have on students. We have not always understood the forces that shape higher education and our roles in it. All too often we have tried to use theories to guide our actions only to be disappointed when they did not work. To complicate matters, we have tried to train others without being able to identify the specific skills that produce effective results or the strategies and techniques that really work time and again. And we have been surprised when our funds and resources have been severely restricted or even eliminated because we lacked the fundamental management skills to establish our accountability within the college and university system. Clearly, we need to unite theory and practice to understand what we do, why we do it, and the most effective way to proceed.

For these reasons, we have commissioned the chapters in this book in an attempt to draw together much of the best thinking in our profession on these critical issues. Other books have described the functions and purposes of student services and still others have reviewed theoretical approaches and conceptual models. Books in other fields have outlined effective management techniques that have been adopted for use in the area of student services. But few, if any, books have focused on identifying, assessing, and evaluating the ideas and competencies that can influence students. We think there is great value in integrating these diverse concerns into a comprehensive handbook, one to be used by the experienced professional or by the beginning graduate student. Chief student services officers, middle managers, staff members, and students in college student personnel and development, as well as those in related graduate programs, will find this integrative perspective helpful. Specific chapters address interests of each of these groups.

In emphasizing both theory and practice, we have organized this book into five major parts, which can be read in any order. The last chapter synthesizes what we have learned about the history, theories, models, and practice of our profession and looks toward a bold, exciting future. The part introductions describe the chapter-by-chapter coverage; the following paragraphs give a general overview of the book's contents.

In Part One, we identify the context of current student services by searching historical roots for the ideas and actions that influenced today's service delivery. We examine present trends in higher education, which will influence how we work with students in the next year, the next decade, and far into the future. The values that guide our current thinking and practice and our attitudes about students have changed over the years. An understanding of this evolution will lead to a better definition of our role, purpose, and function. The chapters in Part One proclaim an appreciation for the efforts of our early professional pioneers, a sense of reality about the issues we face today, and a willingness to plan for the future.

As we thought about the importance of theory to the student services profession, we realized that there is really little theory that we can call our own. Instead, we have bought, borrowed, and stolen our theories from such disciplines as psychology, sociology, and business. Nevertheless, these theories help student services professionals to organize data about our profession, help us explain what we do for others, guide our day-to-day decisions and perhaps, most importantly, help us dream about the future. Rather than present a wide array of possible theories—each with *some* relevance for the student services professional—we have selected a few theoretical ideas to pursue in depth. In Part Two, these theories stimulate questions of how students grow and develop and how they interact with their college environment in ways that either hinder or facilitate their growth.

Practice in student services is based on models or conceptualizations of the appropriate roles for professionals. Such models are general orientations toward what we should be doing in higher education. Unfortunately, the models are often too general. Part Three explicitly delineates several models to facilitate intentional and knowledgeable choices and commitments. Although few student services divisions or agencies utilize only one model, most operate with one of these models as a predominant orientation for practice. By presenting several different models, we hope to encourage innovation and the development of new approaches to the delivery of student services.

Part Four deals with the major skills and competencies required of student services professionals. To work effectively, we must be well trained in an increasing number of sophisticated competency areas. Each individual cannot be trained in all skill areas, but all these competencies should be represented within a division of student services. A review of the needed competencies for effective delivery of services will encourage new goals for personal and professional development.

All managers—from the chief student services officer to the staff member responsible for a specific program—are interested in effective coordination. Part Five offers some new ways to organize and manage programs and services. There is no single "correct" way to manage effectively. Each institution is faced with different challenges and varying resources to meet them. While one institution may need to focus on developing new staff competencies, another may be able to use bright undergraduates in paraprofessional positions. These chapters will help administrators bring about change—effectively and efficiently—through an understanding of sound management and organization.

In shaping the content of this book, we have intentionally avoided discussion of such specific areas or functions as student financial aid, housing, and student activities. The broader scope of the history, theory, models of practice, competencies, and administrative techniques and strategies discussed here will provide student services professionals with the knowledge, attitudes, and skills to work in many areas. To develop student services professionals, we must be prepared to teach and train others. In the final chapter, we outline a curriculum for student services professionals. The curriculum can be used in preparing programs and in staff development and inservice programs. We make some strong statements concerning the student services profession and education for this profession. We hope that our words will facilitate an open dialogue within our field from which a more integrated and effective profession can emerge.

The chapters in this book represent the efforts of many people. We are indebted first and foremost to our contributing authors for the long hours they spent in thinking and writing to bring their ideas to us. Of course, their chapters, prepared for this book by invitation, do not necessarily represent a consensus of opinion. We are also deeply indebted to the individuals who worked with us to not only type and retype manuscripts but to coordinate and manage our professional lives over the long gestation period of this book. To Pauline Harrison, who worked with us for the duration of the project, we offer our gratitude for her excellent typing skills and her helpful editorial comments. At the University of Texas, special tribute goes to Janet Collins, who inherited a great many of the labor pains of producing a manuscript, and to Zora Cary for helping hold everything together during the final stages of finishing the book. To these individuals we owe a great many thanks. Gary Hanson expresses deep appreciation to a most understanding family, who sacrificed many long evening hours and even more Sunday mornings to his absence while he worked on "the book." Finally, we dedicate this book to Philip Tripp, a major influence in the professional and personal lives of both editors. Had it not been for his untimely death, we would have included a substantial contribution from him. For his wisdom, his philosophy, and his humor we are most thankful of all.

August 1980   URSULA DELWORTH
                                                           Iowa City, Iowa

                                                           GARY R. HANSON
                                                           Austin, Texas

Contents

The Authors

URSULA DELWORTH is director of the University Counseling Service and professor of counselor education (counseling psychology and student development programs) at the University of Iowa. She has previously been affiliated with the Western Interstate Commission for Higher Education and Colorado State University.

Delworth received her B.A. degree in political science and education from California State University at Long Beach in 1956 and her M.A. degree in counseling from California State University at Los Angeles in 1962. She worked as an elementary and secondary school teacher and counselor, school psychologist, social group worker, summer camp director, and education director for Anytown, USA. In 1969, she completed her Ph.D. degree in counseling psychology at the University of Oregon.

Active in a number of professional organizations, Delworth is past chair of Commission VII (counseling) of the American College Personnel Association and is a Fellow of the American Psychological Association.

Delworth is the author of more than thirty publications, including *Crisis Center/Hot Line: A Guidebook to Beginning and Operating* (1972), *Student Paraprofessionals: A Working Model for Higher Education* (1974), *Training Manual for Student Service Program Development* (1976), and *Training Manual for an Ecosystem Model* (1976). With Gary Hanson, she serves as editor-in-chief of the quarterly sourcebook, *New Directions for Student Services.*

GARY R. HANSON is assistant dean of students at the University of Texas at Austin, where he is studying the impact of college environments on student behavior. He received his B.A. degree in psychology (1965) and his M.A. (1968) and Ph.D. degrees (1970) in counseling psychology from the University of Minnesota.

Between 1969 and 1977, Hanson worked for the American College Testing Program (ACT). Reflecting his work at ACT, his research publications include an examination of the vocational interests of students in career-oriented educational programs and a longitudinal study of adult students at two-year colleges. Hanson is the coauthor of *Assessing Students on the Way to College: Technical Report for the ACT Assessment* (with N. Cole, 1975). He is a member of the American Personnel and Guidance Association, the American College Personnel Association (ACPA), and the American Psychological Association (APA). Hanson has been chairman of the ACPA Commission IX: Assessment of Student Development, a member of the ACPA Phase III Tomorrow's Higher Education planning task force, and an editorial board review member of the association's *Journal of College Student Personnel.* From 1973 to 1975, Hanson was a member of the APA's Division 17 membership committee, which he chaired during 1975 to 1977. Currently, he serves as secretary for the counseling psychology division.

DAVID A. AMBLER is vice-chancellor for student affairs and associate professor of administration, foundations, and higher education at the University of Kansas, a position he has held since 1977. He was formerly a member of the dean of student's staff at Indiana University and vice-president for student affairs at Kent State University.

JAMES H. BANNING is vice-president for student affairs, associate professor of psychology and of education at Colorado State University. He has served as vice-chancellor for student affairs at the University of Missouri and as program director at the Western Interstate Commission for Higher Education.

ELLEN BETZ is associate professor of psychology and counseling psychologist with the Student Counseling Bureau at the University of Minnesota.

ROBERT D. BROWN is professor of educational psychology and measurements at the University of Nebraska, Lincoln. A prolific writer, he received a special award from the American College Personnel Association for his contribution to literature in student services.

HARRY J. CANON is a counseling psychologist who currently serves as vice-president for student affairs at Northern Illinois University. He has written a number of articles, primarily on staff development, and he serves on the executive committee of the American College Personnel Association.

VAL R. CHRISTENSEN is assistant dean of students at Utah State University, where he serves as director of the student center and student activities.

JOHN G. CORAZZINI directs the Student Development Counseling Center and teaches in the Department of Psychology at Virginia Commonwealth University.

THOMAS B. DUTTON is vice-chancellor for student affairs at the University of California, Davis. He has served as dean of students and vice-chancellor for student affairs at Oakland University and director of research and program development for the National Association of Student Personnel Administrators.

ROBERT H. FENSKE is professor of higher education in the Department of Higher and Adult Education at Arizona State University. He has served as senior research psychologist and director of the Research Institute at the American College Testing Program, as director of research for the Illinois Board of Higher Education, and as faculty member and institutional researcher at the University of Minnesota and the University of Wisconsin.

CECELIA H. FOXLEY is associate professor in the Division of Counselor Education (student development program) at the University of Iowa. Her administrative positions have included acting assistant dean of the College of Education and director of affirmative action at the University of Iowa and coordinator of staff education programs and associate director of student activities at the University of Minnesota.

JUNE GALLESSICH is professor of educational psychology at the University of Texas, Austin. She also teaches in the counseling and school psychology training programs.

SUSAN K. GILMORE is employed in private practice and conducts numerous workshops and seminars on women's issues, career planning, and marital therapy; she also chairs the Oregon board of psychological examiners. For fourteen years she served the University of Oregon as a faculty member, director of doctoral training in counseling psychology, and a staff member with the university Counseling Center.

LOIS A. HUEBNER is currently assistant professor of psychology at Virginia Commonwealth University.

CYNTHIA S. JOHNSON is director of career planning and placement at the University of California, Irvine. She is currently president of the American College Personnel Association.

ROBERT A. KERR is coordinator of memorial union programs and recreation, University of California, Davis.

LEE KNEFELKAMP is associate professor in the Department of Counseling and Personnel Services and faculty associate for research and student development, Division of Student Affairs, at the University of Maryland.

OSCAR T. LENNING is senior associate at the National Center for Higher Education Management Systems. He previously worked for the research services staff of the American College Testing Program.

WESTON H. MORRILL is director of the counseling center at the University of Utah, where he is also professor in the counseling psychology graduate program in the Department of Educational Psychology and clinical associate professor of psychiatry in the School of Medicine. Formerly, he directed the counseling center at Colorado State University.

CLYDE A. PARKER is chairman of the Department of Social, Psychological, and Philosophical Foundations in the College of Education at the University of Minnesota. In the past he has served as the director of a college counseling center and as an assistant dean of students.

SCOTT T. RICKARD is assistant vice-chancellor for student affairs at the University of California, Davis, and lecturer in the Department of Applied Behavioral Sciences. Previously, he was vice-president for Student Affairs at the State University of New York, Stony Brook, and dean of men and assistant professor of education at Willamette University.

GERALD L. SADDLEMIRE has been chairman of the College Student Personnel Department at Bowling Green State University since 1969.

GRANT P. SHERWOOD is director of the Office of Housing and Residence Education and assistant professor of college student personnel administration in the Department of Education at Colorado State University.

CAROLE WIDICK is assistant professor of psychology at St. John's University. She has served as assistant professor on the faculty of special services at Ohio State University.

PART I

*Growth and Status
of Student Services*

A major purpose of this book is to examine the student services profession in terms of who we are, what we do, how we provide our services, and for what purposes. This self-examination should consider our roots—not only in terms of the actual historical evolution of services but also in terms of the ideas that have shaped our thinking. As we look at ourselves, we must likewise consider those many forces that affect higher education, because, if we can identify recurring themes, patterns, and trends that mold our working context, we will use our past to improve our future.

Helping students has not always been the sole responsibility of student services professionals. Long ago, college presidents and faculty members were directly involved in the daily lives of students. As pointed out in Chapter One, we have inherited that responsibility quite by default. How we came to occupy a central role in helping young adults during their college years is a fascinating history. Understanding it provides a perspective for evaluating what we now do. By knowing our past, we may keep and improve what we did well and discard our mistakes. The first chapter in this book provides just such a historical perspective.

Each and every day we work, we make value judgments. We hire and fire staff, spend money, make policy, and make mistakes. The decisions we make are influenced by the philosophy we adopt, and when our philosophy differs from others in our academic community we must defend what we believe. That is much easier when we have explicitly stated it. Although not everyone in our profession subscribes to the same beliefs, we believe our profession shares a common core of ideas. By using these ideas, we should be able to provide a more convincing statement regarding the importance of our existence. The second chapter in this book attempts to identify the key philosophical ideas that have guided and continue to guide our thinking about the delivery of student services.

In the third chapter in Part One, we examine those patterns and trends in higher education that influence the student services profession. Because we never work in a vacuum in the academic community, we need to identify those factors that influence the content and the quality of what we do, particularly those that systematically recur. Such forces may range from changes in the institution's governance structure to national policy regarding student financial aid to changes in budgeting procedures. We must identify these trends not only so we can monitor them for possible changes in direction but also in order to actively change and influence their direction. Our third chapter in Part One begins that identification process.

Robert H. Fenske   1

Historical Foundations

Student services emerged and evolved by default, by taking over necessary and sometimes unpopular tasks abandoned by trustees, administrators, and faculty. It has grown into a ubiquitous but somewhat invisible
empire in virtually every institution of higher education. During one
rather brief period early in this century, it came fairly close to entering
the mainstream of the academic program. In general, however, student
services as a distinct professional role had never become thoroughly
integrated into any of higher education's three principal functions of
teaching, research, and service. By assuming, over the years, a multitude
of student-related roles and activities yet by remaining estranged from
the vital functions of the academic enterprise, student services finds itself
in the peculiar situation of being indispensable but peripheral.

This chapter reviews a number of the historical developments in
higher education that have shaped the present role of student services.
Chapter Two describes the philosophical foundations of current student

Note: The author wishes to thank Louis Attinasi, Katherine Davis, Elizabeth Fisk, and Paul Zuzich for their helpful suggestions. All are doctoral students in the Department of Higher and Adult Education, Arizona State
University.

services practice, and Chapter Three describes and evaluates several contemporary trends and issues regarding the current status and future prospects of student services.

Three developmental themes in the history of American higher education seem particularly relevant for understanding the evolution of the profession. These are (1) the shift in emphasis from religious to secular concerns, (2) the expansion in size and complexity of institutions, and (3) the shift in faculty focus from student development to academic interests. The chapter concludes with a brief chronicle of the development of student services as a recognized profession.

In the early colonial period, several basic aspects of colleges were established that persist to this day. These include the system of governance vested in citizens (first clergy, later laymen) rather than in college faculty, administrators, government officials; the view of students as immature and in need of guidance and supervision (preferably in college residences); and the assumption that college not only prepared students for civic, professional, and business careers but also somehow made them "better," more moral, more humane people.

The Shift from Religious to Secular Concerns

Many historians, drawing on original documents and testimonials, have developed vignettes of the early colleges. These colleges were established in theocratic colonies that felt the need to preserve their own sectarian Protestantism, "dreading to leave an illiterate Ministry to our Churches, when our present Ministers shall lie in the dust" (Morison, 1935, pp. 423–433). Each of the early colonies consisted primarily of one denomination, so the clergy who founded and controlled the colleges on behalf of the colony's congregations staffed both the administration and faculty from within their own denomination. With few exceptions, only the sons of well-to-do colonists were enrolled, in keeping with the rigid class distinctions that were largely preserved before, during, and after immigration (Schlesinger, 1962; Hofstadter, 1973). Because few were allowed to dissent from the predominant sect in each of the colonies (Miller, 1972), there was general support for permeating the students' social and academic life with piety. This process was facilitated by having the students live under the same roof day and night with the president and tutors—all ministers (Brubacher and Rudy, 1976).

It is pointless to argue whether the colonists' colleges were "intended to be theological seminaries or schools of higher culture for laymen" (Brubacher and Rudy, 1976, p. 6). The charters of the only three colleges founded up to 1745 (Harvard, 1636; William and Mary, 1693; and Yale, 1701) made it abundantly clear that they were to be both

(Hofstadter, 1955, pp. 88–89). However, there was no doubt in the minds of the ministers who comprised the trustees, administration, and faculty where the primary emphasis was to be placed: "They maintained that college was a religious society whose basic and chief duty was to train its students to be religious and moral men. The study of nature was to be subservient to the inculcation of religion: The one was only a threshold to the other, and religious instruction therefore was to be emphasized" (McAnear, 1972, p. 464). This pattern of organization, control, curriculum, and staffing continued well into the 1800s. Brubacher and Rudy (1976, p. 27) point out that until "the end of the Revolutionary War, college presidents were almost without exception gentlemen of the cloth. Governing boards, too, abounded with clerics, exclusively at Yale and generally in a majority elsewhere."

Under the pervasive impact of Christian piety as the unifying aim of college education, all functions that might now be called *student services* were carried out by trustees, administrators, and faculty in the name of the colony that nourished the college. Each of the earliest colleges were cloistered microcosms of their respective sectarian communities. Rudolph (1962) describes the essence of the institutional model early colonists borrowed from their English roots: "The collegiate way is the notion that a curriculum, a library, a faculty, and students are not enough to make a college. It is an adherence to the residential scheme of things. It is respectful of quiet rural settings, dependent on dormitories, committed to dining halls, permeated by paternalism" (p. 87). Brubacher and Rudy (1976, p. 39) indicate that this period of collegiality included a heavily moralistic discipline based on orthodox religion. They describe the regime of an apparently typical college of the early nineteenth century: "Everybody had to be in chapel for morning prayers at 6:30 A.M. and 5 P.M. When classes were finished, all students returned to the chapel to hear one of the professors pray for forgiveness for the sins committed since sunrise. All lesson assignments over the weekend were made from the Bible or some theological work, so that the students attended two religious services—a long one in the morning, and a shorter one at 5 P.M." (p. 45).

Surely the religiously oriented college that predominated the American higher education scene for two thirds of its history provided a setting in which student services, although not yet differentiated and professionalized, were at their apex, in the functional sense that they involved all participants and were inseparable from the academic program. Contemplation of these early models tempts one to speculate that, only in a setting in which an absolute unifying principle (such as a specific orthodox religion) permeates all of the life and aims of a college, can student services with its concern for the whole person become a full partner in the academic enterprise. But that source of unity is gone from all but a small minority of present-day colleges, which constitute only a tiny fraction of total U.S. enrollment. "Moral purposes, values, the reality of heaven—these were the focus of the early American college, and there can be no denying that they no longer are central to the academic enterprise" (Rudolph, 1976, pp. 32–33).

Given the almost total immersion in religiosity of the earliest colleges, the direction of change could only be that of decreasing emphasis on religion and piety. The purely sectarian aspect was the first of many strains of religious emphasis to diminish, especially because colonial and post-Revolutionary society rapidly became more pluralistic in every respect.

Consistent with decreased societal concern with religion, many facets of higher education related to religion also changed by the time of the Civil War. For example, the composition of boards of trustees changed from predominantly clergy to laymen; administrators ceased to be drawn primarily from among the clergy; and students became more concerned with higher education as a means to worldly advancement than as a means to spiritual salvation. (The faculty, too, developed other interests in the course of the nineteenth century, as discussed later.)

Expansion in Size and Complexity

In the mid nineteenth century, higher education began to respond to the increasingly pluralistic, secular, and technological societal trends. Widespread death and destruction in the Civil War eroded the concept of an omnipotent God especially benevolent toward Americans. Publication of Darwin's *Origin of the Species* in 1859 and the controversy surrounding it after the Civil War (it was banned on many church-related college campuses) undermined the biblical story of creation and the fundamental authority of revealed scripture that had supported the view of collegiate education as the transmission of established knowledge to young Christian gentlemen.

Probably the most significant organizational development in changing the American college student from "theologian to technocrat in three hundred years" (Rudolph, 1976) was the growth of a public sector as an alternative (ultimately much larger) to the privately supported, church-related college. The public sector was established on a large scale only after the Civil War by the Morrill Land Grant Act of 1862. Although this landmark legislation only initiated the last one third of the history of American higher education, the growth in the public sector has been rapid in recent decades. The last year that enrollments in the private sector equaled those of publicly supported colleges and universities was 1950; the ratio is now nearly five students in public institutions for every private college student.

These developments have a clear genesis in the French Enlightenment, which fostered the ambivalence of Americans in the Revolutionary era toward the establishment of religion as a possibly pernicious influence on the new republican government.

Even though the constitution had clearly proscribed the use of public funds to support any church, the intensely religious society of the early Federalist period had some difficulty in fully accepting the idea. Thus, even though the Northwest Ordinance of 1787 provided land from the public domain "to be given perpetually for the purposes of an university," the same ordinance included the now familiar Third Article of Compact: "religion, morality, and knowledge, being necessary to good government and the happiness of mankind, schools and the means of education shall forever be encouraged" (Rainsford, 1972, pp. 35–46). Despite the precedence set by the Northwest Ordinance in making resources from the public domain available for establishing state universities, the various states in the young republic did not move forcefully to establish them. A number of states chartered universities in the late eighteenth and early nineteenth centuries, but they were generally of collegiate or subcollegiate level and were more private than public in their control (Brubacher and Rudy, 1976, p. 145).

Not until the Dartmouth College Case of 1819 was a publicly supported higher education sector legally prescribed. Essentially the U.S. Supreme Court ruled that an institution of higher education chartered by the state but not supported from public funds could not unwillingly be taken over or controlled by the state, because this would constitute unilateral violation of contract. Because "whoever pays the piper calls the tune," this signaled the end of the use of public funds for private colleges and universities. From that point on, it was inevitable that the states would develop and support colleges and universities controlled by and for public purposes.

Thomas Jefferson's view of the Dartmouth College case was that, when necessary, the state could and should gain control of an institution of higher education in terms of both finance and governance because it comprised a public trust whatever the terms of the charter. Jefferson had earlier been frustrated in attempting to gain control of the second-oldest college in the country (William and Mary) in his home state of Virginia. After failing in both Virginia and New Hampshire to engineer state takeovers of private colleges, he set himself to the task of establishing the first truly state-supported university in the United States—the University of Virginia, established in 1825. It was distinct from all earlier institutions in several important respects.

First, the University of Virginia was explicitly secular and nondenominational; second, it was completely a public enterprise in its finance and governing structure; and, third, it not only gave more advanced instruction than other existing colleges but also offered several curricular choices to its students—a revolutionary concept at that time. The last feature reflected the contemporary need for higher education that was more advanced, practical, and relevant to American society than the standard classical curriculum of the seven liberal arts offered in virtually all other colleges of the time. The year before the founding of the University of Virginia, Rensselaer Polytechnic Institute had been established. The founding of this institute "marked a turning point; it signaled the fact that American life was becoming increasingly complex" (Brubacher and Rudy, 1976).

The founding of these two seminal institutions, plus George Ticknor's abortive attempt to reform and liberalize the classical curriculum at Harvard in 1825, led to the immensely effective conservative counterattack in the Yale Report of 1828 ("Original Papers . . . ," 1829). This document, which was supported by nearly all of the influential church-related colleges of that era, was one of the principal factors in retarding the development of secular publicly supported institutions of higher education for nearly forty years.

The Yale Report effectively convinced the private, church-related colleges that dominated American higher education that they should maintain their narrow, prescribed curriculum and their focus on orthodox Christian piety. It ensured that these colleges would ultimately be superseded by institutions more responsive to the needs of a growing agrarian and industrializing society. Even though parallel and separate kinds of institutions, such as technical institutes of the Rensselaer type, normal schools, and women's colleges, were established during the middle part of the nineteenth century, the traditional church-related colleges continued steadfastly in their old ways.

The states that attempted to follow the lead of Virginia in establishing a state university encountered massive and effective opposition, supported by most of the college-educated leaders of society (virtually all of whom were graduates of private, church-related colleges), and found that their aims could be honored more in wishful ideals than in vigorous, growing institutions. States such as Wisconsin found little widespread support for using its general revenue funds to nurture its new state university founded in 1848. The struggling institution found that it had to accept poorly educated farm boys to fill out its enrollment and then had to place most of these in remedial courses to prepare them for collegiate-level instruction (Nevins, 1962, p. 42).

The persistent and insurmountable problem of the state universities founded after the University of Virginia in 1825 and up until the Civil War was active political opposition and lack of state-provided general revenue funds. Virtually all of the young state universities had to "cope with a suspicious public in the form of well-defined pressure groups. Prominent among these were the proponents of the various organized religions. . . . Religious leaders often resented the trend toward secularization augured by the university. They might even seek by legislative means to hamper a foundation which harbored alien styles of thought and which at the same time drained students from the local colleges operated by the denominations" (Veysey, 1965, p. 15). Several states came close to losing their state universities to these counterattacks. A regent of the University of Michigan warned against sectarianism in 1841: "The history of all collegiate institutions in this country dependent immediately on the State has shown that they have never prospered, as long as they have been subjected to the insolence of desultory legislation. . . . The establishment of a collegiate institution in a free state, and the conducting of its interests, should ever be upon liberal principles, and irrespective of all sectarian predilections and prejudices" (Hofstadter and Smith, 1961, p. 437).

The slow development of the public sector, the adherence of the private colleges to an extremely conservative curriculum, and the effective political resistance to public support for state universities within the state legislatures all built up considerable social and political pressure for the federal government to initiate some action for a more relevant and broadly accessible public sector. These pressures resulted in the Morrill Land Grant Act of 1862, landmark federal legislation that effectively created, for the first time, the basis for a large, significant public sector of higher education. Even though the states failed to fully capitalize immediately on the opportunity and resources provided, the act did establish the precedent of direct federal intervention in higher education in the United States. Veysey (1965, p. 15) claims that despite the Morrill Act "legislatures were always ready to interfere with or curtail the operations of state institutions (as, for example, at Michigan in 1877, when faculty salaries were reduced), and by 1900 only a handful of states had provided outstanding public universities, fit to be compared with the leading private establishments." Nonetheless, by 1900 it was clear that all the states would follow the leadership of California, Michigan, Wisconsin, and others in building their state universities into quality institutions of significant size. By this time, other types of higher education, such as normal colleges, professional schools, and technical institutes, had expanded to additional alternatives for the private college sector. Furthermore, in 1901 the first public junior college was established in Joliet, Illinois, heralding the beginning of a new sector of higher education that would ultimately enroll more first-time students than any other type of institution.

By the 1920s, the outlines of higher education as it exists today were already formed. Nearly every state had committed itself to significantly upgrading its state university or universities in size and quality. Most of these institutions included research and service as a part of their mission. Most states were also further expanding well-established systems of state teacher's colleges, many of which served as general-purpose regional colleges. Furthermore, most states were committed either to expanding local opportunities for higher education through branch campus systems of the state university or to building public junior colleges through an upward extension of high school districts. Private universities continued in their role as highly selective, prestigious institutions, and the private liberal arts colleges were still numerically the largest single segment of higher education, even though most of them no longer had direct church ties. As mentioned previously, the private sector continued to enroll the majority of students until the middle of the century.

The massive and rapid expansion of the public sector, especially after World War II, was due to several egalitarian trends. One was expressed by the President's Commission on Higher Education (the so-called Truman Commission), which published its report in 1947. This commission recommended that racial, ethnic, and financial barriers to opportunity for higher education be removed as soon as possible. It urged the provision of financial aid to students as one way of removing economic barriers. Another egalitarian strategy the commission urged was the proliferation of public junior colleges to provide a network of low-cost commuter institutions.

However, the most direct expression of widening opportunity for higher education was the post-World War II Serviceman's Readjustment Act (the so-called GI Bill). This legislation entitled all veterans to financial support for direct college costs and subsistence on enrollment in an accredited college or university. The majority of the veterans found places at the public, rather than private, institutions. These colleges and universities were more responsive to the urgent need to accommodate on short notice the many hundreds of thousands of young men who wanted higher education and who were reluctant to postpone their opportunity until a later semester or year. A generation later, the veterans turned largely to these public institutions to enroll their own children. Thus, while the private colleges and universities grew slowly and steadily for the most part, the number and size of public colleges and universities burgeoned, especially from 1950 to the present.

The impending tidal wave of students in the early 1960s caused Congress for the first time since the turn of the century to enact legislation of general assistance to institutions of higher education. There was considerable concern by the early 1960s that institutions in the private sector would soon be greatly overshadowed by the mushrooming public colleges and universities. The National Defense Education Act of 1958 provided for several targeted programs that would help build up the nation's mathematics and science education. Some of its titles provided for student loans and institutional assistance that benefited private as well as public colleges and universities. However, the Higher Education Facilities Act of 1963 explicitly helped both sectors for the purpose of accommodating the rapid enrollment increases. It provided loans as well as nonrepayable grants for construction of classrooms, laboratories, libraries, and dormitories.

The Higher Education Act of 1965 contained many titles that were aimed at expanding opportunities for higher education. One of the main emphases was on student financial aid, particularly in the form of loans. It also assisted in the rapid expansion of graduate education to help build up the faculties and other staff needs of colleges and universities.

The 1972 amendments to the 1965 Higher Education Act further expanded the role of federally based student financial aid in support of higher education. The amendments included the new concept of "entitlement," which is intended to meet the Truman Commission's goal of removing financial barriers to entering post-high school education. The principal instrument of entitlement is the Basic Educational Opportunity Grant available to every financially needy high school graduate who is accepted by any public or private postsecondary education institution.

Two overall effects of the 1972 amendments seem to have far-reaching influence on higher education as a whole. First, they carry out the "market model" approach to higher education as developed during the Republican administrations from 1968 to 1976. Essentially, this model provides for a discontinuance of financial support directly to institutions and for a shift to student financial aid. This shift was expected to impress accountability on the institutions, because the student financial aid is "transportable" by the student to any institution of his or her choice. Second, the provisions of the amendments explicitly assist private as well as public institutions through regulations of the student aid program that provide for accommodation of the higher costs at the private colleges and universities. Because the amount of each student grant is responsive not only to the financial need of the student and his or her family but also to the cost at private institutions (typically tuition is at least double that at public institutions), the program channels relatively large amounts of funds to private colleges and universities. Such public student financial aid programs subject private colleges and universities to federal regulations on the receipt of such public funds through students and make them much more sensitive and responsive to students as "consumers" in matters of selectivity for admissions and in tailoring curricula to attract and hold students.

Therefore, although the Higher Education Facilities Act of 1963 was helpful in expanding and renovating private college and university campuses, it unquestionably is the "transportability" feature of the later massive student financial aid programs that has largely maintained the private colleges and universities in the current decade.

The trends outlined in this section resulted in diverse types of institutions that were generally large and emphatically secular (except, of course, for those that are explicitly church related) and that drew students from a wide range of socioeconomic and scholastic backgrounds who were enrolled for decidedly utilitarian and vocational purposes. The latter changes are discussed further in the following section.

Changes in Faculty Involvement in Student Services

Historically, the participation of faculty in what are now called *student services* functions changed from total involvement to detachment. As mentioned earlier, in the early colonial period, when many of the precepts in higher education were established, there was considerable unanimity among the general society, trustees, administrators, and faculty regarding the equal importance of the moral, religious, and academic development of students. This section traces the events and periods related to the gradual disengagement of faculty concern for any mode of student development other than academic.

There are three main roles for academic faculty. First, the *teaching* function is straightforward in its interpretation and has remained the key descriptor and publicly most visible role for most members of college and university faculties. There are many modes of teaching; however, most deal primarily with the transmission of the existing body of knowledge that comprises our humanistic, literary, and scientific heritage. In the most widely accepted role of teacher vis-a-vis student, the college professor is expected to be a master of his specialized subject material and is expected to impart this knowledge effectively. There is implicit in this process an adversary relationship because the transmission of expert knowledge is in one direction, suggesting a major status distinction, and because the teacher is usually required by his or her institution to evaluate or judge the extent to which the student has learned what has been taught. Second, the *research* function is, in a historical sense, a relatively new role for academic faculty, having emerged during the last third of the history of higher education in this country. This function involves exploring and expanding the frontiers of knowledge. Included in this general definition are not only scientific, but also humanistic and literary investigation. Third, as indicated earlier, the development of character and values was originally a central part of the faculty member's role, and for the first two full centuries of higher education's history in this country this function had a thoroughly and explicitly religious tone in the vast majority of the colleges. Knapp (1962, p. 292) has called this role the *"character-developing* function" and described its metamorphosis as follows: "In many instances, the professor was expected to indoctrinate his students with particular articles of religious belief, according to the prevailing conviction that this would foster their development as total persons. With the passage of time, indoctrination in the narrower sense gave way to a more general function of personal counseling and the inculcation of high moral standards." This function evolved further from an active morally prescriptive role to a passive one of "setting a good example for your students" and was finally abandoned altogether as an explicit expectation for most college teachers. However, "lip service is still given to the proposition that the professor should be a builder of character as well as a transmitter of fact and knowledge" (p. 292).

Knapp (1962, p. 292) summarizes well the dynamic interaction among the three functions: "the evolving role of the college professor in America has been characterized by a progressive decline of his character-developing function along with a strong tendency for the research and the informational functions to part company and form two separate callings."

As if to substantiate Knapp's interpretations, a recent, highly regarded book on higher education (Richman and Farmer, 1974) discusses the goal system of professors as including teaching, research, public service, consulting, and administration, with *none* of the related discussion referring to any activity in student development.

A brief narrative of the salient historical events and trends contributing to the "progressive decline" of faculty involvement in student services may be useful.

Many scholars cite certain nineteenth-century developments in higher education organization and curriculum or the emergence of new institutional forms as inaugurating current faculty orientations. However, a good case can be made for the inevitability of faculty disinterest in student development, stemming from the very earliest origins of the colonial colleges: "They developed a peculiar structure which has served as an abiding model, in many respects, for the subsequent development of higher education in America: administrative control was placed in a nonacademic supervisory body and the president, and the faculty occupied a subservient station. This pattern persisted even after denominational universities and colleges in America became secularized, and . . . has become the almost universal pattern in both public and private institutions" (Knapp, 1962, pp. 292–293).

Although Harvard had attempted to set up a policy-making "corporation" of the faculty analogous to the European antecedents of an autonomous guild of scholars, the system was soon aborted (Brubacher and Rudy, 1976, pp. 24–25). The ultimate national model was that established for Yale at its founding in 1701. Principally because of "sectarian desires to maintain religious orthodoxy, the founders of Yale petitioned for a single nonacademic board of control" (Duryea, 1973, p. 19). The leading ministers of the local community who comprised the early governing boards vigorously carried out their mandate to oversee and assist the president in his administrative duties (Leonard, 1956, p. 27).

As American society became more secular and pluralistic, administrative control was delegated more completely and explicitly to the president. This was due at least partly to the loss of consensus on absolute standards of morality and a shift from institutional emphasis on piety to diverse views of culture and learning. In the process, "the development of nonresident control helped to change the president from being either first among equals or spokesman or leader of the faculty into something far different—representative of the governing board and a significant power in his own right" (Rudolph, 1962, p. 167). The result is a pattern of policy making in higher education unique to the United States. Overall goals are not set by governmental agents as in a ministry of education, nor are they set by guilds of those most directly involved in teaching and learning—the faculty and students. Policy is, due to circumstance in the formative years, invested in absentee bodies of laymen. However, as can be verified by examination of any typical college or university charter, the problem is exacerbated by the historical custom of also investing full administrative, as well as policy making, responsibility in the governing boards. Most scholars of American higher education agree that this system became incapable of carrying out its responsibilities in either public or private colleges as society became increasingly secular and pluralistic. An era of powerful and paternalistic presidents emerged and dominated institutions until the twentieth century. Subsequently, faculty gained control of their own activities, and educational decisions were made on a segmented and uncoordinated basis within academic divisions, principally departments.

It is perhaps natural that under these circumstances the faculty would eventually have a common cause with no other constituency in higher education, not even students, when their reward system became tied to individual research efforts recognized and evaluated only within each specialized campus department and within each profession on a national scale. Effectively excluded from policy making by both organizational structure and by lack of unity and interest, faculty generally have a schizophrenic attitude toward the administrators, who not only "manage" them on behalf of the governing authority but also protect them from outside pressures and obtain necessary resources. Faculty attitudes toward students also became increasingly ambivalent as the faculty member's role changed historically from partner in paternalism to individual entrepreneur.

Thus, faculty reorientation began with the gradual fragmentation of the American college's consensus on the importance of Christian piety, the decline in value of the classical curriculum, and the development of public colleges with their attractive technical and scientific programs. Even the most conservative colleges capitulated during the nineteenth century, forsaking both paternalism for their students and the unity of their curriculum (Veysey, 1965, pp. 49, 55).

In the last few decades of the nineteenth century, changes occurred that turned the faculty member, especially in universities, toward research and away from concern with student academic and moral development. These include the development of the elective system in recognition of the irrelevance of the classical curriculum, the formation of academic departments composed of specialists incapable of integrating knowledge with other disciplines, and the development of research-oriented graduate schools superimposed on the liberal arts colleges. The establishment of Johns Hopkins University in 1876 embodied the future direction of all these trends. Based deliberately on German models of research universities, it was designed from the beginning as a "faculty-centered institution" (Rudolph, 1962, p. 271). For the benefit of faculty, the best and brightest students were recruited to assist in research. "The ascendance of research also brought about a new and different view of undergraduate and graduate instruction. To a research man, the more mature student is the more useful. . . . To such a professor, the student becomes interesting as he involves himself either in learning the techniques of scholarly research or in working as an assistant to the professor" (Perkins, 1973, p. 7).

American higher education came to embrace, among other characteristics of the German research university, the concept that students should be free of administrative or faculty supervision of their academic and social affairs. Increasingly, educators were of "the conviction that American colleges and universities should follow the German philosophy of complete disregard for students outside of class" (Cowley, 1949, p. 19). Thus, the changing values of faculty, which had "decade by decade narrowed their definition of students until all that was left was their minds," carried the process further and favored only certain of those minds for their utilitarian value (Rudolph, 1976, p. 31).

Professional societies and specialized research journals were established in great numbers, further balkanizing knowledge and the structure of the university. Scholars soon found that communication across departmental lines was difficult at best and at any rate did not foster specialized research. "The researcher created a private special world for himself" (Veysey, 1965, p. 141). In this hierarchy of values, concern for students' character development is gone, "teaching comes out badly in a typical professor's maximization criteria," and research "is where the high payoff for academics is now at numerous institutions" (Richman and Farmer, 1974, p. 260). This is true especially of the prominent public and private universities that are models to most of higher education and is pervasive in most other institutions, even in those colleges that are avowedly devoted to teaching. In addition to the causative factors mentioned earlier, this value system is fostered by two additional historical accidents that ensured that a research degree (the doctorate) would be the almost universal requirement for a teaching position (Brubacher and Rudy, 1976, p. 192) and that the majority of church-related colleges would become secularized in the period from 1910 to 1920 (Knapp, 1962, p. 295). (Briefly stated, the Carnegie Foundation, in setting up a sorely needed pension fund for college teachers [which later evolved into the Teachers Insurance and Annuity Association] included only institutions without formal religious affiliations, and, of these, demanded that their faculty comprise mainly those with an earned doctorate. Most colleges promptly complied.)

Finally, even if faculty were to undertake a collective effort to restructure their value system to emphasize concern for students or at least teaching, it would seem most difficult to identify any basis or common cause for action. "As the campus has moved from unitary to composite structure, from single to multiple systems of values, from general to specialized work, it has moved away from the characteristics of community," and away from the historic community of scholars (Clark, 1971, p. 241).

In some institutions, faculty have taken collective action, but not for the purpose of reintegrating the curriculum or for reorientation toward student development. The process is called *collective bargain-*

ing, and the focus is on faculty salaries, fringe benefits, and workload. A review of what has happened to concern for student development in the elementary and secondary schools under collective bargaining agreements does not make for optimism in higher education. At those levels, the objectives of bargaining have been toward *less* contact with students rather than more, especially outside of actual classroom teaching, and as much of a reduction in student contact hours of any type as can be obtained. Given the present reward system for college and university faculty, it is not likely that student services will benefit from collective bargaining. In fact, it can be assumed with some certainty that successful faculty negotiations for salary increases and workload reductions will affect student services directly in several ways, none of them very helpful. Essentially, the higher the proportions of the institutional budget rise to meet increased costs resulting from collective bargaining, the more student services budgets will probably be cut. This shift will also probably be accompanied by increased tuition. The cost to the student in both money and services will probably further estrange faculty and students (Shark, 1975, p. 3).

It would be erroneous to assume that most students need, expect, or desire a return to the unitary college of yesteryear with its emphasis on character development and paternalism. They too have reoriented their value system from concern for being saved to concern for being successful (Rudolph, 1976, p. 34). The curriculum of higher education has become resoundingly vocational in response to student demands and expectations and in response to the goals imposed on institutions by funding sources, including government, alumni, trustees, and granting agencies for sponsored research.

How has student services as a profession been influenced by the historical trends just outlined?

A Brief Chronicle of the Student Services Profession

In terms of potential for full integration with the vital functions of higher education, the era of greatest promise and fulfillment for the student services profession seems to have been the period beginning with the end of World War I and ending with the Depression of the 1930s.*

---

*Evidently no comprehensive history of the origins, development and differentiation of the student services profession has been published to date. This seems a notable omission for a profession so large and venerable. A brief tract (Leonard, 1956) exists tracing origin and growth up to the Civil War era, but the profession was hardly established by then. In preparing this section, we have drawn on that work and also reviewed general histories of higher education, journal articles, and other secondary sources.

That era coincided with several positively related developments, including the popularity of a supportive educational philosophy, concern by leading figures in higher education for reintegration of the academic and social development of students, and vigorous, self-confident organizational growth by student services professionals. A period of some disillusionment and inertia followed in the Depression as hard-pressed institutions drastically cut back student services budgets and staff. These setbacks coincided with the prevalence of a new philosophy diametrically and explicitly opposed to student services. Since then, the profession has regained its pattern of significant growth in size but seems to be still searching for ways to become more vitally integrated with the academic enterprise (Mueller, 1961; Brown, 1972; Miller and Prince, 1976). This section provides a very brief description of these developments and their antecedents.

If we can use a working (and somewhat circular) definition of a "student services professional" as one whose main salaried responsibilities are explicitly in those functional areas generally recognized as student-oriented services, we can identify approximately when such responsibilities first emerged.

A whimsical application of this definition would probably identify the first student services professional as "the first tutor at Yale, who was allowed to study for his bachelor's degree, received no salary but subsisted on the fines he collected from the students for presumed disobediences" (Leonard, 1956, p. 29).

As mentioned earlier, the residence halls in the early colleges also contained the classrooms and chapel as well as the sleeping rooms accommodating both the students (often as young as thirteen or fourteen) and the clergymen who were their professors and tutors. "To have a student entirely under their control from the five A.M. rising time until lights out at nine gave them the opportunity they sought to minister continuously to the souls' welfare of their charges. . . . and if a youngster misbehaved, they believed with certainty that they were exorcizing the devil when they whipped him" (Cowley, 1934, p. 708).

Faculty members and administrative officials abandoned these onerous responsibilities as interest in intense religious indoctrination waned. By the mid nineteenth century, when faculty were much more interested in academic affairs than in supervising residence halls, dormitories were more and more left on their own by college officials or were replaced by the new fraternities and sororities. The prototypes of deans of women were established somewhat earlier, to mitigate the supposedly "terrrible dangers" inherent in coeducation, which had begun in Oberlin in 1837. The women charged with supervising such daring activities as unmarried young men and women dining together in a campus dining hall were variously called *principals, wardens,* and *matrons.* Their diligence was successful in having the concept of coeducation ultimately accepted in most states by the end of the nineteenth century (Woody, 1929).

As with housing, academic and social disciplinary activities were at first a responsibility of all administrative and academic officers of the colleges. However, a highly visible instance of differentiation occurred in the late nineteenth century. "Harvard claims the appointment of the first college dean, in 1870. He was a personnel administrator who gave his attention to discipline and the routine mechanics of enrollment, in addition to teaching" (Mueller, 1961, p. 52). Despite his multiple duties, the principal reason for his appointment was to take the burden of discipline off the newly inaugurated president Eliot's shoulders (Brubacher and Rudy, 1976, p. 335). Other institutions soon followed suit, so that by 1900 nearly every sizable men's or coeducational college or university had a dean of men.

The appointment of the first "deans of students" late in the nineteenth century should be viewed in the context of contemporary diversification of other administrative functions in colleges and universities. "The proliferation of administrators . . . [included] first a secretary of the faculty, then a registrar, and then in succession a vice-president, a dean, a dean of women, a chief business officer, an assistant dean, a dean of men, a director of admissions," primarily to "free research-minded scholars from the detailed but necessary work that went into the management of an organized institution" (Rudolph, 1962, pp. 434–435). Thus, student services were separated from the academicians, were professionalized, and became, like business affairs, part of "the administration."

The period of the emergence of the student services profession, from the Civil War to World War I, was one of critical importance to the present role and status of the profession. In response to the concentration of both faculty and administrative concern for only the academic aspects of collegiate life, the students developed their own social and, to some extent, intellectual life. The beginnings of such organizations and activities as the Greek letter societies, intercollegiate athletics, drama, student publications, forensics, and literary societies emerged. The common institutional response to this proliferation of student activities was to hire another student services administrator (Knapp, 1969, p. 56). The trend toward alienation between students and the institution in which they were enrolled extended even to formal religious activities. "By 1880 the various religious denominations were beginning to feel uncomfortable in the new university atmosphere, and from this discomfort developed the university pastorate movement: the assignment of clergymen to work among college students" (Rudolph, 1962, p. 459). The increasing academic specialization of the faculty and "learning for its own sake" seemed more and more remote from the distinctly vocational and utilitarian goals of students around the turn of the twentieth century (Brubacher and Rudy, 1976, pp. 332-333).

Leading educators concerned about the rift between purely academic concerns of the institution and the goals and interests of the students include some of the most eminent in the history of higher education. Daniel Coit Gilman of Johns Hopkins in 1889 appointed the first "chief of the faculty advisors" stating that "in every institution there should be one or more persons specifically appointed to be counselors or advisors of students," and ten years later William Rainey Harper of the University of Chicago indicated that the "scientific study of the student" would be the next great research field in higher education (Cowley, 1949, p. 20). These pioneers in what came to be called the "student personnel movement" were followed by Woodrow Wilson, at Princeton, and A. L. Lowell, who succeeded Eliot as president at Harvard in 1909. In Lowell's inaugural address, he "warned that the recent emphasis upon graduate education and research scholarship was sabotaging the unique function of the American college. Undergraduates must be helped to develop as well-rounded individuals as well as scholars" (Brubacher and Rudy, 1976, p. 335). Wilson attempted to emulate the collegial atmosphere at Oxford and Cambridge in England by developing a Quadrangle Plan at Princeton.

The disruptions of World War I sidetracked the nascent movement temporarily, but following it "the personnel movement received a tremendous impetus all over America. Mental testing and counseling had been developed on a large scale by the army, and as soon as peace came they applied their techniques on the campuses. The field assumed more and more of the aspects of a distinct profession, growing out of the stage of 'sentimentalized intuition' and entering that of systematic differentiation and specialization of personnel functions" (Brubacher and Rudy, 1976, pp. 335-336).

These professional developments were fostered and undergirded by new psychological theories (variously called "organismic psychology," "psychology of the individual," or "the holistic approach") as well as by applications of John Dewey's progressive educational theories to higher education. Such applications included emphasis on meaningful activities, mental and attitudinal testing, and greatly expanded counseling efforts. The thrust of the new approach was summed up in such statements as "Students are developing organisms demanding a personalized learning experience if they are to profit from college" (Wrenn and Bell, 1942, p. 8).

Diversification and professionalization of the student personnel movement during the post-World War I decade included student health services (signified by the formation of the American Student Health Association in 1920), development of placement services (by 1925, nearly half of all large universities had professionally staffed student placement bureaus), and the tremendous growth of intramural and intercollegiate varsity athletics in the "golden age of sports" (Brubacher and Rudy, 1976, pp. 340–346).

The Depression of the 1930s struck a crushing blow to the student personnel movement's attempt to reintegrate academic and character development on the nation's campuses. Because student services not only generated little or no income but were a significant drain on institutional resources, colleges and universities almost invariably cut back or eliminated many student services bureaus and offices for the sake of survival. These moves not only were consistent with financial survival but also coincided with a new philosophical emphasis on an old theme, that of the overriding value of the intellect in higher education as opposed to character or personality development.

The leading exponent of the philosophy antithetical to the student personnel movement was Robert M. Hutchins, and it was of no help to the student personnel movement that he was unquestionably not only a brilliant thinker but also a facile and prolific writer. He railed against the need for the faculty to "be diverted from its proper tasks to perform the uncongenial job of improving the conduct and the health of those entrusted to it" (Hutchins, 1936, p. 11). He satirically evaluated the collegiate life: "Undoubtedly, fine associations, fine buildings, green grass, good food, and exercise are excellent things for anybody. You will note that they are exactly what is advertised by every resort hotel" and called for a repudiation of the need to educate the "whole person" by claiming that "we can do so only if some institutions can be strong enough and clear enough to stand firm and show our people what the higher learning is. As education, it is the single-minded pursuit of the intellectual virtues. As scholarship, it is the single-minded devotion to the advancement of knowledge" (Hutchins, 1936, p. 29).

Dewey and his followers retaliated, stating that the ills of higher education were not to be cured by "monastic seclusion" (Dewey, 1937, p. 104). However, the debate was moot in the depths of the Depression, because most colleges had few or no resources to revitalize their student services. For example, student placement bureaus had little justification when millions were unemployed. At any rate, the debate was interrupted by the upheavals of World War II.

The advent of the GI Bill, with its surging need for academic, personal, and financial advising on nearly every campus in the country, exemplified the postwar trends that breathed new life into student-oriented services of all kinds. By 1958, functional differentiation of student services as they are generally known at present were listed by the prestigious and influential American Council on Education's Committee on the Administration of Student Personnel Work (Feder and others, 1958, p. 16):

- Selection for admission
- Registration and records
- Counseling
- Health service
- Housing and food service
- Student activities
- Financial aid
- Placement
- Discipline

- Special clinics
  - Remedial reading
  - Study habits
  - Speech and hearing
- Special services
  - Student orientation
  - Veterans advisory services
  - Foreign student program
  - Marriage counseling
  - Religious activities
  - Counseling

The number of student services professionals grew large (one scholar estimated at least four on every campus by 1956—Cowley, 1957, p. 21—in the postwar period and continued to mushroom to its present size and dispersion. However, as shown by much of the professional literature in the middle and late 1970s much discontent focuses on the persistent difficulty in becoming totally integrated into the central academic function of colleges and universities. The difficulty seems especially significant in the research-oriented universities of the model type mentioned earlier, where contract research has simply preempted the attention of faculty and academic administrators alike.

The historic development of the student services profession has resulted in a large, highly diversified field of student-related activities that has been and continues to be in a continual identity crisis. We have attempted to portray the historic roots of the trends underlying Brown's assertion (1972, p. 37): "With historical hindsight, it is possible to say that higher education took the wrong fork in the road when it thrust personnel maintenance upon staff with specialized duties." Whether the direction taken is "wrong" or not is perhaps a matter of interpretation or perspective. From the point of view of many faculty, the present arrangement is satisfactory, because it relieves them of many student-related chores. However, there seems little doubt that at present most student services professionals view their segregation from primary academic functions as a troubling issue that continues to evade solution.

References

Brown, R. D. *Student Development in Tomorrow's Higher Education—A Return to the Academy.* Washington, D.C.: American Personnel and Guidance Association, 1972.

Brubacher, J. S., and Rudy, W. *Higher Education in Transition.* New York: Harper & Row, 1976.

Clark, B. R. "Faculty Organization and Authority." In J. V. Baldridge (Ed.), *Academic Governance.* Berkeley, Calif.: McCutchan, 1971.

Cowley, W. H. "The History of Student Residential Housing." *School and Society*, 1934, *40*, 705–712.

Cowley, W. H. "Some History and a Venture in Prophecy." In E. G. Williamson (Ed.), *Trends in Student Personnel Work.* Minneapolis: University of Minnesota Press, 1949.

Cowley, W. H. "Student Personnel Services in Retrospect and Prospect." *School and Society*, 1957, *85*, 18–26.

Dewey, J. "President Hutchins' Proposals to Remake Higher Education." *Social Frontier.* 1937, pp. 103–104.

Duryea, E. D. "Evolution of University Organization." In J. A. Perkins (Ed.), *The University as an Organization.* New York: McGraw-Hill, 1973.

Feder, D., and others. *The Administration of Personnel Programs in American Colleges.* Washington, D.C.: American Council on Education, 1958.

Hofstadter, R. *Academic Freedom in the Age of the College.* New York: Columbia University Press, 1955.

Hofstadter, R. "The Colonial Colleges." In M. B. Katz (Ed.), *Education in American History.* New York: Praeger, 1973.

Hofstadter, R., and Smith, W. (Eds.). *American Higher Education: A Documentary History.* Vol. 2. Chicago: University of Chicago Press, 1961.

Hutchins, R. M. *The Higher Learning in America.* New Haven, Conn.: Yale University Press, 1936.

Knapp, D. "Management: Intruder in the Academic Dust." *Educational Record*, 1969, *50*, 55–65.

Knapp, R. "Changing Functions of the College Professor." In N. Sanford (Ed.), *The American College.* New York: Wiley, 1962.

Leonard, E. A. *Origins of Personnel Services in American Higher Education.* Minneapolis: University of Minnesota Press, 1956.

McAnear, B. "College Founding in the American Colonies." In P. Goodman (Ed.), *Essays on American Colonial History.* New York: Holt, Rinehart and Winston, 1972.

Miller, P. "The Contribution of the Protestant Churches to Religious

Liberty in Colonial America." In P. Goodman (Ed.), *Essays on American Colonial History*. New York: Holt, Rinehart and Winston, 1972.

Miller, T. K., and Prince, J. S. *The Future of Student Affairs: A Guide to Student Development for Tomorrow's Higher Education*. San Francisco: Jossey-Bass, 1976.

Morison, S. E. *Founding of Harvard College*. Cambridge, Mass.: Harvard University Press, 1935.

Mueller, K. H. *Student Personnel Work in Higher Education*. Boston: Houghton Mifflin, 1961.

Nevins, A. *The State Universities and Democracy*. Urbana: University of Illinois Press, 1962.

"Original Papers in Relation to a Course of Liberal Education." *American Journal of Science and Arts*, 1829, *15*, 297–351. (Also published separately by Yale's president, Jeremiah Day, as *Reports of the Course of Instruction in Yale College; by a Committee of the Corporation, and the Academical Faculty*. New Haven, Conn.: Hezekiah Howe, 1828.

Perkins, J. A. *The University as an Organization*. New York: McGraw-Hill, 1973.

Rainsford, G. N. *Congress and Higher Education in the Nineteenth Century*. Knoxville: University of Tennessee Press, 1972.

Richman, B. M., and Farmer, R. N. *Leadership, Goals, and Power in Higher Education: A Contingency and Open-Systems Approach to Effective Management*. San Francisco: Jossey-Bass, 1974.

Rudolph, F. *The American College and University*. New York: Knopf, 1962.

Rudolph, F. "The American College Student: From Theologian to Technocrat in 300 Years." *National Association of Student Personnel Administrators Journal*, 1976, *14*, 31–39.

Schlesinger, A. M. "The Aristocracy in Colonial America." *Proceedings of the Massachusetts Historical Society*, 1962, *74*, 3–21.

Shark, A. R. *Current Status of College Students in Academic Collective Bargaining*. Washington, D.C.: Academic Collective Bargaining Information Service, 1975.

Veysey, L. R. *The Emergence of the American University*. Chicago: University of Chicago Press, 1965.

Woody, T. *History of Women's Education in the United States*. Vol. 2. Lancaster, Pa.: Science Press, 1929.

Wrenn, C. G., and Bell, R. *Student Personnel Problems*. New York: Farrar, Straus & Giroux, 1942.

Gerald L. Saddlemire   2

Professional Developments

Before 1937, student services staff had developed their own statements of purpose in response to (1) forces operating within higher education and (2) the expectations of college presidents. For example, the impetus given to psychological measurement of individual differences during World War I continued on campuses afterward. The expanding mission of higher education led to a diverse curriculum that, in turn, required vocational counselors who could advise students about the emerging career options and new academic majors.

     Some student services staffs prior to 1937 met regularly to discuss the philosophic foundations of their work. Deans of men and women met in national conventions to share concerns and support. Although their duties often included managing services and maintaining order, they also discussed roles and functions specifically intended to implement a humanistic approach to individual students and their development. These discussions of professional roles contributed to the thinking found in later philosophical statements.

     The philosophical ideas that most influenced these early discussions were those of holism, humanism, and pragmatism. Practitioners then as now believed that education needed to reach the whole student; that education should not be offered in fragments to a student conceptualized as a collection of mind-body fragments. Furthermore, they had already rejected the idea (rooted in nineteenth-century German universities that were developing a rigorous academic approach to the teaching of science) that the human seeker after knowledge was somehow subordinate to knowledge itself. Rather, these educators understood that knowledge is found and disseminated *by* human beings; our sciences, like our arts, see through human eyes. Finally, the social services before 1937 were deeply influenced by the pragmatism so deeply rooted in American culture and, in education exemplified by the thought of John Dewey; they felt that thought should guide action and that truth is tested by its practical consequences. Dewey's position that knowledge is a consequence of combining thought and action provided a solid theoretical base for the evolution of a student services approach to involving students in many campus roles and especially for the recent trend toward guiding the development of the whole student.

In 1937, student services staff developed a comprehensive statement of their beliefs, which they accepted as a guide to their professional development: *The Student Personnel Point of View*, published in that year by the American Council on Education (ACE) after a conference on personnel work attended by both practitioners and faculty. The ACE-supported conference defined personnel work, produced a statement of purpose, and listed twenty-three specific services. The results were widely distributed to higher education staff, particularly to student services workers, for whom the report evolved into a charter.

Regarding the holistic, humanistic approach to education, *The Student Personnel Point of View* (American Council on Education, 1937, p. 1) stated that "This philosophy imposes upon educational institutions the obligation to consider the student as a whole—his intellectual capacity and achievement, his emotional make-up, his physical condition, his social relationships, his vocational aptitudes and skills, his moral and religious values, his economic resource, and his esthetic appreciations. It puts emphasis, in brief, upon the development of the student as a person rather than upon his intellectual training alone." It was in this spirit that student services were to be offered. In introducing the list of student services, the report (1937, pp. 3–4) noted that "This philosophy implies that in addition to instruction and business management adapted to the needs of the individual student, an effective educational program includes—in one form or another—the following services adapted to the specific aims and objectives of each college and university." The services listed were as follows:

1. Interpreting institutional objectives and opportunities to prospective students and their parents and to workers in secondary education

2. Selecting and admitting students, in cooperation with secondary schools
3. Orienting the student to his educational environment
4. Providing a diagnostic service to help the student discover his abilities, aptitudes, and objectives
5. Assisting the student throughout his college residency to determine upon his courses of instruction in light of his past achievements, vocational and personal interests, and diagnostic findings
6. Enlisting the active cooperation of the family of the student in the interest of his educational accomplishment
7. Assisting the student to reach his maximum effectiveness through clarification of his purposes, improvement of study methods, speech habits, personal appearance, manners, and so on and through progression in religious, emotional, social development, and other nonacademic personal and group relationships
8. Assisting the student to clarify his occupational aims and his educational plans in relation to them
9. Determining the physical and mental health status of the student, providing appropriate remedial health measures, supervising the health of students, and controlling environmental health factors
10. Providing and supervising an adequate housing program for students
11. Providing and supervising an adequate food service for students
12. Supervising, evaluating, and developing the extracurricular activities of students
13. Supervising, evaluating, and developing the social life and interests of students
14. Supervising, evaluating, and developing the religious life and interests of students
15. Assembling and making available information to be used in improvement of instruction and in making the curriculum more flexible
16. Coordinating the financial aid and part-time employment of students and assisting the student who needs it to obtain such help
17. Keeping a cumulative record of information about the student and making it available to the proper persons
18. Administering student discipline to the end that the individual will be strengthened and the welfare of the group preserved
19. Maintaining student group morale by evaluating, understanding, and developing student mores
20. Assisting the student to find appropriate employment when he leaves the institution

21. Articulating college and vocational experience
22. Keeping the student continuously and adequately informed of the educational opportunities and services available to him
23. Carrying on studies designed to evaluate and improve these functions and services

The report also called for articulation between college and secondary schools; coordination between instruction and student services and among national personnel associations; research on such topics as social development, student out-of-class life, and faculty-student relationships outside class; and a follow-up study of college students (graduates). And, finally, it encouraged student services staff to develop the "service" model and to generate their own statements of purposes and objectives consistent with the philosophic position described earlier and adapted to the local situation.

A decade later, in 1949, E. G. Williamson convened an ACE committee of twelve student services practitioners and professors to review the 1937 document and issue a new statement (American Council on Education, 1949) reflecting social changes and emerging roles for higher education. The report contained three sections: (1) philosophy and objectives, (2) student needs and personnel services, and (3) the administration of student personnel work. Williamson's committee reaffirmed the basic philosophy of the 1937 statement and drew attention to three new goals of higher education:

1. Fuller realization of democracy in every phase of living
2. Expansion of programs for international understanding and cooperation
3. Application of creative thinking to the solution of social problems and to the administration of public affairs

The student services worker was asked to become concerned for the development of students as whole people interacting in social relationships. The report also urged that attention be given to the maturation of students' social and spiritual values. This was a reaction to the participation in World War II to protect values considered basic to the American way of life.

The 1937 and 1949 statements of philosophy and listing of social services were the major guidelines for student services throughout the growth decades of the 1950s and 1960s. Enrollment and staff growth reached the point at which managing functions such as orientation, admissions, financial aid, residence life, placement, counseling, and student activities on the larger campus required staff specialization and statements of philosophy addressed to specific services. In this period, college student personnel were primarily concerned with staff recruitment, department organization, requesting and administering larger budgets, and monitoring and controlling student behavior.

In the early 1960s, a number of behavioral scientists became interested in studying college student behavior. Psychologists, sociologists, and anthropologists (Keniston, Heath, Katz, Clark and Trow, and others) recognized that the interaction between student and the educational environment was a rich field for research. One influential theorist who helped move students services staff from a "services" approach to a developmental approach was Nevitt Sanford. His books, *The American College* (1962), *Self and Society* (1966), and *Where Colleges Fail* (1967), became important resources for student services staff anxious to learn how new theories could modify their own philosophical positions. Sanford frequently spoke at meetings of national student services associations, urging greater attention to the campus as a developmental community that should challenge the student to grow and change. Other theorists also were beginning to pay particular attention to the process of development and change, to assessing student concerns, and to maturation measurements. Different theories and strategies of implementation proliferated, and busy student services practitioners found it hard to keep up-to-date on new developments.

In 1968, the Committee on the Student in Higher Education, supported by the Hazen Foundation and chaired by Joseph Kauffman, dean of student services at the University of Wisconsin, coauthored a report, *The Student in Higher Education* (Committee on the Student in Higher Education, 1968), that provided student services staff with a perspective on the social and psychological influences that shape student attitudes, interests, and activities. The report offered specific recommendations and methods for implementing student development in higher education. Its philosophical assumptions rested squarely on the theoretical work of the behavioral scientists—two of whom, Joseph Katz and Kenneth Keniston, were members of the ten-person Kauffman committee.

The committee introduced its report by challenging colleges to take conscious responsibility for the human development of their students. It said that colleges should be aware that increased sophistication in behavioral sciences has led to an improved understanding of the human development process. It also pointed out that the growing lack of confidence in higher education called for a reexamination of educational procedures. The report asked colleges and universities to take specific steps to educate the whole student, to recognize the wide diversity within the student body, and to stress the development of native talents as well as of areas in which a given student might be relatively weak. Institutions were urged to emphasize the freshman year, in which a flexible, imaginative approach can give students a chance to learn about their educational needs and desires. Every subject matter should be taught in such a way as to take into consideration the developmental needs of the student; furthermore, knowledge of human development generated by the behavioral sciences would help improve the quality of American higher education. The report by the Committee on the Student in Higher Education has been used by chief student services officers as a basis for staff development and as required reading for preparation programs.

Also in 1968, the American College Personnel Association (ACPA) executive committee approved the initial stage, called Phase I, of the Tomorrow's Higher Education (T.H.E.) Project, a planned response to higher education changes that called for examining the future of college student services. A task force was formed, and Robert Brown was commissioned to review and reconceptualize, in writing, the basic assumptions of student services and to describe the philosophical bases for implementing model student services programs on a variety of campuses. The resulting monograph, *Student Development in Tomorrow's Higher Education—A Return to the Academy* (Brown, 1972), was approved by ACPA for publication in the hope that it would stimulate discussion about the philosophical bases of student services.

Brown examines the trends of higher education changes as reported by the Carnegie Foundation, the Hazen Foundation, and the U.S. Department of Health, Education, and Welfare. Woven into this summary is a discussion of the optimum learning environment. Brown argues that the academic dimensions of collegiate life must be humanized by student services educators (as he defines their role). The monograph also reconceptualizes roles, functions, methods, and procedures generally, as they relate to student services educators.

The Brown monograph discusses many innovations that have emerged on campus, often as special programs for small groups of students. He urges using the results of these programs in the academic mainstream, where the majority of students continue to spend their college careers. Teaching-learning centers are suggested to enable faculty to research the learning process, alternative methods of instruction, and possibilities for interdisciplinary sharing. The need for broad change in higher education, Brown points out, can be met by the students services educator, who can collaborate with the academic faculty to promote total student development. Student services staff must recognize that student development is a total campus effort, not the exclusive province of any one segment; should establish direct ties with the academic faculty to support their concern for affective as well as cognitive student development; and must become expert in such areas as learning theory, growth and development, and campus ecology. Brown argues for acceptance of total student development as a goal for higher education and draws attention to the new research in the field.

While the ACPA monograph was in preparation, the Council of Student Personnel Associations in Higher Education (COSPA) charged its Professional Development Commission with updating the guidelines for preparation programs. This commission restated the basic assumptions of the profession and considered a number of position papers prepared by representatives of the major personnel associations, before writing new guidelines. In 1972, the commission (chaired by Alva Cooper) submitted a paper on philosophy and professional preparation, "Student Development Services in Higher Education," to the COSPA council and its constituent groups. After reviewing the feedback, the commission then made limited revisions and issued the new document in March 1975 as "Student Development Services in Post Secondary Education" (Council of Student Personnel Associations in Higher Education, 1975).

The COSPA commission document reported consensus on the following points of view (1975, pp. 1–2):

1. The orientation to student personnel is developmental.
2. Self-direction of the student is the goal of the student and is facilitated by the student development specialist.
3. Students are viewed as collaborators with the faculty and administration in the process of learning and growing.
4. It is recognized that many theoretical approaches to human development have credence, and a thorough understanding of such approaches is important to the student development specialist.
5. The student development specialist prefers a proactive position in policy formulation and decision making so that a positive impact is made on the change process.

The commission report introduces the term "student development specialist" for the first time to identify student services staff, saying that "In general, faculty tend to emphasize content, and student development specialists tend to emphasize process" (p. 3). Moreover, the philosophical assumption of this paper assumes that human beings seek to become free and self-directed through developmental processes and that the student development specialist helps students reach these life goals.

In 1975, "A Student Development Model for Student Affairs in Tomorrow's Higher Education" (American College Personnel Association) reported the outcomes of a conference called to move ahead with Phase II of ACPA's T.H.E. Project. The report outlined a process model for student development and invited student services professionals to submit exemplary programs. Materials submitted to the committee would serve as the basis for a monograph on program planning in student development.

The rationale for student development in the Phase II paper builds on concepts found in Brown (1972) and in both versions of *The Student Personnel Point of View* (American Council on Education, 1937; 1949); for example, "Student development is the application of human development concepts in the postsecondary setting. Human development is a patterned, orderly lifelong process leading to development of self-determination and self-direction, which results in more effective behavior. Development can best be described within the framework of two major constructs: (1) life stages and (2) developmental tasks" (American College Personnel Association, 1975, p. 2). Members of the academic community are urged to learn "to understand the stages of development and related developmental tasks through which those in postsecondary institutions are passing and to develop expertise in the competencies necessary to implement the student development model," so that a developmental learning environment will be realized (American College Personnel Association, 1975, p. 5). This concept of student development is similar to that of the 1975 paper produced by COSPA, an instance of mutual reinforcement that encouraged the two professional committees working as parallel but independent groups.

The response of higher education to the ACPA report is summarized and interpreted by Miller and Prince (1976). In the foreword, Ann Pruitt, president of ACPA, points out that the T.H.E. Project is only one way to individualize higher education, in response to critics who feared that advocates saw T.H.E. as the only viable approach to student services. Miller and Prince (1976, p. 3) offer a definition of student services that they call both a philosophical goal and the means for achieving it: "the application of human development concepts in postsecondary settings so that everyone involved can master increasingly complex developmental tasks, achieve self-direction, and become interdependent." The book describes the process of helping students learn developmental skills and gives specific examples of existing programs. Miller and Prince acknowledge the research and theorizing on development by Erikson, Perry, Kohlberg, Chickering, Piaget, and others, but they place far more emphasis on the process model as a way to show the practitioner how to implement the student development philosophy.

While ACPA and COSPA groups were reconceptualizing the basic philosophy of student services, psychologists and sociologists continued to study changes in students. Clyde Parker, a developmental psychologist, pointed out that the terms "student development" and "development of the whole student" were being used in higher education without an understanding of developmental psychology. He urged, as did the ACPA and COSPA papers, that higher education practitioners and educators in the student services become much more knowledgeable about the increasingly more elaborate and sophisticated theories evolving in the behavioral sciences (Parker, 1978).

Impact of Theory on Social Services Programs

After familiarizing themselves with developmental theory, social services workers must then apply their knowledge to programs. First, they must recognize how theory influences program goals and purposes. Second, practitioners, preparation educators, and the major national associations must continue to reexamine goals in order to clarify objectives, plan programs, and design evaluations consistent with new insights. And managing services for students as listed in the original *Student Personnel Point of View* remains a responsibility.

The impact of student services philosophies on preparation programs has been described in *Perspectives on the Preparation of Student Affairs Professionals* (Knock, 1977). Introducing six position papers on professional preparation, Knock (the editor) traces the development of the philosophic statements and of specific orientations, such as social intervention, process outcome models, and system philosophy, and notes their effect on the field. He also notes that the effort to translate theory into practice has met with only limited success. One of the most telling comments in the books is William Peterson's call for preparation educators to model what they preach; unless educators can model what they preach, they risk sending unprepared students out into the field of student services.

In the early 1970s, when Crookston, Parker, and others called for a more sophisticated understanding of human growth and development, preparation programs began to modify their curriculum. In 1975, COSPA's Commission on Professional Development redrafted a working paper focused on guidelines for preparation, saying that student services specialists should be ready to assume roles as administrators, teachers, and consultants in order to foster student development. This document took the position that it is better to describe desired behavioral objectives for student service staff than to specify courses for preparation programs. The criteria for the objectives suggested were derived from the concept that the student services specialist helps students achieve goals, manage conflict, and become more self-directed and self-fulfilled. Some examples of the objectives given are as follows:

1. To help students move toward goals and to demonstrate the ability to establish a productive counseling relationship with individuals and with groups
2. To assess the status, abilities, and progress shown by students in meeting goals
3. To use principles and techniques for change to facilitate human development
4. To complete a research project that tests a hypothesis related to student behavior or institutional characteristics

The impact of various philosophies or theories on student services is demonstrated in the change the field has seen in typical roles, such as teacher, consultant, intervener, administrator, and researcher. For example, having student services staff teach or coteach academic courses shows the closer relationship between student services and classroom faculty that marks current shifts in orientation. The climate has become favorable for establishing courses in human relations (such as value clarification and career decision making) that relate to development and personal growth. Tollefson (1975) calls for courses with nontraditional (and previously unacceptable) content, such as how to confront and cope with politicians and how to prepare for death.

The role of consultant also becomes more important as student services staff become more aware of human development theory and of strategies to help students examine their goals. Students seek consultation in classrooms, recreation centers, residence halls, and college unions as they explore their own attitudes and purposes and learn to cope with crises. Faculty also show an interest in consultation when they introduce in class new concepts such as values examination, life planning, and self-assessment. Alert student services staff should be prepared to take a proactive, positive approach to the educational process by serving as consultants.

The new emphases on the developed student as a goal and on a new understanding of human development have encouraged student services staff to intervene in students' lives more confidently. Practitioners are also becoming more prone to ask questions about their own professional effectiveness; for example,

1. "How can I discuss a loan application so the student will accept the obligation of full repayment?"

2. "Why, when I used this career counseling approach with a particular freshman, did this student feel good about the career decision he (or she) made?"

3. "How can I find out what style of democratic community can be designed and introduced in the residence hall?"

The answer to each of these questions is determined by the extent of the practitioner's understanding of human development theory. Student services staff no longer respond passively and reactively to such questions and have instead deliberately adopted an interventionist role.

Jones (1978) and Harvey (1974, 1976), in discussing the future roles of student services administrators, point out that the movement away from controlling student behavior opens the door for important educational and developmental contributions to students' lives. The administrative realignment made to allow and encourage such contributions often involves splitting the unit's role into two major areas: student development and student services management. The area of student development emphasizes education and consultation, such as orientation, student activities, academic advising and academic support programs, counseling and health services, and special programs (such as paraprofessional training, leadership training, and drug education). The area of services management emphasizes administration and handles such functions as student discipline, student codes, financial aid, campus security, and recreation.

The administration of discipline is being influenced by new research on moral reasoning. Awareness of the different levels of moral reasoning described by Kohlberg allows staff to help students move to higher levels. This is part of a general movement in higher education to challenge ethical standards on campus; as, for example, in cheating on exams, drug abuse, questionable recruiting practices, and shoddy academic standards.

Student services departments are also responding to new information about adulthood and adult development. For example, older, often part-time students constitute a growing segment of campus enrollment. The institutional response, through policies and programs, shows an awareness that these students differ from the traditional eighteen- to twenty-three-year-olds. Nancy Schlossberg (1978) offers five propositions about adult development that student services departments should consider:

1. Behavior in adulthood is determined by social rather than by biological clocks.

2. Behavior is at times a function of life stage, at others of age.

3. Sex differences are greater than either age or stage differences.
4. Adults continually experience transitions requiring adaptations and reassessments of the self.
5. The recurrent themes of adulthood are identity, intimacy, and generativity.

Student services staff recognize that advocating student involvement on campus encourages student growth and development. The reduction of the age of majority to eighteen gives students full adult rights for their entire college career. Students are aware of their consumer rights on campus. In order to help students contribute to the campus community—a philosophic position that goes back to the personnel point of view—student services staff seek opportunities for involving students in making a wide variety of campus decisions.

The holistic perspective of student services staff makes them useful contributors to research on retaining students. Their direct, personal contact with students gives them a reliable basis for studying causes of student dropout and stopout. They are also aware of the importance of institutional policies and programs that help students leave with dignity and return to an understanding campus.

Another example of the holistic perspective is the attention being given to student health. At Bowling Green State University, incoming students are provided with a questionnaire about their health status and habits. This information is processed by computer, comparing the student with a broad population of the same age. This self-inventory and analysis is then made available to the student, with an upper-class peer advisor to help with the interpretation. This approach encourages student self-awareness and personal responsibility for health habits. On the same campus, student leaders, encouraged by the student services department, have spearheaded the building of a recreation center. The student services support for the project came from the staff's commitment to the well-being of the whole student and the recognition of a need to encourage development of lifelong recreational skills.

Student services staff recognize that facilitating student development should be a total institutional commitment calling for integrating teaching and student services staff. This integration will occur more frequently when existing staff members have had retraining to acquire new skills and to update their understanding of philosophy and theory. Also, new criteria must be established for hiring staff. Recently, national professional associations have provided skill- and competency-updating workshops for staff. In addition, in-service staff training must be undertaken within each department, under the leadership of the chief student services worker.

In the 1970s, ACPA held a referendum on whether or not to change its name to reflect the current concern for student development. The outcome was inconclusive, and the name was not changed, but the resulting discussion served to sensitize a broad segment of higher education, particularly student services, to the importance of developmental theory and facilitating student development.

Also in the 1970s, the American Personnel and Guidance Association (APGA) formed a committee on standards for professional preparation programs, chaired by Robert Stripling. The chief outcome of this committee's work was the initiation of a meeting with higher education accrediting agencies. The agencies were asked to update outmoded standards for student services programs and to standardize guidelines for accreditation as applied by various regional accrediting groups. The committee also supplied the agencies with the names of professionals who could serve on accreditation teams and who were well acquainted with the current philosophy of student services.

Awareness that a new philosophy calls for new competencies has resulted in a number of studies and recommendations. A report prepared for the ACPA executive committee (Hanson, 1977) identifies staff competencies needed to implement the T.H.E. model; the following are strongly endorsed:

1. Goal setting
   - Assess student needs
   - Teach students to take responsibility
   - Help students formulate realistic and attainable personal goals and objectives
2. Consultation
   - Use effective communication skills
   - Facilitate staff development through in-service training
   - Recognize and use others' expertise
3. Milieu management
   - Collaborate with other faculty and staff
   - Be able to bridge the gap between theory and practice in managing programs
4. Instruction
   - Make effective decisions
   - Teach interpersonal communication skills
   - Teach group leadership skills
   - Teach decision-making skills
5. Evaluation
   - Revise programs on the basis of evaluation data

- Write clear, concise memos
- Make realistic conclusions and recommendations
6. Assessment
   - Maintain student confidentiality
   - Communicate effectively on a one-to-one basis
   - Listen to students' perceptions of feelings

This taxonomy of professional competencies provides a basis for reviewing and developing a preparation curriculum.

The Future of Student Services Philosophy

The philosophical ideas likely to influence future student services programs are drawn partly from the original student personnel point of view and partly from the more recent student development theories. Holism, humanism, pragmatism, and individualism remain important, as does the movement to involve students in the campus community as a means for combining thought and action to further development. Peer counselors, resident assistants, university committee members, and work-study staff can learn from their experiences and develop a close identity with the entire campus. Astin's (1977) analysis of student attitudes underscores the fact that involving students in campus activities contributes to positive student attitudes toward the learning environment.

Student services staff will need to be philosophically flexible as new cultures flow into the campus scene. Blacks, Chicanos, Native Americans, and others seek to maintain their cultural identity, unlike earlier immigrants, who often tried to hide their origins. A new wave of refugees from Southeast Asia and increasing numbers of students from the Middle East may arrive, with cultural differences that must be accommodated to prevent conflict and tension. Student services staff will need to understand the new cultures and to help native U.S. students develop sensitivity to and appreciation of other cultures.

A description of future student services functions is offered by a pamphlet directed at students considering the field as a career, issued by the ACPA Commission on Professional Education of Student Personnel Workers in Higher Education. The pamphlet draws attention to the diversity of postsecondary institutions and to the broad spectrum of students they enroll. It notes that student services staff work will be directed toward facilitating each student's full development, whether the student is enrolled for one course or many, whether at the age of seventeen or seventy-one. Readers are also told that a student services specialist in the future will continue to provide one or more of the following functions: consulting, administering, and instructing. Regardless of role, "the student development specialist shares responsibility for humanizing and personalizing each student's higher education. Recognizing that students' problems are often inseparable from institutional problems, he or she should expect to help change the students' institutional environment or to initiate or collaborate with others in bringing necessary change, whenever the environment impedes growth and learning" (American College Personnel Association, 1979, p. 4). The pamphlet advises those who are considering a career in student services to become well acquainted with emerging developmental theories.

Prospective administrators of student development must, moreover, take a leadership role in frequently evaluating the total impact of programs, to ensure that they are in keeping with changing student needs and institutional objectives. They must also make data on students and institutional characteristics available for use in long-term policy decisions and program development.

Finally, the pamphlet offers the following forward-looking descriptions of professional specialized functions:

1. The office of admissions and records is responsible for helping prospective students match their educational needs, interests and qualifications with the offerings of the college.
2. Career planning and placement is available for students and alumni so that they may select a career that provides for personal growth and self-realization.
3. Student housing facilities on campus are designed as living-learning centers, joining academic with out-of-class experiences. Housing accommodates student differences and encourages a wide variety of group experiences.
4. Counseling helps the student acquire self-understanding, relate effectively to the environment, make personal decisions, and take responsibility for individual actions. Counselors must give special attention to marriage, sex, and drug counseling. They must also give input to administrative decisions on the institutional environment and must actively promote positive mental health and human development.
5. The international dimension of student services is advanced by advising foreign students. This field offers unique ways to lead cross-cultural learning experiences. Foreign student exchange programs are arranged.
6. Student activities develop opportunities for leadership education and for a wide variety of skill training workshops. Students are frequently consulted on institutional policies and procedures and will

be even more so in the future. There is increasing research on the effectiveness of student-oriented and -initiated programs.

This booklet is distributed to about 1,200 people per year and is likely to have a strong influence on future student service programs through those who choose this career option.

New statements of student development theories (by Perry, Kohlberg, Chickering, Erikson, Heath, Loevinger, and Holland) have also made a strong impact on preparation programs that is likely to intensify in the future. In the years since the mid 1960s, when Nevitt Sanford discussed the relationship between student development and student services practice, a knowledge explosion has been reflected in those academic departments most helpful in preparing student services staff. For example, Carney Strange and Nancy Evans describe the objectives of a course called "Assessing College Environments," taught at Bowling Green State University. This course focuses on human environments as a subject for observation, description, and systematic inquiry and shows students how to explore theories and apply them in assessing select campus settings. Within an interactionist paradigm, the course "develops an understanding of the influence of the environmental component on human behavior." Students gain an "explicit understanding of select theoretical approaches to the definition and description of human environments." The course also explores the "application of environmental theory to the practice of student development, focusing on the design of campus environments and their influence on student behaviors," and is based on a critical appreciation of environmental research.

Another development that will continue to grow in the future is the provision for workshops to update current practitioners' knowledge of cognitive and psychosocial development and of how students develop. This ensures that the future generation of student services staff will approach their responsibilities somewhat differently from past generations and will be able to join staff whose competencies are continuing to develop on the job. In-service training helps reduce conflict between the new and the old.

Our national commitment to universal access to higher education entails an expansion of academic support services. The basic assumptions and value systems of student services staff make them attractive candidates to fill new positions in developmental education and learning center programs. To do so effectively, they will need an understanding of learning theory (both in the process and in cognitive styles of learning) acquired through preservice and in-service training.

Since the mid 1970s, student services staff have been working closely with and contributing to the work of learning and developmental education centers. As Patricia Cross points out in *Accent on Learning* (1976), major efforts are needed to provide individualized, humanized education for the "new students" who are becoming an ever-larger proportion of many student bodies. Cross anticipates that student services staff will take on the dual roles of diagnostician and program technologist. She also predicts that, as a result of teaching and research associated with the new students, student services staff will considerably increase their professionalism.

The research and program development division of the National Association of Student Personnel Administrators has published a manual, *Planning, Budgeting and Evaluation of Student Affairs Programs* (Harpel, 1976), that discusses management skills needed to implement the new programs and procedures. Particular attention is given to sound management of resources and activities to produce a desired outcome. This emphasis encourages student services staff to enter an era of accountability with appropriate skills. The current stress on accountability, evaluation, and efficiency underscores the need to know how organization of student services can implement student development.

For example, the administration of discipline on campus is a major concern of student services staff. The relationship between disciplinary counseling and Kohlberg's theory of moral development needs to be examined. Smith (1978) discusses ways that moral development can be stimulated on campus. In addition to using this theory in disciplinary matters, Smith (1978, p. 65) says that "the use of moral discussion and the introduction of moral development concepts in training programs, staff and professional development experiences, and in the graduate curriculum can lead to a higher level of moral reasoning and moral behavior in the professional and paraprofessional levels to actively and intentionally function in ways that can facilitate the moral development of college students."

Kohlberg's work should be reviewed carefully because ethical behavior of all subgroups on campus is now being critically scrutinized. Moreover, large numbers of students now reaching college age come from very different home backgrounds than those of previous years. Single and working parents are now typical in most communities. The loosening of ties with parents and the relaxing of behavioral restraints in the home affect college-age students in ways that are not yet fully understood. Student services staff will be encouraging research that will help sensitize them to new modes of behavior. Holistic philosophy and student development theories support research on all aspects of the student experience, both on and off campus.

Finally, all student services professionals need to understand the importance of systematically appraising the future, as discussed by

Frederick Brodzinski in *Utilizing Futures Research* (1979). Brodzinski, the editor, points out that our philosophic commitment to being proactive must be accompanied by systematic consideration of the future to help us cope with no growth in institutions, with vocationalism and consumerism, and with adult students. In addition, Kathleen Plato (1978) reminds us that, although student development theory now guides the profession and seems likely to continue to do so, using only one approach and shutting our eyes to any others will do the future of the profession no good. New theories must be discussed and evaluated as they emerge, and the profession must change accordingly.

Conclusion

This chapter has (1) reviewed the philosophical foundations, theories and principles, and functions of college student services; (2) noted the impact of philosophy on preparation programs; and (3) speculated about the future of college student services. The dynamic nature of the field is evident: To adapt to increasing change, every aspect of the work, programs, and campus interrelationships must be constantly scrutinized and updated. The future of student services will be shaped by emphases on holism, humanism, pragmatism, development of students at all ages and from many cultures, sensitivity to needs, accountability, new research and theoretical contributions, and growing professionalism.

References

American College Personnel Association, Commission XII Professional Education of Student Personnel Workers in Higher Education. *Consider the College Student Development Profession.* Bowling Green, Ohio: Bowling Green State University, 1979.

American College Personnel Association, Tomorrow's Higher Education Project. (T. K. Miller, Chmn.) "A Student Development Model for Student Affairs in Tomorrow's Higher Education." *Journal of College Student Personnel,* 1975, *16,* 334–341.

American Council on Education. *The Student Personnel Point of View.* American Council on Education Studies, Series 1, Vol. 1, No. 3. Washington, D.C.: American Council on Education, 1937.

American Council on Education, Committee on Student Personnel Work. (E. G. Williamson, Chmn.) *The Student Personnel Point of View.* (rev. ed.) American Council on Education Studies, Series 6, No. 13. Washington, D.C.: American Council on Education, 1949.

Astin, A. W. *Four Critical Years: Effects of College on Beliefs, Attitudes, and Knowledge.* San Francisco: Jossey-Bass, 1977.

Brodzinski, F. R. (Ed.). *New Directions for Student Services: Utilizing Futures Research,* no. 6. San Francisco: Jossey-Bass, 1979.

Brown, R. D. *Student Development in Tomorrow's Higher Education—A Return to the Academy.* Washington, D.C.: American Personnel and Guidance Association, 1972.

Committee on the Student in Higher Education. (J. F. Kauffman, Chmn.) *The Student in Higher Education.* New Haven, Conn.: Hazen Foundation, 1968.

Council of Student Personnel Associations in Higher Education, Professional Development Commission. (A. L. Cooper, Chmn.) *Student Development Services in Higher Education.* July 1972.

Council of Student Personnel Associations in Higher Education, Professional Development Commission. (G. L. Saddlemire, Chmn.) "Student Development Services in Post Secondary Education." *Journal of College Student Personnel,* 1975, *16,* 524-528.

Cross, K. P. *Accent on Learning: Improving Instruction and Reshaping the Curriculum.* San Francisco: Jossey-Bass, 1976.

Hanson, G. R. "Stop the Bandwagon . . . ACPA Wants to Get On." Submitted to the ACPA Executive Council and Commission Chairperson. Austin: University of Texas, 1977. (Mimeograph.)

Harpel, R. "Planning, Budgeting, and Evaluation in Student Affairs Programs." *NASPA Journal,* 1976, *14,* i-xx.

Harvey, T. R. "Some Future Directions for Student Personnel Administration." *Journal of College Student Personnel,* 1974, *15,* 243-247.

Harvey, T. R. "Student Development and the Future of Higher Education: A Force Analysis." *Journal of College Student Personnel,* 1976, *17,* 90-95.

Jones, J. D. "Student Personnel Work: Current State and Future Directions." *NASPA Journal,* 1978, *15,* 2-11.

Knock, G. H. *Perspectives on the Preparation of Student Affairs Professionals.* Student Personnel Series, No. 22. Washington, D.C.: American College Personnel Association, 1977.

Miller, T. K., and Prince, J. S. *The Future of Student Affairs: A Guide to Student Development for Tomorrow's Higher Education.* San Francisco: Jossey-Bass, 1976.

Parker, C. A. (Ed.). *Encouraging Development in College Students.* Minneapolis: University of Minnesota, 1978.

Plato, K. "The Shift to Student Development: An Analysis of the Patterns of Change." *NASPA Journal,* 1978, *15,* 32-36.

Sanford, N. (Ed.). *The American College.* New York: Wiley, 1962.

Sanford, N. *Self and Society: Social Change and Individual Development.* New York: Atherton, 1966.

Sanford, N. *Where Colleges Fail: A Study of the Student as a Person.* San Francisco: Jossey-Bass, 1967.

Schlossberg, N. K. "Five Propositions About Adult Development." *Journal of College Student Personnel,* 1978, *19,* 418-423.

Smith, A. "Lawrence Kohlberg's Cognitive Stage Theory of the Development of Moral Judgment." In L. Knefelkamp, C. Widick, C. A. Parker (Eds.), *New Directions for Student Services: Applying New Developmental Findings,* no. 4. San Francisco: Jossey-Bass, 1978.

Strange, C., and Evans, N. "Assessing College Environments." Unpublished paper, College Student Personnel Department, Bowling Green State University.

Tollefson, A. L. *New Approaches to College Student Development.* New York: Behavioral Publications, 1975.

Robert H. Fenske   3

Current Trends

Selected current trends and issues in higher education that significantly influence the student services profession are discussed in this chapter. The unifying theme of this discussion is the existence of a basic perspective held by most student services professionals. As expressed in the profession's own literature, this perspective has two facets. First, the student services profession has persisted in its conviction that education of the "whole person" is the ideal model for higher education regardless of the discouraging outlook for its revival or ultimate implementation. Second, realization of this ideal should be accomplished through a complete melding of the interests and goals of trustees, administrators, faculty, and student services professionals, with driving concern for somehow bringing the last two groups onto common ground.

Introduction and Background

Among the colleges and universities in which the overwhelming majority of student services professionals work, each major type of

Note: The author wishes to thank Katherine Davis, Elizabeth Fisk, and Paul Zuzich for their helpful suggestions. All are doctoral students in the Department of Higher and Adult Education, Arizona State University.

institution seems to have a widely acclaimed normative model toward which much of its change, adaption, and progress is directed. These institutional models are identified by conventional wisdom and folklore (sometimes empirically expressed as polls or surveys); quantitative measures such as size of enrollments, budgets, buildings, and amount of research funds awarded; and qualitative indicators such as Nobel prize winners on the faculty and admissions test scores of students. In the private university sector, such models are exemplified by Harvard, Stanford, and Chicago, while public universities look toward Berkeley, Michigan, and Wisconsin. These models provide more than a mere grail. They provide definitive examples for almost every form of academic striving, whether it be for faculty productivity or mobility, proportion of budget devoted to research, opportunities for snobbery at professional meetings, or even membership in prestigious athletic conferences. More concretely, they provide funding leverage for the many dozens of institutions that loudly proclaim intentions of becoming the Harvard or Berkeley of their particular region.

The existence of these normative models and the striving of many institutions of all types toward their ideals has relevance for the status and prospects of student services. The basis for much of the preeminence of the model universities is the quality and quantity of their graduate education and scholarly research—and these emphases are little concerned with traditional student services functions. In fact, as mentioned elsewhere in this book, the specific rejection or at least avoidance of several historic student services conceptualizations (adjuster, parent, counselor, developer, and manager) by both faculty and academic administrators may indicate a relative deemphasis of student services in many academic "model" institutions. Where such an inverse relationship exists, it may be characterized by such hypothetical statements as "In our college, scholarly research isn't everything, it's the only thing; other functions are strictly subordinate"; "Really high-quality students have little need of 'helping' services for their academic work; their emotional or psychological problems aren't our concern"; or "It doesn't make much sense to have our Nobel prize winning science faculty spending ten hours per week on student-related activities such as advising or discipline, does it?"

Such candid statements are uncommon; but the attitudes they express are not, especially in research-oriented universities and highly selective colleges. Although in the vast majority of higher education institutions student services are generally viewed as more or less necessary, we are emphasizing that "model" colleges and universities undervalue student services simply because they are not viewed as vital to the graduate education and scholarly research functions that dominate those institutions. Most administrative and academic leaders in all higher education institutions (including liberal arts colleges and community colleges) earned their graduate degrees in universities that place relatively little emphasis on student services. Thus, by virtue of the normative influence of the model universities, negative attitudes toward student services tend to be fashionable throughout much of higher education, even in institutions where they might least apply.

In the eyes of many student services professionals, the functions they perform are too often valued by trustees, administrators, and faculty as a somewhat distant second to the primary functions of teaching, research, and service. They sometimes feel that others perceive them engaging in a nebulous array of vaguely "supportive" activities or performing expensive "babysitting," which at best keeps potentially troublesome students quietly occupied and at worst provides opportunities for fomenting trouble through such outlets as inflammatory student newspaper articles or invitations to highly controversial figures to speak on campus.

To balance this somewhat gloomy tableau, it must be recognized that, among the over 3,000 institutions of higher education conforming to our definition, many acknowledged student services to be of central importance and to permeate and undergird all academic and service functions. However, such cases are the exception, not the rule. The type of institution in which these exceptions most commonly exist are private, church-related colleges, especially fundamentalist ones. Perhaps it is no coincidence that these colleges most closely resemble the early colleges in America in that their concerns for the student's spiritual, moral, ethical, emotional, and psychological well-being are inseparable from their concern for academic progress (Pace, 1972).

Education for the "Whole Person"

In a world full of inconsistencies and rapid changes, the student services profession's faithful adherence to the goal of educating the "whole person" is truly remarkable. Dating from clear pronouncements by leading educators around the turn of the century (including Gilman, Lowell, and Wilson, among others) this concept has endured with unusual consistency. As indicated in Chapter One, it was elaborated on both a philosophical and psychological basis in the 1920s and the early 1930s. Successive statements of the "student personnel point of view" sponsored by the American Council on Education in 1937, 1949, and 1958 carried forward the concept to the post-World War II era. The profession's leaders also espoused the philosophy through this period, including Wrenn and Bell (1942), Williamson (1949), and Mueller (1961, see pp. 64–69). Recent and important books on developing models for the profession perpetuate the historic theme in considerable purity; for example, consider Brown (1972, p. 44): "Colleges and universities should establish expectations for students and assess outcomes that cover the broad ranges of human behavior including the intellectual, personal-social, esthetic, cultural, and even the psychomotor dimensions." Tollefson (1975, p. 7) calls for, "a resurgence of concern for the student as a person, for how his needs and interests are being served, and for how effectively the institution is educating him to achieve his personal goals and preparing him for his role in society." And Miller and Prince (1976, p. 169) state, "The mission of the college is to educate the whole student and not only his or her intellect."

An increasingly insistent corollary theme is stated through all of the books and statements just cited. It is often expressed as the need either somehow to make student development an integral part of the academician's goals and reward system or, conversely to bring student development professionals into the central academic arena as a welcome and indispensable part of the curriculum.

Brown (1972, p. 8) commented recently and somewhat plaintively on the profession's view of itself: "Since the end of World War II, student personnel workers have identified themselves as the professional group on campus most concerned about the development of the total student. . . . Is the student personnel worker the only person on campus concerned about student development? . . . Can student development really be fostered effectively without the support and influence of the academic dimensions of college life?"

From the viewpoint of the student services professional, it is no help that the most ambitious and significant reexamination of American higher education since the 1947 Truman Commission gave short shrift to educating the whole person. In its summary report (1973), which analyzed college and university goals in the 1970s and in the foreseeable future, the Carnegie Commission indicated that " 'Totalism' in the campus approach to students is, we believe, neither wise nor possible" (p. 17). The commission took this remarkably forthright stand despite the results of its own national surveys of students. The findings of these surveys placed highest priority on affective and social goals for undergraduate education. "The reaction of undergraduates indicate that they view the college experience as one related to their total developmental growth and not to the cognitive and occupational aspects of their lives alone" (p. 15). Furthermore, the commission acknowledged that "A broader developmental approach to the college experience, going beyond intellectual development alone, is in keeping with new insights in the field of psychology, as, for example, in the writings of Erik Erikson—the college years are an important developmental period, and cognitive and affective activities are closely related to each other" (p. 16).

Nonetheless, the commission directly followed this observation with the following statement: "Yet the campus cannot and should not try to take direct responsibility for the 'total' development of the student. That responsibility belongs primarily to the individual student by the time he goes to college. The primary direct responsibility of the college is to assist with intellectual and skill development" (p. 16).

As I have attempted to show through the historical approach in Chapter One, the current set of priorities of academicians is founded on a reward system that is so fundamentally integrated into the very fabric of higher education that it does not seem vulnerable to change without somehow reconstituting the entire structure and organization. Furthermore, as noted later, some important current trends accentuate the current reward system of academics, although not all do so. Certain trends indicate that it would be more feasible to bring the expertise and cooperative efforts of student services professionals to the aid of faculty than to reorient the entire establishment of higher education. Obviously, this possibility has influenced the models presented by Tollefson and by Miller and Prince, because both include extensive listings of experimental academic and other programs that in various ways involve student services professionals in tandem with academicians.

The apparent goals and concerns of the student services profession outlined earlier were used as a framework for selecting trends to be included in the following listing. Specifically, we selected for consideration those that affect the profession most directly and included only those potentially capable of changing the role and status of the profession.

The trends and issues are organized into three very inclusive categories: (1) organization and structure, including consideration of governance, finance, and certain aspects of the faculty role; (2) students, including characteristics, enrollment trends, and activities; and (3) curriculum and program, including innovations and potential involvement of student services professionals.

We have not included "potential" trends and issues because some, like the doctor of arts "teaching" degree program that has for decades represented a panacea for improving instruction and the academic reward system, seem perpetually on the verge of happening. Nor have we included the very few immutable issues that *never* seem to change. For example, our present system of governance, which was established in another age when it effectively governed institutions that have long since disappeared, led Francis Wayland, president of Brown

University, to ask in 1828, "How can colleges prosper directed by men, very good men to be sure, but who know about every thing except about education? The man who first devised the present mode of governing colleges in this country has done us more injury than Benedict Arnold" (Rudolph, 1962, p. 172).

Finally, we list only established trends, not predictions or forecasts. The latter have been developed by many authoritative organizations (such as the National Center for Higher Education Management Systems, 1972) and by scholars, not always with great accuracy. For example, Mood (1973, p. 39) predicted that new educational technology would radically affect instructional delivery systems, changing higher education "from a labor-intensive enterprise to one that uses capital judiciously." And Brown (1972, p. 13) reported that predominantly student activism would continue its "constant ferment, and uneasy confusion. New movements will come, gain a head of steam, but will not vanish."

Organization and Structure

This section considers the impact of seven organizational and structural trends in higher education on the student services profession.

Centralization of Authority and Loss of Campus Autonomy. This trend applies most directly to the public sector and has been in progress a long time. However, in the 1960s it accelerated in nearly every state and is felt keenly by both faculty and administrators in both two-year and four-year colleges and universities. Most states with extensive public community college systems have developed state agencies to provide varying degrees of funding and regulation for institutions that once answered only to local or county boards. Almost all states now have statewide coordinating boards with purview over four-year colleges and universities. In most cases, such boards also have representation of and purview over private colleges and universities (McFarlane, Howard, and Chronister, 1974). In fact, the federally mandated state "1202 commissions," which exist in all but three states, must represent not only private colleges but also proprietary schools (Fenske and Romesburg, 1975). The loss of campus control over fundamental educational decisions and resources is severe; control is flowing especially to state budget bureaus, coordinating agency staffs, and (the newest develment) statewide "superboards" with statutory governing, coordinating and administrative power, as in Wisconsin and North Carolina.

Implications for student services are not clear, but, as control flows from faculty and campus officials, who have perpetuated the status quo and relegated student services to subsidiary functions, the flow may at the same time create an opportunity for positive changes. This is especially so because control is moving to fewer people—and to people who are less committed to and knowledgeable about current campus power structures and who may also be open to new ideas about the importance of student development.

Growing Influence of the Federal Government. The trend of growing federal influence hardly needs explication for anyone moderately informed about higher education. In a way, it is a macrocosm of the state-level trend and may present some opportunities. In particular, the Carter administration has created a separate department of education with cabinet status. Embedded in this ultimate centralization and the mass of federal dollars is a new potential for change in higher education.

It is axiomatic that expenditure of public funds requires accountability in the form of regulations and evaluation. This is especially true for federal funds appropriated for programs that represent diverse congressional views and are applied to many higher education institutions in a large number of states with inconsistent governing structures. The result has been a massive increase in the institutional burden of interpretation, compliance, and reporting related to federal regulations. This trend is likely to continue and even accelerate with passage of reauthorization legislation in 1980. Most of the proposed titles include new potential for increased regulation. If it is true that "The federal regulatory structure feeds on itself," then the already gigantic mass of regulations will spawn crushing burdens on institutions (Institute for Educational Leadership, 1976, p. 17). These burdens will have to be borne to a significant degree by an expanded student services staff, especially in the areas of affirmative action, consumerism, and financial aid. This new departure could have immense ramifications for student services and for implementation through the new and more powerful bureaucracy.

Shift of Enrollments from the Private to the Public Sector. Most private colleges and universities have problems maintaining enrollments at a desirable level and also have immediate and long-term financial difficulties. Enrollment parity between the two sectors last occurred in 1950 after a continuous 300-year history of dominance by the private sector. At present, the ratio approximates nearly five students enrolled in public institutions for every private institution enrollee. Furthermore, there is every reason to believe that the trend will continue, although it will slow down as the building of new public community colleges nears the saturation point.

Private colleges' reliance on endowment funds devalued by inflation and, increasingly, on student tuition would long ago have driven most of them into insolvency had it not been for two external factors. The most important help has come via state and federal student financial aid applicable at private colleges and universities. Most of the public funds are responsive not only to the extent of financial need of the student, but also to the cost of attending the college (public or private) of the student's choice. Because private colleges have tuition and fees much higher, on the average, than public colleges, disproportionately greater aid funds have accrued to the private sector (Fenske, Boyd, and Maxey, 1979). The second factor reducing the gap in costs between public and private sectors is that state colleges and universities have markedly raised their tuition in the last five years in response to state-level adoption of the "market model" described in Chapter One. Evidently, most state legislatures have become convinced that individual benefits accruing to college graduates should be reflected in higher costs to students.

Private college responses to these challenges and opportunities have included curricular innovations, intensive recruiting of students, and strenuous and successful efforts to obtain student financial aid. Student services professionals are heavily involved in most of these efforts. However, much of the private sector continues to be economically depressed, and maintaining the quality and quantity of student services not related to producing income or increasing enrollments is problematic. Shrinking enrollments in the private colleges and increasing depersonalization of the growing public colleges offer an opportunity for quality, highly personalized student services that is hindered by lack of funds in the private colleges.

Student Financial Aid. Federal and state student financial aid programs now provide over $12 billion, most of which is turned over to colleges and universities in the form of tuition and fees. In response to the availability of these funds, both public and private institutions have markedly increased their tuition, forcing the funding of the aid programs ever higher in a vicious cycle. One effect has, of course, been a dramatic increase in the number of financial aid administrators, enhancing the visibility and activity level of student services on nearly every campus. But another effect is to further entrench the system of budgeting and allocating financial resources on the basis of number of students enrolled and classes attended. It is axiomatic that, as long as the basic financing of the educational program is based on some measure of student time spent in a classroom with an instructor, focus will be on faculty-student ratio, not on the cost of providing education for the "whole person." Student services will thus continue to exist on the largesse of central administration and on direct response to programmatic needs (such as financial aid administration) rather than being built into an integrated budget meeting the needs of holistic education.

Student Evaluation of Teaching. Evidently evaluation of the teaching effectiveness of faculty is a general phenomenon that will exist on many, if not most, campuses for the forseeable future. The continued emphasis on it is one of the few tangible and lasting results of the student activism of the 1960s. It is also related to the persistent difficulty in evaluation of faculty effectiveness and productivity, especially in the teaching function where results are not nearly as quantifiable as research grant dollars or journal articles. On some campuses, student services become involved in the student evaluations of teaching through a testing bureau where expertise and scoring machinery already exists. This places the student services professional in a delicate and potentially vulnerable position. The process of faculty evaluation by students is essentially an adversarial one, and the resident expert and/or technician assisting the process is quite likely to get caught in the animosities inherent in this situation. Student services professionals working to serve student interests, on the one hand, and to become indispensable or at least helpful to faculty on the other could find themselves as unappreciated as the proverbial peacemaker in a family fight.

The Faculty Reward System. There seem to be at least two simultaneous trends, not necessarily countering each other, presently affecting the faculty: the reward system and its relation to other constituencies in higher education. The first is a discernible shift in emphasis from research to teaching. There are several notable exceptions. Although the shift is occurring in most institutions because of the decrease in easily obtainable research funds, some universities, especially those with an established reputation as prominent research institutions, seem to be even more research oriented than before. As grant funds become more scarce, fewer projects are awarded to marginally effective institutions, and proportionately more go to those universities with eminent faculty, facilities, and other resources. In the escalated competition for scarcer research funds, an increasing share of which flows to nonteaching research institutions such as the Brookings Institution and Educational Testing Service, fewer universities acquire significant grant awards. The much larger number of colleges and universities outside of the charmed circle are returning to an emphasis on teaching, although doctoral-degree faculty are reluctant to abandon research activity since the reward system is slow to respond to reorientations of institutional goals. The shift is much encouraged, however, by the pressure for accountability, especially by state legislatures funding the public institutions. Good teaching is a concept easily and naturally comprehended by legislatures and the public they represent, while research is much less so.

Although a return to an emphasis on teaching would seem to create an open climate among the faculty for those who might be helpful (such as student services professionals, for reasons discussed later), other trends indicate a closing of ranks to outsiders—even new faculty. These trends are the tightening of the job market for faculty and the concomitant increase in collective bargaining in higher education. The oversupply of teaching faculty stems from the leveling of enrollment growth beginning in the mid 1970s and from the entrenchment in tenured positions of the large numbers of faculty hired during the enrollment boom of the preceding fifteen years. The continuing oversupply of doctorates quickly absorbs the few faculty openings available for replacement or, more rarely, expansion purposes. And relatively few of these new recruits will move to tenure status at a normal pace, if at all. This situation tends to reduce any possibility for incursions into faculty ranks or even the tendency for the faculties to consider anyone outside the department for assistance in the teaching function that has remained an exclusive faculty prerogative.

The tendencies toward exclusiveness, to define the educational program in terms of classroom teaching by faculty, and the reluctance to view student services professionals as junior partners in the enterprise (much less as fellow faculty) is nowhere illustrated so well as in collective bargaining agreements. The faculty-administrator adversaries have considerable difficulty defining their interface during negotiations. Such difficulties often focus on the departmental or divisional chairperson level in the academic area; categorizing student services professionals as either faculty or administration is much more difficult. Decisions vary, including allocation of student services professionals into a category separate from either faculty or administration (sometimes unceremoniously lumping them with secretarial staff), but they do not preponderantly include such professionals with teaching faculty.

Thus, there are serious qualifications to Brown's (1972, p. 22) assertion that the renewed emphasis on teaching "cannot but help student personnel's relations with faculty."

Budget Cutbacks. Unquestionably, concern about the so-called new depression in higher education (Cheit, 1971) related to declining enrollments and financial problems projected for the years ahead have raised fears about repetition of what happened to "fringe areas" like student services in the Depression of the 1930s. Recent tax referendums in some states have decreased funding for higher education to an extent that promises to rival the depths of the Depression. The Newman reports (1971, 1973) and the more recent series of Carnegie Commission reports have not, in general, been supportive of greatly expanding student services except where they might contribute to financial stability of the traditional academic program. Brown (1972, p. 28) has insightfully pointed to this approach as a potential problem that has more recently accrued special urgency by declining enrollments: "The major focus of many of the recent and significant reports on higher education has been

on numbers, years, degrees, access, options, organization, and finances
. . . little direct attention has been given the impact that the suggested
changes will have on students, except for perhaps getting them in and
out of college easier and more often."

Compounding the potential problem for student services professionals is a new financial conservatism, expressed most dramatically by
the passage of Proposition 13 in California. When such cutbacks in tax
revenues are combined with a renewed emphasis on general education
entailing relatively more institutional resources for basic academic instruction, the prospects for costly student services are discouraging. In
some of the student service areas, particularly those such as counseling
and student activities that cannot demonstrate tangible benefits relative
to their costs, the appropriate slogan for professionals may well be "last
hired, first fired" unless a different basis for their value can be
established.

Students

Enrollment trends and student characteristics are examined in
considerable detail in this section. Retention, the special problems of
commuter students, and activism are also discussed as they relate to student services.

Enrollment Trends. The general leveling trend of the 1970s and
the bleak outlook for the 1980s is too well known to warrant extended
discussion. However, several side issues are of special interest to the
student services profession. The first is a coping strategy pursued by (or
thrust on) higher education; namely, the replacement of decreasing
numbers of traditional students (white, middle-class males) with an
ever-increasing diversity of new students. As discussed later, the latter are
drawn from lower socioeconomic and aptitude levels, different racial
and ethnic groups, and older age brackets and they include more females. Their appearance on the nation's campuses coincides with reduced institutional resources, not only for the private colleges, as noted
earlier, but also for the public sector as state legislatures view higher
education as lower in priority than formerly (Glenny and others, 1976).
This has confronted higher education with the dilemma of decreasing
financial resources to serve an increasing number of students with
greater needs for personnel services such as counseling (Fenske and
Scott, 1973). Somewhat ironically, increasing numbers of the traditional
types of students are attending vocational-technical programs in both
community colleges and proprietary schools where fewer student services are provided, wanted, or needed.

Some years ago, Glenny (1973) predicted that competition for students would become fierce and unbridled. Perusal of any large city newspaper's Sunday edition reveals the media advertising aspect of the competition. Less obvious are the "poaching" or "carpetbagging" activities of troubled public and private colleges as they offer dubious unregulated and unsupervised courses and programs far removed from the parent campus, often in other states. More insidious is the outright misrepresentation of program quality and student costs in efforts to enroll students. Obviously, many such efforts, legitimate or not, involve increasing numbers of student services professionals, whether called "admissions counselors," "high school relations representatives," or some other such designation. There are indications that the era of competition is just beginning. Over the last few years, institutional researchers in colleges and universities have become increasingly interested in developing marketing and enrollment-inducing strategies, as evidenced by technical papers appearing in their national association's annual publication (Fenske, 1976, 1977). At the May 1978 annual Association for Institutional Research forum, no less than twenty-three technical papers on the subject were presented in sessions with such titles as "Enrollment Projections: A Market Analysis Approach" and "Applying Marketing Research and Planning Techniques to College Admissions and Recruiting Processes." Obviously, opportunities for widely varying student services are boundless and challenge programs that prepare professionals responsible for recruiting. In contrast to the potentially lower demand for professionals in areas that do not produce any revenue (such as counseling and student activities, as noted earlier), there may be a brisk demand for recruiters who can deliver live bodies.

Student migration is, curiously enough, one of the least studied topics in all of higher education. The various services needed by students who migrate to institutions from another state are clearly greater than for local students, yet little is known about the extent and motivation for such migration. One of the very few recent studies indicated that the rate of student interstate migration is decreasing and is related to socioeconomic status (Fenske, Scott, and Carmody, 1974), while a companion study indicated that the true migration rates may be obscured by increases in migrating students who quickly establish state residency before enrolling (Carbone, 1974). Because of the radical increase in out-of-state tuition costs imposed by nearly every state, the stakes are high and encourage most migrating students to challenge existing definitions of nonresident status. The regulations and conditions involved in these controversies are so complex and legalistic that many institutions employ student service professionals who specialize in handling these problems. The situation is likely to persist and consequently will offer attractive professional opportunities.

Student Characteristics. One of the most striking recent phenomena in higher education might be called the "graying of the campus," in reference to the rapidly growing proportion of the student body that is older than the traditional undergraduate age span of eighteen to twenty-two. The change is widespread, especially in urban areas and wherever large concentrations of local older students are available. For example, the Maricopa Community College District in Arizona, which encompasses Phoenix and is the third largest in the nation, has in recent years seen the average age of its evening division students increase to over twenty-eight (Maricopa Community College District, 1978). Older adults have special needs, motivations, and apprehensions that heavily involve student services professionals, and their enrollment rate has not yet peaked. Another facet of this phenomenon involves the return to campus of many mid-career professionals and managers who are responding to new certification and upgrading requirements imposed on them by professional associations and employers.

An intriguing potential for new clientele for liberal arts colleges, both private and public, lies in the linkage between (1) the interest of many middle-aged adults in liberal arts, humanistic, and artistic educational programs and (2) demographic projections that show that the size of this age group will increase rapidly in the near future. Many psychological theorists have identified the middle years (thirty-five to fifty) of most adults as the period in which there is a renewed interest in introspection and in integrating knowledge, experience, and personal destiny (Levinson and others, 1978; Neugarten and others, 1964; Vaillant and McArthur, 1972). Most middle-aged people are established in their careers (or beginning new ones) and are no longer heavily involved in rearing young children. In contrast to the drastic shrinkage of the number of eighteen-year-olds in the decades ahead, the number of middle-aged people will almost double during the period from 1975 to the year 2000. Although many educational needs of these adults will center around career-related programs, there will be a significant reservoir of interest in liberal arts and related programs like the humanities and fine arts. Since many of these adults have the time and financial means to pursue their interests, the liberal arts colleges will have an opportunity to serve them and, in so doing, not only survive but persevere in their traditional role rather than switch to different types of programs. In this process, student services professionals will be called on to provide specialized personal counseling for the new adult clientele related to problems of re-entry into formal education. These professionals may even assist in the curricular adaptation necessary to meet the particular academic needs and interests of middle-aged adults.

Federal legislation and categorical financial aid have provided many racial and ethnic minorities with access in the past fifteen years. Of the racial groups, blacks have increased enrollment rates the most, far exceeding those of Spanish-speaking groups and American Indians. Attention by organized minority groups has expanded beyond access to include questions of choice of college and program and, further, to consider the relative quality and outcomes (such as type of career placement) of these educational experiences. In general, teaching faculty have not been anxious to commit themselves to minority programs (Grant and Hoeber, 1978, p. 37).

A quiet revolution has recently occurred in American higher education, and has established a trend that persists. In the 1976–77 academic year, the number of women enrolling as first-time students exceeded that of men for the first time in history. This event had been predicted some years earlier (Fenske and Scott, 1973, p. 46); however, it seems to have caught higher education by some surprise. There have been for many years more females than males in each succeeding high school graduation class, however, the higher education enrollment rates had been lower for females because of societal attitudes giving familial preference to males and because of the lack of financial aid to offset such attitudes. Contributing to the new predominance of female enrollments was the return to education of many middle-aged women, many of whom are actively preparing for entry-level employment in a wide variety of careers. Special student services are often needed by such women, especially personal and academic counseling as well as vocational interest testing.

Widened access to higher education has resulted in the enrollment of increasing numbers of students with relatively poor academic achievement, in terms of rank in high school class, and poor academic aptitude as measured by college admission tests. This trend is discussed later in the context of the consequent growth of remedial, compensatory, and academic orientation programs.

Widening access to include over half of the traditional age group has interacted with the massive programs of student financial aid mentioned previously. Entitlement programs, in particular the Basic Educational Opportunity Grants and the widespread state-level grants have encouraged many hundreds of thousands of young people to seek admission to colleges and universities who would otherwise not have been able to attend because of inadequate financial resources. However, these grants provide only part of the total funds needed, calculated at approximately one half of the total cost of attending college. The remainder is generated through a variable "package" of other resources, including loans, other grants, parental assistance, and employment.

Recent research has shown another, somewhat unexpected effect of the wide availability of financial aid. Many students have used access to such funds to declare early economic emancipation from their parents, throwing the entire burden of support on the grant and loan programs, along with an increased tendency to earn more and work longer hours while in school. Another finding has been that parents contribute less for college expenses of their children than is expected by calculations of formulas based on income and college costs (Boyd and Fenske, 1976, 1977). Thus, many students who receive financial aid work more and receive less from home than is indicated by the formulas used to determine their grants. These factors affect academic efficiency and social life in ways that can be ameliorated by effective student services programs. Student financial aid is the major new thrust in financing higher education in the 1970s, yet programs to specifically prepare student services professionals for these critically important responsibilities are conspicuous by their scarcity.

Retention. The prospect of shrinking enrollments in most colleges and universities has led to a new interest in retaining students through completion of their programs. In dealing with this problem, academic administrators have noted that retaining live bodies already enrolled has much more potential and can be much cheaper than scouring the countryside amid increasing competition for a shrinking number of potential enrollees. For example, if the dropout rate is approximately 50 percent over a four-year program in a student body of 1,000, and if the rate could be reduced by one half, this has the same effect as locating, recruiting, and enrolling 250 new students over that period each year, assuming a consistent rate. Student services of many types can be effective in this process, including counseling, housing, financial aid, and others.

Commuter Students. As mentioned in Chapter One the Truman Commission in 1947 had suggested two principal strategies in widening access to higher education; namely, student financial aid and the proliferation of locally available commuter colleges, especially junior and community colleges. It is unlikely that even the most visionary of the commission members could have foreseen the dramatic growth in number of commuter students since that time. Many urban universities have been established since the early 1960s, and many formerly private or municipal colleges and universities in urban areas have been added to state systems and greatly expanded. However, the major growth factor has been the building of hundreds of public community colleges, which have for many years been the type of higher education institutions with the fastest growth rate. Assuming that nearly all of the community college students are commuters, it is probable that over half of all first-time students in the nation can be classified as commuting students ("Opening Fall Enrollments in 1975, 1976, and 1977," 1978). Such students have special need for services designed to give them a sense of community with their college (as in student unions and activities) and in effective study habits and other coping strategies. Yet it is doubtful that these students are at present adequately served, especially on campuses not specifically designed for commuters or where commuters are mixed with resident students. In many cases, they tend to be on campus only long enough to attend classes, neither seeking nor being offered helpful student services. Little seems to be done in a systematic way to adapt student services to meet this new challenge.

Student Activism. Despite the dire predictions of the early 1970s, student activism as an educationally disruptive process has all but disappeared on most campuses. Replacing it is a widespread indifference on the part of most students to any cause but earning a degree and finding a job. Those who remain active in student government or student organizations tend to be *much* more sophisticated than before, especially in terms of litigation (or at least the threat of it) and working through the legislative system. More permanent student representation on governing boards and campus academic committees has been achieved in the last few years than in any previous period.

Beyond these developments, a recent (August 1978) merger of the two major national student associations creates, for the first time in this country, the potential for a student guild or union of immense power ("Will Merger. . . ," 1978, p. 23). The merger occurs at a particularly auspicious time for an increase in student power. This receptive climate is created at least partly by two recent trends in higher education (1) the "market model" of financing higher education through students as consumers with economic power provided by student financial aid and (2) increasing competition among colleges and universities for the declining number of potential enrollees. Thus, the new U.S. Student Association formed by the recent merger could provide students with group status approaching that of faculty and administration. One can envision a campus student organization ultimately joining faculty and administration at the collective bargaining negotiation table as an equal "party of the third part." These potential developments have positive implications for student services because it can safely be assumed that students would press for improved service of the type provided by the profession.

Whatever the eventual level of power achieved by the newly reorganized student groups, these developments call for responsive levels of sophistication by student services professionals, especially in the area of law and political procedures.

Curriculum and Program

The following discussion of trends and issues in curricular programs relates to opportunities for student services professionals to work more closely with faculty, administration, and trustees. Several curricular trends have been developing for many decades and apparently are still under way. These include continuing fragmentation of what was once a cohesive, unitary program, a steady and inexorable shift away from liberal education toward vocationalism, and increasingly earlier specialization of major field by students. The first two have been discussed in Chapter One, the third will be commented on here briefly. The Carnegie Council on Policy Studies in Higher Education recently sponsored the publication of two important books on the undergraduate curriculum that corroborate all these trends and present new findings on early specialization (Carnegie Foundation for the Advancement of Teaching, 1977; Levine, 1978). In their analysis, the undergraduate curriculum is composed of three main parts: (1) the major field, (2) general education or nonmajor required courses, and (3) electives. They indicate that the first of these components continues to expand at the expense of the other two. Furthermore, the growth of the major is larger than appears in various surveys because departments often require or recommend selection of general education or "elective" courses that are closely aligned with the major. An obvious example would be an engineering college that recommends or requires courses outside the college to be in mathematics, physics, and computer sciences. In some cases, an engineering student has only a few "optional" courses during his or her four-year program.

All these trends have implications for student services, but the need for academic and career interest counseling is particularly pressing for first-year students faced with urgent decisions regarding major field and course selection. A frequent and apparently valid criticism is that such advising usually occurs without benefit of information about the first-year student's vocational interests, background of career experience, or personal preferences and problems. Levine (1978, p. 154) pointed out that "advising divides students into academic, vocational, and personal components and places emphasis largely on the academic, making complete student counseling difficult and in some cases impossible."

Although the trends toward continuing fragmentation of the curriculum and earlier forced choice of major seem inexorable, there are some encouraging signs for those who value general education. Ernest Boyer, former commissioner of the U.S. Office of Education and current president of the Carnegie Foundation for the Advancement of Teaching, has coauthored a seminal book on the need for a core curriculum (Boyer and Kaplan, 1977), and such influential institutions as Harvard and Stanford are recommending changes supporting the expansion of general education. It would seem possible to reinstate some semblance of the former role of general education in the short term by institutional fiat, but the prospects for a permanent status are not bright in the consumer-oriented curriculum now offered by most colleges and universities. Even Harvard, the historic leader in curriculum reform, will evidently experience problems. "Harvard recently revised its core so that students will have to take one or more courses in these five categories: literature and the arts; history; social and philosophical analysis; science and mathematics; and foreign language and culture. The changes have provoked some students. Says Gail Sokoloff, a first-year Harvard student, 'I don't believe Harvard has a right to define what an educated person is.' Adds Eric Fried, a sophomore, 'They shouldn't be telling us what to know when we get out of here. You can't force information down somebody's throat' "("Making College Tougher," 1978, p. 66). The increasingly intense competition for students, lack of consensus on the core content, and the "consumer sovereignty" that prevails at nearly all institutions mitigate against a rebirth of general education.

Innovative Programs in Institutions. There has been almost incessant activity in curriculum experimentation and innovation during the last twenty years, much of which has been funded from external sources. Yet the overall impact of these hundreds of programs has not reversed, stabilized, or even slowed the general trends identified earlier (fragmentation of the curriculum, balkanization and continual subdividing of academic departments, vocationalization, early specialization, student consumerism), nor have they notably changed the mainstream and general parameters of the academic program in higher education. Degrees are still awarded generally on the basis of four years of classroom study on a campus, a practice established in the Middle Ages, with completion dependent on accumulation of degree credits that signify units of time spent in contact with an instructor, a system established over a century ago (Levine, 1978, pp. 156–159).

Many of the innovations have directly addressed problems and shortcomings in the American undergraduate curriculum. As a few notable examples, contract learning counters the decreasing individualization in colleges; cooperative education overcomes the problem of irrelevance; cluster colleges and living-learning centers deal effectively with the bifurcation of students' social and academic life; and programmed and modular instructional systems provide for differences in individual learning rates. Good ideas and energetic innovators have not been lacking in attempts to change and improve the curriculum.

Of more immediate interest to student services professionals are those innovative programs that directly involve their expertise and participation and/or attempt to provide the type of holistic education that represents the goal of the profession. Both Tollefson (1975) and Miller and Prince (1976) extensively list and discuss such programs.

Both the more general curriculum innovations and those related to student services goals have several characteristics in common:

1. They are generally more costly than traditional programs, both in operating expenditures and in staff and faculty time.
2. Nearly all of those that directly involve faculty require diversion from the standard reward system in the sense that Tollefson termed the "expensive luxury" of "wasting time on student involvement" (1975, p. 18) and in the inherent tension in trying to "serve two masters: The students and the journal editors" (Brown, 1972, p. 22).
3. They offer no equally or more appealing alternative to the reward system for faculty other than intrinsic and altruistic satisfactions derived from extended contact with student development.
4. They tend to be short-lived, often extending little beyond the immediate funding cycle of internal or external support.
5. They do not often affect the mainstream of the curriculum, either in goals or practices.

It is not unduly skeptical to note also that students are well aware that long-term involvement in a curricular innovation that does not culminate in standard and easily recognizable degrees, credits, and grades can be counterproductive for career goals and acceptance into graduate schools, those most conservative of all educational organizations. In fact, as I have noted elsewhere, reluctance and withdrawal of student participation have probably been as much to blame for failure of curriculum experiments as have faculty and administrative heel-dragging (Fenske, 1973).

Despite these somewhat gloomy warnings, the current flurry of activity and interest in revitalizing general education, external funding for curricular experiments (notably through the federal Fund for the Improvement of Postsecondary Education), and the student development-oriented programs listed by Tollefson, Miller and Prince, and others signal a continuing ferment that *may* yield significant opportunities for student services professionals to enter the main arena of the academic program.

External Program Initiatives. It is probable that more curricular innovations that have promise of permanency and involve more people are occurring outside of what we have defined as higher education institutions than are occurring within those institutions. They involve two new dimensions: (1) unconventional organizational structures and instructional delivery systems and (2) academic degree credit awarded for personal and occupational experiences as an alternative to the standard classroom basis. The two dimensions are often, but not necessarily, involved in the same program.

No census of these external programs exists at present; however, two organizations have recently emerged that attempt to interpret the activities, especially experiential learning, to the traditional higher education community. One is a unit of the prestigious American Council on Education, the Office of Educational Credit; the other is an autonomous group, the Council for the Advancement of Experiential Learning, which represents over 300 organizations, including colleges and universities, promoting the validation and use of credit for experience.

In terms of organizational structure, the new programs are often aptly described by their names: the Open University, University Without Walls, and the Capital Higher Educational Service. They usually serve mostly adults older than the typical undergraduate age range of eighteen to twenty-two and attempt to deal with the special needs and characteristics of this group. Their programs generally focus on the reluctance or inability of this clientele to be resident on a campus for extended periods or even to travel very far for group meetings or classes. They also relate to the middle-aged or older adults' dissatisfaction with starting "at the beginning" without recognition of past accomplishments. Much of the contemporary literature of higher education deals with these new programs (see especially Carnegie Foundation for the Advancement of Teaching, 1977, and Levine, 1978), but to date there has been little commentary on how they will affect student services professionals. Clearly, many such professionals are needed on the staffs of these programs because a major thrust is diagnosis of prior academic record, nonacademic experiences to be evaluated for credit, and the development of a total "package" leading to a degree or some other acceptable outcome.

What may be of more direct interest is the extent to which these program innovations will ultimately, and sometimes immediately, affect student services professionals in traditional colleges and universities, especially those serving in admissions, records, and counseling. Many of the students now enrolled in these "external degree" programs will arrive on conventional campuses expecting credit for their courses and recognition of their degrees. Furthermore, traditional institutions may well have to set up their own versions of such service programs. For example, the concept of credit for experiential learning is, perhaps naturally, increasingly popular. Levine reports (1978, pp. 218-219), "Thirteen percent of undergraduates report receiving credit for experiential learning or work experience outside college. . . The concept is popular among students. Fifty-five percent would like to be able to earn credit for experiential learning (Carnegie Surveys, 1975-76)."

Because academic departments may well be expected to show a profound lack of enthusiasm for direct involvement in translating social and career experiences into academic credit, the student services professional may serve well in this capacity, even though it may be seen as analogous to a reclamation or recycling center.

Remedial and Compensatory Programs. During each period of rapid expansion in higher education, courses and programs were developed in most institutions to bring incoming students up to the desired level of preparation for "regular" college work. This is as true now in the era of the so-called new student (Cross, 1972) as it was at the inception of the colonial colleges.

To students of the history of American higher education, the current furor over the "lowering of standards" involved in widening access to colleges and universities seems ironic. The same criticisms were made in each expansion era, even when the new additions to the higher education student body only added relatively small increments to a group that represented 5 or 6 percent of the age cohort. The hundreds of colleges established in the early nineteenth century by every major religious denomination offered pioneer children a level of education that was higher learning in name only, because all but a few of their students had completed only a primary education. Even in the early decades of the now-prestigious state universities, in the middle and later periods of the nineteenth century, the *majority* of students were in subcollegiate courses designed to ready them for higher education. For example, at the University of Wisconsin "as late as 1865, only 41 out of 331 registered students were in 'regular' college classes. The rest were in the preparatory department, the 'normal' department, or were classified as 'specials' " (Curti and Carstensen, 1949, p. 187). According to Sizer (1964, p. 36), "As late as 1894 such students still comprised over 40 percent of the entering students in American colleges." The periods of rapid expansion in the 1920s and in the immediate post-World War II era also saw strenuous efforts by the colleges to prepare and upgrade student skills to a collegiate level.

Two basic types of programs or courses are relevant to this discussion. The first might be termed "college-coping" courses designed to acclimatize and socialize the new student to the college environment and its academic demands rather than to overcome educational deficiencies. These, too, have a long history (see Cross, 1976, pp. 24–27) and were periodically very popular, as for example, in helping the G.I. Bill students cope with college. They enjoy current popularity as an aftermath of student activism and the current interest in consumer protection for students. Most often they are offered under the auspices of the student services administration and have little direct or permanent connection with degree credit or academic departments. At Arizona State University, for example, short-term and semester-length courses and programs are offered as orientation to study skills, use of the library, dealing with the bureaucracy, obtaining financial aid, course selection, and so forth. Illustrative is a course entitled "University Adjustment and Survival" and offered to mature women returning to college.

The other type of program not only is widespread among various kinds of higher education institutions but also is the center of a continually swirling controversy that even includes high schools. Generally termed "compensatory education," it includes both remedial and developmental aspects (Levine, 1978, p. 55). The general concept involves preparing students for eligibility to enter academic programs and to enrich the capability of students for academic success in college by overcoming deprivations caused by inadequate prior schooling and home environment.

Three factors seem related to the massive growth in such programs in recent years: (1) the widening of participation in college to include many more students from the middle and lower third of high school rank in ability and achievement; (2) the enrolling of various racial and ethnic groups whose socioeconomic background, cultural alienation, and educational deprivation create intense areas of academic deficiency; and (3) the well-publicized precipitous and continuing decline in admissions test scores. In regard to the last factor, intensive and extensive studies have failed to clearly isolate causes, although consensus seems to be growing that the rise in proportion of low scores is related to the increased numbers of minority and educationally disadvantaged taking the admissions tests. The decrease in "high-end" scores is evidently caused by many interrelated factors. The overall lowering of scores may result from reduced exposure to academic courses in high schools (see Levine, 1978, pp. 69–74).

Whatever the causes, the result has been large numbers of first-time students unprepared to meet the demands of even the most rudimentary first-year courses, especially in mathematics and English. Although this situation was expected to some degree in the community colleges, it arrived at the doorstep of all types of colleges and universities in the late 1960s and throughout the 1970s (Levine, 1978, p. 67). Liberal arts colleges as well as such major universities as Harvard, Columbia, and Minnesota all felt the need to provide compensatory education, and it was "reported that 40 to 65 percent of the incoming freshmen at the University of California were required to take remedial English courses in 1975" (Carnegie Foundation for the Advancement of Teaching, 1977, p. 210).

In view of the extreme specialization and orientation toward graduate education and research of the faculty reward system, it is easy to conjecture about faculty attitudes toward teaching at high school (and sometimes lower) levels in order to remedy past academic deficiencies and prepare prospective students for at least first-year-caliber courses. To paraphrase an old axiom in higher education, enthusiasm for offering remedial courses is in inverse relation to the likelihood of having to teach them. Although few are as blunt as the academician quoted by Cross (1976, p. 27) who warned against "allowing conditions to deteriorate to a point where qualified instructors are forced to dissipate their energies on undeserving students. . . . A college can hardly do very much for students of low academic ability," the fact remains that hardly any activity could be more onerous and less productive of professional advancement than teaching or tutoring in subcollegiate programs. The Carnegie Foundation for the Advancement of Teaching (1977, p. 220) inferred as much when it recommended that the college community should be scoured to find personnel for manning skill development centers, including unemployed new doctorates, advanced undergraduates, faculty members' spouses, retired faculty or schoolteachers, but conspicuously excluded regular departmental faculty. After a national survey, Roueche and Kirk (1973, p. 7) concluded that, although they found that remedial programs "have largely been ineffective," some factors were associated with success, the primary one being that only volunteer faculty are used.

Thus, it would seem that compensatory education offers an unparalleled opportunity for student services professionals to work in tandem in an enterprise essential to the teaching function. Departmental faculty recognize that they necessarily are involved and directly affected by compensatory programs. First, they must deal with the students "remediated" by such programs directly in their regular courses; second, remedial work can hardly be accomplished unless standards are determined. For example, it is difficult to see how the English or mathematics departments could avoid involvement at least to the extent of providing mastery exams in their subjects to determine readiness for regular courses. Where compensatory education comprises remediation or development in academic skills, it encompasses the ken of both teaching faculty and student services professionals: Much individual student diagnosis and counseling is involved as well as teaching and/or tutoring of at least rudimentary subject matter. If current trends are any indication, there will be more compensatory programs in the near future. Furthermore, the trend toward awarding degree credit for remedial courses (Cross, 1976, p. 44) and the fact that student services professionals generally staff the programs bring them into a direct participation with departmental faculty and their academic role, although the relationship is little recognized and even less appreciated by faculty.

Summary

This chapter identifies some contemporary trends and issues that influence the student services professional. The criterion used for selection of trends and issues was their relationship to one or more of the following problems or challenges now confronting the profession. These include (1) alienation from the mainstream academic functions of teaching, research, and service, resulting in little recognition and support from either faculty or central administration; (2) allegiance to the conviction that colleges and universities should develop the "whole person" and the frustration that results from the realization that this conviction generally has little support from others in the institution; and (3) most of the recent changes in higher education further reduce the likelihood that teaching faculty and/or administration will join forces with student services professionals to reinstate a holistic student development approach.

Some of the problem areas seem more than merely persistent; they seem permanent and basically irreversible. It is highly useful to identify such problems so that efforts at amelioration can be better made elsewhere. The historical overview offered in Chapter One helps in discriminating between trends with possibilities for positive change and those that simply confirm established patterns in higher education. For example, the trends since World War II that emphasize research at the expense of teaching and the virtual extinction of faculty concern for noncognitive student development have entrenched the faculty reward system.

Despite this rather depressing litany of significant and persistent problems, several current trends and issues suggest possibilities for improvement, and it is on this note that this chapter concludes.

Foremost among the promising trends is the possibility for making common cause with teaching faculty in the area of remedial and compensatory and of "college-coping" courses for the increasing numbers of students who need them. In this area, faculty would probably welcome the assistance of student services professionals in the diagnosis and remediation of subcollegiate student aptitude and achievement. The most useful strategy in terms of eventual partnership in the academic functions with faculty would be *not* to co-opt such programs but to ensure that they are joint enterprises of the department and appropriate student services divisions. Successful operation of the programs will suggest further cooperation.

Some current organizational changes indicate potential weakening of the present institutional structure, which effectively locks student services professionals out of the primary academic functions. Continuing loss of campus autonomy to system, state, and even federal levels of administration and authority could create an opportunity for renewed interest in student development if, and only if, the higher levels of administration can be effectively persuaded to induce changes in this direction. In effect, this would involve "going over the heads" of campus power groups—always a delicate process, to say the least.

Finally, there seems to be considerable promise in the steady growth of student power, not as an educationally disruptive force but as an effective and legal participant in decision making in higher education. The student services professional should never be in an adversarial relationship with students, who comprise the one other constituency in higher education with similar goals and interests. Because of the growth in student economic power as consumer, the federal laws and regulations protecting their rights, and the impressive political potential represented by the newly merged national organizations, students and the campus professionals who should directly serve them and their interests could form a powerful coalition. The joining of interests of student services professionals and newly powerful organized student groups should create a most encouraging potential for improving higher education.

References

Boyd, J. D., and Fenske, R. H. "Financing of a College Education: Theory Versus Reality." *Journal of Student Financial Aid*, 1976, *6* (2), 13–21.

Boyd, J. D., and Fenske, R. H. *The Illinois State Scholarship Commission Monetary Award Program: A Longitudinal Analysis, 1967–1977.* Deerfield: Illinois State Scholarship Commission, 1977.

Boyer, E. L., and Kaplan, M. *Educating for Survival.* New York: Change Magazine Press, 1977.

Brown, R. D. *Student Development in Tomorrow's Higher Education—A Return to the Academy.* Washington, D.C.: American Personnel and Guidance Association, 1972.

Carbone, R. F. *Students and State Borders.* Iowa City, Iowa: American College Testing Program, 1974.

Carnegie Commission on Higher Education. *The Purposes and Performance of Higher Education in the United States.* New York: McGraw-Hill, 1973.

Carnegie Foundation for the Advancement of Teaching. *Missions of the College Curriculum: A Contemporary Review with Suggestions.* San Francisco: Jossey-Bass, 1977.

Cheit, E. *The New Depression in Higher Education.* New York: McGraw-Hill, 1971.

Cross, K. P. *New Students and New Needs in Higher Education.* Berkeley: Center for Research and Development in Higher Education, University of California, 1972.

Cross, K. P. *Accent on Learning: Improving Instruction and Reshaping the Curriculum.* San Francisco: Jossey-Bass, 1976.

Curti, M. E., and Carstensen, V. *The University of Wisconsin, A History.* Madison: University of Wisconsin Press, 1949.

Fenske, R. H. "Book Review of *The Best Laid Plans.*" *Journal of Higher Education,* 1973, *44,* 655–658.

Fenske, R. H. (Ed.). *Conflicting Pressures in Postsecondary Education.* Tallahassee, Fla.: Association for Institutional Research, 1976.

Fenske, R. H. *Research and Planning for Higher Education.* Tallahassee, Fla.: Association for Institutional Research, 1977.

Fenske, R. H., Boyd, J. D., and Maxey, E. J. "State Financial Aid to Students: A Trend Analysis of Access and Choice of Public or Private College." *College and University,* 1979, *54,* 139–155.

Fenske, R. H., and Romesburg, K. D. (Eds.). *Current Status, Planning and Prospects of the 1202 State Postsecondary Commissions.* Phoenix: Arizona Commission for Postsecondary Education, 1975.

Fenske, R. H., and Scott, C. S. *The Changing Profile of College Students.* Washington, D.C.: American Association for Higher Education, 1973.

Fenske, R. H., Scott, C. S., and Carmody, J. F. "Recent Trends in Studies of Student Migration." *Journal of Higher Education,* 1974, *45,* 61–74.

Glenny, L. A. "A Golden Age for Students, a Precarious Era for Students." Paper delivered at the Special Seminars in Education, American College Testing Program, Iowa City, Iowa, October, 1973.

Glenny, L. A., and others. *Presidents Confront Reality: From Edifice Complex to University Without Walls.* San Francisco: Jossey-Bass, 1976.

Grant, M. K., and Hoeber, D. R. *Basic Skills Programs: Are They Working?* Washington, D.C.: American Association For Higher Education, 1978.

Institute for Educational Leadership. *Perspectives on Federal Educational Policy.* Washington, D.C.: George Washington University, 1976.

Levine, A. *Handbook on Undergraduate Curriculum.* San Francisco: Jossey-Bass, 1978.

Levinson, D., and others. *The Seasons of a Man's Life.* New York: Knopf, 1978.

McFarlane, W. H., Howard, A. E., and Chronister, J. L. *State Financial Measures Involving the Private Sector of Higher Education.* Washington D.C.: National Council of Independent Colleges and Universities, 1974.

"Making College Tougher: Will the Trend Spread?" *U.S. News and World Report,* 1978, *84,* 66.

Maricopa Community College District. *Factbook.* Phoenix: Maricopa Community College District, 1978.

Miller, T. K., and Prince, J. S. *The Future of Student Affairs: A Guide to Student Development for Tomorrow's Higher Education.* San Francisco: Jossey-Bass, 1976.

Mood, A. M. *The Future of Higher Education.* New York: McGraw-Hill, 1973.

Mueller, K. H. *Student Personnel Work in Higher Education.* Boston: Houghton Mifflin, 1961.

National Center for Higher Education Management Systems. *A Forecast of Changes in Postsecondary Education.* (V. Huckfeldt, Ed.) Boulder, Colo.: Western Interstate Commission for Higher Education, 1972.

Neugarten, B., and others. *Personality in Middle and Late Life.* New York: Alberto Press, 1964.

Newman, F. *Report on Higher Education.* Washington, D.C.: U.S. Government Printing Office, 1971.

Newman, F. *The Second Newman Report: National Policy and Higher Education.* Cambridge, Mass.: M.I.T. Press, 1973.

"Opening Fall Enrollments in 1975, 1976, and 1977." *Chronicle of Higher Education,* 1978, *15,* 10.

Pace, C. R. *Education and Evangelism: A Profile of Protestant Colleges.* New York: McGraw-Hill, 1972.

Roueche, J. E., and Kirk, R. W. *Catching Up: Remedial Education.* San Francisco: Jossey-Bass, 1973.

Rudolph, F. *The American College and University.* New York: Knopf, 1962.

Sizer, W. *Secondary Schools at the Turn of the Century.* New Haven, Conn.: Yale University Press, 1964.

Tollefson, A. L. *New Approaches to College Student Development.* New York: Behavioral Publications, 1975.

Vaillant, G. E., and McArthur, C. C. "Natural History of the Male Psychological Health. I: The Adult Life Cycle from 18–50." *Seminars in Psychiatry,* 1972, *4*(4), 415–427.

"Will Merger of Two Big Student Groups Lead to Revival of the 'Movement'?" Chronicle of Higher Education, 1978, *16*, 23.

Williamson, E. G. *Trends in Student Personnel Work.* Minneapolis: University of Minnesota Press, 1949.

Wrenn, C. G., and Bell, R. *Student Personnel Problems.* New York: Farrar, Straus & Giroux, 1942.

PART II

Theoretical Bases of the Profession

The first section of this book presented the philosophical ideas and historical trends that influence the student services profession. Ideas and thoughts alone, however, are not enough to guide our practice. One idea must relate to another in an organized and systematic fashion if we are to use them in our day-to-day work. Although the models to be described in Part Three will help us organize our practice, we need theory as the conceptual cement for our ideas.

Organizing and ordering ideas into theory allows us to accomplish several important tasks. First, theory helps us to organize data, the useful facts that we collect. To use data in our programming efforts from year to year, it is best to store the ideas systematically according to theoretical guidelines. If we have a theory that deals with young adults' social development, we can remember what we learned earlier about the social interaction of men and women if we relate those facts to our theory. This marriage between theory and facts should culminate in a better organization of those bits and pieces of information that we find valuable in our daily practice.

A second use of theory is to better explain to others what we do. A casual observer of our professional activities may have difficulty understanding what we do and, more importantly, why we do it. Theory not only helps explain what we are doing but it also defines our goals and thereby provides a rationale for why we engage in certain activities. When administrators and state legislators ask what we are doing and why we have initiated such services, we should be able to respond more clearly if we use our theory.

Theory also aids our everyday decisions. The details of providing student services raise innumerable questions regarding money, staffing, resources, goals, policies, and politics. Usually, each question will have multiple options, and rarely will there be a right or wrong decision. Value judgments can best be guided by theory, which supplies the boundaries of our options for action and describes the process for achieving our goals.

Finally, theory helps us to dream about the future. Rarely are student affairs professionals content with their current efforts: programs could be improved, costs could be cut, and students could achieve greater satisfaction if only we could design that ideal program or service—an ideal that should arise from theory. Examination of the ideal programs and services that theory suggests will also help us evaluate whether our dreams can become reality.

We believe that student affairs professionals should be familiar with two basic areas of theory. Because we work with students daily, we must understand how they learn, grow, and develop. In Chapter Four, Carol Widick, Lee Knefelkamp, and Clyde A. Parker raise four critical questions that help us compare various theories of college student development. These theories should help us understand how development occurs, how colleges influence student development, what kinds of developmental changes take place in college students, and toward what ends student development should be directed. Each theory that they review provides a slightly different perspective for examining these critical issues. Taken together, these theories stimulate our thinking about the growth and development of college students.

We also realize the importance of a second major theoretical area—educational environments and their impact on students. We sense that certain learning environments have a greater impact on students than others and that we can use theory to design different kinds of environments to meet the needs of students with different learning characteristics. Lois Huebner reviews several major theories and examines how environments affect people, why matching people with environments is important, and how we can best assess environments. Perhaps the most important contribution of Chapter Five is in the strategies that suggest ways to channel the impact of environments on people in maximally effective ways.

Carole Widick
Lee Knefelkamp
Clyde A. Parker

4

Student Development

From the beginning (Paterson, 1928), and reemphasized in *The Student Personnel Point of View* (American Council on Education, 1937), student services professionals adopted a developmental orientation emphasizing responding to the whole person, attending to individual differences, and working with students at their level of development. Yet in the 1960s several members of the profession (Parker, 1973; Penny, 1969) observed that we lacked a knowledge base to guide our developmental philosophy. For example, less than ten years ago Kenneth Keniston (1968, p. 3) said, "We have no psychology apart from the work of Erik Erikson to adequately understand the feelings and behavior of today's American youth." His lament was particularly noteworthy after a decade of extensively studying young adults who attended college. Keniston's comment pointed to the critical gap in our knowledge base; we did not have theoretical models that could effectively describe college students and provide us with a coherent picture of individual development—a theory on which we could base our practice.

In the decade since Keniston's essay, theories and models of college student development have flourished. In a relatively brief period of time, the work of the following theorists was published or, in some cases, reissued: Arthur Chickering (1969), Douglas Heath (1968), Roy

Heath (1964, 1973), Peter Madison (1969), David Hunt (1966, 1970), Lawrence Kohlberg (1969, 1972, 1975). These theorists acknowledge their debt to and refocus our attention on the earlier writings of Theodore Newcomb (Newcomb and others, 1967), Joseph Katz and Nevitt Sanford (1962), Jean Piaget (1964), N. Sanford (1966), and R. W. White (1975), and the early work of Erikson (1963). The writings of person-environment interaction theorists (Pace, 1967; Stern, 1970; Clark and Trow, 1966; Holland, 1966) have also attracted interest and been used with increasing frequency. Most recently, attention has focused on the adult years; Daniel Levinson (1978), Roger Gould (1972), Bernice Neugarten (1964, 1976), and George Vaillant (1977), among others, have presented models of adult development that are important aids to understanding the increasing number of adult learners attending colleges.

Clearly, we no longer lack models of college student development. We have models, many of which represent careful, data-based effort. But we also have several new problems:

1. How to keep up with the knowledge explosion
2. How to make sense of the many models
3. How to translate the models into useful and helpful tools in our work as student services professionals.

This chapter primarily focuses on the second problem: How does one make sense of the many different theories and models that exist? As a starting point, we briefly consider the relationship between developmental theory and our professional practice because, in a way, we "make sense" of theory by using it. Later we will comment briefly on how to transform formal theory into personal theories of action.

Nevitt Sanford is the theorist who has helped us examine the relationship between student development and practice in the broad sense. Sanford's most important writings describe a general process underlying a developmental approach to practice. Sanford has consistently argued that college should be a developmental community that both challenges and supports students.

Development involves an "upending" that brings about new, more differentiated responses. However, if the challenge or disequilibrium is too great, the individual retreats; if the supports are too protective, the individual fails to develop. In essence, the student services professional must create a delicate balance of challenges and supports to encourage student development.

Yet how does one go about such a task? What should be challenged? Toward what ends should one be challenged? What is a challenge? What is a support? Sanford's concepts of challenge and support are a crucial interface between the developing student and the programs we provide. However, if educators are to encourage development, they must know what development is—what changes can, do, and should take place in students and what particular factors challenge and support those changes. From our perspective, the creation of a developmental community requires a theoretical empirical knowledge base to answer these questions:

1. Who is the college student in developmental terms? What developmental changes occur and what do those changes look like?
2. How does the process of development occur? What are the psychological and social processes that cause development?
3. How can college environments influence student development? What factors in the particular and distinctive environment of a college or university can either encourage or inhibit growth?
4. Toward what ends should development in college be directed?

Knowledge in these four areas would give specific and concrete meaning to the task of encouraging student development. Such knowledge would allow us to articulate feasible development goals and design interventions that take into account "where students are" and draw on the processes underlying developmental change. Thus, given the purposes of our profession, the "making sense" of student development theory involves identifying how and to what extent a theory (1) describes the nature of young adult and adult development, and (2) explains the processes developmental change, in a higher education context.

Originally, we turned to the theoretical literature hoping to find or create *the* comprehensive student development theory that would lead us directly to *the* steps involved in creating a developmental community. As we searched the literature, we found different theorists using different language to describe and explain different aspects of development. Our initial immersion in various authors often left us uncertain of the meaning of a given theory and more often befuddled in the attempt to compare and integrate the various models. We found ourselves asking, "What does Chickering mean by the term *vectors?* Are they the same as Erikson's *stages?* Keniston's *sectors?* Are the lines of development set forth by Douglas Heath related to Chickering's vectors or to Loevinger's stages? Are Erikson's stages similar to Kohlberg's stages? Perry's positions? Is type descriptive of people (R. Heath), the environment, or both (Holland)?"

Perhaps the search for a grand design is always ill fated; we did not find nor could we create the comprehensive model of student development. Yet, our search led to a clearer view of the various theories and suggested potential contributions to practice. The different theories can best be seen as a mosaic of necessary pieces. In fact, the theories seem to cluster into five categories or families. Each family of theories shares certain basic assumptions and uses similar constructs to describe development or point to influential factors in development. The five theory clusters are

1. Psychosocial theories
2. Cognitive developmental theories
3. Maturity models
4. Typology models
5. Person-environment interaction models

We believe that each cluster provides a useful vantage point from which to view college students; moreover, these theory clusters outline the parameters that need to be addressed in a student development approach to practice. At this point, it seems valuable to briefly review the distinctive approaches of four of the theory families and suggest how they may relate to each other. Because of their breadth, the person-environment interaction theorists have been described separately in Chapter Five.

Psychosocial Theories

Psychosocial theorists, building on the work of Erik Erikson, suggest that an individual develops through a sequence of stages that define the life cycle. Each developmental phase or stage is created by the convergence of a particular growth phase and environmental demands that pose certain tasks, usually viewed as the learning of attitudes, the formation of a particular facet of one's self, and the learning of specific skills that must be mastered if one is to successfully manage that particular life phase. In general, psychosocial theorists suggest that development follows a chronological sequence; at certain times in life, particular facets of one's personality emerge as a central concern that must be addressed. However, the particular timing and ways in which the concerns are addressed is heavily influenced by the society and culture in which the individual lives. Taking the psychosocial viewpoint, a student services professional would be interested in *what* age the college student is; *what* decisions, concerns, and needs would likely be uppermost in his or her mind; and *what* skills and attitudes he or she would need to develop in order to make those decisions and cope with the various tasks.

Erik Erikson: The Foundation. The thought of Erik Erikson (1963, 1968) provides a foundation for our understanding of psychosocial development. Erikson's early training was psychoanalytic, and his approach reflects that orientation in the emphasis he gives to internal dynamics, particularly ego functioning. Essentially, his view of development focuses on the growth of the ego, an inner organizer that includes one's sense of self.

Yet Erikson's work represents an important extension and expansion of the Freudian model in two respects. In the first place, Erikson views development as a lifelong process. The second expansion is rather obvious but critically important. Erikson emphasizes the social world as an integral aspect of development. He sees development as a "product" of the transactions between an individual's inner realm—for example, feelings, needs, drives, and capabilities—and his or her social environment, with its available roles, rules, demands, and sanctions. For Erikson, ego development—in particular, the emergence of one's sense of identity—requires that we take into account an individual's interpersonal, social, cultural, and historical context.

Erikson conceives human development as an epigenetic process in which "anything that grows has a ground plan, and out of this ground plan the parts arise, each part having its time to special ascendancy, until all parts have arisen to form a functional whole." (Erikson, 1959, p. 52). He suggests that the ego, the inner organizer of one's experience, develops by parts through a sequence of developmental stages. In essence, Erikson assumes development to follow a quasi wired-in master plan. That is, at certain times in life, particular issues become ascendant and reach the point where action is required (a crisis); the ascendance of a particular issue comes about as a result of biological maturation and intellectual growth in interaction with a convergent pattern of societal demands. This interaction leads to a "crisis" or a particular task that must be resolved, thus contributing a "part" to the ego. For example, the typical eighteen-year-old first-year college student has attained physical sexual maturity and is gaining the cognitive capacity to think in increasingly abstract ways, which allows him or her to conceptualize such things as his or her life ten years down the road, the power of society, and the characteristics of an ideal world. Simultaneously, the society through institutions such as parents and the educational system creates new roles and demands certain decisions. The individual can no longer stay home without being considered more than a little odd. Erikson points out that the pattern of maturation meshes with societal demands, raising to top priority the issues of self-definition. At this age, identity becomes the central psychosocial issue; the student must ask and answer the questions "Who am I? What will I be?" Erikson has described eight such psychosocial stages, each with its distinctive issue, crisis, and required developmental task. For Erikson, the resolution of each stage leaves the individual with a basic social attitude about him or herself, an attitude that we most readily recognize as a part of the self-concept. Erikson expresses these attitudes as polarities that reflect successful or unsuccessful handling of the task of each stage.

For our profession, the adolescent and adulthood stages are most important. According to Erikson, the late adolescent or young adult tasks involve the resolution of identity and the forming of intimate relationships. For the mid-life adult, the task involves finding a path through which to contribute to and nurture one's society. If the individual is able to manage the many demands, he or she successively experiences him-or herself and acts as a person who (1) has a consistent, stable identity that is valuable and valued (identity), (2) is able to love without loss of autonomy (intimacy), and (3) is able to invest in and care for the broader society through some productive activity (generativity). However, if he or she is defeated by the demands of these phases the individual adopts orientations that reflect (1) a confused, scattered, inconsistent identity (role diffusion), (2) an inability to care deeply and freely about another (isolation), and (3) an inability-centered focus that blocks the ability to turn outward and care for others' welfare (stagnation).

Erikson's emphasis on the importance of identity-forming tasks during the period of late adolescence makes his model especially useful in the study of traditional college-age individuals. The identity crisis in late adolescence centers on a number of societal demands—in our American society, these are decisions about career and life-styles as well as a number of personal questions regarding one's values and beliefs, marriage, sexual identity, and the nature of commitment. This is often a time when the individual feels an urgency toward action while at the same time experiencing a great deal of confusion and uncertainty.

The identity process is seen as an integration of a great many complexities within the individual; it is more than the sum of the previous stages and requires a conscious synthesis of "old self-images" and new desires and capacities. New experiences and new demands by society combine to make the issue of identity highly complex. Erikson has suggested that identity (and perhaps intimacy) resolution requires that the student (1) experiment with various roles and life-styles, (2) have the freedom to choose activities and experience the consequences of those choices, (3) be involved in what can be seen as meaningful achievement, and (4) have time for reflection and introspection. The individual uses this time to create "new data" about him- or herself; to sort, sift, and integrate that new information with the old; and, finally, to make the commitments that define his or her identity. College can and often does provide a "psychological moratorium" that will allow the student to experiment and reflect in an environment that exists, at least in part, to foster such development.

Of prime importance to the understanding of the stages is the concept of the life cycle. The task of ego development is a lifelong process, in which the individual is continuously involved in coming to terms with the crises of all the previous stages that have led to his or her present sense of self. Each of the stages contains the stages that have gone before and prepares the individual for the stages that come after. It is likely that entrance into a college environment, while calculated to bring forth identity issues with a vengeance, also reraises the earlier issues of trust, autonomy, and industry. At the same time that college students are toying with the question of self-identity, they are looking over their psychological shoulders and wondering if this new world is a safe place where their needs can be met, if they can really do it on their own, and if, indeed, they are as able as their high school grade-point averages suggest. Quite possibly, older, returning students, in encountering an environment with new and different demands, must reexamine the identity issue. In fact, the return to college may reflect societal changes that unsettle adult self-definitions, thus reraising identity questions.

Implications

Erikson's work lays out in a general sense the problems, decisions, and issues that occupy college students. Student services programs and policies need to address and reflect those central issues. In addition, Erikson suggests necessary experiences for coping with the tasks of young adulthood; role experimentation, meaningful achievement, the experiencing of choice, and time and encouragement for reflection. These factors serve as general "prescriptions" that can be used as a frame of analysis for evaluating an ongoing collegiate environment or for changing such an environment. For example, if one were to specifically incorporate experimentation with varied roles, experiencing of choice, and meaningful achievement into residence hall life, what changes would be required? If we wanted to encourage student time for reflection and introspection, how would we structure a campus environment, the academic calendar, or entrance and exit procedures? How could a student activities program be designed to include Erikson's prescription? How could an academic major be so designed? These questions are typical of the type of "help" Erikson provides the practitioner. His work has not spawned much research or particular programmatic efforts, yet he points us to central issues and enables us to ask important questions.

Erikson has broadly outlined psychosocial development delineating eight phases of the life cycle and describing the central issues, developmental crises, tasks, and "outcomes" for each stage. Other theorists have focused on psychosocial development; most can be seen as elaborating or extending a particular aspect of Erikson's general scheme. In the following section, we describe the work of three theorists who have considered the stage of young adulthood, refining and augmenting Erikson's conception of the identity and intimacy tasks. Interestingly, each of the three theorists has examined the late adolescent or young adult from a slightly different vantage point, thus adding in different ways to our understanding of psychosocial growth. Erikson states generally that development emerges from the interaction of the individual in a social context; Kenneth Keniston has specifically examined the sociohistorical context of contemporary college students, articulating its effect in shaping identity issues. Arthur Chickering has related Erikson's stage notions to the collegiate environment. In particular, Chickering has "broken" the identity-intimacy phase of young adulthood into a component set of psychosocial tasks or vectors and identifies aspects of a collegiate environment that affect growth along those component vectors. Chickering provides a relatively specific way of answering the question "What is involved when an individual 'resolves' his or her identity?" James Marcia's work is quite different in focus. Rather than elaborating the issues or tasks of young adulthood, Marcia has attempted to identify individual differences in coping with the identity crises.

As stated previously, a number of theorists have added to and extended our understanding of the middle adult "stages"; for example, Levinson and others (1978), Gould (1972), Sheehy (1976), and Neugarten (1964). Due to limited space, we will not describe the works of these theorists; however, bibliographic references have been included.

Kenneth Keniston. Keniston has recast and refined Erikson's discussion of the identity and intimacy stages in light of the shifting nature of our society. Keniston (1971) asserts that Erikson's term "adolescent stage" is insufficient to describe what happens to college students. He sees the "unprecedented prolongation" of education in our society as a phenomenon that provides opportunities for an extended period of psychological development—in effect creating a "new stage in life." Keniston argues that college students are "neither psychological adolescents nor sociological adults" and prefers the term *youth.*

Keniston's assertion of a new stage of development is of major importance and bears examination. Like Erikson, Keniston believes psychological development results from a complex interplay between "constitutional givens" and societal conditions reflected in family, educational, economic, and political patterns. Erikson's eight stages are postulated to emerge at particular times because of certain regularities in the way individuals grow and the social demands they encounter. Erikson's treatment of adolescence (1963) was based on a social pattern where the majority of individuals entered "adult roles" at or even before age eighteen. In the post-World War II era, however, young people rarely enter those roles before age twenty-five. College attendance has become the normative social experience for young adults. In arguing a new stage of development, Keniston is suggesting that collegiate experience is so distinct in the character, tone, and demands it imposes on individuals that distinct psychosocial tasks and potential gains are created.

In describing the development of "youth," Keniston emphasizes (1) a central theme that occupies the psychic life of the individual, and (2) particular shifts in the way individuals think and behave in several developmental "sectors": moral, sexual, intellectual, and interpersonal. In discussing the sectors of development, Keniston has drawn from the works of other theorists, most notably Kohlberg and Perry; his observations are covered in our treatment of those theorists. It is in his description of the major theme of "youth" that Keniston adds uniquely to our understanding of college students.

Keniston has identified the central theme of this stage of life to be the "tension between self and society." Erikson has suggested that identity is interpersonally "created" yet influenced by cultural parameters. In early adolescence, the process of defining oneself seems to revolve around the individual's aspirations—finding what it is he or she wants to be and do. For the fairly typical college student, the collegiate experience may be the first encounter with societal boundaries. In college, the individual may come face to face with the dynamic tension between what he or she wants and what the world demands; for example, consider the plight of the many preprofessional students aiming for a limited number of slots in medical and law schools. The question is no longer "Who am I?" but "Who can I reasonably be?" Keniston argues that the central task of this age is to find or create congruence between one's self-definition and societal realities. The central theme Keniston presents is certainly not the sole province of youth; however, the issue becomes prominent and compelling at this phase.

As a theorist, Keniston's major contribution rests on his analysis of the social environment of young adulthood. His description of a "new stage" of development with its particular psychosocial theme can alert the student services practitioner to an area that may need attention. Keniston can help us look at our policies and programs from the particular vantage point of the societal pressure on students. How do we help students find a congruence between their needs and societal realities? For example, in the career area, do we counsel students in such a way to help them identify what they want to do in light of the marketplace?

A second value of Keniston's work is that it serves as an example of the process required in understanding college student development. Starting with the broad themes outlined by Erikson, Keniston studied a particular group of individuals and found it necessary to refine the original model. This process of grounding a theory in a particular student population is a necessary component of a student development approach.

James Marcia: Ego-Identity Status. Erikson's discussion of identity resolution is descriptive and often philosophical in tone. The reader finds him- or herself asking a number of questions: "Can identity be partly resolved? Is it a conscious process? Do clear commitments to a career presume 'effective' identity resolution?" In response to these questions, James Marcia (1966, 1976) postulated the existence of different ego-identity statuses that represent styles of coping with the task of identity resolution.

Marcia's original conception of identity statuses drew on Erikson's description of the identity resolution process. Two criteria of identity resolution are (1) the experiencing of crisis, a time of uncertainty and active search, and (2) the making of commitments, particularly in the occupational and value (ideology) spheres. Using these two criteria, four possible identity statuses were derived: the diffused identity, the moratorium, the foreclosed identity, and the achieved identity (see Figure 1).

Starting with a semistructured interview format to identify college student status, Marcia and his colleagues have attempted to identify the particular characteristics of each identity status. The following thumbnail sketches summarize their findings.

The *achieved-identity student* has both experienced a crisis and has made firm commitment in the vocational and value areas. This

Experienced Crisis

		Yes	No
	Yes	Achieved identity	Foreclosed identity
Commitments			
	No	Moratorium	Diffused identity

Figure 1. The Identity Resolution Process

student has a sense of stable and realistic goals and is able to pursue them in the midst of stress. He or she is able to handle changes in the environment and "failure" without major loss of self-esteem. In general, he or she is internally guided and relatively autonomous.

The *moratorium student* is in crisis, actively testing and searching to find his or her path. The identity issue is a conscious concern. This student has ambivalent views about authority, both wanting and resisting external pressures. The student's self-concept and self-esteem appear stable but he or she does evidence more anxiety than the achieved-identity student.

The *diffused-identity student* may be characterized by a "playboy" life-style. He or she appears aimless and disconnected and often seems to actively avoid making or even considering commitments, often appearing to move in response to the environment. The absence of strong characteristics defines this student.

The *foreclosed individual* has made firm commitments without experiencing crisis. Often these commitments reflect parental wishes; the student may be said to have "accepted" his or her identity rather than to be engaging in an active attempt to define and synthesize goals. This student often appears more authoritarian and rigid than students in the other three statuses. Consistently, he or she appears externally guided, and his or her self-esteem is affected by others' judgments.

In general, Marcia's work suggests that students at different ego-identity statuses bring different stylistic approaches to tasks. Achieved-identity and moratorium students are more open, resilient, and flexible; foreclosed students are more closed and rigid. Major differences also exist in the degree to which students act from an internal as compared to an external focus of control.

In one sense, the ego-identity status can be seen as a typology of stable individual differences. However, Marcia suggests that the identity statuses may be a succession of stopping points along the way to resolving the identity crisis. Although the evidence does not provide a clear picture, Marcia (1976) has suggested that individuals may shift through statuses as a set of process steps in accommodating "to each new life cycle issue." An individual may develop an "achieved identity" during college, but that same identity may become "foreclosed" as the individual encounters the demands and challenges of moving into adult life; or, as is more likely, an achieved identity may give way to another period of search (moratorium) as one encounters the demands of adult life. Such reworking of identity issues is consistent with Erikson's model as reflected in Figure 1. Although a particular issue is a crisis at each stage, each of the life issues is reflected and reworked in that crisis.

The fact that students may shift across statuses in a developmental way suggests that the ego-identity statuses do serve as a useful definition of "where students are." Students at different statuses are likely to respond to college in different ways and need different experiences in order to resolve the identity issue. The moratorium student in active search may need assistance in integrating experiences, while the foreclosed student may need stimulation to begin looking more closely at aspirations. Designing programs that respond to those individual differences is an important task for social services workers.

Arthur Chickering: Vectors of Development. One of the most useful contributions to the literature on college student development has been Arthur Chickering's work, which relates Erikson's identity stage to college students and their environments. In *Education and Identity* (1969), Chickering proposes a model of student developmental sources of influence.

Chickering's model was derived from a longitudinal study of thirteen small colleges and drew on the theoretical constructs of Erikson, R. W. White, and Nevitt Sanford. He argues that the central task of college students is the "establishment of identity," yet he suggests (1969, p. x) that "identity is so abstract as to provide only a hazy guide for educational decisions—I have attempted to move identity one step toward greater specificity and concreteness." Chickering then postulates seven vectors that comprise identity development in young adulthood. He suggests that development involves the student in a process of differentiating and integrating thought and behavior in each of the seven vectors. Using the term *vector* in place of *stage,* Chickering points out that *vector* connotes both direction and magnitude. He is careful to mention that the vector's direction is not necessarily linear but may be more appropriately expressed as a spiral. The seven vectors are listed below and briefly described.

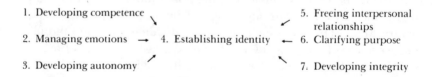

1. Developing competence

2. Managing emotions → 4. Establishing identity ← 6. Clarifying purpose

3. Developing autonomy

5. Freeing interpersonal relationships

7. Developing integrity

Vector 1: Developing Competence. The issue of competence takes center stage at entrance to college. As one talks with first-year college students, one hears various expressions reflecting their underlying concern with competence: "How hard is Chem I?" "How do you meet 'people' here?" or "What does it mean if you get a C on a mid-term?" Chickering views competence as including three distinct abilities: (1)

intellectual skills, (2) physical and manual skills, and (3) social and interpersonal skills. A sense of competence is defined as "the confidence one has in his ability to cope with what comes and to achieve success-fully what he sets out to do" (Chickering, 1969, p. 9).

Vector 2: Managing Emotions. The first task in this vector is for the student to become aware of his or her own emotions and to perceive them for what they are. Then the student may begin to manage and control emotions and to integrate them with decisions and behavior. New patterns of expression and control may be tried, and ultimately the student learns "what can be done with whom, when, and under what circumstances." The two major areas of concern are commonly sex and aggression. Some fairly typical problems seem to derive from an inabili-ty to manage emotions or from an early awareness of previously unrec-ognized feelings. For example, roommate conflicts may reflect an inability to handle angry feelings or a lack of "control" or skill in managing those feelings in a relationship.

Vector 3: Developing Autonomy. Chickering defines *autonomy* as "the independence of maturity" and views the maturely autonomous person as "secure and stable," coordinating behaviors to personal and social ends. Maturity requires (1) emotional and instrumental inde-pendence and (2) recognition of interdependencies.

Emotional independence includes freedom from "continual and pressing needs for reassurance, affection, or approval." Students disen-gage from parents, move to a reliance on peers, and then arrive at a position where they are willing to risk loss of approval in order to stand by their beliefs. Instrumental independence has two components: (1) the ability to carry on activities and to cope with the problems without seeking help and (2) the ability to be mobile in relation to one's needs and desires. The need for instrumental autonomy may be seen in the difficulty many students have in managing time, course work, and financial matters.

Recognition of interdependence is the capstone of autonomy. Students who recognize and accept their interdependencies—with fami-ly, peers, and society—become effectively autonomous individuals. However, as Chickering noted, autonomy requires continual recreation as one moves from one context into another.

Vector 4: Establishing Identity. Identity depends on the first three vectors and fosters change in the final three vectors of development. Chickering states that the complex task of developing identity is the "single major task for young adults." He defines identity as "that solid sense of self that assumes form as the developmental tasks for compe-tence, emotions, and autonomy are undertaken with some success and which, as it becomes firm, provides a framework for interpersonal relationships, purposes and integrity" (Chickering, 1969, p. 80). Chickering notes that establishment of identity in college students seems particularly focused on coming to terms with one's physical appearance and sexuality. Students' struggles to "establish" identity can be seen in their efforts to answer such questions as "Will I ever be stable?" and "What kind of man or woman am I?"

Vector 5: Freeing Interpersonal Relationships. This vector (freeing personal relationships) differs from developing a sense of interpersonal competence in that the major emphasis of this vector involves developing a tolerance for a wider range of individual and ideological differences. The student's tasks are first to recognize differences, then to tolerate them, and finally to appreciate their existence, as reflected in maturely intimate relationships.

Vector 6: Clarifying Purpose. The task of purpose development requires the student to formulate plans and priorities for his or her life and to integrate avocational interests with vocational plans and life-style considerations. Such an integration allows life to have both direction and meaning.

Vector 7: Developing Integrity. The development of integrity involves three overlapping stages: (1) the humanizing of values, (2) the personalizing of values, and (3) the development of congruence. Chickering uses White's (1975) term "humanizing of values" to describe the shift from a dualistic, absolutist view of rules to a more relativistic position in which a connection is made between rules and the purposes they are designed to serve. The next step, personalizing values, is taken when the student recognizes the need to affirm his or her own value system and to act in accordance with it. The final step, congruence, finds the student consistently behaving in accord with values held. Thus the student's life-style becomes one of integrity between beliefs and actions.

Chickering, like Erikson, implies an order among the vectors. The first three are antecedent to and prerequisite for the central vector of identity, and the latter three follow from an established identity. One must first develop a view of oneself suggesting that one is capable, in control, and standing on one's own before one considers how to define oneself. In essence, Chickering suggests that we must first be assured that we can contend with an environment before we can create an identity in the context of that environment. Once that identity is somewhat clear, we turn to the roles through which we will enact that identity—as colleague and friend, as worker, and as man or woman of principles.

Chickering reports the following conclusions about student development along the vectors. First, it was most common for freshmen and sophomores to be dealing with the first three vectors, while the last four vectors were emphasized during the last two years of college. However, individuals at a given college often varied substantially in terms of what vectors were central at entrance to college, and student populations at different colleges appeared widely variant.

Chickering sees the college environment as a source of potential supports and challenges for development. He identifies six major sources of influence:

1. Clarity and consistency of the college's objectives
2. Size of the institution
3. Curriculum, teaching, and evaluation
4. Residence halls
5. Faculty and administration
6. Student culture

In analyzing each influential factor, Chickering identifies its potential developmental role in terms of particular vectors. Underlying his discussion of the six environmental influences are "generic" components, among which are a sense of community that has an identifiable thrust and intellectual climate, opportunities for role experimentation, tasks that involve the student in making choices and exercising independent judgment, and the possibility of significant relationships among individuals from diverse backgrounds.

Chickering's model of student development provides some specific guides for student services practice. First in identifying the seven vectors, he suggests specific issues that a student must master if development is to continue. The vectors can serve to guide the content of programs and policies.

Chickering's model also suggests a particular developmental sequence. Once a student services program has identified "where its students are" in terms of the vectors, programs can be designed to "fit" the needs of the students. For example, a freshman orientation program that focuses exclusively on academic or career planning may "miss" the students; it may need to "back up" in the sequence and emphasize the more immediately crucial vectors of competence and autonomy.

The environmental factors that Chickering identifies as affecting development are important as general considerations. However, they are so global that they do not allow one to translate for a specific small-scale program. In order to create interventions that actually encourage growth along those vectors, one needs to borrow from other knowledge bases that describe how autonomy, purpose, and so on develop.

Cognitive Developmental Theories

In contrast, cognitive developmental theorists describe and explain development from a different vantage point. These theorists employ the structuralist view articulated by Jean Piaget (1964). They see development as a sequence of irreversible stages involving shifts in the process by which the individual perceives and reasons about the world. Basically, this view identifies successive changes in the way individuals think. Most cognitive developmental theorists have focused on identifying the *universal* pattern of stages that individuals go through and, in some cases, the typical ages associated with particular modes of thinking. The process of developmental change is seen as interactive: The individual with his or her way of viewing the world encounters a problem, dilemma, or idea that poses cognitive conflict demanding that he or she "accommodate" or change his or her way of thinking to an "adequate" form. In attempting to work with students using a cognitive developmental perspective, the student services worker would attempt to ascertain *how* students think about particular issues and examine *how* the environment challenges and/or supports such thinking. Theorists included in the cognitive developmental group are Piaget (1964), Kohlberg (1971), Perry (1970), Harvey, Hunt, and Schroder (1961), Hunt (1970), and Loevinger (1966, 1977).

Jean Piaget: The Foundation. Jean Piaget is recognized for his studies of intellectual development in children and adolescents. Kohlberg (1971), among others, credits Piaget with creating the structure for a powerful developmental psychology. We believe that Piaget's primary contribution to student services practice derives from the form of this theorizing or metatheory; for that reason, his description of specific stages of intellectual development is not included; rather, we will emphasize his discussion of the nature of development.

The three fundamental ideas of the cognitive developmental approach (Rest, 1974) were first and most fully explicated by Piaget. His pioneering work established and validated specific developmental principles and constructs employed by all the following three central cognitive developmental theories.

Cognitive developmental theories take what is commonly described as an "information process view" of the individual. A person actively interprets the world outside of him- or herself; that is, he or she selectively attends to stimuli, imposes a "meaningful" order onto the stimuli comprehended, and develops and uses principles and rules to guide behavior and to solve problems. Bieri (1971, p. 178) suggests that the individual's way of processing information is determined by "relatively fixed patterns for experiencing his world . . . patterns which we may refer to as *cognitive structures.*" Other terms that have been used to describe these internal organizing structures are "scheme," "conceptual systems," "personal constructs," "forms," "styles," "plans," and "programs." Whatever the particular label, these models assume that a mediating structure or filter is the major element determining how the person translates and interacts with external reality. From this perspective, an individual's cognitive structure is to be inferred from his or her behavior—not a single behavior but the patterns of behavior, particularly those which reflect thought processes.

Development is a progression through an invariant sequence of hierarchical stages, with each stage representing a qualitatively different way of thinking. Each stage represents a more differentiated and integrated structural organization subsuming that of the previous stage. The goals of development are explicitly contained within these models: The highest stage is an operational definition of human effectiveness in that it spells out the "most adequate" mode of processing information and interpreting stimuli.

Most theorists argue that development is irreversible; changes that involve increased complexity in the cognitive structure simply cannot be undone. The meaning of irreversibility seems to be a psychological view of the idea that "You can't go home again." Once the cognitive structure is expanded to incorporate a wider range of experiences, "home" can only be seen by or through the new, more differentiated, structure.

Development is a product of the interaction between the person and the environment. Both a maturity or readiness within the individual and certain elements in the environment are assumed necessary for growth to occur. In postulating the nature of the change process, the developmentalists appear related to cognitive consistency theorists such as Festinger. They emphasize the role of the environment in creating dissonance or disequilibrium; the individual is confronted by environmental stimuli that cannot be handled by existing constructs, thus pushing him or her to accommodate and alter his or her cognitive structure to admit more complexity. However, too much disequilibrium or challenge can become overwhelming, resulting in fixation at a stage rather than progression to the next stage (Maves, 1972). This is very similar to Sanford's idea about development that we discussed earlier in this chapter.

Among Piaget's important other contributions to cognitive developmental theory are the following concepts. First, development proceeds at an irregular rate. Movement from one stage to the next higher stage involves two growth phases. The first is a readiness phase in which the individual is prepared or, to put it another way, gathers the prerequisites for a higher level of functioning. During this phase, it may appear that the person is at a standstill because there may be little behavioral indication of progress. The second or attainment phase is more obvious; the individual becomes able to employ the reasoning mode characteristic of next-stage functioning.

Even after attaining the next higher stage, the individual may have a limited ability to apply new capabilities in all situations. There exists a process of within-stage development, "horizontal decalage," in which the capacity of the person to use his or her highest-stage operations is gradually expanded to include a wider range of "content" areas. In some cases, it appears that there is a particular order in which cognitive operations are applied to different realms. For example, Piaget has found that children employ certain concrete operations in considering the mass of an object before they can apply those same operations to the weight of an object. Horizontal decalage is a concept that, by incorporating the idea of gradual change, modifies the idea of development as a series of steps from stage to stage.

An important contribution of Piagetian theory has been the identification of an attitude or "state of mind" that appears to accompany some phases of developmental progress. An egocentrism, an extreme self-consciousness, seems to arise when a person takes on a novel task; for example, the mode of thinking or "operations" of a new stage. Piaget has identified three major eruptions of egocentrism in the process of intellectual development. Two occur during the childhood, while the other appears in adolescence as a by-product of the transition to formal operational or abstract thought. A major part of the developmental process includes "decentering"—shifting the focus from self to the larger world.

The cognitive developmental models of Harvey, Hunt, and Schroder (1961), with subsequent refinement by David Hunt (1966, 1970), Jane Loevinger (1966, 1976), Lawrence Kohlberg (1969, 1971), and William Perry, Jr. (1970), are particularly valuable as a way of viewing the student in higher education. Although the four models share the same assumptions and theoretical constructs, they differ in range and focus. Harvey, Hunt, and Schroder's original model proposed four stages of conceptual functioning in regard to interpersonal relationships. More recent work, particularly that of David Hunt, has used the term "conceptual level" to describe a hierarchical sequence of increasing cognitive complexity in the way an individual construes the world. More than the other theorists, Hunt has attempted to develop approaches that "match" an instructional environment to the way a person reasons about the environment. Hunt's most recent work reflects an individualized, transactional approach for working with individuals. Loevinger's model of ego development is the most comprehensive; for Loevinger, each stage of development reflects a core structure manifest in a particular cognitive style, a distinct intrapersonal concern, an interpersonal orientation, and an approach to moral issues. Loevinger's original research focused on women across the life span; thus, her model can be used reliably with an adult population. Kohlberg's work, the most widely researched and disseminated, focuses on stages of moral development and emphasizes approaches to moral education. The Perry scheme, based on a college student population, describes stages in the way individuals view knowledge and values.

Space does not permit coverage of each of the theorists. We have selected the work of Kohlberg and Perry to exemplify the cognitive developmental approach. It is our belief that these two theorists are most directly useful in a college context.

William Perry, Jr. Using research conducted with Harvard undergraduates from 1954 to 1968, William Perry, Jr., and his associates have derived a scheme that is appropriately classified as a cognitive developmental framework focusing on intellectual and ethical development. Nine positions or stages comprise the Perry model. Each of these positions represents a qualitatively different mode of thinking about the nature of knowledge. The scheme describes nine steps that move a student from a simplistic, categorical view of knowledge to a more complex, pluralistic view in which knowledge and truth can no longer be equated. Perry contends it is a developmental sequence of "personal epistemology."

Perry's work suggests that the student's idea about the nature of knowledge determines his or her perceptions of the teacher's or other authority's role and of his or her own role as a learner. These perceptions ultimately lead to considering the nature of existence and to confronting questions such as "What is truth?" "What is to be valued?" and "What gives life—my life—meaning?" In this sense, intellectual development and identity development are two sides of a coin, intellectual progress leading into the task of examining one's place and commitments in the world.

The nine positions may be grouped into four more general categories for purposes of discussion.

Dualism. Positions 1-3 represent a view of the world of knowledge that is dualistic—right or wrong, good or bad. For the student at these positions, concepts such as "truth," "importance," and "correctness" are external givens; the learner views him- or herself as a receptacle ready to receive truth. For this student, answers exist; the college student's task is to find and master them. At all three positions, the student would view him- or herself as having minimal right to use his or her own opinions and would have developed little capacity for handling academic tasks that require one to deal with conflicting points of view.

Multiplicity. In Position 4, a plurality of points of view or evaluations for a topic or problem is acknowledged. This plurality is perceived as an aggregate of factors without internal structure or external relations. Thus, anyone has a right to his or her own opinion. No criteria has yet been established to evaluate the merits of one opinion against another. The following examples of students' responses illustrate the way of thinking: "Things can be a hundred different ways. Both sides can bring in a ton of evidence to support their views. Both are equally right. Everybody is right."

Relativism. Positions 5 and 6 describe movement to a recognition of knowledge as relative and contextual. In this sequence, all knowledge and values are disconnected from the concept of rightness or truth. With Position 5 emerges the capacity to think in complex analytic ways; at this point, the student can identify assumptions, draw implications, and evaluate points of view. The individual can think about thought (metathought); the capacity for metathought is intertwined with the capacity for detachment and an objective examination of one's way of thinking. At this position, students are "brought" to consider the meaning of their existence. If there is no truth, no "right" theory, then what of one's own beliefs, values, and goals—is there no right answer for anything? With relativism of knowledge may come the loss of old signposts and the experience of being lost and alone in a chaotic world. Yet, movement along Positions 5 and 6 brings an awareness that much of what "truth" he or she "creates" will emerge from the student's own experience and judgment as well as from external factors.

Commitment in Relativism. During Positions 7, 8, and 9, the student gradually accepts the responsibility of the pluralistic world and acts through commitment to establish identity. Perry (1970) found two components to commitment. The first is a coming to terms with the content of one's commitment by selecting a particular career, a set of values, or a stance toward marriage. The other aspect of commitment appears to be based on the individual's recognition that within him- or herself are many diverse, conflicting personal themes. This second aspect of commitment seems to involve defining one's style of identity. During this phase, students undertake to find their particular balance point on the various polarities important to them—being controlled versus being impulsive, being a contemplative versus being an activist, being a realist versus being an idealist. Initial commitments to a major or career are often sophisticated attempts to narrow one's world sufficiently to rediscover some degree of certainty. Usually such specialization confirms relativism and various adages such as "The more you learn the less you know."

The developmental progress of many students reflects delays. Perry identified three types of delay: temporizing, retreat, and escape. Temporizing represents a pause at any of the positions and is an important consolidating or readiness-building process. At certain times, students are not ready to leap headlong into change but seem to need time out to prepare for growth. Retreat is a regression to or entrenchment in dualism. This may result from insufficient psychological strength to cope with the anxiety and uncertainty inherent in the relativistic framework and/or a reaction to a highly threatening environment; for example, expecting college classes to be lectures and finding oneself in the midst of discussion and encounter groups. Escape defines the behavior of individuals who seem to avoid taking on the personal responsibility necessary for commitment and who are, for the time being, "hiding out" in relativism.

Perry, like Piaget, views developmental change to come about through encounters with the world that raise "cognitive dissonance." As the college student bumps repeatedly into information or ideas that do not fit with his or her assumptions about the world, disequilibrium occurs, requiring accommodation of changes in those assumptions. At dualistic positions, uncertainty and diversity of viewpoints seem to handle reality better. Perry's study suggests that the inherent relativism of knowledge reflected in most course work and in a diverse student population has that disequilibrizing effect.

Students in multiplicity position perceive the world as an aggregate of conflicting views, an emphasis on critical thinking skills may encourage the shift to ordered thinking that characterizes the relativist position. The movement from relativism to the making of personal commitments is a different type of journey, more emotional than cognitive; it can neither be forced nor hurried. For Perry, this shift requires the support of a community that recognizes the importance and difficulty of making commitments in a relativistic world.

The pattern of development that Perry describes has not been extensively studied or validated on other student populations; however, the scheme seems to have a certain face validity—many college students report that they quite clearly recognize themselves in Perry's descriptions. The scheme may describe a general pattern of change for many aspects of a college student's life; some evidence (Knefelkamp and Slepitza, 1976) suggests that individuals follow this general sequence in their thinking about careers.

This model of development clarifies the meaning of reasoned mental goals. The long-range objective of helping students make reasoned personal commitments is certainly consistent with the philosophy of the student services profession. However, as the scheme suggests, students develop through a sequence.

Perry's work also points to factors that may be important in designing programs. Individuals at different stages of development have quite different characteristics and may prefer different environments in which to learn, grow, and be at ease. The central point is that the nature of intellectual development is such that we should pay as much attention to processes we use as to content.

Lawrence Kohlberg. The work of Lawrence Kohlberg extends and expands Piaget's cognitive developmental theory into the domain of moral reasoning. Kohlberg has developed a hierarchical stage theory of how individuals reason about the moral issues and decisions in their lives. As a cognitive stage model, it is based on the three assumptions made by Piaget and discussed earlier.

Kohlberg's model (1971) consists of three major levels of reasoning (preconventional, conventional, and postconventional or principled). Each of these levels consists of several specifically defined stages as described below. These levels represent an orderly expansion of an individual's sense of self in relation to others (from egocentric, to sociocentric, to allocentric) and in the different primary considerations used in making moral decisions, as illustrated in Figure 2.

At the preconventional level, the individual is responsive to cultural rules and levels of good and bad, right or wrong, but he or she interprets the labels in terms of either the physical or hedonistic consequences of action (punishment, reward, exchange, or favors) or the physical power of those who enunciate the rules and labels. The individual's concept of what is moral comes directly from parent or authority definitions of right and wrong because the individual lacks the cognitive structure to either generate or consider alternatives and lacks the affective repertoire to empathize with others.

At the conventional level, the individual preceives the maintenance of the expectations of his or her family, group, or nation as valuable in its own right, regardless of immediate and obvious consequences. The attitude is not only one of *conformity* to personal expectations and social order but also of loyalty to it, of actively maintaining, supporting, and justifying the order, and of identifying with a person's intent in an action and not just whether the action violates the letter of a law or rule.

The postconventional individual makes a clear effort to define moral values and principles that have validity and application apart from his or her own identification with groups. The individual is now capable of abstract thought processes and is thus able to consider how consequences of actions are related and what degree of personal responsibility one has for them.

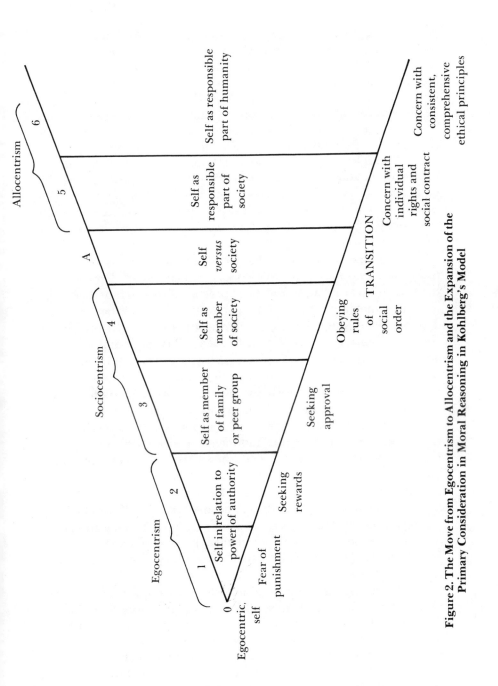

Figure 2. The Move from Egocentrism to Allocentrism and the Expansion of the Primary Consideration in Moral Reasoning in Kohlberg's Model

The longitudinal research supports the theoretical hypothesis that moral development proceeds through the stages just described (Kohlberg, 1969). Moreover, cross-cultural studies have led Kohlberg and his associates to conclude that this particular sequence of stages is universal, although the rate of progress through the stages varies depending on the stimulation available in the cultural environment (Kohlberg and Turiel, 1971). As a result of his longitudinal studies, Kohlberg has found that most of the adult population operates within the stage four level of moral reasoning. Studies have shown that 20 to 25 percent of the adult population operates on the principled levels (Kohlberg, 1972). Because the structure of the social environment can either promote moral development or cause it to "fixate" at a certain stage, the elements of the culture encourage "conventional" ways of thinking about moral issues.

One aspect of the Kohlberg model is its compatibility with educational interventions. Kohlberg's work is really understood in two parts: the attempt to build and validate a universal theory of moral development and the attempt to build an educational model that promotes development through the stages. The educational model involves deliberately presenting the student with disequilibrizing moral dilemmas and experiences and with lengthy discussions in which the educator interjects reasoning that is one stage above the student's. Research has shown that students tend not to be able to understand reasoning at more than one level above their own, hence the intervention is designed to present a developmental stimulus that is not overwhelming. It is this general process that is used in Kohlberg's model. He also has written that the schools cannot promote the advancement of moral reasoning unless they, too, operate at levels that model and promote greater complexity of reasoning in the students. The work of Mosher and Sprinthall (1971), Erickson (1975, 1978), and Blatt and Kohlberg (1975), in "deliberate psychological education" has brought this educational intervention to the classrooms of elementary and secondary schools. Straub and Rodgers (1978) have used this same type of approach with college students.

As with all developmental models, Kohlberg's stages provide a means of describing students so that expected behavior can be more in line with actual behavior. Not infrequently faculty expect students to behave in postconventional ways, although research indicates that most students are not capable of such thought, let alone such action. Discipline procedures in higher education have often been construed as being educational when in fact they have been widely misunderstood by students and by faculty. With the help of Kohlberg's model, one could begin to organize a set of disciplinary procedures that were tuned to students' developmental level and thus truly educational in nature.

For those who accept the purpose of education as broader than either intellectual or vocational and including values, ethics, and morals, the model presents a possible direction. Work already under way in deliberate psychological education, the "just community," and similar efforts offer models that may possibly apply to higher education as well.

As mentioned earlier in this chapter, Sanford was among the first to describe a developmental community. He recognized the importance of challenge and support as ingredients of such a community. Kohlberg's attempt to present challenges at one stage above that of a person's present level of functioning is an explicit effort to make the challenge optimal. Further research with this model of change is likely to give us much information about how to encourage development.

Maturity Models

In using the different psychosocial and cognitive developmental models, one finds oneself considering particular facets of the student. Yet student services workers deal with the whole student, individuals who simultaneously think, value, relate, and wonder about themselves. Theorists who attempt to construct models of maturity, such as Douglas Heath, describe in a comprehensive way the often simultaneous changes involved in development. These writers are synthesizers who attempt to specify the total developmental picture and hence may provide an umbrella that subsumes the specific, more narrowly focused, developmental models. These maturity models suggest the long-range comprehensive goals that a student services program may use as a frame of reference. For us, the substantive work of Douglas Heath represents a maturity model that links the other models of college student development.

Douglas Heath's work centers on the idea of maturity. Drawing on education and psychological thinkers, he has created a model that comprehensively delineates the many components involved in the maturing process. Heath's view of maturity considers the person in terms of four "self systems" and five growth dimensions. Heath suggests that maturation involves movement along the five growth dimensions in each of the four areas of the self. In maturing, one becomes more able to think and analyze, to understand and care for others, connect the different streams of one's experience, to maintain and persist, and to act without external guidance. In combining the growth dimensions and self systems, Heath emerges with a matrix that represents the domain of maturing. We have generated statements for the twenty categories of the matrix; these statements outline the characteristics of a mature person (see Table 1).

Self Systems	*Growth Dimensions*
1. Intellect	1. Becoming more able to represent experience symbolically
2. Values	2. Becoming allocentric or other-centered
3. Self-concepts	3. Becoming integrated
4. Interpersonal relationships	4. Becoming stable
	5. Becoming autonomous

Taking this conceptual map as a starting point, Heath has addressed the following questions in a series of cross-cultural longitudinal studies (Heath, 1965, 1968, 1977):

1. Does the model accurately outline the general changes that occur as an individual moves into adulthood?
2. Is there a consistent pattern in maturation? For example, is there a sequence of movement along the growth dimensions and self system?
3. What maturation pattern occurs during the traditional college years, and what factors in the college environment facilitate those changes?

Based on his original study of Haverford college students, Heath found the following. First, the model does provide a good picture of the types of changes that occur as individuals become adult. Haverford seniors were more "mature" than freshmen on nearly all dimensions. Second, the pattern of growth was consistent for most students. Major changes were initiated during the first half of the freshman year. Heath provides extensive data on the various changes students go through. The results are too complete to review in detail here. However, a statement that appears in *Growing Up in College* (Heath, 1968, p. 176) is a summary of the maturing process: "Is there an orderly sequential development to the maturing process in young adults? Our hunch is that there may be, and that it is initiated by induced instability, to which the person responds with increased awareness and more allocentric and integrative adaptive attempts. Eventually, an adaptive solution is evolved that stabilizes and begins to function more autonomously. This sequence occurs at different rates in different sectors of personality. The developmental process is completed first in the maturation of intellective-cognitive skills, next in the same-sex and then opposite-sex personal relationships. The maturing of a person's values tend to follow the stabilization of his personal relationships. The maturing of the self-concept takes longer and goes through more transitional stages, eventuating in a stable integration with the person's values."

Table 1. The Mature Personality

	Intellect	Values	Self-Concept	Interpersonal Relationships
Becoming able to symbolize experience	Able to evaluate one's own thought	Awareness of one's own belief	Awareness of self; accurate insights, self-analysis	Able to reflect about relationships; able to analyze why others act or feel certain ways
Becoming allocentric (other-centered)	Thoughts are logical; tied to social reality	Centered on people; tolerant and altruistic	Ability to see self as similar to others; empathy	Caring for others; ability to love, capacity for intimacy
Becoming progressively integrated	Able to solve problems systematically; creative syntheses, coherence in thought	Workable world view; coherence in value commitments	Congruent self-image; realistic view of self	More openness, able to be wholly with another; capable of reciprocal, mutual, and cooperative relationships
Becoming stable (resistant to disruption or threat)	Thoughts stay organized; able to function consistently	Clear, sustained commitment to set of values	Stable view of self; certainty, resilience	Enduring friendships; commitment to specific other
Becoming autonomous	Use of data less imprisoned by bias	Independence of mind; integrity in belief and behavior	View of self as responsible; not overly reliant on others' perceptions	Relationships reflect autonomy, not sacrifice integrity for "belonging"; nonmanipulative

Third, overextended development in one self area seems to result in inhibited growth in that area and a turning to other areas. Haverford students tended to be overly intellectual; the confrontation with the college environment appeared to redirect their concern to their interpersonal relationships.

Finally, maturing is not and probably cannot be completed during the college years. The sequential nature of such development appears to preclude attaining a stable and autonomous self-concept and value orientation in that period of time.

The maturing changes that occurred in college, "expanding awareness, deepening tolerance and caring for others, more stabilized values and self-concepts" were encouraged by a number of elements in the college environment. In agreement with many other observers of the college scene, such as Chickering and Perry, Heath suggests that the principal sources of impact are interpersonal (roommates, close same-sex friends) and intellectual and academic determinants (the mission and atmosphere of the college in a broad sense, courses that focus on values, and faculty who are models of maturity).

Heath's approach to understanding college student development starts with a model that describes the end points of development. A specific model that effectively describes a "mature" person can and should have meaning for our professional practice in a number of ways. Our task is to nurture personal growth, and students are moving toward these characteristics; Heath thus provides us with a comprehensive set of developmental goals.

More specifically, his research indicates a particular pattern of maturational change that occurs with young adults in a college context. Growth seems to occur first in the area of intellect, then in the interpersonal realm, and finally in the more intrapersonal sectors, involving one's self-concept and values. Heath's work may suggest that student services programs may best function by supporting such a pattern of growth.

In addition, Heath's work suggests that not all growth is possible during the traditional college years; thus, the model allows us to be more reasonable in our expectations.

As a theorist of development or maturity, Heath's major limitation lies in his description of the growth process. Although he points to factors in the college environment that appear to aid growth, his model lacks a well-articulated conception of the underlying processes that allow one to become more capable of symbolic thought, more stable, integrated, and so on. We do not know whether these capacities are inherent and will emerge "naturally"; if they are "learned," like patterns of reinforcement; or if they reflect some other underlying process of cognitive and behavioral change. Without a feasible explanation of how the maturing changes come about, we are limited in our ability to structure a developmental environment.

Typology Models

As stated earlier, some theorists have emphasized stable individual differences that may interact with general patterns of development. Many writers have concentrated on psychological typologies; characteristic differences in the way individuals perceive and respond to situations. Some typologies have focused on cognitive style (Witkin, 1962), others have, more broadly, emphasized personality functioning (Myers-Briggs, 1962). We have chosen Roy Heath's model of temperamental differences (1964) to exemplify the contributions of this theoretical approach. Heath's work is one of the few typologies derived in a college context that describes the interaction of the individual differences and psychosocial development.

Other typologies exist that emphasize sociological differences among individuals. In fact, much of the socialization research that has investigated the impact of college on students used sociological criteria, such as socioeconomic status and parental educational level (Feldman and Newcomb, 1969). We have chosen to describe the ideas of Patricia Cross as an example of sociological frame of reference for viewing student differences. Cross may best aid us in recognizing the need to put all developmental models currently in use to the test of whether or not they are appropriate and applicable for students who are outside the typical white, middle-class, academically well-socialized eighteen- to twenty-two-year-old group.

Patricia Cross: A Sociological Approach to Student Differences. The work of Patricia Cross represents a sociological view of student differences. Cross suggests that presently "new students" (Cross, 1971, 1976) are entering our colleges and universities in large numbers and that these students have different characteristics and needs from their predecessors. The term "new student" can be misleading, because there have always been new students in American higher education and each successive new student population has managed to adapt to the environment. And, at times, the environment has been modified by the presence of these students. Hence, we may have a tendency to dismiss Cross' call for attention because we are not fully aware of the characteristics of the students who meet her definition of "new student."

Cross argues that today's new student has unique characteristics that institutions of higher education are not prepared to address. The new student has appeared on the scene as a result of an attempt by the institutions to reach a wider range of society. Thus, these students would not have had access to higher education as recently as fifteen years ago. Cross defines the new students as those students who

1. Score in the lowest one third among national samples of high school students taking the traditional academic ability tests
2. Have had difficulty performing traditional academic tasks, and for whom present forms of education do not seem to be appropriate

Although a substantial number of the new students are from minority groups, most are Caucasians whose fathers and mothers work at blue-collar jobs. Regardless of their ethnic origin, these students are the first generation in their family to attend college. They have generally not been successful in high school, attaining averages of C or below. Many are being swept into college by society's emphasis on college degrees as a way to a better life. Often they are less interested in learning for learning's sake and see education as an instrumental path to a vocationally and economically enhanced position in life. As Cross suggests, their most distinguishing characteristics are their low test scores and their low performance on other measures that predict academic success in college. Although the new students are relatively diverse and no single approach to meeting their needs is sufficient, we do know that they are

1. Less academically motivated than their "traditional" peers
2. Apt to associate the learning environment with the threat of failure
3. More attuned to concrete learning environments than to abstract ones
4. More comfortable in social and interpersonal tasks than in academic ones
5. Less able to perform well the academic tasks of reading and writing than are their "traditional" peers
6. More in need of consistent and concrete feedback on performance than are their peers
7. More directly vocationally oriented than their peers
8. More likely to come from a family with no previous experience in higher education; hence they have not been socialized to the norms of higher education institutions.

These students present a challenge not only to higher education institutions but also to the appropriateness and validity of student development models that have been based on the "traditional college student." Hence we must be prepared to conduct research that will enable us to identify and acknowledge the limitations of the original models, but we must also be careful not to dismiss the models too hastily. Rather, we would benefit from a careful analysis of the constructs of each theory to determine the usefulness of each as a general human development model and thus applicable to these students as well. And some models may be more helpful than others. This may be particularly true of the cognitive models and their implications for classroom and instructional design, the area of most vulnerability for the new student.

Roy Heath: Personality Typologies. The work of Roy Heath (1964, 1973) serves both as a reminder of the importance of individual differences and as a descriptive model of how those differences can affect an individual's movement toward maturity. Our work with the model has convinced us that its apparent simplicity (three types of personalities capable of moving toward an idealized description of maturity) is deceptive. Rather, it is a complex model that offers practitioners a useful way of conceptualizing the differences among the students with whom they work. The model is based on Heath's own intensive case studies of thirty-six Princeton male undergraduates as they progressed through their four years in college in the early 1950s. Since the model is based on a small number of men from a single institution, the appropriateness of this theory for women is unclear.

The model is based on the interfacing of two primary dimensions. The first dimension is "ego functioning" or maturity level of the individual, "the manner in which the self interacts with the world, achieves its satisfaction, and defends itself from threats to its survival" (Heath, 1973, p. 9). The individual is conceptualized as being able to move through a series of three developmental maturity levels (low, medium, high) on the way to achieving an idealized level of maturity referred to as being a "reasonable adventurer." The second dimension is individual style or type, the person's basic temperamental approach to life. Heath conceptualized three basic personality types, based on the manner in which the individual regulates the "dynamic tension" between the inner, instinctual, feeling self and the outer, more rational self. Each type proceeds toward maturity in his or her own individualistic manner, but each one has an equal chance of achieving the maturity level of the reasonable adventurer. Thus the model assumes the need to integrate developmental (maturity) level with temperamental style (personality type) in order to achieve a holistic picture of the self.

Heath's concept of maturity level is similar to the stage concept we have discussed in previous sections. He conceptualizes a sequential and hierarchical continuum that begins with the lowest level of ego functioning and proceeds through the medium level. The characteristics of individuals at each level are qualitatively different with respect to manner in which they regulate their behaviors, feelings, thought processes, and actions. The developmental levels assume Erikson's (1968) epigenetic principle that each is built on the strengths and achievements of those that have come before and that each contains a preview of and is an enabler of the levels that follow. An individual cannot skip a level in that model, although individuals do proceed at varying rates.

One of the major contributions of Heath's model is its attention to the importance of individual differences. Everything about his work calls our attention to this vital aspect of the students with whom we work. Yet, in his attention to the differences among us Heath is mindful of commonalities, shared characteristics with others, and the fact that those shared characteristics can be used to place students in meaningful group classifications, such as "types." He has defined the types in his model according to the "kinds of personality patterns that the individuals may manifest" (Heath, 1973, p. 58). Individual differences are manifested in three types of patterning behaviors. The types are defined by the different "patterns" in the way an individual regulates impulses. The three personality types are based on the manner in which the individual regulates the "dynamic tension" between the inner, instinctual feeling self and the outer, more rational self. The placement of the three primary types along a continuum is determined by the degree to which the impulse regulation system allows the instinctual and the rational worlds of the self to be aware of and interact with one another. Individuals differ with respect to the degree of porosity of their regulation systems; that is, how much awareness the system allows. "There are differences between persons in the functional limits of the filter capacity range. . . . I suspect that the limits of one's filter capacity is a reflection of what is generally called one's *temperament* or *inherent disposition*" (1973, p. 58). The three types and their locations along the continuum are Type X, constricted filter capacity (located at the left of the continuum); Type Y, semiconstricted (located in the center); and Type Z, porous filter (located at the right). These three primary types are characterized by differing defense systems, dispositions toward the motive behind social involvement, sources of reward and punishment, environments that challenge or support, attitude toward self, manner in which students tend to interact with both people and environments, and the very tasks that they find either appealing or frightening.

Although Heath discusses only three primary types, his use of a *continuum* reminds us that individuals could be placed anywhere along the temperamental line depending on the degree of constrictedness or porosity of their filter systems.

The temperamental continuum is widest at the lowest maturity level. Individuals manifest the most pronounced differences across typologies at this level, hence the lower a person is on the developmental dimension, the easier is the judgment on temperament. As the person becomes more mature, he or she exhibits fewer stereotypic characteristics of his or her type and more of the mature forms of his or her stylistic approach to the world. Types maintain their individualistic qualities and do *not* merge into one "supertype." The reasonable adventurer reflects the stylistic variations of each of the types, but those variations are less pronounced than at the lower developmental levels as a result of the maturing process.

The *Type X* person has difficulty responding to his or her inner self and being aware of inner feelings. At the *lowest level of ego functioning,* the individual's emotional self is unconsciously "embedded" deep within, resulting in an unawareness of who he or she is and how he or she really feels. This lack of knowledge about self produces the following characteristics:

1. A need to avoid entanglements and commitments by maintaining a neutral position or stance (after all, if you do not know who you are or how you feel about something, it is frightening to contemplate taking a public stance)
2. A tendency to be a passive participant in both relationships and academic world
3. A tendency to depend on an authority figure for answers and solutions to dilemmas
4. A need to deny negative thoughts and feelings and to see only the positive aspects of a situation
5. A fear of risk taking and change
6. A strong need "to belong" and to help relationships be harmonious and free of conflict

The *medial Xs* have begun to be more self-aware and have begun to learn how to cope with conflict in relationships and diverse opinions in the academic, social, and work worlds. Although their first impulse is to seek the opinions of others or to avoid taking a stand, they are learning to think and act more independently. They remain in the peacemaker or maintenance role in a group but are growing in confidence in their ability to confront or to disagree. They are getting in touch with both positive and negative feelings and are just beginning to accept the legitimacy of existence of those feelings.

The *high level Xs* have become more aware and integrated. They not only recognize the array of feelings but also have accepted them as a legitimate part of themselves. While still most comfortable when receiving structure and guidance from an authority figure, high-level Xs have become capable of independent thought and action. The motive behind being a peacemaker is now to facilitate the accomplishment of tasks as well as to maintain peace. Conflict remains stress producing, but it is no longer viewed as always negative and always to be avoided. High-level Xs have begun to develop both the skills and the courage to initiate and to lead as well as to receive and to follow—although they very carefully pick the time and place to do so. Skills as a watcher and observer are well honed and are now beginning to be strategically directed.

The *Y type's* semiconstricted filter system allows more awareness of feeling state than is true of the more constricted X. However, this partial awareness results in the Y's distrust (and even fear) of those impulses and in active, conscious effort to avoid confronting the impulse life by engaging in an intense level of activity. The Xs have a strong need to facilitate and keep peace; the Ys have an inordinate need to achieve and to assert themselves on the world. Frequently characterized as being at war with the world, they are really at war with themselves, convinced of their own lack of self-worth and desperately wanting the affection and approval of others. *Low-level Ys* are "pseudoselves" striving to be composites of all the successful things they think others want them to be. In their impatience to succeed and their profound fear of failure, they are often insensitive to the feelings of others. Afraid of their own feelings, they deny feelings in others. The low-level Y is characterized by dichotomies: Thinking is good, feeling is a waste of time; change is good, status quo is bad; leading is good, following is bad; one either achieves complete success or one is a failure. Although low-level Ys represent themselves as thinking, rational, objective people, they are not introspective or insightful. The medial Ys have begun to experience the legitimacy of viewpoints that differ from their own, and hence they no longer hold quite so firmly to their dichotomous rules. They are more sensitive to and forgiving of themselves and others, more able to relax, to laugh at themselves, to be free to not achieve in every endeavor. They have begun to believe that others value them for their own sakes and not just for their achievements. The *high-level Ys* remain achievement oriented but also risk participating in activities for fun or for new experiences. Some of the rigidity and sharp, defensive edges are gone, so the high-level Ys can more effectively express emotions and empathize with the emotions of others. Although they still prefer the thinking mode, feeling has become legitimate. They no longer insist that their rules should be for everyone, because others have become legitimate.

The Z type's filter system is the most porous, and the Z is often characterized by impulsiveness and variable moods. The *low-level Zs* are aware of their impulses and feeling states but are neither insightful about nor in control of them. They are at the mercy of feelings and impulses. As such, they often have difficulty completing tasks because their attention is captured by something new or they become bored and lack the self-discipline to continue. Although the low-level Ys are orderly to the point of rigidity, Zs are free spirits who foil any and all attempts at scheduling and structuring. The low-level Zs often have communication difficulties because they often cannot make themselves understood—their jumble of ideas, thoughts, and feelings come pouring out in a seemingly unconnected manner. It is almost as if they trip over themselves in their efforts to get everything said. The low-level Zs' academic and interpersonal efforts are often sporadic, confusing themselves as well as their teachers and friends. The low-level Zs alternate between feeling lonely and misunderstood and feeling unique, original, creative, and capable of anything and everything. The *medial Zs* have begun to learn how to control and regulate impulses so that they are more consistent performers in social and academic realms. They are more able to express their inner feelings in a manner others can understand and respond to. Still subject to wide variations of mood, they are more aware of what triggers moods and how they can behave so that they are more in control. The *high-level Zs* have learned to direct their creativity in ways that promote completing a project and to provide structure that enables others to more easily understand them. They have also learned to protect themselves from people who are not attuned to their open sensitivity and vulnerability. And they have discovered the consistent aspects of their personalities, which serve as the cores around which their idiosyncratic characteristics revolve.

The *reasonable adventurer* is Heath's term for an individual who has reached the level of mature, integrated ego functioning. The reasonable adventurer is characterized by six attributes:

1. Intellectuality
2. Close friendships
3. Independence in value judgments
4. Tolerance of ambiguity
5. Breadth of interest
6. Sense of humor

Heath describes reasonable adventurers as individuals who have integrated their instinctual and rational selves and have a confident sense of being able to act in the world. They possess a wide array of behaviors and skills and are able to react appropriately to almost any situation. They are reasonable, thoughtful, and accepting of others and their different perspectives and values. They communicate well and are sensitive to others. Reasonable adventurers are able to be both independent and interdependent in action and decision making. They are characterized by an ability to find or develop ways to satisfy themselves and by a personal resourcefulness that enables them to look forward with confidence to a future of exciting possibilities. Although highly integrated, the reasonable adventurer is also highly individualistic and does not conform to any one behavioral mode. Stylistic characteristics remain.

It is important to remember that being a reasonable adventurer is not an end point. Rather, it is having achieved a perspective on a mature way of functioning in the world that enables one to continue to explore and experience, as Murray of the movie *1,000 Clowns* would say, "all the marvelous possibilities."

Heath notes that the three types of students tend to respond to different sources of support and challenges for growth. His model provides important information for the practitioner responsible for designing interventions deliberately constructed to provide the balanced, development-enabling challenge and support. For each type, one can ask a series of specific questions that should help in designing programs: (1) "What are the sources of support for each type?" (2) "What are the sources of challenge?" and (3) "What are the relevant content areas based on the most difficult developmental tasks for each type?"

Heath's model also helps us to focus on ourselves as administrators. How do we put people together in task groups, for example? If we assume that the three types in combination cover the skills necessary to complete any project (strengths in organization, innovation, and communication) and the weaknesses to doom a project (hesitancy, obstinacy, inconsistency), we would need to select fairly mature individuals from all three types to ensure that they could work together to capitalize on the strengths of our staff (student and professional) and to not expect them all to be able to do all things.

However, Heath's model reminds us that an individual is fully capable of learning those skills and behaviors of other types but that the tendency is to avoid venturing into those foreign areas. Hence, our staff development committees might well be able to use Heath's model as an analysis and then as a training tool. An analysis of almost any student services position (again, student or staff) reveals that we want the individual to be able to be as outstanding a communicator as the mature X, as able an organizer as the mature Y, and as creative and innovative as the mature Z. Yet we place in those positions real people who will be able to be outstanding in some of the areas but rarely in all of them. Can we do a specific analysis of the tasks of the job and then design our staff development programs to help individuals learn those additional skills that are really demanded and on which their job performance reports depend?

Finally, the Heath model may prove to be a useful tool for self-assessment. What are our individual strengths and weaknesses; what are the developmental tasks that we find difficult? Where can we seek to enhance our range of skills and abilities? What do we reward or punish in others, and is that a result of our style and not necessarily of their performance?

On Using Theory

The use of theory to implement practice and intervene in the development of college students, has been described as a dilemma, a paradox, and a problem (Parker, 1977). The dilemma of using theory is that theory building requires the abstraction of a few elements from the whole of the human experience while intervention and practice require concrete and specific behavior in complex situations. To create a researchable model of how a person develops, we must choose and select those parts we wish to study and ignore the rest of the person, but the practitioner must work with the whole person in real-life situations. If we attempt to preserve that wholeness, we cannot handle the complexity in our conceptual models. Thus, the dilemma is that our practice is too complex for theorizing and our theories are too simple to be useful in practice.

The paradox of using theory to help students grow and develop is that we must deal with two true, but contradictory, conditions: the nature of theory is such that it does not lead directly to practice, but the nature of our practice is such that it does not proceed without theory. One way to deal with this paradox is to distinguish between formal and informal theory. By formal theory, we refer to the explicit conceptualization of the basic elements of a given phenomenon, the hypothesized relationships among those elements, and the procedures by which those relations may be validated. By informal theory, we refer to the body of common knowledge that allows us to make implicit connections among the events and persons in our environments and to act upon them everyday. Everyone has informal theories; they relate only two or three elements, seem unconnected with one another, and contain propositions of what is valuable. These mini-theories are such a part of our everyday life that we rarely think of them as theories, yet they guide what we do. Whether we retain our informal theories as guides to future action depends on whether our experience validates what we believe. Typically, we do not systematically test our informal theories, but we accept what supports our view and ignore other data that do not. Formal theories are necessary because they act as counterforces to our highly personal world. Formal theory allows us to test, in a systematic manner, what we know about student development in a general way. Each formal test advances our knowledge about students and incorporation of this knowledge into our personal world makes it possible for us to implement our practice with individuals.

By distinguishing between formal and informal theory, we can identify three strategies for using theory in practice. One strategy is to use formal theory in working with broad conceptual issues at the level of the college. Parker (1977), for example, describes a consulting project in which Perry's theory of cognitive development was used as a guideline to collect useful data about students, faculty, and the college setting. The purpose of the data collection was to determine if faculty were teaching at the developmental level of their students. The data were used in a diagnostic way to show that students expected to learn the facts and to be taught by faculty who knew the right answers to important questions. Students also expected to be rewarded for learning the facts presented and faithfully reproducing them on examinations. In short, students were using Perry's dualistic and multiplistic modes of thinking. However, faculty wanted students to use a variety of data to analyze problems, to bring together disparate pieces of knowledge into integrated syntheses, and to make important judgments. Most faculty members were at relativistic and highly committed modes of thinking. Perry's formal theory allowed student services professionals to identify the mismatch and show groups of faculty the need to change the way they taught some students.

A second way to use theory is to combine some elements of formal and informal theory to work with groups of relatively homogenous students. When a group of students is similar with respect to particular needs or characteristics, activities can be planned with those characteristics in mind. Also, when students are similar, a formal theory can be helpful in setting goals for a group and determining effective procedures to reach those goals. Informal theory can be used to design the specific steps required to carry out the general procedures. Over time, we all develop a repertoire of techniques that we know will work in a given situation and it is the utilization of these day-to-day skills that is guided by our informal theories. The difficulty with implementing the second strategy is that in most settings students are not similar; they are highly diverse and do not fit into any general model. The real world requires that we respond to individual students, a process best approached using the third strategy.

Because formal theory has guided research and data collection, we have come to view students as highly diverse individuals in need of emotional, social, intellectual, and value development. They come from a wide variety of backgrounds and have divergent interests. From our research in the student services profession, we know much about the average student; unfortunately, we never have the opportunity to work with him or her. There is no "average" person. However, if our common knowledge is sufficiently broad, we can enter into the diverse world of students' personal constructs to form meaning from what they say as individuals. This ability to adapt oneself to each individual has been called *reading* and *flexing* by Hunt (1970). That is, as professionals we must be sufficiently adaptable to read the student cues and to flex in reaction to the particular needs of the person and the situation. We can do this by using many theories to understand and assist individuals. In essence, we can consciously pick and choose selected elements from a variety of theories to understand where students may be developmentally. With that understanding as a foundation, we can utilize our informal theories to select whatever strategies and techniques have helped us in the past to facilitate student growth and development.

On Reflection

This chapter is longer than we thought might be necessary to meet the purpose of this handbook. Yet, when we consider the complexity of each person we know, it becomes apparent that no single theory can encompass the commonalities and differences of human functioning. Even the theories described here do not do that. There are far more social psychological theories current in professional circles than we have included here. We have limited ourselves to representative theories of college students or elements of personality development that have special relevance to college students. We believe that our framework of psychosocial, cognitive, maturity, and typology theories, together with the person-environment interaction models discussed in Chapter Five can be useful to a practitioner or researcher in the area of student services. We hope you will find it so.

References

American Council on Education. *The Student Personnel Point of View.* American Council on Education Studies, Series 1, Vol. 1, No. 3. Washington, D.C.: American Council on Education, 1937.

Bieri, J. *"Cognitive Structures in Personality." In H. Schroder and M. Suidfield (Eds.), Personality Theory and Information Processing.* New York: Ronald Press, 1971.

Blatt, M., and Kohlberg, L. "The Effects of Classroom Moral Discussion Upon Children's Level of Moral Judgment." *Journal of Moral Education,* 1975, *4*, 129–161.

Chickering, A. *Education and Identity.* San Francisco: Jossey-Bass, 1969.

Clark, B. R., and Trow, M. "The Organizational Context." In T. M.

Newcomb and E. K. Wilson (Eds.), *College Peer Groups: Problems and Prospects for Research*. Chicago: Aldine, 1966.

Cross, K. P. *Beyond the Open Door: New Students to Higher Education*. San Francisco: Jossey-Bass, 1971.

Cross, K. P. *Accent on Learning: Improving Instruction and Reshaping the Curriculum*. San Francisco: Jossey-Bass, 1976.

Erickson, V. L. "Deliberate Psychological Education for Women: From Iphegenia to Antigone." *Journal of Counselor Education and Supervision*, 1975, *14*, 297-309.

Erickson, V. L. "The Development of Women: An Issue of Justice." In P. Scharf (Ed.), *Readings in Moral Education*. Minneapolis: Winston Press, 1978.

Erikson, E. *Identity and the Life Cycle: Psychological Issues*. New York: International Universities Press, 1959.

Erikson, E. *Childhood and Society*. (2nd ed.) New York: Norton, 1963.

Erikson, E. *Identity: Youth and Crisis*. New York: Norton, 1968.

Feldman, K. A., and Newcomb, T. M. *The Impact of College on Students*. San Francisco: Jossey-Bass, 1969.

Gould, R. "The Phases of Adult Life: A Study in Developmental Psychology." *American Journal of Psychiatry*, 1972, *129*, 521-531.

Harvey, O. J., Hunt, D. E., and Schroder, H. M. *Conceptual Systems and Personality Organization*. New York: Wiley, 1961.

Heath, D. *Explorations of Maturity*. New York: Appleton-Century-Crofts, 1965.

Heath, D. *Growing Up in College: Liberal Education and Maturity*. San Francisco: Jossey-Bass, 1968.

Heath, D. *Maturity and Competence*. New York: Gardner Press, 1977.

Heath, R. *The Reasonable Adventurer*. Pittsburgh: University of Pittsburgh Press, 1964.

Heath, R. "Form, Flow, and Full-Being—Response to White's Paper." *The Counseling Psychologist*, 1973, *4*(2), 56-63.

Holland, J. L. *The Psychology of Vocational Choice: A Theory of Personality Types and Model Environments*. Waltham, Mass.: Blaisdell, 1966.

Hunt, D. E. "A Conceptual Systems Change Model and its Application to Education." In O. J. Harvey (Ed.), *Experience, Structure and Adaptability*. New York: Springer, 1966.

Hunt, D. E. "A Conceptual Level Matching Model for Coordinating Learner Characteristics with Educational Approach." *Interchange*, 1970, *1*, 68-72.

Hunt, D. "Teacher's Adaptation: 'Reading and Flexing' to Students." *Journal of Teacher Education*, 1976, *27*, 268-275.

Katz, J., and Sanford, N. "The Curriculum in the Perspective of the Theory of Personality Development." In N. Sanford (Ed.), *The American College.* New York: Wiley, 1962.

Keniston, K. "Social Change and Youth in America." In K. Yamamoto (Ed.), *The College Student and His Culture.* Boston: Houghton Mifflin, 1968.

Keniston, K. *Youth and Dissent.* New York: Harcourt Brace Jovanovich, 1971.

Knefelkamp, L. L., and Slepitza, R. A. "A Cognitive Developmental Model of Career Development and Adaptation of the Perry Scheme." *Counseling Psychologist,* 1976, *6*(3), 53–58.

Kohlberg, L. "Stage and Sequence: The Cognitive Developmental Approach to Socialization." In D. Goslin (Ed.), *Handbook of Socialization Theory and Research.* Chicago: Rand McNally, 1969.

Kohlberg, L. "Stages of Moral Development." In C. M. Beck, B. S. Crittenden, and E. V. Sullivan (Eds.), *Moral Education.* Toronto: University of Toronto Press, 1971.

Kohlberg, L. "A Cognitive-Developmental Approach to Moral Education." *Humanist,* 1972, *6,* 13–16.

Kohlberg, L. "The Cognitive-Developmental Approach to Moral Education." *Phi Delta Kappan,* 1975, *10,* 670–677.

Kohlberg, L. "Counseling and Counselor Education: Developmental Approach." *Counselor Education and Supervision,* 1975, *4,* 250–255.

Kohlberg, L., and Turiel, E. "Moral Development and Moral Education." In G. Lesser (Ed.), *Psychology and Educational Practice.* Chicago: Scott Foresman, 1971.

Levinson, D., and others. *The Seasons of a Man's Life.* New York: Knopf, 1978.

Loevinger, J. "The Meaning and Measurement of Ego Development." *American Psychologist,* 1966, *21,* 195–206.

Loevinger, J. *Ego Development: Conceptions and Theories.* San Francisco: Jossey-Bass, 1976.

Loevinger, J., Wessel, R., and Redmore, C. *Measuring Ego Development.* Vols. 1 and 2. San Francisco: Jossey-Bass, 1970.

Madison, P. *Personality Development During College.* New York: Addison-Wesley, 1969.

Marcia, J. "Development and Validation of Ego-Identity Status." Journal of Personality and Social Psychology, 1966, *3*(5), 551–558.

Marcia, J. "Studies in Ego-Identity." Unpublished manuscript, Simon Frazier University, 1976.

Maves, P. B. "Religious Development in Adulthood." In M. Strommen (Ed.), *Research on Religious Development.* New York: Hawthorn Books, 1972.

Mosher, R. L., and Sprinthall, N. A. "Deliberate Psychological Education." *Counseling Psychologist,* 1971, *4,* 3–82.

Myers-Briggs. *Myers-Briggs Type Indicator.* Princeton, N.J.: Educational Testing Service, 1962.

Neugarten, B. *Personality in Middle and Later Life.* New York: Atherton Press, 1964.

Neugarten, B. "Adaptation and the Life Cycle." *Counseling Psychologist,* 1976, *6*(1), 16–20.

Newcomb, T. M., and others. *Persistence and Change.* New York: Wiley, 1967.

Pace, C. R. *Analysis of a National Sample of College Environments.* Washington, D.C.: U.S. Department of Health, Education, and Welfare, 1967.

Parker, C. A. "With an Eye to the Future." *Journal of College Student Personnel,* 1973, *14,* 195–201.

Parker, C. A. "On Modeling Reality." *Journal of College Student Personnel,* 1977, *18,* 419–425.

Paterson, H. F. "The Minnesota Student Personnel Program." *Educational Record,* Supplement no. 7, 1928, *9,* 3–40.

Penny, J. F. "Student Personnel Work: A Profession Stillborn?" *Personnel and Guidance Journal,* 1969, *47,* 958–962.

Perry, W., Jr. *Forms of Intellectual and Ethical Development in the College Years: A Scheme.* New York: Holt, Rinehart and Winston, 1970.

Piaget, J. "Cognitive Development in Children." In R. Ripple and V. Rockcastle (Eds.), *Piaget Rediscovered: A Report on Cognitive Studies in Curriculum Development.* Ithaca, N.Y.: School of Education, Cornell University, 1964.

Rest, J. "Developmental Psychology as a Guide to Value Education: A Review of Kohlbergian Programs." *Review of Educational Research,* 1974, *44* (2), 241–259.

Sanford, N. *The American College.* New York: Wiley, 1962.

Sanford, N. *Self and Society.* New York: Atherton Press, 1966.

Sheehy, G. *Passages—Predictable Crises of Adult Life.* New York: Dutton, 1976.

Stern, G. G. *People in Context.* New York: Wiley, 1970.

Straub, C., and Rodgers, R. "The Student Personnel Worker as Teacher: Fostering Moral Development in College Women." Paper presented at the national convention of American College Personnel Association, Detroit, March 1978.

Vaillant, G. *Adaptation to Life.* Boston: Little, Brown, 1977.

White, R. *Lives in Progress.* (3rd ed.) New York: Dryden Press, 1975.

Witkin, H. A., and others. *Psychological Differentiation.* New York: Wiley, 1962.

Lois A. Huebner   **5**

Interaction of Student and Campus

Since the time of Aristotle, a major question that has vexed philosophers has been the relationship between an individual and the environment. In a very real sense, this question lies at the core of philosophy and of all social services, because without understanding how people and their environments are related we cannot understand the most basic issues of human behavior: knowledge, feeling, and action—in short, existence. How does one know one's world? How does one affect one's world? How does the world affect the individual?

     Individuals do not act in isolation, so it has become popular to speak of "person-environment interaction." Student services professionals rally around the banners of student ecology, environmental intervention, and systems change agentry. Having discovered the theoretical short-sightedness and practical limitations of totally intrapersonal models, we now want to manipulate the way in which students interact with their environment to aid their development. The student services literature of the past five years might suggest that we are in the middle of such a revolution. But our zeal and fervor, unfortunately, are considerably ahead of our knowledge or technology. Before we can develop reasonable, effective interventions, we must know what manipulations of which variables produce what effects in which people with what certainty and risk. And we must know how individuals will repond to these efforts. We are nowhere near such specification.

This chapter, then, is devoted to extending our knowledge of the person-environment transaction. It begins with a brief overview and critique of the interactionist perspective. We critically review five promising approaches to assessing person-environment interaction and then review the research literature on person-environment congruence. To help the reader move from theory to practice, we present and critique several methods of assessing how individuals interact with their environment. In the final section, we explore the application of data and theory to interventions in the university setting.

The Interactionist Perspective

The idea that people act within contexts that influence their behavior is not recent; it has, in fact, appeared in the literature of psychology and sociology for years. Historically, three theoretical positions have been used to explain person-situation variance—"personologism," "situationism," and "interactionism" (Ekehammar, 1974). Personologism explains behavior in terms of individual attributes (or traits) that allow or cause people to act in a fairly consistent fashion in a variety of situations. Behavior is seen as largely internally directed. The opposing view, situationism, views behavior as chiefly influenced by the environment or context in which it occurs. Thus, individuals are expected to behave inconsistently (or discriminately) in differing situations. The third position, interactionism, hypothesizes that a person's attributes interact with situational variables to motivate and direct behavior. Behavior is thus a function of both the individual and the environment.

Although the interactionist perspective is often seen as a contemporary phenomenon, it can be traced (Ekehammar, 1974) back to Kantor (1926), who wrote that "no biological fact may be considered as anything but the manual interaction of the organism and the environment" (p. 369). However, despite these early beginnings and the ensuing theoretical work of such men as Tolman (1935), Angyl (1941), Murray (1938), and Murphy (1947), empirical investigations of the interactionist hypothesis failed to materialize and the position dropped from the forefront of interest. The vast majority of psychological research emphasized the contributions of either the person or the environment in producing behavior. For example, the rise of behaviorism as an important psychological theory resulted in much research documenting the power of the environment in producing and controlling behavior. Theoretical formulations by Mischel (1968) and studies by Douglas (1964), Friedlander and Greenberg (1971), Moos (1973b), and Wolf (1966) demonstrated that properties of the environment may account for more of the variance in behavior than measures of trait qualities or even biographic and demographic background data (Insel and Moos, 1974).

As Ekehammar (1974) points out, research on the interactionist hypothesis was not directly testable using correlational and factor analytic methods. However, developments in experimental methodology, especially analysis of variance techniques, made possible the direct examination of the relative contributions of the person (P), the situation or environment (E), and the $P \times E$ interaction. This examination led to findings such as those reported by Endler, Hunt, and Rosenstein (1962) that, with respect to inventories of anxiousness, interactions among modes of responses, situations, and persons are more important in producing variations in behavior than are any of the individual sources of variance alone. Other studies (Bishop and Witt, 1970; Endler and Hunt, 1966; Moos, 1968; Raush, Dittman, and Taylor, 1959; Sandell, 1968) supported these findings and the interpretation of the superiority of the interactionist perspective in accounting for human behavior. This methodological advance paved the way for the reemergence of the interactionist perspective in theory and research (Bowers, 1973; Endler, 1973; Mischel, 1973).

Based on preceding evidence, the interactionist perspective is the most compelling of the three models proposed to explain person-situation variance (Ekehammar, 1974). Although this chapter focuses on theories of the environment, remember that environments impinge on *people*—people with widely differing abilities, goals, expectations, and attitudes. And people are part of the environment and impose their own idiosyncratic interpretations and meanings on the environment. The impact of any environment is always mediated by person attributes.

Mischel (1976) has developed a promising conceptualization to account for the greater and lesser coercive or unitary effects of environments. He has identified attributes of the environment that result in its being "powerful"—having maximal treatment effects—and thus affecting most people similarly and attributes that result in the environment being "weak"—minimal treatment effects—wherein person variables have considerable impact upon behavior. Individual settings or situations can be positioned along this powerful-weak continuum to indicate the differential contributions of both person and environmental characteristics in the initiation and direction of behavior.

An active issue in the measurement of the environment concerns whether the environment should be defined by objective, directly measurable attributes—behaviors, physical characteristics, observable events— or whether it should be defined by characteristics that are subjectively experienced by participants or observers—the psychological environment, for example. Some theorists have taken a primarily objective approach (for example, Barker, 1968; Sommer, 1969); others have opted for a primarily subjective approach to the environment (for example, Jessor, 1956, 1958; Magnusson, 1971; Pace, 1969). Pervin (1968) makes the point that, although either end of this objective-subjective continuum can be easily defended, investigators' preferences ought to be contingent on evidence indicating which methods are preferable in given circumstances. Until such evidence is presented, he cautions, both kinds of data should be gathered whenever possible; both contribute to the perspective on the environment. The objective environment includes numbers of inhabitants, average number of hours spent studying, and the content and frequency of conversations; it affects and reflects the experiences of its inhabitants. Theorists who adopt an objective approach assume that a valid theory of behavior cannot be based on subjective self-report about the meaning of the physical environment (Walsh, 1973). Individual subjective impressions of the environment are rejected in favor of operationally defined and concrete, discrete, environmental variables or stimuli. But individuals and groups hold subjective perceptions about these objective, observable facts (for example, the setting is crowded or uncrowded; scholarship is or is not emphasized). Such perceptions also influence the experiences of the setting's inhabitants (French and Kahn, 1962; Pace, 1969). Those who adopt the phenomenological or subjective approach base their work on the principle that "the physical world can affect the individual only through his or her perceptions or experiences of it" (Walsh, 1973, p. 2). Hence, the psychological environment, not the physical environment, determines the way in which the individual responds or behaves.

A rapprochement between these two orientations can be made by comparing individuals' perceptions with related observable or objective indexes, especially those mediated by subgroup membership or other person attributes. Such comparisons can uncover some significant dynamics that operate in the setting (see, for example, Huebner, 1975). The integration of these two approaches, in fact, seems critical for a thorough understanding of any setting.

Sources of Environmental Impact

Many different aspects of the environment affect human functioning. Moos (1976) classifies the variables as (1) *the physical environ-*

ment, including the manmade and the natural environment—the architectural environment, weather, and geography, for example, and (2) *the social and psychological environment*—for example, behavior settings, social climate, organizational structure and functioning, and characteristics of milieu inhabitants. The social or psychological environment can be further differentiated as either an organizational attribute, which exists objectively and independently of the individual (Barker and Wright, 1955; Forehand and Gilmer, 1964; James and Jones, 1974), or as an individual attribute, which is a summary evaluation of events and characteristics and the perception of them (Jackson and Levine, 1977; Schneider, 1973; Shader and Levine, 1969).

Major Theories of Environmental Impact

Walsh (1973) delineates the formal requirements of psychological theory as: comprehensiveness, clarity and explicitness, operational adequacy, inclusion of known findings, parsimony, and generation of empirical research. Applying these criteria, he concludes that there are no true theories of person $\times$ environment interaction; at best only hypotheses, partial theories, or orientations have been presented. This view is reinforced by Proshansky, Ittelson, and Rivlin (1970).

In evaluating what he considers the five best attempts at theory-building—those by Holland, Stern, Barker, Pervin, and the subcultural approaches—on the basis of the formal criteria, Walsh awards "adequate" ratings only to Holland, for clarity and explicitness, operational adequacy in describing man, and parsimony; to Barker for inclusion of known findings; and to Stern for operational adequacy in the treatment of man. Surprisingly, no theories provided an adequate operational definition of the environment. No theories of the environment or of $P \times E$ interaction rival the more sophisticated theories of the person. Fortunately, there are theoretically and heuristically useful models that describe how the environment affects its inhabitants. Five orientations will be outlined here, with the most promising examples of models and theories in each category described briefly.

Behavior Settings. In the first orientation, people are influenced by the operation of behavior settings. Roger Barker is the primary theorist representing this approach. In his book, *Ecological Psychology* (1968), Barker maintains that environments select and shape the behavior of people who inhabit them. People tend to behave in highly similar ways in specific environments, regardless of their individual differences. Wicker (1972) uses the term "behavior-environment congruence" to describe the dynamic interaction between the inhabitants of a given setting and other aspects of the setting that produce homeostasis.

This approach has spent considerable effort on identifying and describing behavior settings. Behavior settings are basic and naturally occurring environmental units consisting of "one or more standing patterns of behavior," with the surrounding environment similar in form to the behavior (Barker, 1968, p. 18). The surrounding nonpsychological environment (the place-thing-time constellation) is called a "milieu," and it is defined as physical and independent of behavior or of perceptions (Barker and Wright, 1978). The behavior-milieu parts are called "synomorphs." A behavior setting constitutes a collection of such synomorphs and includes four factors: (1) physical components, (2) overt behaviors, (3) temporal properties, and (4) the relationship between behavioral and nonbehavioral factors (Gump, 1971; Moos, 1976). Examples of behavior settings might be a baseball game, a lecture, or a church service.

Barker suggests that behavior settings have great coercive power over the behaviors that occur within them. Research, however, has demonstrated that the influence of behavior settings is more complex than simply "demanding" certain isomorphic behaviors (Moos, 1974a). A potent contributor to behavioral variations is the number of people available in a setting to perform the essential functions of that setting. Thus, environments may be classified as underpopulated, optimally populated, or overpopulated. The population status affects the frequency, intensity, origin and termination of forces that impinge on a setting's inhabitants (Barker, 1968) and thus affects their functioning (see Wicker and Kirmeyer, 1976; Willems, 1967, 1969).

Although behavior setting theory is commonly identified with the objective approach of the study of person-environment (P-E) relationships, Barker and his colleagues attend to the phenomenological aspect of the environment by introducing the concept of "psychological habitat" (Wright, 1978). The psychological habitat is what people see and "how" they see it—the psychological meaning of their observations. The subjective or psychological meaning is approached, however, through a characteristically "objective" procedure of observing the present behavior of the person, the sequential context of the behavior, and the characteristics of present behavior settings and objects (Wright, 1978).

Barker's theory is one of the more systematic to appear and seems to be logically sound. In addition, his theory has stimulated research in organizational and work environments, groups, communities, and educational settings (Barker and Wright, 1978). Results of this research generally support Barker's formulations on overt behavior. However, the theory has a number of weaknesses. As noted by Walsh (1973), Barker has not conceptualized or operationalized his views of the individual, although he does concede that the individual must be considered when predicting behavior. In this sense, his model is situationist rather than interactionist. A strength of the position is its multidimensional quality—defining behavior settings in terms of places, objects, behaviors, and time. Its weakness is the sparse attention given to the individual.

Barker's theory also lacks any direct or significant assessment of the perceived environment. Walsh (1973), for example, further criticizes the lack of correspondence between Barker's definitions as used by field researchers. Wicker (1972, 1973), however, has recently attempted to remedy this problem by reformulating these concepts for field use.

Perhaps the most compelling criticism of behavior setting theory is that it is very complex, too specific, and too cumbersome—all of which may well mitigate against its use. "The proliferation of terms, details, and operations would discourage all but the most tenacious researcher" (Huebner, 1975, p. 39).

Environmental Press and Personal Needs. A second conception of how the environment influences people uses the notions of environmental press and personal need and is represented by the work of George Stern. Its three main assumptions are that (1) behavior (B) is a function (f) of the person (P) and the environment (E): $B = f(P \times E)$ (Stern, 1964); (2) the person is represented in terms of needs, which are inferred from self-reported behaviors (Walsh, 1973) and which refer to organizational tendencies that unify and direct a person's behavior (Stern, 1964); and (3) the environment is defined in terms of press and is inferred from the aggregate of self-reported perceptions or interpretations of the environment (Walsh, 1973; Stern, 1964). The concept of press thus provides an external situational counterpart to the internalized personal need (Stern, 1964).

Stern (1970) defines two dimensions of the person-environment relationship. The first is congruence–dissonance, and Stern hypothesizes that a relatively congruent P-E relationship (a stable and complimentary combination of need and press) would produce a sense of satisfaction and fulfillment. A dissonant P-E relationship may result in discomfort or stress, which in turn might eventuate in modification of the press, withdrawal of the participants, or, perhaps, tolerance of the dissonance.

The second dimension is related to the amount of personal growth possible for an individual in a setting, a concept Stern labels "anabolic-catabolic." An anabolic need-press situation tends to stimulate self-actualization, while a catabolic need-press pattern hinders self-enhancement and self-actualization.

Walsh finds fault with both Stern's theoretical constructs and his operational definitions of those constructs. Others have noted that research on need-press congruence does not support the theory for the outcome of achievement and satisfaction (Raab, 1963; Keith, 1965; Lauterback and Vielhaber, 1966). Moreover, little research has been done using both need and press measures, and what has been done suggests that the scales may not actually measure parallel or corresponding need-press pairs at all (Saunders, 1969; Stricker, 1967).

A major limitation in Stern's theory relates to the assumption that needs may be inferred from preferences for activities. Walsh points out that it is not clear whether self-reported preferences are useful estimates of actual behaviors. At any rate, Stern does not include any measurements of the occurrence, frequency, or intensity of behaviors in concrete situations. Selvin and Hagstrom (1963) suggest that Stern's press measure does not discriminate between public belief and private behavior or between fiction and nonfiction. Rather than guess the feelings or behaviors of others, students should be asked to describe their own feelings and behavior. Feldman and Newcomb (1969) criticize the lack of attention to the physical or objective environment and to the impact of press on behaviors (Feldman and Newcomb, 1969). Final limitations of Stern's theory include the insufficient attention paid to learning and change and to need development. Walsh (1973) also criticizes Stern for failing to explore the impact of the direction of need-press noncongruence, noting that it may make a significant difference whether individual's needs are stronger than press or whether press variables are more potent than needs.

Person-Environment Transactions. A third model for understanding the processes through which environments influence people has been proposed by L. A. Pervin (1968). According to Pervin (1968, p. 581), behavior can best be explained in terms of "objects in a causal interconnection of one object acting upon the other" (interactions) and "objects relating to one another within a system" (transactions). There are, for each individual, both interpersonal and noninterpersonal environments that suit or fit that individual's personality characteristics. A match between an individual and the environment contributes to higher performance and satisfaction and less stress, while poor fit decreases performance and increases dissatisfaction and stress. Pervin further hypothesizes that, ideally, the congruence of individual and environment should not be exact but should present opportunities for change and personal growth.

Pervin (1968) defines both the individual and the environment subjectively, according to the perceptions of setting inhabitants (for example, about self and ideal self or college and ideal college) and their reactions to those perceptions (for example, satisfaction).

Pervin's transactional model is grounded in the cognitive balance orientation articulated by Argyris (1969). The specific assumptions underlying Pervin's model are related to the discrepancies between the individual's perceived actual self and ideal self. These assumptions (Pervin, 1968; Walsh, 1973) are that

1. Individuals find large discrepancies between their perceived actual selves and ideal selves to be both unpleasant and painful.
2. Individuals are positively attracted to objects in the perceived environment that have potential for moving them toward their ideal selves. Conversely, individuals are negatively disposed toward stimuli that have potential for moving them away from their ideal selves.
3. Similarity of the individual to objects of importance is desirable when the individual's actual self and ideal self are highly discrepant.

Pervin's main hypothesis is that individuals perform better and are more satisfied in environments that tend to reduce the discrepancy between their perceived actual selves and their ideal selves (1968).

Pervin's transactional theory also can be criticized on a number of grounds (Walsh, 1973). Although the psychological significance of the environment for individuals is measured and although Pervin states that the individual is influenced by the objective environment, he never defines the environment in an objective or physical sense and makes no attempt to aggregate individual perceptions or arrive at a consensus about the "actual" psychological environment. Thus Pervin's operational definition of the environment differs from his theoretical statements about it.

Pervin's theory also ignores the function and relevance of personality variables. The theory is also more descriptive than explanatory and does not attend to the development of self-concept or ideal-self-concept or to notions such as change and learning.

Research generated by this model is sparse, and there are virtually no data concerning the model's applicability to noncollege populations. The extant research, however, does support the congruency-satisfaction hypothesis.

A final criticism concerns Pervin's confusing interchangeable uses of the terms *interaction* and *transaction* (by definition not equivalent). Although his model is not truly transactional, it is interactionist.

The Human Aggregate. The environment may also affect people via the composition of the human aggregate. That is, the major defining characteristic of an environment is closely related to the people who inhabit it: their attributes, their behavior, their goals, and so on. John Holland (1966, 1973) has contributed the most extensive body of research using this position. He defines the environment in terms of the (self-reported) vocational preferences, academic majors, or occupations of members of a population. According to Holland (1973, p. 9), the people in a given vocational group "will create characteristic interpersonal environments." Each environment is described by a six-point code that relates it (in terms of similarity) to each of six "model environments."

Personality is characterized via vocational choice (or preference), based on Holland's assumption that members of a vocational group tend to have somewhat similar personalities and histories of personal development and tend to respond to similar situations in similar ways. Holland is concerned with the degree of fit or congruence between person and environment and hypothesizes that a good fit contributes to vocational satisfaction, stability, and achievement.

The similarities among personality types, among environments, and between types and environments are ordered according to a hexagonal model; psychological similarities and differences are direct functions of the distance between points on the hexagon. Personality or environment types that are similar fall closer together on the hexagon than do less similar types.

Holland states four formal assumptions:

1. People may be described by their resemblance to one or more personality types (clusters of personal attributes) that may be used to measure the person. The six basic types, corresponding to vocational choices, are realistic, investigative, social, conventional, enterprising, and artistic. Resemblance to these types is a product of a person's life history.
2. Environments may be characterized by resemblance to one or more of the six model environments, which correspond to the six personality types. Thus, environmental models are defined in terms of the situation or atmosphere created by the people who dominate them.
3. Each personality type searches for an analogous environment.
4. Congruent person-environment relationships lead to predictable and understandable outcomes with respect to vocational choice, stability, and achievement; personal stability and development; and creative performance.

Holland makes use of two additional constructs in studying person-environment relationships: (1) *consistency*—similarity of primary and secondary personality characteristics or environment orientations, such as realistic-investigative (consistent) types versus conventional-artistic (inconsistent) types, and (2) *differentiation*—degree to which a person or environment resembles just one type of model. Satisfaction is theoretically related to these two constructs as well: People having more consistent and more highly differentiated personality patterning generally are more satisfied.

In terms of evaluation, Holland's assumptions are, for the most part, both consistent and explicit. In addition, the theory seems to hold up well in light of empirical research (Helms and Williams, 1973; Walsh, 1973) and has been tested on a wide variety of people (Holland and Gottfredson, 1976). Walsh, however, questions the logic behind some of the assumptions, noting, for example, that "the evidence supporting the supposition that interest inventories are personality inventories is certainly not conclusive" (1973, p. 91). Other criticisms are that the theory is primarily descriptive, not explanatory (although this criticism is nicely countered by Holland and Gottfredson, 1976), that neither the perceived nor the physical environment is assessed, and that the theory does not significantly attend to the issues of learning and change or to the process of personality development. Finally, the classification of occupations may differ for the different devices used to assess the type and many important personal and environmental contingencies that lie outside the scope of the typology (Holland and Gottsfredson, 1976). The theory is, however, truly interactionist and operationalizes both person and environment.

Social Climate. In the final model to be presented, the environment has been hypothesized to affect people via the construct of organizational or social "climate." Industrial and organizational psychologists frequently use this approach and have refined both the measurement and understanding of these concepts (see for example, James and Jones, 1974; Gavin and Howe, 1975).

Outside of the industrial and organizational area, Rudolf Moos has perhaps been the one most responsible for advances in the study of social climate and its impact, which Moos (1974a, p. 3) sees as extending to "attitudes and moods . . . behavior . . . health and overall sense of well-being, and . . . social, personal and intellectual development."

Moos' approach is based on the theoretical work of Murray (1938), Lewin (1936), and Stern (1964, 1970). His focus is the perceived climate, which he measures via respondents' descriptions of the usual patterns of behavior that occur in their setting plus their own perceptions of the environment. Moos thus measures (Murray's) consensual beta press (Gerst and Moos, 1972).

Moos and his colleagues at the Stanford Social Ecology Laboratory have studied the social climate in eight different types of environments and from this have empirically generated three broad categories or
clusters of dimensions (Moos, 1974b; Insel and Moos, 1974): *relationship*
(how people affiliate, their mutual support), *personal development* (the
potential or opportunity in the environment for personal growth and
the development of self-esteem), and *system maintenance and change*
(the extent to which the environment is orderly and clear in its expectations, maintains control, and responds to change). These dimensions are
similar across the eight environments studied and also appear in the
analysis of other organizational climate, according to Insel and Moos
(1974). They conclude that these three categories of dimensions "must
all be accounted for in order for an adequate and reasonably complete
picture of the environment to emerge." (p. 186).

Although Moos' research has to date been primarily concerned
with describing environments or, to a lesser extent, describing the effects
of environments on people (for example, recent research relates environmental dimensions to affective, attitudinal, and behavioral outcomes), his model is in theory interactional and calls for the study of the
link between people and environments, including P-E matches (Cowen,
1977a). His approach now appears to be broadening as published research attends more to P-E interactions and as he begins to consider the
impact of the "human aggregate," organizational structure, the physical environment, and so forth on the social climate and on human
functioning (Moos, 1976).

Moos' major work is more recent than that of the other theorists
mentioned and consequently has not been subject to the same critical
review. However, his model seems to be limited by its singular focus on
the phenomenological or psychological environment, to the exclusion
of physical or other objective characteristics. The reliance on the concept
of social climate as the moderator of environmental impact also seems
narrow, because research indicates that there are other significant sources
of impact as well.

Moos also does not provide a detailed conceptualization of the
person, although he does discuss the contribution of the interactionist
researchers to the study of person influences on behavior (Moos, 1976).
Although Moos' theory is interactionist in orientation, he has failed to
translate this into his own research, and thus his studies are largely
situationist in perspective.

Moos has used his model in a diverse set of situations and has
shown consistencies in underlying climate dimensions across these settings (Moos, 1979). His model also seems to have considerable heuristic
value. Most research has studied relationship dimensions, however, and

more research needs to be done on system maintenance and change and on personal development.

A Summary. The five quasi-theoretical approaches to studying person-environment interactions and the environment's impact on its inhabitants presented here represent some of the most useful and interesting models developed to date. However, several additional approaches have been widely used and deserve mention (Moos, 1974a): (1) the definition of objective ecological variables or dimensions by which the environment can be classified (for example, meteorological and physical design characteristics); (2) the description of dimensions of organizational structure or organizational functioning and its effects on individual and group behavior; and (3) identification of functional or reinforcement properties of the environment that maintain particular behaviors. Walsh (1973, p. 188) concludes that "the area of person-environment interaction is a long way from having a theory that may be considered a full-fledged general theory."

Person-Environment Congruence

Person-environment congruence is a major conceptual tool used by a cross-section of theorists to predict behavior and understand the person-environment relationship. This concept and the research conducted to explore its concomitant has provided some links between differing theoretical approaches, including the five just described. A good fit between persons (their needs, attitudes, goals, and expectations) and the environment (its press, demands, supports, and the characteristics of its inhabitants) is generally hypothesized to have a positive impact, promoting satisfaction, productivity, performance, achievement, personal growth, and so on while poor fit creates stress. A promising refinement of this proposition has been made by Pervin and other theorists but has not been tested in reported research. This refinement concerns the differential impact of maximal or perfect congruence versus optimal or imperfect congruence. There is some conceptual support for the notion that a degree of misfit, or optimal incongruence, enhances personal growth and is to be preferred over a perfect fit between person and environment.

Because a number of the theories we reviewed earlier focus on the individual and the setting as part of one total situation, the "goodness-of-fit" between the two (congruence) has been a popular research topic. Because various researchers give the concept of congruence differing operational definitions, the results generated from the major orientations are presented by researcher.

Holland defines person-environment (P-E) congruence as the match between personal orientation (type) and model environment. Results of his research (1968) on P-E congruence suggest two tentative theoretical rules about congruence and satisfaction: (1) students tend to be more satisfied the more closely they resemble the dominant pressure(s) in their environment, and (2) students probably report more satisfaction in colleges that exhibit heterogeneous profiles (Walsh, 1973). In addition, in accord with Holland's theoretical orientation, if an individual possesses an accurate perception of self and reality, he or she is more likely to select environments congruent with his or her personal orientation (Holland, 1962; Holland, Gottfredson, and Nafziger, 1975; Osipow, Ashby, and Wall, 1966). Holland also predicts that congruent P-E relations should tend to stimulate achievement, satisfaction, and the reinforcement of successful coping behavior. Brown (1968), Holland (1968), Morrow (1971), Nafziger, Holland, and Gottfredson (1975), and Williams (1967) likewise found support for Holland's prediction that congruent person-environment relationships are positively related to satisfaction. Finally, studies by Walsh and Russel (1969) and by Walsh and Lewis (1972) support Holland's theory with respect to the reinforcement of successful coping behavior.

Stern defines P-E congruence as a close fit between the needs of an individual and the press of the environment. Research related to this model has been reported for the outcome measures of achievement, satisfaction, and student-college fit. Stern's hypothesis that need-press congruence tends to be associated with greater achievement was not confirmed (Keith, 1965; Landis, 1964). Several studies, in fact, found that low need-press congruence stimulated achievement (Kirkland, 1967; Lauterbach and Vielhaber, 1966; Pace, 1964). Results from studies using a satisfaction measure are mixed: Two studies failed to find any significant relationship (Keith, 1965; Raab, 1963), and one study lent some support to the hypothesis that need-press congruence is related to greater satisfaction (Landis, 1964).

The study of student-college fit as it relates to need-press congruence (Stern, 1962a, 1965) indicates that when need and press scale (or factor) means are related across schools, rather than across people, relationships emerge that suggest some congruence between the average level of student need and prevailing environmental pressure. These findings were taken to indicate that students characterized by a certain need pattern tend to be found at institutions with appropriate press.

According to Pervin, P-E congruence is a match between the individual (ideal self-concept or actual self-concept) and the individual's perception of the environment. Pervin carried out four studies on the relationship between P-E congruence and satisfaction. In three of these studies (Pervin, 1967b; Pervin and Rubin, 1967; Pervin and Smith, 1968), results supported the hypothesis that congruence (small discrepancies between self and college, self and students, college and ideal college, self and "eating club," and ideal self and "eating club") is related to satisfaction.

A fourth study (Pervin, 1967a) was designed to test the hypothesis that the college is perceived as moving the individual toward his or her ideal self if the college is rated between the self and the ideal self (S–C–IS) and that satisfaction is then reported. The secondary hypothesis was that the college is perceived as pulling the individual farther from the ideal self if it is rated on one side of the self and the ideal self is on the other side (C–S–IS) and that dissatisfaction would be reported. The first prediction was not supported: Relationships between scale values and satisfaction ratings were low. The second hypothesis was supported, however. Pervin draws the implication that students may be more aware of and sensitive to cognitive inconsistency than they are to cognitive consistency. Thus, they are more likely to support and express their dissatisfaction than to report satisfaction.

Bauer (1975) examined student satisfaction and performance related to congruence between perception of self and perception of the environment. Performance was significantly correlated with P-E fit when the environment was defined either by students as a group or by the faculty. Satisfaction with academic aspects of the school was also related to the congruence between self and perceived environment.

Pervin (1968) reviews a number of research studies (from a variety of theoretical perspectives) related to the impact of P-E congruence and incongruence. He states (p. 57) that "a number of studies show that a fit between the personality characteristics of one individual and those of another, or between an individual and the social climate created by a group of individuals, leads to high performance." Research supporting this conclusion has been reported by Smelser (1961), Amison and Flanders (1961), Grimes and Allinsmith (1961), Beach (1960), and McKeachie (1961).

The relationship between P-E fit and increased satisfaction has also received some empirical support (Brophy, 1959; Douvan and Kaye, 1962; Funkenstein, 1962; Lott and Lott, 1965; Sanford, 1962). Relationships between student personality variables, the work setting, and student performance were also substantiated (Bay, 1962; Katz and Sanford, 1962; Malleson, 1959; McConnell and Heist, 1962; Patton, 1955; Snyder, 1966). According to Claunch (1964), grades reflect the interaction between the student's mode of operation and the tasks set by the environment.

The concept of congruence can also be used to study the relationship of incidence of mental illness or other dysfunction to population characteristics (such as race, ethnic group, social class, age, place of birth, and religion) using the notion of minority and majority subgroup membership. According to Moos (1976, p. 309), "there is some evidence that groups who are not congruent with their communities, either racially or ethnically, may have higher rates of disorder than their counterparts living in areas where they are congruent with the majority." Such results are noted for rates of schizophrenia relative to blacks and whites (Faris and Dunham, 1939), for juvenile delinquency and diagnosed mental illness for blacks and whites (Klee, and others, 1967), for severe psychiatric disorders relative to Italians in Italian versus non-Italian communities (Mintz and Schwartz, 1964), and for hospitalization rates for people who were incongruent versus those who were congruent with their communities on such characteristics as age, marital status, and place of birth classifications (Wechsler and Pugh, 1967).

The most common explanation for these findings related to congruence with one's community is that incongruent groups experience greater social isolation than other (more congruent) residents. Bell (1961) has reported some empirical support for this isolation hypothesis.

This review indicates that the research on person-environment congruence, however defined, supports the following general relationship: Congruence is related to satisfaction, achievement, successful coping behavior, and better performance. Conversely, lack of congruence has been related to mental illness, delinquency, and hospitalization. In addition, people tend to seek out environments congruent with their own significant personal qualities.

Methods of Assessment

Person-environment assessment is not yet a very sophisticated science nor a very advanced art. A variety of instruments have been developed and standardized, however, and can be used to measure certain aspects or qualities of environments. Menne (1967) has classified these instruments into three basic (although not independent) types: demographic, perceptual, and behavioral. A fourth—multimethod— has been identified by Hyne (1973). In addition, as we have seen, a number of theorists have conceptualized person and environment as interdependent parts of one situation and hence have attempted to measure both with similar or parallel operation. Therefore, in the description of assessment instruments that follows, when such companion person measures have been developed to accompany a given environmental measure, that is indicated, and the person measure is briefly described as well.

The Demographic Approach. The demographic approach is largely descriptive and, in a university environment, is concerned with such variables as institutional size, ability level of students, number and rank of faculty, student-faculty ratio, and number of library books. Holland's Environmental Assessment Technique, or EAT (Astin and Holland, 1961) measures eight such variables: total number of students, average intelligence of students, and the institution's score on each of six model environment scales. The person measure companion to the EAT is the Vocational Preference Inventory, or VPI (Holland, 1965), on which students indicate which of 160 occupations they find appealing. Based on the pattern of responses, each individual is designated as a certain personality type using a three-point code. A more complex person measure also used in conjunction with the EAT is the Self-Directed Search (Holland, 1971), which uses students' activities, competencies, projected occupations, and self-ratings to assess their resemblance to each personality type. Other examples of the demographic approach to environmental assessment include the factor analytic studies of Astin (1962) and of Richards, Rand, and Rand (1965) and the Master Institutional File of Craeger and Sell (1968).

The Perceptual Approach. The perceptual approach to environment assessment is the best developed and most widely used and involves obtaining responses to a series of descriptive statements, yielding a global characterization of the institution in terms of certain scales or factors. This technique may be used to compare the perceptions of various constituent subgroups or may be modified to obtain perceptions of the "expected," "actual," or "ideal" environment (Morrill, 1973).

Pervin used this approach in designing the Transactional Analysis of Personality and Environment, or TAPE (Pervin and Rubin, 1967), which requires that respondents rate each of several concepts (such as self, ideal self, college, ideal college, faculty, administration, students) on fifty-two scales using an eleven-point semantic differential. Thus, students supply data for both person and environment measurement on one form.

Moos also adopted this perceptual methodology in constructing his series of parallel environmental scales (for example, the Classroom Environment Scale, Moos and Trickett, 1974, and the University Residence Environment Scale, Moos and Gerst, 1974). Each of these scales contains a number of subscales that measure the relationship, personal development, and system maintenance and change dimensions of the environment. (Not all scales have each type of subscale, however.) These scales assess "similar underlying patterns in a wide variety of social

environments" (Moos, 1976, p. 5). A more recent description and application of these scales is provided by Moos (1979).

The perceptual approach was used by Stern and his colleagues as
well in developing several measures of environmental press, collectively
called the Syracuse Indexes. Included are the College Characteristics
Index (Pace and Stern, 1958), the High School Characteristics Index
(Stern, 1970), the Organizational Climate Index (Stern, 1970) and the
Evening College Characteristics Index (Stern, 1970). Each of these instruments consists of 300 items that measure thirty kinds of press, each
parallel to an analogous personal need scale (from the Activities Index,
Pace and Stern, 1958). Respondents indicate, via true or false responses,
whether the described activities, policies, procedures, attitudes, and
impressions are characteristic of their school. Thus the environment is
defined as collectively perceived and measured based on activities that
occur or are perceived to occur there. The Activities Index, measuring
personal needs, also consists of 300 "like-dislike" items. There are ten
items for each of thirty need scales, which are based on Murray's
classification.

Other well-known perceptual instruments include the College
and University Environment Scales, or CUES (Pace, 1964; Pace and
Baird, 1966), the Institutional Functioning Inventory (Peterson and
others, 1970), and the Institutional Goals Inventory (Educational Testing Service, 1972). A brief description of the content and psychometric
characteristics of all of these perceptual instruments is provided in an
excellent overview by Baird and Hartnett (1980).

The Behavioral Approach. In the behavioral approach, specific,
observable constituent behaviors are studied as guides to the institutional climate or environment. This approach is not well developed, but a
few instruments seem promising. McDowell and Chickering's (1967)
Experience of College Questionnaire has students report their concrete
experiences and behaviors in several general areas—academics, extracurricular activities, relationships with peers, student-faculty relations,
and religious experiences and activities. The Inventory of College Activities, or ICA (Astin, 1971a, 1971b) is designed to describe and measure
some of the important differences among the environments of undergraduate institutions. Students respond to sixteen items that gather
information about their history, career goals, and college experience and
to four questions that require student evaluation of their college's atmosphere. Other methodologies in this genre include unstructured student interviews (Bloom, 1971; Carruth and Comer, 1972) and
participant-observer debriefings (Eddy, 1959; Kennedy and Danskin,
1968).

The Multimethod Approach. The multimethod approach actually is a conglomerate of the previous techniques and thus may combine demographic, perceptual, and behavioral approaches in an attempt to gather a variety of relevant information in a single administration. Two instruments that employ this approach are the College Student Questionnaire, or CSQ (Peterson, 1968), which measures attitudinal and biographical information about students, and the Questionnaire on Student and College Characteristics (Centra, 1970), which measures perceptual and behavioral data for the purpose of providing information to prospective students about the environment at various colleges and universities.

An Evaluation. The major focus of published person-environment assessment instruments has been on describing, classifying, and/ or differentiating institutions; that is, on making interinstitutional comparisons. Thus an instrument is administered on a campus, and the results are compared with profiles of other, similar colleges. An alternative, and more programmatically useful, strategy is to study the unique features of and relationships within one given institution; that is, to make an entirely ipsative assessment of intrainstitutional variables. Baird (1971, p. 85), in commenting on the usefulness of campus assessment measures for making program or other administrative decisions, noted that "more attention has been devoted to gathering general knowledge than to developing measures of high utility" in campus decision making. He called for a reversal in this trend, urging test developers to "develop instruments and information systems that could be the basis for individual and institutional decision."

Each approach surveyed here has both advantages and disadvantages for decision making, as well as regarding the more usual issues of reliability, validity, norms, standardization, and so on.

The demographic approach (as reviewed by Morrill, 1973) has the advantages of using information that is verifiable and readily available so that widespread comparative research is facilitated. Demographic variables are also easily manipulated during environmental interventions. However, the integration of these data is ambiguous and perhaps arbitrary, and sources of impact within a university are difficult to specify. In addition, demographic measures tend to be stable over time (for example, test-retest reliability of five or six scales of the EAT over six years ranged from .80 to .97), so environmental changes that have occurred may not be reflected. The demographic approach, then, appears to be most useful in providing data to augment and clarify results from other types of assessment (Hyne, 1973; Morrill, 1973).

The perceptual approach has several advantages (Hyne, 1973; Morrill, 1973), including sensitivity to person-environment change, straightforward interpretation, less need for representative sampling (Centra, 1970), and the availability of several published, psychometrically adequate instruments. Morrill (1973) cites the following possible drawbacks of perceptual measures: (1) they may reflect only the perceived environment and not necessarily the "actual" environment; (2) students' reports may be biased or inaccurate because of an "image lag," a selected and limited perspective, or a tendency to "overrate" the institution; and (3) perceptual measures generally fail to provide specific information about sources of impact or press within the environment.

Morrill's concerns show that there is some disagreement over the accuracy with which perceptual measures may reflect the objective environment. Centra (1968) also mentions the possibility of "image lag" and a tendency toward "overrating the institution." Austin (1970) warns about the bias introduced by a sample's limited perspective. And theorists in the area of organizational climate note the influence of individual (person) variance in perceptual descriptions and caution against assuming accuracy of perception (Guion, 1973; James and Jones, 1974). Nevertheless, research on the Syracuse Indexes led Stern (1964, p. 167) to conclude that (1) "perceptions of institutional environments are not a function of the personal characteristics of the participant (McFee, 1961; Stern, 1962b); (2) perceptions of the environment by experienced participants are consensual—respondents from the same institution are more alike in their perceptions of the institution than in their perceptions of themselves (Stern, 1962a, 1962b); and (3) the consensual perception of the environment reflects the objective environment (Pace and Stern, 1958)."

Care must be taken to distinguish between (1) perceptions that are designed to, or do, reflect objective environmental characteristics and (2) perceptions that are designed to, or do, reflect the personality characteristics of inhabitants (Jackson and Levine, 1977). This requires further work in delineating the interaction of personality variables and perceptual responses (under what circumstances and how they interact) and the differentiation of the various types of press or environment that can be measured.

The behavioral approach provides accurate and detailed accounts of activities within a setting, which Chickering (1972, p. 142) sees as providing "immediately useful and powerful information for program planners and decision makers." It can also pinpoint issues specific to a particular campus that may be missed by other approaches (Hyne, 1973). A disadvantage noted by Centra (1970) is the "crucial" need for representative sampling.

Analysis of the issues presented earlier, augmented with more detailed critiques by reviewers such as Hyne (1973), Morrill (1973), and

Huebner (1975), lead to the following conclusions. First, environments must not be viewed as monolithic; rather, subenvironments and subgroups must be identified and studied independently and in relation to each other. In this regard, Moos (1976), Cowen (1973), and Anastasi (1967) have urged the creation of a taxonomy of environments to aid both in further research and in interventions. Second, descriptive instruments designed to make interinstitutional comparisons are inadequate for decision making for intervention purposes. Instead, diagnostic instruments (Centra, 1968) yielding "data about the causes or sources of pressure that influence the environment" (Morrill, 1973, p. 45) must be used. Third, locally developed instruments may likely prove more useful than standardized instruments in planning and evaluating environmental intervention (Aulepp and Delworth, 1976; Austin, 1970; Oetting, 1976a, 1976b), and their use should be encouraged. A sound argument for using standardized instruments for similar intrainstitutional applications was made by Baird (Baird and Hartnett, 1980) and provides an interesting contrast in perspective. Fourth, multiple measures and multiple approaches must be employed and integrated to achieve a more complex and complete understanding of environments and P-E relationships (Centra and Linn, 1970; Chickering, 1972; Huebner and Corazzini, 1978; Huebner and Paul, 1978). Fifth, relationships between the "objective" environment and the "perceived" environment must be further delineated, along with relationships between "perceptions" and personality factors (James and Jones, 1974).

Wicker (1972, p. 613) summarizes succinctly the basic thrust of this position: "Research must reflect the interdependence of the man-environment relationship. Studies must not treat persons or settings merely as objects to be measured, but rather as interacting components of a system. Complexities must be grappled with, even at the expense of certain niceties of research design."

Alternative Assessment Strategies. Ekehammar (1974) offers several timely suggestions for applying new measurement techniques to the study of the person and the environment. One method that has been employed is analyzing one selected response variable (such as anxiety) for a sample of persons observed in different situations. A factor analysis of correlations among situations across people may be used to obtain a taxonomy of situational dimensions (for example, see Ekehammar, Magnusson, and Ricklander, 1974; Endler, Hunt, and Rosenstein, 1962; Frederiksen, 1972; Sakoda, 1952).

A second method is to observe a sample of individuals in different situations, in each of which a sample of several reactions (and especially their patterns) is measured. Collapsing data across individuals, computing correlations among situations across reactions, and then factor analyzing this correlation matrix yield factors that according to Frederiksen (1972) can constitute the categories in a taxonomy of situations. A related but more sophisticated method is a three-mode factor analysis that essentially produces, simultaneously, situation factors, response factors, and person factors (for example, see Frederiksen, Jensen, and Beaton, 1972; Levin, 1965).

Ekehammar's final suggestion is an elaboration of Magnusson's (1971) notion that the method of "similarity estimation," followed by multidimensional scaling techniques, could be effective in studying the psychological situation or environment. In this method, subjects give direct estimates of situational similarity for each pair of situations presented. The multidimensional scaling analysis then indicates which factors individuals use in their perceptions of the stimulus situations. To date, the situational factors identified using this method have been labeled (interpreted) as active, passive, positive, negative, and social (Ekehammar and Magnusson, 1973; Magnusson, 1971; Magnusson and Ekehammar, 1973).

A measurement technique that has been specifically designed for use in the study of person-environment interactions (Huebner and Corazzini, 1978) is the Environmental Referent (ER). The ER is designed to provide specific, concrete data on situations identified as particularly stressful (or growth producing). Respondents are asked to provide written descriptions of factors (referents) that cause them to experience the identified situation as stressful and incongruent (or growth-producing and congruent). They may also be asked to indicate how they have coped or dealt with the situation or what could be done to improve the situation. Responses may be analyzed in a variety of ways (Aulepp and Delworth, 1976; Huebner, 1975) to isolate particularly dysfunctional environmental features or aspects and activities that aid successful coping, as well as to identify those individuals who may find adaptive and positive methods for dealing with poor environmental circumstances. A major function of this assessment tool is to provide the kind of detailed and concrete information about what is "wrong" so that corrective interventions may be instituted. Although of recent origin, this technique shows a good deal of promise and would most likely be classified in the "multimethod" category. The major drawback to its use is its cumbersomeness in terms of respondents' time and data analysis.

Intervening in Person-Environment Interaction

Understanding as we now do the contribution of person-environment interactions to the determination of behavior and other outcomes, it seems appropriate to channel this understanding into our efforts as student services professionals. The major implication seems to be that interventions may be directed toward individuals, toward their settings (or the environment), and toward the points of intersection between the person and the environment, as well (Paul and Huebner, 1977). We need to fit environments and students together, facilitate appropriate and responsible use of the environment by students, increasing accurate and speedy communication between the two, and make each more responsive to the needs, requirements, and structures of the other, in a truly ecological sense.

Pressure to move in these directions has been building and increasing for at least a decade. In 1967, Oetting suggested that counselors assume a developmental role aimed at both the student and institution. One aspect of this role is determining whether students are able to use the college environment for personal, intellectual, or social development. Related functions involve providing programs that either prepare the student to engage and use the environment or create changes in the environment so that the developmental experiences students need are available. This perspective has been more fully elaborated by Morrill and his associates (Morrill and Hurst, 1971; Morrill, Ivey, and Oetting, 1968; Morrill, Oetting, and Hurst, 1974) who have defined three roles for counseling psychologists, including "to contribute to, support, modify and enhance the learning environment; to facilitate maximum utilization of the learning environment by students; and to study the student, the learning environment and their interaction as a means of providing the necessary data base for the implementation of roles one and two" (Morrill, Oetting, and Hurst, 1974, p. 355). An important notion was that interventions should be directed not only toward students knowledgeable or hurt enough to seek and find help but also toward all students.

Several task forces of the Western Interstate Commission for Higher Education (WICHE) have reported "innumerable mismatches" between the campus environment and organization and the requirements of campus members (Western Interstate Commission for Higher Education, 1973). They urge that a high priority be given to finding people and methods to "map out mismatches" to build environments and structural organizations that will better fit student developmental needs and faculty and staff needs.

The interest in broadened and expanded roles that encompass students, the environment, and their interaction has been accompanied by interest in the prevention of emotional as well as academic distress and by an orientation toward development and positive mental health or programming to facilitate the normal growth of normal people (Kelly, 1974; White, 1973). Terms such as *organizational development, primary prevention, community involvement, outreach, paraprofessionals,* and *consultation* have become commonplace. There has also been an interest in, as well as a felt necessity for, greater involvement with the university's major functions, so that counseling and student functions may be better integrated into the mainstream of university aims and activities.

Although there is much discussion and exhortation, it is difficult to assess exactly how much is actually being attempted in these areas and with what success. Based on several assessment efforts and some informal data gathering at national conventions and from the literature (for example, Cowen, 1977a, 1977b; Lewis and Lewis, 1977; Morrill and Banning, 1973), it does not seem that efforts in these emerging areas are proceeding as quickly or successfully as had been anticipated.

However, as we have outlined this general environment orientation, a number of types of interventions seem possible, and some efforts are being made in most of these categories. Figure 1 depicts a number of dimensions along which interventions might vary. First, either the environment or the person may be the focal point or target of the intervention. Also, both may be considered simultaneously. A second major dimension is the theoretical perspective taken: whether the intervention is based on concepts of positive mental health or on dysfunction. There is also a "level of analysis" dimension, indicating concern with either the individual (or his or her personal environment), group (and its environment), or community or institution (and the total environment). Within each cell, we may also have either research (and related theory) or programmatic activities. For example, Blocher (1977) reviews research on the learning environment and describes seven "necessary conditions" for structural change (learning) to occur: involvement, challenge, support, structure, feedback, application, and integration. Although these dimensions seem to hold as abstractions for the general "community" level and offer the "elements of a schema by which to analyze and improve the quality" of the learning environment, Blocher notes that individual students have unique needs, strengths, and so on, and hence envisions "an infinite number of classroom environmental profiles with differential loading on each variable, depending on student characteristics and desired outcomes (Blocher, 1977, pp. 354–355). Iscoe (1974) and Kaswan (1973) make similar efforts to describe the necessary environmental conditions for a "competent community" and for individual "psychological effectiveness," respectively. Efforts to identify and rate the severity of life changes or life stress (Holmes and Rahe, 1967) have also captured attention recently. Studies in the epidemiological mold have attempted to identify and describe the distribution patterns of various dysfunction types in the population and then to hypothesize about their causes.

Theoretical Orientation

		Positive Mental Health Concepts		*Dysfunction Concepts*	
		Research	*Programs*	*Research*	*Programs*
	Unit				
Environment	Group				
	Community				
Target					
	Unit				
Person	Group				
	Community				

Figure 1. A Model for Classifying Ecologically Oriented Interventions

In terms of the educational setting, the description of psychosocial dimensions of classroom environments and their relation to student behavior, achievement, performance, and affect has received attention from researchers (Kleinfeld, 1973; Pulvino and Hansen, 1972; Walberg, 1969a, 1969b; Walberg and Anderson, 1972). So, too, have the effects of teaching or testing methods on different types of students (Amison and Flanders, 1971; Beach, 1960; Claunch, 1964; Grimes and Allinsmith, 1961), the relationship between student and college environmental variables and dropout rates (Douvan and Kaye, 1962; Funkenstein, 1962; Pervin, 1967a; Summerskill, 1962), evaluations of curriculum by student interactions as related to performance (Katz and Sanford, 1962; Malleson, 1959; McConnell and Heist, 1962; Snyder, 1966), mode of information presentation and student motivation (Bay, 1962; McKeachie, 1961; Patton, 1955), and school size or under- and over-manned status and student participation rates, and student participation rates and achievement (Baird, 1969; Barker and Gump, 1964).

Attempts to study and then intervene (for example, "action research") in the environments of residence hall floors (Daher, Corazzini, and McKinnon, 1977), a medical school (Huebner, 1978), and the university as a whole (Conyne, 1975) have also been described. Other interesting interventions may involve increasing the accuracy, salience, and timeliness of information communicated to students (Paul and Huebner, 1977); making available self-help and self-administered vocational inventories and information (Holland and Gottfredson, 1976), and funneling "marginal students" into undermanned subenvironments.

Person-oriented interventions and research have also been changing according to this ecological orientation. There have been innumerable studies of the possible biological and psychological factors involved in emotional disorders and in learning abilities and styles. A more recent emphasis has been oriented toward identifying adult stages of development, including the progression of moral and intellectual development (Kohlberg and Mayer, 1972; Loevinger, 1976; Perry, 1968). These efforts have contributed to interventions in the structure of learning situations and in methods of teaching designed to produce changes in cognitive development and to the whole area of "deliberate psychological education" (Sprinthall, 1975). Other ventures, such as research on student problem-solving strategies (Goldfried and D'Zurilla, 1969) and on behavioral self-control techniques (Mahoney and Thoresen, 1974), as well as the area of affective education, are gaining increased momentum, and attempts to teach such skills are gaining acceptance. Courses on coping strategies (Dooley and Catalano, 1977) and competency-based life skills of all kinds (such as assertion, interpersonal relating, life planning, effective parenting, communication skills, and career decision making) are also taking their place as academic course content and counseling outreach activities.

There has also been an interest in adaptability concepts (Beiser, Feldman, and Egelhoff, 1972), anticipatory guidance (Heller and Monahan, 1977), as well as in the ability of some people to convert stress into growth-producing experiences (Finkel and Jacobsen, 1977). And teaching environmental negotiation skills is beginning on several campuses. In regard to this, Moos (1975) has suggested interventions aimed at teaching people to better select their settings and to transcend environmental pressure when necessary.

In a move the preceding review might suggest, Cowen (1977b) quotes from Kessler and Albee's 1975 analysis of the area of primary prevention, noting that "nearly everything, it appears, has implications for primary preventions, for reducing emotional disturbance, for strengthening and fostering mental health" (1975, p. 560). A problem, however, is that we student services professionals, like everyone else, have narrower competencies than Cowen's "nearly everything," and it is easy to overstep those competence boundaries. Recognizing this dilemma, Cowen identifies two clusters of variables that have been demonstrated to affect mental health outcomes and that are also within the purview of psychologists. He urges that we concentrate our preventive efforts on the analysis and modification of social environments and on competency building, and he suggests that we proceed with "concrete, here-and-now, do-able 'baby steps,'" rather than amorphous, gargantuan, boundary-busting "save the world non-do-ables" (Cowen, 1977b, p. 489). This seems like good advice for campus student services in general.

References

Amison, E., and Flanders, N. A. "The Effects of Direct and Indirect Teacher Influence on Dependent-Prone Students Learning Geometry." *Journal of Educational Psychology*, 1961, *52*, 286–291.

Anastasi, A. "Psychology, Psychologists, and Psychological Testing." *American Psychologist*, 1967, *22*, 297–806.

Angyl, A. *Foundation for a Science of Personality.* New York: Commonwealth Fund, 1941.

Argyris, C. "The Incompleteness of Social-Psychological Theory: Examples From Small Groups, Cognitive Consistency, and Attribution Research." *American Psychologist*, 1969, *24*, 893–908.

Astin, A. W. "An Empirical Characterization of Higher Educational Institutions." *Educational Psychology*, 1962, *53*, 224–235.

Astin, A. W. "Two Approaches to Measuring Students' Perceptions of Their College Environment." *Journal of College Student Personnel*, 1971a, *12* (3), 169–172.

Astin, A. W. *Manual for the Inventory of College Activities.* Minneapolis: National Computer Systems, 1971b.

Astin, A. W., and Holland, J. "The Environmental Assessment Technique: A Way to Measure College Environments." *Journal of Educational Psychology*, 1961, *52*, 308–316.

Aulepp, L. A., and Delworth, U. *Training Manual For An Ecosystem Model.* Boulder, Colo.: Western Interstate Commission for Higher Education, 1976.

Austin, M. *Methods for Surveying Opinion Among University Students and Faculty.* Seattle: Bureau of Testing, University of Washington, 1970.

Baird, L. L. "Big School, Small School: A Critical Examination of the Hypothesis." *Journal of Educational Psychology*, 1969, *60*, 253–260.

Baird, L. L. "The Functions of College Environmental Measures." *Journal of Educational Measurement*, 1971, *8* (2), 83–86.

Baird, L. L., and Hartnett, R. T. "Directory of Leading Instruments for Assessing Campus Environments." In L. L. Baird, R. T. Hartnett, and Associates, *Understanding Student and Faculty Life: Using Campus Surveys to Improve Academic Decision Making.* San Francisco: Jossey-Bass, 1980.

Barker, R. G. *Ecological Psychology: Concepts and Methods for Studying the Environment of Human Behavior.* Stanford, Calif.: Stanford University Press, 1968.

Barker, R. G., and Gump, P. V. *Big School, Small School.* Stanford, Calif.: Stanford University Press, 1964.

Barker, R. G., and Wright, H. F. *Midwest and Its Children.* New York: Harper & Row, 1955.

Barker, R. G., and Wright, H. F. "Standing Patterns of Behavior." In R. G. Barker and Associates, *Habitats, Environments and Human Behavior: Studies in Ecological Psychology and Eco-Behavioral Science.* San Francisco: Jossey-Bass, 1978.

Bauer, G. E. *"Performance and Satisfaction as a Function of Person Environment Fit."* Unpublished doctoral dissertation, University of Missouri, Columbia, 1975.

Bay, C. "A Social Theory of Higher Education." In N. Sanford (Ed.), *The American College.* New York: Wiley, 1962.

Beach, L. R. "Sociability and Academic Achievement in Various Types of Learning Situations." *Journal of Educational Psychology,* 1960, *51,* 208–212.

Beiser, M., Feldman, J., and Egelhoff, G. "Assets and Affects: A Study of Positive Mental Health." *Archives of General Psychiatry,* 1972, *27,* 545–549.

Bell, W. "The Utility of the Shevky Typology for the Design of Urban Sub-Area Field Studies." In G. Theodorson (Ed.), *Studies in Human Ecology.* New York: Harper & Row, 1961.

Bishop, D. W., and Witt, P. A. "Sources of Behavioral Variance During Leisure Time." *Journal of Personality and Social Psychology,* 1970, *16,* 352–360.

Blocher, D. H. "The Counselor's Impact on Learning Environments." *Personnel and Guidance Journal,* 1977, *55,* (6), 352–355.

Bloom, B. L. "Strategies for the Prevention of Mental Disorders." In J. Glidwell and M. Brown (Eds.), *Community Issues in Contemporary Psychology and Preventive Mental Health.* New York: Behavioral Publications, 1971.

Bowers, K. S. "Situations in Psychology: An Analysis and a Critique." *Psychological Review,* 1973, *80,* 307–336.

Brophy, A. L. "Self, Role, and Satisfaction." *Genetic Psychology Monographs,* 1959, *59,* 263–308.

Brown, R. D. Manipulation of the Environmental Press in a College Residence Hall." *Personnel and Guidance Journal,* 1968, *46* (6), 555–560.

Carruth, J. F., and Comer, P. E. "Outreach by Structured Interview." In W. H. Morrill (Ed.), *Preliminary Report: Outreach-Developmental Programs in College Counseling.* Grant No. R01 MH 18007. Washington, D.C.: National Institute of Mental Health, 1972.

Centra, J. A. "Studies of Institutional Environments: Categories of Instrumentation and Some Issues." In C. Fincher (Ed.), *Institutional Research and Academic Outcomes: Proceedings of the Eighth Annual Forum of the Association for Institutional Research,* 1968.

Centra, J. A. "The College Environment Revisited: Current Descriptions and a Comparison of Three Methods of Assessment." *College*

Entrance Examination Board Research and Developmental Reports. RDR-70-71, No. 1. Princeton, N.J.: Educational Testing Service, 1970.

Centra, J., and Linn, R. L. "On Interpreting Student's Perceptions of Their College Environments." *Measurement and Evaluation in Guidance,* 1970, *3* (2), 102–109.

Chickering, A. W. "Undergraduate Academic Experience." *Journal of Educational Psychology,* 1972, *63* (2), 134-143.

Claunch, N. C. "Cognitive and Motivational Characteristics Associated with Concrete and Abstract Levels of Conceptual Complexity." Unpublished doctoral dissertation, Princeton University, 1964.

Conyne, R. K. "Environmental Assessment: Mapping for Counselor Action." *Personnel and Guidance Journal,* 1975, *54* (3), 150–155.

Cowen, E. L. "Social and Community Interventions." In *Annual Review of Psychology.* Palo Alto: Annual Reviews, 1973.

Cowen, E. L. "Baby-Steps Toward Primary Prevention." *American Journal of Community Psychology,* 1977a, *5* (1), 1–22.

Cowen, E. L. "Psychologists and Primary Prevention: Blowing the Cover Story." *American Journal of Community Psychology,* 1977b, *5* (4), 481–489.

Craeger, J. A., and Sell, C. L. "The Institutional Domain of Higher Education: A Characteristics File." *American Council on Education Report,* 1968, *4* (6), entire report.

Daher, D. M., Corazzini, J. G., and McKinnon, R. D. "An Environmental Redesign Program for Residence Halls." *Journal of College Student Personnel,* 1977, *18,* 11–15.

Dooley, D., and Catalano, R. "Money and Mental Disorder: Toward Behavioral Cost Accounting for Primary Prevention." *American Journal of Community Psychology,* 1977, *5* (2), 217–227.

Douglas, J. W. B. *The Home and the School.* London: MacGibbon and Kee, 1964.

Douvan, E., and Kaye, C. "Motivational Factors in College Entrance." In N. Sanford (Ed.), *The American College.* New York: Wiley, 1962.

Eddy, E. D. "The College Influence on Student Character: An Exploratory Study in Selected Colleges and Universities Made for the Committee for the Study of Character Development in Education." Washington, D.C.: American College of Education, 1959.

Educational Testing Service. *The Institutional Goals Inventory.* Princeton, N.J.: Educational Testing Service, 1972.

Ekehammar, B. "Interactionism in Personality from a Historical Perspective." *Psychological Bulletin,* 1974, *81,* 1026–1048.

Ekehammar, B., and Magnusson, D. "A Method to Study Stressful Situations." *Journal of Personality and Social Psychology,* 1973, *27,* 176–179.

Ekehammar, B., Magnusson, D., and Ricklander, L. "An Interactionist Approach to the Study of Anxiety." *Scandinavian Journal of Psychology*, 1974, *15*, 4-14.

Endler, N. S. "The Person Versus the Situation—A Pseudo Issue? A Response to Alker." *Journal of Personality*, 1973, *41*, 287-303.

Endler, N. S., and Hunt, J. McV. "Sources of Behavioral Variance as Measured by the S-R Inventory of Anxiousness." *Psychological Bulletin*, 1966, *65*, 338-346.

Endler, N. S., and Hunt, J. McV. "S-R Inventories of Hostility and Comparisons of the Proportion of Variance from Persons, Responses and Situations for Hostility and Anxiousness." *Journal of Personality and Social Psychology*, 1968, *9*, 309-315.

Endler, N. S., Hunt, J. McV., and Rosenstein, A. J. "An S-R Inventory of Anxiousness." *Psychological Monographs*, 1962, *76* (17, entire issue).

Faris, R. E. L., and Dunham, H. W. *Mental Disorders in Urban Areas.* Chicago: University of Chicago Press, 1939.

Feldman, K. A., and Newcomb, T. M. *The Impact of College on Students.* San Francisco: Jossey-Bass, 1969.

Finkel, N. J., and Jacobsen, C. A. "Significant Life Experiences in an Adult Sample." *American Journal of Community Psychology*, 1977, *5* (2), 165-175.

Forehand, G. A., and Gilmer, B. V. "Environmental Variation in Studies of Organizational Behavior." *Psychological Bulletin*, 1964, *62*, 361-382.

Frederiksen, N. "Toward a Taxonomy of Situations." *American Psychologist*, 1972, *27*, 114-123.

Frederiksen, N., Jensen, O., and Beaton, A. E. *Prediction of Organizational Behavior.* New York: Pergamon Press, 1972.

French, J., and Kahn, R. "A Programmatic Approach to Studying the Industrial Environment and Mental Health." *Journal of Social Issues*, 1962, *18* (3), 1-47.

Friedlander, F., and Greenberg, S. "Effects of Job Attitudes, Training and Organization Climate on Performance of the Hard-Core Unemployed." *Journal of Applied Psychology*, 1971, *55*, 287-295.

Funkenstein, D. H. "Failure to Graduate from Medical School." *Journal of Medical Education*, 1962, *37*, 585-603.

Gavin, J. F., and Howe, J. G. "Psychological Climate: Some Theoretical and Empirical Considerations." *Behavioral Science*, 1975, *20*, 228-240.

Gerst, M., and Moos, R. "The Social Ecology of University Student Residences." *Journal of Educational Psychology*, 1972, *63*, 513-522.

Goldfried, M. F., and D'Zurilla, T. J. "A Behavioral-Analytic Model for Assessing Competence." In C. D. Spielberger (Ed.), *Current Top-*

ics in Clinical and Community Psychology. Vol. I. New York: Academic Press, 1969.

Grimes, J. N., and Allinsmith, W. "Compulsivity, Anxiety, and School Achievement." *Merrill-Palmer Quarterly,* 1961, *7,* 247–271.

Guion, R. M. "A Note on Organizational Climate." *Organizational Behavior and Human Performance,* 1973, *9,* 120–125.

Gump, P. V. "The Behavior Setting: A Promising Unit for Environmental Designers." *Landscape Architecture,* 1971, *61,* 130–134.

Heller, K., and Monahan, J. *Psychology and Community Change.* Homewood, Ill.: Dorsey Press, 1977.

Helms, S. T., and Williams, G. D. "An Experimental Study of the Reactions of High School Students to Simulated Jobs." Research Report No. 161. Baltimore: Center for Social Organization of Schools, Johns Hopkins University, 1973. (ERIC Document Reproduction Service No. ED 087 822.)

Holland, J. L. "Some Explorations of a Theory of Vocational Choice: I. One- and Two-Year Longitudinal Studies." *Psychological Monographs,* 1962, *76* (26), entire issue.

Holland, J. L. *Manual for the Vocational Preference Inventory* (6th rev. ed.) Palo Alto, Calif.: Consulting Psychologists Press, 1965.

Holland, J. L. *The Psychology of Vocational Choice: A Theory of Personality Types and Model Environments.* Waltham, Mass.: Blaisdell, 1966.

Holland, J. L. "Explorations of a Theory of Vocational Choice: VI. A Longitudinal Study Using a Sample of Typical College Students." *Journal of Applied Psychology,* 1968, *52,* 1–37.

Holland, J. L. *The Self-Directed Search.* Palo Alto, Calif.: Consulting Psychologists Press, 1971.

Holland, J. L. *Making Vocational Choices: A Theory of Careers.* Englewood Cliffs, N.J.: Prentice-Hall, 1973.

Holland, J. L., and Gottfredson, G. D. "Using a Typology of Persons and Environments to Explain Careers: Some Extensions and Clarifications." *The Counseling Psychologist,* 1976, *6* (3), 20–29.

Holland, J. L., Gottfredson, G. D., and Nafziger, D. H. "Testing the Validity of Some Theoretical Signs of Vocational Decision Making Ability." *Journal of Counseling Psychology,* 1975, *22,* 411–422.

Holmes, T. H., and Rahe, R. H. "The Social Readjustment Rating Scale." *Journal of Psychosomatic Research,* 1967, *11,* 213–218.

Huebner, L. A. "An Ecological Assessment: Person-Environment Fit." Unpublished doctoral dissertation, Colorado State University, 1975.

Huebner, L. A. "Counseling Interventions: An Organizational-Interactional Approach." *The Counseling Psychologist,* 1977, *7* (2), 69–73.

Huebner, L. A., and Paul, S. C. "The Assessment of Environmental

Quality." In T. O'Riordan (Ed.), *Resource Management and Environmental Planning*. New York: Wiley, 1978.

Huebner, L. A., and Corazzini, J. G. "Ecomapping: A Dynamic Model for Intentional Campus Design." *Journal Supplement Abstract Service*, 1978.

Hyne, S. "Institutional Assessment in Outreach Counseling: A Comparison of Two Techniques." Unpublished master's thesis, Colorado State University, 1973.

Insel, P. M., and Moos, R. H. "Psychological Environments—Expanding the Scope of Human Ecology." *American Psychologist*, 1974, *29* (3), 179–186.

Iscoe, I. "Community Psychology and the Competent Community." *American Psychologist*, 1974, *29* (8), 607–613.

Jackson, J., and Levine, D. "Treatment Environment and Staff Ideology in Two British Mental Hospitals." *American Journal of Community Psychology*, 1977, *5* (3), 307–319.

James, L. R., and Jones, A. P. "Organizational Climate: A Review of Theory and Research." *Psychological Bulletin*, 1974, *81* (12), 1096–1112.

Jessor, R. "Phenomenological Personality Theories and the Data Language of Psychology." *Psychological Review*, 1956, *63*, 173–180.

Jessor, R. "The Problem of Reductionism in Psychology." *Psychological Review*, 1958, *65*, 170–178.

Kantor, J. R. *Principles of Psychology*. Vol. 1. Bloomington, Ind.: Principia Press, 1924.

Kantor, J. R. *Principles of Psychology*. Vol. 2. Bloomington, Ind.: Principia Press, 1926.

Kaswan, J. "Change, Interdependence and Predictability: Necessary Conditions for Psychosocial Effectiveness." Position paper prepared for a symposium on the Division 27 Task Force Report on Community Psychology and Preventive Mental Health, annual meeting of the American Psychological Association, 1973, Montreal, Canada.

Katz, J., and Sanford, N. "The Curriculum in the Perspective of the Theory of Personality Development." In N. Sanford (Ed.), *The American College*. New York: Wiley, 1962.

Keith, J. A. "The Relationship of the Congruency of Environmental Press and Student Need Systems to Reported Personal Satisfaction and Academic Success." *Dissertation Abstracts*, 1965, *25*, 7081.

Kelly, J. C. *Toward a Psychology of Healthiness*. Paper presented at meeting of the Western Psychological Association and the Icabod Spencer Lecture, Union College, Schenectady, New York, May 2, 1974.

Kennedy, C. E., and Danskin, D. G. "Research Frontier: Pilot Phase of a Research Project Studying Student Development." *Journal of Counseling Psychology*, 1968, *15* (1), 98–100.

Kessler, M., and Albee, G. W. "Primary Prevention." *Annual Review of Psychology*, 1975, *26*, 557–591.

Kirkland, M. C. "An Investigation of the Characteristic Needs, Beta Presses, and Certain Resultant Behaviors of Selected Auburn University Freshmen." *Dissertation Abstracts*, 1967, 8272B.

Klee, G. D., and others. "An Ecological Analysis of Diagnosed Mental Illness in Baltimore." In R. Monroe, G. Klee, and E. Brody (Eds.), *Psychiatric Epidemiology and Mental Health Planning*. Washington, D.C.: American Psychiatric Association, 1967.

Kleinfeld, J. S. "Classroom Climate and the Verbal Participation of Indian and Eskimo Students in Integrated Classrooms." *Journal of Educational Research*, 1973, *67*, 51–52.

Koffka, K. *Principles of Gestalt Psychology*. New York: Harcourt Brace Jovanovich, 1935.

Kohlberg, L., and Mayer, R. "Development as the Aim of Education." *Harvard Educational Review*, 1972, *42* (4), 449–496.

Landis, H. L. "Dissonance Between Student and College Variables Related to Success and Satisfaction." *Dissertation Abstracts*, 1964, *25*, 1047.

Lauterbach, C. G., and Vielhaber, D. P. "Need-Press and Expectation-Press Indices as Predictors of College Achievement." *Educational and Psychological Measurement*, 1966, *26*, 1965–1972.

Levin, J. "Three-Mode Factor Analysis." *Psychological Bulletin*, 1965, *64*, 442–452.

Lewin, K. *Principles of Topological Psychology*. New York: McGraw-Hill, 1936.

Lewis, M. D., and Lewis, J. A. "The Counselor's Impact on Community Environments." *Personnel and Guidance Journal*, 1977, *55* (6), 356–358.

Loevinger, J. *Ego Development: Conceptions and Theories*. San Francisco: Jossey-Bass, 1976.

Lott, A. J., and Lott, B. E. "Group Cohesiveness as Interpersonal Attraction: A Review of Relationships with Antecedent and Consequent Variables." *Psychological Bulletin*, 1965, *64*, 259–309.

McConnell, T. R., and Heist, P. "The Diverse College Student Population." In N. Sanford (Ed.), *The American College*. New York: Wiley, 1962.

McDowell, J. V., and Chickering, A. W. *The Experience of College Questionnaire*. Plainfield, Vt.: Project on Student Development, 1967. (Mimeograph.)

McFee, A. "The Relation of Students' Needs to Their Perceptions of a College Environment." *Journal of Educational Psychology*, 1961, *52* (1), 25–29.

McKeachie, W. J. "Motivation, Teaching Methods, and College Learning." In M. R. Jones (Ed.), *Nebraska Symposium on Motivation.* Lincoln: University of Nebraska Press, 1961.

Magnusson, D. "An Analysis of Situational Dimensions." *Perceptual and Motor Skills,* 1971, *32,* 851–867.

Magnusson, D., and Ekehammar, B. "An Analysis of Situational Dimensions: A Replication." *Multivariate Behavioral Research,* 1973, *8,* 331–339.

Mahoney, M. J., and Thoresen, C. E. *Self Control: Power to the Person.* Monterey, Calif.: Brooks-Cole, 1974.

Malleson, N. "Operational Research in the University." *British Medical Journal,* 1959, *1,* 1031–1035.

Menne, J. W. "Techniques for Evaluating the College Environment." *Journal of Educational Measurement,* 1967, *4,* 219–225.

Mintz, N., and Schwartz, D. "Urban Ecology and Psychosis: Community Factors in the Incidence of Schizophrenia and Manic-Depression Among Italians in Greater Boston." *International Journal of Social Psychiatry,* 1964, *10,* 101–118.

Mischel, W. *Personality and Assessment.* New York: Wiley, 1968.

Mischel, W. "Toward a Cognitive Social Learning Reconceptualization of Personality." *Psychological Review,* 1973, *80,* 252–283.

Mischel, W. *Introduction to Personality.* (2nd Ed.) New York: Holt, Rinehart and Winston, 1976.

Moos, R. H. "Situational Analysis of a Therapeutic Community Milieu." *Journal of Abnormal Psychology,* 1968, *73,* 49–61.

Moos, R. H. "Sources of Variance in Responses to Questionnaires and in Behavior." *Journal of Abnormal Psychology,* 1969, *74,* 405–412.

Moos, R. H. "Differential Effects of Psychiatric Ward Settings on Patient Change." *Journal of Nervous and Mental Disease,* 1970, *5,* 316–321.

Moos, R. H. "Conceptualizations of Human Environments." *American Psychologist,* 1973a, *28,* 652–665.

Moos, R. H. *Military Company Environment Manual.* Palo Alto, Calif.: Social Ecology Laboratory, Department of Psychiatry, Stanford University, 1973b.

Moos, R. H. "Systems for the Assessment and Classification of Human Environments: An Overview." In R. H. Moos and P. Insel (Eds.), *Issues in Social Ecology.* Palo Alto, Calif.: National Press Books, 1974a.

Moos, R. H. *Ward Atmosphere Scale Manual.* Palo Alto, Calif.: Consulting Psychologists Press, 1974b.

Moos, R. H. *The Human Context: Environmental Determinants of Behavior.* New York: Wiley-Interscience, 1976.

Moos, R. H. *Evaluating Educational Environments: Procedures, Measures, Findings, and Policy Implications. San Francisco: Jossey-Bass, 1979.

Moos, R. H., and Gerst, M. *University Residence Environment Scale Manual*. Palo Alto, Calif.: Consulting Psychologists Press, 1974.

Moos, R. H., and Trickett, E. J. *Manual: Classroom Environment Scale*. Palo Alto, Calif.: Consulting Psychologists Press, 1974.

Morrill, W. H. "Institutional Assessment and Counseling Outreach." Grant application to Department of Health, Education, and Welfare, Public Health Service, 1973.

Morrill, W. H., and Banning, J. H. *Counseling Outreach: A Survey of Practices*. Boulder, Colo.: Western Interstate Commission for Higher Education, 1973.

Morrill, W. H., and Hurst, J.C. "A Preventive and Developmental Role for the College Counselor." *Counseling Psychologist*, 1971, *2* (4), 90-95.

Morrill, W. H., Ivey, A.E., and Oetting, E. R. "The College Counseling Center: A Center for Student Development." In J. D. Heston and W. B. Fricks (Eds.), *Counseling for the Liberal Arts Campus*. Yellow Springs, Ohio: Antioch Press, 1968.

Morrill, W. H., Oetting, E. R., and Hurst, J. C. "Dimensions of Counselor Functioning." *Personnel and Guidance Journal*, 1974, *52* (6), 354-360.

Morrow, J. M., Jr. "A Test of Holland's Theory of Vocational Choice." *Journal of Counseling Psychology*, 1971, *18*, 422-425.

Murphy, G. *Personality: A Biosocial Approach to Origins and Structure*. New York: Harper & Row, 1947.

Murray, H. A. *Explorations in Personality*. New York: Oxford University Press, 1938.

Nafziger, D. H., Holland, J. L., and Gottfredson, G. D. "Student-College Congruency as a Predictor of Satisfaction." *Journal of Counseling Psychology*, 1975, *22* (2), 132-139.

Oetting, E. R. "Evaluative Research and Orthodox Science." Pt I. *Personnel and Guidance Journal*, 1976a, *55* (1), 11-15.

Oetting, E. R. "Planning and Reporting Evaluative Research." Pt II. *Personnel and Guidance Journal*, 1976b, *55* (2), 60-64.

Osipow, S. H., Ashby, J. D., and Wall, H. W. "Personality Types and Vocational Choice: A Test of Holland's Theory." *Personnel and Guidance Journal*, 1966, *45*, 37-42.

Pace, C. R. *The Influence of Academic and Student Subcultures in College and University Environments*. USOE Cooperative Research Project 1083. Los Angeles: University of California, 1964.

Pace, C. R. *College and University Environment Scales Technical Manual*. (2nd ed.) Princeton, N.J.: Educational Testing Service, 1969.

Pace, C. R., and Baird, L. "Attainment Patterns in the Environmental

Press of College Subcultures." In T. M. Newcomb and E. K. Wilson (Eds.), *College Peer Groups: Problems and Prospects for Research.* Chicago: Aldine, 1966.

Pace, C. R., and Stern, G. G. "An Approach to the Measurement of Psychological Characteristics of College Environments." *Journal of Educational Psychology,* 1958, *49* (5), 269–277.

Pace, W. T. "Profiles of Personal Needs and College Press of Negro Teacher Trainees." *Dissertation Abstracts,* 1962, *22,* 3748.

Patton, J. A. "A Study of the Effects of Student Acceptance of Responsibility and Motivation on Course Behavior." Unpublished doctoral dissertation, University of Michigan, 1955.

Paul, S. C., and Huebner, L. A. "Multiple Perspectives: Intervening with People in their Contextual Systems." Unpublished manuscript, University of Missouri, Columbia, 1977.

Perry, W. G. *Patterns of Development in Thought and Values in a Liberal Arts College.* Final Report Project No. 5-0825. Washington, D.C.: Office of Education, Bureau of Research, 1968.

Pervin, L. A. "Satisfaction and Perceived Self-Environment Similarity: A Semantic Differential Study of Student-College Interaction." *Journal of Personality,* 1967a, *35,* 623–634.

Pervin, L. A. "A Twenty-College Study of Student X College Interaction Using TAPE: Rationale, Reliability, and Validity." *Journal of Educational Psychology,* 1967b, *58* (5), 290–302.

Pervin, L. A. "Performance and Satisfaction as a Function of Individual-Environment Fit." *Psychological Bulletin,* 1968, *69* (1), 56–58.

Pervin, L. A., and Rubin, D. B. "Student Dissatisfaction with College and the College Dropout: A Transactional Approach." *Journal of Social Psychology,* 1967, *72,* 285–295.

Pervin, L. A., and Smith, S. H. "Further Test of the Relationship Between Satisfaction and Perceived Self-Environment Similarity." *Perceptual and Motor Skills,* 1968, *26,* 835–838.

Peterson, R. E. *Technical Manual: College Student Questionnaires.* (rev. ed.) Princeton, N.J.: Institutional Research Program for Higher Education, Educational Testing Service, 1968.

Peterson, R. E., and others. *Technical Manual: Institutional Functioning Inventory.* Princeton, N.J.: Educational Testing Service, 1970.

Proshansky, H., Ittelson, W., and Rivlin, L. (Eds.). *Environmental Psychology: Man and His Physical Environment.* New York: Holt, Rinehart and Winston, 1970.

Pulvino, C. J., and Hansen, J. C. "Relevance of 'Needs' and 'Press' to Anxiety, Alienation, and GPA." *Journal of Experimental Education,* 1972, *40,* 70–75.

Raab, W. E. "Congruence and Dissonance Between Need and Press in

Determining Satisfaction in the University Environment." *Dissertation Abstracts*, 1963, *24*, 1923.

Raush, H. L., Dittman, A. T., and Taylor, T. J. "Person, Setting, and Change in Social Interaction." *Human Relations*, 1959, *12*, 361–378.

Richards, J. M., Rand, L. M., and Rand, L. P. *A Description of Junior Colleges*. Iowa City, Iowa: American College Testing Program, 1965.

Sakoda, J. M. "Factor Analysis of OSS Situational Tests." *Journal of Abnormal and Social Psychology*, 1952, *47*, 843–852.

Sandell, R. G. "Effects of Attitudinal and Situational Factors on Reported Choice Behavior." *Journal of Marketing Research*, 1968, *5*, 405–408.

Sanford, N. (Ed.). *The American College*. New York: Wiley, 1962.

Saunders, D. R. "A Factor Analytic Study of the AI and the CCI." *Multivariate Behavioral Research*, 1969, *4*, 329–346.

Schneider, B. "The Perception of Organizational Climate: The Customer's View." *Journal of Applied Psychology*, 1973, *57*, 248–256.

Selvin, H. C., and Hagstrom, W. O. "The Empirical Classification of Formal Groups." *American Sociological Review*, 1963, *28*, 399–411.

Shader, R. I., and Levine, F. M. "Staff-Patient Interaction Patterns and Opinions About Mental Illness." *Social Science and Medicine*, 1969, *3*, 101–104.

Smelser, W. T. "Dominance as a Factor in Achievement and Perception in Cooperative Problem Solving Interactions." *Journal of Abnormal and Social Psychology*, 1961, *62*, 535–542.

Snyder, B. R. "Adaptation, Education, and Emotional Growth." In L. A. Pervin, L. E. Reik, and W. Dalrymple (Eds.), *The College Dropout and the Utilization of Talent*. Princeton, N.J.: Princeton University Press, 1966.

Sommer, R. *Personal Space*. Englewood Cliffs, N.J.: Prentice-Hall, 1969.

Sprinthall, N. (Ed.). *Counselor Education and Supervision*, 1975, *14*, (1, entire issue).

Stern, G. G. "Environments for Learning." In N. Sanford (Ed.), *The American College*. New York: Wiley, 1962a.

Stern, G. G. "The Measurement of Psychological Characteristics of Students and Learning Environments." In S. J. Messick and J. Ross (Eds.), *Measurement in Personality and Cognition*. New York: Wiley, 1962b.

Stern, G. G. *Scoring Instructions and College Norms: Activities Index, College Characteristics Index*. Syracuse, N.Y.: Syracuse University Psychological Research Center, 1963.

Stern, G. G. "$B = f(P,E)$." *Journal of Personality Assessment*, 1964, *28* (2), 161–168.

Stern, G. G. "Student Ecology and the College Environment." *Journal of Medical Education*, 1965, *40*, 132–154.

Stern, G. G. *People in Context: Measuring Person-Environment Congruence in Education and Industry.* New York: Wiley, 1970.

Stricker, G. "Interrelationships of Activities Index and College Characteristics Index Scores." *Journal of Counseling Psychology,* 1967, *14,* 368–370.

Summerskill, J. "Dropouts from College." In N. Sanford (Ed.), *The American College.* New York: Wiley, 1962, 627–657.

Tolman, E. C. "Psychology Versus Immediate Experience." In E. C. Tolman, *Collected Papers in Psychology.* Berkeley: University of California Press, 1951.

Walberg, H. J. "Social Environment as a Mediator of Classroom Learning." *Journal of Educational Psychology,* 1969a, *60,* 443–448.

Walberg, H. J. "Predicting Class Learning: An Approach to the Class as a Social System." *American Educational Research Journal,* 1969b, *6,* 529–542.

Walberg, H. J., and Anderson, G. J. "Properties of Achieving Urban Classes." *Journal of Educational Psychology,* 1972, *63,* 381–385.

Walsh, W. B. *Theories of Person-Environment Interaction: Implications for the College Student.* Iowa City, Iowa: American College Testing Program, 1973.

Walsh, W. B., and Lewis, R. O. "Consistent, Inconsistent, and Undecided Career Preferences and Personality." *Journal of Vocational Behavior,* 1972, *2,* 174–181.

Walsh, W. B., and Russell, J. H., III. "College Major Choice and Personal Adjustment." *Personnel and Guidance Journal,* 1969, *47,* 685–688.

Wechsler, H., and Pugh, T. "Fit of Individual and Community Characteristics and Rates of Psychiatric Hospitalization." *American Journal of Sociology,* 1967, *73,* 331–338.

Western Interstate Commission for Higher Education. *The Ecosystem Model: Designing Campus Environments.* Boulder, Colo.: Western Interstate Commission for Higher Education, 1973.

White, R. W. "The Concept of the Healthy Personality. What Do We Really Mean?" *Counseling Psychologist,* 1973, *4* (2), 3–12.

Wicker, A. W. "Processes Which Mediate Behavior-Environment Congruence." *Behavioral Science,* 1972, *17* (3), 265–277.

Wicker, A. W. "Undermanning Theory and Research: Implications for the Study of Psychological and Behavioral Effects of Excess Populations." *Representative Research in Social Psychology,* 1973, *4,* 190–191.

Wicker, A. W., and Kirmeyer, S. "From Church to Laboratory to National Park: A Program of Research on Excess and Insufficient Populations in Behavior Settings." In S. Wapner, B. Kaplan, and

S. Cohen (Eds.), *Experiencing the Environment.* New York: Plenum, 1976.

Wicker, A. W., McGrath, J. E., and Armstrong, G. E. "Organization Size and Behavior Setting Capacity as Determinants of Member Participation." *Behavioral Science,* 1972, *17,* 510.

Willems, E. P. "Sense of Obligation to High School Activities as Related to School Size and Marginality of Student." *Child Development,* 1967, *38,* 1257–1258.

Willems, E. P. "Planning a Rationale for Naturalistic Research." In E. P. Willems, and H. L. Raush (Eds.), *Naturalistic Viewpoints in Psychological Research.* New York: Holt, Rinehart and Winston, 1969.

Williams, J. E. *Conflict Between Freshmen Male Roommates* (Research Report No. 10-1967). College Park, Md.: University of Maryland Counseling Center, 1967.

Wolf, R. "The Measurement of Environments." In A. Anastasi (Ed.), *Testing Problems in Perspective.* Washington, D.C.: American College of Education, 1966.

Wright, H. F. "Psychological Habitat." In R. G. Barker and Associates, *Habitats, Environments, and Human Behavior: Studies in Ecological Psychology and Eco-Behavioral Science.* San Francisco: Jossey-Bass, 1978.

PART III

Models for Practice

Our identity as student services professionals is clearly a mix of many components—the context of higher education, the theories that undergird our work, and the specific skills and knowledge we bring to our mission on campus. A key component, perhaps the crucial one for defining our identity, is the use of general models for practice, or role orientations, in student services. In most of our literature, as well as in our preparation programs, these roles are vaguely defined or only briefly explored. The jump all too often is from theory to specific competency. The "glue" that holds context, theory, and skills together is a model of practice, a sense of our own unique role orientation. Such models of functioning provide general orientations for our work in higher education.

Every student services professional harbors a sense of role, a model that holds together all the various activities that fill each day. And from time to time thinkers in our field have called either for a recommitment to an existing model or for a change to a newer model. Yet rarely is it clear just what models predominate in our field. Such models are not explained in a way that leads to a choice among them by the individual student services professional or by divisions of student services. The four chapters in this section represent an effort to (1) label the predominant models, (2) explain and clarify each, and (3) illustrate the relevance and need for each in student services.

In our literature and practice of the past thirty years, three models stand out: (1) surrogate parent and/or disciplinarian; (2) administrator; and (3) counselor. Although the first role, that of surrogate parent, was predominant in early periods (see Part One), it is no longer relevant for our profession. Changes in higher education and in society, as well as our own growing distaste for this role, have produced a milieu in which students are expected (and generally themselves expect) to be treated as adults. There is no doubt that a "flavor" of this surrogate parent model remains in our field, expressed sometimes by parents who hope we will take over their role as their son or daughter enrolls on our campus, sometimes in institutional policy or procedure, and sometimes in our own need to nurture or control. But even though remnants of it exist, the model is no longer central and viable.

The other two more traditional models, administrator and counselor, remain viable today. In Chapter Six, David Ambler develops the administrator model, emphasizing the current challenges in this role. Some readers may think this chapter does not apply to them, because they do not have official administrative responsibilities. Yet Ambler addresses several issues that we believe all professionals in the field will find useful. The counselor role, however, is one with which many student services personnel identify but which many also find difficult to explicate. In Chapter Seven, Ellen Betz reviews the historical roots of this orientation and then specifies its current relevance for a wide variety of professionals in our field.

In Chapters Eight and Nine, Robert Brown and James Banning present the newer models of student development educator and environmental manager, respectively. Both models assert a need for new ways to look at ourselves, our students, and our campuses. Brown sees student services professionals as educators who bring a solid theory and concept background to helping students develop personally, intellectually, physically, and esthetically. Banning advocates actively assessing our campus environments and providing "routes" (such as programs or organizational changes) to enhance the fit between students and various aspects of campus communities.

None of these four models or orientations claims exclusive adherence. Each offers a unique, important perspective for understanding and articulating our role. How much of each role or model we adopt depends on individual perceptions and philosophy, specific interests, talents and jobs, and, certainly, the nature and mission of the institutions and agencies in which we work. In presenting and explaining these central models, we hope to help each student services professional understand and then intentionally select those portions of the models that fit his or her own practice.

David A. Ambler 6

The Administrator Role

In 1970, Clyde Parker proposed that the student services profession divorce itself from its traditional administrative and service roles and link up with the central academic functions of higher education as student development consultants and researchers. James F. Penny's reaction was to ask, "Who's minding the store?" (1970). Their exchange epitomizes an unnecessary dichotomy that has plagued the student services field almost since its inception. The debate centers on the question of whether we are "educators" with a systematic body of knowledge based on theoretical constructs or whether we are "practitioners" just "minding the store" of ancillary but necessary services for students. The debate is unfortunate because the arguments are always presented in the extremes; the dichotomy is unnecessary because it is possible to be both.

The administrative model, which this chapter explores, is based on the premise that the student services profession is an administrative, service-oriented unit in higher education that provides many facilitating and developmental activities and programs for students. A historical perspective on the debate surrounding this administrative model and the forces that have shaped the administrative role can help improve understanding of the substance of this role: its rationale, functions, and elements.

History

The dichotomy in the student services profession between "administrator" and "educator" has become acute with higher levels of specialization, diminishing resources, and increasing emphasis on accountability; but it also reflects the historical factors and movements that gave rise to the student services field. Appleton, Briggs, and Rhatigan (1978, p. 13) identify the early sources of the split as follows: "It is likely that few administrators understand that our work emerged from three separate sources: the dean of women, the dean of men, and the personnel worker. Their vestiges are still apparent in the existence of three major national organizations (NAWDC [National Association of Women Deans and Counselors], NASPA [National Association of Student Personnel Administrators], and ACPA [American College Personnel Association]. Anyone doubting the influence of history should be advised of the several efforts to merge these three organizations. The inability to accomplish any merger can be traced to various conditions, but a dominant reason surely is the function of history."

These positions reflect the major source of the debate. Early deans of men and women were identified with the administration of colleges and universities and with the enforcement of institutional regulations. Personnel workers were not; they came from a variety of academic movements—educational psychology, measurement and testing, vocational guidance, and mental health—and they were perceived less as disciplinarians than as counselors of students.

A number of authors suggest that this dichotomy was unreal and unnecessary and assert that the profession—like a political party—was broad enough to accommodate various concerns and viewpoints. It can be open, they suggest, to the developmental concerns of the behavioral scientist as well as the desires for effective management of services of the personnel dean. In summarizing his objections to what he perceived as Parker's reconceptualization of student personnel work, Penny (1970, p. 5) noted that "Most campuses need the kinds of functions and the kind of competencies that the student development center and its specialists propose to make available. Most campuses *also* need effective personnel program administration."

In 1972, the Commission on Professional Development of the now defunct Council of Student Personnel Associations in Higher Education (COSPA) outlined a philosophy encompassing both the "service" and "developmental" aspects of student services. In diplomatic language, the council introduced the phrase "student development services in higher education" as an inclusive term for the many areas usually included in student personnel programs (Commission on Professional Development, Council of Student Personnel Associations in Higher Education 1972, p. 2). It defined the purposes of student services work in behavioral and developmental goals but conceded that they are accomplished through administrative, instructional, and consultative roles. Different members of the profession perform their responsibilities through one or some combination of these roles. Through this document, COSPA recognized the need for a multidisciplinary curriculum in training new professionals, whose demonstration of basic values, consistent with those of the profession, is as important as any skills acquired in training.

Three other historical facts are important in order to understand the unique administrative role of the student services profession in higher education. First, the commitment of the United States to extend higher education to as wide a segment of the population as possible brought a large and extremely diverse student body to colleges and universities, and highly developed student services were essential (Brubacher and Rudy, 1958, p. 338).

Second, the traditional concern of colleges for values and the development of "character" found new support in the early twentieth century when efforts were made, after years of neglect, to wed the curriculum and extracurriculum. Thus early personnel deans were appointed to provide services that met the developmental needs of the "whole" student.

Third, as the profession emerged in the twentieth century, the theory of bureaucratic organization—developed by the German sociologist, Max Weber—was just beginning to influence the structure of American colleges and universities. Developed as a reaction to the excesses of the industrial revolution, this theory introduced the concepts of specialization of function, rational hierarchy of authority, efficiency, and effective management. The student services field did not escape these ideas, which so dramatically shaped the character of American institutions, academic as well as commercial and governmental.

The diversity and numbers of students; the assumption of responsibility for extracurricular services, and the growth of institutional bureaucracy thus describe how the complex portfolio of student services emerged. Concern for impact on the educational environment and the need for efficient management of these rapidly expanding services tied the profession to the administrative structure and introduced the position of the "chief student services officer."

Rationale

The rationale for the administrative model of student services can be stated in five assumptions that reflect both the historical roots of the profession and current realities:

1. The effective development and delivery of services and programs is the historical and legitimate basis of the profession and is its only viable means to accomplish its educational goals for students. To abandon our role of providing essential services and of managing them to achieve desired institutional outcomes would result in our demise. Colleges and universities could not afford us or—worse yet—tolerate us if we were not related to our basic service functions.

2. There is no inherent conflict or dichotomy between the profession's administrative orientation and its educational and developmental goals. Resolving conflict between society and the individual is an important function of democratic leadership—on or off the campus. Tension between the individual and the group is in itself educational. In his efforts to focus higher education on individual student development, Clyde Parker (1971, p. 405) says, "I have become less concerned with whether this becomes the new identity for student personnel, is contained within the framework of student personnel, or is part of the larger system of the university." I hope he is wrong. Students see us as administrators, but they also see us as models. The fact that they do not recognize us as teachers is a testimony to our current lack of effectiveness in that role.

3. In order to affect desired educational outcomes, student services must be effectively managed and coordinated with academic programs and services. If student services cannot be justified by their contribution to the educational mission, they should probably be abandoned to private entrepreneurs or the students should be allowed to fend for themselves. By linking the classroom and the campus, student services provide the students with some reality referents to test their scholarly constructs. This assumption about the relationship between academic programs and student services was noted by Miller and Prince (1976) in their principles for a student development organization. They state that "Collaboration among student affairs staff members, faculty members, and students is essential to the success of the student development program. . . . The institution's commitment to student development is directly proportional to the number of these collaborative links between the student affairs staff and the faculty" (Miller and Prince, 1976, p. 155).

4. Identification with the administrative structure permits student services to influence policy formulation and resource allocation to effect its educational goals. Policies, procedures, and resources are the

life blood of any institution; the ability to influence their development and use is real power. The involvement of the chief student services officer in policy decisions can affect the climate for inquiry, create or reduce factors that contribute to student persistence, and protect or violate student citizenship rights. The chief student services officer can help keep the institution honest in its obligations to students.

5. The administrative model provides the student services profession with the greatest flexibility for responding to student and institutional needs and with the ability to reach large segments of the student population. Because the administrative model relates to the management function of directing resources to achieve desired outcomes, it does not prejudice the needs or the process. It can alter, abandon, or add services according to identified contemporary trends such as the consumer movement, the lowering of the age of majority, or *Dixon* v. *Alabama* and the consequential popularity of lawyers as student services professionals.

Historically, we have claimed that each student is unique, with unique needs and that he or she is responsible for his or her own development. It follows that not all students have the same need of our assistance. The administrative model recognizes that fact while permitting the student services worker to specialize in satisfying needs identified in the total student population. Under this arrangement, we are not limited by a prescribed set of developmental tasks or predetermined solutions.

Functions of Administration

Concern for the efficient management of the educational enterprise dates back to the early parts of this century, although the systematic study of higher education only gained prominence after World War II. Management functions have been stated in a number of ways. Luther Gulick dissected the management process into the functions of planning, organizing, staffing, directing, coordinating, reporting, and budgeting with his "POSDCORB" formula (Gulick, 1937). Edward H. Litchfield (1959), former chancellor of the University of Pittsburgh, wrote of the management process in higher education as consisting of programming, communicating, controlling, and reappraising.

We have changed the nomenclature, redefined some of the procedures, and become more conscious of their daily applicability, but the basic management functions remain unchanged. Any effective chief student services officer can undertake planning, organizing, motivating, executing, and controlling. They are standard items on the daily routine. These management activities apply at every level in the administrative structure and are found in every service or program in the taxonomy of student services. They may be most evident in such service units as student records or financial aids, but they are equally useful and necessary to counseling, career guidance, and student activity units.

A number of processes for planning and resource use have been developed more recently. Planning, programming, and budgeting systems (PPBS), management by objectives (MBO), and other such planning schemes hit the campuses in the late 1960s and early 1970s as enrollments and resources peaked and began to decline. Calls for economies, long-range planning, and better use of resources gave these new management systems some degree of credibility on campus. Although some people touted these industrial and government systems as saving higher education in the latter quarter of the century, others continued to resist any efforts to quantify educational outcome or measure educational "productivity." More sane administrators recognized these evaluation systems as useful, new approaches to the management systems adopted in business, government, and education after the industrial revolution and saw that the conscious and systematic application of these systems to higher education in general and student services in particular held great promise for the profession. Richard L. Harpel (1978, p. 20) believes their use is absolutely essential: "As both a professional and a manager . . . the student personnel administrator must be prepared to demonstrate the contribution of student services to the aims of the institution and to adapt these services as needed on the basis of pointed, objective assessments of effectiveness and efficiency."

A number of contemporary members of the profession have contributed to these newer definitions of the management process in student services, but Harpel has perhaps contributed most to our understanding of their applicability. In a manual prepared for the NASPA Institute of Research and Development (NIRAD), Harpel (1976) outlined a management and evaluation sequence for student services. It is a system that permits both educational achievement and management effectiveness to be evaluated. The major functions and guidelines of Harpel's system are as follows:

1. *Identification of a need or problem.* Define the need to be met by a comprehensive and accurate description of the target population to be served.
2. *Assessing Environmental Constraints.* Planning must include a description of the environment and those social, economic, political, and legal constraints on the ways the needs of the target population can be met.

3. *Stating Goals.* Goal statements should be long-range, abstract statements describing ideal results, and their development and review should include as many members of the organization as possible.
4. *Stating Objectives.* Objectives should describe some terminal condition or behavior. (How do you know when you get there?) Objectives should define some criterion of acceptable performance. (How much of what is enough?)
5. *Plan of Action.* Activities should bear a direct, logical relationship to the goals and objectives of the organization.
6. *Program Structure.* The program structure should describe an organization in terms of clusters of activities performed to achieve stated goals, illustrating both what is done in the organization and why.
7. *Budgeting.* A budget should be a plan that allocates resources, orders and gives priority to various activities, and relates resources to outcomes.
8. *Evaluation.* Evaluation should include both measures of activity and measures of impact, which, when related to objectives and costs, will describe the effectiveness and efficiency of programs.

Readers can find additional information and guidelines in Chapter Seventeen, by Dutton and Rickard. Whatever system is used, sound definition of and adherence to management functions remains a basis for the administrative role in student services.

Elements of the Program

Every good student services staff member knows that administration is a process, not an end in itself. The effective student services administrator uses basic management functions (described earlier) to integrate various program elements to achieve goals. The development of students as self-functioning individuals and the realization of their own personal and academic goals are the desired outcomes of all we do as educators and managers.

Certain elements needed to achieve those outcomes are common to all student services programs regardless of size, scope, purpose, or organization of the college or university. From the perspective of the administrative model, these elements are (1) students, (2) services, (3) structure, (4) staff, and (5) sources.

Students. Ever since student services emerged as an organized unit of higher education, students have been an integral part of the program. They have never been viewed as "customers" or the end "product" of our bureaucratic machinery. Almost everything we do, we do *with* students. The high regard for and the devotion to students that has characterized this profession is perhaps its most significant contribution to the unique character of higher education in America. It has served to keep higher education aware of its special role of educating the individual in and for a free society.

This is an historical commitment and mission for student services. The original statement of the "student personnel point of view" by the American Council on Education in 1937 and its restatement in 1949 made it clear that the student was seen as an active participant in the educational process: "The concept of education is broadened to include attention to the student's well-rounded development—physically, socially, emotionally and spiritually, as well as intellectually. The student is thought of as a responsible participant in his own development and not as a passive recipient of an imprinted economic, political, or religious doctrine, or vocational skill. As a responsible participant in the societal processes of our American democracy, his full and balanced maturity is viewed as a major end-goal of education" (American Council on Education, 1949, p. 1).

Those who criticize the identification of student services with the administrative elements of higher education accuse us of often neglecting this commitment to the student's education for the sake of institutional order and harmony. They point to our lack of theory, poor record of assessing student needs, and the hodgepodge of unrelated services that constitute our programs. There is some merit to their criticisms. Harpel (1978, p. 22) noted, "Given that the institution's purpose is derived from the needs of its constituents, the lack of attention to needs analyses within higher education is astonishing. Even when someone tries to find out what students need, subjective judgments and public opinion are often substituted for systematic inquiry."

A dynamic administrative model of student services, however, provides for constant reassessment of student characteristics and needs. Clyde Parker (1971) doubted that such assessment was possible in the traditional organization of student services, yet it is encouraging to note the more recent incorporation of student development concepts and research programs within the administrative structure. Knowing student needs is essential to an effective student services program and is compatible with institutional goals.

There are several different organizational models for structuring a student services research program. Which model is used depends on such factors as staff competencies, available resources, and the institution's structure and commitment to organizational research. Three possible arrangements for student research would be (1) within each office of the division of student services, (2) as a separate office of the division, or (3) as a part of or in cooperation with an institutional research office.

Each arrangement has its own problem and promise. There is some merit in creating an ethic in which each office is responsible for researching its own effectiveness. Yet such research may be biased, may lack coordination with other units, or may fail to assess student development from a broader perspective. A separate office for research within a division of student services can promulgate a comprehensive student assessment program as well as an effective management and program evaluation system. It frequently is unable, however, to secure institutional resources and commitment. Teaming up with an institution-wide research effort has two major advantages: (1) resources as well as credibility are easier to secure and (2) the assessment program can command the attention of academic programs, student services, and other university elements that affect student development. The major disadvantage of this approach is the danger that the research on students and program effectiveness may not be used for measuring educational outcomes but may be used strictly for cost-benefit analysis.

In Chapter Nineteen, Robert Kerr gives a number of suggestions and examples related to this area. Whatever system is used, the student remains the key element. The administrative model permits us to *know* students and thereby to be better able to meet their needs.

Services and Programs. The student services administrator is frequently asked a sometimes embarrassing question: "What do you do?" What we do is not always readily apparent. Because we are neither "teachers" nor "administrators," student services workers frequently respond by enumerating the various kinds of services and programs we offer, hoping that the educational role will be implicit if not self-evident. "What we do" follows logically after identifying student needs; student services and programs are the primary means by which the profession accomplishes its goals and organizational assignments.

Some models of student services are based on complete professional control of the scope and definition of its function in the university. In the administrative model, however, the content and assignments of the student services unit are determined by the institution's purpose, philosophy, and organizational structure. The student services unit is viewed as one of many subdivisions, related to the organizational whole and institutional goals. Indeed, this model frequently shows a variety of functions shared among units. Examples include housing, shared with the business office; financial aids, with the comptroller; and admissions and records, with academic administration.

Because the content of the student services program in this model is controlled by institutional rather than professional considerations, it provides the greatest latitude in defining the scope and extent of the services offered. Student services may have activities assigned to it that are somewhat foreign to the profession or distasteful to the staff, such as intercollegiate athletics, alumni affairs, and the university security program. And, as in most political systems, the skill and effectiveness of the student services leadership—more than professional requirements—dictate whether the unit has a limited or comprehensive role in the institution's mission.

Developing a comprehensive service taxonomy is vital to the functioning of the administrative model; structuring or clustering services promotes program and management effectiveness. In a major survey for the federal government, Ayers, Tripp, and Russell (1966) identified the primary student services and programs under four main functions:

1. Welfare functions such as counseling, testing, health services, financial aids programs, placement, and alumni relations
2. Control functions such as admissions, records, discipline, and living arrangements
3. Activities functions such as cocurricular and extracurricular programs, student government, student publications, student unions and cultural programs
4. Teaching functions such as orientation programs, foreign student programs, remedial clinics, and other special informal educational services in residence halls and elsewhere in the college community

Others have designed different but useful program classifications. Hershenson (1970) suggested four different function categories: internal coordinating, orienting, supportive, and educational. But perhaps the most useful taxonomy of student services comes in the program classification structure (PCS) of the National Center for Higher Education Management Systems (NCHEMS) of the Western Interstate Commission for Higher Education (Myers and Topping, 1974).

The PCS system provides for eight major functional units in higher education. In the original definitions of student services, six categories are identified: (1) student services administration, (2) social and cultural development, (3) counseling and career guidance; (4) financial aid administration, (5) student auxiliary services, and (6) intercollegiate athletics (Myers and Topping, 1974). Recent modifications have added student recruitment, admissions, and records as a seventh major category. The PCS system is the most widely used system for comparative studies because its categories and definitions are sufficiently broad, yet specific enough, to permit inclusion of virtually every defined student service. It is also useful for planning organizational structures, strategies, and evaluation.

If services and programs follow the identification of student needs, then evaluation is the logical next step in the process. Yet the lack of systematic evaluation of student development and program effectiveness continues to plague this profession. It remains to be seen whether contemporary theories and models will substantiate our achievements. One thing is sure: The coming decades of diminished resources will demand that student services demonstrate their contribution to the institution's goals and welfare.

Structure. Bureaucratic organization is an American way of life. Although the size and complexity of contemporary corporate life may seem negative, it is successful (or lacks any equally successful substitutes). Many have criticized the corporate model for higher education; nevertheless, it has allowed us to provide advanced education to most Americans.

Student services must be effectively organized to accomplish their mission. They must be appropriately clustered, staffed, and supervised. Lines of authority and communications must be established and operational guides and parameters identified. Staff titles, training, and compensation must properly motivate people to work together on the unit's programs and services. Through effective coordination of administrative efforts, student services helps achieve the institution's goals.

There has been little systematic study of student services structures. Crookston and Atkyns (1974) surveyed a cross section of institutions across the country and found three major plans dominating the field: (1) a centralized, line-staff structure with all program and service units reporting to the chief student services officer; (2) a decentralized structure with programs clustered in three or more operational or budgetary units (each unit supervised by a middle manager with the chief student services officer providing overall planning and direction for the program); and (3) a less-common, decentralized plan with two operating units divided between educational programs and administrative services.

The most common structure for student services has been the horizontal or "flat" organizational pattern, in which all major services report to the chief student services officer. This pattern has worked well for the small college or in situations where the program is limited or the unit head is not considered a major institutional officer. Unfortunately, this pattern is also found in many large, complex universities where the unit head is expected not only to direct the student services program but also to serve as an institutional leader. Clearly, some other pattern is needed if the program is to be an integral part of the institution. In Chapter Seventeen, Dutton and Rickard describe the advantages of a multidimensional model for more complex universities and systems.

No one organizational pattern can be imposed on student services programs. However, one can suggest factors to be considered in organizing or reorganizing a program: size and scope of the services, the organizational pattern of the institution, the administrative philosophy and style of the president, the internal and external governance system, the diversity and competencies of the professional staff, the resource base, and, finally and importantly, the preferences of the chief student services officer, who is ultimately responsible for the effectiveness of the program.

Staff. Operating with students through the structures and services of the student services program is the staff of competent professionals. Nothing is accomplished without them. Their degree of effectiveness, availability to students, morale, and personal welfare must be a daily concern of the chief student services officer.

The administrative model calls for a wide variety of professional specialists to perform its various tasks. Unlike other models, it welcomes individuals from a large array of disciplines and professions; mobility within the structure depends more on level of training and performance than on the kind of training. Although specialization is a chief staff characteristic, common attributes such as organizational commitment, behavioral modeling, and interunit cooperation and collaboration are encouraged and rewarded. The specialized training of staff members notwithstanding, in this model each person performs his or her task through administration, instruction, consultation, or some combination of these roles.

Regardless of the structure, scope, or size of the student services programs, three levels of staff are evident in the administrative model: administrative, managerial, and program. These three classifications refer to what is commonly called the "professional" staff. In addition, there are many technical, clerical, paraprofessional, student, and skilled and semiskilled workers.

The category of administrative staff is reserved for the chief student services officer and middle-level administrators who coordinate major program areas in the larger, more complex programs. The title of vice president for the chief student services officer usually signifies institution-wide involvement and responsibility. Some deans of students, with corresponding duties, however, report directly to the president. A more recent development has been personnel deans with specialized responsibilities for administering a cluster of services. Titles used with this category of administrative staff include the deans of admissions and records, student development, and student life. The chief administrative officer and the middle management personnel come from diverse specialties. Some come from traditional counseling or student services training programs, while a growing number are graduates of higher education or educational administration programs. And some come from disciplines unrelated to student services, having been selected for personal qualifications or circumstantial reasons.

Most service units within the student services division are headed by individuals who carry the title of "director" or "coordinator." They are the management staff: a diverse group of middle managers who frequently share little with respect to professional training and interests. They range from medical doctors directing health services and business managers supervising housing programs to the more traditionally trained student services worker, who may coordinate student activities or run the admissions program. In the administrative model, however, these individuals share common management responsibilities in terms of personnel policies, budgeting procedures, and program management and evaluation. It is the responsibility of the chief student services officer to achieve a high degree of administrative effectiveness and functional interdependence within this group.

Undergirding the organization are the program or professional staff, who deal in direct instructive, consultative, or administrative service to students. These people also reflect a wide range of training and specialization. They are usually the youngest and most energetic workers in the organization. Many of them enter student services out of some positive experiences as an undergraduate with either service staff or campus life. Certain student services require a high degree of specialization in the program level staff, while others can effectively use individuals from student services training programs or other related disciplines. Still others enter the profession as much for personal skills they possess as for the degrees or training they have received. Services requiring specialized training at this level include health services, counseling programs, psychological testing, food services, and legal and consumer advising programs. Most other services attract generalists and provide much on-the-job training.

Staff development is most crucial at this level. A young staff member can easily get "locked into" a position if concern for his or her professional mobility is not expressed early on. It is easy to become "tagged" as a residence hall specialist or an activities person if opportunities to explore other career options are not provided on the job. In Chapter Twenty-One, Harry Canon explores staff development programs.

Entry-level workers are the backbone of the profession, yet they are frequently asked to carry the burden with litle experience or supervision. They often have titles that do not reflect what they do and are branded as "bureaucrats" or "cogs" in an unresponsive system. They are usually the poorest paid members of the team in both dollars and attention. Chief student services officers need to make regular contact with these people.

Sources. Volumes have been written about the financial and other resources for higher education. Not much, however, has been said about the funding of student services in our own literature. However, we do not here intend to explore the complexities of finance for higher education and/or student services, although it is extremely important to the effective functioning of the administrative model. We will limit our comments to identifying sources of funds for student services.

Sources for the support of student services programs in almost any college or university can be categorized as general, restricted, or user generated. General fund support for student services is the largest single source. Monies from this source are usually not designated for specific functions and come from tuition and fees, endowments, unrestricted gifts, and, if applicable, government allocations. They are used to fund many regular services and to pay for salaries, operating expenses, and equipment. Restricted funds are usually of two types: (1) fees collected from students for a specified purpose and (2) designated gifts or grants. Residence hall charges or student activity funds are the best examples of restricted fees. Financial aid from federal or private scholarships is the most frequently specified money. More recently, user charges have increased as a means of funding certain services. Food services on campus have traditionally been funded in this manner, but now a number of charges for other services are being made to students and other users. Health services and placement activities are two prime examples. User fees have either been forced on the student service program or adopted reluctantly when no other option—save eliminating the service—is available.

It is a major responsibility of the chief student services officer to secure the necessary financial and other resources for programs. He or she must be skilled in budgeting and accounting and must demonstrate those competencies to others in the administrative structure. A good student services officer knows how to skillfully blend the different kinds of funds available. Johnson and Foxley, in Chapter Eighteen, address the issue of generating financial resources at the middle management level.

One note of advice: Chief student services officers must be well versed in higher education finance. Only in recent years have we included courses on this subject in training programs. Staff members are well advised to enroll in business, finance, and economics courses to supplement their other training.

Summary

Student services has traditionally and historically been an administrative unit in higher education. Yet its role has been unique: While providing essential services in support of the academic mission of the institution, it contributes significantly and directly to student education and development. Thus, there should be no real or perceived dichotomy with respect to the role of student services work in higher education. Its service-oriented function should be as clear to the practitioner today as it was to the authors of the *Student Personnel Point of View* in the 1930s.

Functioning within the administrative system gives us the greatest latitude for responding to student needs and institutional purpose. Our survival depends most heavily on our ability to deliver these essential services in a manner that clearly demonstrates that they make a difference to the students and the institution. We need to get on with the business of "minding the store."

References

American Council on Education. American Council on Education Studies, *The Student Personnel Point of View*. Series 1, Vol. 1, No. 3. Washington, D.C.: American Council on Education, 1937.

American Council on Education. American Council on Education Studies, *The Student Personnel Point of View*. Series 4 (Student Personnel Work), Vol. 13, No. 13. Washington, D.C.: American Council on Education, 1949.

Appleton, J., Briggs, C., and Rhatigan, J. *Pieces of Eight*. Portland: National Association of Student Personnel Administrators Institute of Research and Development, 1978.

Ayers, A., Tripp, P., and Russell, J. *Student Services Administration in Higher Education*. Washington, D.C.: U.S. Department of Health, Education, and Welfare, 1966.

Brubacher, J. S., and Rudy, W. *Higher Education in Transition*. New York: Harper & Row, 1958.

Commission on Professional Development, Council of Student Personnel Associations in Higher Education. *Student Development Services in Post Secondary Education*. 1972.

Crookston, B. B., and Atkyns, G. C. "A Study of Student Affairs: The Principal Student Affairs Officer, the Functions, the Organization of American Colleges and Universities, 1967–1972 (A Preliminary Summary Report)." Paper presented at the National Association of Student Personnel Administrators Conference, Chicago, April 1974.

Gulick, L. "Notes on the Theory of Organization." In L. Gulick and L. Urwick (Eds.), *Papers on the Science of Administration.* New York: Institute of Public Administration, 1937.

Harpel, R. L. "Planning, Budgeting and Evaluation in Student Affairs Programs: A Manual for Administrators." *NASPA Journal,* 1976, *14* (1), i-xx.

Harpel, R. L. "Evaluating From a Management Perspective." In G. R. Hanson (Ed.), *New Directions for Student Services: Evaluating Program Effectiveness,* no. 1. San Francisco: Jossey-Bass, 1978.

Hershenson, D. B. "A Functional Organization of College Student Personnel Services." *NASPA Journal,* 1970, *8,* 35-37.

Litchfield, E. H. "Organization in Large American Universities." *Journal of Higher Education,* 1959, *30,* 353-364, 489-504.

Miller, T. K., and Prince, J. S. *The Future of Student Affairs: A Guide to Student Development for Tomorrow's Higher Education.* San Francisco: Jossey-Bass, 1976.

Myers, E. M., and Topping, J. R. *Information Exchange Procedures Activity Structure.* Technical Report No. 63. Boulder, Colo.: National Center for Higher Education Management Systems, Western Interstate Commission for Higher Education, 1974.

Parker, C. A. "Ashes, Ashes . . . " Paper presented at the American College Personnel Association Convention, St. Louis, Missouri, March 1970.

Parker, C. A. "Institutional Self-Renewal in Higher Education." *Journal of College Student Personnel,* 1971, *12*(6), 405-409.

Penny, J. "Who's Minding the Store?—Reactions to 'Ashes, Ashes . . . '" Paper presented at the American College Personnel Association Convention, St. Louis, March 1970.

Ellen Betz   7

The Counselor Role

Each year, student services graduate students across the country enroll in courses in counseling and psychology, often including a supervised counseling practicum. Although it might appear that these students are preparing to become professional counselors, this is not their goal. Rather, they seek to maximize their effectiveness in future roles and relationships as student services professionals. The skills, perceptions, and understandings of the counselor have proven to be a solid base for improving understanding of oneself and others and for increasing interpersonal effectiveness.

The purpose of this chapter is to describe the counseling approach in student services work. This approach has developed out of training and practice in counseling psychology and is one of the most successful conceptual bases for work in the field. The chapter is organized in three parts. The first section is basically historical, detailing the major philosophical ideas and methods that characterize the approach as defined, first, by Edmund G. Williamson, by a number of other thinkers and practitioners. This section is followed by a description of the counseling approach as practiced today in the preparation of student services professionals. The third and last part of the chapter describes some major applications of the counseling approach in student services roles and relationships.

Historical Background

The counseling approach to student services originated with Edmund G. Williamson, formerly counseling psychologist and dean of students at the University of Minnesota. As early as 1939, Williamson pointed out in his book, *How to Counsel Students*, that counseling "is the basic type of personnel work with individual students and serves to coordinate and focus the findings and the efforts of other types of [student personnel] workers" (p. 36). In this and later writings, Williamson (1950, 1957, 1961) further explained his belief that the counseling approach is universally applicable to the various functions of the student services worker, providing a core from which all of these services can develop.

Williamson's counseling approach was characterized by strong philosophical beliefs regarding the purpose of education and, accordingly, of student services. Williamson (1950, p. 38) believed that "the basic purpose of education is not only to train the intellect but also to assist students to achieve those levels of social, civic and emotional maturity which are within the range of their potentialities." He saw student development as the major function of the student services worker. Counseling is education, he stated, its purpose being to supplement academic work through "a comprehensive program geared to the strategic objective of helping each individual to select and grow toward personal goals, of which one is the full development of each individual member of our democratic society" (Williamson, 1950, p. 4).

Williamson's belief in the potential and worth of each individual was indicated in his emphasis on recognizing the individual's ability to think and to solve problems by rational means (Williamson, 1961). He also urged the counselor to use rational methods of working with the student, rather than following intuition alone. In reaction to a period when brief counseling contact was too often characterized by uniform advice giving, he urged workers to gather facts and to consider them carefully, rather than rushing to advise. He and John Darley presented a set of rational procedures for counselors to use with students:

1. *Analysis.* Assembling factual information about the student, based on such data as the student's records, test scores, and case history information—to acquire dependable information, rather than making counseling decisions based solely or largely on subjective impressions
2. *Synthesis.* "Summarizing and organizing of the data from analysis in

such a manner as to reveal the student's assets, liabilities, adjustments, and maladjustments" (Williamson, 1950, p. 101)
3. *Diagnosis.* Interpreting the data and coming to conclusions regarding the student's problems, their characteristics, and causes
4. *Prognosis.* Making predictions regarding the probable outcome of the problems, a step that facilitates considering the total situation and needed actions
5. *Counseling.* Steps taken by the counselor and the student to bring about a better adjustment
6. *Follow-Up.* Steps taken to determine the effectiveness of the counseling and/or the further needs of the student for assistance

Williamson also urged that students be taught as much as possible of the growing knowledge regarding human beings and their psychological functioning. He said that student services workers must be the "principal educators," conveying to students information about the facts and principles of psychotherapy, testing, and human development. In particular, Williamson urged that counselors and students learn to use psychological tests accurately and to the advantage of the student. The psychologically trained person recognizes that carefully developed methodology is more trustworthy than untested, unvalidated conversations, interviews, or common sense (Williamson, 1961).

Reviewers have often assumed that Williamson's emphasis on the value of rational processes indicated a lack of concern for less rational aspects of human functioning. Although Williamson (and the society as a whole) dealt less openly in the 1940s and 1950s with these facets of individual behavior, they certainly were not disregarded in his writings. He recognized the potential problems of using the rational "technologies" within an interpersonal relationship and urged that counselors keep in mind at all times the basic importance of maintaining a personal relationship with the student. He described the ideal counseling interview as a warm, caring relationship characterized by a focus on the individual, a centering on the individual's life and development.

Others in the field have also made significant contributions. Foremost among these is Donald G. Paterson, in his own right a major contributor to both counseling and student services. Paterson viewed research as fundamental to a sound program of student services. Coming from a background of experience in personnel and measurement, Paterson believed that many student problems in higher education could be approached from a scientific perspective. In one of his earliest projects, he followed up a first-year testing program begun in 1919 and established test score standards for student selection at the University of Minnesota. Paterson's major contributions to student services work included his studies in individual differences, his development of tests and methods of evaluating student aptitudes and interests, and his emphasis on objectivity and research.

Following in Paterson's footsteps, Ralph Berdie applied counseling ideals to student services concerns through his early and numerous studies of college student variables, long before the restive 1960s when college administrators began seriously to concern themselves with student attitudes. Berdie (1944) investigated students' satisfaction with college, the first of a long series of studies of college student characteristics of concern to the student services worker (for example, see Berdie and Sutter, 1950; Berdie and Layton, 1952).

In more recent years, Clyde Parker (1966) has reiterated Williamson's belief that education as a counselor is important preparation for the student services worker. He points to the "dual concepts of the dignity of the individual and his [or her] interdependency" (Parker, 1966, p. 260) as a basis for student services work. Parker (1966) states that each student services worker needs skills pertinent to his or her areas of specialization but that counseling training develops major skills: sensitivity to others, skills in interpersonal relationships, interviewing skill, ability to analyze objectively an individual's strengths and weaknesses, awareness of the individual differences between people, the ability to identify peoples' learning difficulties, and knowledge of how people learn.

Parker's work in recent years has emphasized developmental concerns of college students (Parker, 1978). In this connection, he brings together both the counseling and developmental approaches, proposing that measures of students' status on Perry's (1970) cognitive dimension be used, along with knowledge of aptitudes, in designing instruction and classroom environments (Parker, 1975). One of Parker's present aims is to develop a program that will help faculty "in the personalization and individualization of their teaching in an effort to promote the development of college students" (Parker and Lawson, 1978, p. 425).

Rogers (1942, 1961) has made a major contribution in emphasizing a "client-centered" approach to counseling and in identifying specific dimensions of counselor effectiveness. His work in identifying warmth, genuineness, and positive regard in effective counselors has led to further research, specification, and teaching of these skills (Carkhuff, 1969; Egan, 1975).

Today's Counseling Approach in Student Services

Williamson's visions have today been incorporated into student services programs throughout the country. The counseling approach is now so deeply ingrained in the typical college and university that it is difficult to determine its specific dimensions. Nonetheless, we need to begin the process of definition, to develop a description of the counseling model that can be analyzed and discussed as the basis for revision and further development.

The counseling approach is described as it is practiced today in the preparation of student services professionals. This approach contains many contributions from other disciplines, notably education and psychology.

Philosophical Beliefs. First and all-important, the counseling approach is a set of beliefs about people and life. Without clearly understood beliefs and values, the student services worker experiences uncertainty and uncomfortable variability, both in what he or she chooses to do and in how that choice is carried out on the job. Hopefully too, clarity regarding one's own beliefs enables the student services worker to take a more active role in influencing the attitudes and beliefs of the university and/or college commuity.

The counseling approach takes a positive position regarding human growth and development. It holds that humans develop in interaction with the environment and that learning can continue throughout life. The belief that adult human beings can indeed continue to learn and grow is basic to effective student services. This position encourages people in their attempts to learn and grow.

The counseling approach holds too that humans are basically good, that they want to contribute in a positive way in their lives. The writings of Williamson are persistently positive regarding human potential. Another major contributor to this position is Carl Rogers, whose thinking and writing are built on a belief in the human drive to grow, to move "in a basically positive direction" (Rogers, 1961, p. 26). The student services worker who is grounded in the counseling approach sees his or her role as one of furthering this positive life force, facilitating the natural desire to be competent and to grow.

Following closely the confidence in human potential is the belief that the purpose of education includes the development of the total person, not the intellect alone. It includes also an active belief in the potential reality of the democratic ideal, the right of every person to full development and use of talents, to equal opportunity, respect, and dignity. Our belief in these goals is indicated by our own behaviors with the individual student, by our willingness to work with all types of students and with all types of programs, and, above all, by our willingness to speak up in the university community for the rights of all students to a full range of development experiences. The intellectual elitism that pervades many campuses is difficult to confront, because humanistic beliefs regarding human development are frequently equated, although erroneously, with less intellect. Accordingly, those who hold humanistic orientations are sometimes devalued by others and in establishing budgets. The vocal student services worker can make a positive contribution to the philosophy of the campus through his or her contacts with individual students and through conscious efforts to influence the values of leaders in the educational environment.

Closely related to the belief in the right of people to full development is the recognition and acceptance of individual differences. The English biologist Francis Galton (1869) first attempted to apply the principle of individual variability to the understanding of human beings. Individual differences were further explored through the testing movement, which dominated the first half of the present century and resulted in the development of numerous and useful tests of such human characteristics as abilities, interests, and personality. In these early studies, no particular judgmental position was intended regarding the value of various scores obtained by different individuals. Nevertheless, the ensuing societal inference was that certain human characteristics, or degrees of same, were to be judged either "good" or "bad." Thus, rather than facilitating the acceptance of individual differences, the testing movement may have inadvertently brought about an overemphasis on certain human characteristics, particularly intelligence, and a tendency to denigrate persons having the "less desirable" test scores. Certainly, the use of test scores to help people understand themselves did not indicate a lack of respect for the characteristics of any individual. Nonetheless, acceptance rather than criticism of individual differences is an attitude that has yet to be learned by many people in our culture. Teaching such acceptance can be an important goal in the work of the student services professional.

True acceptance of individual differences allows a nonjudgmental attitude toward the differences among people, cultures, and groups of different races, sex or sexual preferences, and religions. Such acceptance helps us deal with both our own and others' foibles and idiosyncracies. It helps us recognize the dangers of overemphasizing conformity with its concomitant, frequently crippling fear of "what other people think." Acceptance of individual differences allows the individual to try out ideas and to take chances, both of which are basic to the full and creative development of oneself. Our lack of acceptance of individual differences underlies our criticism of others and of ourselves and underlies our fear of criticism or ridicule by others. It is closely related to human problems in relationships and overall adjustment. Acceptance of individual differences is a basic value in the counseling approach. It can provide a conscious teaching goal for the daily work of the student services professional. Through his or her informal comments and through modeling, in addition to more formal campus programming, the student services worker can teach students to accept themselves and others, to appreciate rather than depreciate differences. The end result can be more comfortable, creative individuals, freed for the long-term process of self-development.

Perhaps the most difficult of all of the philosophical beliefs underlying the counseling approach is the belief in the right of each individual to hold his or her own values and the right to indicate what they are. We are forever hampered by the fact that we almost always believe that our own values (at least in some areas) are indeed the "right" ones. Yet, if we do not believe in anything, or recognize in which areas we have particularly strong values, our effectiveness as student services workers will be reduced. The values discussed earlier in this section are basic to the counseling approach to student services work; at the same time, however, we must accept the fact that others have a right to hold values that differ from ours.

Counseling Knowledge and Skills. A background in psychology and counseling produces a worker with advanced interpersonal skills and valuable knowledge regarding human behavior and dynamics. Much of that learning can be of particular importance in the human interactions involved in student services. So much has been learned in recent years, however, that it is impossible to describe that content fully in this chapter. Accordingly, only a summary of the highlights can be included here. The major topics reviewed are (1) knowledge regarding human learning, (2) theories of career and life planning, (3) skills in using psychometric data, and (4) communication and perception skills.

A most important area of relevance to the student services worker is knowledge regarding how people learn. Our formal, primarily didactic educational system was developed long before we reached our present level of knowledge about human learning. Although people do indeed learn from lectures and from memorizing, these are not the only ways in which educational processes can be conducted successfully. The extensive literature on conditioning, initiated by the work of Skinner (1953), is directly relevant. The importance of reinforcement, the effects of punishment, and the effects of different schedules of reinforcement, for example, have direct and important implications for student services workers. Knowing the effects of anxiety on human learning and knowing how to control or desensitize anxiety, such as described by Wolpe (1966), is also important for people who work with people. Bandura and his associates (Bandura and Walters, 1963; Bandura, 1966) have made clear that people also learn by modeling the behavior of others and by observing the consequences of that behavior. The behaviorists have also taught counselors to question assumptions regarding the "meaning" of an individual's responses to a given stimulus. Through developing an understanding of learning principles, the worker discovers that no human act, in and of itself, is necessarily "abnormal." Instead, people are capable of responding in many ways to stimuli in their environments, and no single response has any single explanation.

Knowing the many ways in which people learn gives student services workers an advantage in planning their work. It provides them with ideas for alternative teaching strategies to help students learn, both in individual contacts and in group programs. Although didactic-type programming is always possible for some educational goals, other approaches may be more effective. Every student services worker, even those not directly involved in group programming with students, can teach students through the modeling and conditioning modes and thus can directly further student development. Additionally, knowledge of how people learn reduces the tendency to categorize people and facilitates the recognition and acceptance of individual differences.

The counseling approach also teaches knowledge and skills of importance in helping students learn how to manage their career and life planning. For example, building on the work of Erikson (1950), Donald Super (1957) has taught counselors the importance of attending to the total developmental process in helping people with career decisions. He pointed out that careers, rather than resulting from a single decision at one point in time, are the ongoing outcome of a sequence of decisions continuing throughout a lifetime. Super emphasized that careers represent an implementation of the individual's self-concept (Super and others, 1963), an idea that has helped both counselors and clients understand more fully the motivations underlying some of their decisions.

The use of objective psychometric data is one way of helping students to know themselves. The person who is well trained in the use of tests has a healthy respect for the valuable knowledge that can be obtained from tests. At the same time, however, this worker knows the limitations of tests and does not attribute unrealistic qualities to them. He or she has learned various ways of using test information: In one case, the worker may use the test data to validate what the individual has already discovered about himself or herself; in another case, the personal experiences of the client may be used to help validate test information. The student services worker who understands test usage can supplement the work of the professional counselor, clarifying students' expectations regarding tests, helping to clear up misunderstandings regarding a student's own test scores.

The counselor's interpersonal skills are also of critical importance to the student services worker. Carl Rogers (1942) first pointed out a method by which counselors' listening could be sharply improved. By teaching the counselor to follow the client's expressed feelings, reflecting feelings as well as content, Rogers simultaneously taught counselors to listen. The student services worker who is trained in the counseling approach is a skilled and conscientious listener who, to the extent possible, allows a great deal of time and freedom for the student to express ideas fully. He or she spends much time with the individual student, and during that time the student spends much time talking, while the counselor listens. Both feelings as well as facts will emerge as appropriate material. Carkhuff (1969), Ivey (1971), Kagan (1975), and Egan (1975) have developed specific methods to teach these listening and response skills to counselors and other helpers.

Counseling training also sharpens the perceptions of the student services worker. The trained counselor learns to note the human cues that indicate how a person is feeling: the sounds of stress in the individual's voice, the clenched hand, the rapping foot, the meaningful pauses, to name but a few of the many indicators. Training improves not only the perceptions but also the ability to interpret them with accuracy. The counselor learns to test his or her perceptions, to recognize the difference between hypotheses about people and facts. The counselor's perceptiveness can be used to help the student express what he or she is feeling or thinking. This, in turn, can help the student understand and manage himself or herself more effectively. Skills in perception alert the worker to unexpressed and sometimes serious areas of concern. They help the worker recognize people who can be helped by referral to others in the campus community. Like most other skills, perceptive skills can be misused; the counseling approach, however, emphasizes (1) the use of these skills to aid in the development of the client and (2) the avoidance of their use to establish power or authority over the student.

Attitudes Toward Oneself. In addition to developing counseling knowledge and skills, training in the counseling approach can strengthen the worker's own personal and interpersonal adjustment. An important objective of training in the counseling approach is the strengthening of attitudes toward oneself. Every person, in the process of growing up, develops some attitudes or beliefs that inhibit or retard growth and development. In each of us, there are areas where important learning has been incomplete. Healthy self-attitudes can enhance the counselor's own continuous learning. In turn, these attitudes can help the worker provide an atmosphere that will optimize client learning and can set an example for the student client to model.

Healthy attitudes toward the self include the recognition and acceptance of one's own strengths and weaknesses. Self-acceptance facilitates the individual's ability to face up to his or her inadequacies as well as to the adequacies, with lessened anxiety or defensiveness. With self-acceptance, the counselor can seek and use help from others and can give help without diminishing the other person. Without self-acceptance, the counselor is unlikely to be able to help others develop it in themselves. Openness about oneself helps to reduce such problems as defensiveness, posturing, or projection, and at the same time, as a by-product, seems to help build one's own self-acceptance.

Closely related to the goal of openness is another important value held by workers representative of the counseling approach: the belief in basic honesty as a style of life—honesty in relationships with others, directness and nonmanipulative communications, openness with other people. Rogers' (1957) term *genuineness* expresses effectively the overall impact of this philosophical base. Our early training in conformity, our desire to impress others and to do well, and our own attitudes and fears regarding inadequacy all tend to cause us to simulate total assurance when our real feelings are somewhere short of such confidence. We deny our fear, doubt, and ignorance although these are a part of each of us much of the time. Such covering up of feelings may seem to protect us from criticism but it also increases the self-doubts of the students we work with and the manipulativeness of everyone around us. Certainly there is a time and place for performing "confidently" despite fear, for withholding full expression of our doubts in all places at all times. With these qualifications, however, the counseling approach holds a strong belief in the value of genuineness and openness and encourages a continued effort toward living accordingly.

Self-analysis as a way of life is another valuable asset of the counseling approach. Most likely it too is a by-product of learning to be a counselor and, accordingly, of using some counseling skills on oneself. Obviously, self-analysis, like other skills, can be carried too far. In moderation, however, it produces a continuous educational process for the counselor and contributes a spirit of adventure and a desire for learning to every counseling or student services relationship.

Applications to Student Services Functions

Much of the knowledge and many of the skills discussed in the previous section were originally applied in the process of professional counseling. In practice today, some student services workers actually do provide counseling services and thus can use their skills and knowledge directly in counseling with students. Many other workers, however, have other student services functions and use their counseling skills less directly. With these skills, the worker can gather information more effectively, can learn more about the real needs of the students with whom he or she works, and can use this knowledge to provide more effective services.

Referral. The student services worker can often be a critical link in helping students use counseling services. Many students, perhaps almost all of them, are afraid to go to a professional counselor. Many have only vague ideas about what happens in counseling, and they wonder what counselors are like. They worry that their problems may be an indication of mental illness. They need to express their fears aloud, to be able to talk to someone who will keep their concerns confidential but will fully accept them as individuals. The student services worker who is trained in the skills and knowledge of the counselor and known by the students to be a person who likes and respects people can be the ideal "first step." The worker, in turn, can help the student to accept what he or she is experiencing, to build up confidence and self-respect, and to discover that there are other good people on the campus who can help with the next step, counseling. Thus, the student services worker gradually develops the student's readiness for counseling. If possible, the worker will refer the student to a specific counselor, one known to the worker to be helpful and effective. Thus, the student moves into counseling with a confidence that can make a substantial difference in his or her ability to gain from the experience. In the referral process, the counseling-trained student services worker again has an important advantage: He or she knows what to look for in counselors and how to be maximally helpful in preparing the student for the counseling experience.

Once counseling has commenced, the student services worker can continue to provide support and encouragement for the student. On occasion, the student will want to talk over the counseling experience or to work through some remaining detail. Here, however, the worker moves into a more difficult terrain. There is no simple answer to the question of what support is and when it begins to infringe on the counseling relationship. At times the worker may be tempted to talk over the student's situation with the counselor, but this is where the student's right to confidentiality begins. The worker is ethically bound, as is the counselor, to protect the student's confidentiality rights; no such contacts should be initiated without the full, freely given consent of the student.

Direct Support of Students. Although some contacts of the student services worker will result in a counseling referral, there will be many more student contacts where the worker provides the informal, day-to-day support and help, without a counseling referral. This is an important, ongoing function of the student services worker. Tyler (1969) points up the need in our urban society for what she calls "incidental counseling," the informal but attentive counsel and support that used to be provided by the family doctor, minister, or teacher who has known the individual for a period of time. Bergin and Lambert (1978) have reported evidence that such helpers may well have been responsible for the fact that some young people were able to overcome their pathological home environments while their siblings were not able to do so. The good listener, the stable model, the adult who believes in a person's individual worth can unquestionably make a difference in people's lives. That role is a familiar and important one for the student services worker, and counseling skills are helpful.

In at least one area, the student services worker sometimes has an important advantage over the professional counselor. In institution- or organization-based jobs, such as residence halls, student unions, and orientation programs, the student services worker often has ongoing contacts with students that take place in the students' own interpersonal environments, rather than being limited to office contacts. Working in these settings, the student services worker frequently can observe a student's relationships with others. He or she may be on hand when the student confronts a difficult situation and reacts to the resultant stress. By observing the student in real-life experiences, the student services worker can often assess the student's strengths, needs, and problems more quickly and sometimes more accurately than the office-bound counselor. This can make an important difference in the process of establishing rapport, confronting the key problem, and taking specific and appropriate action.

Direct Programming. Another application of the counseling approach lies in direct programming with students. Most undergraduate students today need and want to improve their ability to get along with people. They need to learn how to listen, how to be open about themselves, and how to express themselves without becoming abrasive. These skills are basic to both interpersonal and career success, and they are skills that can be taught by the counseling-based student services worker, informally as well as formally. The counseling-trained worker in the financial aid area, for example, can serve as a model for the students he or she works with and can incorporate communications skills or decision-making skills into individual or group training sessions on money management, budget planning, or on financial communications with parents. The residence halls worker can encourage or facilitate the organization of communications, career-planning, or decision-making workshops within the residence halls. In some cases, time constraints require that the actual training be given by others, but the counselor worker will still be a more helpful enabler because of his or her counseling skills.

Relationships with Other Workers. A counseling background can facilitate almost every interpersonal interaction. Thus, the relationships of the student services worker with his or her own associates should benefit from counseling training. A good place to start might be with the worker's supervisory relationships. Obviously, even if both supervisor and supervisee have the benefit of counseling training, there will be times, situations, and people with whom the relationship will be strained. For one thing, student services workers and their supervisors get tired and frustrated like everyone else; no one can always be attentive, listening carefully, fully accepting, and thoroughly informed.

Nevertheless, counseling background on the part of either or both of the principals can be helpful. When the relationship seems to be going badly, the student services worker can fall back on counseling skills and attitudes to evaluate the situation, to think about what may be going wrong, what action might be most helpful. Counseling training often helps the worker postpone self-centered explanations and doctrinaire positions. It can help the worker assess his or her own concerns, needs, and defenses. It provides skills to facilitate the full expression of ideas and feelings. The counseling-trained worker values openness and encourages and models it in the relationship. He or she values directness and strives to avoid manipulation. Counseling training certainly does not guarantee that all will go smoothly in supervisory relationships, but it should make for a significant improvement. Perhaps its greatest contribution will be noticed across time, after many contacts and much work together. Relationships with supervisors, like those with clients and like those with one's other associates, grow strong over time. Nothing less should be expected of supervisory relationships.

Consulting Roles. Another setting where the student services worker's counseling background will be helpful is in the worker's role as a consultant, whether working directly with leaders of student organizations or with staff members from other campus or community agencies. As a consultant, the worker may provide certain technical information, assist in the development or evaluation of current programs, help in clarifying issues, and assist in the search for solutions to present problems, among other potential assignments. The trained staff member has the counselor's special skills and knowledge, all of which can help the worker to improve working relationships and thus the effectiveness of services.

Summary

The counseling approach to student services work grew out of the belief, first presented by E. G. Williamson (1939), that counseling is basic to all student services functions. As carried out in student services programs today, the counseling approach is based on intensive training in both counseling and psychology. It results in the development of the worker's interpersonal skills and provides specialized knowledge about human dynamics. It has a direct and significant effect on the person's understandings and beliefs about others and about him- or herself. It provides tools that can be used to help others develop their own interpersonal skills and their own self-management. In addition, the counseling approach provides a philosophical base, a set of beliefs that underlie each effort, each interpersonal contact, and that can be extended actively to have an impact on the total university or college environment. Whether these skills are used regularly and directly, as in professional counseling, or indirectly, as in other student services functions, they can form the basis for effective, informed, and comfortable functioning as a student services professional.

References

Bandura, A. "Behavioral Modification Through Modeling Procedures." In L. Krasner and L. P. Ullman (Eds.), *Research in Behavior Modification.* New York: Holt, Rinehart and Winston, 1966.

Bandura, A., and Walters, R. H. *Social Learning and Personality Development.* New York: Holt, Rinehart and Winston, 1963.

Berdie, R. F. "The Prediction of College Achievement and Satisfaction." *Journal of Applied Psychology,* 1944, *28,* 239–245.

Berdie, R. F., and Layton, W. L. "Predicting Success in Law School." *Journal of Applied Psychology,* 1952, *36,* 257–260.

Berdie, R. F., and Sutter, N. A. "Predicting Success of Engineering Students." *Journal of Educational Psychology,* 1950, *34,* 184–190.

Bergin, A. E., and Lambert, M. J. "The Evaluation of Therapeutic Outcomes." In S. L. Garfield and A. E. Bergin (Eds.), *Handbook of Psychotherapy and Behavior Change.* New York: Wiley, 1978.

Carkhuff, R. R. *Helping and Human Relations.* Vols. 1 and 2. New York: Holt, Rinehart and Winston, 1969.

Egan, G. *The Skilled Helper: A Model for Systematic Helping and Interpersonal Relating.* Monterey, Calif: Brooks/Cole, 1975.

Erikson, E. *Childhood and Society.* New York: Norton, 1950.

Galton, F. *Hereditary Genius: An Inquiry into Its Laws and Consequences.* London: Macmillan, 1869.

Ivey, A. E. *Microcounseling: Innovations in Interviewer Training.* Springfield, Ill.: Thomas, 1971.

Kagan, N. *Interpersonal Process Recall: A Method for Influencing Human Interaction.* East Lansing: Michigan State University Educational Publication Services, 1975.

Parker, C. A. "The Place of Counseling in the Preparation of Student Personnel Workers." *Personnel and Guidance Journal,* 1966, *45,* 254–261.

Parker, C. A. "Developmental Instruction and Student Personnel Work." Paper presented at Office of Student Affairs Seminar, University of Minnesota, March 20, 1975.

Parker, C. A. (Ed.). *Encouraging Development in College Students.* Minneapolis: University of Minnesota Press, 1978.

Parker, C. A., and Lawson, J. M. "From Theory to Practice to Theory: Consulting with College Faculty." *Personnel and Guidance Journal,* 1978, *56*(7), 425–427.

Paterson, D. G. "Student Personnel Service at the University of Minnesota." *Journal of Personnel Research,* 1925, *3,* 449–453.

Paterson, D. G., Gerken, C. A., and Hahn, M. E. *The Minnesota Occupational Rating Scales and Counseling Profile.* Chicago: Science Research Associates, 1941.

Perry, W. J. *Intellectual and Ethical Development in the College Years.* New York: Holt, Rinehart and Winston, 1970.

Rogers, C. R. *Counseling and Psychotherapy.* Boston: Houghton Mifflin, 1942.

Rogers, C. R. "The Necessary and Sufficient Conditions of Therapeutic Personality Change." *Journal of Consulting Psychology,* 1957, *21,* 95–103.

Rogers, C. R. *On Becoming a Person.* Boston: Houghton Mifflin, 1961.

Skinner, B. F. *Science and Human Behavior.* New York: Macmillan, 1953.

Super, D. E. *The Psychology of Careers.* New York: Harper & Row, 1957.

Super, D. E., and others. *Career Development: Self-Concept Theory.* New York: College Entrance Examination Board, 1963.

Tyler, L. F. *The Work of the Counselor.* (3rd ed.) New York: Appleton-Century-Crofts, 1969.

Williamson, E. G. *How to Counsel Students.* New York: McGraw-Hill, 1939.

Williamson, E. G. *Counseling Adolescents.* New York: McGraw-Hill, 1950.

Williamson, E. G. "Editorial Note." *Journal of Counseling Psychology,* 1957, *4,* 262.

Williamson, E. G. *Student Personnel Services in Colleges and Universities.* New York: McGraw-Hill, 1961.

Wolpe, J. "Direct Behavior Modification Therapies." In L. E. Abt and B. F. Riess (Eds.), *Progress in Clinical Psychology.* Vol. 7. New York: Grune & Stratton, 1966.

Robert D. Brown   8

The Student
Development Educator
Role

By definition, the student development educator is knowledgeable about theories and practices in learning and development that relate to intellectual, emotional, cultural, moral, physical, and interpersonal dimensions of life. He or she trained to work with individual students, groups of students, and others who interact with students to (1) assess students' developmental status and diagnose their developmental needs, (2) help students determine appropriate goals and experiences, (3) design and implement programs intended to foster development, (4) evaluate each student's developmental progress, and (5) record this attainment.

The Meaning of Student Development

The term *student development* in the preceding definition of the student development educator's role refers to what a few decades ago was called the "whole student." Among student services professionals, the "whole student" consisted primarily of social and personal dimensions (such as leadership skills) that were influenced by life outside the classroom in student activities, student government, and residence hall life. For some professionals today, the two expressions mean essentially the same, and some suggest that the profession is simply conjuring up new jargon. However, implicit in the use of "student development" are two meanings generally not associated with the term "whole student." First, there is a tie to the burgeoning theoretical and data-based literature on human development, particularly that which focuses on young adults. This has led to conceptualizations concerned with stages of development, intervention strategies and environmental factors that affect development, and the relationship between cognitive and personal development. Chapters Four and Five have explicated these theories and their implications. Although more research is necessary to validate various theories of development, people who use the term "student development" often have a theoretical foundation. Second, the notion of intentionality is also involved for many student developmentalists. They see the individual student as an active agent in the developmental process, and they assume that it is possible to program experiences that can assist development.

For nearly a decade now, the specific content of student development has remained amorphous. Student development *toward* what or *for* what has, in fact, not been considered. If there has been a focus, it has been on interpersonal skills, but most often the focus has been as nonspecific as "self-direction." It is time for student development to have a content, one that recognizes all facets of potential development. To initiate what is hoped will become a full-blown dialogue on this question, a broad outline of potential dimensions will be presented.

The dimensions of student development include (1) personal identity, which includes having a sense of purpose, a value system, and a vocational (in the broad sense of that term) purpose; (2) interpersonal development, which includes communication skills, ability to understand and empathize with others and to give others emotional support, and group interaction skills; (3) intellectual and academic skills, which permit the individual to engage in lifelong learning; (4) aesthetic development, which includes both an awareness of the arts and some sense of personal skill in both appreciation and creation; and (5) physical recreation skills, which, like aesthetic development, include both appreciation and participation.

These dimensions need expansion and refinement. They are somewhat unique in emphasizing the importance of the aesthetic and physical recreation skill development dimensions if the student development movement is not only to provide theory and intentionality but to also remain true to its "whole student" roots.

Higher education has not systematically fostered the personal growth of students. It sometimes happens—even intentionally. However, for the most part, although college catalogues espouse personal growth as a clear intent, it has remained essentially a paper commitment. There is support for providing student services—at least some of them. Certainly, most institutions have sought to make residence halls living-learning communities, to provide personal counseling services, to monitor student activities, and to provide many other services that make the learning environment more humane and productive. But, in contrast to their sometimes ambivalent concern with all aspects of student development, they have emphasized above all others the one facet of intellectual and academic growth. There are variations in the extent of flexibility and rigidity of their expectations, but for the most part the pattern is clear and consistent. Generally, it looks something like this: The institution expects students to prove they have certain academic competencies or at least have had related experiences prior to entrance to the college. This includes a high school diploma, which is sometimes sufficient. However, often the college also expects the student to have successfully completed several units of particular course work, such as English and mathematics. If the college is selective, there will be entrance examinations on which a certain level of attainment is required. Within the college, there may be another set of requirements, with higher examination scores needed for entrance into some programs and different course prerequisites, such as more math for some or a foreign language for others. Sometimes the student may be admitted to the program without all the prerequisites, with full admission contingent on removing the deficiencies within a specified period of time.

At many institutions, the student is subjected to a battery of tests after he or she arrives on campus. These tests are used diagnostically to assess strengths and weaknesses and prescriptively to place students in certain speech, English, and math classes. If students pass the admission and testing hurdles, they are free to enroll in the college courses of their choice. However, the choice is governed by certain general requirements for all students and specific course requirements for an academic major. For the most part, as long as students persist and pass all the necessary courses they leap over the academic hurdles in college life rather smoothly. Some institutions require a final comprehensive examination in the major field, but for the most part the student accumulates the necessary credit hours and graduates. Performance in each course, at least as it is evaluated by professors on the traditional A to F grade scale, is duly recorded on an academic transcript. This transcript serves several purposes. It provides the institution with a record of the student's progress through the prescribed or selected courses, and it provides students, their employers, and graduate and professional schools with indexes of the students' academic achievement.

This pattern of expectancies and behaviors is outlined in Table 1 and compared to the pattern of expectancies and behaviors in the area of personal developmental growth. The area of personal growth essentially has no counterpart in the pattern or range of activities that make up the program for intellectual and academic development. The best that can be said for personal development is that the avenues are sometimes available—the opportunities may be there—but they are certainly not systematic.

In light of research findings and examination of available opportunities for systematic student development, the answer to the question, "Why are student development educators needed?" is that college experience *can* make a difference in all facets of student development but colleges do not program for most aspects with the intensity nor as systematically as they do for intellectual and academic development. Student development will not make further headway in higher education until other facets of development become a formal and systematic expectation by each institution. Until institutions establish programs comparable to those designed for intellectual and academic development, student development at large will remain incidental, if not accidental. That is, if student development is to be anything other than a utopian concept in the minds of a few theorists and a multitude of self-styled student development educators, a significant transformation must occur.

A viable and potentially powerful role for the student development educator lies within a system that would either parallel or be integrated with the academic and intellectual system described in Table 1. The system itself may range from one loosely parallel to the academic system and requesting only voluntary student involvement to a process that the institution requires of all students. The roles and functions of the student development educators between these systems would vary only slightly. What are some roles and activities?

Five major activities that involve the student development educator working either directly with students or with others who have direct contact with students parallel the responsibilities listed in the definition of the student development educator at the start of this chapter. These activities include (1) assessing current developmental status, (2) establishing goals for students, (3) program planning and instruction, (4) evaluating and recycling, and (5) recording student progress. This model is not unique. Some portions have existed, at least as an ideal, for several decades in instructional contexts. Every teacher trainee has been taught that instruction should be based on where the students are, that

Table 1. Institutional Policies and Activities Related to
Intellectual, Academic, and Personal Development

Policy/Activity Area	Intellectual-Academic	Personal Development
1. Institutional commitment	College catalogue states institutional goals and purposes	College catalogue states institutional goals and purposes but may not refer to specific personal development goals
2. Admission requirements	A. Specified prerequisite experiences and certification (diploma, specific courses)	A. No prerequisites, although some private institutions may require references
	B. Entrance examination	B. No assessment
3. Program planning	A. Diagnostic testing and advising	A. No assessment of current student status
	B. Prescribed general education course requirements.	B. Some courses and experiences available
	C. Prescribed course requirements for academic major	C. No requirements
	D. Established number of course hours and grade points for graduation	D. No requirements
4. Instruction and evaluation	A. Planned sequence of courses	A. No planned program
	B. Progress evaluated after each course and sometimes comprehensively	B. No systematic evaluation
	C. Some advising available throughout program	C. Counseling and advising available
5. Progress recorded	A. Academic transcript maintained	A. No record kept
	B. Grade point and test scores on national tests on file	B. Letters of reference occasionally reflect growth and status

goals should be specific, and that instruction should be based on a task analysis.

Interest in applying an instructional model involving assessment, goal setting, and evaluation for fostering student development has gained momentum. Potential roles as diagnosticians and programmers were noted several years ago (Brown, 1972). Parker (1973) adapted the instructional model to include teacher and learner goals, noting how each can contribute to the planning. Miller and Prince (1976) presented one of the most extensive discussions of this model and its implications for student development educators.

These adaptations are quite useful. They prompt us to think more systematically about goals and programming, and they highlight the need for evaluation. A major fault lies not with the models but with proposed implementation that appears to depend almost entirely on voluntary student involvement. Parker suggests that students and the teacher have equal power in the decision making. Miller and Prince refer extensively to "collaboration" between the student and the student development educator throughout the process. Assuming equal power is neither an accurate reflection of reality nor an ideal. One of the major differences between these models and the version proposed here is that the directed student development model would be integrated into the entire college program and would be on a par with the academic program, including not only assessment but also record keeping. Students would be expected to progress in development, just as they are currently expected to do in academic areas. Parker and Morrill (1974, p. 163) have suggested that student development proponents have been "shortsighted" in making development "synonymous with humanism." They offer examples of specific programming as alternatives to what they characterize as the "ambiguous, amorphous, idealistic rhetoric of humanism" (p. 166). Unfortunately, the alternatives they offer, including test anxiety reduction programs, crisis switchboards, and student characteristics surveys, although worthwhile in themselves, can hardly be said to systematically promote student development. Believing that students and teachers have equal power and that a hodge-podge of programming will significantly affect student development is not as realistic as working to integrate developmental goals and programming into the mainstream of academic planning, assessment, and evaluation.

Figure 1 presents the schema for directed student development in terms of the activities of the student development educator. It includes four consultant specialist roles: measurement, counseling, programming and learning, and evaluation. These experts are available for special program planning and services. However, it is anticipated that the student development educator is involved with the student throughout the process and also has skills in all four areas. The educator is ideally a generalist, serving as the mentor for a student throughout the process, which consists of a few basic tasks: assessing developmental status, establishing goals, programming experiences, and evaluating and recording student progress.

Assessing Developmental Status

The developmental status of each student is determined on enrollment and a profile constructed of a student's relative strengths. Assessment is formal and informal and takes many forms. The activities and attainments of the student prior to enrollment make up a significant portion of the developmental profile. Some aspects of physical recrea-

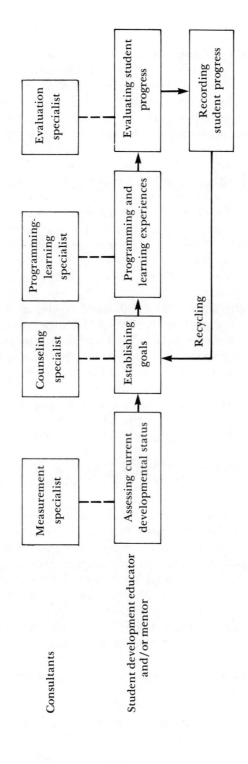

Figure 1. Schema of Roles and Activities for Student Development Educators

tion skills, for example, are certified by recreational directors and high school coaches. Students are asked to demonstrate their physical fitness through a series of skill exercises that demand endurance, strength, and flexibility. Proficiency in potential leisure-time sports is assessed. A paper-and-pencil test is used to assess knowledge of the nutritional value of foods and appropriate diet and exercise programs.

The students participate in special life-planning workshops designed to provide an opportunity to determine the certainty of their current career choice and how it relates to other life-style interests and needs. Problem-solving and leadership skills are assessed by observing students in a variety of contexts calling for groups and individuals to accomplish tasks, solve problems, and establish team objectives and responsibilities. Cultural and aesthetic awareness are assessed primarily through questionnaires that determine knowledge, extent of activities, and indications of skills in such areas as photography, crafts, and the performing arts.

Emotional maturity and moral development are two areas that may be more controversial as dimensions to be assessed and growth to be required. They are also areas in which assessment strategies are far from perfect. Some institutions may be in a position to be more bold and experimental in both programming and assessment in these areas. Further development and research such as that being done by the Cooperative Assessment of Experiential Learning program (Knapp and Sharon, 1975) and that using instruments such as the *Student Development Task Inventory* (Prince, Miller, and Winston, 1974) are of some assistance.

Assessment is indeed a formidable task, but it need not be impossible. The flexibility inherent in the process permits institutions to develop assessment strategies congruent with their own resources and schedule. Institutions can establish assessment centers and have students spend three days to a week during the summer for a combination assessment and orientation period. Some institutions prefer to spread the assessment over the course of the first semester or the entire first year. Others prefer to do no initial screening but expect students to complete a series of courses and experiences during their first two years that would be analogous to general education courses, with the option of excusing students from required activities if they can demonstrate proficiency.

In assessing large numbers of students, pitfalls common to routine diagnostic academic testing must be avoided. Too often the students are herded into a large room to complete an extensive battery of tests, which are then processed and the students placed in certain remedial or advanced classes on the basis of the test performance. The process is generally mechanical, if not inhumane. Determining developmental levels could quite easily become a similar assembly-line activity. However, it is quite important that it not be reduced to a computer analysis with an automatic printout of a profile, such as the biorhythm readings now available in arcades and airport terminals. It is important that the students not be passive throughout the process; they must be active as well as being acted on. Students must have an awareness of the full meaning of the assessment process. It should be experienced as something that is happening *with* them rather than *to* them, something they are helping to shape rather than solely being shaped by.

In some ways, the assessment process might be equated with a spiritual retreat. The retreat is usually entered into with anxiety and vulnerability. In a testing situation, the goal is to get by, to pass the test. A minimal hope in some situations is to not make a fool of oneself, and seldom does one feel any sense of oneness with self. In the context of retreat, however, participants are involved in determining who they are. It is not a question of "passing" but rather one of "growing." Spiritual perfection is always something beyond accomplishment, but the retreat not only provides people with an updated picture of themselves and who they are but also provides the opportunity for developing a renewed image of who they may become.

The spiritual retreat usually occurs at significant periods in life. For the medieval knight, it took place before going into battle; for the monk or nun, before taking vows. However, the retreat is not necessarily a single event; it can be periodic, even ongoing. The same is true for the developmental assessment process. It is at least an annual process during the college years. It is itself a skill development activity, because it is not only an opportunity for students to gain a picture of where they are now but also a process that fosters the ability to engage in self-assessment in the future. This ability can be one of the more important developmental tasks for college students.

If the analogy of the spiritual retreat holds for the assessment process itself as a period of rediscovery of self, then perhaps the analogy of the retreat leader also holds for the role of the student development educator in this context. This is clearly an instance in which the educator must collaborate with other campus specialists, as noted earlier, in a consulting role rather than a referral role. The kind of expertise called for in this aspect of the model is not readily found within the student services profession. People responsible for assessment should select appropriate instruments and procedures. They need an extensive knowledge of measurement theory and need to be particularly skilled in devising and working with techniques other than the traditional paper-and-pencil tests.

There are many areas of human behavior and many skills for which there are few, if any, measurement devices. Current assessment tools and techniques in the area of student development are gross—sometimes satisfactory for assessing group performance but of limited value for determining individual status and growth. Despite this, implementation of a full-fledged developmental model that includes assessment is becoming more sophisticated and sure. Refining old procedures and instruments and developing new ones must be done along the way.

Establishing Developmental Goals

It is no longer possible and perhaps even not desirable to attempt to promote the development of a new Renaissance person for the twenty-first century. The image of the Renaissance person is of one alert to the important events and artifacts of the arts, sciences, and humanities; what sometimes is characterized as knowledgeable and "well-rounded." Today it is readily accepted that it is impossible for a person to have more than superficial breadth in all of the arts and humanities, much less the sciences. The likes of a Leonardo Da Vinci or even a Jefferson or Franklin will never be seen again. However, today a new Renaissance type may be emerging. The new definition of the well-educated person is not made in terms of factual knowledge across the breadth of disciplines alone but demands a deeper look into the core of human experience. Wisdom and virtue are composed of knowledge but also entail how well that knowledge is used. Adequate problem-solving skills, for example, are now viewed as critical whether the individual is working on an engineering task or a personal behavior management task.

A great deal of emphasis has been placed on what is referred to as "collaborative" advising as opposed to "prescriptive" advising (Crookston, 1972; Miller and Prince, 1976). The former is seen as a joint effort of the adviser and the student to arrive at goals and specific courses of action that are in the student's best interests. The student is viewed as a consenting adult who voluntarily enters into the advising relationship, in this case for the purpose of goal setting, and is thus an equal partner. The prescriptive role, however, is characterized as authoritarian, not developmental. This dichotomization fails to recognize that either extreme has its weaknesses. Certainly, a purely authoritarian approach without consideration of where the student is developmentally and without appropriate input from the student is not good But a different kind of mistake is made if the students are permitted to be their own dietitians in the developmental cafeteria. Many educators have the notion that, if they give students free choice, ultimately the students will make the right choice. There will be temporary setbacks, but in the long run it will all work out for the student. This viewpoint is mistaken. Some students do survive and even thrive in such an environment, but many do not.

The student development educator provides structure and guidelines for the selection of developmental goals. These may take a form comparable to those often provided for academic development when students are expected to choose courses within selected broad categories, such as humanities, science, arts, and literature. The courses are not often easily categorized but the framework exposes students to the knowledge, heritage, and formats of several disciplines. In the case of student development, some goals are also established by the institution. These are broad goals derived from the institution's specific mission. Thus, one college may have a generic goal related to leisure time or personal development goals, under which sports, reading, crafts, and other pursuits would be listed. The student is free to select any two or three specific areas. Another institution may believe that physical recreation skills should be required of everyone, and the students are free to choose whether they pursue badminton, tennis, golf, bowling, or some other sport.

Other goals are determined by the specific academic major and/ or professional aspirations of the student. Leadership and managerial skill development are critical in the area of business management. Counseling and interpersonal skills are essential for a student pursuing a helping profession.

Finally, personal goals are a third source for the selection of specific developmental goals. A student who is planning to take over a family business but who also has a high need for expression may want to select goals that promote development of skills in creative areas, such as crafts, writing, or painting. Another may wish to explore opportunities for altruism available in volunteer activities.

The role for the student development educator here is one of adviser and counselor in exploring the institution's options available to each student. The goals defined by the institution as those which it expects of all students must be explained to and specified for the student. The variety of options within each of the broad goals must be clearly delineated, and avenues by which the student can obtain the necessary experiences and competencies must be apparent. A plan must be developed that helps the student know which goals should assume primary focus and when. The student must be aware of the need to accomplish short-term goals along the path to long-term goals. This may be specified in writing, in something comparable to a college academic bulletin, but if the program is highly individualized then consultation with an adviser or mentor is critically important.

A role more comparable to that of counselor is called for when the student must determine developmental goals related to career aspirations and determine steps needed to foster emotional maturity. This may require more personalized assessment of a student's own resources and goals and decisions addressing more intimate aspects of the individual's life.

Program Planning

Each institution should have at least four avenues available for students through which they can attain the necessary skills, competencies, and perspectives. These would include (1) academic course offerings, (2) specific courses in human development offered for credit or noncredit, (3) experiential field learning, and (4) informal campus options. Because the role of the student development educator varies with each of these avenues, I will elaborate on each avenue briefly.

Traditional academic courses can and should provide students with the opportunity to understand themselves as well as the world better. They can stimulate students to dig deeper into themselves as well as into the content. They can provoke students into considering entirely different viewpoints from those they have held before. Of course, an important factor is what is taught and how it is taught. History can give the student a perspective that helps him or her develop identity. Psychology can be taught in a manner that enables the student to understand him- or herself as well as others. Chickering (1976) describes how the study of history, philosophy, science, literature, and drama relate to moral and ethical development. The courses do not have to be radically changed, nor do the instructors need to become therapists in order for the course experience to have a dramatic impact on the student. Too little research has been attempted to examine what impact a few minor modifications in teacher style, assignments, and class discussions might have on maximizing the developmental impact of an academic class.

Second, courses in human development have existed on college campuses for years. Too often, however, their basic purposes have been forgotten in an effort to give them some semblance of academic respectability. For example, courses in marriage and the family have been available for several decades. One of the course objectives is to promote or improve the marriages and family relations of the students enrolled. Many such courses have languished, in the same way as did music and art appreciation in the past. The content is seldom related directly to where the students are, the presentation is essentially lecture, and assessment consists of knowing appropriate names, dates, and authorities presented in the textbook. Gerontology is a subject of growing interest across the country and is a prominent research topic, but it could suffer the same fate. College students may learn about growing old, but do they learn how they might relate to the old in a more humane fashion or how they might themselves grow old gracefully?

Courses in human development hold promise for the future of student development on the college campus scene. The content is more directly related to the students, and the staff may be receptive to focusing on the personal growth of their students as well as what cognitive knowledge they gain. There are at least two, not mutually exclusive, forms this avenue may take. One is for academic credit. Courses in marriage, human relations, family life, and others can be taught in such a way as to directly affect students' personal beliefs, styles, and at least awareness of the options open to them. There can also be noncredit opportunities. Extension offerings made available in a workshop format can be staffed by student development educators as well as by staff from psychology and human development departments. These course experiences could be offered on a fee basis. A number of universities now offer planned task-oriented experiences focused on assertiveness training, marriage enrichment, and life planning. These are seen as acceptable service activities for university staff and may someday be recognized as appropriate parts of regular academic offerings, if not full-fledged independent courses themselves.

The value of off-campus learning experiences either prior to college or while attending college has gained increasing acceptance (Keeton, 1976). A host of real-world experiences are now seen to play a valuable role in students' learning. For years, these experiences were for the most part limited to the curricula of neophyte professionals. For example, we had the student teachers practice teaching in their last semester. Now we have first-year prospective teachers visit classrooms and help children. Today, field experiences are a vital part of programs for sociology, political science, health service, and a host of other academic majors. Experiential learning holds a promise for developmental learning that is limited only by the imagination and availability of staff.

Finally, encouraging informal campus experiences has been the primary avenue for student development on campuses for the past 200 years. It includes student government, campus newspapers, organizations, supervisory roles in residence halls, participation in student activities, intramurals, and all of the other avenues for student involvement in what has been traditionally referred to as *extracurricular activities*. These opportunities remain and in fact may flourish under the proposed student development model. As they now exist, they provide valuable experiences for what might be characterized as the campus joiner. They also contribute significantly to the larger campus community through the services, organizations, and entertainments that they foster and provide.

A major limitation, however, of these activities is that they seldom provide opportunities for novices. Most college campus leaders played leading roles in high school, and so it becomes a case of the rich getting richer. The student with the assertiveness and confidence that comes from previous success becomes more polished and skillful, the accomplished musician has an audience, the experienced actor or actress has a platform, and the practiced debater has a forum. The true neophyte has no audience, platform, nor forum. Incidences of the shy, average student becoming president of the student body are rare enough to be labeled fairytales.

Under the proposed model, students can contract with their mentor to try out different activities that involve them in administrative and leadership positions. In fact, the base of decision making regarding student life can be broadened extensively so that more opportunities for students to assume leadership responsibilities are possible.

The role of the student development educator in this programmatic aspect of the model varies depending on the instructional or learning environment. The educator can serve an entire group of faculty as a general curriculum consultant or as a consultant to individual faculty members. An enlightened faculty may want to examine their entire curriculum from a developmental perspective. Available research and theory do not have the answers to the many questions that a concerned and interested faculty member may have, so the consultant role requires expertise that enables student development educators to help design local research to answer these questions. The curriculum can also be examined for gaps, for the need for new courses.

Individual instructors who are committed to fostering student development in their specific courses welcome expert assistance. The student development consultant provides advice regarding what specific assignments such as personal journals, cooperative writing ventures, group projects, and instructional strategies might be most appropriate. The student development educator can also become involved with the actual instructional process itself as appropriate team-teaching situations develop. Some of these activities involve the specialist in ongoing relationships with particular departments and professors in such a way that this becomes a regular part of that person's job assignment. In other instances, the consulting activities are phased out as the department and individual faculty members attain some expertise themselves. Such a program has existed on the University of Nebraska-Lincoln campus for several years. Attempts have been made to design first-year science and social science courses that take into consideration whether students are in a formal operations or a concrete stage of cognitive development (Tomlinson-Keasey and Eisert, 1978).

In this phase of the model, student development educators find themselves also serving directly as instructors in both formal and informal, credit and noncredit instructional settings. The opportunities include offering courses on the psychology of personal adjustment, through the psychology department; on the implications of literature for understanding the self, through the English department; or on assertiveness training, through the extension division. The student services staff at many institutions are already involved in similar activities, primarily providing noncredit workshop experiences. A shift from the informal, noncredit option to the more formal credit option would present role conflict problems for the student development educator who is now serving as an instructor. In the academic setting, the process becomes more formal, and some form of evaluation is necessary, even if only a pass–fail or pass–incomplete distinction is required. This shift to an evaluative role is uncomfortable for some staff but can be kept congruent with student development goals.

Evaluating Student Progress

Earlier, it was suggested that the period of initial assessment should be a period of self-exploration and self-discovery for the student, in a setting that is warm and supportive, as well as challenging yet nonthreatening. The period of evaluating whether the student has achieved institutional and personal goals, should also be viewed as a period of reflection and renewal. This may be a difficult mood to establish. The ease with which it is accomplished depends on the contingencies that are established. Are there grades? Do certain goals have to be accomplished prior to graduation? If the model proposed is to function in similar ways as do the academic requirements, then it follows that students are expected to demonstrate attainment of objectives either by completing related experiences or by demonstrating proficiency in the related skill. Although it is doubtful that pressure can ever be completely eliminated, we can think of ways in which the anxiety might be reduced. If the entire model has been operationalized on a campus, it is quite likely that an integral part of the system is continual evaluation along the way, rather than evaluation only at significant terminal points. This makes any one evaluation less threatening and also provides at least the potential that evaluation is seen as a developmental activity itself.

The evaluation process should indicate that a contract has been fulfilled and a skilled or competency level demonstrated. It should also provide for redirecting the student to reassess the value of the original goal or to try again. Even if the goals have been completely met and contracts fulfilled, part of the evaluation activity involves exploration of the next step for the student. This is an opportunity for the student development educator to move beyond what happens in the academic arena, where, although the degree is often seen as terminal, in reality learning continues, hopefully for a lifetime. The fostering of continued personal growth is built into this model because it leads to self-evaluation and self-direction.

Recording Student Progress

The final act in the process involves recording the student's progress on a developmental transcript. The transcript itself may take many forms. Each institution probably uses one consistent with the options selected throughout the model, or it uses a patchwork quilt representative of all the options the institution provides and permits. If, for example, the institution decides to have students engage in experiences and to have evaluations consist primarily of indications of completion rather than attainment of proficiency levels, it probably uses some form of an experiential checklist. If it expects students to demonstrate specific competencies within each developmental area, then a competency checklist may be used that reflects both attainment of the competency and the level of attainment achieved. In other settings, some sort of narrative or a portfolio may be most appropriate (Brown and Citrin, 1977).

Depending on how institutionalized the developmental transcript is, the student development educator can interpret an individual's transcript to others as well as either maintaining it or helping the student maintain it. Graduate schools, professional schools, and employers may all have an interest in the students' developmental accomplishments. The safeguards and privacy rights now protecting the academic transcript apply here as well, but there can be innumerable instances in which the student may find it helpful to release some of the records, if not all. A record of what the students have actually done and what they actually can do may be of interest and eventually have more meaning than a letter or numerical grade that summarizes academic attainments.

Conclusion

The proposed model, including description of activities for the development educator, is unique in that it assumes that human development is a required part of the collegiate experience. This may well be idealistic, but it is not impossible. Some forms and elements already exist on a few campuses. It is more likely to flourish in some campus environments than others. It is unrealistic, however, to try to implement a mandatory program without a good deal of preparation and pilot efforts. The functions and roles described for the student development educator do not contradict the worth of other roles. No one role should be *the* role. It is a mistake to assert that all student services workers should be developmentalists, or campus ecologists, or change agents, or whatever. The roles should be complementary rather than alternative. Cynics may suggest that a developmental role is probably the most idealistic—but there are worse things to be called.

Implementing the proposed model has significant implications for the training of student development specialists if they are to fulfill the specified roles. Counseling and working with groups have been the traditional training background for student service workers. The proposed model demands a broader and in some instances a deeper knowledge background for the developmental specialist. Some of these needs are discussed in greater detail in other chapters, but they should be noted here.

Measurement and evaluation become a more critical knowledge base for the proposed activities than is currently true in traditional models. Student development educators must be fully aware of the available and developing assessment instruments and techniques. They should also be flexible enough and creative enough to adapt and devise procedures that fit the unique setting of the particular institution and its students. At least a basic acquaintance with research and program evaluation strategies is necessary. It is unlikely that there is going to be any significant breakthrough in the availability of funding for major research efforts, so whenever possible solutions must come from field studies. Knowledge about development of college-age students and adults is also an important core. Of course, counseling skills remain important.

For some, the title "student development educator" or "student development specialist" is an all-encompassing term. It may be some time before the exact terms or phrases are sorted out. The working definition is a new starting place. However, regardless of what student personnel workers call themselves, they can make a difference. Fighting for developmental programming is an uphill battle, despite public support for the ideas and intents, especially if new programming calls for new funds. Although the support presently is precarious, we can now systematically program for student development. The real world of budget restrictions and staff cuts must be recognized, but it does not have to be accepted nor viewed as a limitation. Commitment to student development must become one of the "basics" to which we are all returning.

References

Brown, R. D. *Student Development in Tomorrow's Higher Education: A Return to the Academy.* No. 16. Washington, D.C.: American College Personnel Monograph Series, 1972.

Brown, R. D., and Citrin, R. "A Student Development Transcript: Assumptions, Uses, and Formats." *Journal of College Student Personnel,* 1977, *18,* 163–168.

Chickering, A. "Developmental Change as a Major Outcome." In M. T. Keeton and Associates, *Experiential Learning: Rationale, Characteristics, and Assessment.* San Francisco: Jossey-Bass, 1976.

Crookston, B. B. "A Developmental View of Academic Advising as Teaching." *Journal of College Student Personnel,* 1972, *13,* 12–17.

Keeton, M. T., and Associates. *Experiential Learning: Rationale, Characteristics, and Assessment.* San Francisco: Jossey-Bass, 1976.

Knapp, J. E., and Sharon, A. *A Compendium of Assessment Techniques.* Princeton, N.J.: Cooperative Association of Experiential Learning; Educational Testing Service, 1975.

Miller, T. K., and Prince, J. S. *The Future of Student Affairs: A Guide to Student Development for Tomorrow's Higher Education.* San Francisco: Jossey-Bass, 1976.

Parker, C. "With an Eye to the Future." *Journal of College Student Personnel,* 1973, *14,* 195–201.

Parker, C., and Morrill, W. "Student Development Alternatives." *Journal of College Student Personnel,* 1974, *15,* 163–167.

Prince, J. S., Miller, T. K., and Winston, R. *Student Development Task Inventory.* Athens, Ga.: Student Development Associates, 1974.

Tomlinson-Keasey, C., and Eisert, D. C. "Can Doing Promote Thinking in the College Classroom?" *Journal of College Student Personnel,* 1978, *19,* 99–105.

James H. Banning

9

The Campus Ecology
Manager Role

The management of the campus ecology is an emerging role for the student services worker. Management per se is certainly not a new role for student services, but the concepts of milieu and campus ecology do extend traditionally accepted management activities. This emerging role of managing campus ecology is best described in Crookston's (1975, p. 46) definition of milieu management: "It is the systematic coordination and integration of the total campus environment—the organizations, the structures, the space, the functions, the people and the relationships of each to all others and to the whole—toward growth and development as a democratic community. In furtherance of human development theory the relationship of the whole milieu with all its parts, and vice versa, must be symbiotic, or mutually enhancing or growth producing. Thus as the individual and the group contribute to the total community they give the community the capacity to create the conditions that contribute to the enhancement of the individual and the group." However, many student services workers may be hesitant to assume the role of manager because the term "appears to mean manipulation and coldness, rather than the warmth they expected when they entered a field characterized by helping relationships" (Miller and Prince, 1976). This reaction may appear confusing, because the field has generally accepted the concept of student services administration. To many, the concept of administration connotes far more "coldness" in its concern for the implementation of policies, procedures, and regulations.

Historically, the only portion of the campus that student service programs have attempted to manage are the individuals who comprise the student body. These efforts have been primarily applied directly to the student as an individual. The dominance of this approach was documented by a 1971 survey that concluded that, at universities in western states, 60 to 78 percent of all staff time in counseling services is spent in working with individuals through individual and group counseling strategies (Banning and Aulepp, 1971). Another study of 220 programs across the country (Morrill and Banning, 1975) indicated that 83 percent of the programs were aimed at individual students, 8 percent at campus associations, 6 percent at primary groups on campus, and 2 percent at the institution as a whole. Observation leads to the same conclusion when viewing other student services, such as recruitment, admissions and registration, advisement, student activities, residence halls programs, health services, financial aids, and placement and career planning. Almost all the strategies used to serve students have been developed to serve the individual student and have not generally offered a systematic way of serving students by managing the campus ecology.

This concentration of effort on the individual student stems directly from the conventional perspectives that have guided, and that in a large part continue to guide, student services. Banning and Kaiser (1974) labeled these perspectives as the "unenlightened perspective," the "adjustment perspective," and the "developmental perspective." The unenlightened perspective views the student in stress as a "bad actor" or as a person in the wrong place. Therefore, out of a general theory of paternalism and authority, strategies to discipline or remove the student are developed. The adjustment perspective views the student in stress as being ill or deficient in some manner. A treatment strategy such as counseling or psychotherapy is seen necessary in order to keep the student functioning on campus. Various theories focusing on individual psychodynamics have been developed to guide this treatment strategy. Finally, the developmental perspective, although more positive in outlook, still focuses on the individual student. The student in stress is seen as being "immature" or at least in need of further development. Programs targeted at such individuals are then developed and guided by theories relating to development in late adolescence. Although these three perspectives overemphasize working with the individual student, they are not without merit. Not all students belong on campus, some students need individual psychological attention, and certainly many students are involved in a number of critical developmental tasks while on campus. However, all three perspectives are one-sided. They all focus on the necessity for the individual student to adjust, and they fail to address the broader need for the campus to change.

The failure to address broader change strategies is related to two phenomena: (1) the adoption of the medical model by "helping" professions and (2) the universities' perception of their role *in loco parentis.* Historically, the prevailing strategy for all "helping fields" has been the medical model, in which individuals are defined as ill and in which appropriate treatment follows the diagnosis. Treatment is also focused on curing the individual or at least helping the individual to cope. In the medical model, treatment is only initiated when individual patients present themselves or are referred to the person who dispenses aid. The individual must become symptomatic before interventions are begun. Proactive or prevention measures aimed at conditions outside the individual are not in concert with the passivity of the model. By focusing only on symptomatic individuals, the scope of interest is also reduced, and little time is directed toward other elements in the environment. As a result, the intervening agency becomes isolated from the patient's total milieu. Given this model for "helping," it can be readily seen how the work of student services has been influenced to work primarily with individual students.

A second phenomenon influencing the focus on the individual student has been the concept of *in loco parentis.* For many years, universities have maintained that they occupy the role as students' parents away from home. As noted by Banning and Kaiser (1974), parents seldom look on their children as being a part of a community or an ecology but are more likely to see them as individuals. Universities, like parents, often fail to see the need to change themselves in order to produce a better relationship with their students. These perspectives and historical phenomena have led student services to focus on managing only the student and have distracted from the examination of the campus environment in which students are imbedded. Consequently, some serious ethical concerns have arisen.

By giving almost total attention to encouraging individual students to adjust, the work of student services programs maintains the status quo. If, in managing student services, universities assume that the factor that is deficient is the student, all of their efforts may be aimed at helping the individual adjust or accommodate to a defective campus environment (Banning and Kaiser, 1974). Similar concerns have been raised in the field of mental health, where the "helping" work has also been primarily focused on the individual. Nidorf (1970, p. 21), in writing about campus mental health centers, points out the need to go beyond individual intervention strategies and to look at the total campus community: "To prevent personal and social ills requires social change of a qualitative nature—not just quantitative treatment additions. Unfortunately, in any social institution, qualitative changes are hard to come by. The change agent, by its very nature, must be political. It must be able to influence the many dimensions of vested interest maintaining the status quo. An ideal model for such an agent—a model that has been tested and approved effective—is the comprehensive mental health agency." Even in the field of psychiatry, where the influence of the individual treatment perspective has been so strong, the same concern is being raised by Farnsworth (1970, pp. 471–472): "Accusations of exhibiting political bias, having a moral point of view, or being a social engineer must be expected. Psychiatrists generally, and college psychiatrists particularly, must have *some* point of view if their efforts are not to be futile. The bias of the college psychiatrist is explicitly toward freedom, independence, integrity, sincerity, humane attitudes, and the development of sound and effective methods for coping with the conflicts and ambiguities common to all who strive to improve the human situation. To sit idly by without attempting to direct social change in the direction of improvement rather than disintegration in the good human relations is an abdication of wisdom and common sense and unworthy of the traditions of psychiatry." If student services is to free itself from the role of pacifying and maintaining the status quo, it must direct its energies toward the management of campus ecology. The qualitative nature of the campus environment must be examined. The position of student services must not be "to sit idly by" and make no attempt to manage the campus for the improvement of student growth and development. The ecological relationship between students and environment must be recognized. An ecological approach helps to correct the overemphasis on working with individual students.

Ecology and the Campus Environment

The word *ecology* stems from a Greek word meaning "house" and was used in early scientific works to denote habitat. Ecology has come to represent the generic term for the scientific study of organism-environment interaction (Sells, 1966). Insel and Moos (1974) point out that the term *ecology* is most often used to refer to the natural habitats of animals, while the concept of *human ecology* encompasses the domain of social scientists who are interested in the distribution of human populations. The term *social ecology* is used by Insel and Moos (1974) to denote the view of humanity interacting with both physical and social environment. Banning (1978) developed the concept of *campus ecology* to describe the interaction between the college student and the campus environment. For Insel and Moos (1974), social ecology has an explicit value orientation because it is concerned with helping people function at maximum effectiveness. The same is true for campus ecology, in which there is an explicit value for promoting maximum personal growth. The concept of campus ecology does not rule out or even deemphasize the concern for the individual student, but the ecological perspective does bring back into focus the concept of campus environments. The concern of student services under the ecological perspective includes the total ecology, the student, the environment, and, most importantly, the transactional relationship between the two.

This interest in environments and their effect on individuals is not new. Its historical roots are well documented by some outstanding psychologists (Barker, 1968; Brunswick, 1955; Lewin, 1936). Out of Lewin's framework, Murray (1938) developed the interaction scheme between the needs of human beings and those of the environment. The impact of this thinking reached the managers of university programs in part through the work of Pace and Stern (1958), when those researchers began to study the climate or atmosphere associated with campus environments through the College Characteristics Index. By their definition, the environment included such areas as student-faculty relationships, rules and regulations, methods, and facilities. The measuring and characterizing of campus environments was significantly furthered by the work of Astin and Holland (1961) and again by Astin (1965, 1968). Feldman and Newcomb (1969) noted the impact of the college environment on students and gave further impetus to the study of campus environments. A major help in understanding the person-environment interaction is the work of Walsh (1973). He organized the significant person-environment research that had direct applications for the college environment by reviewing five theoretical approaches: Barker's behavior setting theory, the subcultural approach, Holland's theory of personality types and model environments, Stern's need-press theory, and Pervin's transactional approach. An introduction to and critique of these theories is presented by Huebner, in Chapter Five.

The most recent summary addressing the processes of measuring and structuring the campus environment to facilitate improved outcomes is presented in the work of Baird (1976). The notion of managing the campus environment in order to benefit student relations is appearing more frequently. Crookston (1975) suggested that milieu management could serve both as a concept integral to student development and as an emerging key role of student services. Likewise, in writing about the future of student services, Miller and Prince (1976) included environmental management as a role appropriate for the profession. Delworth and her colleagues recently reported on the implementation of this approach on several western campuses (Delworth and others, 1975). The concept of environmental management for specific areas within student services is also gaining support. Conyne (1975) illustrates the usefulness of environmental assessment in mapping consultation activities for campus counseling centers. Environmental management strategies in residence halls have also proved useful (Schroeder and Freesh, 1977). As noted, this interest in campus environments and their impact on the student has a significant history, but the utility of the concept of ecology as an organizational framework for student services is only now emerging.

The ecological perspective can serve as a framework from which to view a full range of intervention strategies, not just environmental or milieu management. For example, Rappaport (1977) uses an ecological approach to discuss sources of social intervention strategy. Four intervention strategies are present when one is attempting to adjust the ecological relationship between individuals and their environment: individual, group, associational, and institutional interventions. This configuration is quite similar to the cube framework presented by Morrill, Oetting, and Hurst (1974). The importance of this work for student services is that it helps to view the campus in its totality and places the possible strategies in perspective. For example, if a campus is well designed for growth and development for the majority of the students, but a few students are not benefiting, then the intervention strategy may be to help those students to adjust or cope or be more comfortable in fitting in. Although many strategies for accomplishing this goal—such as counseling, advising, psychotherapy—are traditional adjustment strategies, in the ecological framework they are not implemented until the impact of the overall campus design has been determined. Individual intervention is not used to treat every problem, but it is used in situations that warrant it. If, however, the problems within the campus appear to be related to particular groups, the strategy for improving the ecological balance for the campus may well include working with the ill-fitted groups. Several approaches are used with different types of small groups and their various problems, such as couples therapy, communications training groups, and sensitivity groups. Problems may not be associated with individual or within primary groups but may evolve out of organizations that do not adapt to the campus structure. This could be dealt with by using systems-centered consultation, organizational development strategies, and other methods relating to social organizations. Finally, campus problems may be stemming not from students or small groups of students or from organizations but from the campus as an institution. The attitude of the campus's administration, faculty, and staff toward students; the institution's value orientation; its policies; or other factors may produce a poor ecology for student growth and development. Interventions at the institutional level emerge as the appropriate treatment under these conditions. Major social change strategies may be needed to create new institutional values and policies. Morrill, Oetting, and Hurst (1974) also present a framework that helps to put into perspective the choice of strategy, including target, purpose, and method of intervention. From this perspective, student services can respond to the ecological relationship between students and the campus environment and not be limited to changing or serving individuals. The concept of ecology not only provides a theoretical backdrop and an organizational framework for intervention strategies but can also serve as the key concept in determining the purposes and goals of student services programs on specific campuses.

The Ecosystem Model

Student services managers who apply the ecological perspective help ensure that a campus encourages maximum growth and development of the students. The practitioner who intends to employ this perspective must be able to perceive working models. Perhaps the most helpful translation from perspective to working models in light of actual student services work on campus was the contribution of the task force developed by the Western Interstate Commission for Higher Education (1973) and presented by Banning and Kaiser (1974) and Kaiser (1975) as the ecosystem model. The ecosystem model is based on the ecological perspective and provides a methodology to design and manage the campus ecology. Included in this approach is a systematic way of viewing the campus termed the *ecosystem design process*. The seven basic steps in the process are as follows (Western Interstate Commission for Higher Education, 1973, p. 7):

1. Designers, in conjunction with community members, select educational values
2. Values are then translated into specific goals
3. Environments are designed that contain mechanisms to reach the stated goals
4. Environments are fitted to students

5. Students' perceptions of the environment are measured

6. Student behavior resulting from environmental perceptions is monitored

7. Data on the environmental design's success and failures, as indicated by student perceptions and behavior are fed back to the designers in order that they may continue to learn about student-environment fit and design better environments.

The steps of the design process are interdependent, so planning arrangement of a campus can begin at any of the steps. If the campus is yet to be constructed, the process of campus design would start with Step 1 (the selection of educational values) and continue on through the final step (feedback). Such an opportunity is quite rare, because most campuses have been established for a number of years, and the goals and values of the institution have been selected or at least published in various institutional documents. Therefore, the design process would more likely begin at Step 5 (measuring students' perceptions of the campus) and then move from these perceptions to other steps in the process in order to map out the existing ecological relationships between the environment and students. The technology available to carry out the measurement and monitoring in Steps 5 and 6 is developing rather rapidly. Keating (1974) outlines a number of available environmental assessment instruments that can aid campus administrators at these steps. However, Keating has pointed out that it may often be necessary for campus personnel to design one or more of their own instruments in order to obtain information peculiar to a particular campus and in forms usable in specific redesigning. Aulepp and Delworth (1976, 1978) also suggest a number of assessment strategies that can be used in a team approach to environmental assessment. The importance of this assessment information, from whatever sources, is that it can be used to map out specific elements in the ecology that cause students to be distressed or dissatisfied. In other words, by managing environmental referents (specific elements in the environment) an ecology can be developed to promote maximum growth and development of students. This assessment process may also lead to the conclusion that the original values and goals selected by institutions no longer are appropriate and that selecting new values and goals becomes the management task. Or it may be found that the original goals and values remain quite appropriate but that the programs and policies related to these goals need revision. If so, the management task becomes the development of new programs and policies to attain the original institutional goals. Successful management of the campus ecology under any condition depends on how well the managers carry out the remainder of the seven steps in the design process.

The design or management processes can be implemented at different levels of the campus ecology. The macro-level design is concerned with ecology that includes large numbers of individuals; the micro-level design focuses on specific campus groups; and the third level of the ecosystem model, termed "life-space design," is concerned with the individual imbedded in the total campus ecology.

As student services becomes involved in managing the campus ecology to promote optimal growth and development, it can be helped by the methodology of the ecosystem design process. This includes the systematic assessment of the campus in terms of whether the goals and purposes of the campus (optimal growth and development of students) are being served by the campus structures (policies, programs, and services). Student services management can focus at any and all levels (macro-, micro-, and life-space).

The Ecosystem Model and Student Development. The ecosystem model is greatly enhanced by being coupled with the concept of student development. Of particular importance to this coupling is the work of Blocher (1974, 1978). Blocher points out that there is increasing evidence that developmental processes are not automatic but must be purposefully triggered and carefully nurtured by the environment if full growth and development is to be reached. Blocher goes on to suggest that the ecology related to individual development can be characterized as containing three subsystems or structures: opportunity, support, and reward. The opportunity structure is represented by the set of tasks, problems, or situations in the environment that the person negotiates to exert mastery or control and thereby gain competency. The support structure is the set of environmental resources available to people for coping with the environment. For Blocher, the support structure includes two kinds of resources: "These are the affective, or relationship, resources and the cognitive structures available. Relationships networks that touch the student allow stress reduction to occur through the operation of factors of warmth, empathy, acceptance and involvement of others. . . . In addition to relationships, there are important cognitive structures that allow for impressed coping with stress. These involve understanding, assessing, predicting, and labeling" (Blocher, 1974, p. 364).

The reward structure refers to those properties and contingencies of the environment that reward effort. For example, if the rewards offered in an environment are arbitrary and unrelated to effort, then the growth-sustaining ecological balance may be destroyed. When coupling the concepts of ecology and student development, student services must design and manage the opportunities, resources, and rewards within the campus ecology that affect student development. The utility of this merger becomes even more evident when the process for designing the ecosystem (presented earlier) incorporates student development concepts.

Steps in the Model

Step 1: Valuing. Faculty, students, and staff of the campus collectively develop the values of the environment or qualities of the environment that relate to the behaviors intended for the inhabitants of the environment. Within the student development framework, these behaviors considered desirable might be the major development "vectors" postulated by Chickering (1969) as summarized by Miller and Prince (1976, pp. 11–12):

1. *Achieving competence.* This involves the development of intellectual and social abilities as well as physical and manual skills. The sense of competence is defined as the confidence individuals have in their ability to cope with what comes and to achieve successfully what they set out to do.

2. *Managing emotions.* The young adult's initial task is to become aware of personal feelings and to recognize that they provide information relevant to contemplated behavior or to decisions about future plans. As a larger range of feelings is fully expressed, new and more useful patterns of expression and control can be achieved.

3. *Becoming autonomous.* Mature autonomy requires both emotional independence (freedom from continual and pressing needs for reassurance and approval) and instrumental independence (the ability to carry on activities and cope with problems without seeking help from others and the ability to be mobile in relation to one's needs). Simultaneously, the individual must accept interdependence, recognizing that one cannot receive benefits from a social structure without contributing to it, that personal rights have a corollary social responsibility.

4. *Establishing identity.* Identity is confidence in one's ability to maintain inner sameness and continuity; to reach this state, one must understand one's physical needs, characteristics, and personal appearance and must be sure of sexual identification and sex-appropriate roles and behavior.

5. *Freeing interpersonal relationships.* As one matures, one should be able to express greater trust, independence, and individuality in relationships, becoming less anxious and defensive and more friendly, spontaneous, warm, and respectful. De-

veloping tolerance for a wide range of people is a significant aspect of this task.

6. *Clarifying purposes.* To develop purposes, an individual must formulate plans and priorities that integrate avocational and leisure-time interests, vocational plans, and life-style considerations.

7. *Developing integrity.* This task involves making one's values both more personal and more human. One examines and selects "a personally valid set of beliefs that have some internal consistency and provide a guide for behavior." At the same time, one drops a literal belief in the absoluteness of rules and adopts a more relative view. Then one must also develop congruence; that is, begin to act in accordance with these personal values.

A campus that selects these vectors as desirable values has taken the first step in the ecosystem design process of selecting educational values. A similar set of outcomes is suggested by Lenning and his colleagues (1975) in the following developmental areas: academic, intellectual and creative, personality and adjustment, motivational and vocational, social, aesthetic and cultural, and moral, philosophical, and religious.

Step 2: Goal Setting. Environmental values (developmental vectors) are translated into specific goals. Some campuses may wish to develop higher priority for certain developmental tasks than for others, and this would be reflected in the goal statements. For example, a vocationally oriented institution might emphasize achieving vocational competence more than would a college of liberal arts. At this step, the concepts associated with the field of "management by objectives" may be very useful in moving from a value statement to specific objectives.

Step 3: Programming. The goals and objectives of Step 2 are translated into programs or activities. Important to the structure of these programs are the concepts of opportunity, support, and reward. A variety of programs should be provided to allow students to undertake critical development and in which sufficient support and appropriate reward exist to encourage growth and development.

Step 4: Fitting. Because of the range of individual needs, the programs must fit the campus to the student. Some programs may be fitted at a macro-level, where the needs of most can be handled by a single uniform program. Other programs, however, may need tailoring to specific groups with a micro-level approach. Finally, a life-space program may be needed, such as individual counseling.

Step 5: Mapping. Student perception of the campus is measured and compared with the original goals developed by the campus. This is a mapping process. If students are to benefit (develop) from the opportunities, supports, and rewards of a planned campus ecology, clearly they must be able to perceive and use the programming of the campus.

Step 6: Observing. The student's behavior in the campus environment is monitored or observed and compared with the perception of the campus environment and the goals of the campus. If the design is working, there should be a high correspondence among behavior, perceptions, and goals.

Step 7: Feedback. All of the information and data gathered are fed back through the design process in order to review the previously selected values. Appropriate changes may also be initiated to help ensure intended outcome.

The coupling of the ecosystem design process and the student development model is summarized in Table 1.

Table 1. A Management Template for Campus Ecology (Blank)

	Ecological Structure		
Developmental Vector	*Opportunities*	*Support*	*Reward*
Achieving competence			
Managing emotions			
Becoming autonomous			
Establishing identity			
Freeing interpersonal relationships			
Clarifying purposes			
Developing integrity			

The management template for campus ecology, combining the ecosystem design process and the student development model, may be applied at any or all the levels of analyses. As a mapping aid, its application may reveal that the campus has relatively few opportunities for certain development vectors. Some opportunities may be present but, because either affective or cognitive support is lacking, they cannot develop successfully. Or, if a task's reward structure is random and indirect, successful negotiation of the task is difficult. Many possible combinations lead to poor design. With three levels of design, the picture becomes quite complex but to successfully manage the campus ecology this complexity must be considered. On a typical campus, several opportunities are available for developing physical competence (defined here as increased athletic competence). Each of the five opportunities noted is associated with a support structure. Material support is the equipment, facilities, space, and so on necessary for a certain activity. Affective support includes students' relationships with peers or with faculty members. Cognitive support is instruction and information. A classification system for a reward structure is more difficult to develop, so several items that reflect how students benefit from activities are listed in Table 2.

Table 2. A Management Template for Campus Ecology (Example)

Ecological Structure

Developmental Vector	*Opportunities*	*Support*	*Reward*
Achieving physical competence (increased athletic competence)	1. Free play	Material	Internal reward
	2. Physical education classes	Material, cognitive, affective	Grades
	3. Club sports	Affective	Peer approval, status
	4. Intramurals	Material, affective	Peer approval, status
	5. Intercollegiate athletics	Material, cognitive, affective	Peer approval, status, identity, job training, scholarship

When all the ecological structures are outlined in relationship to the developmental vector, the campus ecology related to the vector becomes apparent. For example, each of the five opportunities listed on the template has associated with it a support and reward structure. A campus's opportunities for free play require primarily material support such as basketball and tennis courts, running tracks, playing fields, and equipment checkout facilities. To the degree the free-play activity is designed as a group effort, the possibility of affective support increases. For the individual jogger or weight lifter, the primary reward may be personal satisfaction. Within the physical education class, a student can expect material, cognitive, and perhaps affective support, in addition to a tangible grade. Organized club sports (such as soccer and chess) on most campuses are supported primarily by those who enjoy the sport. Material support may be also present, but universities are unable to provide the necessary equipment and facilities. Intramurals usually receive institutional support in the form of equipment, facilities, and personnel. Intramural teams formed from living units or departments develop an *esprit de corps,* but rarely receive instruction. The prestigious place that intercollegiate athletics maintains on some campuses is evident in Table 2. The best equipment and facilities and the best coaching available on campus are reserved for the intercollegiate athletic program. The personal relationships that develop through personal recruiting, common dining facilities, and athletic housing complexes create a very strong affective support system. Most unique to intercollegiate athletics, however, is the elaborate reward or benefit structure. Peer approval, status, and identity on campus are often not paralleled by success in any other field. And only intercollegiate sports offer scholarships and potential future employment.

Table 2 is referred to as a management template because the student development associated with the vectors can be managed by adding and removing opportunities and by rearranging the support and reward structure. For example, if the intramural activities were removed, there would be fewer rewards available in peer approval and status.

The analysis of the management template thus far has been a micro-level approach. A micro-level or group analysis could be developed by looking at how the ecological structures fit women in contrast to men. Until the passing of recent federal legislation, the campus ecology for developing athletic competence has been extremely limited for women. Another micro-level analysis could consider how to increase athletic competence for the physically handicapped. A life-space analysis is also possible. Take, for example, a student with few social and physical skills who would like to learn how to play tennis. The ecology outlined in Table 2 may not be adequate. The least threatening situation is provided by free play, but very little instruction is associated with this opportunity. The threat of poor grades may also discourage the student from becoming involved in formal physical education classes. Obviously, the level of skill needed for club, intramural, and intercollegiate sports would not allow for the entry of a novice. Changes or management of the ecology would have to occur to fit the socially and physically limited student. For example, perhaps a residence hall staff member could offer informal instruction in tennis for those residents who wish to learn, thereby adding a new program opportunity to the ecological structure. Or this student might enroll in a physical education course on a noncredit basis, thereby changing the reward structure. Management of the campus ecology for student growth and development requires a similar analysis for all developmental vectors that institutions select as valuable (Step 1 of the ecosystem design process). Managing campus ecology for student development therefore depends on information about students' activities.

Organizing the Management of the Campus Ecology

The informational and analytical functions needed to manage campus ecology can be organized through a campus design center (WICHE, 1972; Kaiser, 1975; Fawcett, Huebner, and Banning, 1978). In essence, the campus design center emerges as an implementing concept for managing the campus ecology. "The mission of the Campus Design Center is to provide a dynamic linkage between students as consumers and the environmental settings as providers of student development opportunities. The goal of the center is to identify, redesign, or design opportunity support and reward structures within the environment to assist students in their mental, social, and physical development. To achieve that goal the center will function to (1) provide multiple mechanisms for identifying potential student-environment misfit . . . (2) provide comparative information to students, and institutional programs . . . and (3) provide a process for campus involvement, including establishment of new environments designed to facilitate total student development" (Fawcett, Huebner, and Banning, 1978, p. 41). The presentation of the campus design center by Fawcett and his colleagues is very structured and detailed. The important point is not the structure of the center but the fact that the concept does allow for the development of a mechanism to assist in the student services role as manager of the campus ecology. The emphasis on the importance of the concept of the center rather than on a specific structure is clearly noted (Fawcett, Huebner, and Banning, 1978, p. 35): "Establishing a design center is itself a case study in ecosystem design. The creation of such a locus of activity with the characteristics mentioned earlier is not an isolated event, but rather, must be approached with a recognition of the unique aspect of the campus environment in order to capitalize upon positive elements (that is, individual predispositions to support change) and to avoid or ameliorate negative elements (that is, faculty distrust, administrative territoriality). In its embryonic stage, the campus design center might begin as a mode of thinking or "mind set" within a single individual or groups of individuals on campus who share the common thought: in a healthy community, it is not only the individual who must adjust to the environment but also environments which must be adjusted to meet individual needs."

The concept of the design center helps not only to organize the management of the campus ecology but also to address the critical questions, "Who designs?" Kaiser (1975, p. 36) points out the need for community participation: "Successful campus design depends upon participation of all campus members including students, faculty, staff, administrators and regents. The ecosystem model offers a participatory design strategy. It is based upon the conviction that all people impacted by a space have the moral right to participate in its design."

Full participation of all who are involved in the campus's ecology is also a reasonable response to the ethical questions raised in the intentional management of an environment (Conyne and others, 1977). These authors note that "The notion of intentional campus environmental design for the purposes of prevention and the enhancement of student development, while being mandated from several corners, poses significant changes from traditional counselor functions. And these changes have a number of serious implications for individual counselors and for the field as a whole. Not the least of these is the question of ethics. Applied to environmental design, several complex issues arise, including those of freedom vs. control, privacy, competence, political positioning, value systems, and participation" (Conyne and others, 1977, p. 17). The authors conclude "If one advocates the intentional design of campus environments, then ethical issues such as the above must be addressed within the context of full participation of environmental members. The satisfaction of this stipulation should hedge against the possibility of a select few controlling the behavior of many. Under these conditions, intentional design should increase the probability of personal freedom" (p. 23).

Implications of Campus Ecology Management

Campus ecology management calls for a shift in perspectives and attitudes of student services personnel. The historical concern directed toward individual students must be broadened to include the total campus ecology. The new attitude or "set" should include providing and designing opportunities, supports, and rewards to foster full student development. Although this endeavor can be carried out in a variety of ways, a systematic framework must be developed in order to analyze information so that ecological change can be designed and managed. An attitude of participation must accompany the new concern for the total ecology. All campus members must be encouraged to participate to avoid the impersonal manipulation of many by a select or self-appointed few. The campus ecology perspective also calls for new knowledge and skills. The task of implementing such a perspective will be difficult because of the strong traditional training in individual intervention skills. We need to examine concepts from a wide range of disciplines for their usefulness in helping to understand the campus ecology. Student services must truly become multidisciplinary. This challenge is most clearly stated by Conyne and others (1977, p. 12): "Training programs might strive to recruit and produce graduates who could be characterized as high-profile, initiating, and system-change focused, supplanting the more prevalent model, which can be characterized as low-profile, passive, and person-change focused."

Even though the ecology management perspective calls for a major shift in attitude, skills, and training of student services workers, the promise it holds for the development of campus environments that promote optimal growth is substantial. The ecology of today's campuses holds the key to the future quality of all environments in society, just as today's students will ultimately design our society (Banning, 1978).

References

Astin, A. W. "Effect of Different College Environments on the Vocational Choice of High Aptitude Students." *Journal of Counseling Psychology*, 1965, *12*, 28–34.

Astin, A. W. *The College Environment*. Washington, D.C.: American Council on Education, 1968.

Astin, A. W., and Holland, J. L. "The Environmental Assessment Technique: A Way to Measure College Environments." *Journal of Educational Psychology*, 1961, *52*, 308–316.

Aulepp, L., and Delworth, U. *Training Manual for an Ecosystem Model*. Boulder, Colo.: Western Interstate Commission for Higher Education, 1976.

Aulepp, L., and Delworth, U. "A Team Approach to Environmental Assessment." In J. H. Banning (Ed.), *Campus Ecology: A Perspective for Student Affairs*. Portland, Oreg.: National Association of Student Personnel Administrators, 1978.

Baird, L. L. "Structuring the Environment to Improve Outcomes." In O. T. Lenning (Ed.), *New Directions for Higher Education: Improving Educational Outcomes*, no. 16. San Francisco: Jossey-Bass, 1976.

Banning, J. H. (Ed.). *Campus Ecology: A Perspective for Student Affairs*. Portland, Oreg.: National Association of Student Personnel Administrators, 1978.

Banning, J. H., and Aulepp, L. "University Community Mental Health Services Survey." In *Program Activities and Student Utilization of Campus Mental Health Facilities in the West*. Monograph No. 3. Boulder, Colo.: Western Interstate Commission for Higher Education, 1971.

Banning, J. H., and Kaiser, L. "An Ecological Perspective and Model for Campus Design." *Personnel and Guidance Journal*, 1974, *52*, 370–375.

Barker, R. G. *Ecological Psychology: Concepts and Methods for Studying the Environment of Human Behavior.* Stanford, Calif.: Stanford University Press, 1968.

Blocher, D. H. "Toward an Ecology of Student Development." *Personnel and Guidance Journal,* 1974, *52,* 360–365.

Blocher, D. H. "Campus Learning Environments and the Ecology of Student Development." In J. H. Banning (Ed.), *Campus Ecology: A Perspective for Student Affairs.* Portland, Oreg.: National Association of Student Personnel Administrators, 1978.

Brunswick, E. "The Conceptual Framework of Psychology." In *International Encyclopedia of Unified Science.* Vol. 1, Pt. 2. Chicago: University of Chicago Press, 1955.

Chickering, A. W. *Education and Identity.* San Francisco: Jossey-Bass, 1969.

Conyne, R. K. "Environmental Assessment: Mapping for Counselor Action." *Personnel and Guidance Journal,* 1975, *54,* 151–154.

Conyne, R. K., and others. "The Environment as Client: Considerations and Implications for Counseling Psychology." Paper presented at 85th annual meeting of American Psychological Association, San Francisco, September 1977.

Crookston, B. B. "Milieu Management." *National Association of Student Personnel Administrators Journal,* 1975, *13*(1), 45–55.

Delworth, U., and others. "Designing Campus Ecosystems: Panel Presentations." *National Association of Student Personnel Administrators Journal,* 1975, *13*(1), 40–44.

Farnsworth, D. L. "College Mental Health and Social Change." *Annals of Internal Medicine,* 1970, *73,* 467–473.

Fawcett, G., Huebner, L. A., and Banning, J. H. "Campus Ecology: Implementing the Design Process." In J. H. Banning (Ed.), *Campus Ecology: A Perspective for Student Affairs.* Portland, Oreg.: National Association of Student Personnel Administrators, 1978.

Feldman, K. A., and Newcomb, T. M. *The Impact of College on Students.* San Francisco: Jossey-Bass, 1969.

Insel, P., and Moos, R. "Psychological Environments: Expanding the Scope of Human Ecology." *American Psychologist,* 1974, *29,* 179–189.

Kaiser, L. R. "The Long-Term Care Administrator as a Planner of Institutional Environments." Paper presented at National Symposium on Long-Term Care Administration Education, New Orleans, January 23, 1973.

Kaiser, L. R. "Designing Campus Environments." *National Association of Student Personnel Administrators Journal,* 1975, *13*(1), 33–39.

Keating, L. A. *Environmental Assessment Instruments: An Aid for Campus Administrators*. Boulder, Colo.: Western Interstate Commission for Higher Education, 1974. Mimeographed.

Lenning, O. T., and others. *The Many Faces of College Success and Their Non-Intellective Correlates*. Iowa City, Iowa: American College Testing Program, 1975.

Lewin, K. *Principles of Topological Psychology*. New York: McGraw-Hill, 1936.

Miller, T. K., and Prince, J. S. *The Future of Student Affairs: A Guide to Student Development for Tomorrow's Higher Education*. San Francisco: Jossey-Bass, 1976.

Morrill, W. H., and Banning, J. H. "Counseling Outreach Programs on the College Campus." In B. L. Bloom (Ed.), *Psychological Stress in the Campus Community: Theory, Research and Action*. New York: Behavioral Publications, 1975.

Morrill, W. H., Oetting, E. R., and Hurst, J. C. "Dimensions of Counselor Functioning." *Personnel and Guidance Journal*, 1974, *52*, 354–359.

Murray, H. A. *Exploration in Personality*. New York: Oxford University Press, 1938.

Nidorf, L. J. "Community Mental Health Model Applied to Student Personnel Work." *Journal of College Student Personnel*, 1970, *2*, 19–27.

Pace, C. R., and Stern, G. G. "An Approach to the Measurement of Psychological Characteristics of College Environments." *Journal of Educational Psychology*, 1958, *49*, 269–277.

Rappaport, J. *Community Psychology: Values, Research and Action*. New York: Holt, Rinehart and Winston, 1977.

Schroeder, C. C., and Freesh, N. "Applying Environmental Management Strategies in Residence Halls." *National Association of Student Personnel Administrators Journal*, 1977, *15*(1), 51–57.

Sells, S. B. "Ecology and the Science of Psychology." *Multivariate Behavior Research*, 1966, *18*(11), 131–144.

Walsh, W. B. *Theories of Person-Environment Interaction: Implication for the College Student*. Iowa City, Iowa: American College Testing Program, 1973.

Western Interstate Commission for Higher Education (WICHE). *The Ecosystem Model: Designing Campus Environments*. Boulder, Colo.: Western Interstate Commission for Higher Education, 1973.

PART IV

Essential Competencies and Techniques

Student services professionals are asked to work at increasingly complex jobs that require very sophisticated knowledge and skills. We are asked to design programs, administer services, supervise staff, analyze budgets, evaluate programs, assess students, and consult with faculty. It is nearly impossible to teach all that is needed to perform these many tasks in any given graduate training program. Most in-service staff development training programs can only begin to scratch the surface. That leaves conscientious professionals scrambling to learn what they need to know as best they can—usually with limited resources.

What is needed, we believe, is a systematic identification and classification of competencies essential for effective delivery of services. Not all professionals either want or need to master all these competencies; not all preparation programs teach all of them. Within any given division of student services, however, it is important to have a combination of staff members who possess a reasonably high degree of expertise in the designated competencies. We follow Delworth and Yarris (1978, p. 2) in defining competencies. As these authors point out, "to be competent, the staff member needs certain kinds of knowledge, certain attitudes, emotional qualities, and particular skills. So we might think of competence as a combination of cognitions, affect, and skills." Thus, we view skills as one component of the larger domain of competence.

In organizing this part of the book, we identified four critical basic competency areas: (1) assessment and evaluation, (2) teaching or training, (3) consultation, and (4) counseling. These four competencies, in varying combinations, comprise three important and more complex competency areas: program development, environmental assessment and redesign, and paraprofessional training. These areas represent a fundamental "core" that we believe is necessary to maintain a vital and dynamic division of student services. To help readers understand the importance of these competencies, we have asked the authors of the following chapters not only to identify critical knowledge, attitude, and skills but also to explain how, when, and why these attributes can be used. Each competency relates to one or more of the models or roles for professional practice described in Part Three. Depending on the chosen model for a given division or unit, some competencies are focal, and others are less important.

In the first chapter of this part (Chapter Ten), Oscar Lenning examines both assessment and evaluation competencies. Lenning considers assessment as one component of evaluation: It precedes and leads to the judgments made in an evaluation but its role and activities are not the same as for evaluation, nor are its required competencies necessarily the same. To clarify the distinctions between assessment and evaluation skills, Lenning discusses general procedures for conducting student assessments and then presents special issues in doing various kinds of assessments. He also describes the evaluative process in detail and presents several strategies for evaluating student services. The last section of his chapter outlines specific skills that student services professionals need to conduct sound student assessment and program evaluation.

Teaching and training others has long been an important competency for student services professionals to master. In Chapter Eleven, Gary Hanson examines the process of teaching and training and the factors that influence it, with the goal of identifying specific skills that help others learn. The diversity of the educational audience, in terms of educational background and preferred learning styles, and the context of the teaching situation are two critical factors that define the boundaries of the teaching process. Within these boundaries, Hanson identifies teaching and training as a five-step process. Each step includes many key skills, attitudes, and feelings that teachers should acquire. In the final section of his chapter, Hanson summarizes these competencies into four main categories and discusses why they are important for student services professionals to develop.

Counseling has long played a central role in the student services profession, although the specific competencies it requires have not always been clearly defined. The purpose of Chapter Twelve is to delineate counseling knowledge and skills, discuss their importance, and provide examples of their application. In it, Susan Gilmore explores the purpose of counseling in the college setting, describes an eclectic model of counseling and the associated skills needed to implement it, and then shows how these skills can be applied in student service settings. Using a conceptual model to focus on needed skills, Gilmore identifies three broad categories of interventions to deal with three types of counseling problems: choice, change, and confusion reduction. Specific competencies needed to intervene with certain kinds of problems are then readily identifiable. The strength of this approach is the relative simplicity with which the various components are interrelated.

Student services professionals can make significant contributions to the educational community, so we must understand the process of consultation and the competencies needed to do it well. In Chapter Thirteen, June Gallessich (1) develops a rationale for student services staff consultation; (2) describes various consultation services we can offer to faculty, staff, administrators, and student organizations; (3) differentiates consulation from other student services; and (4) identifies critical consultation skills needed by effective student services consultants. Perhaps the most important aspect of her chapter is her description of strategies to be used in acquiring consultation skills.

The last three chapters present complex competency areas or practice models that build on the competencies of assessment and evaluation, teaching and training, counseling, and consultation. Some combination of the "core" competencies discussed earlier is necessary for successful work in the three practice areas presented next.

In Chapter Fourteen, Weston Morrill uses the dimension of counselor functioning (cube) model as a focus for thinking about educational programs for students. He indicates how choice of purpose (remedial, developmental, or preventative) and target (individual, primary group, associational group, or institution) directly influences the remainder of the program-planning process. His chapter provides a framework and also a step-by-step process for developing and implementing a wide variety of programming experiences. Morrill's model draws heavily on the professional role of student developer proposed by Brown but contains elements of the other three roles as well.

As a basis for both programmatic and other interventions, in Chapter Fifteen Jack Corazzini advocates use of an environmental redesign model. In his AIDE (assessment, intentional design, and evaluation) model, Corazzini proposes an ongoing assessment process that constantly samples changing population needs in the campus community. Such an assessment leads to design processes that provide currently needed programs, organizational changes, and other adjustments in an agency or institution. An important part of the model is the evaluation of redesigns, which is then fed back through the assessment process. Although the model draws directly on Banning's professional role of environmental manager, it also implies some adherence to the administrator and student developer roles addressed by Ambler and Brown.

A specific example of a program that can affect students both as deliverers and receivers of service is the paraprofessional training model outlined by Grant Sherwood in Chapter Sixteen. He addresses both the rationale for such programs and the specific process necessary for an effective program in this area. All the basic competencies presented in Chapters Ten to Thirteen are needed, and the model clearly fits with any or all of the professional role orientations discussed in Part Three. Thus, effective paraprofessional programming emerges as a complex set of concepts, roles, and competencies. Sherwood shows us how to succeed in this area and also why investment in paraprofessional training can have an immense, exciting payoff for professionals, students, and our campuses as a whole.

Our hope is that these competencies and practice models will make sense to our readers in terms of the philosophy, theories, and role orientations already discussed. We must master the competencies addressed in these seven chapters in order to make real contributions to the campus community and the lives of students.

Reference

Delworth, U., and Yarris, E. "Concepts and Processes for New Training Role." In U. Delworth (Ed.), *New Directions for Student Services: Training Competent Staff*, no. 2. San Francisco: Jossey-Bass, 1978.

Oscar T. Lenning   **10**

Assessment and Evaluation

Traditionally, a chapter on assessment and evaluation would occur last in a part of a book like this because such activities would be considered to follow the functions discussed in the next chapters. Assessment and evaluation cannot be very effective or have a major impact on improving those functions, however, if they are after-the-fact activities. In fact, assessment and evaluation planning should occur along with the very earliest planning for an operational program, whether it is for student services or some other kind of program, to ensure that all the needed data are collected at the appropriate time prior to and during the operational phase. Therefore, it is appropriate that a chapter on assessment and evaluation occur first in this part of the book.

An example of a problem that early planning prevents, lack of baseline data, is discussed by Anderson, Ball, Murphy, and their associates (1975, pp. 42–43) as follows: "Evaluations are frequently undertaken without adequate baseline data. Sometimes, through lack of foresight, an evaluation is not envisaged until after the program is in operation. In other instances, a program is considered so urgent that it is implemented before an evaluation can be planned and baseline data obtained; some of the War on Poverty programs begun in the 1960s fall

Note: Special appreciation is hereby expressed to Philip E. Beal for critiquing this chapter and providing helpful suggestions.

in this category. For whatever reason of neglect or priority, when baseline data are unavailable evaluation results are likely to be equivocal and
to stimulate considerable argument and confusion about whether the
program was effective."

Some Useful Distinctions

Before discussing the strategies and procedures involved in assessment and evaluation, several basic conceptual classifications should
be made. The activities to be discussed in the later sections can be
usefully grouped according to these differentiations.

Assessment Versus Evaluation. One component of evaluation (no
matter what type of evaluation) is assessment. Assessment precedes and
leads to the judgment or evaluative component of evaluation.

In some cases, evaluators gather their own data on which judgments are to be based; in other cases, they use data gathered and analyzed
by others. The roles and activities are not the same for assessment as for
evaluation, nor are the needed skills and competencies the same. This
section discusses the differences.

The term *assessment* was made popular in the late 1930s by Henry
Murray and his associates, who used it to mean the appraisal of individuals. We can assess a person's physical and emotional characteristics,
personality, needs, behavior, competencies, development, performance,
educational and occupational progress, readiness for further education,
quality of life, and so forth. This can be done in general, or in terms of
the person's role, such as his or her role as a student or as a teacher.
Because of Murray, counselors and other student services personnel have
tended to associate assessment with individuals and evaluation with
groups and programs. Furthermore, they have tended to think strictly in
terms of assessing students, whereas it is just as legitimate and pertinent
to assess themselves—their needs, their skills, their attitudes and interests, their professional readiness, their performance, and so forth. Analogous to this self-assessment is Menges' (1973) model for assessing the
readiness of teachers for professional practice.

Higher education authors outside student services have often
applied the term *assessment* to groups and programs—for example, see
Baird's (1974, 1976) discussion of assessing educational environment,
Doi's (1974) "assessing faculty effort," Lasell's (1974) conducting "assessment of internal decision events," and Clark, Hartnett, and Baird's
(1976) "assessment of the dimensions of quality in doctoral education."
Assessment is also discussed within even larger contexts than programs,
such as a total educational institution, a total educational system in a
state or the nation, and a community or society at large—for example,

the assessment of enrollment patterning, educational environment, educational quality, educational impacts, and service to the community. Outside education, we hear about assessing costs and ecological impact.

Many people in education seem to equate assessment with evaluation; for example, Dressel (1976) and Lasell (1974). Yet some equate assessment with measurement; for example, Harrocks (1964). And then there are those who equate evaluation with measurement, such as May (1975), who defines guidance program evaluation as "the measurement of what is valued." Others, including myself, take an intermediary position and view measurement as a component of assessment, which is in turn a component of evaluation.

The word assess is closely related to *assay*, which means "to examine, test, or analyze." Murphy (1975, p. 27) pointed out that, "in its derivation, the word *assess* means 'to sit beside' or 'to assist the judge.' " From such a perspective, *assessment* refers to gathering data, transforming data so that they can be interpreted, applying analytical techniques, and analyzing data in terms of alternative hypotheses and explanations. Based on such assessment, judgments about value, worth, and ways to improve can be made—the evaluative process. Therefore, for the purposes of this chapter, an assessment study includes measurement and analysis, while an evaluation study includes measurement, analysis, and judgment. One cannot have assessment or evaluation without measurement and analysis of some kind.

Another way to say the same thing is to use Popham's (1975) definition of measurement as "status determination" and evaluation as "worth determination." Then, based on the preceding discussion, assessment *links* status determination to worth determination.

Formative Versus Summative Evaluation. The traditionally accepted form of assessment and evaluation is intended to provide evaluative evidence to suggest whether a program should be continued as is, terminated, or revised. Scriven (1967) coined the term *summative* for this activity because it focused on the program in terms of the end-of-period or end-of-tryout status and is intended to provide a summary value judgment about the worth or usefulness of the program and its activities.

A potentially more useful concept of evaluation than summative was referred to by Scriven (1967) as "formative." Formative evaluation also results in judgment, but its primary focus occurs during the development and operation of the program. Formative activities focus on a continual assessment and evaluation, suggesting how the program should be modified in order to improve it. Thus planning for this type of evaluation at an early stage of program development is especially crucial.

Both summative and formative evaluation depend on data. Some of the same data usefully serve both types of evaluation, but summative evaluation needs additional data that assist value judgment while formative evaluation needs additional data that assist understanding. Scriven pointed out that summative evaluators should be unbiased, independent, outside people without a vested interest in seeing that that program succeeds (it does not have to be someone outside the institution, just someone outside the program who has no vested interest in the program) and who can thus be objective and matter-of-fact about the matter.

Formal Versus Informal Evaluation. Another distinction that should be made is between formal and informal assessment and evaluation. Stake (1967, p. 523) made this distinction well when he indicated that informal evaluation depends on "casual observation, implicit goals, intuitive norms, and subjective judgment" while formal evaluation is very systematic, making use of formalized, concrete goals and depends on "checklists, structured visitation by peers, controlled comparisons, and standardized testing of students." Informal evaluation can provide effective and penetrating insight but can just as often be superficial and distorted. Thus Stake, in 1967, suggested that rational judgment requires formal evaluation. He later changed his position, however, and now supports the use of a systematic form of informal evaluation that he calls "responsive evaluation," defined (Stake, 1973, p. 5) as follows: "Responsive evaluation is less reliant on formal communication, more reliant on natural communication. . . . It is evaluation based on what people do naturally to evaluate things: They observe and react. . . . Subjectivity can be reduced by replication and operational definition of ambiguous terms even while we are relying heavily on the insights of personal observation."

Responsive evaluation allows the evaluator to respond to both current and emerging issues and to adjust easily to changing conditions. A major focus is on observing the program in action. Thus, Stake suggests that responsive evaluation is preferred in formative evaluation when monitoring is desired and no particular problems are projected and in summative evaluation when an understanding of the program's activities, strengths, and shortcomings is desired. Yet strictly formal evaluation, which Stake refers to as "countenance" or "preordinate" evaluation, is preferred when the purpose is to see if goals have been reached or promises kept and to test predetermined hypotheses and issues.

The position taken in this chapter is that the formality or informality of the evaluation activities depends on the purpose, situation, and context of the evaluation. For example, political attitudes and traditions within certain groups of citizens lead to a trust of firsthand, subjective, and experiential data and a distrust of scholarly data collected through formal and standardized measurement instruments. Where evaluation results are meant to speak to such a subpopulation, carefully collected subjective data may be called for even if the purpose is to see if goals have been reached or promises kept.

Goodrich (1978, pp. 631–632) offered an additional useful perspective on subjectivity in evaluation: "The very word *evaluation* denotes judgment about the value of something and therefore makes manifest our final reliance on subjectivity no matter how much objectivity is attributable to the data upon which the judgment is based. Indeed, we must begin to question the desirability, let alone the possibility, of even gathering data which warrant the term *objective* as it is commonly understood. . . . Our concern to establish evaluation as a scientific activity has had the following result: We limit ourselves to what we think we can measure well and so often focus on the trivial parts of a program. In the meantime, we turn our backs on the larger considerations, which arise from the fact that both evaluation and the programs to which it is directed take place within a social system and therefore are affected by the fundamental stuff of social systems."

Individual Versus Group Evaluation. Through assessment and evaluation, counselors and instructors appraise individual students' status and readiness and make judgments about needs, progress, diagnosis, and so forth. They also often use such activities to help students understand themselves and their needs, strengths, behavior, achievements, and so forth.

In contrast to individual evaluation, group evaluation results are used to make decisions about programs. Program decisions include those related to planning, management, evaluation, and policy development. Because the focus of this chapter is on assessment and evaluation *related to student services programs*, the primary emphasis throughout the chapter is on group evaluation.

Assessment Strategies and Considerations

I have elsewhere (Lenning, 1977a) discussed eight uses of student assessment by student services personnel. Three of them are definitely evaluation functions: grading, promoting, and granting merit awards; evaluating efficiency and effectiveness; and evaluating innovations. The others are less evaluative in nature: planning learning experiences, counseling and advising students, diagnosing student problems, appraising student readiness, and classifying and categorizing students. Assessments can also be conducted by students—of themselves, their needs, environments, activities, and achievements. Assessing people other than students—such as staff, graduates, and members of the community—can also be important.

This section first discusses general procedures for conducting formal assessments. Then, the focus shifts to special considerations for different kinds of assessments, such as of individuals versus groups and by self versus by others.

General Assessment Procedures. Payne (1974) proposes seven generally accepted stages or steps in assessing cognitive and affective learning that I judge to be applicable to all kinds of assessment. Payne's terminology has been used to form five headings for this section: (1) specifying detailed goals and objectives, (2) designing the assessment system, (3) selecting measures and data-gathering methods, (4) collecting data, and (5) using the data. Each of these tasks will be discussed from the perspective of a student services worker.

Specifying Goals and Objectives. To be useful, goals must be transformed into concrete, observable, precise terms. Too often student services program goals are broad and vague abstractions, such as "to promote maximum development of the total self," "to promote self-actualization," and "to develop realistic and independent decision making."

Conrad (1974) has outlined a number of purposes goals may have. Although he was talking about university goals, the same points can be made about program goals: (1) they are standards against which to judge program success, (2) they provide a source of legitimacy for the activities of the program, (3) they define and order program needs, (4) they define the units of program outcomes, (5) they identify the program's clientele, and (6) they define the relationship between the program, the institution of which it is a part, and society.

Such goals must be clear and precise to effectively guide actions to accomplish ends for students, a course, a program, or an institution. Transforming goals into concrete ends or objectives to be achieved is difficult. For an example of one way to do it, see my (Lenning, 1977b, pp. 15–25) application of a new, comprehensive outcomes taxonomy to this process. As indicated there, additional, more detailed taxonomies, such as Bloom's (1956), may be needed to get the specificity required at the program level. I (Lenning, 1977c) have provided an in-depth review of several dozen such detailed classifications in the cognitive, affective, and psychomotor domains that may be useful for this purpose.

The task of reaching maximum agreement among various staff members and constituents, concerning goals and priorities is also difficult. It may sometimes call for special consensus-rendering techniques, such as the Q-sort or the Delphi techniques, if give-and-take discussion does not yield enough agreement.

What we assess must relate to the goals and objectives of the program or individuals being assessed. Two types of program goals exist. The first, outcome goals, focuses on the results that the program is intended to achieve. The other type of goals, process goals, refers to how the outcome goals are to be achieved—the personnel, money, time, activities, techniques, methods, and tools used to achieve particular outcomes.

Designing the Assessment System. Once the goals and objectives for the assessment are specified, work can begin on developing the strategy and procedures to be used for accomplishing those goals and objectives. Success rests on an integrated, detailed, well-thought-out assessment design.

First, we must outline the purposes of the assessment and then delineate the context in which the assessment is to take place. The context includes factors within the program, institution, or other environments that either *assist* the assessment effort or *constrain* it. Examples of such factors are the attitudes and values of staff or students, political pressures and situations, financial and staff resources available, time and space considerations, baseline data already available, the diversity of the students using various student services, and so forth. Third, we must outline the specific questions that need to be answered by the assessment concerning particular problem-solving, decision-making, or other purposes. Next, decisions should be made and recorded concerning the information needed to answer the questions; available indicators and measures; relevant and feasible data sources; whether sampling should be used and what kind; data-gathering and analysis strategies and procedures to collect the proper data and convert them into pertinent information; the data interpretation strategy; and feedback procedures for getting the information out to decision makers and concerned others in an effective manner that promotes use. Finally, factors such as assessment costs and how the entire plan fits into an integrated system should be considered and necessary refinements or modifications made.

The design must be realistic and feasible in terms of the costs and effort required and must effectively generate the information needed to answer the pertinent decision makers' questions. It must provide a rationale concerning which specific groups of students, other people, and entities such as the environment should be assessed. How the assessment strategy and procedures vary by group or area should also be ascertained. For example, assessing *older* students' academic competencies using a standardized psychometric instrument designed for and normed on teen-age college students is clearly inappropriate unless it has been tested and found to be valid for them also.

The design of an assessment system for a student services program or for individuals should be tailored specifically to the situation at hand. One may usefully borrow ideas from another program or institution, but care should be taken to customize design to the local situation. The same is true of standardized models, such as the General Integrative Model developed by Pottinger and Klemp (1975, 1976).

Selecting Measures and Data-Gathering Methods. In selecting measures and indicators, reliability and validity are important criteria. So are factors such as ease and cost of data collection, ease of scoring and tabulating, appropriateness to the analytic procedures and tests that are planned, and so forth.

Let me illustrate the importance of such factors. I recently heard about a new test battery that had been used with reported success and that seemed to have adequate reliability plus good validity in measuring "real-life" competencies. I was consulting on the evaluation of a non-traditional program emphasizing the development of such competencies, and I recommended that this battery be tried out. Fortunately, the people who were consulting me tried it out on a pilot-test basis because, even though it admirably met the reliability and validity criteria, it was extremely difficult for their people to administer and score. Yet I have talked to people on other campuses where the administration and scoring procedures worked quite well. This case illustrates the importance of trying out measures and data-gathering procedures ahead of time with small pilot samples of respondents similar to those in the study before the final decision is made to use them in the full assessment study.

Standardized paper-and-pencil instruments are often used in student and program assessments, but, although they may have good reliability and validity for what they purport to measure, they often do not measure what is specifically of concern in the program. A good example of this is the Watson-Glazer Critical Thinking Appraisal. It has excellent validity on the ability to reason critically in a passive manner, and it has good reliability. However, its validity is low for measuring the ability to apply that critical thinking proactively in "real-life" situations, as in managing social confrontations. When considering a standardized instrument, one should examine an actual copy, supporting manuals, and reviews in Buros (1972) and other available sources (such as the journals *Measurement and Evaluation in Guidance, Educational and Psychological Measurement,* and *NCME Measurement in Education)* for assurance that it is appropriate for local needs.

To get a paper-and-pencil instrument that measures specifically what is desired, one often must construct one's own. There is an abundance of excellent texts on measurement theory and the development of norm-referenced tests and questionnaires, offering variety for both experienced as well as inexperienced instrument developers. Whenever possible, locally developed instruments should build on similar ones developed elsewhere. Lange, Lehmann, and Mehrens (1967) have shown that revising items takes less time, effort, and expense than developing them from scratch. Great care must be taken, however, to modify the instrument appropriately for the new context. Locally developed *criterion-referenced* instruments that focus on absolute levels of performance or mastery should always be considered as an alternative to norm-referenced instruments (see Gronlund, 1973, for help in developing such instruments).

Most measures and indicators are more reliable and valid in some contexts than in others. Furthermore, all measures have both weaknesses (some more so than others) and strengths. Therefore, whenever feasible, multiple measures and indicators should be used for a particular learning outcome.

Assessments have traditionally been limited to paper-and-pencil tests, questionnaires, and interviews for data collection, even though a variety of other methods are practical, valid, reliable, and cost effective for particular purposes and contexts. I found (Lenning, 1978a) fifty different data collection methods in the literature that were recommended for assessments of various kinds. Knapp and Sharon (1975) reviewed a number of methods that can be used instead of, or to supplement, traditional methods.

Specific precautions must be taken when collecting and using data for various kinds of measures. For example, Thelin (1976, p. 133) emphasizes that unobtrusive measures "have to be considered in clusters and tied to a conceptual framework if they are to be of significance for institutional monitoring." Unobtrusive measures—such as increased attendance at campus plays and art displays after a demonstration program on appreciation of the arts sponsored by the office of student services in the dormitories—can be quite useful and revealing if such cautions are observed. See Webb and others (1966) for a helpful, in-depth discussion about unobtrusive measures.

Often it is possible to use data collected for other purposes (for example, from student transcripts, administrative files, and community records), which some have called "secondary data." Usually we think we need new data for an assessment study, but it may not be necessary. Boyd and Westfall (1972) provide criteria for determining when particular secondary data are acceptable for a particular situation and use, and they also discuss how to avoid pitfalls in using such data (it is very easy to misuse secondary data).

As was true for indicators and measures, and for the same reasons, multiple data collection methods are desirable whenever feasible. That this can be feasible and cost effective was shown by the learning assessment system developed and implemented at Empire State College (Palola and Lehmann, 1976). Multiple data collections supplement standardized and local test score data with student self-reports, instructor observations, writing samples, and administrator observations.

Collecting Data. The proper measures and data collection methods are of no avail if one does not plan well and use care in the actual data collection. For example, a poorly worded cover letter sent out with a questionnaire can easily cut the response rate in half or more; so can sending students the questionnaire shortly before mid-term exams. Much time, money, and frustration can be saved if one takes pains to have well-designed interview forms, written instructions to read for test administrators, careful selection of samples, questionnaire items free of bias, well-designed pilot tests to try out procedures ahead of time, procedures for maximizing response rate (such as showing the need for such data and promising—and giving— respondents feedback about the results), sensible coding and data-formatting rules; careful editing procedures; and so forth. The appendixes of Micek, Service, and Lee (1975) provide many helpful suggestions in this area.

Analysis, Interpretation, Reporting, and Application. Most assessment studies rely exclusively on the use of simple descriptive statistics such as means, standard deviations, and tabulations and cross-tabulations of frequencies and percentages. Much useful information can be obtained from such simple statistics, especially if they are profiled graphically and patterns of similarities and discrepancies across information items and across groups are examined. Means by themselves can be quite misleading if the frequency distributions are not also examined. Also, response bias should be analyzed in questionnaire and interview studies.

It is often useful to make comparisons across groups when group differences on other characteristics (for example, input variables) are taken into consideration. Although "eyeballing" across groups and profile analysis can be revealing, such procedures may need to be supplemented with statistical tests such as t-tests, chi-square, analysis of variance, correlational analysis, and discriminant analysis. In planning the study, the staff member and the analytical design expert should consider the analytical designs proposed by Campbell and Stanley (1963) and the nine evaluation design types proposed by Oetting and Cole (1978), which have been explained by Hanson and Lenning (1979). In addition, many helpful resources discuss the selection and use of statistical methods (for example, Tatsuoka and Tiedeman, 1963; Siegel, 1956).

In outcome studies, change in status is often of concern. However, most analysts now agree that change scores or average score changes of the same individuals should not be used in such analyses. Rather, they advise comparing students' final status to the final status of other students who have the same initial ability. For comparison across groups, this can be accomplished by random appointment to each group initially, by group assignment through stratified random paired matching on input level, by comparing across similar initial-level strata, or by sophisticated statistical adjustments to posttest scores that effectively equate initial levels (for example, analysis of covariance).

Interpretation and use of data are crucial in an assessment study, and too often data results are applied ineffectively. If the assessment data are to have any impact, the data users must be identified early in the assessment-planning process, before conducting the study. Input should be solicited from them concerning their specific concerns and what assessment information would help them make decisions. Such input serves a primary role in determining what study groups, data, and analyses are desired for the study. Once analyses are completed, brief, concise reports tailored to each user's information needs should be sent to them. Graphical presentation can often be helpful in such reports. One interesting and potentially useful way of making these reports attention getting is through a "peer group-intergroup" model proposed by Alderfer and Holbrook (1973) and used by Hecht (1977). In this model, selected college staff prepare "action-oriented" written and oral responses to the evaluation data for presentation to other college staff *at their levels*.

Special Considerations for Different Kinds of Assessment. The general steps outlined in the preceding section apply to the assessment of both groups and individuals. For individuals, however, they apply in a much more informal, subjective way than is true of groups. Furthermore, an important difference is that for individuals the instruments used must have much higher reliability coefficients (in the 0.8–0.9 range versus as low as 0.6 for groups) to be useful.

Another dimension with differential considerations is the assessment of students versus nonstudents. Usually, one is interested in assessing different factors for students than for nonstudents. Second, the assessing of students often involves the use of standardized paper-and-pencil instruments, such as achievement and ability tests, whereas most nonstudent assessments of interest to student services workers do not make use of such instruments. For an illustration of nonstudent assessment, see May (1975), where two types of assessment of staff member competence (he called it *evaluation*) in the guidance setting are discussed.

In assessing individual students, student services workers (especially personal counselors) have been considered experts for many years. However, the traditional focus on student services personnel assessing students is being replaced in many quarters by helping students assess themselves. As outlined by Miller and Prince (1976, pp. 48–49), the goal of assessment for student development "is to help students understand their current patterns of behavior, emphasizing positively the specific skills they have instead of the ones they lack. From this base, all students can move toward increased self-direction. . . . Assessment programs must be designed with students rather than for or about them; therefore, only information that can directly increase students' self-understanding or improve their self-direction need be collected. The primary focus of many student assessment efforts has been to help student affairs workers better understand their 'clients.' Although this objective is desirable, it has tended to create volumes of information about students that is rarely used directly by them."

Miller and Prince offer much good discussion focusing on how to conduct such self-assessment. They do not limit this "assessment for student development" to individuals, however. They define it as "the process through which *students, groups,* and *organizations* systematically acquire and use data from a variety of sources to describe, appraise, and modify *their own development.* Thus, this method differs from the more traditional approaches in its purpose, in what is assessed, in the techniques used, in the way it is implemented, and in the role the student affairs practitioner plays" (p. 47, italics in original).

Assessment of certain types of factors has produced separate areas of specialization. A good example is "needs assessment," where discrepancy between "what is" and "what should be" is a primary focus. Needs assessment is also noteworthy in that there is a serious definitional problem among assessors concerning what is a "need" (Lenning 1978b; Lenning and McAleenan, 1979). Other areas of specialization within assessment include assessment of ability, achievement, personality, goals, values, interpersonal functioning, and organizational functioning.

The Evaluative Process

Whereas much has been written in the professional literature about the assessment process as it relates to evaluation, relatively little has been written about the evaluative (judgment) process. Furthermore, what has been written tends to see the latter more as an art (for which procedures would be useless) than a science.

The evaluative process involves taking the synthesis of assessment results and alternative interpretations of those results, and applying the interpretations to making judgments or decisions about value and worth of a service, activity, or program and its possible deletion, replacement, modification, or revision. In addition, the process often involves making a judgment or decision about the best ways to bring about improvement. The evaluative process can be carried out by a single person, the evaluator. Often more effective, however, is a group process involving a judgments team or committee; for example, see Harshman and Reinert (1979).

Applying results from an effective assessment process can lead to value judgments with much utility. Krumboltz (1974) was one author who discussed the need for better evaluation in terms of benefits to student services workers, specifically counselors. He said that better evaluative judgment—he uses the term *accountability*—can lead to benefits for counselors as follows: Such judgment "would enable counselors to obtain feedback on the results of their work; select counseling methods on the basis of demonstrated success; identify students with unmet needs; devise shortcuts for routine operations; argue for increased staffing to reach attainable goals; [and] request training for problems requiring new competencies. . . . By learning how to help clients [through evaluation] more effectively and efficiently, counselors would obtain: more public recognition for accomplishments; increased financial support; better working relationships with teachers and administrators; acknowledged professional standing; [and] the satisfaction of performing a constantly improving and valued service" (pp. 639–640).

Similar benefits could also accrue to other areas of student services if a sound system of evaluation (assessment and follow-up judgment) were implemented. Krumboltz noted several criteria that such a system should meet that especially relate to the evaluative or judgment process. As suggested by Krumboltz, one's values enter into the evaluative process, and one must thus take care that the goals for process and outcomes results have been defined clearly and agreed on by all concerned parties. Similarly, it cannot be overemphasized how important it is to apply the evaluative process results to decisions about program continuation, discontinuation, and improvement rather than to blame, condemn, or punish. Finally, Krumboltz cautions that, in making the judgment about whether the benefits of a student affairs activity outweigh the costs, staff accomplishments must be stated in terms of important student behavioral change, not in terms of staff effort and activity expended (which are costs rather than accomplishments).

How common it is to equate expenditures such as effort and activities to accomplishments is well illustrated by Wickline (1971, p. 8): "If one sat in on congressional hearings today, he would find that, in justifying the expenditures in education, people still talk primarily about how the money has been spent, what kind of materials and equipment have been purchased, the number of children who have been served and the number of teachers who have been involved. They talk very little about what has been accomplished."

Scriven (1971) points out an important role differentiation that should be made about the evaluative process: (1) evaluating the goals of the program versus (2) evaluating whether and how well the program goals have been achieved. Formal program evaluation studies have almost always focused on judging the worth of the program and/or how to improve the program, without considering the worth of the goals. However, an evaluator should also evaluate the appropriateness and worth of the program goals. Scriven indicates that the goals should be evaluated prior to evaluating the attainment of those goals; if it is a poor goal, it matters little whether the goal was achieved. Evaluating the appropriateness of goals involves agreed-on, objective criteria for what constitutes a good goal. Unlike the evaluation of goal achievement, goal evaluation does not involve data derived from measurement; goals cannot be measured as can achievement. Instead, according to Scriven, the welfare of the consumer and society should be important criteria in evaluating goals.

Scriven made an additional noteworthy point concerning program goals—that the evaluator should *not* focus so intently on whether the program goals have been achieved that there is a failure to notice significant unintended program outcomes that have taken place. According to Scriven, one should definitely look for evidence of unintended outcomes and be open to considering equally such evidence with evidence of accomplishment or lack of accomplishment pertaining to the program goals. The importance of this admonition is demonstrated by my and my associates' finding (Lenning and others, 1977) that unintended outcomes can be positive as well as negative and can have as much or more evaluative impact on program planning as the intended program outcomes. Even negative outcomes, which many people wish to ignore, should be considered because they can suggest important modifications that are needed in the program.

In reaction against the commonly accepted strategy of devoting *all* evaluative attention to the outcomes intended or planned for the program, Scriven (1972) developed a model that identifies significant program impacts of any kind, whether they are implied by the program goals or not. He called this model "goals-free evaluation." Scriven's idea is that an outside evaluator should be brought in and should deduce what appears to be the program's goals based on his or her observations. Only then should the evaluator talk to the program staff about their intended program goals. Scriven does not downgrade the importance of program goals for evaluation, as the following quote (1971) indicates: "The statement of goal narrows our problem to manageable size. We can't apply all possible tests to every sample in order to look for all possible effects. We check in the general area where the shot was aimed, keeping our eyes open for any side effects."

Another useful formulation pertinent to the evaluative process is Scriven's distinction between what he calls "secondary" or "intrinsic" evaluation and "primary" or "payoff" evaluation: evaluation of the means used to bring about desired end results versus evaluation of those end results. He suggests that secondary evaluation is fine if we can make a solid link between the secondary indicator and the primary payoff; otherwise, primary evaluation is essential. However, by doing both types of evaluation in the same study, understanding is increased, and we have greater assurance that our judgments are reliable. Intrinsic and payoff evaluation both can be applied in formative evaluation as well as in summative evaluation.

The evaluative or judgment process is essentially a logical exercise much like (1) putting a puzzle together; (2) a meteorologist predicting the weather based on information about various conditions; (3) a detective solving a crime based on evidence gathered, analyzed, synthesized, and assimilated; (4) a doctor or mechanic making a diagnosis; or (5) an electronics technician trouble-shooting an electronic circuit. The important things are, in an orderly and systematic manner, to

- Consider all the evidence available, and look for patterns
- Decide on all the plausible alternatives implied by the evidence
- Determine weights and probabilities based on the pattern of evidence plus experience and knowledge
- Arrive at a judgment, considering the pattern of evidence, weights, and probabilities

Related to these activities is a general five-step procedure, taken from Scriven (1971), for conducting the evaluative process: (1) identify and value the intended goals of the project or program, using ratings of such things as social utility, necessity for the goals at this point in time, and the number of people who will be benefited if the goals are met; (2) value the program's effectiveness, where effectiveness is not restricted to the stated or implied goals; (3) relate value to the program costs (here Scriven uses a twelve-point checklist involving installation versus maintenance costs, dollar versus psychic costs, per-student versus per-system costs, and so forth); (4) relate value to the program availability and practicality; and (5) produce an overall summary report regarding judgments, recommended actions, and their justification. Scriven was talking to professional evaluators when he presented this list, but it is also relevant for other evaluators. Note that, in following this five-step procedure, program benefits are related both to program process and costs.

Strategies for Evaluating Student Services Programs

In their excellent book of readings and comment pertaining to the theory and practice in educational evaluation, Worthen and Sanders (1973, p. 1) open with a serious charge that unfortunately may still be true: "Evaluation is one of the most widely discussed but little used processes in today's educational systems. This statement may seem strange in the present social context where attempts to make educational systems accountable to their publics are proliferating at a rapid pace . . . yet, despite these trends toward accountability, only a tiny fraction of the educational programs operating at any level have been evaluated in any but the most cursory fashion, if indeed at all. Verbal statements about evaluation and accountability? An abundance. Genuine evaluation of educational programs? Unfortunately rare."

This statement applies to student services programs as much if not more than to other areas of education. Student services goals for students often tend to be imprecise, vague, illusory, and difficult to measure. Student services programs usually emphasize affective development, while formal instructional programs usually emphasize cognitive development, which is much easier to measure. Counselors and other student services people also perhaps have more aversion to empirical data and analysis than do academicians involved primarily in research and scholarship.

However, for their programs to retain support, student services personnel must do a more effective and concrete job of communicating to others the important and central benefits students can gain from their programs and must provide factual evidence of such benefits occurring. Furthermore, they must demonstrate that their activities and programs are both efficient and effective. Only through effective program evaluation can such evidence be developed, and such evaluation must begin with a clear and concrete delineation of activity and program goals and objectives.

Burck and Peterson (1975), with tongue-in-cheek cynicism, discuss seven of the most common evaluation strategies, or models, used in student services. Each of them is not really program evaluation at all, according to Burck and Peterson. These "models" are

1. The Sample-of-One Method, which involves discussing the problem with one or two colleagues and arriving at a consensus
2. The Brand A versus the Brand X method, which compares nonequivalent "apples versus oranges" groups
3. The Sunshine Method, which solely provides evidence of program quantity and extensive client exposure to the program
4. The Goodness-of-Fit Method, which establishes how standard the program is and how well it fits into established procedures
5. The Committee Method, which involves a group of people connected with the program discussing and reaching consensus on the program's effectiveness and writing a report for those in authority that points out and extolls its merits
6. The Shot-in-the-Dark Method, in which clear objectives are lacking for the program or evaluation is entirely divorced from program goals so evaluation involves a random search for any kind of impact that might be possible
7. The Anointing-by-Authority Method, in which nationally recognized consultants are brought in to confirm preordained findings through talking with the "right people" and whose name and status legitimize those findings in the eyes of those in authority

The one thing that all these common (and they are common) approaches have, in addition to being poor evaluation, is that none of them tries to objectively determine the real outcomes of the program.

A number of evaluation strategies or approaches, developed by evaluation theorists and practitioners in the area of curriculum development, provide viable alternatives to meet distinct conditions and situations and have aspects or components that student services program evaluators should consider. Worthen and Sanders (1973) reprinted original writings by a number of these strategy developers that they felt had made important contributions to evaluation practice and could provide frameworks for such practice. After each reprint, they separately discussed each strategy in terms of potentials and limitations and then used a chart (pp. 209–220) to compare the models on twelve factors or dimensions: (1) definition, (2) purpose, (3) key emphasis, (4) role of the evaluator, (5) relationship to objectives, (6) relationship to decision making, (7) types of evaluation, (8) constructs proposed, (9) criteria for judging evaluation studies, (10) implications for evaluation design, (11) contributions to the design of evaluation studies, and (12) limitations and possible misuses of the approach.

One strategy I strongly favor and that has not really been emphasized by any of the theorists concerns the desirability of a holistic phase followed by a focused phase. The holistic phase is diverse and "broad band" in focus and examines many different factors at one time. Focused and more in-depth or detailed "narrow-band" follow-up of obvious problem areas is then called for as a part of the overall process.

House (1978) differentiates eight categories of evaluation strategies on the basis of their proponents, their major audiences, on what they assume consensus, the methodology used, the outcome or purpose, and the typical questions asked. For example, the typical questions associated with each category are as follows (p. 12):

- Systems analysis: Are the expected effects achieved? Can the effects be achieved more economically? What are the most efficient programs?
- Behavioral objectives: Are the students achieving the objectives? Is the staff producing?
- Decision making: Is the program effective? What parts are effective?
- Goal free: What are all the effects?
- Art criticism: Would a critic approve this program?
- Accreditation: How would professionals rate this program?
- Adversary: What are the arguments for and against the program?
- Transaction: What does the program look like to different people?

On the basis of his study of the various strategies, House reported that the primary factors in understanding the strategies are their ethics, their epistemologies, and their political ramifications.

A more subjective analysis (Popham, 1975) suggests that there are four general classes of educational evaluation strategies, with a varying evaluative focus on (1) goal attainment, (2) worth or improvement suggested by intrinsic criteria, (3) worth or improvement suggested by extrinsic criteria, and (4) facilitating decision making.

Goal Attainment Strategies. Strategies for attaining goals focus attention on program goals and objectives and on how well these are attained. In the simplest form (Tyler, 1942), the important program goals are expressed in terms of specific, concrete behaviors that can be observed or measured; for example, "Can clearly state and defend his or her philosophy of life in a debate with other students." Then a way to measure each behavioral objective is decided on that will give attainment feedback to the students as well as to the program managers.

A modification of the behavioral objective approach (Metfessel and Michael, 1967) involves ordering the goals into a hierarchical arrangement from broad outcomes at the top to specific component outcomes at the bottom. Then, for each outcome deemed important enough, multiple criteria measures of effectiveness are selected and applied.

A more recent approach formulated by Hammond (1973) goes far beyond either of the preceding two by applying a multidimensional structure showing interactions that can remind staff of important program factors that might be overlooked if the structure were not used. This model was developed specifically as an approach for evaluating innovations, and the structure is represented graphically by a cube. Each of the three axes of the cube represents a dimension: (1) the "behavioral dimension" lays out the behavioral objective outcomes desired, which are separated into Bloom's cognitive, affective, and psychomotor categories plus a "perceptual behavior" category; (2) the "institutional dimension" consists of all significant staff and student groups involved in the program, each subdivided according to various demographic and personal description variables; and (3) the "instructional dimension" is divided into categories that describe program resources, methodology, content, organization, time, and so forth. Central to this approach are

- Stating the program objectives in terms of the behavior that will be accepted as evidence the client has achieved the objective, the conditions under which the behavior will be expected to occur, and the level of performance that is acceptable
- Assessing the behavior described in the objectives
- Analyzing the results within factors and the relationships between factors, to arrive at conclusions based on actual behavior

Hammond (1973, p. 67) says the following about his structure and its application: "The structure developed provides a framework to produce factors that have a direct influence on a given innovation. The factors created by the interaction of one variable from each of the dimensions may be studied in any depth desired. . . . In most cases, the study of a given factor will be determined by time, availability of tests and procedures, and the needs. . . . Once the forces affecting a given innovation have been identified and placed in a structure which permits an analysis of the interaction of these forces, the next step is that of placing the structure in a working model for evaluation. . . . Sound evaluation procedures require that the process begin with the current programs. Before attempts at innovation are made, adequate baseline data is required to make those decisions which determine the direction of the change process."

Because personnel have limited evaluation skills, Hammond proposes that the process at the beginning evaluate only one area of the program. With such a precaution and effective training, he contends, local staff can conduct all aspects of the evaluation throughout the program.

As suggested by House's questions, goal achievement strategies are designed to provide evidence related to student achievement of objectives and how well the staff is producing. In the formative evaluation sense, one also gathers evidence to suggest ways in which the student achievements and staff productivity can be improved.

Intrinsic Criteria Strategies. In the intrinsic criteria strategy for evaluating programs, the benchmarks for judging how well the program is functioning are in the mind and experience of the evaluator. It is subjective and observational in activity and format but can have fair reliability and validity if the questions to be answered and the observations made are stated in specific, concrete terms. Referring back to House's list of questions again, this type of evaluation addresses the following: "Would a critic approve this program? How would professionals rate this program? What does the program look like to different people?" Examples of this type of approach are the personal judgment, the critic, and the accreditation models that make use of self-study, visitations, annual reports, and panels of expert judges. Although most institutions perhaps do not really try to use accreditation study data for program improvement, the accreditation bodies are verbal proponents of such application of the data.

In another approach of this type, the focus is on the student services program as a complex array of human players and a multitude of factors all interacting in an on-going and dynamic process. The difficult task of perceiving accurate and meaningful patterns of interaction—and of judging vitality, effectiveness, and efficiency of the dynamics—involves a process called *transactional analysis* (Rippy, 1973). It requires a perceptive and knowledgeable person experienced in the type of activity involved in the program. Informal analyses, such as the case study, are the primary method of such a strategy. Variations have been developed, however, that are quite formal and structured. An example is the *interaction analysis* approach to evaluating student-faculty verbal interaction in the classroom developed at the Northwest Regional Educational Laboratory (Flanders, 1973). Interaction analysis involves a formal classification of specific, observable, verbal interactions; intensive training in observing, interpreting and recording interactions within the classroom; and either a manual or computerized system into which the classroom observer can store a record of the observed interactions for later analysis.

Stake's (1973, 1975) responsive evaluation (discussed at the beginning of this chapter) is, in effect, a transactional model. As Stake has indicated, informal evaluation such as this sacrifices some measurement precision, although the reliability is adequate if one stays at a concrete observational level. However, as Stake contends, the loss in measurement precision is compensated by the gains, over more formal approaches, in the value of the findings to those involved with the program. Stake (1973, p. 6) says about his model,

> An educational evaluation is responsive evaluation (1) if it orients more directly to program activities than to program intents, (2) if it responds to audience requirements for information, and (3) if the different value perspectives of the people at hand are referred to in reporting the success and failure of the program. . . . To do a responsive evaluation, the evaluator of course does many things. He makes a plan of observations and negotiations. He arranges for various persons to observe the program. With their help, he prepares brief narratives, portrayals, product displays, graphs, and so on. He finds out what is of value to his audiences. He gathers expressions of worth from various individuals whose points of view differ. Of course, he checks the quality of his records. He gets program personnel to react to the accuracy of his portrayals. He gets authority figures to react to the importance of various findings. He gets audience members to react to the relevance of his findings. He does much of this informally, iterating, and keeping a record of action and reaction. He chooses media accessible to his audiences to increase the likelihood and fidelity of communication. He might prepare a final written report; he might not—depending on what he and his clients have agreed on.

Extrinsic Criteria Strategies. As the name implies, the extrinsic criteria strategies involve the collection and presentation of formal, objective evidence of program functioning and worth. Judgments are based on how the program compares to similar programs on the same factors and/or how the program rates compared to some absolute standard that is logical, objective, and agreed-on by relevant people.

Referring once again to House's list of questions, extrinsic criteria evaluation includes emphases such as the following: "What are the arguments for and against the program? Are the expected effects achieved? Can the effects be achieved more economically? What are the most efficient programs?"

Wolf's (1975) application of the concept of a jury trial to educational evaluation is clearly an external criteria strategy. In a jury proceeding, objective evidence is presented by advocates on either side to an impartial group, which makes a judgment about the worth of the program. As in a jury trial, a "judge" is present to ensure consistency and fairness in the proceedings. Wolf (1975, p. 186) contends that his "judicial evaluation" (or "adversary evaluation" as it is more commonly referred to) "demands that the evaluation focus on relevant and significant issues as determined by a broad variety of persons involved in or affected by the program." The adversary approach has subsequently received mixed reviews (Arnstein, 1975; Popham and Carlson, 1977; Jackson, 1977; Thurston, 1978).

The approach of this type that probably has the most potential relevance to the evaluation of student services programs is Stake's (1967) "countenance or preordinate evaluation." For this approach, Stake suggests that description and judgment are the two major activities in program evaluation and that they should be many-faceted, comprehensive activities focusing on all aspects of the program. His strategy distinguishes among three types of data necessary for both description and judgment: *antecedent* data (input conditions and characteristics not part of the program that may relate to outcomes), *transaction* data (interactions and encounters between the clients and program, including program personnel, that constitute the program process), and *outcome* data (short- and long-term consequences of the antecedents and transactions on the clients, the program and its components, and other people or entities). A matrix with twelve cells describes the data that should be collected for the evaluation; antecedents, transactions, and outcomes form the vertical axis, and intents (goals and objectives), observations of outcomes, standards that the clients expect, and judges' perceptions of program value form the horizontal axis. The matrix is vertically split into a description section and a judgment section.

Concerning the *description* section of the matrix, *intents* includes program effects that are planned for or intended, desired, hoped for, and anticipated and those that are feared. A major problem for the evaluator is to deduce the intentions for the program and transform them into concrete, usable data. *Observations* include descriptions of surroundings, events, behaviors, and consequences, gathered by direct observation and by instruments such as "inventory schedules, biographical data sheets, interview routines, check lists, opinionnaires, and all kinds of psychometric tests."

During the analysis phase, the focus is on discovering for each row of the matrix how much of what was intended actually happened (the amount of congruence and discrepancies between intents and observed occurrence) and also on examining the relationships (or contingencies) among antecedents, transactions, and outcomes across both the intended and observed dimensions. In addition to the congruence and contingency comparisons of descriptive data already discussed, Stake stressed the importance of examining whether the program plan (intents) logically relates or conforms to the philosophic background and basic purposes of the program; whether the intents constitute a plausible and well-thought-out plan for implementing the program rationale.

Concerning the *judgment* section of the matrix, Stake indicated that a holistic view is imperative but is not being taken in most current evaluation efforts within education. As he stated it, "it is a great misfortune that the best-trained evaluators have been looking at education with a microscope rather than with a panoramic view finder" (1967, p. 538).

The descriptive data on the program, discussed earlier, can be judged with respect to sets of absolute standards or criteria of what the antecedent, transactional, and outcome intentions and observations should be (*absolute comparison*), each set conforming to the view of a relevant reference group or point of view. The other possibility is to judge the data with respect to the same data for similar programs elsewhere (*relative comparison*). In doing the judging, the evaluator assigns a weight of importance to each set of standards he or she considers to have relevance and determines the program data on which to make comparisons. Based on relative and/or absolute judgment, the evaluator arrives at "an overall or composite rating of merit" and specifies limitations and qualifications that apply to this rating. He or she then develops recommendations regarding the program decisions of concern (continue the program as is, terminate the program, or modify the program in particular ways).

Stake (1967) made it clear that not everything he proposed must be done in one massive effort. Furthermore, because of available evaluation resources many evaluation efforts devote all of their resources to only certain areas of programs and to particular types of data (for example, intended versus actual outcomes). And Stake makes it clear that the process for narrowing down the focus should also be deliberate and formal.

Decision Facilitation Strategies. The emphasis throughout this chapter has been on going beyond value or worth to practical program decisions. This type of strategy especially emphasizes this additional step. In terms of House's list given earlier, it focuses on questions such as "Is the program effective?" and "What parts are effective?"

The earliest, and by far the most influential, approach of this type is Stufflebeam's CIPP (context, input, process, and product) evaluation. Stufflebeam and his associates (1971, p. 40) introduced a new definition and focus for evaluation: "Evaluation is the process of delineating, obtaining, and providing useful information for judging decision alternatives." In addition, they set forth four separate types of evaluation, each of which primarily influences one of four major types of decisions:

Evaluation Type		*Decision Type*
Context Evaluation	→	Planning Decisions
Input Evaluation	→	Structuring Decisions
Process Evaluation	→	Implementing Decisions
Product Evaluation	→	Recycling Decisions

Each type of evaluation and decision is described in Table 1. In this approach, the decision maker is provided with continual feedback, which may cause him or her to reconsider earlier decisions.

Alkin (1969) developed an approach that is very similar to Stufflebeam's in purpose and operation but that involves five types of evaluation and five types of decisions. He separates Stufflebeam's process evaluation into "program implementation" and "program improvement" and also uses systems assessment (context), program planning (inputs), and program clarification (products).

Another major approach to evaluation for decision making is "discrepancy evaluation," a term made popular by Provus (1971) in his strategy for evaluating *ongoing* educational programs. (The purpose he espoused for evaluation was to determine whether the program should be improved, maintained, or terminated.) His approach involves three general procedures, five program development stages, and three content categories. The three general procedures are (1) to agree on and define program standards and objectives, (2) to identify any discrepancies between observations made about particular aspects of the program and what should be the case according to the program standards and objectives, and (3) to use the discrepancy information to identify program weaknesses and feed it back to the program developers to guide program modification and problem solving. The five program stages are: (1) design adequacy, (2) installation fidelity, (3) process adjustment, (4) product assessment, and (5) program comparison (cost-benefit analysis). The three content categories are input, process, and output. As a basis for his approach, Provus also focused on teamwork between the program developers and evaluators and on the necessity for continuous communication between the evaluator and the program staff.

The discrepancy evaluation concept can usefully be carried beyond the definition of discrepancy favored by Provus. For example, I am a strong proponent of profile analysis, in which the patterns of similarities and discrepancies among program factors within and across program dimensions are studied to identify not only weaknesses but also

Table 1. A Two-Dimensional Matrix Relating Stufflebeam's Four Types of Decisions and Associated Evaluation Strategies

	FOCUSES ON	
	End Results	*Means of Obtaining Results*
Intentions	*Planning decisions.* Decisions about the setting to be served, the program ends or outcomes intended, and whether or not program mission, goals, and objectives should be changed	*Structuring decisions.* Decisions about sources of support and the means to be used to achieve the desired outcomes, including decisions about methods, content, organization, personnel, schedule, facilities, and budget
NO	*Context evaluation.* Developing a rationale for determination of program objectives, identification of potential methodological strategies, and development of proposals for outside funding through identification and analysis of (1) needs and opportunities; (2) problems and constraints related to those needs and opportunities; (3) discrepancies between actual and intended inputs and outputs; (4) baseline information regarding actual, probable, and possible program operations and accomplishments; (5) internal and external environment philosophies, values, attitudes, goals, priorities, politics, economics, demographics, traditions, practices, and so on; (6) technological advances in the field; and (7) strategies, operations, and results obtained in similar programs elsewhere	*Input evaluation.* Determining if outside assistance is required to meet the program objectives, how the objectives should be selected operationally, the overall program strategy to employ, and the best use of available resources to meet program goals effectively and efficiently through identification and analysis of (1) availability of human and material resources and capabilities for the program; (2) sources of possible additional resources, likelihood of obtaining such support, and the probable kinds and amounts of support; (3) relevance, effectiveness, feasibility, and economy of alternative solution strategies and procedural designs that are available to the program; and (4) numbers and characteristics of entities—such as students or other client groups—that are intended to be served, acted on, and/or modified by the program

Implementing decisions. Operational decisions pertaining to utilization, control, modification, and refinement of the program procedures and design

Product evaluation. Measuring and interpreting program process and outcome attainments during and at the end of each program cycle, through (1) defining program objectives in concrete, observable, and operational terms; (2) identifying or developing indicators and measures, and associated interpretational criteria; (3) collecting data for the indicators and measures specified; (4) comparing the measurement and indicator data to either absolute or comparative standards selected as the criteria to be met; (5) interpreting the outcome results obtained, through relating them to the context, input, and process information gathered in the other three types of evaluation; and (6) making judgments about program worth and/or how program outcomes can be improved through program modification

Recycling decisions. Decisions to continue, terminate, refine, revise, or refocus the program; based on the attainments achieved

Process evaluation. Identifying and predicting (based on program operation) defects in procedural design or its implementation, servicing the operational decisions built into the program design, and determining the extent to which program procedures are operating as intended, through (1) continuously monitoring and identifying staff and student interactions, communication channels, logistics, adequacy of program resources, amount of consensus among program staff and participants about the purposes of the program, sources of problems, unanticipated bottlenecks and other problems, and so on; (2) providing the information needed to make the operational decisions specified by the program plan; and (3) recording program process events and activities as they occur and relating them to what was projected in the program design, for indications of why the program objectives are or are not being met

Actualities

FOCUSES

Source: Abstracted from Stufflebeam and others (1971, pp. 79–84, 218–235).

strengths on which improvement can be built. Perhaps such discrepancy evaluation should be referred to as "profile" or "pattern" evaluation in order to distinguish it from the concept and approach popularized by Provus.

Conclusion: Staff Skills and Competencies Needed

The preceding discussion of procedures and strategies for conducting assessment and evaluation implies a number of skills and competencies that student services assessors and evaluators should have in order to be effective, with the requirements varying according to the strategy endorsed. Some skills are important for all approaches, however, such as the ability to ask the important questions, to think logically, and to communicate effectively.

Scriven (1971) makes the following statement: "Evaluation requires almost all of the skills known to man in order to be done well; although it is also true that we will do it in our amateur kind of way, sometimes quite successfully, whenever we buy a new washing machine or decide on a new automobile. It's worth remembering that those tasks which we all do as individuals are done with extreme care and quite demonstrably better by semitechnical skilled personnel, ranging from Tom McCahill down to the staff of consumer reports." In his discussion, Scriven emphasizes a number of specific skills for becoming competent in evaluation; for example, the ability to conceptualize and the ability to work together with others as a team. Scriven also concluded that some evaluation problems, but not a majority, require considerable sophistication in statistics (a statistician could be brought in for such cases). Other skills and competencies mentioned include the ability to do moral and political analysis; an understanding of game theory; the ability to formulate goals in a way that makes it possible to determine later if they were achieved; the ability to form, clarify, and communicate about behavioral objectives; the ability to link what is observed in field tests to language; general knowledge about the program being evaluated and the practices relevant to that field; the ability to formulate alternative hypotheses; the ability to identify concretely and specifically what one is evaluating; and the ability to evaluate options and to make balanced, practical judgments about their desirability and feasibility. Scriven claimed that all of these skills are important but that the most crucial one is the one here listed last.

In the late 1960s, the American Educational Research Association (AERA) approved the formation of a task force on training educational resource and research-related personnel, consisting of experienced researchers and evaluators. Evaluators constituted one group of research-related personnel on which the task force focused, and the initial activity consisted of listing "essential" practitioner skills, which were refined on the basis of interviews with several dozen expert practitioners who administer such efforts. Rather than focus on evaluation in general, as Scriven did, the task force members directed their attention at the skills needed to implement one particular strategy, the decision-facilitation strategy developed by Stufflebeam and his associates that has been very popular during the past decade, as discussed earlier. Furthermore, they differentiated the skills needed for the four different types of evaluation that make up that strategy (Worthen and Byers, 1970, pp. 26–30).

Owens (1977) focused on the program evaluation skills needed by busy administrators, who are far more representative of the typical student services worker than is a professional evaluator. Interestingly, the skills Owens emphasizes are similar to the ones emphasized by Scriven and by the AERA task force, and they cover the following broad array of abilities.

- To identify the purposes and audiences for one's evaluation
- To prepare a basic description of the program and its activities to be evaluated
- To refine educational objectives in terms of who will do the action, what the activity is, the criteria for judging successful objective attainment, and the conditions under which the activity will be conducted
- To write worthwhile objectives (clearly, emphasizing important skills and processes, and providing a challenge that at the same time is achievable) and to determine which objectives are most critical to evaluate
- To describe the resources and processes to be used in achieving one's objectives
- To specify the alternative decisions likely to be made about a program
- To state evaluation questions clearly and concretely
- To establish evaluation guidelines consistent with funding availability, local concerns, administrative policy, and ethical principles
- To identify available resources for conducting the evaluation
- To specify pertinent data sources
- To determine appropriate ways to measure selected processes and outcomes
- To select and apply instruments in terms of reliability, validity, and usefulness
- To establish and apply criteria for the selection of an evaluation specialist

- To prepare a basic evaluation plan for collecting, analyzing, and reporting data and transforming it into information
- To make judgments regarding various types and formats for evaluation reporting
- To apply various types of evaluation findings

All these skills and competencies are important for the assessment and evaluation of student services programs. However, the amount of emphasis on each depends on the assessment and evaluation strategy one chooses to guide such efforts (as mentioned earlier) or on the combinations of strategies and procedures from various strategies that are integrated into one's personal framework. For example, Stake's responsive evaluation does not need skills in the formal measurement of outcomes and in statistics. Rather, it emphasizes such skills as interpersonal relations, negotiation, natural observation and communication, and the ability to portray and narrate. Conversely, Stake's preordinate evaluation emphasizes such things as developing formal objectives; transforming those objectives into concrete, systematic data requirements selecting formal instruments and using them plus formal observation procedures to gather the needed data; and using analyses of various kinds (including sophisticated statistical techniques where appropriate) to compare actuality to intentions on antecedent, transaction, and outcome variables.

Concerning statistical analyses, Stake would not expect the evaluator to be a statistician. The evaluator would need to know enough about statistics, however, to be able to intelligently choose and communicate with a statistics expert when needed for the project and to appropriately interpret and apply any statistical data that are gathered.

Which assessment and evaluation approaches one chooses depends on many factors, including the evaluator's philosophy and skills. It is quite appropriate to use components from several different models to form one's own eclectic model, as long as it is well thought out and logically sensible in relation to the evaluator, the program, and the context. Furthermore, the same evaluator may often need different approaches for different programs and contexts.

One additional skill that has not yet been mentioned is very important to planning an evaluation study: One should be able to explore the potential costs and benefits of the evaluation process itself. This should be done in probable terms and long enough in advance of the evaluation that the evaluation process can be modified if necessary.

Stufflebeam and his associates (1971, pp. 27–30) discussed eleven criteria that evaluation of the evaluation plan should meet: (1) *internal validity*, close correspondence between the evaluative information and the phenomena it represents; (2) *external validity*, generalizability of the information; (3) *reliability*, consistency and replicability of the information; (4) *objectivity*, publicness of the information; (5) *relevance*, purposes of the evaluation that are served; (6) *importance*, high-priority information highlighted; (7) *scope*, comprehensiveness; (8) *credibility*, amount of trust and integrity in the evaluation and evaluator perceived by pertinent others; (9) *timeliness*, information provided when needed; (10) *pervasiveness*, evaluative findings disseminated to all persons who need it; and (11) *efficiency*, evaluative time, cost, and personnel.

In applying these criteria to evaluating an evaluation plan, remember that social and personal values from many and diverse sources influence the content of the evaluation, no matter how careful and skilled one is and how objective one tries to be. Smith (1977) discusses the major sources of value influence on evaluation activities and identifies four approaches for clarifying the values present in any evaluation effort: (1) identifying and stating publicly *all* relevant value positions; (2) clarifying the evaluator's role; (3) explicitly incorporating different values into the study by conducting comparative analyses; and (4) actively searching out conflicting value positions to ensure coverage of the full range of potentially influential values.

A final point should be emphasized: *The comprehensiveness of assessment and evaluation implied in this chapter is an ideal that often involves more than the time, the financial resources, and the political restraints present, allow.* Furthermore, it is crucial for the reader to understand that the total evaluation for a program should not be attempted all at once and that feasibility (with respect to fiscal resources, time, staff expertise, the political environment, and so forth) must be a primary consideration in designing the evaluation plan—along with the needs of the program, the purposes the evaluation is to serve, what methods and activities will be effective, and so forth. An ongoing program evaluation plan should be cyclical, with differential phases totaling several years before the cycle is repeated. During the year that a particular segment of the program is being evaluated in depth, simple monitoring techniques such as those discussed by Hecht (1977) should be used to keep one's "finger on the pulse and gross health" of the other areas of program functioning. If assessment and evaluation activities are well-planned and spaced appropriately, such activities can contribute greatly to program improvement, support, and accountability. Although this chapter has provided many suggestions for conducting evaluations for student service programs, readers interested in additional practical assistance should see Hanson (1978) and Kuh (1979).

References

Alderfer, C. P., and Holbrook, J. *A New Design for Survey Feedback. ED 078 598.* Bethesda, Md.: ERIC Document Reproduction Service, 1973.

Alkin, M. C. "Evaluation Theory Development." *Evaluation Comment,* 1969, *2,* 2–7.

Anderson, S. B., Ball, S., Murphy, R. T., and associates. *Encyclopedia of Educational Evaluation: Concepts and Techniques for Evaluating and Training Programs.* San Francisco: Jossey-Bass, 1975.

Arnstein, G. E. "The Outcome." *Phi Delta Kappan,* 1975, *57,* 188–190.

Baird, L. L. "The Practical Utility of Measures of College Environments." *Review of Educational Research,* 1974, *44,* 307–330.

Baird, L. L. "Structuring the Environment to Improve Outcomes." In O. T. Lenning (Ed.), *New Directions for Higher Education: Improving Educational Outcomes,* no. 16. San Francisco: Jossey-Bass, 1976.

Bloom, B. S. (Ed.). *Taxonomy of Educational Objectives.* Handbook 1: *Cognitive Domain.* New York: McKay, 1956.

Boyd, H. W., and Westfall, R. *Marketing Research.* (3rd ed.). Homewood, Ill.: Irwin, 1972.

Burck, H. D., and Peterson, G. W. "Needed: More Evaluation, Not Research." *Personnel and Guidance Journal,* 1975, *53,* 563–569.

Buros, O. K. *The Seventh Mental Measurements Yearbook.* (2 vols.). Highland Park, N.J.: Gryphon Press, 1972.

Campbell, D. T., and Stanley, J. C. "Experimental and Quasi-Experimental Designs for Research on Teaching." In N. L. Gage (Ed.), *Handbook of Research on Teaching.* Chicago: Rand McNally, 1963.

Clark, M. J., Hartnett, R. T., and Baird, L. L. *Assessing Dimensions of Quality in Doctoral Education: A Technical Report of a National Study in Three Fields.* Princeton, N.J.: Educational Testing Service, 1976.

Conrad, C. "University Goals: An Operative Approach." *Journal of Higher Education,* 1974, *45,* 505–515.

Doi, J. I. (Ed.). *New Directions for Institutional Research: Assessing Faculty Effort,* no. 2. San Francisco: Jossey-Bass, 1974.

Dressel, P. L. *Handbook of Academic Evaluation: Assessing Institutional Effectiveness, Student Progress, and Professional Performance for Decision Making in Higher Education.* San Francisco: Jossey-Bass, 1976.

Flanders, N. A. "Interaction Analysis: A Technique for Quantifying Teacher Influence." ED 088 855. Bethesda, Md.: ERIC Document Reproduction Service, 1973.

Goodrich, T. J. "Strategies for Dealing with the Issue of Subjectivity in Education." *Evaluation Quarterly,* 1978, *2,* 631–645.

Gronlund, N. E. *Preparing Criterion-Referenced Tests for Classroom Instruction.* New York: Macmillan, 1973.

Hammond, R. G. "Evaluation at the Local Level." Address to the Miller Committee for the National Study of ESEA Title III, 1967. In B. R. Worthen and J. R. Sanders (Eds.), *Educational Evaluation: Theory and Practice.* Worthington, Ohio: Jones, 1973.

Hanson, G. R. (Ed.). *New Directions for Student Services: Evaluating Program Effectiveness,* no. 1. San Francisco: Jossey-Bass, 1978.

Hanson, G. R., and Lenning, O. T. "Evaluating Student Development Programs." In G. Kuh (Ed.), *Evaluation in Student Affairs.* Washington, D.C.: American College Personnel Association, 1979.

Harrocks, J. E. *Assessment of Behavior.* Columbus, Ohio: Merrill, 1964.

Harshman, C. L., and Reinert, P. C. *A Model for Assessing the Quality of Non-Traditional Programs in Higher Education.* St. Louis: St. Louis University, 1979.

Hecht, A. R. "A Summary of the Moraine Valley Community College Evaluation System." Unpublished paper, Moraine Valley Community College, Palos Heights, Ill., 60463, 1977.

House, E. R. "Assumptions Underlying Evaluation Models." *Educational Researcher,* 1978, *7,* 4–12.

Jackson, G. "Adversary Evaluation: Sentenced to Death Without a Fair Trial." *Educational Researcher,* 1977, *6,* 2.

Knapp, J., and Sharon, A. *A Compendium of Assessment Techniques.* Princeton, N.J.: Educational Testing Service, 1975.

Krumboltz, J. D. "An Accountability Model for Counselors." *Personnel and Guidance Journal,* 1974, *52,* 639–646.

Kuh, G. (Ed.). *Evaluation in Student Affairs.* Washington, D.C.: American College Personnel Association, 1979.

Lange, A., Lehmann, I. J., and Mehrens, W. A. "Using Item Analysis to Improve Tests." *Journal of Educational Measurement,* 1967, *4,* 65–68.

Lasell, W. L. "Product Evaluation as a Way of Thinking." *American Vocational Journal,* 1974, *49,* 25–26.

Lenning, O. T. "Assessing Student Progress in Academic Achievement." In L. L. Baird (Ed.), *New Directions for Community Colleges: Assessing Student Academic and Social Progress,* no. 18. San Francisco: Jossey-Bass, 1977a.

Lenning, O. T. *The Outcomes Structure: An Overview and Procedures for Applying It in Postsecondary Education Institutions.* Boulder, Colo.: National Center for Higher Education Management Systems, 1977b.

Lenning, O. T. *Previous Attempts to Structure Educational Outcomes and Outcome-Related Concepts: A Compilation and Review of the Literature.* Boulder, Colo.: National Center for Higher Education Management Systems, 1977c.

Lenning, O. T. "Assessing Student Educational Progress." *AAHE College and University Bulletin,* 1978a, *30,* 3–6.

Lenning, O. T. "A Conceptual Framework for Identifying and Assessing Needs in Postsecondary Education." Paper presented at the Annual Forum of the Association for Institutional Research, Houston, Texas, May 21–25, 1978b.

Lenning, O. T., and McAleenan, A. C. "Needs Assessment in Student Affairs." In G. Kuh (Ed.), *Evaluation in Student Affairs.* Washington, D.C.: American College Personnel Association, 1979.

Lenning, O. T., and others. *A Structure for the Outcomes of Postsecondary Education.* Boulder, Colo.: National Center for Higher Education Management Systems, 1977.

May, R. D. "Guidance Program Evaluation—The Counselor's Role." ED 120 595. Bethesda, Md.: ERIC Document Reproduction Service, 1975.

Menges, R. J. *Assessing Readiness for Professional Practice.* Evanston, Ill.: Center for the Teaching Professions, Northwestern University, 1973.

Metfessel, N. S., and Michael, W. B. "A Paradigm Involving Multiple Criterion Measures for the Evaluation of the Effectiveness of School Programs." *Educational and Psychological Measurement,* 1967, *27,* 931–943.

Micek, S. S., Service, A. L., and Lee, Y. S. *Outcome Measures and Procedures Manual.* (Field review ed.) Boulder, Colo.: National Center for Higher Education Management Systems, 1975.

Miller, T. K., and Prince, J. S. *The Future of Student Affairs: A Guide to Student Development for Tomorrow's Higher Education.* San Francisco: Jossey-Bass, 1976.

Murphy, R. T. "Assessment." In S. B. Anderson, and others (Eds.), *Encyclopedia of Educational Evaluation: Concepts and Techniques for Evaluating Education and Training Programs.* San Francisco: Jossey-Bass, 1975.

Oetting, E. R., and Cole, C. W. "Method, Design, and Implementation in Evaluation." In G. R. Hanson (Ed.), *New Directions for Student Services: Evaluating Program Effectiveness,* no. 1. San Francisco: Jossey-Bass, 1978.

Owens, T. R. *Program Evaluation Skills for Busy Administrators.* Portland, Ore.: Northwest Regional Educational Laboratory, 1977.

Palola, E. G., and Lehmann, T. "Student Outcomes and Institutional Decision Making with PERC." In O. T. Lenning (Ed.), *New Directions for Higher Education: Improving Educational Outcomes,* no. 16. San Francisco: Jossey-Bass, 1976.

Payne, D. A. *The Assessment of Learning: Cognitive and Affective.* Lexington, Mass.: Heath, 1974.

Popham, J. W. *Educational Evaluation.* Englewood Cliffs, N.J.: Prentice-Hall, 1975.

Popham, J. W., and Carlson, D. "Deep Dark Deficits of the Adversary Evaluation Model." *Evaluation Researcher,* 1977, *6,* 3-6.

Pottinger, P., and Klemp, G. *Final Report to the Fund for the Improvement of Postsecondary Education.* ED 134 540. Boston: McBer, 1975.

Pottinger, P., and Klemp, G. *Concepts and Issues Related to the Identification, Measurement, and Validation of Competence.* ED 134 539. Boston: McBer, 1976.

Provus, M. *Discrepancy Evaluation for Educational Program Improvement and Assessment.* Berkeley, Calif.: McCutchan, 1971.

Rippy, R. M. *Studies in Transactional Evaluation.* Berkeley, Calif.: McCutchan, 1973.

Scriven, M. "The Methodology of Evaluation." In R. Tyler, R. Gagné, and M. Scriven (Eds.), *Perspectives of Curriculum Evaluation.* AERA Monograph Series on Curriculum Evaluation, No. 1. Chicago: Rand McNally, 1967.

Scriven, M. "Evaluation Skills." Washington, D.C.: American Educational Research Association, 1971.(Audiotape.)

Scriven, M. "Pros and Cons about Goal-Free Evaluation." *Evaluation Comment,* 1972, *3,* 1-4.

Siegel, F. *Nonparametric Statistics for the Behavioral Sciences.* New York: McGraw-Hill, 1956.

Smith, N. L. *Sources of Values Influencing Educational Evaluation.* Research Evaluation Department Report, No. 7. Portland, Ore.: Northwest Regional Educational Laboratory, 1977.

Stake, R. E. "The Countenance of Educational Evaluation." *Teachers College Record,* 1967, *68,* 523-540.

Stake, R. E. "Program Evaluation, Particularly Responsive Evaluation." Paper presented at "New Trends in Evaluation," conference, Göteborg, Sweden, October 1973.

Stake, R. E. *Evaluating the Arts in Education: A Responsive Approach.* Columbus, Ohio: Merrill, 1975.

Stufflebeam, D. L. "Evaluation as Enlightenment for Decision-Making." In W. H. Beatty (Ed.), *Improving Educational Assessment and an Inventory of Measures of Affective Behavior.* Washington, D.C.: Association for Supervision and Curriculum Development, National Education Association, 1969.

Stufflebeam, D. L., and others. *Educational Evaluation and Decision Making.* Bloomington, Ind.: Phi Delta Kappa, 1971.

Tatsuoka, M. N., and Tiedeman, D. V. "Statistics as an Aspect of Scientific Method and Research on Teaching." In N. L. Gage (Ed.), *Handbook of Research on Teaching*. Chicago: Rand McNally, 1963.

Thelin, J. R. "Beyond the Factory Model: New Strategies for Institutional Evaluation." *College and University*, 1976, *51*, 161–164.

Thurston, P. "Revitalizing Adversary Evaluation: Deep Dark Deficits or Muddled Mistaken Musings." *Educational Researcher*, 1978, 7, 3–8.

Tyler, R. W. "General Statement on Evaluation." *Journal of Educational Research*, 1942, *35*, 492–501.

Webb, E. J., and others. *Unobstrusive Measures: Nonreactive Research in the Social Sciences*. Chicago: Rand McNally, 1966.

Wickline, L. W. "Educational Accountability." In E. W. Roberson (Ed.), *Educational Accountability Through Evaluation*. Englewood Cliffs, N.J.: Educational Technology Publications, 1971.

Wolf, R. L. "Trial by Jury: A New Evaluation Method." *Phi Delta Kappan*, 1975, *57*, 185–187.

Worthen, B. R., and Byers, M. L. *An Exploratory Study of Selected Variables Related to the Training and Careers of Educational Research and Research-Related Personnel*. ED 110 441. Washington, D.C.: American Educational Research Association, 1970.

Worthen, B. R., and Sanders, J. R. (Eds.). *Educational Evaluation: Theory and Practice*. Worthington, Ohio: Jones, 1973.

Gary R. Hanson   **11**

Instruction

Teaching students in classrooms, residence halls, student activity centers, and all kinds of informal, noncredit courses has long been part of our professional history, as the earlier chapters by Fenske, Saddlemire, and Brown in this handbook have illustrated. But our teaching has not been restricted to students. In becoming more professional, we have had to teach and train ourselves and our colleagues through preservice and in-service staff development activities. Knowing how students learn and the conditions that facilitate their growth, we have taught teachers how to teach through faculty training workshops. Hence, the question is not *whether* we should teach, for we have a rich heritage of doing so—one we will probably continue for some time. Rather, our emphasis must be on *how* we should teach. What makes for good, effective teaching? What ideas, attitudes, and skills help others to learn? The purpose of this chapter is to answer those questions—to identify effective teaching skills.

The Context of Our Teaching

Almost everyone agrees that student services professionals engage in training their colleagues. But, beyond such training, do we teach?

Most assuredly. Crookston (1972) has defined teaching as any experience in the learning community in which student and teacher interact, provided the experience contributes to the growth and development of the individual, group, or community and provided the experience can be evaluated. And Lenning (1977) reminds us that college instruction includes more than what happens in the classroom. It involves all planned program activities that contribute to student learning, in or out of class and on or off campus. Thus, whether we realize it or not, we teach students, our colleagues, and other faculty members and administrators.

Because our teaching role is so broad, we must find some way to focus on our most important teaching skills. One way to do so is to examine the nature of the educational audience we teach. Who, for example, are our students today, and how do they typically learn? A careful analysis of these students not only helps establish the domain of our teaching activities but also highlights the skills we need in order to teach them well. A second way is to consider the conditions of an effective learning environment. Teaching includes much more than the communication of facts and ideas: It involves sharing attitudes, feelings, and emotions. And learning can be enhanced by providing an educational setting that is stimulating, exciting, and fun. The environment we establish for teaching has a great impact not only on how well we teach but also on how well our students learn and thus should be a major consideration in identifying essential teaching skills.

Diversity Among Students. Today's college students are not only increasingly diverse in terms of their demographic characteristics such as age, sex, ethnicity, physical mobility, and socioeconomic status—characteristics that frequently influence the way they learn—they also differ with respect to learning or cognitive styles. If we have discovered anything at all in the last fifty years of higher education, it is that people learn at different speeds, with greater and lesser amounts of supervision, and at varying levels of complexity. To teach well, we must use skills that match the individual's learning style. The goal of this section is to describe students and others we teach in terms of demographic characteristics and cognitive learning styles and, from this description, to identify key skills that help this diverse audience learn better.

Diversity of Educational Background. Traditionally, a college education was something men obtained, usually young white men from upper and middle socioeconomic classes. Beginning in the 1970s, however, many students began to attend college who had simply never before had the opportunity. One major characteristic of these students was that they were less academically able than traditional students. These new students, as defined by Cross (1971), scored in the lowest third among national samples of college-bound students on traditional tests of academic ability. Most of their parents were blue-collar workers who had never attended college. Few of these students had been successful in high school, and their primary motivation for attending college was a better job and a better life than that of their parents. College teachers were not ready for students with poor academic preparation. As Fenske noted in an earlier chapter, student services professionals now have a rare opportunity to provide developmental education to enhance the academic skills of these new students.

Other new students were older than average. From 1972 to 1974, for example, the number of students older than thirty-five increased by 30 percent (Campbell and Hanson, 1979). Lenning and Hanson (1977) found differences between older and younger students with respect to abilities, grades, attrition, self-perceptions, aspirations, goals, competencies, job values, satisfaction with college, expressed needs for help, and work outside school. Shriberg (1980) also analyzed in detail the unique educational needs of returning adult students. These students have been away from traditional academic routines, and consequently they may learn at different speeds, for different reasons, and at a different level of intensity. They confront their teachers more directly. Returning adult students are more active participants in the learning process, and as teachers we must respond accordingly.

A particular challenge for student services professionals who teach comes from the increasing number of handicapped students who have and will continue to enter college in greater numbers now that the 504 laws have opened the doors (Tuscher and Fox, 1971). Schmidt and Sprandel (1980) expect not only that handicapped students will enter college in greater numbers but also that they will pursue a wider variety of careers, feel less different from other students, participate in campus activities more, and by their presence stimulate teachers to consider new ways to teach. The content of college instruction may need to be expanded for handicapped students because many of them have come from residential schools where they had little opportunity to learn basic living skills (Bryan and Becker, 1980). Thus, they have been socially isolated, had a limited academic preparation, lacked vocational and social models, and had little opportunity to practice social interaction skills or day-to-day decision-making skills. Perhaps one of the greatest challenges in our work with other faculty will be to teach them to provide practical experiences within academic courses to enhance the daily living and learning skills of handicapped students.

Another major demographic change in today's college student population is the increased numbers of minority students attending college. Volumes have been written documenting the particular educational needs and interests of minority students (for example, see Astin and others, 1972), and I will not try to summarize the results here. Rather, I will use the results of one or two recent studies to illustrate the needs of these learners. Pitcher and Hanson (1979) reported the results of a multi-ethnic student needs assessment at the University of Texas at Austin. Blacks, Mexican Americans, and Anglo students expressed different levels of concern regarding 63 specific items within six general categories: financial, academic, career, environmental, interpersonal, and minority concerns. On items dealing with specific academic and classroom problems, the ethnic minority students were generally more concerned with their lack of high school academic preparation and their ability to study and do well on tests than were Anglo students. These high levels of concern over academic skills may negatively affect their ability to learn. Additional research by Munoz and Garcia-Bahne (1978) also supports the notion that Mexican American students must deal with higher levels of stress in college than do Anglos. Teachers who work with these students must learn to recognize the symptoms of stress, particularly when it interferes with students' ability to learn. In addition, students from different ethnic backgrounds bring with them a rich array of new and different ways that they learn. Cultural pluralism in higher education can be used to enhance the learning of all students, if teachers are willing to recognize the academic strengths that come from such varied backgrounds (Gonzalez, 1978; Ramirez, Cox, and Castenda, 1977).

Another major educational audience we can expect to teach and train, through service and in-service staff development activities, are paraprofessionals and our professional colleagues. Because our desire to develop programs frequently leaps ahead of both dollars and available teachers, a popular strategy is to train and hire paraprofessionals, undergraduates, graduate students and new student service professionals to provide the needed services (Fulton, 1978). Also, skills and competencies for successful program intervention have not been taught in most graduate-level preparation programs. Despite the fact that the required skills are readily taught and learned through in-service training, few staff development programs have been established in student services organizations (Baier, 1979). According to Miller (1975), only one higher education institution in five has a formal policy concerning in-service staff training. Clearly, there is a strong need for teaching professional skills in counseling, group advising, leadership training, group dynamics, social psychology of late adolescence, student subcultures, higher education, finances, and human relations (Baier, 1979). Later in this chapter, I will briefly describe several approaches to teaching and training these skills. For now, it is important to recognize that teaching and training our colleagues and students to effectively deliver student services involves a major educational audience. And teaching people with widely differing levels of professional preparation represents a considerable challenge.

Diversity of Learning Styles. As noted earlier, not all students learn the same material at the same rate or the level of performance. Obviously, one technique does not work with all students, rather, it is important to choose teaching techniques that match a student's learning characteristics. As Cross (1976, p. 112) points out "We all have characteristic 'styles' for collecting and organizing information into useful knowledge." Some people approach learning tasks in very systematic and structured ways, while others use more intuitive strategies. Neither approach is more correct, or easier, or more beneficial for all students. Such individual differences in learning style are important, however. Cognitive styles, as psychologists have come to call variations in approach to learning, influence "how students learn and teachers teach; and . . . how students and teachers interact in the classroom" (Witkin, 1973, p. 1). Because cognitive style represents an important dimension of the educational interaction between teacher and student, I have provided a brief description and definition and will attempt to analyze the importance of cognitive style for the teaching process

The term *cognitive style* does not refer to any one trait or characteristic of students. In fact, many cognitive styles have been identified. Messick (1970) identified at least nine such dimensions that have been systematically studied and that can be briefly described as follows:

1. *Field independence versus field dependence* emphasizes differences between analytical and global ways of perceiving and dealing with objects. The field-independent person approaches tasks analytically, separating each element from its perceptual background. Field-dependent individuals approach situations more globally, seeing the whole instead of the parts.
2. *Scanning* refers to how extensively and intensively individuals attend to objects in their environment as well as to the time span of their awareness and how vividly they perceive a particular experience. Some attend to or "scan" a simple object or event very intensely for a long time, while others scan many things less intently for shorter periods.
3. *Breadth of categorizing* represents the degree to which individuals categorize objects or events, using a very expansive or a very restricted set of descriptors.
4. *Conceptualizing styles* is the way individuals categorize perceived similarities and differences in objects and events, using many differentiated concepts or relatively few. This dimension also involves the way people approach the formation of concepts by using either descriptive or functional characteristics.

5. *Cognitive complexity* refers to individual differences in the way people tend to construe the world, particularly social behavior, in terms of multidimensional and abstract terms or in unidimensional and relatively simple terms.
6. *Reflectiveness versus impulsivity* indicates the speed with which individuals select and process information. Impulsive people tend to respond quickly with the first thought that comes to mind, while reflective individuals ponder their responses at length.
7. *Leveling versus sharpening* represents variations in ability to memorize information. Leveling individuals tend to blur similar memories and to merge perceived objects or events with similar but not identical previous experiences. Sharpening individuals tend not to confuse similar objects and may perceive differences as greater than they really are.
8. *Constricted versus flexible control* refers to how susceptible individuals are to distraction and cognitive interference. Individuals with a constricted cognitive style are more susceptible to distraction than those with a flexible control.
9. *Tolerance for incongruous or unrealistic experiences* affects the degree to which individuals are willing to accept perceptions that vary with their experience.

These brief definitions of various cognitive styles indicate that people see and make sense of their immediate world in vastly different ways. People attend to different aspects of their environments, use different approaches to solving problems, construct relationships between objects and events in very consistent and distinctive patterns, and process information at different rates and in personally consistent ways. As Cross (1976) suggests, an individual is consistent in the way he or she behaves cognitively across a wide variety of tasks and situations. These consistent ways of acting broadly influence many aspects of the individual's personality and behavior—perception, memory, problem solving, interests, social behavior, and learning behavior in the classroom. The implications of cognitive style for how we teach are crucial and are examined in more detail later.

In an attempt to define the boundaries of teaching, I have identified two dimensions of student diversity, with respect to (1) demographic characteristics such as age, ethnicity, sex, and ability level, and (2) preferred learning styles. Effective teachers must have diagnostic skills to assess the ways in which students differ along these dimensions. Teachers must be able not only to assess the strengths that students bring from diverse demographic backgrounds and their preferred learning styles but also to plan and implement teaching strategies that capitalize on these strengths. Then they must evaluate which strategies work well for which students. Assessment, planning, implementation, and evaluation skills all require a sensitivity to and an understanding of who is being taught. Teachers ought to define the limits of their teaching activities and develop their skills according to who is being taught.

The Teaching Environment. The importance of the environment for teaching has been recognized at least since the work of John Dewey (1916). Research on how learning environments actually affect student learning has followed four primary lines. Kohlberg (1972) and his associates have identified the conditions necessary for stage changes within his six-stage scheme of moral development. Second, Loevinger (1976) and her associates have examined stages of ego development and the relationship of ego development to cognitive growth in the broad sense of personality development. Third, Harvey, Hunt, and Schroeder (1961) have focused on the effects of learning environments on conceptual levels and belief systems. Fourth, Perry (1970) has studied cognitive growth during the college years and identified nine positions within four general stages of growth. All these researchers have contributed to our understanding of conditions that facilitate cognitive learning. Blocher synthesized the major contributions from these four lines of research and identified seven major elements that contribute to a cognitive, growth-producing learning environment. Blocher (1978, p. 19) feels that these seven elements "contribute to the acquisition and maintenance of new ways of thinking, and consequently of feeling and acting that are qualitatively different from preceding patterns." These conditions help teachers understand factors that can be manipulated in a learning environment.

First, teachers must establish a condition of *involvement*. Students must actively engage the learning environment in such a way that they risk important psychological values such as self-esteem, approval of significant others, or important aspects of their self-concept. Second, teachers must establish a condition of mild tension or disequilibrium in the learning process—a *challenge* condition. They must stimulate students with novelty, complexity, abstractness, ambiguity, and intensity. The major goal for teachers in challenging is to optimally mismatch the learner with the requirements for mastering those aspects of the environment that lead to such intrinsic rewards as feelings of competence and control. A third condition that facilitates learning is *support*. In an effective learning environment, the student experiences a high degree of empathy, caring, and honesty from other human beings. Fourth, teachers must also learn to establish a condition of *structure*. In a structured learning environment, the learner is given examples or a model of effective performance slightly more advanced than that he or she is currently using. The learner must be able to observe such models of performance, see that they facilitate learning a new task, and witness the rewards of learning. A fifth condition teachers must learn to build is that of *feedback*. An opportunity to practice using new ways of thinking and to receive clear and immediate information regarding the performance level relative to the demands being made is very critical. The sixth major condition is that of *application*. The learner must be able to actively practice new concepts, attitudes, and skills in a variety of new learning situations that allow problem solving and decision making. The last major condition is that of *integration*. This condition provides for time to reflect on recent learning experiences so they can be reconciled and assimilated with past learning experiences. Teachers must establish a safe, reflective, unhurried atmosphere in which students can review, critically examine, and evaluate new learning.

Blocher (1974) has shown that most learning environments consist of three important subsystems, each capable of providing optimal levels for one or more of the central conditions just described. The three subsystems are (1) the opportunity subsystem, (2) the support subsystem, and (3) the reward subsystem.

The opportunity subsystem provides the major learning tasks such as readings, reports, laboratory experiments, and projects and also provides for the social psychological elements of role and status. Thus, learners are given the opportunity not only to deal with specific intellectual tasks such as a reading assignment but to also assume certain roles such as class leader, evaluator, helper, or critic. The conditions of involvement and challenge can be developed through these intellectual tasks and roles. According to Blocher (1978, p. 21), "the opportunity subsystem allows each learner to engage in intellectually demanding tasks within social roles that can result in enhancement of self-esteem and status." Creative use of opportunity subsystems also facilitates integration by providing for reflective, introspective learning environments. The privacy and intimacy needed to integrate important learning experiences can best be initiated within flexible opportunity subsystems. A critical skill for teachers to develop is the ability to analyze a given learning environment to determine whether an opportunity subsystem is providing involvement, challenge, and integration. Teachers must also develop the skill to create new and innovative learning opportunity subsystems. To do this, they must blend intellectually demanding tasks with the opportunity to learn new social roles within the learning environment, and with an atmosphere that allows time for reflection and integration.

The support subsystem provides conditions of structure and support in a learning environment. Positive learning experiences are threatened by high levels of ambiguity, complexity, and abstractness. A well-developed support subsystem helps the learner deal with threatening situations by providing techniques to deal with ambiguous, complex, and abstract concepts. That is, a structure is provided for processing information. For example, an economic theory might be used in the classroom to structure an individual's understanding of economic inflation. By using the theory to organize and process (structure) information about inflation, the learner feels less threatened and more easily learns this abstract concept. When the learner is ego involved and challenged, he or she is also vulnerable to failure. Naturally, the support subsystem of any learning environment must provide a relationship network that communicates empathy, caring, and honesty so that the learner can understand and express doubt about his or her ability to learn new material and can move beyond fear of failure. In some learning environments, the support subsystem may provide interpersonal training skills to help establish relationship networks.

The conditions of feedback and application can be developed through the reward subsystem. Teachers should try to create a condition where clear, accurate, and unambiguous information can be given to an individual about his or her performance in relation to a specific learning objective. The reward value of feedback is particularly high when the learner is also involved and challenged. When involvement in a challenging task is high, information about improved performance is intrinsically rewarding. The reward subsystem can also be used to foster application. The condition of application facilitates new learning by rewarding it under natural circumstances. Teachers must avoid developing a reward subsystem that only provides for external rewards in artificial and temporary environments. Long-term learning that generalizes across a wide variety of learning situations is best facilitated by providing intrinsic rewards to learners in practical settings where their application of the learned material can be evaluated and clear, concise feedback provided.

As teachers and educators in the student services profession, we can contribute significantly to all three environmental subsystems. As Blocher (1978) suggests, student services workers can work closely with academic departments to design curriculum and help students select involving and challenging programs. Opportunities to reflect on and integrate new learning experiences can be facilitated by consulting and by training learners in group leadership skills, both in and outside the classroom. Perhaps student services professionals can make the greatest impact on learning environments in the area of support. Supportive relationships in the college and university learning environment can be built by teaching human relations within residence halls, student unions, and fraternities and sororities. Through career counseling, job placement, and volunteer service efforts, we can provide the necessary and important condition of application so that new learning can be intrinsically rewarding and meaningful.

The Teaching Process

In the previous section, I discussed who student services professionals teach and the factors teachers can manipulate to design effective learning environments. Although both topics influence the type of skills teachers may need and help define limits on the search for effective teaching skills, I did not explore the actual process of teaching. In this section, I first discuss *how* teaching is done and then identify what skills are needed to do it well. Although the content of what is taught may dictate the development of certain teaching skills, my primary purpose is to identify generic skills that can be used in many content areas. Specialized skills, strategies, and techniques are identified if they have the potential for wide application. Because I have established broad limits regarding who is taught and the context of teaching, my examination of the teaching process is not restricted to classroom activities but focuses on a variety of teaching efforts in which student services professionals participate.

Descriptions of the classroom teaching process (Orlich and Associates, 1980), training models used for staff development (Delworth and Yarris, 1978; Meade, 1978; Moore and Delworth, 1976), and procedures developed for microteaching by Allen and Ryan (1969) lead to a clear model of the teaching process. All these methods are based on a systems approach, in that the teaching process can be represented as a combination of components that work together in a particular sequence to accomplish a given teaching goal. The common elements are (1) defining the goals and objectives for a given teaching activity, (2) planning the instructional activity, (3) selecting and implementing appropriate techniques to accomplish the teaching task, (4) assessing mastery of the learning task, and (5) evaluating and redesigning the teaching process in view of the learner's performance.

Defining Goals and Objectives. The teaching process typically begins with an exploration of what teaching ought to accomplish. That is, what characteristics will learners have if the teaching has been effective? Inherent in this exploration is an understanding of the goals and mission of the institution in which the teaching activity takes place and an understanding of the students' educational goals. Both institutional and personal goals may be influenced by state and federal legislation; for example, the Section 504 laws for the handicapped, the National Defense Education Act of 1958, and Title IX, to mention only a few. Teachers must balance federal, state, institutional, and student goals with their own personal goals for teaching. Therefore, we must sift through a multitude of goals and establish priorities. There are no right or correct goals, nor are some goals always better than others. Goals provide an opportunity to state our values and philosophy more explicitly, so we must carefully consider what we hope to accomplish through teaching. Then we can select the most valuable goals to take precedence during teaching. As teachers, we must keep in mind that goals are not taught but are used to provide a framework within which content, skills, processes, and attitudes can be taught. Goals are simply abstractions that inspire action. As such, goals are never attained—rather, objectives that stem from them become the means by which we pursue our goals.

A second important skill for teachers is to write specific objectives for what they want to accomplish. Well-written objectives give clear guidelines for achieving specific outcomes because they explicitly state the precise behaviors students must exhibit as the result of instruction. Second, objectives also give the learner an idea of what is expected and may even motivate accomplishment. Students who are aware of the teaching objectives are less confused about what to learn. One caveat needs mention, however: Writing behavioral objectives is *not* an educational panacea that resolves all learning problems. The primary, and perhaps only, reason objectives are useful is that they communicate the exact intent of a teaching activity. They do not replace good teaching techniques or good interpersonal skills. Objectives are based on the assumption that learning consists of changes in the learner's observable behavior and that these changes can be measured and monitored over a period of time. The use of objectives also assumes that most individuals can master any learning activity at an acceptable level if given sufficient time and appropriate experience and practice.

Although objectives may be written in a variety of styles, generally three elements are stated: (1) an observable behavior or performance by the learner, (2) the conditions under which learning is to occur, and (3) a minimal level of mastery. In writing objectives, teachers should use active verbs, such as *name, list, write,* and *compute,* to indicate how the learner should perform and what should be done or produced. The conditional elements prescribe the conditions under which the learner must perform and generally include materials to be used, how the performance may be accomplished, time elements (when relevent), and location for the activity. The third element, the criterion measure, usually states the minimal performance level that is acceptable, thereby giving the learner an idea of what is expected. This element is the most difficult to write because the teacher must know what a reasonable minimum standard would be for a given group of learners.

Delworth and Yarris (1978) have shown how one aspect of the goal—"Student service staff members should evaluate the services they provide to students"—can be translated into an objective dealing with the cognitive component of understanding the purposes of evaluative research. Such an objective may be written as follows: "Using the six purposes of evaluation presented in the recent staff development workshop" (the condition of the objective), "student services staff will be able to list" (the performance required) "at least three specific purposes for conducting an evaluation of their student service department" (the criterion of performance). A more detailed discussion of how to write objectives and of the purposes they serve is available in Mager (1975) and Duell (1978). Limitations and several cautions regarding behavioral objectives are described by Fisher (1978), Melton (1978), and Shenkman (1978), which are recommended reading.

Planning the Instructional Activity. Once general teaching goals have been selected and specific objectives written, the next step is to develop a plan to accomplish each objective. This plan typically involves a *task analysis* of the particular sequence in which material should be presented and the appropriate level at which to begin. Then the teacher can select teaching techniques and strategies that present the material in a sequence that facilitates learning and that begins at a point that is understandable to the learner. Orlich and Associates (1980) cite two important purposes that sequencing instruction accomplishes. The first is to isolate knowledge (a fact, concept, generalization, or principle) so that the learner can understand the unique characteristics of the information or to isolate a thinking process so the learner can master the process under varying conditions. The second purpose is to relate the knowledge or process to a larger body of organized knowledge. Isolating what is being taught helps to make the learning activity more manageable, while relating the information makes learning more meaningful. The content of certain subjects (such as mathematics) has traditionally been sequenced so that successive learning experiences build on the preceding ones in an orderly manner. Recently, Gagne (1970) emphasized that the process of thinking should be sequenced so that the introduction of cognitive material goes from the simple to the concrete to the complex to the abstract. For example, the first step in presenting information is to make a simple statement of fact in familiar terms. The second step proceeds to the concrete by using many examples to illustrate the fact. From the concrete stage, additional variables can be introduced, new criteria added, and relationships among facts explored. The purpose of this step is to make the thinking process more complex by getting students to apply the information, using additional related facts and examples. The last step in this sequence is to introduce students to a higher level of abstraction by having them generalize or explain the information learned earlier or to predict further facts. The process outlined by Gagne is only one of several approaches to sequencing instruction. For example, Widick and Simpson (1978) have used Perry's (1970) cognitive learning theory to organize and sequence a college history course. The theories advanced by Loevinger (1976) on ego development, by Kohlberg (1969) on moral development, and by Chickering (1969) on college student development also can be used to sequence teaching activities related to developmental learning. The important point is to systematically analyze how students learn certain kinds of information and to determine an appropriate sequence for its presentation.

The second major function in planning an instructional activity is determining at which level the learner should begin. Most learning activities can be categorized into levels (in this respect, sequencing and categorizing content into levels are related). The major distinction is that sequencing concerns the process of learning, while identifying levels of learning concerns content. To identify the most appropriate place to begin, the different content levels must be described and arranged into some meaningful order. Over the years, several systems of classification—called *taxonomies* when the classes are arranged hierarchically—have been developed. Much of higher education can be categorized into three areas: cognitive, affective, and psychomotor. The cognitive domain, in which the majority of college teaching is conducted, concerns knowledge and the development of intellectual skills and abilities. Students services professionals are more likely to teach in the affective domain, which is concerned with attitudes, interests, and values, or in the psychomotor domain, which deals with manipulative and motor skills. The following brief description of several taxonomies shows how they can be used to structure the content of any learning domain.

One of the most widely used cognitive taxonomies was developed by Bloom (1956). His taxonomy classified cognitive behavior into six categories ranging from the fairly simple to the more complex behaviors:

Level	*Cognitive Behavior*
Knowledge	Remembering, memorizing, recognizing, and recalling
Comprehension	Interpreting, translating, and describing in one's own words

Application	Problem solving and applying information to produce the same result
Analysis	Breaking something down to show how it is put together and finding the underlying structure of information
Synthesis	Creating an original, unique product
Evaluation	Making value decisions about issues and resolving differences of opinion

As in most taxonomies, behaviors are arranged hierarchically: Learning at the higher levels depends on mastery at the lower levels.

To organize and classify instructional objectives in the affective domain, Krathwohl, Bloom, and Massia (1964) established five major categories:

- *Receiving (attending)*—being open and sensitive to stimuli in the environment
- *Responding*—acknowledging that messages or stimuli have been received
- *Valuing*—internalizing the concept of "worth," accepting that some values are preferable to others, and making a commitment to act on one's values
- *Organization*—ordering and classifying values into an abstract, conceptual system that leads to development of a value system
- *Characterization by a value or value complex*—acting in a manner consistent with internalized values; words and actions entirely consistent with one's value orientation

Although this taxonomy does not have the simple elegance of Bloom's, it does provide a way to analyze teaching objectives that deal with attitudes, emotions, and feelings. Good teachers have been incorporating affective goals into their curriculum for a long time, and such taxonomies encourage them to be sensitive to affective components of learning. Lenning and others (1976) developed a classification system that combines cognitive and affective domains within the context of higher education (Table 1). This system provides a very broad picture of the many student characteristics that can be changed by college instruction and also represents the general goal of developing the "whole " student.

At the planning stage, such taxonomies not only help decide at which level to begin the teaching process but also serve several other useful planning purposes. A taxonomy also provides a range of possible objectives in any subjective area. A close examination of taxonomy

**Table 1. A Taxonomy of Student Characteristics
That Can Be Changed by College Instruction**

Aspirations	Desires, aims, and goals
	Dislikes, likes, and interests
	Motivation or drive level
	Other aspirational outcomes
Competence and skills	Academic skills
	Citizenship and family membership skills
	Creativity skills
	Expression and communication skills
	Intellectual skills
	Interpersonal, leadership, and organizational skills
	Occupational skills
	Physical and motor skills
	Other skills
Moral Satisfaction, and affective characteristics	Attitudes and values
	Beliefs, commitments, and philosophy of life
	Feelings and emotions
	Mores, customs, and standards of conduct
	Other affective outcomes
Perceptual characteristics	Perceptual awareness and sensitivity
	Perception of self
	Perception of others
	Perception of things
	Other perceptual outcomes
Physical and Psychological characteristics	Physical fitness and traits
	Physiological health
	Other physical or physiological outcomes
Personality characteristics	Adventurousness and initiative
	Autonomy and independence
	Dependability and responsibility
	Dogmatism and authoritarianism
	Flexibility and adaptability
	Habits
	Psychological functioning
	Tolerance and persistence
	Other personality characteristics
Status, recognition, and certification	Credit recognition
	Image, reputation, or status
Social roles	Affiliations
	Avocational and social roles
	Career and vocational roles
	Citizenship roles
	Family roles
	Friendships and relationships
	Other roles

Table 1 (continued)

General knowledge and   Knowledge and understanding of general facts and
understanding   terminology
                               Knowledge and understanding of general processes
                               Knowledge and understanding of general theory
                               Other general knowledge and understanding
Specialized knowledge   Knowledge and understanding of specialized facts
and understanding   and terminology
                               Knowledge and understanding of specialized
                                   processes
                               Knowledge and understanding of specialized
                                   theory
                               Other specialized knowledge and understanding

Source: Lenning and others (1976), pp. 16–17.

categories helps a teacher balance many possible objectives. Because sequencing activities and content are closely linked, a taxonomy also allows the teacher to build a series of learning experiences that match appropriate content with the learning process. When this is done, a third major purpose of taxonomies is accomplished; that is, the instructional process is individualized for students who enter the learning situation with different skills and abilities, start at different points in the taxonomy, and proceed through a sequence of activities at very different rates. Finally, such taxonomies also help the teacher select strategies and techniques that coincide with written objectives—the next major step in the teaching process.

Selecting and Implementing Appropriate Teaching Techniques. The fact that students are able to learn by using quite different cognitive styles suggests that teachers can increase their effectiveness by helping students "match" their learning styles with course content and teaching techniques. A critical skill that teachers need is the ability to assess or "map" an individual's preferred learning style and then to develop appropriate teaching techniques.

Cross (1976) refers to four kinds of matches that can be made between students and an institution's learning resources. Placing students in a conflict situation, so that they are forced to develop in an area where they are relatively weak, is called a *challenge match.* Correcting a student's weakness is called a *remedial match,* and designing teaching strategies to build on a student's strengths to compensate for certain deficiencies by using a more highly developed skill is called a *compensatory match.* A fourth kind of match builds on students' unique strengths (such as music, mathematics, or art) and is a *capitalization match*. These four kinds of matches allow several different strategies to help students learn. Even though cognitive styles are consistent, extend over long periods of time, and are fairly resistant to change, it is worthwhile not only to diagnose a student's preferred cognitive style but also to teach the student a variety of learning strategies to use in different situations.

In reviewing the research literature on cognitive styles, Cross (1976) identified nine major implications for educational practice:

1. Teachers and students should gain insight into cognitive learning styles in order to better match students' styles with an institution's resources.
2. People are probably happier and more productive if they are learning by a method compatible with their style. But teachers must be aware of the different kinds of matches possible between learning style and the institution's resources. Rather than automatically matching techniques with student learning styles, they should be flexible in determining the type of match so that the goals of the student and the institution are both met.
3. No one teaching method should be used for all students in all subject areas. Some techniques work better with certain kinds of students than with others; again, a flexible approach is crucial.
4. Because most students must learn certain subject areas and skills, teachers should devise cognitive strategies to teach in new and creative ways.
5. Teachers must be aware of the rewards that reinforce students with different cognitive styles. Inappropriate rewards reduce the effectiveness of teaching techniques.
6. Institutions should offer major courses using teaching strategies that complement a variety of learning styles. Students should be able to choose alternative teaching techniques.
7. More attention should be given to cognitive style in long-range planning, such as career planning. The stability of cognitive styles makes them especially useful for long-range planning.
8. Teaching techniques should use *capitalization* matches to build on the particular strengths of students.
9. Because much knowledge associated with cognitive style is incomplete and tentative, teachers should remain open to new teaching strategies and should remain flexible in using new ideas.

The last point is especially important. At least in the immediate future, there are no "right" answers about which techniques best facilitate learning for students who prefer certain learning styles. Individuals process information differently, attend to different aspects of their environment, solve problems using different strategies, and construct relationships using different techniques. Therefore teachers must be aware of the individual differences in learning style if they hope to teach effectively.

Different teaching techniques require widely different skills to implement. In this section I examine the four categories of teaching strategies and techniques developed by Delworth and Yarris (1978). These four areas cover nearly all teaching activities and provide a useful way to analyze which techniques might be most appropriate for a given objective.

The first category—materials and demonstrations—includes many traditional teaching techniques, such as simple lectures, written materials such as book manuals and articles, audiovisual techniques, and modeling. All these methods require teachers to organize and present factual material systematically, and communication between teacher and learner is primarily in one direction. Much individualized instruction, as summarized by Cross (1976), uses these kinds of techniques. For example, programmed instruction, computer-assisted instruction, computer-managed instruction, self-paced modules, the audiotutorial approach, and personalized systems of instruction all require that the content of what is being taught be specified in learning objectives; that small, sequenced units of material be developed for presentation; that students achieve a certain level of mastery; and that students learn at their own speed. Another important feature of these techniques is that individuals receive immediate feedback and evaluation of their learning activities. Greater detail regarding the development of self-paced learning modules and videotaped training tapes is provided by Barr (1978), and techniques for developing manuals and other written materials are described by Rickgarn (1978).

A second major category of teaching techniques deals with how teachers interact with students. After lectures, the second most frequently used teaching technique is that of questioning and discussion. To use such techniques effectively, teachers must use different kinds of questions as well as techniques that facilitate group discussions, such as group process training, simulation tasks, and role playing. Cognitive, affective, and psychomotor taxonomies of teaching objectives provide a useful framework for developing questions and small group exercises.

Orlich and his associates (1980) have identified three basic kinds of questions—convergent, divergent, and evaluative—that correspond to different levels of cognitive behavior suggested by the Bloom taxonomy. Convergent questions help students focus on a central theme and usually elicit short responses from students—typically, yes or no answers. Such questions focus on lower levels of knowledge and comprehension. In contrast, divergent questioning evokes student responses that vary greatly, are longer and more involved, and rarely are either right or wrong. Responses to such questions reflect higher levels of application, analysis, and synthesis. A divergent question that might be used in teaching residence hall staff the importance of administrative policy is "What would happen if our residence hall had no rules?" Responses to this question would vary and would reflect rather high levels of reasoning. The third kind of questioning technique— evaluative—is a variation of the divergent question with one added component: Individuals are asked to evaluate or make a judgment with respect to a particular set of criteria. Such questions not only demand higher levels of thinking but also demand that teachers help students develop a logical basis for making value judgments. Hence, this questioning format may increase interaction between teacher and learner.

For the most part, lectures, self-paced learning modules, and various questioning techniques emphasize either presentation of material or interaction between the learner and the teacher. Individuals also learn from interacting with each other, and small group discussion techniques are especially effective in facilitating such learning. An extensive literature exists on the purposes of small groups, how they can be established, how they work, and what outcomes can be expected. Although consideration of all of these aspects is beyond the scope of this chapter, I will summarize several important elements of small group discussions as they relate to teaching. A group discussion typically involves a few individuals who discuss a common topic for the purpose of introducing, exchanging, and evaluating information toward some specific goal or objective. To facilitate this style of learning, teachers must be sensitive to the fact that group discussions typically follow a routine pattern. Knowledge of this sequence can help teachers use the technique effectively. Schmuck and Schmuck (1971) have shown that group members establish their place in the group and develop levels of trust before effective communication begins. During the next stage, one or more members of the group become more influential; a primary group task is to ensure that one or two influential members do not dominate the discussion. A third stage involves setting goals and procedures for attaining them. This stage is usually highly productive and allows group members to evaluate their progress toward attaining objectives. In the final stage, the group has attained high levels of trust, can analyze its own problems, and can prescribe appropriate corrective action. This process allows the group to generate enthusiasm for the topic and continue the discussion effectively. Details on how to design and structure small group experiences are given by Pfeiffer and Jones

(1975), and Orlich and his associates (1980) thoroughly examine various small group discussion methods. Many of these methods involve group interaction techniques such as role playing, simulation games, and team-building exercises.

A third major teaching technique focuses on skill building and involves the concepts of microteaching developed by Allen and Ryan (1969). Although it was developed for specific classroom purposes, the general procedure has been applied to other skills such as the training of counselors (Ivey, 1971).

Microteaching consists of four important elements: identifying objectives, modeling, feedback, and practice. This technique shows the individual how to perform a given task and how to analyze his or her own performance, and then gives each person a chance to practice the learned behaviors. The most significant feature of this skill-building technique is its emphasis on scaled-down experiences. Class size, lesson length, and teaching complexity are all reduced to short, intensive learning experiences. Allen and Ryan (1969) describe fourteen primary teaching skills that can be taught using this procedure. Meade (1978) also discusses five human development training models that vary this general procedure to teach effective communication and interpersonal skills. All these descriptions provide additional insight into how skill-building techniques can be used to teach various affective as well as cognitive skills.

The fourth category of teaching techniques deals with learning activities that most typically occur outside the classroom. Students may be assigned to visit various work settings to observe skilled workers. By observing effective workers model the desired behavior, students are better able to integrate material they have been taught. In a second type of learning experience outside the classroom, the student participates in an actual work setting under close supervision. Work experience allows students to apply their knowledge and skills in a practical setting and to receive valuable feedback regarding their performance. A third out-of-class teaching technique requires students to keep daily or weekly diaries or logs of their thoughts and feelings regarding their learning experience. Not only does this give students a chance to analyze their affective behavior about a particular learning experience but teachers also often gain valuable insight and feedback about the learning process and the student's perception of the teacher's role.

Assessment and Evaluation of the Mastery of Learning Objectives. Once learning objectives have been specified, decisions regarding the sequence and content of material have been made, and teaching has been done, the next step is to assess students' learning. Using written objectives that include clearly stated behaviors, conditions under which the learning should take place, and minimal standards of performance allows teachers to determine whether or not the minimal standards have been met and gives important assessment information. Variations in stated conditions may have interfered with the learning or the standards may have been set at an inappropriate level if the learning objective was not accomplished. Assessing mastery can involve two major kinds of assessment identified by Lenning in the preceding chapter: formative and summative. Formative assessment and evaluation of learning provides feedback *during* the learning experience. For example, short instruments testing the skills students are asked to acquire can be used to provide "corrective" feedback so that learning does not stagnate but continues to proceed through a given sequence. Many teaching techniques that incorporate the microteaching process described by Allen and Ryan (1969) or the training models suggested by Meade (1978) and Moore and Delworth (1976) use formative assessment and evaluation techniques to help students master their learning objectives. Traditionally, assessment procedures are paper-and-pencil tests but many formative assessment procedures can best be accomplished through creative verbal questioning, video- and audiotaped sessions, peer review, and small group discussions. Usually, formative assessment is used not to grade the final learning product but to help students master the objective. Records indicating where in the learning process students had the most trouble can be used in the last stage of the teaching process—that of evaluation and redesign.

Summative assessment and evaluation require that a judgment be made regarding whether a learning objective has been accomplished. Such assessments typically occur *after* the learning experience has been completed. Although individual objectives can be assessed in terms of mastery, it is especially important that the summative evaluation also review the total teaching plan to ensure that critical steps have been learned to the required standard. Hence, an analysis of the entire range and scope of learning objectives is necessary. Again, sequence and a content taxonomy, developed earlier, are absolutely critical.

One caveat should be made about assessment. Written objectives do indeed define the assessment process and procedures that must be used, but teachers should realize that there are two limitations. First, assessment is based on minimal standards, and assessment information may need to be enriched and/or expanded to fairly represent all that a student learned. Second, written objectives provide information about an individual's performance with respect to specific objectives, and, ideally, teachers help all students master all the objectives. At the least, teachers should know what percentage of a class has actually mastered each important objective. The limitation is that normative information is simply not available. In learning situations where not all students can continue to advanced levels, teachers may need to rank order students to select students for continued instruction. Some argue that in theory only assessment for mastery is needed but in fact time, money, and resources may limit who may continue a learning process. If and when that happens, teachers must be aware that procedures used for assessing and evaluating mastery of objectives do not suffice for selection decisions. Different assessment instruments and procedures are needed, and teachers should know the purposes and functions of both types even though they may routinely rely on one of them.

Evaluation and Redesign. The last step is evaluating teaching effectiveness and using that information to redesign teaching. The process of evaluation was detailed in Chapter Ten (by Lenning) and is not repeated here. However, several key issues are reiterated and their implications for teaching noted.

When evaluating teaching, teachers not only must make evaluative judgments regarding whether or not their instructional goals have been accomplished but also must judge whether or not their goals were worth accomplishing. The latter evaluation is frequently overlooked. Value judgments must be made with respect to whose goals are pursued, who benefits from the instruction, who pays for the teaching process, and whether the time and energy spent produced any worthwhile change in student knowledge, attitudes, or skills.

Both summative and formative evaluations help teachers judge the worth of their teaching. Formative evaluation helps them understand the sequential nature of teaching. As teaching unfolds, teachers must collect data that support or refute their selection of a given technique to teach a particular objective or set of objectives. Little is known about which techniques work best for which students under which conditions. The formative evaluation process should provide data to judge appropriate sequence of instruction and entry level. Such evaluation also should provide data regarding the rate at which students have assimilated learning. The primary value of formative evaluation is that it can be used to modify teaching as it develops. Changes in entry level and in sequence, style, and rate of presentation can be made at many points in the process. Formative evaluations and using the results effectively, however, require advanced planning and a commitment to making evaluation an integral component of teaching.

Summative evaluations of teaching provide very different kinds of information because they emphasize outcomes. They focus on the question "What did students learn as a result of your teaching efforts?" A summative evaluation must collect data that reflect both level and scope of mastery. Some learners may acquire knowledge in great depth but only in a very limited domain, while other students may learn more superficially but across a broad content domain. Evaluation requires that teachers judge the relative worth of these various outcomes. A written plan that includes the goals of teaching makes these judgments easier, but the teacher must also be sensitive to unexpected findings that may have either positive or negative implications.

Teaching Skills

The focus of this entire chapter has been on examining the teaching process and identifying skills that facilitate learning. The diversity of the educational audience, as well as the context in which we typically teach, also affect teaching skills.

Four categories of skills seem to emerge from our review of the teaching process: (1) assessment, (2) planning, (3) implementation, and (4) evaluation. Each consists of many subskills. This section is not intended to provide an exhaustive list of teaching skills but to suggest a few of the more critical ones. As student services professionals become involved in teaching, they will acquire new, creative, and innovative skills. This discussion provides a foundation on which to build skills.

Assessment Skills. Assessment skills are needed throughout the teaching process. Teachers should begin by assessing the demographic background of their audience to determine how it might affect teaching. As the educational audience becomes more diverse, teachers must be particularly sensitive to the unique strengths of different individuals and to their new and different learning strategies. Hence, assessment of skills involves not only the ability to measure and assess background characteristics that influence the student's ability to learn but also sensitivity to and awareness of the learning strengths that derive from our pluralistic society. Another important skill is the ability to assess levels of educational preparation. Teachers must be able to use information about past education in order to build on students' strength and identify potential weaknesses. A certain level of sophistication is needed to interpret and analyze test scores, self-report information, and previous academic grades. Teachers must also be able to assess goals, aspirations, expectations, and other noncognitive needs students may bring to the learning situation, because teachers must incorporate these factors into planning. Identifying student motivations also can be used to plan and implement specific teaching strategies.

The ability to assess preferred learning styles is a skill that is still very undeveloped. Considerable more research and experience is needed. Nevertheless, teachers should begin to assess students' cognitive styles. Because our educational audience is diversifying dramatically, it is even more important to plan and implement teaching techniques that match individual learning styles. Finally, teachers must be proficient at assessing mastery of learning objectives. A critical skill is the ability to specify criteria for mastery. Defining what is expected for which students and under what conditions allows more effective assessment of mastery.

Planning Skills. The second major category of teaching skills includes all activities that teachers do *before* they actually interact with learners. The first critical skill in this category is the ability to identify local, state, and national priorities. Teachers must also identify the educational values of individual learners. All these diverse educational values must be balanced against the teachers' own set of values in order to establish specific teaching goals. Deciding which goals to pursue requires that priorities be established and the relative importance of various values and goals be made explicit. A necessary skill for choosing appropriate teaching goals is knowing and understanding possible outcomes. Goals should clearly state what is expected to happen as a result of teaching.

Another aspect of planning is developing a taxonomy of educational objectives. By reviewing values, goals, and possible outcomes, teachers can define the scope of objectives. Developing a taxonomy allows teachers to emphasize some objectives over others and to present a balanced program of instruction. Once a good taxonomy has been established, teachers may begin to write specific objectives for each teaching task. The skills required for writing objectives include the ability to state the specific behavior required, to understand the conditions under which behavior is expected to occur, and to detail appropriate levels of mastery. Having clearly stated expectations, teachers can analyze the teaching activity to determine the best entry level and the most appropriate sequence for material. Clearly stated objectives also help teachers match students learning styles to learning activities. This matching skill is particularly critical for teachers to develop.

Another important skill in the planning process is identifying conditions that can be established to help students learn. Teachers must be able to challenge students, provide necessary support, and provide structure so that instruction does not overwhelm or frighten students. Teachers must also be able to provide open, honest, and constructive feedback. Giving students the opportunity to practice what they have learned allows them to integrate previous learning experiences with new challenges. Establishing these conditions within the learning environment can mean the difference between a successful learning experience and an unsuccessful one.

Planning for effective teaching also requires the skill to identify unique and innovative opportunities and stretch the learner's imagination. Moreover, the teacher must diagnose and provide emotional and attitudinal support at appropriate times. Perhaps one of the most important planning skills is the ability to structure rewards that motivate students to learn. Different students learn at different rates of speed and degrees of effectiveness, depending on the kind of reward provided. Recognizing individual differences and reward expectations helps teachers to facilitate learning.

Implementation Skills. Perhaps one of the most exciting aspects of teaching is testing educational plans developed in the early stages of teaching. With educational goals defined and specific objectives written into an organized plan, teachers can begin to interact with their students. The strategies and techniques that teachers use probably make the most difference in how well students learn. A high degree of interpersonal skills is required to establish the planned conditions of involvement, challenge, support, structure, feedback, application, and integration in the learning environment. Much teaching activity traditionally involves direct communication between the teacher and the student. Teachers not only must communicate verbally and nonverbally to the students but must also receive messages from the students. The interpersonal skills training mentioned earlier is a way to acquire the necessary skills of attending, receiving, responding, and valuing. Teachers can also communicate with their learning audience through written materials such as manuals, articles, and books. The ability to write clear directions outlining what is required is a very critical skill. As education becomes more involved with advanced technology, teachers must also develop skills in using media, computers, videotapes, and television.

One of the most critical skills for implementing a teaching plan is a high level of expertise in questioning students about what they have learned. Teachers should be able to discriminate between the different kinds of questioning techniques described earlier.

Because much teaching occurs within group settings, it is imperative that teachers understand small group discussion techniques and dynamics. Teachers must be able to intervene appropriately in the group process and be able to diagnose if and at what point a discussion group is running into trouble. Learning by interacting with student peers can be a very potent technique provided that teachers understand its advantages and disadvantages.

Finally, teachers must be able to use skill-building techniques as a teaching tool. They must be able to write objectives, model learned behavior, provide constructive feedback, and design learning experiences that provide the opportunity to practice and apply what has been modeled. Modeling is particularly useful for teaching specialized skills that can be developed in relatively short, intense learning situations. Perhaps the most difficult implementation skill is the ability to select an appropriate teaching strategy for a given student. When teachers can use a variety of techniques and skills applicable to a particular teaching objective, implementing a teaching plan is much easier.

Evaluation Skills. Broadly speaking, evaluation skills can be reduced to two very broad domains. First, teachers must be able to evaluate how well students master particular learning objectives, and, second, they must be able to evaluate how well they have achieved their own teaching objectives. Teachers must continually make value judgments about the worth of educational goals and objectives. As the educational climate within the institution, community, or the nation fluctuates, teachers must be flexible enough to redesign their teaching process. One very necessary component of the evaluation skill category is commitment to evaluation. Evaluation must begin at the assessment and planning stages and must continue throughout as well as after the teaching. When teaching has been completed, teachers must step back and ask, "What have I accomplished?" To do this well, teachers must know and understand the basic elements of the evaluation process, be able to collect meaningful information, and, perhaps most importantly, be able to interpret information from a variety of sources that speak to the effectiveness and thoroughness of which they have done their jobs. As accountability demands become more intense, teachers must acquire the skill to disseminate evaluations of their teaching effectiveness. Good evaluation properly communicated to other individuals interested in the educational process helps them understand what students learn in your educational setting. The most important person to communicate that information to, of course, is yourself. You can best improve your teaching by taking a careful look at what you have and have not accomplished with your students.

References

Allen, D., and Ryan, K. *Microteaching*. Reading, Mass.: Addison-Wesley, 1969.

Astin, H. S., and others. *Higher Education and the Disadvantaged.* Washington, D.C.: Human Service Press, 1972.

Baier, J. L. "Competent Staff: The Crucial Variable." In M. J. Barr and L. A. Keating (Eds.), *New Directions for Student Services: Establishing Effective Programs*, no. 7. San Francisco: Jossey-Bass, 1979.

Barr, M. J. "Self-Paced and Videotaped Training Innovations." In U. Delworth (Ed.), *New Directions for Student Services: Training Competent Staff*, no. 2. San Francisco: Jossey-Bass, 1978.

Blocher, D. H. "Toward an Ecology of Student Development." *Personnel and Guidance Journal*, 1974, *52*, 360–365.

Blocher, D. H. "Campus Learning Environments and the Ecology of Student Development." In J. H. Banning (Ed.), *Campus Ecology: A Perspective for Student Affairs*. Cincinnati, Ohio: National Association for Student Personnel Administrators, 1978.

Bloom, B. *Taxonomy of Educational Objectives: The Classification of Educational Goals*. Handbook I: *Cognitive Domain*. New York: McKay, 1956.

Bryan, W. A., and Becker, K. M. "Student Services for the Handicapped Student." In H. Z. Sprandel and M. R. Schmidt (Eds.), *New Directions for Student Services: Serving Handicapped Students*, no. 10. San Francisco: Jossey-Bass, 1980.

Campbell, M., and Hanson, G. R. *Ecological Analysis of the Psychological and Social Adjustment of Adult University Students*. Research Report Series. Austin: Office of the Dean of Students, Universiy of Texas, 1979.

Chickering, A. W. *Education and Identity*. San Francisco: Jossey-Bass, 1969.

Crookston, B. B. "A Developmental View of Academic Advising as Teaching." *Journal of College Student Personnel*, 1972, *13*, 12–17.

Cross, K. P. *Beyond the Open Door: New Students to Higher Education*. San Francisco: Jossey-Bass, 1971.

Cross, K. P. *Accent on Learning: Improving Instruction and Reshaping the Curriculum*. San Francisco: Jossey-Bass, 1976.

Delworth, U., and Yarris, E. "Concepts and Process for the New Training Role." In U. Delworth (Ed.), *New Directions for Student Services: Training Competent Staff*, no. 2. San Francisco: Jossey-Bass, 1978.

Dewey, J. *Democracy and Education*. New York: Macmillan, 1916.

Duell, O. K. "Overt and Covert Use of Objectives of Different Cognitive Levels." *Contemporary Educational Psychology*, 1978, *3*, 239–245.

Fisher, K. M. "What's Wrong with Behavioral Objectives?" *Journal of College Science Teaching*, 1978, *7*, 297–300.

Fulton, D. R. "Teaching Staff to Be Trainers." In U. Delworth (Ed.), *New Directions for Student Services: Training Competent Staff*, no. 2. San Francisco: Jossey-Bass, 1978.

Gagne, R. M. *The Conditions of Learning*, 2nd ed. New York: Holt, Rinehart and Winston, 1970.

Gonzalez, A. "Psychological Characteristics Associated with Biculturalism Among Mexican-American College Women." Unpublished doctoral dissertation, University of Texas, Austin, 1978.

Harvey, O. J., Hunt, D. E., and Schroeder, H. M. *Conceptual Systems and Personality Organization.* New York: Wiley, 1961.

Ivey, A. *Microcounseling: Innovations in Interviewer Training.* Springfield, Ill.: Thomas, 1971.

Kohlberg, L. "Stage and Sequence: The Cognitive Developmental Approach to Socialization." In D. P. Goslin (Ed.), *Handbook of Socialization Theory and Research.* Chicago: Rand McNally, 1969.

Kohlberg, L. "A Cognitive Developmental Approach to Moral Education." *Humanist,* 1972, *6,* 13-16.

Krathwohl, D. R., Bloom, B., and Massia, B. B. *Taxonomy of Educational Objectives: The Classification of Educational Goals.* Handbook II: *Affective Domain.* New York: McKay, 1964.

Lenning, O. T. "Assessing Student Progress in Academic Achievement." In L. Baird (Ed.), *New Directions for Community Colleges: Assessing Student Academic and Social Progress,* no. 18. San Francisco: Jossey-Bass, 1977.

Lenning, O. T., and Hanson, G. R. "Adult Students at Two-Year Colleges: A Longitudinal Study." *Community/Junior College Research Quarterly,* 1977, *1,* 271-287.

Lenning, O. T., and others. *A Structure for the Outcomes of Postsecondary Education.* Boulder, Colo.: National Center for Higher Education Systems, 1976.

Loevinger, J. *Ego Development: Conceptions and Theories.* San Francisco: Jossey-Bass, 1976.

Mager, R. F. *Preparing Instructional Objectives.* (2nd ed.) Belmont, Calif.: Fearon, 1975.

Meade, C. J. "Interpersonal Skills: Who, What, When, Why." In U. Delworth (Ed.), *New Directions for Student Services: Training Competent Staff,* no. 2. San Francisco: Jossey-Bass, 1978.

Melton, R. F. "Resolutions of Conflicting Claims Concerning the Effect of Behavioral Objectives on Student Learning." *Review of Educational Research,* 1978, *48,* 291-302.

Messick, S. "The Criterion Problem in the Evaluation of Instruction: Assessing Possible, Not Just Probably Intended Outcomes." In M. C. Wittrock and D. E. Wiley (Eds.), *The Evaluation of Instruction.* New York: Holt, Rinehart and Winston, 1970.

Miller, T. K. "Staff Development Activities in Student Affairs Programs." *Journal of College Student Personnel,* 1975, *16* (4), 258-264.

Moore, M., and Delworth, U. *Training Manual for Student Services Program Development.* Boulder, Colo.: Western Interstate Commission for Higher Education, 1976.

Munoz, D., and Garcia-Bahne, B. *A Study of the Chicano Experience in*

Higher Education: A Final Report. San Diego: Center for Minority Group Mental Health, 1978.

Orlich, D. C., and Associates. *Teaching Strategies: A Guide to Better Instruction.* Lexington, Mass.: Heath, 1980.

Perry, W. G. *Forms of Intellectual and Ethical Development in the College Years.* New York: Holt, Rinehart and Winston, 1970.

Pfeiffer, J. W., and Jones, J. E. *A Handbook of Structured Experiences for Human Relations Training.* 5 vols. La Jolla, Calif.: University Associates, 1975.

Pitcher, G., and Hanson, G. R. "A Comparison of Problems Perceived by Three Ethnic Groups of Students at a Large University." Unpublished paper, Office of the Dean of Students, University of Texas, Austin, 1979.

Ramirez, M., III, Cox, B. G., and Castenda, A. "The Psychodynamics of Biculturism." Unpublished paper, University of Santa Cruz, 1977.

Rickgarn, R. I. "Manuals: Their Development and Use in Training." In U. Delworth (Ed.), *New Directions for Student Services: Training Competent Staff,* no. 2. San Francisco: Jossey-Bass, 1978.

Schmidt, M. R., and Sprandel, H. Z. (Eds.). *New Directions for Student Services: Serving Handicapped Students,* no. 10. San Francisco: Jossey-Bass, 1980.

Schmuck, R. A., and Schmuck, P. A. *Group Processes in the Classroom.* Dubuque, Iowa: Brown, 1971.

Shenkman, H. J. "Beyond Behavioral Objectives: Behavioral Processes." *Journal of Reading,* 1978, *22,* 113–116.

Shriberg, A. (Ed.). *New Directions for Student Services: Providing Student Services for the Adult Learner,* no. 11. San Francisco: Jossey-Bass, 1980.

Tuscher, J., and Fox, G. G. "Does the Open Door Include the Physically Handicapped?" *Journal of Rehabilitation,* 1971, *37* (5), 10–13.

Widick, C., and Simpson, D. "Developmental Concepts in College Instruction." In C. Parker (Ed.), *Encouraging Development in College Students.* Minneapolis: University of Minnesota Press, 1978.

Witkin, H. A. *The Role of Cognitive Style in Academic Performance and in Teacher-Student Relations.* Princeton, N.J.: Educational Testing Service, 1973.

Susan K. Gilmore 12

Counseling

Counseling is one of the cornerstone skills in student services. A basic understanding of, and minimal competence in, counseling is required and useful for nearly all student services positions, and we can all do a better job if and when we apply these skills. However, all too often we overlook or ignore application of these skills in our day-to-day functioning. The purpose of this chapter is to remind the student services professional of the purpose of counseling, to describe an eclectic model of counseling and the associated skills, and then to show how such skills can be applied in student services settings.

The Purpose of Counseling

All the diverse life circumstances that prompt a person to seek the assistance of a counselor can be sorted into one of these three categories: (1) choice—the person has reached a point where some decisions must be made; (2) change—the person wants something about his or her pattern of actions, thoughts, and/or feelings to be different; (3) confusion reduction—the way the person has structured experience and assigned meaning to his or her life is no longer working—not much seems to matter or make any sense anymore. The manner in which these three purposes are incorporated in an eclectic model of counseling and the necessary skills required to achieve these purposes are described in a later section.

These three purpose categories can be seen as three potential counseling contracts, and a separate intervention strategy associated with each one:

Purpose	Intervention Strategy
Choice	Rational planning and decision making
Change	Behavior modification
Confusion reduction	Perceptual and cognitive restructuring

Choice. Choice is one of the existential realities of being a separate, unique individual. A human being cannot choose to not make choices. In the extreme cases, humans can adopt very passive, indifferent, undirected postures in relation to the way they spend their time and energy, but even then they cannot escape the fact that they are choosing such a posture and that they could choose otherwise. Of course, not all things are possible for humans, and there are limits on what an individual can choose. We always make choices among limited possibilities, and in many cases, such as extreme poverty, profound physical disability, stigmatization, and prejudice, the limits on choice are irrational, unnecessary, or unjust. Nevertheless, individuals cannot escape choosing their response to the limited possibilities that confront them. Making choices is a defining characteristic of humanness.

The hazard that goes with the emphasis on choices and decisions is overrationality. Counselors who see their role in this way may unconsciously try to avoid any contact with deeper levels of motivation, unreflectedly accepting at face value clients, initial formulations about what they want, and why they want it. Thus their approach to complex and difficult decisions may be superficial and unhelpful, and the public they should be serving may come to regard counseling as a futile exercise.

Unfortunately, the general public tends to use a "disease model" interpretation of anyone's seeking counseling for any reason; that is, students are viewed as emotionally ill, and the purpose of counseling is to cure them of their sickness. Whereas there is very little you can do to make sweeping changes in the way the general public views counseling, counselors, and clienthood unless you have access to the mass media, you *can* make certain that you personally do not harbor such a view and that you do not subtly communicate that you expect counselees to be very sick and troubled. At any developmental state, seeking counseling for making choices ought to be viewed as normal, natural, appropriate, and sensible. *The purpose of such counseling is to facilitate wise choices of the sort on which the person's later development depends.* Counseling should not be *just* for people who are anxious, unhappy, or unable to cope with the circumstances of their lives. In our complex and rapidly changing society, all individuals must make choices fraught with important consequences for their future, and they should not have to prove they have become psychologically dysfunctional in order to qualify for a counselor's help. Depth of understanding and the interest in the full complexity of people that is characteristic of psychotherapy at its best should be built into every counseling relationship. Superficiality has no place in this endeavor; there are no "routine" cases.

Change. All successful counseling involves change in the sense that things are different at the close of successful counseling from what they were at the beginning. If a student has made some choices or plans or established some goals or determined the direction to be headed, certainly we could say change has occurred. However, change as it is being used to identify this second category of purposes has a much narrower meaning, and it does not include anything and everything that might be different from the beginning to the end of counseling. An easy way to understand change as a counseling purpose is in terms of a counselee wanting to do, think, or feel some specific thing more often or less often or in some situations but not others. The contract negotiated between the counselor and the student is designed to change specific actions, thoughts, or feelings so that they occur more frequently or less frequently or under one set of conditions but not under other conditions. At present, the counselors and/or psychotherapists who are clearly most effective in changing behavior are those who work with their clients to create situations in which the clients learn new ways of acting, thinking, and feeling. Often, such counselors are referred to as "behavior modifiers"; their primary function is teaching.

Ullmann's (1969, pp. 68–69) definition of behavior modification offered in the early days of the behavior modification movement has never been surpassed for clarity and simplicity:

> The model that in my opinion most closely fits the work of the behavioral therapist is that of teacher. The teacher helps people change in ways that will have presumably favorable consequences. The object is the engendering of skills. This is more than conformity; a good teacher aims not only for solution to a set of problems; that is, rote memory, but also for an approach to future problems; that is, creativity.
>
> Every therapist is faced with another human. Every therapist endeavors to help. Every therapist shares certain role characteristics such as training, social recognition, and the like. The

behavioral therapist maneuvers. *These are in addition to and do not replace interviewing skills. . . .*

For the client, the behavioral or educational model means that he is treated as a normal human being, who under certain limited and specifiable conditions, acts in a manner that does not serve him well and therefore is changeworthy. He is not a "phobic" or a "schizophrenic" or a "sexual deviate." He is a worthwhile person who serves himself and his community well the vast majority of the time, but who, in certain restricted situations, emits behaviors that he himself or others find upsetting and wish to change. The first point, then, is that there is a basic respect for people implied in the very model. The second point is that the client has the same obligations as any student: to work with his teacher. The teacher has the responsibility of effective lesson design, reinforcement of good performance, and pacing the stimuli to fit the student's needs and growth.

All of these procedures have in common a direct, tutorial approach by the therapist rather than an indirect approach in which some hypothesized internal personality construct is altered prior to changed overt behavior. Behavior therapy or behavioral counseling is not the use of any single technique but rather a way of thinking about the helping relationship that in operation leads to the use of a selection of techniques based on psychological principles. Finally, new techniques are being constantly introduced and older procedures are constantly being modified. Again, behavioral therapy is not the use of specific techniques, but the application of general principles or effective independent variables in experiments from learning and social psychology laboratories. . . .

That behavioral procedures are not that simple does not mean that procedures cannot be specified; it does mean that there is a technology that must be learned and that a set of good intentions and new words are not enough. [Italics added]

We are a long way from knowing what techniques to apply to help bring the desired changes for every student who seeks counseling and/or psychotherapy. However, we are no longer in a position where one approach works about as well as another, and thus counselors and therapists are free to choose whatever procedures they happened to learn or that suit their personal styles best. Personal comfort with a procedure is no longer an adequate or an ethically justifiable basis for planning how you will assist a client change. The evidence is strong and clear that behavioral approaches to counseling and psychotherapy, as opposed to other approaches such as insight, result in far greater success when change is the purpose of counseling and/or psychotherapy. Whenever you are faced with clients who want and need to change their behavior, either you need to know to whom you can refer them for behavioral counseling and/or psychotherapy, or you need to have acquired sufficient skills and competencies in behavioral theory and techniques in a recognized training institution, so that you can assist them directly. Talking with them and hoping that when they get a few insights things will straighten out is no longer a viable alternative for anyone but a well-meaning but untrained layperson who is given neither professional status nor money for being a good friend.

Confusion Reduction. The third and final category of counseling purposes within which counselors and students negotiate contracts is called *confusion reduction* and is more far-reaching and complex than simple "clarification," which is the first step toward negotiating any counseling contract. That is, confusion reduction is more than the initial phase of all counseling interactions. It is true that in the beginning of a counseling interaction, which eventually becomes defined as a choice situation or as a change situation, there may be considerable confusion that must be clarified and eliminated. The communication process between counselor and counselee is designed to bring about such clarification and eliminate any confusion so that choice or change can be accomplished. However, there are several kinds of distressing life circumstances in which neither choice nor change, as we have defined them earlier, are called for—and yet the student experiences a profound and pervasive sense of confusion. As a separate category of counseling purpose, confusion reduction is most closely tied to inadequacy of the structure with which an individual is attempting to perceive and understand daily life.

Each of us has a complicated set of assumptions, built up from our own life experiences, that concern what it takes to get along at work, with other people and in relation to oneself. For most people, many, and maybe even most, of those assumptions would be difficult to state clearly and simply. Nevertheless, that set of assumptions about life in general, together with perceptual and cognitive mechanisms each of us has developed to perceive and understand specific daily events, bring order, consistency, and predictability into each of our lives. The set of assumptions plus the perceptual and cognitive mechanisms provide the structure by means of which we function in our daily lives. If for some reason, the set of assumptions and/or perceptual and cognitive mechanisms we have developed do not seem to work any more or have somehow vanished, we experience a tremendous amount of confusion, which usually interferes seriously with our daily functioning.

When individuals feel very confused and report that they just cannot seem to function as they would like to, it may mean that they are facing some choices that, once made, will result in their being able to function again. It may mean that they need to make some changes that, once accomplished, will result in their being able to function again. However, it also could mean that the person has suffered the loss of part or all of the basic structure for living and only a process of building a new structure or rebuilding the old structure will reduce the person's confusion sufficiently to restore functioning. When such individuals seek counseling assistance, the purpose is to become less confused so they can function again. The restructuring process that will accomplish such confusion reduction must necessarily deal with the basic assumptions about life in general, especially the basic assumptions about work, relationships, and aloneness. And it must necessarily deal with peoples' perceptual mechanisms whereby they represent the events of daily living to themselves.

You, as a counselor, must ascertain whether the confusion a client is expressing is associated with choices or changes, which are yet to be made, or whether the confusion is associated with inadequate basic personal structure; the process of counseling ought to be different in each case. If confusion is merely an outgrowth of unmade choices, then negotiating a contract to engage the client in a rational decision-making process is what is required of the counselor. If confusion is an outgrowth of unrealized changes, then negotiating a contract to engage the client in a process of modifying behavior is what is required of the counselor. But, if confusion is an outgrowth of inadequacy of structure in the client's life, then what is required of the counselor is negotiating a contract that will engage the client in a process of building a new structure or rebuilding an old structure. Confusion reduction, the third and final category of counseling purposes, applies to those students who seek counseling because the structure (the set of basic assumptions and the perceptual cognitive mechanisms) with which they make sense out of life is no longer adequate and so they feel confused and unable to function as they would like to.

Two types of human experience that frequently include loss of structure and therefore lead to profound confusion are briefly outlined in this section. If counselors are aware of the kinds of circumstances that often result in structure loss and confusion, they are more likely to discern when a particular student's primary purpose in seeking counseling is confusion reduction. They will more quickly negotiate a confusion reduction contract designed to engage the counselee in an effective restructuring process. The outline shown in Table 1 provides clues for detecting confusion reduction as the primary counseling purpose. Not everyone who experiences one or more of the following things will require confusion reduction counseling. Also, a person who could definitely benefit from confusion reduction counseling would not necessari-

**Table 1. Clues for Detecting Confusion Reduction as the Primary
Counseling Purpose**

I. Loss of structure through major life change

    A. Sudden onset—structure obliterated

        1. *Self:* physical disability; for example, loss of arm or leg, facial scars, heart attacks

            Drug-induced psychological changes; for example, recurrent hallucinations, addiction

            Personal failure; for example, expelled from school, bankruptcy, sexual impotence, frigidity

            New or unfamiliar role demands; for example, older sister to brand new baby brother, retirement, return to school after many years, share room for first time

        2. *Significant others:* no longer accessible; for example, death, divorce, moved away, serious illness

        3. *Setting:* move to a new neighborhood, community, or state

            Job change; for example, desk work after being a field man

            Changes in institution; for example, old, downtown church razed

    B. Gradual onset—structure eroded

        1. *Self:* aging and/or chronic disease

            Retarded youngster facing increasing school demands

            Skills becoming obsolete with increased automation

            Inability to form close personal relationship

        2. *Significant others:* diminishing contact with previously close friend or family member

            More accelerated job advancement of friend

            Growing independence of one's children

            Aging parents

            Gradual reduction in previously commonly held values among family and/or friends

        3. *Setting:* policies governing job role and activities gradually redefined and revised

            Church doctrine revised and reinterpreted

            Small town becoming a city

            Increasing crime and violence in previously safe neighborhood

II. Loss of Structure through personal examination and evaluation of previously distant events

    A. Refocusing of time perspective; for example, long-range career planning, contemplating one's own death, increased knowledge of history

Table 1 (continued)

B. Expansion of personal world; for example, increased knowledge of or contact with other cultures, religions, sociopolitical systems

C. Increased knowledge of self; for example, insight into egocentric or self-aggrandizing motives, awareness of one's own sexuality, shift in appraisal of personal strengths and weaknesses

ly have experienced any of the preceding. However, it bears repeating that the counselor who has some awareness of the kinds of circumstances that frequently result in structure loss and confusion is better equipped to discern the need for confusion reduction counseling.

When people experience major changes in their lives or begin examining new ideas previously very foreign to them, they typically pass through a period of ambiguity and uncertainty—a period of confusion— before they are able to sort things out and make whatever choices or changes seem necessary and/or possible. However, for some people the confusion never ends. They often begin doubting many of their basic assumptions about life and distrusting their own perceptions of reality. In some cases, the individual's assumptions and perceptions are quite appropriate and accurate; in some cases, the individual's assumptions and perceptions are fallacious and distorted. Regardless of the accuracy and trustworthiness of the assumptions and perceptions from your point of view, if the individual lacks confidence in them and is thus very confused your task as a counselor is to help him or her build a new, more adequate life structure or rebuild the old structure, which may be adequate if the person had confidence in it. Except in cases of marked disorganization and dysfunction, you and the counselee make the judgments concerning the desirability and/or necessity of building a new structure.

People who are drawn to counseling as a profession often abhor putting other people into the categories of some classification system. However, it is impossible not to sort and classify people in some way. The very fact that counselors use *language* to understand the person being counseled means that the person is being described some ways and not others; that certain characteristics, but not others, are being attributed to the person; and so on. Avoiding evaluation and classification is impossible; what is important is that the classification system being used does not demean the person being described and, more importantly, serves well our purposes of helping that person. Even if our categorizing were humane and respectful as well as consistent and reliable, unless we actually *do something different* as a result of differentiating among choice, change, and confusion reduction such differential diagnosis is useless and may be destructive.

Most counselors, as they become seasoned and mature, realize there is no one way, approach, method, or strategy to achieve the various purposes of counseling just described. In time, most professional people who help others become more eclectic; that is, they recognize that some approaches accomplish some goals better than others and that some people in some situations can use a particular strategy well that is utterly useless in other situations, even though the people appear to be facing the same struggle.

Even though it makes good sense to become increasingly eclectic and most skillful counselors do become increasingly eclectic, there are some serious objections to this tendency, which need to be recognized. Eclecticism invites inconsistency and disorganization and patchwork theorizing. It can be mistaken for an antiintellectual, antiscientific subjectivism that flies under a flag of "do whatever feels right." Eclecticism may foster dilletantism in those who are unwilling to expend the additional time and energy required to become competent with a comprehensive set of technical tools but are curious enough about the content to dabble with various forms of psychological intervention. Finally, eclecticism has not stimulated research or evaluation, and those who embrace eclecticism are, thus, not encouraged or expected to engage in research and/or evaluation in the manner that characterizes some specific systems; for example, Rogerian counseling and behavioral counseling. Perhaps more serious than the obvious loss of information and understanding that such research and evaluation from an eclectic framework would bring is the loss of a posture, an attitude, a mind set within eclectic counselors that is actively evaluative, self-critical, and open to new ways of viewing their work.

A Framework for Eclecticism

Table 2 presents an eclectic theoretical model that has been offered as structurally and functionally adequate for a counselor practicing in any setting. As is evident from the outline, the process of counseling involves two interrelated but distinguishable activities: appraisal and intervention. Depending on a counselor's setting, these activities might be called *diagnosis and treatment, assessment and therapy,* or *analysis and action.* Basically, counseling must include (1) "understanding what is and what needs to be" and (2) "making something happen."

Counseling Skills and Competencies

Depending on a counselor's skills and experience and credentials, the counselor may carry out the entire process of appraisal and intervention, refer the student immediately, or handle some aspects while refer-

**Table 2. Outline of the Tyler-Gilmore Framework for
Appraisal and Intervention**

I. Appraisal with the person

   A. Individual interview
   B. Personal journals and other writings
   C. Photo life history
   D. Self-report following self-observation
   E. Reports of significant others
   F. Observations in natural settings
   G. Medical examination
   H. Legal status evaluation
   I. Economic assessment
   J. Standardized psychological tests

II. Intervention with the person

   A. Choice: Rational planning and decision making

      1. Appraising the challenge
      2. Surveying alternatives
      3. Weighing alternatives
      4. Deliberating about commitment
      5. Adhering despite negative feedback

   B. Change: Behavior modification

      1. *Neutralizing tactics:* For example, systematic desensitization, flooding, imagining, imploding, relaxation, hypnosis, meditation, yoga

      2. *Acquisitional tactics:* For example, modeling, role play, behavioral rehearsal, coaching, videotape self-confrontation, shaping, cuing

      3. *Self-management tactics:* For example, self-instruction, covert sensitization, self-reward, Premack principle, incompatible responses, ritualizing, stimulus control

      4. *Contingency management tactics:* For example, behavioral contract, token economy, punishment, negative reinforcement, sheltered workshop, half-way house

   C. Confusion Reduction: Perceptual and cognitive restructuring

      1. *Life history review and projection:* photo life history, personal journals, diaries, logs, scrapbooks, school yearbooks, interview people from past times and places, visit places from the past, draw life line, visualize aging, write out eulogy

      2. *Reattribution tactics:* rational restructuring, cognitive relabeling, Rational Emotive Therapy (RET), role reversal, Kelly's fixed role therapy, dance therapy, music, art

      3. *Bibliotherapy tactics:* novels, plays, poetry, biography and autobiography, philosophical and spiritual writing; film and books

Table 2 (continued)

4. *Professional relationship tactics:* understanding and acceptance,
   learning laboratory, counselor-therapist self-disclosure, advice, temporary assumption of responsibility for client, hospitalization

ring the student for other aspects. Table 3 is a description of the
professional competencies of an entry-level counseling psychologist;
that is, the minimum for someone at the highest level of competence.
Counselors who are not licensed and cannot represent themselves as
"psychologists" to the public are not expected to possess all the diagnostic and treatment competencies presented in Table 3.

Student services workers who have the appropriate credentials
and possess all the competencies presented in Table 3 are able to appraise, intervene with, or refer anyone who walks through the door. At
the other end of the continuum are student services workers who need
competencies at least through Number 5 under "Appraisal" but who
probably refer most people who walk through the door. In most student
services settings, an immeasurable service could be provided to large
numbers of students if student services staff would view themselves as
"diagnosticians" whose task it was to carefully appraise a situation and
make an excellent referral. Hence, they should strive to develop appraisal competencies.

Dimensions of Skillful Referral. In order to execute an excellent
referral, the counselor must understand very well the person to be
referred and must, above all, understand the person's purpose—"What
wants or needs to be different?" "In what direction does this person
need/want to move?"

Moreover, the counselor must have developed a personal connection with a network of resources in the community. Firsthand knowledge of and experience with resource people, places, and information are
imperative. If a counselor is new in a community, excellent referral takes
longer; the counselor is less efficient, but it can be done. The position
that a new counselor takes is "Somehow, somewhere in this community
is what we need—we just have to find it!"

A student services counselor can maintain an ongoing relationship with many students as, again and again, the worker is called on to
make a referral based on a thorough knowledge of the student and the
student's situation and purpose.

It would be a very unusual student services counselor who had
sufficient training, experience and/or scheduled time to carry out the
full array of counseling interventions. But it would be difficult to
overstate what a positive difference it could make to a student to know a

Table 3. Professional Competencies Expected of an Entry-Level Counseling Psychologist

A. *Appraisal*

Specific objectives

1. Differentiate among psychotic, neurotic, and characterological patterns of dysfunction

2. Differentiate suicidal and non-suicidal patterns

3. Differentiate between dysfunctional and developmental patterns (between pathology and possibilities)

4. Identify possibility of organic processes; for example, perceptual and motor dysfunction, hormonal imbalance, minimal brain damage, seizures, metabolic disturbance

5. Assess level of anxiety

6. Assess an individual's intellectual ability

7. Assess an individual's vocational interests

8. Assess an individual's situation: what is facilitating and what is blocking the person from accomplishing his or her purposes

9. Evaluate whether or not the individual's goals are compatible in terms of your competence, time

Specific procedures

1. MMPI and other standardized measures of psychological dysfunction; Mental Status Examination; DSM II

2. Predictive indicators of suicide, ability to monitor unstable situation during appraisal period

3. Concepts and indicators of positive mental health, developmental states, personal growth in contrast to pathology, problems, and deviance that are evident in interview

4. Internalized base rates and norms for different ages, sexes, classes, ethnic backgrounds, and so on; observation of person's movement; mental status examination, review of medical and psychological history

5. Interview; standardized tests; consultation with significant others

6. Standardized tests; internalized norms and base rates for various ages, educational levels, ethnic backgrounds; review records and observation of others

7. Standardized vocational interests and aptitude tests; knowledge of occupations and careers; freedom from sex, age, ethnic biases regarding career possibilities; career decision-making model

8. Functional analysis of behavior; setting observation; journal keeping; consultation with other professionals; report of family friends

9. Self-knowledge regarding competence, personal resources, ethical standards, and

Table 3 (continued)

and energy, obligations to supervisors and to other clients, and
your personal ethical code
10. Articulate those presenting situations that are appropriate to
refer rather than accept
11. Delineate an intervention strategy
and an estimated time expectation, as a result of the appraisal
process

moral beliefs; willingness and
ability to accept the limitations
thereby imposed
10. Knowledge of referral sources;
willingness to refer
11. Formulate a working model of
the person; identify the purpose, expectation and/or goals
of intervention; relate the intervention strategy and tactics to
outcomes desired; present the
plan in nontechnical lan-
guage, avoiding jargon

B. *Intervention* (using the array of tactics presented in Table 2.)

Choice: Rational planning and decision making

1. Help an individual gather and organize accurate, relevant information
   necessary in order to develop a career plan (such as ability, interest, aptitude, values, labor market information)
2. Help with resumé preparation
3. Help an individual organize a job search
4. Teach effective job interview skills
5. Develop an array of community contact people who are knowledgeable
   about and willing to discuss various career fields
6. Help an individual gather and organize accurate, relevant information
   necessary in order to develop a plan about a relationship (for example,
   marriage, divorce, leave home, place parent in nursing home)
7. Help an individual gather and sort information necessary to make a difficult, emotion-laden decision (for example, disclose homosexual orientation, abortion, leave career and family, life-style shift, disown a child)

Change: Behavior modification

1. Anxiety reduction techniques; for example, systematic desensitization,
   relaxation training, hypnosis, meditation, yoga, implosion, RET, assertiveness training, guided fantasy
2. Help a person establish a self-modification program to reduce the frequency and/or intensity of certain behaviors; for example, weight gain,
   smoking, social anxiety, procrastinating, unwanted thoughts
3. Help a person establish a self-modification program to increase the frequency and intensity of certain behaviors; for example, studying, exercising, praising a child, encouraging supervisees
4. Help adults use contracting and self-contracting to modify behavior—
   their own and others
5. Teach behavior shaping through contingent positive reinforcement to
   parents and teachers
6. Help a parent and/or teacher develop and implement a contingency
   management program for a child
7. Help individuals acquire new behaviors through modeling, role play,
   behavioral rehearsal, and videotape self-confrontation

Table 3 (continued)

Confusion Reduction: Perceptual and cognitive restructuring

1. Help individuals temporarily organize their shattered, fragmented lives following a structure loss (for example, death, move, job change, divorce)
2. Make appropriate referrals to other professionals: medical, legal, economic, spiritual, educational practitioners
3. Effectively handle your recommendation for hospitalization
4. Decrease polarization among small groups of people (family, faculty)
5. Increase collaboration among a small group of people

Additional Professional Activities

1. Effectively handle reporting of child abuse
2. Evaluate the outcome of individual cases
3. Evaluate the overall impact of your professional efforts
4. Help with monitoring your professional colleagues

student services counselor (1) with whom the student feels very comfortable, (2) by whom the student feels well understood and accepted, (3) in whose information and judgment the student has confidence, and (4) to whom the student is encouraged to return for ongoing consultation.

A Case Example. An example will illustrate how an eclectic framework facilitates the counselor's work and how different counseling strategies using a wide variety of skills and competencies are needed depending on the focus of the counseling purpose: change or confusion reduction. Let us say that a thirty-four-year-old woman and two children walk into a student services office. She states she needs to see a counselor because she has been recently widowed and has to make a living. She speaks in a too-soft, high-pitched voice, makes limited eye contact, and repeatedly tugs at her too-tight skirt while trying to contain a set of very active twins.

If her grief has not been prematurely suppressed and there has been sufficient time to reorganize her life without her husband, then her widowhood may not be a counseling focus. If, however, this major loss has not been dealt with emotionally, socially, economically, and organizationally—whether the relationship was positive or negative or mixed—she will undoubtedly need to focus on what this fragmenting loss means to her and her children. Confusion reduction counseling would likely involve a complete life history interview, including (1) a picture of her abilities, interests, expectations, and values prior to marriage; (2) a history of the marriage and of its strengths and weaknesses; (3) a fantasy projection of her future as she presently regards it—her hopes and fears for her family, her work, and herself; and (4) an assessment of her financial and medical condition. Together, this woman and her counselor would reconstruct her present world to help her (1) understand herself and her situation so that she can speak of it constructively to herself and others and (2) regain a sense of her life as meaningful and worthwhile.

In the event that she has already dealt with the loss of her husband—emotionally, socially, and economically—and has come to the conclusion that she now needs most additional training in order to engage in psychologically and economically rewarding work, then choice counseling is what is needed. Information about her abilities, interests, style, work experience, the local labor market, personal financial resources, educational opportunities, supportive other people, obligations, and so on must be carefully gathered, sorted, and brought to bear on the possibilities open to her. A branching plan, plus tactics for implementing the plan, together with a time schedule would be the likely outcome of rational planning and decision making in this case.

Finally, it is possible that the woman just described is no longer fragmented by her loss when she enters the student services office, and she may also know exactly what education and training she wants and needs to pursue. It may be when this women presents herself she needs three things: (1) coaching on how to manage small children while trying to return to school, (2) study skill building in reading, listening, note taking, test taking, and paper writing, and (3) anxiety reduction for test taking and speaking in class. Obviously, behavior modification is the preferred strategy if these are the woman's circumstances. If fragmentation and existential crisis, characteristic of confusion reduction, are the case, then not only does behavior modification have nothing to say, but trying to speak that dialect also may offend and hurt her. If, however, she needs skill building and neutralizaion of her fears, the last thing that will be helpful is encouraging her to confront the existential aspects of academic skill deficits and being scared to take a test.

The general strategy and pattern of intervention for a particular case vary depending on whether the purpose of counseling is conceptualized as choice, change, or confusion reduction. However, no matter what the purpose of counseling—choice, change, or confusion reduction—some of the same counseling tactics will be used to achieve those different purposes. If a counselor is unaware of, unskilled with, and/or unwilling to refer to someone who is skilled with the three separate intervention strategies (rational planning and decision making, behavior modification, and perceptual and cognitive restructuring), then there is no point in differentiating among the three purposes. If thinking in terms of the three purpose categories does not result in approaching and intervening in different ways, it is difficult to justify the existence of a three-category system to differentiate among counseling purposes.

In order to negotiate an appropriate contract for choice, change, or confusion reduction, counselors need (1) a general working knowledge of people and their situations; (2) skills in establishing a working relationship with people of wide-ranging ages, circumstances, ability levels, value systems, and life-styles; (3) competence with a diverse array of intervention tactics (counseling techniques); and (4) adequate time and energy to carry out the intervention.

To describe the counseling relationship as "contractual" is simply to say that both counselor and student have agreed to do something together; they both know what the "something" is; each one expects to do a significant part and expects the other person will contribute significantly to making something happen. Together they formulate the contract that describes their purpose, and together they continue working to fulfill their contract.

The advantages of viewing the purpose of counseling in terms of a contract that is negotiated between the counselor and the student are:

1. The purpose of counseling becomes the mutual concern of the counselor and the student; both the counselor and the student become responsible for formulating a statement of their purpose in meeting. Stating their mutually agreed-on purpose as a contract to be fulfilled fosters an attitude of joint responsibility for the counseling process selected to fulfill the contract.
2. The purpose of counseling becomes explicit; both the student and the counselor have a clear understanding of why they are meeting and what they can expect of one another. Explicitly stating their mutually agreed-on purpose as a contract to be fulfilled allows and encourages both the counselor and the client to evaluate their progress toward fulfilling the contract.

The contracts that specify how particular students and particular student services counselors collaborate may range as widely as from "You tell me clearly what information you need, student, and I, your student services counselor, will tell you where to go for accurate, relevant information" to "You, student, meet with me regularly, open your entire life—values, beliefs, abilities, interests, circumstances, and so on— and I, your student services counselor, will help you reorganize and restructure your whole world." The individual student services counselor, together with his or her supervisors, must decide on the appropriateness of contracts, taking into account the student's needs and purposes, the student services counselor's competencies and commitments, and the agency's purposes and constraints. It can be exciting and challenging and rewarding, but it is never simple.

Reference

Ullmann, L. P. "From Therapy to Reality." *The Counseling Psychologist,* 1969, *1*(4), 68–69.

June Gallessich   **13**

Consultation

Student services professionals have generally overlooked the possibilities for expanding their impact on students through consultation with other campus organizations. The purpose of this chapter is to develop a rationale for student services staff consultation and to identify and explore related issues and problems. The chapter begins by describing the consultation services that we might offer to faculty, staff, administrators, and student organizations. Next, consultation is defined and differentiated from other forms of service and other professional relationships. The special problems of the "in-house" consultant and their implications for student services professionals' consultation is followed by a description of the crucial consultant skills and suggests methods by which student services professionals can attain these skills. Legitimization, entry, and contractual and ethical issues also are addressed. Underlying the discussions in this chapter is the assumption that the basic responsibility of student services professionals is to provide direct services to students and that consultation should not be regarded as a substitute for these primary functions but rather as an expansion of them.

As our profession develops and we continue to reexamine and redefine our roles and functions, we are discovering new possibilities for serving students through consultation. We are finding that in some cases we can help students most by going beyond the roles of "adjuster," "parent," and counselor to collaborate with the faculty, staff, and administrators who are in continual contact with students and who have profound impact on student welfare and development. We have always acknowledged that the major sources of many student problems are environmental, but our philosophy, knowledge base, and skills have emphasized student adjustment rather than environmental adjustment and change. We might greatly expand our impact if we think in terms of multiple sources of problems and explore a variety of avenues for solutions. The chapters on environmental assessment and redesign describe the processes of searching for the sources of problems and for the loci and the strategies that offer the most promising solutions. In most cases, the origins of problems are complex, and complete solutions are rare. Sometimes the most efficient solutions are traditional direct student services. And in many situations other leverage points may be closed to our intervention overtures. Yet student services staff should carefully assess student needs and, prior to allocating resources, consider the advantages and disadvantages of an array of services, including consultation, to meet these needs.

We have many competencies that can be valuable in helping other campus organizations increase their helpfulness to students. We have a great store of substantive knowledge. We are experts on students. We are knowledgeable in such areas as adolescent development, student and campus characteristics, and student's personal and academic problems. We know how to create, implement, and evaluate programs. We have research skills and are knowledgeable about campus administrative structures, political issues, and on- and off-campus resources for students. We have also learned process skills from our work with students that are useful in consultation—we *are* experts in the helping process. We are experienced in problem solving and conflict management, and we are skilled in organizing and leading student groups. These competencies can enhance our consultation services to student-related organizations.

But consultation offers us more than a means of helping other individuals and organizations serve students more effectively. As a result of collaborative interactions with other staff and faculty, we can gain enriched and expanded perspectives of the campus as a total system, important data for the planning, administering, and implementing of our student services.

Types of Consultation

Consultation objectives and processes vary. Consultation can be a medium through which student services staff help others through case consultation regarding individual student's problems. In case consultation, the major objective is to help the consultee cope more effectively in a specific case; a second objective is to increase the consultee's knowledge and skills for increased competency in future work. For example, an engineering professor may ask the dean of student's office for assistance in understanding and responding to the special needs of a physically handicapped student who is having trouble taking lecture notes and executing laboratory and library assignments. Student services professionals can provide useful information about the needs of handicapped students and about resources that are potentially valuable to both student and the professor. This consultation might also increase the professor's confidence in working with this student and with other students with special problems. Similarly, a resident assistant in a first-year student dormitory may seek guidance from the counseling center staff in working with a homesick, unhappy student who refuses to seek counseling. In the consultative process, the counselor's training and experience can help the young resident assistant understand the troubled student and increase his or her guidance skills. In consultation, the assistant might learn more about adolescent development, peer-counseling techniques, campus-wide resources, and methods for creating a healthful dormitory environment. As a result of consultation, the resident assistant would be better prepared for future work with students.

In either of these situations, consultation regarding individual "cases" may lead to consultation regarding groups of students. The engineering professor may ask for assistance in managing several handicapped students or perhaps in helping foreign students or female students adjust to the departmental demands. The professor may ask other professors in his or her department to join for conferences in which the consultant works with groups of faculty or staff regarding common student concerns. The resident assistant in the situation just described may ask for assistance with other troubled students or in managing entire groups of residents or for information regarding programs, activities, and other resources of interest to students. Subsequently, the dormitory staff might ask for group consultation regarding student problems and development.

Student services professionals also may be asked to consult by providing *systematic information or training* to faculty or other on-campus or off-campus student-concerned groups. I am describing here those workshops, discussion groups, seminars, and so forth that are held not for students but for those who serve students, such as student leaders, faculty, and staff. Workshops and informal seminars led by student services professionals can contribute to the effectiveness of these groups.

We may have opportunities to present seminars or workshops for departmental faculty, campus community religious organizations, heads of student organizations, or to the staff of YMCA or foreign students' centers. The content might be drawn from numerous areas, such as needs of special groups of students, the "senior syndrome," stages in student development, optimal conditions for growth, indexes of poor mental health, how to interview troubled students, changing student mores, and campus community resources.

The extensive experience of student services staff in planning, implementing and evaluating their own programs is especially valuable in another indirect service—*program consultation*. This service is different from student services program development activities, in which we work within our own organization to plan and staff various programs. Leaders of a student society may want help, for example, in surveying its members' needs or in designing, implementing, and evaluating programs to meet identified needs. Similarly, a dormitory staff may want help in developing recreational programs for their residents. Departmental faculty may ask for help in planning a career-advising program. A graduate school may want help in planning activities to include spouses as a means of alleviating student marital tensions related to graduate school enrollment. Some student services professionals have extensive expertise not only in evaluation but also in research and can help other campus groups design methods for gathering and analyzing data to answer important questions.

Yet another consultative service is *organization consultation*—working with groups and organizations with the objective of improving their functioning. The focus of the consultation may be on processes such as leadership, team development, conflict management, goal setting, or decision making or on organizational objectives, structure, and roles. Organizational consultation may be requested by the governing bodies of such organizations as a cooperative housing council, a fraternity, the student senate, a minority students' association, or the Young Democrats or Republicans club.

On some campuses, student services professionals may at times be asked to service at an even more abstract level through *policy consultation*. Our opinions may be sought by administrators of various campus organizations in formulating or revising policies affecting students. For example, the executive committee of an academic department may consult with the dean of students' office regarding the creation of a policy regarding cases of academic dishonesty. A Panhellenic group may want to discuss membership and discipline policies with this office. An academic dean may seek input from the student dean in regard to proposed changes in academic and job workload limits. An official may want consultation with student services staff in regard to setting curfew hours or restricting student organizations from using certain areas for meetings or changing policies to favor disadvantaged groups. A Dad's or Mom's club may want us to help formulate criteria for scholarship awards.

Definitions of Consultation

These examples illustrate some of the consultative activities in which student services professionals might be involved. These diverse services share several generic characteristics that distinguish them from our other services. All are *indirect* ways of serving students. Although the ultimate objective of consultation, as in all student services, is to foster students' development, in the consultant role the student services professional does not work directly with students but through consultees, other professionals, or members of campus groups. Thus, the student services consultant interacts with faculty, staff, and student leaders with the objective of increasing their effectiveness with students.

The consultative relationships described are quite different from other work relationships. Unlike administration or supervisory relationships, in which one person has authority over the work of the other, the *consultant and consultee relate as coequals,* and the consultee's participation is voluntary. Although either the consultee or consultant may initiate the relationship, the consultee retains the right to reject the consultant's ideas and may terminate the relationship at any time. Furthermore, *the responsibility for decision making and implementation belongs to the consultee.* The consultant cannot require disclosure of information and does not evaluate the consultee's work. Consultation appears similar in some ways to teaching and indeed often includes explicit education objectives, but the material covered in consultation is either information specifically requested by the consultee or information that the consultant thinks might be relevant and useful in the consultee's situation. The consultant does not, of course, evaluate the consultee's learning. Consultation differs from counseling in that the *focus is limited to the consultee's work situation.* Problems of personal life are outside the boundaries of consultation. The focus may be on a number of levels from individuals to groups, programs, organizations, and policy.

"In-House" Consultation Issues

So far, these definitions of consultation are compatible with our other roles and functions. But in some ways, consultative involvements create special conflicts for us. Typically a consultant is not an ongoing member of the consultee's organization but is externally based and assumes a neutral stance in intraorganizational conflicts. The student services consultant, however, is internal or "in-house," an integral part of the consultee's system. Furthermore, internal consultants are members of a particular subsystem with values and priorities that may, at times, conflict with those of other subsystems. These memberships greatly complicate the consultative process and in several important ways are likely to affect the quality of services.

The perceptions of the internal student services consultant are probably more constricted or system-bound than those of external consultants. Although the internal consultant's background may provide extensive, valuable information related to consultee concerns, his or her system membership imposes perceptual limitations similar to those of the consultee. The student services consultant therefore lacks the objectivity that only physical, psychological, and social distance can bring and may not be able to serve the important function of bringing to consultees a fresh, objective viewpoint on their system in time and space.

Secondly, as a member of a particular subsystem of the university, the student services consultant views campus phenomena from a particular perspective. Student services professionals are trained and employed to serve students; a student-oriented perspective, as opposed to academic or general administrative orientations, pervades our values, attitudes, and behaviors. When consulting with other components within the university, we appropriately view problems in terms of student needs, while consultees often have greater concerns for maintaining standards associated with their particular sectors. Thus, all student services consultation inherently contains potential for conflict. The assumption of the consultant neutrality does not hold in these situations. The extensive implications of this subgroup membership for values conflicts in intracampus consultation are little understood and confuse both consultants and consultees. For example, in consulting over problems of a failing student, the academic constituency might place the highest value on preserving performance standards while the student services person will likely place the highest priority on the student's needs for growth and for educational opportunities. Regarding student violations of rules, the administrative consultee may be most concerned with upholding regulations, while the student services person probably places the highest priority on the student's need for growth and for educational opportunities. The administrative consultee may be most concerned with upholding regulations, while the student services consultant is most concerned with student welfare and development. Even in consultation with other student services organizations, a student services consultant discovers conflicting priorities. The efficient management of student resident halls is at times incompatible with certain student needs, such as for self-expression and self-government.

Consulting in these conflict situations has the potential for all concerned to gain more comprehensive views of problems and for the generation of solutions in which diverse needs are integrated. But differences in perspectives and priorities can lead to tensions. The student services consultant must be alert to this problem and must be prepared to make difficult decisions as to his or her priorities. A choice must be made between student or consultee needs. In some cases, the student services professional may decide to abandon the consultative role and to become a student advocate. In other cases, the prospect of long-term gains for students through consultation may persuade the student services person to continue to work within the bounds of the consultant role. In either case, an especially sensitive issue will be confidentiality. One of the major characteristics of consultation is the confidentiality of all information emanating from the client organization. For ethical reasons, consultees should, of course, be informed of any conflicts that might bias the consultant's perceptions and input. Once an advocacy position is taken, the relationship becomes adversarial rather than collaborative, and it is usually difficult to reestablish the trust needed in consultation. Decisions related to value conflicts within consultative relationships are crucial and should be carefully considered by the entire student services staff involved. Hopefully, as student services professionals increase their contact with other campus organizations, the different values, perceptions, and needs will be better understood. The increased information may facilitate more satisfactory compromises or integrative solutions that incorporate the needs of all constituencies.

Finally, consultants ideally are economically, socially, and emotionally independent of the consultee system and may take risks that their consultees cannot. But, because the student services consultants receive their income from the university and, in addition, are embedded in the university's social system, they may feel restricted in speech and actions. Service to consultees may be limited to those issues that do not threaten social and professional relationships and job security.

Complications related to the in-house consultant's role conflicts can be reduced by early, frank acknowledgment of their existence and by thoughtfully confronting and working through issues. Student services professionals *can* minimize the biases related to their system membership by periodically bringing in external consultants and by increasing their competencies in some of the areas described later in this chapter. Moreover, not all of the effects of the in-house status of the consultant are negative. Consultees benefit from the student services consultant's in-depth knowledge of the campus and continuity of commitment.

Critical Consultation Skills

We can greatly increase our effectiveness as consultants by developing competencies that were not included in our traditionally oriented training programs. First we need to broaden the framework we use to formulate problems. We tend to perceive campus phenomena from a limited perspective, consistent with our training, experience, and skills. We are likely to see problems in terms of student adjustment, developmental problems, or deficits, and we may view the external sources of problems as beyond our influence. If we wish to collaborate with other campus agencies, we must understand from a systems view the complex and interacting variables affecting student life. This approach can help us identify general issues and relationships among variables that are not apparent from one domain or from a situation-specific perspective. Temporal patterns can be observed that are useful in understanding sources of current problems and in predicting long-range problems. The systems approach can help us interpret the reciprocal interplay of campus and community forces.

Two examples of common referrals will illustrate the systems approach to understanding problems of students. A faculty member contacts a counseling center staff member regarding the failing performance of several minority first-year students. The professor expects to refer these students to the reading and study clinic for what are perceived to be student deficits. Instead of stopping with this definition, we could collaborate with the professor to study the situation in a more systemic way, to discover contextual forces that might be contributing to the failures. For example, we might help the faculty member understand the students' backgrounds and goals and their reasons for enrollment in college. We would want to identify not only academic pressures on these students but also social and financial stresses. Also, pressures on faculty might be relevant. The background of this particular faculty member could be of importance. We would want to use a systems approach to help the professor integrate and interpret information gathered from these and other domains.

Similarly, when a sorority officer contacts a student dean about several pledges drinking heavily, the dean might suggest that the students be referred for discipline and/or counseling, assuming that the primary sources of the problem are individual and psychological. But, from a systems approach, the presented "problems" could be examined in relation to a number of factors. Of interest might be the society's history and goals, orientation activities and socialization processes, leadership, formal and informal bases of influence, communications patterns, governance rules, and campus forces outside the sorority itself that affect members' behaviors. Thus, to be maximally helpful in consultation with other organizations, we need first to be able to go beyond our usual perspectives to comprehend problems from their viewpoints and from a "gestalt."

Therefore, we need to add to our competencies knowledge of social systems and of organizational processes such as communications, conflict, and decision making. We need to understand the bases, uses, and implications of formal and informal power. We need to be aware of the campus cultural and educational history and of the trends affecting life on campuses today and those which will be salient tomorrow. We need knowledge of the local, state, and national forces affecting campus life. We need to learn how to organize and interpret large quantities of information in systemic ways.

Student services professionals can learn broader concepts for assessing student concerns from a variety of courses available on most campuses. Courses related to social systems, general systems theory, organizational sociology, and organizational psychology are found in many management, educational administration, sociology, social psychology, and government departments. Independent study through readings in books and journal articles can supply the needed background (see, for example, Buckley, 1968; Demone and Harshbarger, 1974; Hall, 1972; Hasenfeld and English, 1975; Katz and Kahn, 1978; Miller and Rice, 1967; Perrow, 1970).

Another barrier to expanding our roles comes from our limited *intervention concepts and strategies,* which, of course, complement our traditional diagnostic framework. A systems approach to understanding student problems is of little value if we are unable to think in terms of systems change; we need a conceptual framework for interventions that includes an array of possibilities, strategies not only for changing students but also for changing some of the organizational behaviors that have harmful consequences for students. For example, in our example of the failing minority students, the most likely diagnosis might be student "maladjustment" or "deficit," and this diagnosis is probably an accurate, although partial, explanation of the problem. Given our usual orientation to intervention, we would likely decide that the remedy should be individual counseling or tutoring. Given a systems interpretation, we might still want to provide direct remedial services to these particular students; in addition, we would open up a wide range of interventions for consideration, emanating from a careful review of problem sources. We might want to suggest that university recruitment activities at high schools from which these and similar students come be monitored to ensure that realistic information is provided to prospective students. Or we might help faculty establish summer tutorial programs for incoming students with weak academic backgrounds or might consult with faculty regarding curricular modifications for the first semester for disadvantaged students. Or we might intervene to reduce the social shock and isolation often experienced by minority students. We could, for example, work with minority student leaders to establish networks of advanced students to contact entering first-year students prior to their arrival on campus in order to arrange needed social support.

A systems diagnosis of the drinking problem example could also extend the number of viable interventions. Case consultation with sorority officers and advisers regarding the individuals involved and the organization as a whole might increase our understanding of problem sources and of structural methods for remediation or prevention. Leaders of social organizations might be interested in special programs led by student services professionals to provide information as to adolescent development, indexes of serious problems, skills in guiding students, and resources for referrals. Or student services staffs could help social organizations develop their own programs to better prepare officers to facilitate their members' social and emotional development.

It is easier to find resources for diagnosis of systems than for extending our intervention skills. Most of our training programs and publications stress direct services. Some campuses, however, have courses in consultation theory and process and include supervised field placements in which graduate students practice case and/or organizational consultation in human service agencies. The National Training Laboratories (1979) offer workshops in consultation and organization development. National, state, and regional professional organizations such as the American Personnel and Guidance Association, the Americal Psychological Association, and the Association of College Unions International frequently schedule workshops on consultation and other interventions at their conventions. Student services staff can also arrange for their own inservice training in different types of interventions.

Readings can help student services professionals extend their conceptual framework for interventions. A number of writers have compared the theoretical bases of contrasting intervention strategies (Blake and Mouton, 1976; Caplan, 1970; Chin ar d Benne, 1968; Crowfoot and Chesler, 1974; Hornstein and others, 1971). Other writers describe the application and underlying concepts of singular intervention approaches (Argyris, 1970; Beckhard, 1969; Beisser and Green, 1972; Merry and Allerhand, 1977; Schein, 1969; Walton, 1969).

In addition to a systems approach to diagnosis and intervention, we need to increase our competencies in building and maintaining cooperative relationships with peers. Student services staff have high levels of skills in traditional vertical helping relationships. The interpersonal skills required for consultation are not, for most of us, easy to learn and apply. We are accustomed to working from an authority position, based on our office, our status, on our control of information and sanctions, and on our age and experience. As consultants, we cannot be successful if we are parental or judgmental. We must shift from an expert role to an egalitarian one; this shift from vertical to horizontal positions often involves difficult unlearning. It is usually easier to work from an expert role and in controlling positions. The collaborative skills cannot, like the competencies described in the preceding sections, be acquired through readings, attending seminars, or brief workshops. The well-learned advice giving, directive behaviors tend to persist. Laboratory training and supervised experiences in ongoing consultation activities are most helpful in establishing and supporting the needed changes in our behaviors.

A fourth area of competency needed for successful consultation is that of evaluation (see Chapter Ten). When we serve students directly, we have simple measures for at least rudimentary evaluations of our impact, such as the number of students using our services, their follow-up ratings of our services, persistence in school of students with whom we work, and the number of new programs we offer. Consultative impact, although it may be more extensive than direct services numbers of students affected and in significance of influence, is more difficult to measure. We need to have on our staffs professionals who have the critical skills for accountability through evaluation of services.

Home-Base Support

Finally, even if student services professionals have skill and knowledge in systems concepts and a wide range of intervention skills, they are unlikely to be successful in sustained consultation efforts without a strong support system. Consultation requires a shift from the security of our offices and of our traditional modes of operation to settings and services that are less familiar and in which we have little control. We risk rejection and failure. Even when we are highly successful, we do not receive the immediate gratification that comes from direct service roles. Rewards in consultation are more remote not only in terms of space but also in terms of time; they are usually vicarious and long-term, at best. Consultation is often intellectually stimulating but emotionally draining, so consultants need emotional support. They also need conceptual support from peers who can join in discussing systems analyses and in critiquing consultation processes and underlying assumptions. Would-be consultants also need time allocated to pursue consultation. The home base—the student services staff—must decide whether or not consultation will be an integral part of the service delivery program. If the decision is made to move in this direction, there must be a corresponding commitment in terms of incentives, guidance, encouragement, and training of professionals involved.

Student services staffs that decide to offer consultative services may want to obtain the needed knowledge and skills by arranging their own inservice consultation training. Curricular topics and methods of preservice consultation training for doctoral-level professional psychologists have been described (Gallessich, 1974). A five-step training sequence for in-service consultation training for master's-level school counselors was reported by Gallessich and Ladogana (1978) and is derived from evaluations of pilot programs. A study guide for mental health consultants suggests activities and readings for self-directed training (Beisser and Green, 1972) that are relevant for student services professionals.

Legitimization Issues

Attaining critical skills and home-base support does not ensure student services professionals of consultation opportunities. Sanction for the consultation role must come from consultees and is not as readily earned as sanctions for student support services. Obtaining credibility for "in-house" consultation is especially difficult. Student services professionals are much more likely to be recognized and used as consultants on other campuses than on their own. Part of the legitimization difficulty comes from the interagency tensions described earlier. Each agency promotes its own unique values and is alert to conflicts of interests with other groups. Competitive, territorial attitudes may block cooperative efforts. Therefore, student services' consultative overtures may be regarded with suspicion. Status barriers present another set of problems. Academicians on some campuses prefer to discuss problems only with other academicians. Given the realities of campus politics, the first sanction for consultation is most likely to come from other service organizations or from student organizations rather than from the academic sector.

Even the "external" professional is not always granted immediate sanction as a consultant but must demonstrate usefulness and trustworthiness in other roles first. Gerald Caplan (1970), an eminent mental health consultation theorist, trainer, and practitioner, observed that legitimization of consultative roles typically occurs in stages. In the first stage, consultants work in traditional referral or liaison roles and, with their agencies, provide direct assistance to individuals whom consultees refer for services. Later comes the role of staff educator; still later, the consultant is trusted with "cases," then with programs, and finally with organizational and administrative concerns. Legitimization in consultant roles, according to this view, does not occur until acceptance in familiar direct service roles is established.

Student services professionals who wish to extend their services across campus but find themselves blocked by lack of sanction or credibility may find Caplan's notion of sequential steps of legitimization helpful. Rather than seeking entry in campus agencies as consultants in the more advanced stages described by Caplan, we need first to review our performance in traditional roles. If we are not successful and visible in direct student services and as resources for referrals from other campus professionals, our capacities for helping other people solve their student-related problems will be suspect. From a secure base of effective services such as information, guidance and counseling, and programming, we can begin to initiate contacts to explore the possibilities of helping members of other services and departments solve student problems.

Consultation Entry

On-campus consultation by student services professionals should always be conducted under staff aegis. There should be weekly opportunities for consultants to discuss their work with other student services staff members to ensure careful review of activities and to ensure that consultation remains a staff commitment rather than an individual one. Individual consultation services should be carefully coordinated. Team approaches are preferable to individual consultation and increase the consultative information base, objectivity, and psychological support.

"Entry" into the various campus organizations should be the culmination of extensive student services staff planning and clarification of consultation goals and priorities. Background information should be gathered about potential consultee agencies, including their goals and operations, current issues and problems, and past and present use of student services. Newspapers, journals, university documents, and the experiences of long-term, senior staff members can supply helpful background material. The appropriate contact person, the organizational "gatekeeper," should be identified and an appointment made for specified purposes and times. A preinterview letter confirming the appointment and objectives is helpful.

Establishment and maintenance of rapport is critical to the effectiveness of consultation. The consultant is, in a sense, a guest in a "foreign land" and must be especially sensitive to the host organization's norms and procedures. The consultant should be punctual and reliable in keeping appointments and must observe organizational protocol. The consultant's behaviors as well as verbal statements give consultees cues on what to expect from the relationship. The collaborative dimension that is basic to consultation should be clearly communicated in words and in behavior; consultees often misunderstand this aspect of consultation. Ideally, consultative interviews are highly collaborative and interactive.

Consultant and consultee should participate in setting the agenda for each interview. In initial conferences, information exchange is the major task. The following are typical topics in preliminary phases of consultation:

1. *Objectives of the interview*
   a. The consultant acquaints consultees with the various services available from student services. A brief overview might be accompanied by illustrations of services that might be least known and that might be useful in this particular organization.
   b. The consultant explores (1) the extent to which student services, and consultation services in particular, might be useful to the consultee organization and (2) the extent to which the consultee organization is interested in these services. The consultant needs to get some notion of the concerns of the consultee organization and the support within the organization for a consultative approach to problem solving. The consultant needs to identify any people who, in addition to the "gatekeeper," should be contacted before decisions are made on the use of student services consultation.
2. *Definitions of the consultation role and relationship.* The consultant describes major dimensions of consultation such as (a) an indirect service to students, (b) focus on helping consultees solve work-related problems, (c) a collaborative relationship between consultant and consultee, and (d) any special commitments of the consultant that might either enhance or interfere with the consultee organization's goals.
3. *The consultant's background of training and experience and qualifications for consultation with the consultee agency.* If the organizational gatekeeper is seriously interested in consultation, it will need information on the consultant's professional qualifications, training, and experiences relevant for consultation.

The information exchange phase may be concluded in a few minutes, or it may require several interviews. If at the end of this preliminary stage both consultant and consultee are interested in consultation, a second phase of the entry process begins. During this period, consultee concerns are extensively explored. Potential consultative services are more thoroughly elaborated. Various ways of fitting services to consultee needs are discussed. Successful progress through this phase culminates in a contract, an informal agreement for consultative services.

Contracting for Consultation

Many consultants fail to explicate the consultation "contract." Consequently, both consultant and consultee are uncertain as to the exact objectives and boundaries of the relationship. If the objectives and methods of the consultation and the responsibilities of both parties are not clearly defined, all concerned are likely to be confused and dissatisfied. Furthermore, in the absence of specified goals the impact of consultation cannot be evaluated. This problem is associated with the general failure of human service organizations to clarify goals and priorities and the bases on which decisions are made (Hasenfeld and English, 1975; Demone and Harshbarger, 1974). Some of the consultation dimensions on which explicit agreement is needed are the following:

1. *A definition of the consultee's problem or concern to be addressed through consultation*
2. *Clearly stated objectives.* An objective, for example, might be for the consultee to help a single student "survive" the first year of college. The objective might be to increase the skills of a group of resident assistants in leading fall orientation activities. The objective might be to help leaders of a social organization work together more effectively or to help administrators determine the consequences of current policies regarding student workload and course load limits. An objective might be to help minority students organize or to provide information on the needs of older students to department heads.
3. *Strategies to be used in consultation.* The strategies selected to reach the consultation objectives are stated, including procedures and expected outcomes. Any anticipated risks should be clarified.
4. *Criteria and methods for evaluating consultation.* Criteria and methods for evaluating the impact of a consultative service should be specified. In addition to a final evaluation, it is often helpful to set a date for a midpoint review and evaluation with the possibility of renegotiating the consultation contract.

5. *The identity of the consultees, the people who are to work with the consultant*
6. *The commitment of consultant and consultee in terms of duration of contract and time to be allocated weekly*
7. *The responsibilities of each party in implementation and evaluation of services*
8. *The location for consultation activities*
9. *Conditions and limitations of confidentiality*

Contracting is usually a continuous process because objectives and strategies may change as the data base generated from consultation increases. The consultant is responsible for the explication and maintenance of a feasible, ethical contract. Consultants should not accept contractual conditions that appear to be inappropriate or contradictory to the organizational goals and interests.

Ethical Issues

Ethical problems are inevitable in consultation practice. Even with knowledgeable and careful planning, all contingencies and issues cannot be anticipated. Often the surface concerns first encountered in consultation obscure deeper organizational problems. However, ethical dilemmas can be greatly reduced by awareness of common pitfalls and by continual surveillance for potentially sensitive situations. Professional codes provide helpful guidance to consultants. Probably the best single means of preventing ethical problems is to exercise great care in contractual deliberations discussed earlier in this chapter. The consultant should be sure not only that contractual terms and implications are clear to the administrators involved in contract agreements but also that this information is known to all consultees who are involved in consultation activities. The consultant should be certain that his or her behavior is congruent with the contract. Regular monitoring of consultation services through discussions with consultees should prevent serious ethical problems from arising.

One common ethical blunder occurs when the consultant goes beyond the boundaries of the consultation agreement. Consultants frequently experience pressures to become involved in organizational problems and processes that are not within the contractual boundaries. For example, a student services professional may be asked to lead a workshop on leadership skills for officers of a campus student organization. In the workshop discussions, two consultees become involved in an angry dispute and ask the consultant to intervene. Ethically, the consultant cannot comply with this request, for it involves intrastaff conflicts outside the agreed focus of consultation. Contractual changes should be made only through careful review with the organizational gatekeeper.

Another ethical problem arises when a consultant undertakes services for which he or she lacks adequate training and experience. Consultees are often unaware of the different specialty areas and levels of competency of student services professionals, and they may ask for services—workshop leadership, diagnosis of problems, or program expertise—from a staff member who lacks the appropriate qualifications. The consultant who agrees to provide services for which he or she lacks proper training and experience commits a serious ethical error.

Breaches of confidentiality sometimes occur in consultation, usually because of consultant ignorance of the confidential nature of the material or from carelessness. In one case, a consultant may divulge confidential information about one individual or subgroup to another individual or subgroup within an organization. In another case, a consultant may disclose client organizational problems to external individuals or groups. In either case, these confidentiality breaches could have disastrous consequences for the client organization.

Sometimes consultants unwittingly collaborate with administrators in exploitative processes. For example, an administrator may ask a student services consultant for his or her opinion of a staff member with whom the consultant has been working to develop a special program. Answering this question violates the confidentiality of the consultation relationship. In another situation, an administrator may request a consultant to join him or her and his or her staff in an "open" discussion of staff problems. The consultant, simply through his or her presence, or by explicit encouragement, may foster staff candor. In this situation of assumed safety, staff members may expose feelings or problems that might subsequently be used in administrative evaluations. The consultant is responsible for informing consultees of potential risks in consultation-related activities and for helping consultees monitor their disclosures.

References

Argyris, C. *Intervention Theory and Method*. Reading, Mass.: Addison-Wesley, 1970.

Beckhard, R. *Strategies for Organization Development*. Reading, Mass.: Addison-Wesley, 1969.

Beisser, A., and Green, R. *Mental Health Consultation and Education*. Palo Alto, Calif.: National Press, 1972.

Blake, R., and Mouton, J. *Consultation*. Reading, Mass.: Addison-Wesley, 1976.

Buckley, W. (Ed.). *Modern Systems Research for the Behavioral Scientist.* Chicago: Aldine, 1968.

Caplan, G. *The Theory and Practice of Mental Health Consultation.* New York: Basic Books, 1970.

Chin, R., and Benne, K. D. "General Strategies for Effecting Changes in Human Systems." In W. G. Bennis, K. D. Benne, and R. Chin (Eds.), *The Planning of Change.* New York: Holt, Rinehart and Winston, 1968.

Crowfoot, J., and Chesler, M. "Contemporary Perspectives on Planned Social Change: A Comparison." *Journal of Applied Behavioral Science,* 1974, *10*(3), 278–303.

Demone, H. W., and Harshbarger, D. (Eds.) *A Handbook of Human Service Organizations.* New York: Behavioral Publications, 1974.

Gallessich, J. "Training the School Psychologist for Consultation." *Journal of School Psychology,* 1974, *12*(2), 138–149.

Gallessich, J., and Ladogana, A. "Consultation Training Program for School Counselors." *Counselor Education and Supervision,* 1978, *18* (2), 100–108.

Hall, R. H. *Organizations, Structure and Process.* Englewood Cliffs, N. J.: Prentice-Hall, 1972.

Hasenfeld, Y., and English, R. A. (Eds.). *Human Service Organizations.* Ann Arbor: University of Michigan Press, 1975.

Hornstein, H. A., and others. (Eds.). *Social Intervention.* New York: Free Press, 1971.

Katz, D., and Kahn, R. L. *The Social Psychology of Organizations.* (2nd Ed.) New York: Wiley, 1978.

Merry, U., and Allerhand, M. E. *Developing Teams and Organizations.* Reading, Mass.: Addison-Wesley, 1977.

Miller, E. J., and Rice, A. K. *Systems of Organization.* London: Tavistock, 1967.

National Training Laboratories Institute. *1979 NTL Programs.* Rosslyn Station, Arlington, Va.: National Training Laboratories Institute, 1979.

Perrow, C. *Organizational Analysis: A Sociological View.* Belmont, Calif.: Brooks/Cole, 1970.

Schein, E. *Process Consultation.* Reading, Mass.: Addison-Wesley, 1969.

Walton, R. E. *Interpersonal Peacemaking: Confrontations and Third Party Consultation.* Reading, Mass.: Addison-Wesley, 1969.

Weston H. Morrill **14**

Program Development

A college has created day-long workshops to help students assess their personal goals and present roles and to develop realistic short-term objectives related to their long-term priorities. The workshops are held in residence halls, with psychology graduate students as group leaders. But the overall response to the workshops is small—only nineteen students participate, despite announcements in the campus newspaper and in the residence halls. The workshops are judged successful in meeting their basic objectives with the few students who attend. But should the workshops be repeated or changed so recruitment is more successful?

  At another institution, through newspaper and class announcements, students have been invited to participate in group sessions of systematic desensitization plus directive counseling to overcome test anxiety. Thirty-two students express interest in the program, but only ten eventually participate. With them, the program effectively reduces

Note: The projects, directed by Weston H. Morrill at Colorado State University, were completed under Grant No. 1 RO1 MU 18007 of the National Institute of Mental Health.

measured anxiety and increases their grade-point averages. But how can staff time be better used to meet this evidently infrequent but nonetheless serious need among students?

At another university, a program has been implemented to help new commuting students become active in the university community and avoid feeling like alienated, second-class citizens. Groups of students have met to discuss the problems they are confronting and to work out solutions, but the program has not been able to change their self-depreciating attitudes and behavior. Can other attempts solve the problem?

On another campus, a "study skills circus" is held, based on the observation that the typical student's life is like a three-ring circus of study, occupation, and family or social life. Sessions with circus-like names are held over a two-day period by counselors and faculty on ways students can develop consistently rewarding study strategies, and the sessions result in significantly higher grades and increases in the amount of academic work students complete. But a program involving parallel series of achievement training groups, designed to help students economize on time and effort in organizing their work and play activities for the greatest payoff in grades, fails to produce effects different from a control group that receives no training. Why the difference?

These five programs illustrate ways that student services administrators are trying to make the best use possible of available resources despite limited staff. Program development is an approach designed to respond to this crunch by maximizing the potential impact of professionals. Programs are planned, structured learning experiences designed to meet the needs of students. These needs may be remedial, developmental, or even preventative in nature, and interventions planned to meet these needs may be aimed at both individuals and environments (Morrill and Hurst, 1971).

It is becoming increasingly apparent that we can no longer afford the luxury or the potential ineffectiveness either of designing programs that meet low-priority or nonexistent needs or of dealing with all student needs on an individual basis. Many authors suggest that there are common developmental experiences from which most students could benefit. These can be provided more economically, efficiently, and perhaps more effectively by designing programs for groups of students rather than for individuals. Drum and Figler (1973, p. 56) suggest that we can "develop programs which anticipate the developmental tasks of . . . . students. By making these programs available to correspond with the students' *teachable moments*, the counselors can find it easier to intervene in the lives of their students."

Drum and Figler (1973, p. 41) indicate that programs can be characterized by (1) a focus on groups of students; (2) an attempt to isolate and center on a particular developmental need; (3) an explicit structure indicating the length of the program, sequence of topics, and the need being fulfilled; and (4) an advertising and marketing plan for the program that sufficiently motivates the target group to participate. A fifth area should be added: a plan to carefully evaluate the program to determine if and how well it is meeting its objectives. Lewis and Lewis (1977, pp. 11-12) raise these provocative questions relevant to the design of such interventions:

1. To what extent is the individual capable of resolving the issue through personal change?
2. What resources in the environment are available to help the individual grow?
3. To what extent does the solution really rest in the environment instead of the individual?
4. How can the counselor and/or the counselee act to bring about the necessary changes in the environment?

This chapter focuses on the development of programs designed to enhance individuals in those situations in which it is determined that issues can either be resolved through personal change (Question 1) or through the use of resources (Questions 2-4). By using a systematic behavior change approach, it is possible to anticipate in a program, some of the developmental needs of students and to do so in a way that provides information that can be used to make decisions regarding the utility, maintenance, or elimination of the programs.

Moore and Delworth (1976) present a systematic approach for program development that consists of several stages. Each stage concentrates on a different aspect of program development, with one stage leading to the next. This approach results in a program that has been carefully planned to ensure that it is needed, has specific objectives that can be monitored to determine if desirable results are achieved, and on which data for decisions about continuation or modification are available. Table 1 presents an outline of a program development model, adapted from Moore and Delworth. The following sections discuss each stage and task in detail.

Stage I: Initiating the Program

There are six steps to take in initiating the program. The steps are generally consecutive, but planners often find that they are working on two steps at once or moving back to rethink an earlier step in light of their work on subsequent steps.

Table 1. A Program Development Model

Stage I: Initiating the Program

Step 1. *The germinal idea.* The idea for the content area of a program is identified. (This may come from the subjective experience of a need by a professional, a request by a member of a target population, or from a more formal ecomapping assessment.

Step 2. *The initial planning team.* A small group of people interested in or concerned about the idea being considered are brought together to begin the initial planning.

Step 3. *Assessment: Needs and resources.* This stage involves collecting data regarding the need for programs, searching the literature for research and program data, and identifying resources available in the environment.

Step 4. *Identifying alternative program targets and purposes.* This is a process to stimulate alternatives through a type of brainstorming.

Step 5. *Program selection.* After considering the assessment data and the identified alternatives, a program direction is selected.

Step. 6. *Development of a full planning team.* Once a direction is identified, the planning team is expanded to include other individuals.

Stage II: Planning Program Objectives, Delivery System, and Evaluation Methods

Step 1. *Selecting program goals and specifying behavioral objectives.* The goals of the program are stated explicitly and the specific behavior change objectives specified.

Step 2. *Development of the training methods on delivery system.* This step involves planning the training procedures and tasks that the planning team thinks will best achieve the program objectives with the available resources.

Step 3. *Planning the method of intervention.* Based on the planning in Step 2, the planning team must determine who will deliver the training and how the training will be offered.

Step 4. *Planning for program evaluation.* This step involves developing the evaluation instruments, methodology, and design to determine if the program meets its objectives.

Step 5. *Preparation for pilot test.* This step deals with the detailed planning necessary for conducting a pilot program.

Stage III. The Presentation and Evaluation of a Pilot Program

Step 1. *Program publicity.* This task involves acquainting potential consumers of the program with the pilot program.

Step 2. *Implementation of pilot program.* This step involves carrying out the selection of participants and offering the program.

Step 3. *Assessment of evaluation data and decisions about program future.* Based on the subjective feedback and objective data about the effects of the pilot program, decisions about the future of the program are made.

Table 1 (continued)

Stage IV: Program Refinement

Step 1. *Refine training procedures and materials.* Based on feedback data from pilot, the training materials and procedures need to be reviewed and refined.

Step 2. *Planning for continued evaluation.* Continued evaluation is necessary because of changing conditions and circumstances.

Step 3. *Training of trainers.* Many mature programs may use peers, volunteers, paraprofessionals, or allied professionals as trainers. A process for selecting and training these individuals is needed.

Step 4. *Offering program on a regular basis.* Continuing the program with the target population and conducting an ongoing evaluation of the program's needs, effectiveness, resources, and priorities.

Source: Adapted from Moore and Delworth (1972, 1976).

Step 1. The Germinal Idea. The idea for a program can come from many sources. An idea may emerge from the subjective experience of a need by professionals based on contacts with many people over a long period of time, or it may be generated through a formal assessment of needs of served populations. An idea may begin as a request by students, faculty, or administrators for programs in a particular area. Drum and Figler (1973) and Glidewell (1971) suggest the importance of programs that anticipate the developmental tasks that students face. Lewis and Lewis (1977) recognize the existence of common crises that are particularly stressful for people and around which programs could be developed. Ideas for programs could come from any of these sources. Following the steps of this program development model provides the means for translating the germinal idea into productive programs. Too often, programs have been developed because professionals had an interest and/or skill repertoire in a particular area but had not assessed the needs or priorities of the target populations with whom they worked. An idea resulting from the interests of a staff member can be the basis for a valid program. The important consideration, however, must be the needs of the populations served, not the interests and "hobbies" of the professionals. Drum and Figler (1973, p. 121) suggest three sources of information that can be used to establish an accurate hierarchy of problems for a given institution: (1) the students themselves; (2) important others, such as faculty members, lay helpers, natural student advocates, and parents; and (3) past records about students. Likewise, a Western Interstate Commission for Higher Education (1972, p. 6) publication on consultation indicates that "any mental health problem on campus must first be felt or sensed by an individual or a group. Mental health facilities need to develop sensors that will detect needs. In many instances, the sensor will be an individual. Paraprofessionals working in programs out and around the campus are generally excellent sensors of concerns and conditions that affect life on campus. Students visiting facilities provide important sensory input. Campus publications and ad hoc activities also serve as sensors for the detection of needs. There are a multitude of people and events which serve as sensors. It is important for the consultative process to use information consciously to detect needs and identify trends while individuals, groups, institutions, and community interact."

Step 2. The Initial Planning Team. Once an idea has been identified that seems to have potential for program development, a small group of people who have interest in or concern for the area of program interest are brought together to begin the initial planning. For a number of reasons, a team approach is recommended rather than a single individual working alone. A team can represent a number of viewpoints and stimulate more creative solutions. People affected by an idea, who thus are in a position to support ideas they help create rather than to resist ones that are thrust on them, can be included on a team. And a team can bring together a number of individuals with different competencies and skills needed in the program development process. For example, to stimulate career exploration in the residence hall, students could include counselors, career services or placement staff, academic advisers, and certainly residence hall advisers and students.

Although the specific criteria for selecting initial planning team members depend on the germinal idea, the following are salient issues suggested by Moore and Delworth (1976). They propose that the team members should have an interest in the idea and that their involvement in the program should help members achieve their own personal or job objectives. In addition, they suggest that there should be administration representatives who have some involvement with the idea. The team should also have individuals who have special knowledge and skills as well as individuals representing some diversity across faculty, students, and administrators. An initial planning team should be used, and then a full planning team should be assembled after some initial work has pinpointed more precisely the direction of planning. Other authors have detailed some of the important process and procedures that enhance the planning team's cohesion and productiveness (Moore and Delworth, 1976; Drum and Figler, 1973).

Step 3. Assessment: Needs and Resources. One of the first tasks of the planning team is to carry out three phases of an assessment process. The first phase involves the clear demonstration that a need exists. Many professionals spend hours developing and presenting workshops only to find that there is not much response to the offering. One example was the test anxiety reduction program described earlier in this chapter. Although the program had a great deal of face validity for the professionals who had prepared and presented it and although considerable effort went into publicity, only ten students participated. The students may not have recognized this as an area of need for themselves. Thus, some assessment of need or interest early in the process would have saved considerable planning. The program on evaluating student needs through structured interviews, also described earlier, provides insight into problems faced by many professionals. The hypotheses developed by professionals on the basis of their contacts with students in general did not hold up.

The second phase of the assessment process, once a need has been established, involves searching the literature for research and program data related to the germinal idea. These data are essential for specific planning of program delivery methods and for evaluation in later stages of development. The third phase of the assessment process consists of identifying available environmental resources. Are there other such programs already being offered? If so, is another one needed? If another program seems to be needed, are resource people available who are expert in the area of the program idea and who would be useful additions to the planning team?

Step 4. Identifying Alternative Program Targets and Purposes. Once the program team has determined that a clear need exists, it undertakes a brainstorming process to generate ideas about the delivery of a relevant program. Many program suggestions can be generated for any germinal idea. Professionals tend to always develop the same type of program for every germinal idea. Most often, programs are aimed at individual students who are defined as having problems. Although appropriate in many instances, this is a very limited perspective. The intervention model developed by Morrill, Oetting, and Hurst (1974a) can stimulate divergent thinking about what type of program might be developed. The model presented in Figure 1 suggests alternative targets, purposes, and methods of intervention that are useful in developing program suggestions.

The first two dimensions of the model are of primary importance in this stage of planning; the third dimension is important in the second stage and is discussed later. Brainstorming at this level may identify the need for more than one program to address different targets or purposes. For example, focus on the purpose dimension. The purpose dimension has three classifications: remedial, preventative, and developmental. The team should brainstorm remedial, preventative, and developmental program possibilities. Remedial programs address deficits or problems

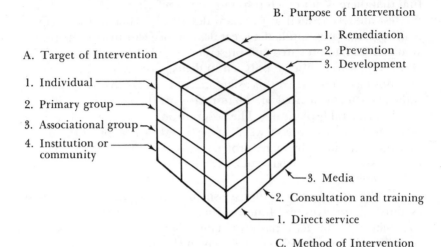

B. Purpose of Intervention
1. Remediation
2. Prevention
3. Development

A. Target of Intervention

1. Individual
2. Primary group
3. Associational group
4. Institution or community

3. Media
2. Consultation and training
1. Direct service

C. Method of Intervention

Source: This figure © 1974b by Weston H. Morrill, Eugene R. Oetting, and James C. Hurst, and is reproduced with their permission.

Figure 1. Dimensions of Counselor Functioning (Cube)

concerning people or negative aspects of the campus environment. Preventative programs anticipate that future environmental demands will be greater than many in the target population can successfully handle and are thus aimed at teaching target individuals the skills they need to successfully meet environmental demands (developmental tasks) or, if the environmental demands are counterproductive, are aimed at reducing the demands. Developmental programs do not contain a problem element but suggest activities that enhance or enrich people and/or their environments. The brainstorming team should recognize the possibility of several program ideas in each of these dimensions.

The target dimension of the model also suggests a number of alternatives for program development. Programs developed for primary groups focus on two or more people with an ongoing, close, interdependent relationship, such as couples, roommates, or families. When the program is developed for associational groups, the consumers are groups of people associated because of similar interests, needs, or goals. Where the target is an institution or community, the consumers can be all people who perceive themselves as affected by the institution or who have power or influence to change aspects of the institution in the idea area. Table 2 presents an example of various program ideas across both different targets and purposes (Moore and Delworth, 1976).

Table 2. Examples of Programs to Raise the Level of Academic Achievement Among Students Who Live in Campus Housing as Suggested for Various Combinations of the Cube's Target and Purpose Classifications.

Target	Purpose		
	Remediation	Prevention	Development
Individual	Learning skills for students with less than a 2.0 grade-point average	Series of learning skills workshops at each residence hall for identified high-risk students	Offer in residence halls special learning modules for advanced writing and reading skills
Primary group		Prepare and distribute to couples in married student housing a manual on "How to Set Up a Study Corner"	Offer workshop on helping your partner graduate
Associational group	Learning skills that utilize group interaction for members of a residence hall whose average has fallen below a 2.0 grade-point average		
Institution or Community	Train residence hall assistants on how to better identify and refer marginal students to learning skills programs	Train residence hall assistants about study environments and how these can be implemented in residence halls	Training program also achieves this purpose

Source: Adapted from Moore and Delworth (1976, p. 14), reproduced with permission.

Step 5. Program Selection. The program selection step requires the integration of the data and ideas generated in Steps 3 and 4. Planners should compare the suggested programs' purposes and targets with those of already existing programs in order to avoid overlap and to identify the greatest needs. Obviously, resource constraints must be considered in planning. With these issues in mind, the planning team makes decisions about the specific program direction and about the program's future. At this point, the planning team has developed a proposal that a program be developed in a specific idea area for a specific target and for a specific purpose. The decision to continue is based on the availability of required resources and the willingness of some individual, agency, or group to sponsor the program. With the decision to continue, the full planning team is assembled, and the planning process moves into the second stage.

Step 6. Development of a Full Planning Team. Once the commitment is made and a direction is identified, the planning team is reformulated as a full planning team. New members who collectively possess the skills necessary for completing the program development process may need to be added, and some of the initial planning team members may want to leave. Moore and Delworth (1976) recommend that at least four categories of personnel be represented on the planning team: (1) professionals in the field in which the program is being developed; (2) allied professionals who bring relevant expertise from professions outside the program area; (3) paraprofessionals (students or other nonprofessionals) who are given special training to conduct some of the tasks usually performed by professionals; and (4) target population members representing the intended consumers of the program. In addition, including representatives from several administrative areas encourages efficient use of resources in the broad area of student services. Moore and Delworth (1976, p. 17) suggest that "perhaps the greatest benefit of a team effort is the mutual support and encouragement that members can give each other in the sometimes slow and difficult parts of the rather long process." They further suggest (p. 19) that the following core skills and characteristics are desirable in a team member:

1. The ability to make commitment to attend regular team meetings and to complete additional tasks outside the meetings
2. The ability to work as a team member regarding both task and group processes
3. Specific skills in one or more of the following:
   a. Knowledge of program subject area
   b. Familiarity with population for which the program is being developed

c. Evaluation and research skills
d. Communication and writing skills
e. Process and observer skills

Stage II: Planning Program Objectives, Delivery System, and Evaluation Methods

Steps 1 through 4 involve planning (1) objectives for the program, (2) delivery system, and (3) methods of evaluation.

Step 1. Selecting Program Goals and Specifying Behavioral Objectives. An extremely important but often overlooked process in developing programs is making explicit goals that are implicit in the program's purpose. This is accomplished in a three-step procedure adapted from Weigel and Uhlemann (1975) in setting behavior change objectives for therapy groups. The first level of specification is to identify the broad general goals for the program. These are obtained by asking the question "What is (are) the broadest mission(s) of the program?" Moore and Delworth (1976) recommend brainstorming to identify goals. They give the following example (p.23): "What is the broadest mission for a high-risk freshman learning skills program? . . . To improve skills that freshman students need to succeed academically in college." The second level of the goal-setting process involves restating each general goal in terms of the behavior that students would display if they had achieved the general goal. Often there are several behaviors that the students could display if they had achieved one general goal; each becomes a general objective of the program. Again using the brainstorming process, the second stage is achieved by answering the question "How would program participants behave differently if they achieved the general goal?" From the preceding example, Moore and Delworth (1976, p. 23) generated the following answers to the question "How would program participants in a freshman learning skills program behave if they gained the skills needed to succeed academically in college?"

1. Participants will be able to organize their time so that they can get enough studying done and still have some social and recreation time.
2. Participants will be able to give their professors regular positive and negative feedback.
3. Participants will be able to take objective examinations without blocking anxiety.
4. Participants will be able to write term papers in an organized and clear fashion.

The third level of the goal-setting process is critical to the specific planning of the program delivery system. In this stage, the planning team should restate each general objective as several behavior change objectives. These latter objectives are increasingly specific and are obtained by answering the question "What specifically will be happening if participants accomplish the general objective?" According to Moore and Delworth, the task here is to define the scope of the desired behaviors by specifying as many of the following as possible: the time, the place, the person, or the context or setting of the accomplishment. The following examples of behavior change objectives for the second general objective are given by Moore and Delworth (1976, p. 24):

1. Participants will speak up in a designated class every day at least twice to give their reactions about the lecture.
2. Participants (after class) will orally give one of their professors some specific compliment or positive feedback about some aspect of the lecture or lab they liked privately.
3. Participants will at least once every day ask a lecturer to clarify some point that was not clearly presented.
4. Participants will practice giving negative feedback to one professor every week in writing, then practice saying it to a friend, and then give it to the professor—feedback about some aspect of the way the class is taught.

This three-level goal and behavioral objective framework is critically important, yet deceptively simple to implement. Planners tend to express goals in vague, nonbehavioral terms. Developing clear behavior objectives greatly enhances the probability of success, facilitates the evaluation planning, and enhances the ability of the delivery system to achieve the program goals.

Step 2. Development of the Training Methods or Delivery System. This step involves designing the specific training procedures and tasks that the planning team thinks will best achieve the program objectives given the available resources. The behavior change objectives identified in Step 1 provide the basis for selecting and developing the training tasks necessary for their achievement. The information gathered as part of the literature search in the first stage, initiating a program, is also important in this step. The planning team can evaluate previously developed training programs in light of the behavior change objectives identified for the current program and can determine for which objectives they will need to develop their own unique training tasks. Again, a number of training tasks are brainstormed; the final selection of tasks is based on a judgment by the planning team about which tasks are most likely to achieve the objectives with available resources. The following examples of training procedures were developed for the behavior change objectives presented earlier (Moore and Delworth, 1976, p. 27):

1. A didactic presentation outlining the difference between assertive and aggressive behavior
2. A small group exercise where class members practice *discriminating* between assertive and aggressive reactions to professors
3. A role-playing exercise where class members verbally practice giving assertive feedback to mock professors (positive or negative) in a wide range of situations
4. Diary or log of each student's progress kept on behavior objectives
5. Partner chosen by each student from the class, who will be communicated with daily about the student's accomplishments of behavior objectives

Step 3. Planning the Method of Intervention. Based on the planning in Step 2, the planning team must determine who will deliver the training and how the program will be offered. The method dimension of the cube model presented in Figure 1 (Morrill, Oetting, and Hurst, 1974a) is useful in this step of the planning. Although the specific goals and training plans may dictate to a large extent the method of intervention, the dimensions of the cube suggest that, in addition to offering the program themselves, student services professionals might consult with and/or train others to conduct the actual training. In addition, it is possible to prepare training modules and programs using media (television, audio recorders, programmed textbooks, and computers) in the presentation of programs.

The first classification in the method dimension, *direct service,* involves the professional staff personally training the consumers. This is the preferred method of intervention when training requires the expertise, credibility, and status of professionals. Many programs might best use the direct application of skills by professionals; however, professionals are not always the trainers of choice. It is important to consider the limited professional time available and the potential multiplier effect of their impact by using professionals to train and consult with the people who actually present the program. This second classification of the method dimension, *training and consultation,* suggests the use of peers, paraprofessionals, or allied professionals to deliver the training to consumers. Here the deliverers are usually trained and supervised by professionals. This method is useful when resources are scarce and professional time is limited. It is also preferred when training is enhanced by the special rapport or influence that peers or allied professionals can establish with consumers. Another method that should be considered is the use of *media*. Many training programs or modules can be presented through the use of media, thus allowing greater dissemination, easier continuation, and less professional time. Media can involve the use of television, computers, audio recorders, programmed textbooks, or written manuals. The delivery method also can integrate all three forms of intervention. Again, the alternatives suggested by each form open the planning process to more creative solutions. If the program involves paraprofessionals, peers, or allied professionals, this step must also include planning for the selection and training of these individuals. It is essential to determine what skills these people will need to establish behavior change objectives, and to develop training procedures. If media interventions are to be used, specific training materials are developed in this step.

Step 4. Program Evaluation and Design. The critical step of program evaluation and design is often overlooked in program planning (Morrill and Banning, 1973), yet it is possibly the most important. If the goals of the program have been carefully stated and translated into behavior change objectives (Step 1 of Stage II), this step is relatively easy. Where it has not been done, the step is difficult if not impossible. The planning team (or a consultant to the team) must identify or create instruments to measure the behavior change objectives. These may be directly administered instruments such as attitude tests, self-reports, or personality or behavioral tests, or they may be more indirect or unobtrusive measures such as observer reports or dropout rates. Once the instruments have been developed, the team must select a research design that allows control of enough variables that the team can say with some confidence that any changes found can be attributed to the program. This type of applied program evaluation does not allow the strict controls that experimental research provides; however, efforts should be made to apply as strict controls as possible in the pilot testing. Moore and Delworth (1976, pp. 75–77) suggest some commonly used research designs in a technical appendix.

Step 5. Preparation for the Pilot Test. This step involves completing detailed planning necessary for conducting a pilot test. The major planning tasks have already been completed. The need for the program has been demonstrated; the program's purpose, target, and method of intervention have already been completed. The need for the program has been demonstrated; the program's purpose, target, and method of intervention have been established; the program's goals have been specified in terms of behavior change objectives; and the training procedures and means of evaluating outcomes have been developed. Therefore, as indicated by Moore and Delworth (1976, p. 38) the final preparation steps should be:

1. Assign the remaining tasks to be completed so as to best use all personnel involved in the program.
2. Set criteria for program participants.
3. Determine the number of participants that the program's pilot test will accommodate.
4. Review all program, training, and evaluation materials for final approval.
5. Develop pilot program schedules, time-line charts, or other desired administrative materials.
6. Recruit candidates to be trainers, schedule interviews, and select trainers if the chosen method of intervention and the system of delivery require this as a prerequisite for the program's pilot test.

Stage III: Presenting and Evaluating a Pilot Program

The goal of the planning team in this third stage is to be able to make an informed decision about whether the program should be continued on a regular basis, whether it should be revised, or whether it should be dropped. In the five examples of programs presented earlier, the decision after the pilot testing was to continue or expand two of the programs, to eliminate or reassess two other programs, and to continue and expand one aspect of the fifth program and eliminate one other aspect of the program. From these few examples, it is obvious that this pilot-testing phase is critical. Without it, several programs might have been continued when they needed to be either extensively revised or eliminated. In addition, there could not have been as much confidence and support for the successful programs had they not been evaluated.

Steps 1–3 describe tasks concerning publicity, pilot testing, and making decisions about the future of the program, based on evaluative data.

Step 1. Program Publicity. The most carefully devised program will not be successful if the potential consumers are not aware of it and do not take advantage of it. Two programs described at the start of the chapter did not attract enough consumers. This may have reflected incomplete assessment of need but may also have resulted from inadequate publicity. The publicity should inform intended consumers why they might be interested, some of the specific benefits they might derive from their participation, as well as the time and place of the program.

Step 2. Implementation of Pilot Program. Actually selecting participants and offering the program on a pilot basis culminates all the planning to this point. There are three major tasks at this stage of the program. These are (1) recruiting and selecting the participants for the pilot test, (2) establishing the controls dictated by the evaluation research design, and (3) administering the evaluation procedures. Moore and Delworth (1976, p. 41) suggest these five specific tasks for team members:

1. Use a plan for the publicity needed to recruit participants.
2. Choose a selected sample of participants.
3. Set up a control group or groups.
4. Assign member(s) of the team to oversee the administration and collection of evaluation data.
5. Assign member(s) of the team to conduct any training required at this stage by the team's chosen method of intervention. At the minimum, this will entail the careful preparation for and/or rehearsing of each training task to be offered by professional personnel when a direct service method of intervention is used. When a consultation and training method is used for the pilot test, then planning team members will have to undertake the training procedures dictated in their design of the delivery system.

Step 3. Assessment of Evaluation Data and Decisions about Program Future. After the pilot test, the planning team will need to consider the evaluation data and decide whether the program should be continued and, if so, what changes or modifications should be made. The team should review both subjective and objective data in relation to each specific goal and behavior objective and should decide whether the program should be continued or discontinued. The evaluation data may suggest needed changes or modifications. Thus, the program development model branches at this point, depending on the decision. If the decision is to continue, then the process moves on to Stage IV; if the decision is to abort, the process moves back to the first stage to develop a new idea or to Stage II to develop an alternative delivery system.

Stage IV: Program Refinement

Step 1. Refine Training Procedures and Materials. Using feedback from the pilot program, the team should review and, where necessary, refine and polish training materials. Data may suggest modifying some procedures or adding audio, written, or visual materials to strengthen the program. Some procedures may be superfluous and can be dropped from the program with little impact on outcomes.

Step 2. Planning for Continued Evaluation. Continued evaluation is necessary for a number of reasons. Changing conditions and circumstances may alter need for the program or even alter program outcomes. Any redevelopment or modification of the program may change outcomes; therefore, continued assessment must be planned. As a program matures, different personnel may affect program outcomes; also, the newness of a program, the involvement of the planners, and the excitement may produce spurious evaluations of data because of the special attention the program receives at first. All these issues make it important that the planning team develop plans for continued evaluation, using as powerful a design as feasible.

Step 3. Training of Trainers. Eventually, many mature programs may use peers, volunteers, paraprofessionals, or allied professionals as trainers in programs so that the professional staff are free for other purposes. Often professionals are the trainers or implementers during the pilot testing and the early life of programs, but others may be incorporated into the program as time goes on. When this occurs, careful consideration must be given to selecting and training nonprofessional trainers: What skills do they need to have? How are they to be given these skills? Who is to train them? And who is to supervise the continuing program?

Step 4. Offering Program on a Regular Basis. When all of the preceding tasks have been completed, the planning team is ready to offer the program on a regular basis. Some individual or group must assume ongoing coordination and supervision with continuous attention to publicity details, selecting and training trainers, room scheduling, and collecting and disseminating evaluative data. The need and continued support for the program must be continually monitored in light of changing priorities. No program remains completely viable over an extended period of time without requiring some changes, modifications, and perhaps reconceptualizations. Moore and Delworth (1976, p. 51) indicate that to maintain a program the planning team should periodically answer the following questions with supporting data:

1. Is there still a demonstrated need for the program?
2. Do the current delivery system procedures still accomplish the program's intended objectives?
3. Have the target, program personnel, level of training, or implementation changed enough so that an objective reevaluation of the program is necessary?
4. Are staff resources and funding still adequate to maintain the program?
5. Has priority for the program changed?

Conclusion

This chapter has presented strategies and techniques associated with program development. Too often professionals have not carefully used an empirically based model and thus have achieved questionable results. Program development is not unlike good applied research. The term *research* creates anxiety for some people; sometimes the trauma associated with writing a thesis creates resistance to doing research, yet we need to think in research terms in all that we do. Research provides us with a systematic means of answering important questions about what we are doing: for example, "What are the needs of those I am concerned about serving? Is there a group of individuals who could profit from a systematic program? Does the program I have developed really make a difference or do I need to seek some other way? And, if the program goals are achieved, is it worth the cost?" We cannot avoid the questions, and seeking the answers can be a stimulating and productive experience.

References

Drum, D. J., and Figler, H. E. *Outreach in Counseling.* New York: Intext Educational Publishers, 1973.

Glidewell, J. "Priorities for Psychologists in Community Mental Health." In Division 27, American Psychological Association, Task Force on Community Mental Health., *Issues in Community Psychology and Preventive Mental Health.* New York: Behavioral Publications, 1971.

Lewis, J. A., and Lewis, M. D. *Community Counseling: A Human Services Approach.* New York: Wiley, 1977.

Moore, M., and Delworth, U. *Initiation and Implementation of Outreach Programs.* Technical Report No. 2, Grant No. MH 18007, NIMH. Fort Collins: Colorado State University, 1972.

Moore, M., and Delworth, U. *Training Manual for Student Service Program Development.* Boulder, Colo.: Western Interstate Commission for Higher Education, 1976.

Morrill, W. H., and Banning, J. H. *Counseling Outreach: A Survey of Practices.* Boulder, Colo.: Western Interstate Commission for Higher Education, 1973.

Morrill, W. H., and Hurst, J. C. "A Preventative and Developmental Role for the College Counselor." *Counseling Psychologist,* 1971, *2*(4), 90–95.

Morrill, W. H., Oetting, E. R., and Hurst, J. C. "Dimensions of Counselor Functioning." *Personnel and Guidance Journal,* 1974a, *52,* 354–359.

Morrill, W. H., Oetting, E. R., and Hurst, J. C. (Eds.). *Nine Outreach Programs.* Final Report, Grant No. MH 18007, NIMH. Fort Collins: Colorado State University, 1974b.

Weigel, R. G., and Uhlemann, M. R. "Developing Individualized Behavior Change Goals with Clients." *Journal of Contemporary Psychotherapy,* 1975, 7, 91–95.

Western Interstate Commission for Higher Education. *Consultation: A Process for Continuous Institutional Renewal.* Boulder, Colo.: Western Interstate Commission for Higher Education, 1972.

John G. Corazzini **15**

Environmental Redesign

If a student services program is to serve students effectively, it must actively adapt to the challenges and unique needs that each generation of students brings to college. This chapter offers a model of environmental redesign that hopefully will help student services workers respond to this responsibility.

The following section describes and discusses the AIDE (assessment, intentional design, and evaluation) model of assessment and redesign. Core components of the model are described, and information is provided to acquaint the reader with the issues involved in forming a work team. A design center is proposed, and six assumptions to the formation of a centralized assessment agency are enumerated and discussed. Finally, implications of the model are reviewed.

Elements of Redesign

A primary goal for most divisions of student services is the promotion of student growth and development in a fashion that is integrated with the academic arm of the university. Traditionally student services has responded to student needs by offering general programming, on the assumption that needs are somewhat constant across time and population. This programming has been offered to assist students as they attempted to matriculate through the university.

More recently there has been a greater appreciation for the effect environments have on people. Environments have certain characteristics and are major factors in a student's educational success or failure. When student needs and campus resources effectively match, the probability of dysfunctional stress is reduced. When the environment is mismatched with student needs, stress and frustration usually increase, and the environment must adapt. AIDE offers a system that allows student services personnel to intentionally redesign their campus environments to increase the fit between student needs and campus resources.

The AIDE model has three basic components: (1) assessment, (2) intentional design, and (3) evaluation. Each component is integral and interlocks with the other two components. AIDE is similar to traditional student services work in that it suggests programming as one way of meeting student needs. It is different in that it assumes that student needs change, that environments can and sometimes must change, and that science can help the student services worker both identify student-environment mismatches as well as find information about the effectiveness of the planned interventions.

Assessment. The last six or seven years have been marked by more emphasis on student needs assessment for student programming. Although many different terms have been used—such as "need assessment," "ecomapping," and "environmental assessment"—the construct has remained consistent: identifying the mismatch or area of incompatibility and programming for greater confluence between students and their environments.

The first step is to identify the target population. This is difficult because student populations are constantly changing. Age, for example, is an important variable. It is no longer safe to assume that the typical undergraduate is twenty-one years old. As we enter the 1980s, it is anticipated that more and more mature women and men will pursue courses of study at colleges throughout the country. This will alter the characteristics of many student populations. Planning for these students is imperative if colleges wish to maintain their enrollment. By knowing the population, it is possible, for example, to plan refresher courses and study help sessions for the returning student. Other demographic considerations include answers to the following: "Do the students live on campus? Are they from urban or rural backgrounds? Do they commute? What is their income? Do they hold full-time or part-time jobs? Are there identifiable subgroups within the population (such as handicapped, veteran, ethnic minority, and foreign)?" Gathering all available identifying data is the first step toward a successful assessment and redesign.

Once the population can be described, one can then ask what it needs. Typical static administrations offer standard student services packages that were relevant ten years ago and are expected to be so ten years hence. Even on such campuses, there are innovations; they are not, however, the product of systematic study and foresight but often result from (1) federal legislation, (2) student agitation, or (3) the particular interest or expertise of a staff member. These do not usually lead to effective programming. An institution must constantly gather information about student needs if it is to know what programming is necessary. The student services worker uses systematic ongoing assessment to identify student-environment mismatches.

There have been a variety of approaches to assessment. The more typical have used a questionnaire approach that yields gross scale scores about a number of environmental factors. More typical instruments are the College and University Environment Scales (CUES) and the College Survey Questionnaire (CSQ), which yield scores on such indexes as satisfaction with major, cultural sophistication, scholarship, and community. A handy guide to environmental assessment instruments of this type is included in Aulepp and Delworth's *Training Manual for an Ecosystem Model* (1976). The guide, written by Keating, includes such helpful information as instrument cost, format, administration, and reliability.

Although the preceding measures do yield important information about the environment, it is very difficult to redesign from the type of scores they generate. Moreover, the same instrument cannot be used to provide data on the unique differences and problems of different campus environments. For these reasons, it is often necessary to design one's own instrument.

In building an instrument, it is important to use techniques that will ensure that the instrument can yield data concerning specific campus mismatches or points where the student population and the campus environment are identified as incompatible. The Environmental Satisfaction Questionnaire, or ESQ (Corazzini, Wilson, and Huebner, 1977), is essentially a series of techniques for designing an appropriate instrument. It has two parts. Part I is typical of more traditional need assessment instruments. Statements such as "Freshmen do not feel isolated on this campus" are followed by a five-point Likert-type response from "strongly disagree" to "strongly agree." Respondents are asked to answer a series of statements by circling their response and then coding it in a box provided at the right.

Each campus assessment team should develop specific ESQ items to capture the unique mismatches of the particular environment. By carefully selecting the content of these items, the questionnaire developer can avoid the problems that other measures have in gathering information about possible mismatches in a particular environment. This suggests that the assessment team must identify potential sources of incongruence between students and their environment by carefully interviewing representatives of various groups within the larger population, reviewing past research studies, and studying sources of unobtrusive data found in such agencies as academic advising or health centers. These are then reduced to the most parsimonious list, and only those relevant to the particular study are chosen for Part I of the ESQ. Students then are asked to respond to these items in a five-point Likert-type format from "strongly disagree" to "strongly agree"; their response tells the environmental assessment team if this *possible* mismatch is in fact real.

Part II of the ESQ is used to gather more data on items that have been validated as sources of incongruence in Part I; that is, respondents answer "strongly disagree" (1) or "disagree" (2) to the items (mismatches are keyed in the negative direction). In Part II, the respondents are asked to provide environmental referents for the "incongruent items": (1) "What things in the environment have caused this?" (2) "How have you responded?" and (3) "What would you do to change things?" A content analysis of the items in Part II, means from Part I, and percentages of the population that score "strongly disagree" or "disagree," for each item, give the environmental assessment team the data it needs for redesign purposes. Table 1 contains some typical environmental referent data, analyzed by content, for the item "My adviser has been helpful to me." For further information on the development and use of this particular form of environmental referents, the reader is directed to Corazzini, Wilson, and Huebner (1977); for other environmental referent formats, see Aulepp and Delworth (1976).

Data collected periodically from questionnaires of this type allow the team to monitor trends in student-environment interaction. In a recent study at Colorado State University, information was collected about the counseling center and compared to that gathered two years earlier. There was approximately a 10 percent gain in dissatisfaction toward the center by respondents to the questionnaire over the two-year period. If a traditional questionnaire alone had been used, this would have been the only data reported. Fortunately, environmental referent data were collected suggesting that the reason for this increased dissatisfaction was a rising religious emphasis and interest among students, which they had translated into seeking solutions to problems by prayer or from religious leaders. Knowledge of the referent data allowed the counseling center staff to respond proactively by assessing and fostering their relationships with the campus ministry as one response, albeit indirect, to providing the students' mental health needs.

Table 1. Possible Student Responses to the ESQ in Three Categories

What things exist or have happened to make you feel this way?	*How have you responded to this feeling or situation?*	*What could be done to change or improve the situation?*
"Advisers are too biased in their assistance toward their own department. They want you in their department."	"He told me to sign his name to all my papers; he doesn't care, so I do it."	"Have more advisers."
"I don't have an adviser."		"I don't know."
"He is very prejudiced against women studying in agriculture."	"As a Freshman, I feel that my adviser has not done anything to help with my major. Probably because he is not a civil engineering adviser."	"Inform advisers of students' perceptions of them and their advice."
		"Not sure. This could be an individual rather than a general problem."
"He has an empty folder with my name on it. He is too busy with research."	"Talked with professors in my own field instead."	"Match advisers with students interested in adviser's field."
"Past experience with advisers at large schools."	"Going to department instructors, getting information, and making my own decisions."	"Don't know. I suppose it was my fault."
"My adviser's office is six miles off campus, and I don't have a car."	"Stopped seeing him. Talked to other professors to find answers to my questions."	"Help from other faculty."
"In my department, there isn't a single adviser for preregistration. Everything is impersonal."	"Quit seeing him for now."	"I don't have the slightest idea."
		"Provide more than one adviser for each student."
"I've had so many advisers (three) that it's easier to do things myself."	"Go to individual teachers who would comprehend my position."	"Stress to faculty members that students are more important than their research."
"My adviser and all advisers are worthless."	"I have never talked to an adviser."	"Be sure new students get one."

Probably one of the most unused but valuable sources of data are unobtrusive measures (Webb and others, 1966). Unobtrusive measures can indicate mismatches (or matches), can be used without active participation, and often are unknown to the constituents in an environment. Grade-point averages, dropout rates, number of applicants for financial aid, and costs for repairing damages to residence halls are but a few examples of unobtrusive measures. Unobtrusive measures are powerful research tools for the environmental assessment team because they are, in contrast to questionnaire data, real-life indicators of behaviors. Because these measures already exist, they can also be readily used for pretest-posttest comparisons.

For example, staff members at the counseling center at Colorado State University recently collaborated with the person in charge of academic withdrawal from the university to use the withdrawal process to identify potential mismatches between students and the Colorado State campus environment. Students who had decided to withdraw from the university were required to do so formally. After some examination of the process, the team decided to develop a student withdrawal form and print it to be read by an optical scanner. The form included demographic data (age, sex, college, major, and so on), a list of four major reasons (financial, health, personal, scholastic) for withdrawal, and twenty-four more choices included to allow the student to be more specific about the reason. With this format tied to a computer program, the office of academic withdrawal was able to identify who was leaving what part of the university for what reason at what time. Using optical scan sheets required no extra staff work; on the contrary, it saved a secretary approximately two weeks of work time because lists that were usually typed were generated by a computer from the data on the optical scan sheets. Ongoing assessment of student withdrawal allows trends to be identified and interventions planned. The intervention team could intervene by circulating the results of this assessment to deans and other relevant university personnel.

A third method of assessment is the interview, structured or unstructured. In a study of two western universities (Western Interstate Commission for Higher Education, 1972), an unstructured interview was used as one part of an elaborate assessment of mismatches between students and their respective campus environments. The unstructured interview substantiated the testing results and added previously untapped information.

Although it is not my intention to exhaustively discuss here the merits and methodologies of interviewing, it may be useful to note some of the diverse ways that an interview may be conducted. A telephone interview is one of the easiest and quickest ways that an environmental assessment team can gather information about one or two probable mismatches in a particular environment. By using volunteers to call randomly selected residents about a particular issue, in a matter of twenty-four hours the assessment team can have information from which to program or otherwise intervene. This technique may be criticized because it discriminates against those who have no phones, but it can be very effective in concert with other methods of collecting data. Alternative interviewing strategies include having a cadre of people "in the street" randomly interview students in key traffic areas. Again this research can be faulted for its lack of randomness, but as one of several sources of data it is quite acceptable.

Naturalistic observation is a fourth method that can be used by the environmental assessment team. Just as organizations and groups use trained consultants to observe functioning and diagnose difficulties, so too can observers be trained to unobtrusively detect mismatches between an environment and its inhabitants. Although this is a relatively new concept, it is possible to train people to recognize both functional and dysfunctional student-environmental interactions, thereby providing a diagnosis based on real events in their natural settings.

The assessment process itself can heighten or lessen the confluence between students and their environment. One phase of the assessment process should focus on identifying specific subgroups (traditionally, ethnic minorities and women) that may be mismatched with the environment. A second step is to identify the source of the incongruence. The ESQ technique is helpful in this process. This technique, however, assumes that the person can read, can read English, is sighted, and can write. Foreign and disabled students may experience greater incongruence as a result of this assessment process than without it. The assessment team should sensitize itself to the issues of the subpopulation and should not contribute to existing difficulties.

Intentional Design. Once the mismatches have been identified, the process of bringing people needs and campus resources together begins. One method through which this union might be effected is program development. (Program development has also been discussed by Morrill in Chapter Fourteen.)

Program development linked to assessment and to the identification of student-environment mismatches provides the student services worker with a valuable redesign tool. In the past, many programs have, in large part, developed out of the goodwill or expertise of a particular staff member. Moreover, programs are often offered across entire populations when not the entire population is incongruent with its environment. This type of programming inhibits full delivery of service.

Assessment provides a scientific basis for program development by helping the student services worker identify both the mismatch and the population that experiences it. For example, a typical complaint for many students is a lack of academic advising assistance from faculty. Studies of student needs can support this hypothesis on a particular campus and can identify whether all students or only a particular subgroup have difficulty in this area. In an ongoing assessment project at Colorado State University, academic advising was found to be a particular source of incongruence between many students and their environment. Complaints about it were substantiated through assessment. Further investigation, using indexes such as class and college, revealed that students of two colleges were extremely displeased. Instead of offering a peer advising program for all students, it made more sense to focus the intervention only on disappointed students.

This approach has a number of advantages. People and institutional resources, which are becoming more and more limited today, are more efficiently used, and those who need the university services have a greater opportunity of receiving them. Furthermore, it should be pointed out that administrators, deans, and faculty like to hear about the good things that they do. It is politically advantageous at a number of levels not only to identify problems but also to point out successes. An alternative intervention is to suggest that the faculty who were having difficulty get together with successful faculty. The latter could then act as resource consultants. This would allow them to feel good about what they had done as well as to provide support and assistance to their academic colleagues rather than to leaving them dependent on an outside student services group.

Once the mismatch has been identified, the population targeted, and the program responses developed, it is necessary to pilot-test and evaluate the programming effort. This often missed or omitted step is vitally important. Again taking the example of academic advising problems, we must find out if a peer advising program will in fact lessen student-environment incongruence. If the program accomplishes what the designers intended, then full implementation can follow; if the program goal is not attained, adjustments or reprogramming can then take place.

This particular assessment and design model constantly samples changing population needs. Student services divisions often presuppose a constant set of student needs. This has led to a set of institutionalized agencies and offices, which in turn has precipitated a rather rigid approach to programming. Personnel and functions have been locked into a system, thus making it very difficult for them to change and adapt. Essential to the model I am proposing is attaching time limits to a program. Some programs by their very nature have a shorter institutional life than others. A program should only be maintained while it meets a need and is effective. Ongoing assessment provides information on needs; ongoing evaluation provides data on effectiveness. For example, a grief program instituted for the friends of a dead student is a very short-term project of only a few months' duration, while a program designed to provide study skills for returning students might last for years. Programming should always be in flux, subject to new identified needs and evaluation, and programmers should be flexible enough to dissolve a program when there is no evidence to support its continuation.

An example from another university illustrates this last point. During the 1960s, students were concerned about their interpersonal skills and very much affected by the encounter-type activities spawned by the human potential movement. This led to the development of a communication skills workshop in response to this particular need, based on encounter experiences; for example, trust falls and trust walks. This program was highly successful in its early years, but in the early 1970s student needs changed and responsiveness to the program waned. After several years of failure, this program was dropped. Coincidentally, a new program was developed based on a different set of goals and a more structured format and initiated by a particular staff member. This program was targeted to build social skills in dating behavior, and it recaptured the student interest lost with the passing of the communication skills workshop. Although this second program was developed, the transition was neither planned nor anticipated. Effective ongoing assessment could have been used to predict this and other changes in the student needs and values. The anticipatory nature of the model contributes in large part to its proactive nature. Table 2 provides program examples that could be developed to respond to specific mismatches.

Not all student-environment adjustments are appropriate for program development intervention. Some environmental changes are more appropriately accomplished directly with a policy or architectural modification. For example, students across the nation have been feeling the financial recession and have complained about it (Corazzini and Wilson, 1975–76). One program response to the students' financial plight was a survival budgeting class. Administrative and policy decisions can also respond to this student-environment mismatch. An alternative proposed by students at one university was the elimination of student athletic fees; another was a less expensive meal plan for the residence halls, on the premise that students would not be required to eat every meal in the dining hall.

Besides policy changes, there is also a category of interventions that includes specific changes in the existing physical environment, accomplished either by altering something that already exists or by adding something new. There are countless ways that the environment

**Table 2. Typical Program Development Rationales with Samples of
Precipitating Mismatches and Program Interventions**

Program Rationale	Precipitating Mismatch	Program Example
1. Providing new, not previously offered services	Poor faculty advising program	Development of peer advising program using paraprofessionals
2. Teaching students how to tap resources already existing in the campus environment	Complaints of financial stress	Survival course for students in financial need designed to help students identify financial resources in the campus environment
3. Teaching faculty and administration how to bring resources to students	Complaints about not having certain resources on a campus when in fact they do exist	Sensitivity training or communication skills workshops for student services personnel, especially those who most come in contact with students
4. Teaching skills necessary for students coping with developmental or other similar needs	Expressed concern by student assistants about their inability to respond to students who have lost significant others	Student assistant training in grief work for loss

can be adapted to eliminate this type of mismatch. If students have visual disabilities, for example, their environment may be improved by adding braille signs to office doors and elevators, while those who need wheelchairs may benefit from curb cuts and access ramps. The physical design of an environment is an important factor to consider when determining why a student or group may be incompatible with an environment. Carefully planned architectural modifications can significantly increase the congruence.

A student assistant in one residence hall recently asked the counseling center to provide a resident environment adaptation program (REAP), a program designed to help students make their living environment more congruent with their needs. She stated that the students on the floor for which she was responsible felt isolated and did not have much interaction with students on other floors and the 'bad' feelings were growing. Some residents were being openly sarcastic with each other, and others were saying they would not return to this particular floor. Consultants worked with the student assistant and floor residents to identify mismatches and take corrective steps. A key mismatch in the physical environment was identified. The residents had all asked to be part of a mixed-sex floor, and, although men and women both lived on the same floor, they did not perceive themselves as being on a mixed-sex floor. The REAP consultants noticed that the floor plan consisted of two horseshoes facing each other. At the foot of each horseshoe was a heavy fire door, and between them was an open space with elevators. The men lived in one horseshoe and the women in the other, which effectively segregated them and frustrated their goal for living on this floor; namely, to live and interact with the opposite sex. Coincidentally with this discovery, the housing staff offered materials and assistance to any residents who wanted to construct a lounge on their floor. The students on this floor chose to build their lounge in the open area between the two horseshoes. This brought the residents to a central but neutral area, facilitated interaction, and reduced negative feelings because they were able to pursue the primary goals of this living experience. It was also very important that people from both horseshoes be involved in designing and building the lounge. By working together, they both invested in the lounge concept as well as developed a community spirit.

When deciding on a response to a perceived need, one should be aware that there is not one right solution; often there are many. An intervention can be called successful when students are more congruent with their environment after there has been an attempt to modify it. When the environmental team begins to redesign, brainstorming is an effective technique that increases team cohesion while providing a plethora of very creative alternatives. Once the team evaluates the list of ideas, there are usually several that can be used and that will be successful. By choosing a response that is both timely and well thought out, the mismatch can be reduced, and, hopefully, the students' educational experience will be enhanced.

Evaluation. The third intrinsic component of the process model is evaluation. Just as assessment is essential to identify the targets for programmed interventions, evaluation is necessary to assess its success or failure. It is imperative to ask, "Does the intervention (program) make a difference?" With the data gathered from ongoing evaluation, the redesign team knows if the intervention is successful, partly successful, or needs to be totally replanned because it does not lessen the mismatch between students and their environment. The evaluation data goes through a feedback loop process from program to administrator and back into the program again.

With each intervention, the evaluation plan must be decided on before implementation. Often evaluation has been an afterthought, unplanned and poorly executed. It has been thought a luxury to be indulged in only if a student needed a research project or an administrator needed data for a political purpose. More positive attitudes toward evaluation must be cultivated or the best-intentioned programming may go for naught.

We are traditionally slow to assess or evaluate our interventions. Often, if it feels good then it is thought to be right. Today, however, we cannot afford to be so slipshod or intuitive. In the first place, unsuccessful programs are maintained that only perpetuate environmental problems. If we allow them to continue, we contribute to the production of educational casualties as well as block a more successful intervention. Moreover, assessment demonstrates to governing boards and others that the dollars for student support services are being spent efficiently and effectively. Evaluation is an instrument for survival, rather than a luxury that can be dallied with and discarded when time, effort, or expertise is lacking.

Evaluation expertise is an important skill for the redesign team. It is an emerging, complex skill relevant in its own right but also particularly salient today because of tightening budgets and accountability. "Each of the steps involved in completing an evaluation study is a point of vulnerability which, if not sturdily constructed, will create an end result that is invalid and unusable" (Struening and Guttentag, 1975, p. 3). Although it is helpful if the evaluator is also a researcher, ability and experience in research does not necessarily suggest that the person is able to conduct adequate evaluation. Evaluation data, unlike research, is used for making decisions about programming and, in the AIME model, for judging the success or failure of a specific campus redesign. The evaluator must also be politically astute because the decision making is done in a political context, and its ramifications reach far beyond the immediate situation. Those wanting to review the basic issues of evaluation as well as learn about some "how to" rules will find enlightening two articles prepared for the *Personnel and Guidance Journal* by Oetting (1976a, 1976b). Among countless other sources, two should be pointed out: (1) a two-volume work entitled *Handbook of Evaluation Research* (Struening and Guttentag, 1975) and (2) *Evaluation: A Form for Human Service Decision-Makers,* an experimental magazine published by the Minneapolis Medical Research Foundation in collaboration with the National Institute of Mental Health. Both are excellent resources for the evaluator. Chapter Ten in this book also offers valuable ideas and strategies.

The Work Team

Throughout this chapter, I have made numerous references to the assessment and redesign team. What are some of the purposes and the composition of such a team?

If students and environments are to benefit mutually, they usually must achieve congruence. This means both must change—but people do not like to be changed, and the less involved they are in diagnosing "their" problem the more apt they are to thwart attempts at changing them. More successful campus-student modifications follow self-diagnosis and planning. This suggests that the assessment and design team be composed of representatives from the different components of the environment affected by or involved in the assessment or redesign program.

The first suggestion in formulating the work team is to make it representative of the population you wish to serve. This population can be a new group charged specifically with campus redesign, or it can be an ongoing group, such as a mental health advisory board, that receives as a new charge responsibility for assessment and redesign.

The redesign team is composed of people from the environment and functions as consultant to the university community. As in traditional consultation models, legitimacy and high administrative sanction for the consultation are imperative. The charge must be clear, and the team must experience itself as owning the model and its implementation. Again, power is a very important issue. If the redesign team does not experience itself as being in charge and having a mandate to implement the model, it will become frustrated, fracture, and eventually dissolve itself.

The team must also legitimate itself with the population. Representativeness does not in itself legitimate the team as a friendly change agent that is understood and accepted as working to improve the total environment. The team must decide early how to keep the favor of all parties involved in the redesign process. One helpful way to accomplish this is by being very open with the population about the assessment and redesign process. Publishing reports in the campus journal, sending newsletters and reports to key people, making media presentations, requesting feedback in an ongoing manner from the total community, and holding open forums are but a few ways that this openness may be achieved.

One must also address expertise needs and campus politics. Evaluation has already been highlighted as one necessary skill. Others include (1) environmental assessment and redesign; (2) program development; (3) consultation skills; (4) organizational change theory; (5) group theory; (6) computer programming; (7) campus history, organization, and politics; and (8) knowledge and sensitivity to human rights. Grant writing, although not absolutely necessary, may also be an asset. People with these skills can be tapped individually, or a particular department such as anthropology, sociology, or psychology can be asked to help. It is not absolutely necessary that these individuals be included as members of the team. Their expertise must be acknowledged, however, and the individual must be included at least as a consultant. Also, selecting team members has political implications. This in part parallels the representation issue. The difference lies in both identifying and asking people with power to be a part of the team. These people may, but not necessarily, be the same ones representing specific groups. The power they have may be formal, through administrative appointment, or informal. Both sources must be considered. Often a person with informal power may be a more important asset than one with invested power.

Of course, team size is important. If *all* the preceding suggestions for representativeness are followed, the team will be a very large group, which may often be unwieldy and become dysfunctional. A good size to work with is eight to twelve; smaller groups are also workable, but larger ones should be discouraged (Aulepp and Delworth, 1976). If it becomes difficult to keep work teams down to a reasonable number, alternative formats can be employed. For instance, a nucleus steering committee can be in charge of several work teams linked together (Sexton, 1970). Aulepp and Delworth (1976) discuss work team formation and provide additional assistance to expedite this process.

The Design Center Concept

To begin the process of environmental design, an ongoing and centralized assessment procedure must be established. In a 1972 publication by the Western Interstate Commission on Higher Education (WICHE), it was suggested that universities interested in environmental assessment, or "ecomapping," as it is sometimes called, establish a central agency to continuously collect information that can be used to identify areas of matches or mismatches between students and their environments. The agency would have a permanent staff as well as office space and equipment and would provide the university with a source of programs and other interventions to decrease student-environment mismatches.

A number of principles or assumptions underly the establishment of such a central agency. First, as mentioned earlier, students are always changing, and new points of incongruence arise while old ones become assets to the system. Second, if assessment is diffused throughout a division of student services, then resources (such as money, expertise, and people) are used inefficiently. Thirdly, a centrally established agency can be sanctioned by the university community, thus allowing for better communication and acceptance of the data collected.

Some elaboration of this latter point is required. There has been some debate among proponents of the environmental management approach as to the location of an assessment and redesign center within a university administration. Some suggest it have a staff relationship to the college president, others prefer it to be within a division of student services, and yet others think it is the domain of a counseling center responsible for the mental health of a university community. I prefer the first position. My reasoning is based on a consultation principle; namely, that the probability of succeeding with a system intervention increases the higher up in the administrative hierarchy one is able to intervene. In some aspects, sanction is equivalent to power, and in this case it is more powerful to be at the presidential level than to be buried as a unit in student services. This is particularly important given the past history of student services and its relation to the academic arm of the university. Academic deans are more apt to become involved if the agency head reports directly to a president of the college as opposed to a vice-president of student services or a counseling center director.

A fourth assumption suggests that funneling data into a central agency from diverse points within the campus environment enables the environmental assessment team to draw a comprehensive picture of student-environment interactions, including areas of congruence as well as incongruence.

Both matches and mismatches between students and their environment should be identified. Some proponents of environmental assessment, myself included, have been criticized for focusing only on what is going wrong in the campus community. I suggest that the environmental assessment team look also at what goes well. To respond only to negative interactions is to respond only to part of the community. In many cases, good interactions exist that if supported or strengthened could do more than a new program could. Politically, as mentioned earlier, administration and faculty like to hear what goes well rather than what is wrong with "their" system, and it bodes well for the assessment and design agency that starts off with this type of feedback. It is much easier to hear criticism from someone perceived as an ally than from someone who is seen as consistently rocking the status quo.

In the fifth place, the assessment and design center team is not responsible for making all the interventions suggested by its ongoing data collection process. It should have both staff and administrative sanction to make certain select interventions. Although it might appear to be more expeditious to have both staff and responsibility for all interventions, solutions produced independent of the concerned populations would only be temporary, and the problems within the system would remain. If changes or adjustments are to be truly effective, the point of the system that is incongruent must also be responsible for adapting. Leaving the responsibility with each university component diffuses the design process throughout the entire community. Engaging the many and various individuals, agencies, or departments throughout the university heightens the probability of successful redesign.

Because responsibility is spread across the entire university community, the design center team must employ a number of techniques in facilitating intentional campus design. First and foremost, the team should adhere to the basics of consultation and the consultation process. Second, the team should be aware of a number of possible intervention strategies. These strategies may lie anywhere along a continuum from a very active direct intervention by the design center staff itself to a less active and more indirect intervention, such as a survey or data feedback technique used in organizational change. Between the two differing approaches lie a multitude of strategies depending on the staff's expertise, style, ingenuity, and resources.

Finally, the sixth assumption states that the central design center concept need not be initiated with one executive decision or at one point in time. The concept of assessment and design is relatively new and foreign to most university officials. Education regarding the process and its impact on the total educational experience is imperative. One sure way to educate the entire college community and especially those in positions of power is to demonstrate the effectiveness of the model with manageable but maladaptive student-environment interactions.

Implications of the AIDE Model

This chapter began with a discussion of how student populations and their needs are constantly changing. Effective student services respond to students and their needs as they emerge. This demands flexibility on the part of the student services administration and personnel. A full implementation of the process model of assessment and redesign can provide the structure to achieve this goal.

One step in establishing this process is to create a center for campus assessment and redesign. All agencies and programs would be created in response to assessed needs. No one agency would be established on a permanent basis. Instead, the mandate to the unit would be for a specific time period, renewable only if the mismatch persisted and the program was evaluated as successful. Personnel would understand that their appointments were temporary; they would not be rehired unless another project for which they were competent was beginning. This model is based on an organizational style of project management

(Sexton, 1970) and is not without problems, especially those of staffing and of setting time limits.

Project management is recommended by a number of advantages, but it also raises some problems. The personnel problem is particularly difficult, but it is not insoluble. In many respects, many divisions of student services have been operating informally on a project management basis. As new needs have arisen on campus, coordinators or specialists in these areas have been hired. For example, many universities are now hiring specialists in programming for women, minority, and handicapped students or individuals with background in Greek life or veterans' affairs. When specific positions have not demanded the full attention of the person hired for them, that time was often released to allow the person to begin new endeavors and respond to other needs in the campus community. Commitment to this process would be a commitment to formalizing the project management approach as well as working through the very complex personnel issues that are involved. A further aid to facilitate this procedure would be retraining—modifying the traditional benefits package by providing ongoing in-service training.

Conclusion

The model presented here is based on the knowledge that students change and so do their needs. When students experience a mismatch between their needs and a university resource, stress often occurs, which leads to problems for the student, the university, or both. Effective student services work is flexible and proactive in collaborating with the academic arm of the university to educate students.

Student services workers are clearly challenged to help make education a dynamic and growing experience for students. Effective programming and change based on real student needs can help them meet this challenge. Any problems with model implementation are soluble. Those who are responsible for student services must decide if they will meet the challenge and offer truly versatile and effective service or if they will rest content with the status quo.

References

Aulepp, L., and Delworth, U. *Training Manual for an Ecosystem Model.* Boulder, Colo.: Western Interstate Commission for Higher Education, 1976.

Corazzini, J., and Wilson, S. "Students, the Environment, and Their Interactions: Part 2." *Student Development Series* (Colorado State University), 1975–76, *13* (2, entire issue).

Corazzini, J., Wilson, S., and Huebner, L. "The Environmental Satisfaction Questionnaire: A Guide to Assessment and Program Development. *Journal of College Student Personnel,* 1977, *18*(3), 169–173.

Oetting, E. R. "Evaluative Research and Orthodox Science: Part 1." *Personnel and Guidance Journal,* 1976a, *55*(1), 11–15.

Oetting, E. R. "Planning and Reporting Evaluative Research: Part 2." *Personnel and Guidance Journal,* 1976b, *55*(2), 60–64.

Sexton, W. P. *Organization Theories.* Columbus, Ohio: Merrill, 1970.

Struening, E. L., and Guttentag, M. *Handbook of Evaluation Research.* Beverly Hills, Calif.: Sage, 1975.

Webb, E., and others. *Unobtrusive Measures: Non-Reactive Research in the Social Sciences.* Chicago: Rand McNally, 1966.

Western Interstate Commission for Higher Education. *The ecosystem model: Designing campus environments.* Boulder, Colo.: Western Interstate Commission for Higher Education, 1972.

Grant P. Sherwood　　　　　　　　　**16**

Allied and Paraprofessional Assistance

The allied and paraprofessional model represents a relatively new approach to providing or expanding student services at the college and university level. The concept of using students to help professional staff in their job responsibilities is not new. For years, housing as well as admissions administrators have employed undergraduates in various orientation, advising, and administrative functions. Faculty members, campus ministers, and a wide assortment of professionals in fields other than student services have been consistently involved in various aspects of student services. What has been severely lacking, however, is the notion that there should be an organized, thoughtful process of integrating these allied or paraprofessionals into the institutional work setting. In essence, a plan or model is needed that defines the purpose, goals, and objectives of using allied and paraprofessionals. The time is ripe to concentrate on such a plan. Full-time staff face zero or minimal growth possibilities, although services are in increased demand. Systematic use of allied and paraprofessionals promises improved services to students, higher staff morale, and increased productivity on a cost-efficient basis.

What roles can these additional resources play in our work? Let us start by defining the terms *paraprofessionals* and *allied professionals* in the student services setting. *"Paraprofessionals* [are] persons without extended professional training who are specifically selected, trained, and given ongoing supervision to perform some designated portion of the tasks usually performed by the professional. This does not include offering of support services, such as clerical, as the major function. Paraprofessionals are involved in the central activity of the agency with which they are associated, such as counseling [and] orientation. They are employed to work in a specific area for which they are qualified because of their specific skills. They are generally members of the indigenous population, or the population being served. In higher education, they are therefore students, undergraduate or graduate. Paraprofessionals generally receive some remuneration for their services" (Delworth, Sherwood, and Casaburri, 1974, p. 12).

"Allied professionals . . . differ from paraprofessionals in basically two respects: experience and level of education in a particular profession. Allied professionals are defined as administrators, faculty members, campus clergy, or professionals from the community who become involved and are trained to offer a special student service. Advanced graduate students are considered allied professionals as well. Reimbursement for such allied professional services varies greatly. Commonly, allied professionals trade their free service for a personal growth experience or for advancement of their own professional goals. Equally common on campus is the release of time of the allied professional from regular assignments for involvement in the additional service function. There are times, however, that the expertise of this type of specialist is so fundamental to the proposed program that involvement must be procured and monetarily reimbursed" (Delworth and Aulepp, 1976, p. 1).

I believe that allied and paraprofessionals can be productively used in every student services area or unit. Indeed, it seems clear from the literature that student paraprofessionals, if not allied professionals, have been so used. Counseling and career centers use paraprofessionals to lead programs and workshops in such areas as test anxiety, life planning, assertion skills, and resume writing. Both allied and paraprofessionals staff crisis phone lines and centers at a number of colleges and universities. Orientation programs employ undergraduate paraprofessionals as advisers and use advanced graduate students and faculty members as trainers, consultants, and organizers for orientation activities. Residence halls offer many opportunities for students to work as hall staff and often for faculty members and others to provide leadership, training, and special programs as allied professionals. Admissions and financial aid offices often employ paraprofessionals for specific functions, such as recruitment and interviewing. Tutoring programs are generally composed almost entirely of allied and paraprofessionals.

Unfortunately, the research on paraprofessional effectiveness in these many roles is limited, and research on allied professionals is virtually nonexistent. Brown (1965, 1972, 1974) and Zunker and Brown (1966) give the strongest positive evidence. Their research indicates that student paraprofessionals are as effective as professionals in academic adjustment counseling. Upcraft (1971) demonstrated the effectiveness of undergraduate students working as academic advisers.

Clearly, additional research on the effect of services offered by allied and paraprofessionals is needed. Research on paraprofessionals in community and other agencies (Gartner, 1969; Ellsworth, 1968; Carkhuff, 1969) indicates that paraprofessionals *can* be effective in providing services and that the large number of seemingly successful programs, both within and outside higher education, cannot be overlooked.

The basic role for allied and paraprofessionals in student services is thus to provide services to students. The model advocated in this chapter, however, views such personnel more broadly. We see the goals of a paraprofessional program as follows:

1. To maximize the cost effectiveness of any program without decreasing the quantity or quality of services offered
2. To build on the inherent value of peer identification between those offering and those receiving the service
3. To free professional staff members for training, development, and planning activities by using allied and paraprofessionals to help provide direct services to students
4. To enhance the professional's and the agency's image and to help establish more regular, long-term contacts with the student population

Goals 2 and 4 are especially relevant for student paraprofessionals; Goals 1 and 3 are played by both allied and paraprofessionals. These goals can be realized by paying careful attention to all phases of the model presented in this chapter.

The model has four stages: (1) institutional preparation, (2) position and personnel selection, (3) staff training, and (4) program evaluation. These stages are sequential, and each stage is interrelated to others and to any or all of the four goals of a paraprofessional program.

Institutional Preparation

Institutional preparation refers to assessing existing professional attitudes and interests of the staff; evaluating the availability of financial, human, and physical resources; and planning, developing, and selling the new program. The initial reception institutional staff give to using allied and paraprofessionals is a key determinant of its ultimate success or failure.

In many instances, staff and students may agree that the student services offered do not address major campus issues. Many services exist because of tradition, without due consideration of need or purpose. Minimal thought is often given to allocation of staff time, use of funds, and duplication of existing programs. Communication among departments is thus minimized, and each service area appears content to live with the status quo, resulting in reduced output and creativity.

The paraprofessional model can help overcome these obstacles. More specifically, the following questions need to be addressed: "Are programs meeting the perceived needs of the academic community and the real needs of the student population? Is staff wasting time on functions that make minimal contributions because of budget cutbacks? Can student feedback be used more effectively in making administrative decisions? And, finally, are departments or agencies in the student services willing to relinquish certain professional responsibilities to trained students and allied professionals in order to provide more developmental time to the administrator?" Institutional preparation thus becomes a relatively complex issue that must be addressed very early in the planning stage.

Planning Team. A planning team should be established to define specific program goals and objectives and to assess current institutional needs. The team should consist of student services professionals, faculty, administrative staff outside the student services field, and students or allied professionals. The latter three groups may be initial team members or may be added to the planning effort once team goals and objectives have been established. Moore and Delworth (1976) state that the planning team must

1. Take the initial idea and make it a student services commitment
2. Develop a written explanation of how the use of allied or paraprofessionals supports the established goals of the student services division
3. Demonstrate through assessment that the paraprofessional model is both needed and understood in the particular setting
4. Identify resources crucial to the program's operation

Further commitment from the team is more long range and involves developing specific department goals, an appropriate delivery system, evaluation procedures and a potential pilot program. Often the team names a program coordinator to assume major responsibility for implementing the program.

Professional Attitudes. The program will clearly never get off the ground if it does not have philosophical support from the division leader (for example, the vice-president or dean). If the impetus to start the program does not come from the divisional leadership level, it is at least important that the leader become involved very early in the planning stages. The planning team must see that they have the support and appropriate involvement from the chief officer in the division. An orientation for department or agency heads should also be set up, to explain the program objectives and to alleviate anxieties. Initially, some professionals may totally reject this model, arguing that it represents an administrative ploy to reduce departmental budgets for professional salaries. Still others may deny that students, even with adequate training and supervision, can offer quality services. These challenges are to be expected. The planning team at this point must identify its bases of support within the division and begin the program with these agencies. The ideal is to have the whole division actively participating.

Resources. The resources needed for developing the paraprofessional program fall into three categories: financial, human, and physical.

Financial Resources. Financial resources are necessary for obvious reasons. The paraprofessional by definition is not a volunteer, although the allied professional may be. A list of basic operating expenses generally includes paraprofessional salaries, operational costs, equipment and supplies, training materials, lease of facilities, and professional expenses.

It is reasonable to expect the program to *cost* money for perhaps the first six to twelve months. That is, the professional time spent in planning and initial implementation of the program will be roughly equivalent to time spent in direct delivery of services, so that paraprofessional salaries and other costs are additional expenses. Over time, professional time invested in the program will decrease to a cost-effective level. An example is as follows:

Activity A
(totally offered by professionals)

- 100 hours of service at $10 per hour   = $1,000

Activity B
(similar service offered by professional + trained paraprofessional)

- 10 hours of professional service at $10 per hour   = $100
- 120 hours of paraprofessional service at $4 per hour   = $480
- 10 hours of professional supervision and consultation
  at $10 per hour   = $100
                                                                                      $680

In this example, total *hours* devoted to the activity increase, but total professional time and cost substantially decrease. Of course, programs vary in the amount of savings realized through use of paraprofessionals. The important idea to remember is that the savings are not realized immediately, so that planners must commit themselves to an initial financial investment.

The planning team should identify various funding sources. The financial aid office is a starting point to review current student wage levels and to determine available state, federal, and private funding sources. A centralized funding model can be used if all potential positions are to be funded through one agency in charge of total program coordination. However, the individual department that uses paraprofessionals often funds the positions directly from its operating budget. This decentralized funding source is particularly relevant for those operations financed by auxiliary monies. Generally a combination of these two plans is best. Other funding sources that should be investigated are federal and state research grants, foundation or corporate grants, financial support from local business interests, and compensation in kind, such as room, board, academic credit, or tuition waivers.

Human Resources. The paraprofessional program is people-oriented. The program not only serves a specific student population but also involves dedicated staff who ultimately deliver the service. Professional time involved in selection, training, supervision, and evaluation is considerable, particularly in the early stages. This time commitment decreases in direct proportion to the increased productivity of the fully functioning paraprofessional staff.

One group of staff who play an active resource role in the program are the secretarial and clerical personnel. Because the paraprofessionals will be actively involved in the central function of a service, they will be cooperating with the office support staff. Secretarial staff are typically the initial contact with students. Thus, it is important that their attitudes and relationships with total agency staff be positive. They also offer particularly crucial support for paraprofessional staff. Together they form a close working relationship in which the paraprofessional depends extensively on the skills and experience of secretarial personnel.

The role that professional supervisors play in administering this program is critical. The professional's commitment, training and supervisory skills, and ability to evaluate performance are vital. The planning team and ultimately the coordinator of the paraprofessional program should very carefully assess individual strengths and weaknesses and design ways to increase professional competencies. Delworth and Aulepp (1976, p. 42) have identified four basic characteristics of qualified professional supervisors.

1. Maturity
2. Generally good organizational ability and work habits
3. Flexibility and interest in learning new skills
4. Competency in areas in which they will work with paraprofessionals

A fifth characteristic might be termed supervisor motivation—a dedication to work with subordinate staff to improve the services offered.

Moore (1974, pp. 309–311) describes other critical supervisory skills as the abilities

1. To assess the paraprofessional's beginning skill level
2. To teach the paraprofessional how to make use of supervision
3. To teach the paraprofessional the necessary skills for successful completion of the job
4. To help the paraprofessional deal with the ambivalence and anxiety of the job
5. To help the paraprofessional identify and eliminate overextension

The time and attention spent by supervisors can significantly enhance the paraprofessional's input. A primary goal of the paraprofessional model is improved feedback to the system. Thus, the professional has a significant listening role as supervisor. And the professional must make every effort not to use organizational structure, red tape, and jargon, which all frustrate input from paraprofessionals.

Finally, the professional must systematically design a peer support base for the allied or paraprofessional. The opportunity to discuss issues, concerns, and operating procedures in a peer group is important. This sense of community among paraprofessionals is an essential complement to the professional's supervisory role.

Physical Resources. Physical resources are often overlooked in the success of paraprofessional programs. However, the lack of such essentials as office space, supplies and equipment, and program areas can handicap efforts.

The physical needs of a paraprofessional must be considered. A base of operation for the paraprofessional needs to be identified that does not conflict with the general needs of the office. Housing paraprofessionals and professionals together in the same office is rarely a viable alternative. Often the paraprofessional's status within the office is determined by the type of accommodations provided. Before confirming positions, the professional must also check availability of equipment and supplies related to the paraprofessional's job. A phone, duplicating facilities, production supplies, and other equipment are generally needed.

Finally, by the nature of their position, many paraprofessionals need additional program space. For example, a paraprofessional might be in charge of a career-planning workshop for the placement office. The size and purpose of this responsibility dictates the need for expanded program space. Space needs should be determined before responsibilities are assigned.

Selection

There are two distinct selection responsibilities in the paraprofessional model: choosing specific positions and selecting people to fill them. Both processes are critical.

Position. Often the team decides to begin by using allied or paraprofessionals in only one type of position (for example, as residence hall advisers or as tutors). A more comprehensive model may also be developed, in which various student services agencies or departments may design two or more specific positions for paraprofessionals. In the latter case, the planning team must evaluate requests from the various student services departments on the basis of predetermined criteria. These criteria should be generated in terms of the program goals.

Each agency requesting paraprofessional assistance should submit a standardized application form. In general, the proposal should answer the following questions: "Does the position described involve the allied or paraprofessional in the central function of the agency? Has a specific, clear job description been established? Are the basic skills necessary to assume this position specified? Is the professional supervisor specified, and is there some understanding of commitment on his or her part? Are the proposed means of training, supervision, and evaluation specified in detail? Are supportive resources available in the agency?"

Once data from all agencies submitting requests have been analyzed, the planning team can begin to select positions. Then it can rank order positions and secure final approval from the chief administrative officer in the division, if necessary. As the programs become more established, a selection team composed of a wide range of paraprofessionals and professionals from the division can annually select positions and provide evaluation.

Personnel. We can identify some of the core characteristics of successful allied professionals and paraprofessionals by referring to solid programs throughout the country. Some "baseline" characteristics are:

1. Familiarity and experience with the institutional setting in order to make appropriate referrals, decisions, and contributions

2. The ability to handle the dual roles of paraprofessional and some other role, such as student or faculty member in terms of both general flexibility and time management
3. The ability to communicate effectively with a diverse population
4. The ability to exercise personal confidence in a variety of leadership capacities
5. The ability to understand and actively promote the philosophy of student services and the specific unit

Application materials should highlight these basic characteristics. The screening process should give applicants the opportunity to provide both oral and written comments about these characteristics.

Job expectations should be detailed for each position available, thereby allowing applicants to indicate specific programs of interest. For efficiency and fairness' sake, applications can be accepted at one central location on an ongoing basis. This helps to establish an "active pool" from which to select qualified candidates. The student services agencies employing allied or paraprofessionals should establish the selection process in advance. Some successful techniques are role-playing real-life situations, review of written recommendations, group interviews, written tests of communication and discrimination, academic progress and success, and on-the-job prehiring performance evaluations. If criteria such as grade-point average, age, or class standing are used, this should be made very clear on the general application materials.

Some promotion of allied and paraprofessional positions may be necessary to attract qualified applicants, particularly in the first year. It helps to articulate the positive benefits of serving in these positions:

General
1. Ability to contribute directly to improving the student services system
2. Development of personal skills related to personal growth, maturity, and self-confidence
3. Feeling more sense of community with the institution in general
Paraprofessionals
1. Direct work experience, which often opens doorways to full-time professional employment
2. Earning money while attending school
3. Supplementing academic studies with direct experience
Allied professionals
1. Opportunity to learn new skills applicable to their chosen professional field
2. Increased exposure to students in a different work setting

Staff Training

There are several goals of the total training program. Basically, we are attempting to get the allied and paraprofessionals functioning successfully in their assigned responsibilities. This means the paraprofessional must develop a sense of identity with the agency and must acquire skills needed to perform assigned tasks. Training is a dynamic process that begins in the initial stages of employment and progresses systematically throughout the contract period. It is the responsibility of the professional supervisor to identify paraprofessional needs and to develop the training methodology and techniques to serve these needs. Two general vehicles can achieve these goals: core training and job-specific training.

Core Training. There is an essential body of knowledge or expectations that all paraprofessionals in student services should be expected to know and understand. This "core" of the student services division comprises acknowledged commitments of our profession: developing a sense of community; behaving with openness, honesty, and trust; being able to organize and administer; being able to understand and interpret existing policies and procedures; adhering to professional ethics; and understanding and developing "helping relationships."

These skills or attributes are not assumed. Paraprofessionals need to gain insights into these areas and to relate these to their specific job responsibilities. Riessman (1967) and Carkhuff (1971) view core training as having two desirable effects on the participants: (1) eliminating negative habits, due most of the time to inexperience or poor judgment, and (2) teaching basic skills that are interpreted as helping and positive.

To develop consistency throughout the program, it is strongly suggested that this training be done as a group process, involving all paraprofessionals and as many supervisors as possible. This process should occur early in the employment stage and should use available professional talent (including academic faculty). Core training can be accomplished in a structured class for academic credit or in a retreat format.

Job-Specific Training. As the adjective "job-specific" implies, these skills are taught at the agency level by the professional supervisor. The professional must begin by referring to the detailed job description produced before the application process. The supervisor identifies needed skills and designs a training program based on expectations and necessary skills. For example, a paraprofessional being trained to function as a staff member in the career services office may need to (1) interview candidates effectively; (2) understand the community resources related to job placement; and (3) instruct students in resume preparation. The supervisor's responsibility is to establish training programs to meet these listed needs. These may include (1) practice interview sessions, possibly using videotape feedback; (2) presentations by community leaders, with field trips designed to give firsthand observation at various personnel offices; and (3) practice sessions designed to review and research effective ways of writing resumes.

The trainer should write well-defined, behavioral objectives for the paraprofessional. Progress toward these objectives should be evaluated routinely and feedback given to the paraprofessional.

The following steps, adapted from Delworth, Sherwood, and Casaburri (1974, p. 23), are applicable to the job-specific training role of the professional supervisor when a specific skill is being taught:

1. Break the skill down into small sequential steps.
2. Explain the goals and method of training and skill, and tell the allied or paraprofessional what he or she will be taught and why.
3. Describe the first step in learning the skill.
4. Demonstrate the first step.
5. Give the trainee an opportunity to try the first step either in a role-playing or real-life situation.
6. Give feedback on performance.
7. Repeat Steps 5 and 6 until an acceptable performance level is achieved
8. Discuss process with trainee.

The opportunity to be creative with training methodology and techniques is almost limitless. Some formats supervisors might want to explore are (1) role playing and group simulation, (2) workshops and retreats, (3) academic course lectures, (4) written materials (for example, programmed learning manuals), and (5) audiovisual presentations.

Finally, it is important to remember that trainers are successful not only because of what they teach but also because of how their acts are interpreted. Training is clinical, in that the professional must understand the reality of a situation through observing, listening, and seeing how its parts are interrelated. In assuming the role of both trainer and supervisor, one must come to grips with the fact that one's behavior and attitude are constantly on display and that supervision and training require the ability to make tough decisions related to one's own personal philosophy.

At Colorado State University, in the Office of Housing and Residence Education, we have prepared a statement related to the Residence Hall Staff training of paraprofessional staff. The following excerpt from the Training Manual (1977) illustrates how goals and objectives are conceptualized:

Staff Development and Training

Introduction

Staff development and training is an ongoing process, which begins with initial orientation and training sessions and continues throughout the year. Each of you brings to this process your own skills and abilities, which reflect your past experiences.

Staff development and training is a vital aspect of our Housing and Residence Education program. If we expect to provide the best possible living environment and services for students, staff must be able to respond to the many diverse problems/concerns and tasks generated within the halls. How well we perform depends on how well we prepare. Below is a list of general training goals, which you should review before developing or participating in our staff training program.

Paraprofessional Staff Training Goals

1. To clarify the role or respective positions within the Housing and Residence Education system:
   a. Organizational overview
   b. Office of Housing and Residence Education philosophy and goals
   c. Position job description
   d. Supervisor's expectations of you and your expectations of supervisor
2. To develop the following skills basic to the staff helping role:
   a. Communication skills
   b. Ability to understand one's limits as a helper
   c. When it is necessary to refer
   d. Awareness of crisis and emergency situations and how to respond to them appropriately
3. To develop an understanding of the concept of programming and its relationship to your position and Office of Housing and Residence Education philosophy
4. To transmit necessary information relative to all administrative responsibilities of each position (such as opening, desk, and duty tasks)
5. To develop a code of ethics for paraprofessional and professional staff behavior
6. To develop an organizational team concept which takes into account varying group strategies; for example, conflict, cooperation, compromise, cohesion and identity
7. To acquaint staff with existing policies and procedures, and to identify areas which need further development
8. To assimilate information about campus and community resources and services which are necessary for
   a. Student development in the residence halls
   b. A successful referral service for students

9. To develop an understanding of one's individual values and
   how they affect one's ability to assist students in their development
10. To provide an opportunity for staff to explore and identify
    specific areas of interest which will lead to personal and pro-
    fessional development

These goals will primarily be accomplished through four
major aspects of our staff development and training program: (1)
fall orientation and training sessions; (2) in-service training; (3)
an academic course for student assistants and (4) staff retreats.

Evaluation

Evaluation is a predetermined, planned phase of the total paraprofessional model. Evaluation method should focus on the key elements
of the model:

1. To increase credibility and accountability within the academic community
2. To provide feedback to both professionals and allied or paraprofessionals about progress on performance
3. To assess changes in total agency and division productivity and morale as a result of using allied or paraprofessionals
4. To determine if specific goals and objectives regarding the delivery of
   services to students were accomplished
5. To decide which programs merit continued support

Data on each of these issues must be gathered from a variety of
sources: the allied or paraprofessional, professional supervisors,
members of the planning team, office personnel who work with and
enjoy the benefits of paraprofessional services, and, ultimately, the
students being served. All these sources should be assessed at predetermined intervals to provide feedback about the model application. It is
particularly important to discriminate between program and personnel
in evaluation. All too often a program is eliminated because of personnel deficiencies, not because of its potential contribution to student
services.

Delworth and Aulepp (1976) underscored the necessity of discussing evaluation among planning team members to conceptualize an
overall approach. They concluded that the evaluation plan must
include

1. Decisions on what is to be evaluated and monitored
2. A sequence for evaluating various components

3. Methods of evaluating each component
4. A schedule describing how often and when each component will be evaluated
5. Decisions regarding who will be responsible for the evaluation of each component
6. Decisions regarding how and to whom evaluation and monitoring data will be reported

Differing techniques for gathering data are available in the evaluation process. A list of these methods follows, showing the relationship between the position evaluated, criteria considered for evaluation, and the actual method employed. For sake of brevity, three basic components of the model are analyzed—the paraprofessional, the professional supervisor, and the services offered. These are only some examples of data collection. Oscar Lenning delineates evaluation strategies more fully in Chapter Ten.

What or Who Is Evaluated	*Evaluation Criteria*	*Evaluation Methodology*
Paraprofessional	Motivation and interest in position	Supervisor assessment
	Skill development	Self-assessment
	Accomplishment of goals	Ratings from students served
	Ability to effectively use resources	Feedback from other paraprofessionals and support staff
Professional supervisor	Commitment to program	System coordinator assessment
	Supervisory skills	Self-assessment
	Development of training program	Feedback from other supervisors and supervisee
	Ability to set priorities	
Service offered	Quality of products	Contact log
	Changes in behavior or attitudes	Student attitude questionnaire
	Numbers served	Time and efficiency studies
	Time and money expended	Direct observation
		Statistical analysis of behavioral objectives using pre- and posttests
		Budget analysis

Other functions that should be evaluated in depth are the selection process, the training process (both core and job specific), planning team effectiveness, the system coordinator's role, and ongoing community perceptions of the paraprofessional program.

As student services professionals, we have often been lax in developing solid research and evaluation programs to support what we do and why we do it. The paraprofessional model will succeed only if there is a total commitment to research each step in the process and to redesign procedures accordingly.

Summary

This chapter proposes and documents various ways to adapt the allied and paraprofessional model in student services. I have generalized its application to the many agencies termed "student services," because paraprofessional skills can be used in all departments that meet the student needs on campuses today. It is outmoded to think of paraprofessionals as only capable of filling the live-in residence hall positions or serving as campus tour guides for the admissions office. Creative application of their skills has proven successful in less traditional areas, including (but not limited to) student orientation, academic assistance, counseling center programs, student activities, financial aid, career planning, health center programs, and food service operations.

It is important to stress that allied or paraprofessional positions are designed to complement rather than displace professional staff. The basic goal of an allied or paraprofessional program is to maintain or increase student services without increasing costs. Student paraprofessionals in particular can also allow more student input to the student services unit and enhance student identification with that unit.

Whether we choose to use either paraprofessionals or allied professionals to help provide services depends on a number of factors, including the skill level necessary to complete the job, compatible allied professions available within the institution, and the funds available to attract qualified people. Generally speaking, a combination of allied and parapersonnel is the ideal staffing pattern. The age, level of education, and maturity the allied professional brings to the student services setting often directly complements the enthusiasm and peer relationship inherent in the paraprofessional groups.

The needs of students on campuses are constantly changing, so we professionals must also redesign programs to respond to this change. The allied and paraprofessional model is a practical attempt to address this issue.

References

Brown, W. F. "Student-to-Student Counseling for Academic Adjustment." *Personnel and Guidance Journal,* 1965, *18,* 821–830.
Brown, W. F. *Student-to-Student Counseling: An Approach to Moti-

vating Academic Achievement. Austin, Texas: Hogg Foundation for Mental Health, 1972.

Brown, W. F. "Effectiveness of Paraprofessionals: The Evidence." *Personnel and Guidance Journal,* 1974, *53,* 257–263.

Carkhuff, R. R. *Helping and Human Relations.* Vols. 1 and 2. New York: Holt, Rinehart and Winston, 1969.

Carkhuff, R. R. "Principles of Social Action in Training for New Careers in Human Services." *Journal of Counseling Psychology,* 1971, *18,* 147–151.

Delworth, U., and Aulepp, L. *Training Manual for Paraprofessional and Allied Professional Programs.* Boulder, Colo.: Western Interstate Commission for Higher Education, 1976.

Delworth, U., Sherwood, G., and Casaburri, N. *Student Paraprofessionals: A Working Model for Higher Education.* Student Personnel Series No. 17, American College Personnel Association. Washington, D.C.: American Personnel and Guidance Association, 1974.

Ellsworth, R. B. *Nonprofessionals in Psychiatric Rehabilitation.* New York: Appleton-Century-Crofts, 1968.

Gartner, A. *Do Paraprofessionals Improve Human Services: A First Critical Appraisal of the Data.* New York: New Careers Development Center, New York University, 1969.

Moore, M. "Training Professionals to Work with Professionals." *Personnel and Guidance Journal,* 1974, *53,* 308–312.

Moore, M., and Delworth, U. *Training Manual for Student Service Program Development.* Boulder, Colo.: Western Interstate Commission for Higher Education, 1976.

Riessman, F. "Strategies and Suggestions for Training Non-Professionals." *Community Mental Health Journal,* 1967, *3,* 103–110.

Residence Hall Staff Training Manual. Fort Collins, Colo.: Office of Housing and Residence Education, Colorado State University, 1977.

Upcraft, M. L. "Undergraduate Students as Academic Advisors." *Personnel and Guidance Journal,* 1971, *49,* 827–831.

Zunker, V. G., and Brown, W. F. "Comparative Effectiveness of Student and Professional Counselors." *Personnel and Guidance Journal,* 1966, *44,* 738–743.

PART V

Organization and Management

The job of the administrator and manager in student services has become increasingly complex during the past decade. New tasks and demands have arisen from campus disturbances, increased accountability, and developments in the field. Administrators must deal with the expectations of top-level campus administrators, academic faculty, their own staff members, student services colleagues, governing boards, and student consumers. In addition, these varying constituencies are increasingly better organized and more assertive in expressing their needs and demands. Clearly, student services administrators at all levels need much more "know-how" to effectively perform their roles. The chapters in Part Five provide both an overview and a selective, in-depth presentation of the knowledge and skills administrators need. Although the first chapter is aimed primarily at chief student services administrators in complex systems, we believe middle managers will find it helpful as well. The remaining four chapters should be of equal value to top administrators, directors of student services units, and staff members who have or hope to have some management responsibilities. Graduate students may find it helpful to familiarize themselves with the main concepts in each of the chapters.

In Chapter Seventeen, Tom Dutton and Scott Rickard share their expertise in organizing and managing a student services system or division. Their central thesis is that an effective system is built on an understanding of and interface with the mission of the institution, on solid assumptions regarding student services, on appropriate organizational structures, and on effective management processes. They give a lucid and helpful presentation of the multidimensional organization structure for complex systems.

Concerns and specific tasks of middle managers—that is, directors of student services units—are addressed by Cynthia Johnson and Cecelia Foxley in Chapter Eighteen. They focus on practical strategies for goal setting, management information systems, and resource management. Johnson and Foxley's ideas are well tested and should prove useful to the frequently overwhelmed and frustrated director, as well as to those agency staff members who have specific management roles. They include some particularly helpful advice on time management.

In Chapter Nineteen, Robert Kerr outlines concepts and models for evaluating student services systems and entire agencies. His examples from various institutions provide a focus for administrators who are just beginning to attend seriously to evaluation, as well as for those who are making their evaluation processes more effective.

Staff development is the key to "pulling it all together," now that staff turnover has declined. Harry Canon's ideas and work in this area are well known and respected. In Chapter Twenty Canon presents a solid rationale and model for staff development and specific suggestions on building an effective program. Canon also challenges us to look beyond maintaining and improving narrowly defined professional skills. He believes we can use staff development to acknowledge and respond to our roles in the larger missions of the student services division and of the college or university itself.

Concepts and models are necessary but not sufficient for effective administrative work. In Chapter Twenty One Val Christensen outlines a superb set of practical guidelines for "getting the job done." They provide the best road map we have seen for ensuring positive changes in our work as administrators. Val presented his guidelines during a WICHE conference in 1976, and they have become part of the treasury of unpublished gems for many of us since then. We are pleased to be able to share them now with a larger audience of administrators and student services professionals.

The blend of concept, models, and practical strategies in Part Five provides a basis for administrative competency. We believe that serious attention to these ideas will result in increased managerial effectiveness and satisfaction, which in turn will increase the impact of student services on campus.

Thomas B. Dutton
Scott T. Rickard

17

Organizing
Student Services

A number of challenges for higher education in general and student service administration in particular must be met in the decade ahead; among them are conflicting views of purpose, demands for access and educational programs responsive to particular needs, greater scrutiny of expenditures, inflation, steady-state or declining enrollment, growing litigation, and increasing federal and state legislation designed to protect student consumers, employee rights, and the public interest, as well as to maintain health and safety standards. To cope with these critical problems, institutions need to clarify purposes, rights, responsibilities, and internal governance processes; examine how they are organized and managed; and make necessary adjustments in their management systems. Effective management is particularly important today because of the increased complexity of institutions and because of the external and internal demands they face.

Student services administrators must therefore deal with an array of difficult questions: "What are appropriate organizational assumptions for student services systems? What are key organizing principles for these services? How can systems be managed more effectively? And what is a viable role for the chief student services officer?" This chapter grapples with these questions in order to help administrators do their work more effectively and with greater satisfaction.

We begin by looking at organizational assumptions and discuss principles for building the organizational structure. We then focus on the advantages of a multidimensional model before turning, in the last section of the chapter, to the management of the system and especially to the role of the chief administrator.

Organizational Assumptions

All systems, or organizations, are based on assumptions about human behavior, values, and ways of operating. Such assumptions form the basic philosophy of student services. It is important to make these assumptions or philosophical bases explicit, for several reasons. To the degree that assumptions are examined, understood, and clarified, the student services program and organization contribute more effectively to institutional goals. Administrators often accept assumptions that are in vogue without fully analyzing them. For example, with the waning of various *in loco parentis* functions during the 1960s and 1970s, many student services programs have moved their emphasis from control and reaction to student development. We need to ask whether student development programs merely restate the "personnel point of view" or if they represent a new approach based on different assumptions about student growth and management practice.

There are practical and politically important reasons why educational and organizational assumptions should be stated as explicitly as possible. During the recent retrenchment in higher education, several student services programs were the victims of budgetary reductions and in some cases were virtually eliminated. Most campuses face declining or limited enrollment in the 1980s, coupled with rising inflation and increasing costs as they attempt to balance current budgets. In this age of renewed concern for accountability, programs will increasingly be asked to justify their existence. Programs that have a clearly defined educational rationale increase probability of their survival as well as their effectiveness in responding to student needs.

Core Assumptions. We see at least three core assumptions in student services. These concern how human beings work best, the ties between the institution and its components, and the pragmatic nature of our organizations.

The critical element in management is people. People create organizations to accomplish goals that could not be achieved without cooperation. Recognizing that cooperative effort is essential to fulfill vital needs motivates people to accept compromises, forswear individual aims, and obey the requirements of the social order (Audrey, 1970, p. 72). Moreover, achievement of goals requires the creation of large-scale organizations (Kast and Rosenzweig, 1973). To understand and improve performance of such organizations, people have developed the systems approach. Churchman, Ackoff, and Arnoff, (1957, p. 7) define a system as an "inter-connected complex of functionally related components." Richman and Farmer (1974) characterize the university as "a continuously importing-transforming-exporting system." More specifically, they describe a university as "a set of interdependent parts that together make up a whole because each contributes something and receives something from the whole which, in turn, is interdependent with some larger environment" (Richman and Farmer, 1974, p. 5).

Regarding assumptions about the tie between the institution and its components, as a subsystem of the larger campus management system the student services organization must function as an integral part of the system to effectively contribute to institutional goals. Student services has no standing in its own right; it has only one valid reason for existing—to serve the goals of the institution. Accordingly, the context for student services must be institutional purposes, philosophy, and values.

Regarding the pragmatic nature of organizations, there is no management system that is suited to all institutions or set of individuals. Effective systems must be shaped in relation to institutional mission and character and the available human talent. Successful management must be pragmatic. Managers and others in the organizations must be free to exercise judgment about what will work in concrete situations and to alter short-range goals and means in order to accomplish long-range goals.

Educational Assumptions. Additional assumptions regarding learning, education, and the nature of the campus learning environment guide student services activities. First and foremost is the belief that valuable learning can take place outside formal classroom activity. Student residences, cultural and artistic programs, student organizations and activities, recreational programs, and athletics are potential settings for learning. This position, promulgated by any number of educators and educational groups, including the Carnegie Commission on Higher Education in *Priorities for Action: Final Report of the Carnegie Commission on Higher Education* (1973), holds that a constructive learning environment should provide planned learning experiences not only in intellectual but also in cultural, artistic, personal, and recreational areas.

A second belief about education is that effective action in influencing student learning depends on cooperation with the faculty. It is no more valid for student services staff to expect to effectively deal with a student's personal development independent of his or her academic life than it is for a faculty member to think that a student's life outside the classroom does not affect his or her academic growth.

Third, student services staff also value and encourage contributions made to the campus by students from various cultural, socioeconomic, and experiential backgrounds. The vigor and vitality of the institution depends to a large degree on the quality, as well as the diversity, of its students. Efforts to attract, enroll, and retain ethnic and low-income minority students, as well as older students, are an important part of the campus educational program. In this same vein, equal access and opportunity for both men and women students continue to be very important. Continuing efforts are needed to ensure equal access for both sexes to student services and to encourage full participation in a wide variety of activities.

Student services activity is also guided by the assumptions that individuals differ with respect to the ways and rates in which they learn. Some learn most effectively through reading and private reflection, while others need direct experience and involvement in practical situations. Some students excel at memorization, and others function best at analysis and synthesis. Efforts to facilitate learning require an awareness and comprehension of differences in learning style.

Finally, we tend to believe that the learner must actively participate in the learning process. Primary responsibility for learning rests with the individual. Certainly, learning can and should be facilitated by the teacher, adviser, or counselor, but the individual learner must be able to experiment, synthesize, and use knowledge gained for solving problems and completing concrete tasks. Therefore, programs are designed to respond to individual needs, learning habits, and levels of development; to encompass a wide range of activities, both curricular and extracurricular; and to facilitate the integration and application of knowledge.

The organization of the student services program is thus a system of learning support services designed to help students clarify and attain their educational objectives. This system complements the institutional program by providing services that focus on the total development of the student. The core organizational and educational assumptions provide a philosophy on which to build the structure of the student services organization.

Organizing Principles

A critical question facing all administrators is how to build an organizational structure that will realize these goals most effectively. We believe that the principles and guidelines discussed in this section will help administrators design such a structure.

Stimulating Creativity. The organization must be responsive to the goals and needs of the people who work in it. Stimulating creativity in its members is a challenge in all organizations. Hierarchical organizations are necessary to achieve goals in complex settings, but with their cumbersome bureaucracies and communication difficulties, they tend to work against creativity. To cope with this reality, organization members must recognize the worth and importance of the individual and develop specific strategies to stimulate people to extend and stretch themselves in their work, to interact with different parts of the organization, and to see the larger perspective. They also need to accept candor, spontaneity, and individual differences and to recognize the human drive to maintain some control over one's own life. According to Likert and Likert (1976, p. 5), "The highest levels of creativity are found in those organizations which deliberately stimulate innovative-mindedness by encouraging diversity and differences among persons engaged in tasks where imaginative thinking yields valuable results."

It is normal for individuals in the organization to want to influence decisions that affect them and to feel that they have some measure of control over their role and work in the organization. To create organizations that recognize and reinforce these realities is extremely difficult in complex institutions, but it is possible if appropriate use is made of recent research. Likert and Likert (1976, p. 8) concluded that new knowledge growing out of social science research can be used to create, within social and political institutions, "the structure and decision-making processes to enable all persons in the institution to exert influence commensurate with their contribution upon decisions affecting them." The organization must stimulate people to interact because this enhances achievement of objectives. Both informally and formally, people must pool their talents to complete tasks aimed at achieving institutional goals.

Agreement on Purposes. Maintaining unity of purpose through all levels and segments of the organization is a basic challenge in hierarchical structures, where work has been divided into small units with specific roles and responsibilities. Assigning specific tasks to units is essential if the required work is to be completed, but it also tends to differentiate functions, isolate units from one another, and diffuse the overall goals of the organization. To the extent units do not identify with overall goals, they tend to serve their own needs rather than those of the total organization. Richman and Farmer (1974, pp. 192–193) have described this problem as *suboptimization:* "Most people try to suboptimize in organizations—they try to make their groups perfect, no matter what happens to the total organization. If every group is trying to do this, with more or less success, the result is extensive suboptimization, with the overall organization functioning much less smoothly and efficiently than it might." When organizational and unit goals are unclear, overlap unduly, or compete, the potential for suboptimization is increased. To avoid this problem, considerable time must be devoted to clarifying goals at all levels and the roles that units play in contributing to the mission of the total organization.

Unity of Command and Delegation of Authority. There must also be unity of command. Someone must be in a position of ultimate responsibility and accountability. How this process functions and who is responsible for what decisions must be clear to staff at all levels. Middle managers need to be clear on what decisions they can make and are responsible and accountable for making, which decisions require consultation with the chief student services administrator, and which the chief administrator makes with or without consultation. Written delegations and assignments, reviewed annually with the principal parties, should be routinely meshed into the fabric of the organization. One way to ensure that delegation and assignment of work is clear and up-to-date is to annually review position descriptions. Although authority to act can be delegated, ultimate responsibility cannot be reassigned. In the final analysis, a higher-level official can be held accountable for the misdeeds of a lower-level officer. Accordingly, some senior officers delegate on paper but in reality retain virtual control, thereby constricting the freedom of subordinates to complete complex assignments creatively.

Grouping of Functions. The organization must group similar functions in order to facilitate team building and coordination of effort. Obviously, it is not always possible to group functions in a rational manner, because of personnel or political problems, but a concerted effort should be made to do so. Rational grouping can result in improved coordination, clarity of direction, use of resources, and service to students. Of course, there are constraints on grouping: The grouping cannot be too large, and the units must be reasonably compatible and physically located relatively close together.

One fairly typical grouping of functions is as follows:

1. Academic support (admissions, registration, advising, and learning assistance)

2. Recreation and culture (athletics, creation programs, concerts, and lectures)
3. Financial assistance
4. Housing and food service
5. Mental health (counseling and psychiatric care)
6. Physical health and safety
7. Special student services (services to disabled, foreign, and disadvantaged students)
8. Student activities and governance
9. Research and needs assessment

The major responsibility for services within any one of these groupings is usually assumed by a particular unit or office, but effective functioning requires that each unit be aware of all other services and assist in them when appropriate.

Line and Staff Roles. Both line and staff roles are needed in complex organizations. Line officers supervise, coordinate, and carry out the basic program, while staff officers aid them in this task by conducting critical analytical or evaluation studies. Among line positions, those of general management (involving planning, organizing, staffing, directing, and controlling functions) can be distinguished from specialized roles (involving such functions as counseling, teaching, and providing financial aid). Both management and specialized services are necessary and must be provided. The critical tasks are allocating resources to each and integrating management and direct service. In varying degrees, most line officers perform both general management and specialized functions, but the higher the manager's position in the organization the more likely available his or her time will be devoted to management than to education and direct service.

Guidelines. Specifically, organizational structures to achieve institutional aims should:

1. Be consistent with institutional purposes, goals, philosophy, traditions, values, and style
2. Facilitate the interaction of human talent, the circulation of ideas and information, and the pooling of human resources in policy development, planning, and other vital organizational tasks
3. Take into account the expertise, experience, needs, and attitudes of staff
4. Provide for clear and consistent delegation of authority and assignment of duties and provide for line, staff, management, and specialized service roles and functions
5. Accommodate a reasonable span of control for line administrators

6. Group similar functions together under a middle manager or coordinator, keeping the distance between the chief student services officer and line units as short as possible, and offering specific strategies to keep the senior officer in touch with the line units.

Organizational Models

Any number of organizational models exist to carry out the student services mission. In some institutions, student services operate as one division under academic affairs. In such arrangements, academic faculty are often heavily involved in student services work. In small or less complex institutions, the cell model, which clusters specific activities and holds small groups of professional staff and/or academic faculty responsible for such activities, is common. Two distinct organizational models have emerged in large, more complex institutions. Both assume a staff of student services professionals and a chief administrative officer (a vice president, or dean, and so forth). The first is the traditional hierarchical model or pyramidal structure, focused on delegation of authority, assignment of tasks, accountability, and vertical and horizontal compartmentalization. The second is the matrix model, in which an individual or unit has responsibility for more than one activity or function, authority is delegated from more than one source, and decision making is multidimensional (Meyer, 1977, p. 6). These basic forms of organizational structure can be combined to achieve the advantages of each. The basic hierarchical structure with clear lines of authority and assignment of work can be retained but team organization can be used to cut across reporting lines and to bring together the essential talent to solve problems, develop policy, and make important decisions. The result is a multidimensional organizational model that provides both vertical and lateral linkages. The model has clear potential for improving communications, use of human talent, and decision making.

Overview of the Multidimensional Model. The essential characteristics of the multidimensional organization are as follows:

1. Members recognize that complex tasks cut across functional lines, that individuals with the appropriate expertise must be brought together in teams to complete complex tasks, that an individual or unit has responsibility for more than one program, and that authority is delegated from more than one source (because functional reporting lines are crossed) and, accordingly, that team members may report to a different manager, depending on the task.
2. The hierarchical structure, with its delegation of authority, assignment of tasks, and accountability, has clearer delegation and defini-

394   Student Services

tion of work and more effective performance by subordinates because of the degree of delegation, the trust shown by higher-level managers, and the improved coordination, integration, and communication that results.

3. The assignment of work is decentralized to the appropriate level of expertise in order to marshal the necessary talent to complete specific assignments.

4. Specific strategies and structures are created to facilitate cross-functional activity, integration of effort, and communication.

To function well, the multidimensional model must involve careful planning, organizing, communication, and implementation. Moreover, top-level managers must believe in the system and act to reinforce it. They must provide leadership to develop necessary detail in the system and must encourage people at lower levels to take initiative and to think creatively. Senior administrators should not undermine an otherwise effective system by interfering in team assignments, in violation of delegated authority, and should trust the teams to do what is required.

In applying this multidimensional model to the university, with its unique character and mission, history, and values, one must remember that the hierarchical arrangement is an integral and necessary part of institutions and the structure through which authority flows. Most complex academic institutions have two distinct lines of delegation—administrative and academic. Administrative staff typically are delegated authority over budget, planning, personnel, student discipline, and general campus management, while the faculty or academic staff have authority over courses, curricula, and standards for admissions and graduation. This dual delegation has resulted in bifurcated structures that complicate management and require strategies to bring diverse units together in the decision-making process and educational enterprise. For the learning process to be effective, student services and academic affairs must closely cooperate in jointly sponsored programs designed to meet the diverse needs of students.

The multidimensional approach allows staff to facilitate coordination and integrate effort, both laterally and vertically. The model's operational value is that student services units can interact directly with other administrative units, academic departments, or student groups without going through the vice president. Although it is necessary to separate operations from policy development, after policy is fixed units should be free to interact without involving superiors. This model, of course, can be used to develop policy, but at some point policy proposals must move to a higher level for approval. Specific mechanisms to facilitate effectiveness of the multidimensional model include work groups, task forces, and advisory committees. Each is discussed briefly here in the following sections.

Work Groups. In complex organizations, with overlapping jurisdictions, it is not possible to delineate precisely who has what authority. Moreover, talent in one segment of the organization can be useful in making decisions or completing tasks in another. A cross-functional work group can cope with overlapping jurisdictions and can pool talent across reporting lines. Work groups are permanent structures designed for developing and carrying out policy in a functional area that crosses administrative lines of authority. They are composed of individuals from units whose administrative activities or responsibilities will be affected by the group's decisions. Each member of the work group participates in making decisions and can commit his or her unit to action. The chairperson, as the administrator responsible for the primary functional area, is held accountable for the decision and its implementation.

An example of a cross-functional work group that cuts across a number of organizational structures is in the area of admissions. Admissions is important to diverse segments of the institution, and successful implementation involves many different units. The work group responsible for ensuring that admissions relate to the campus academic plan might well be chaired by the chief executive officer of the campus and consists of the vice presidents for academic affairs and student services; any other administrator who may coordinate admissions, registration, and financial aid; the director of admissions; the director of institutional planning and analysis; and the chairperson of the academic senate committee on admissions. The president, as chairperson of the work group, is responsible for the decisions of the group.

An example of a work group within the student services organization could be an educational opportunity program work group, created to increase coordination of the various units—such as admissions, financial aid, counseling, advising, and learning assistance—involved in efforts to help disadvantaged students. An educational opportunity program requires a matrix approach in management: Information flows horizontally across departmental lines, and all units participate in developing and implementing policy in order for the total program to effectively serve students. A work group for such a program might consist of the coordinators of admissions, financial aid, and registration; key staff from the learning assistance center and counseling center; and the directors of student relations and other units involved in the program and might be chaired by the principal student services administrator.

Such work groups have the advantage of bringing together key people from the units that either play a critical role in the program or feel the impact of decisions made in the process. All work group members participate in and are simultaneously informed of decisions.

Task Forces. Another cross-functional device is the task force, designed to handle short-term and specialized problems. When an important problem arises, a task force can be appointed, with temporary authority for decisions assigned to one person in a functional area. Staff are brought together across functional lines, if necessary, to secure the best talent for the task. When the task force has completed its work and filed its report with the appropriate administrative officer, its recommendations, if approved, are assigned to a functional unit or to a work group for implementation.

Advisory Committees. As noted previously, membership on work groups is limited to administrators who have responsibility for making and implementing decisions, while task forces consist of individuals who have the necessary expertise to solve a particular problem or complete a specific assignment. Obviously, by definition these bodies exclude representatives from important segments of the institution. This problem can be solved by using advisory committees consisting of students, faculty, and staff. These bodies advise the administrators, who have the legal authority to make final decisions. Because the administrators cannot give up ultimate responsibility for decisions, the committees can only be advisory. Still, they play a vital role in decision making by providing a mechanism for communicating, identifying needs and concerns, and recommending action. In some cases, advisory committees help administrators determine recommendations that are passed on to the president or governing board of the institution for decisions.

For the advisory committee system to be effective, it must be formalized; that is, the role and purpose of the system and membership of individual committees, selection and training of members, communication channels, reporting relationships, and means of evaluation must be clarified and stated in writing. The administrator whom the committee is advising must provide staff support to ensure that the committee receives the information required to make intelligent judgments. Moreover, the administrator must seriously consider the advice received to the extent possible; there is nothing more demoralizing to a committee than to study a problem and then have the advice ignored or rejected. It is important to note, however, that the administrator ultimately responsible for the decision must retain final authority. Sometimes committees fail to take all factors into account or arrive at conclusions inconsistent with the best interests of the institution. When an administrator modifies or rejects a committee proposal, he or she should carefully explain the reason for the action to the committee.

In order to ensure effective input from students, it is important to include sufficient numbers of students from many segments of the campus. A single student, or two or three students, can be intimidated by a large number of faculty or administrators on a committee. This problem can be overcome by balanced representation of students, faculty, and staff.

Good communication is necessary to make the multidimensional model work effectively. Work groups, task forces, and advisory committees facilitate communication but managers must make a conscious and continuing effort to make the process of communication work both laterally and vertically. Formal councils, periodic staff, and other meetings also help. Basically, there are three critical factors in achieving effective communication: (1) building a system of communications through work groups, committees, staff meetings, and other mechanisms; (2) a commitment by top management to communicate; and (3) sufficient openness and flexibility in the system to stimulate informal human interaction.

Example of the Multidimensional Model. The complexity of the educational setting and the delegation of authority to the primary administrator for student services largely determines the type of organization developed. Where the number of functional areas is within a reasonable span of control, it is possible for line managers of units to report directly to the chief student services officer. In complex institutions, it is not uncommon for this officer to have a wide range of responsibility. Figure 1 presents an example of the student services organization for a large, complicated university. In view of the many units and personnel in the organization, it has been necessary to group similar functions together. Obviously, a flat line organization with all unit heads reporting to the chief student services officer is unworkable. The organization simply could not function, because the vice chancellor could not effectively supervise so many unit heads and still complete other essential management tasks. When line units reporting to the vice chancellor are reduced, more time is available for policy development, coordination, planning, evaluation, budget development, and interaction with other senior administrators, faculty, and student leaders.

For this model to function successfully, groupings of similar functions must be directed by line coordinators to facilitate teamwork, cross-unit communication, and sharing of resources. Although the coordinators are essential, their use also presents a problem; that is, the chief student services officer is removed by one level from the line units. Some organizational structures by their very nature further limit contact between the chief officer and line units by having middle management coordinators report through an assistant or associate to the chief officer. Because of the distance thus created between line unit and chief officer,

Figure 1. Student Services Organization Chart for a Complex University

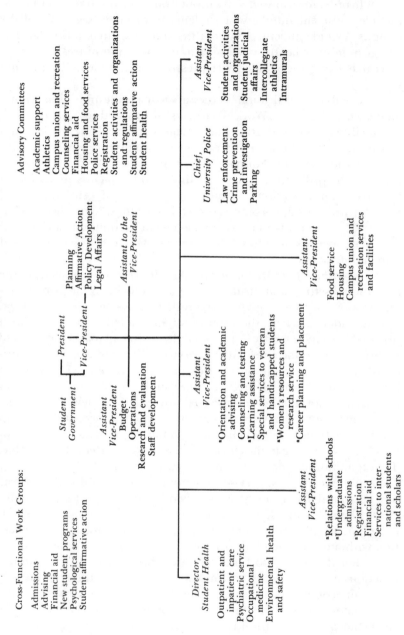

Cross-Functional Work Groups:

Admissions
Advising
Financial aid
New student programs
Psychological services
Student affirmative action

Advisory Committees

Academic support
Athletics
Campus union and recreation
Counseling services
Financial aid
Housing and food services
Police services
Registration
Student activities and organizations
and regulations
Student affirmative action
Student health

President

Student ————— *Vice-President* ——— Planning
Government   Affirmative Action
                                          Policy Development
                                          Legal Affairs

                           Assistant to the
                           Vice-President

Assistant
Vice-President

Budget
Operations
Research and evaluation
Staff development

Chief,
University Police

Law enforcement
Crime prevention
and investigation
Parking

Assistant
Vice-President

Student activities
and organizations
Student judicial
affairs
Intercollegiate
athletics
Intramurals

Assistant
Vice-President

Food service
Housing
Campus union and
recreation services
and facilities

Assistant
Vice-President

*Orientation and academic
advising
Counseling and testing
*Learning assistance
Special services to veteran
and handicapped students
*Women's resources and
research service
*Career planning and placement

Director,
Student Health

Outpatient and
inpatient care
Psychiatric service
Occupational
medicine
Environmental health
and safety

Assistant
Vice-President

*Relations with schools
*Undergraduate
admissions
*Registration
Financial aid
Services to inter-
national students
and scholars

*The administration of these functions involves both student affairs and academic affairs.

specific strategies are needed to combat problems of communication, morale, and mistrust that can develop because of lack of personal contact.

Although groups of units are coordinated by middle managers in a preferred hierarchical structure for large, complex institutions (such as shown in Figure 1), the distance between the line units and the chief student services officer is shorter and direct contact with units is easier. But even with this arrangement, the chief officer must make a concerted effort to maintain contact with line staff to gain a sense of what is working, what is not, and changes that should be considered. Contact can be facilitated through unit visits, staff meetings, and working with small groups of staff on specific problems. The model represented in Figure 1 also centralizes planning, evaluation, and budgeting. The line units play an important role in these areas, but the responsibility for coordination and direction of these functions rests with the vice president.

The Student Role

The role of students in student services presents a critical challenge because they have no, or very limited, delegated authority. Moreover, students' tenure is limited, their interests and needs are varied, and usually they have no single entry point into the decision-making process.

Why should students be involved in decision making? The response to this question will determine the quality and form of student participation. There are at least three primary reasons for involving students in governance: (1) students are affected by most of an institution's decisions; they have the right to be consulted, (2) the "student" point of view is essential to the development of good decisions, and (3) students can learn from taking part in governance. Through interaction and exchange of views, the students, faculty, and administrators can build a sense of trust and credibility that is essential in governance within a university.

A major problem in developing mechanisms for student involvement is that the administration and faculty, on the one hand, and student government officers, on the other, have quite different views of how decisions should be made. Faculty have the delegated authority to make academic judgments, while administrators have the delegated authority for administrative decisions. Superimposed on formal administrative and faculty bureaucratic structures are collegial models of decision making that emphasize civil and orderly consultation, debate, and deliberation. "The elected officialdom of student government, in contrast, is built largely on advocacy, and political models, [are] based on win-lose tactics and often confrontation techniques" (Regan, 1978, p. 20).

In complex multicampus systems of higher education, student governments tend to emphasize political pressure at the highest decision-making levels and in state government—the levels where critical policy and budgetary decisions are finally made. However, "administrative and faculty power is decentralized to campus-wide, college and departmental levels" (Regan, 1978, p. 21). This discrepancy in the focus of power occasionally results in conflict and a breakdown in cooperative decision-making structures at the campus level. Administration and faculty assume that the emphasis should be on interaction at lower levels, where the basic work on a decision is done, whereas student government officers may favor intervention at the highest levels of governance. Another problem is that student leaders participate in discussions at lower levels but go directly to the trustees or state government if they are not satisfied with campus decisions. This tends to anger administrators and faculty, who feel that student leaders have the unfair advantage of participating at the departmental or campus level and then skipping to the top, where they attempt to achieve ends that were rejected at lower levels. Given the bureaucratic structure with its chain of command, administrators and faculty do not have the same opportunity.

The university governance system is based on the assumption that the emphasis is on communication, interaction, and rational debate in decision making. For this system to work, trust and credibility among the participants must be established; they must be committed to the model of free and open consultation and consensus in solving problems and conflicts. Therefore, decision makers must be skilled in intellectual exchange, group dynamics, and conflict resolution rather than confrontation politics.

It is difficult to find a suitable model for student involvement that copes with the problems associated with the different decision-making methods and styles of administration, faculty, and student government, but Likert and Likert (1976) have developed an approach that has merit. The Likert model consists of linkages with various segments on the campus. Student representatives from living groups, academic departments, student governments, and other groups are linked to administrative and faculty bodies by overlapping, face-to-face problem-solving groups. Members have overlapping membership in two or more groups, providing for communication and exchange of information and ideas. Figure 2 illustrates this type of arrangement.

Following sound organizational principles, making use of more complex approaches such as the multidimensional model, and involv-

Figure 2. Linking Pin System

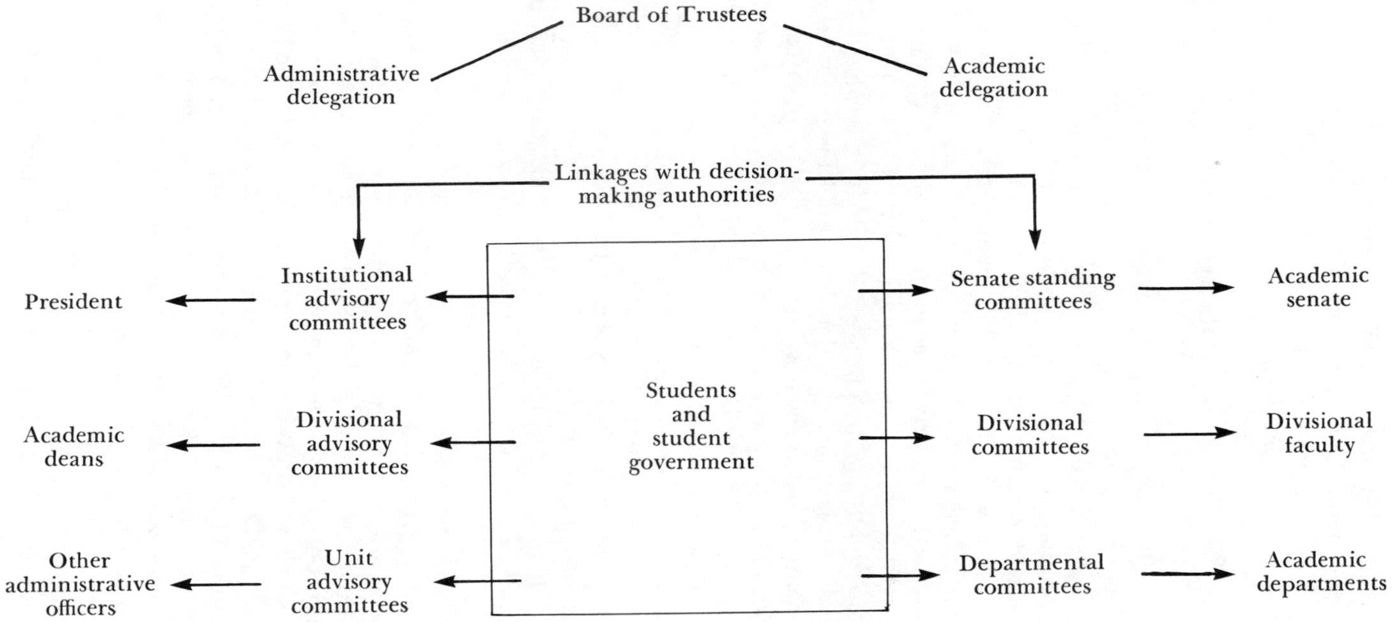

ing students productively are important in building an effective student services program. Sound management of the system helps realize the potential of the principles and organizational structure on which an ongoing operation is based.

Management

It is essential that the management system be shaped to the mission, philosophy, values, and style of the institution. Management is a process created for only one purpose: to facilitate the achievement of institutional goals. It is a means, not an end; it is a vehicle than can only be justified or retain vitality as long as it serves the educational mission of the institution. Unfortunately, management systems tend to become ends in themselves, serving the narrow purposes of those within them or failing to change direction as institutional goals change.

The complexities of human behavior and academic institutions are too great to be encompassed by any one theory of management. Various scholars have considered the problems associated with a unifying theory of management with varying degrees of success. Thought on how to best manage human resources includes the traditional or bureaucratic, human relations, systems, political, and contingency schools. Regardless of the theoretical basis for action, a basic set of functions must be attended to: planning, setting policy, and execution or action. The three are not mutually exclusive nor sequential but it is helpful to delineate the broad outlines of each function in order to understand the management task more fully.

Planning. The most basic of all management functions is planning, because it is staff activity at all organizational levels (Koontz and O'Donnel, 1972). The level of position and degree of delegated authority determine the extent of staff involvement. Although everyone engages in planning, the chief student services officer and other key management associates are concerned with a broader spectrum of activities and must coordinate the planning of the total organization. Planning is essentially decision making, determining what to do , how to do it, when to do it, and who is to do it. Without planning, activities would be left to chance.

Planning can be formal or informal and long- or short-range. Steiner's (1972) informal or intuitive-anticipatory approach of short-range planning, generally used by an individual administrator, may or may not result in a written set of plans and usually has a short time horizon. This personalized approach is based on the individual's past experience, intuition, and reflective thinking. In contrast, in the formal system—a more organized approach based on a set of well-defined procedures—plans are often written statements based on research and analysis. These two different approaches to planning occasionally clash or create conflicts within the staff and organizational subsystems when staff are not aware that two planning systems are simultaneously at work. Ideally, the two approaches should not conflict but should complement each other.

Fuller (1976) has discussed a number of desirable characteristics of planning in academic institutions, which include a concern for process as well as outcomes. The first trait is assessment of fundamental values and assumptions. Student services administrators should identify explicit assumptions about a desirable learning environment, because they cannot ignore the importance of the learning process in planning. Secondly, in developing operational objectives the planning process should (1) determine specific and diverse institutional objectives, (2) candidly assess the institution's ability to accomplish these objectives, (3) project specific programmatic ways to accomplish objectives within available resources, and (4) develop an evaluative mechanism that measures the strengths and weaknesses of existing programs and weighs the priority needs for program changes. Thirdly, meaningful planning must be based on data collection and analysis. The fourth characteristic is determination of priorities and implementation strategies. Planning processes that do not determine priorities are quite literally academic.

Budgeting is a critical part of planning. Administrators must first of all understand that budget formats reflect management assumptions or philosophy. The primary budget formats are line item; performance; planning, programming, and budgeting systems (PPBS); and zero-base budgeting (although at this point the latter form is more theoretical than practical). The line-item budget emphasizes accounting and control, provides extreme accountability, and is input oriented. Performance budgeting classifies expenditures by functions, activities, or projects and develops work-cost measures to facilitate the efficient performance of prescribed activities. PPBS is planning oriented by providing data on the costs and benefits of alternative ways of attaining proposed objectives and by providing output measures to determine whether objectives have been accomplished. Zero-base budgeting is a process whereby the total allocation of resources is regularly reexamined in relationship to goals, programs, and projected priorities.

Chief student services officers rarely have free choice of a budgeting format. To the extent they do have choices, however, their decisions can affect their planning processes. For example, there are several advantages to program budgeting. Such a format can be helpful if one is interested in knowing the costs of various program areas and cost per student contact in the various programs. A performance budgeting format involves translating the workload of a unit into meaningful program categories. For example, the programs of a counseling center may be categorized as individual counseling, group counseling, training, consulting, testing, research, and management. Each counselor's work is summarized annually under the various categories. Student contact information for each category can help determine the cost per student contact in each program area as well as the cost per program. In summarizing output, this format can be useful in a variety of ways. It indicates the two criteria of organizational competence (Huse and Bowditch, 1973, p. 310): (1) organizational efficiency, defined as the amount of resources an organization uses to produce a unit of output, and (2) effectiveness, or the degree to which the organization realizes its goals and objectives. In conjunction with measures of student needs and organizational effectiveness, performance budgeting data can provide valuable information for program planning. A note of caution and qualification in using a performance budgeting format: Summarizing the activities of various professional staff in a series of numbers can be dehumanizing unless staff are involved in the process of determining program priorities. If staff are involved, performance budgeting can be a useful tool for improving the quality of planning.

No single budget format or technique can provide all the answers needed for planning in our increasingly complex institutions. The need for multiple budget formats as a necessity of life and a hedge on survival is readily apparent in multicampus systems where systemwide administrations often require budgets to be reported in functional categories that may not serve the needs of individual campuses. State and federal agencies may also require different budget-reporting formats that are of limited value to campus administrators. The ability to move easily from one budget format to another is an essential skill of the competent administrator.

Policy Determination. Solid planning processes allow the administrator to set priorities and determine policy. The term *policy making* can refer to the level of discrete policy statements made by the chief student services officer as well as to the general statements made by an administrator that guide the thinking and action of subordinates. Thus, setting program priorities can be viewed as one aspect of policy making, although it is also part of the planning process.

The primary factors involved in determining program priorities are assessing student needs, clarifying unit goals, evaluating programs, availability of resources, and the campus academic plan. Because student needs are constantly changing, it is impossible to rank order programs from most important to least important with any degree of permanence. Consequently, priorities are constantly reviewed within the planning system of the university, and policies are redetermined in light of changing priorities.

Policy Execution. Action is based on strategies that reflect the broad, overall conception of the organization and that include the general program of action and deployment of resources to accomplish goals. Strategies often remain in the head of an administrator and are shared informally if at all. However, in this new era of accountability and fiscal restraints, strategy statements need to be stated clearly and often in writing so that decision makers can fully understand the rationale behind a particular organizational structure. Although specific action plans can and should be delegated, those with responsibility for the total student services enterprise must assert the basic overall strategies to be followed, based on planning and policy-making processes that include wide input and consultation.

The Administrator's Role

Management systems do not function well unless they are guided intelligently by administrators. In a university student services department, the chief administrator's formal role is specified by the delegation of authority from the university president, who defines the roles and functions performed and the territory supervised. Because the degree of delegation varies from institution to institution, the role of the administrator varies as well. To a great degree, then, the institution and those who act for it determine the nature and scope of the administrator's role in realizing institutional goals. In addition to and quite apart from the formal prescription of role and functions are the informal expectations imposed by the trustees, presidents, other senior administrators, faculty, and students. As is true of any senior administrative officer, conflicting pressures and expectations converge on the chief student services officer, making it difficult to perform effectively and to maintain a clear sense of direction and sanity.

The challenge facing the administrator is to be aware of the determinants of behavior and to sort out those that contribute to success in the context of one's beliefs and values. Because there is no one way to respond to all of the conflicting demands and expectations, an administrator must decide which stimuli will, in fact, direct action and which will be rejected. In making this decision, it is important to start by assessing one's beliefs and values. Obviously, such factors as status, financial reward, and security influence behavior. Although it is very difficult to separate these considerations from beliefs and values, in the final analysis one's dignity and self-worth are measured by the degree to which beliefs and values determine behavior. As May states (1975, pp. 13–14), "an assertion of the self, a commitment, is essential if the self is to have any reality" and "a man or woman becomes fully human only by his or her choices and his or her commitment to them." Institutional goals, philosophy, traditions, values, style, and formally and informally defined roles must, to a reasonable degree, be compatible with personal beliefs and values. For example, an institution that encourages great freedom to students to determine their own direction in curricular and extracurricular programs might be a very satisfying place to work for a person with a similar philosophy but unproductive for someone with a different view.

Another factor that impinges on the administrator's behavior is others' perceptions of values, role, and job effectiveness. Misperceptions of beliefs and what the administrator actually does can negatively affect the quality of work performed. Self-perceptions of student services administrators do not always coincide with those of others in the academic community. A 1970 National Association of Student Personnel Administrators study of assumptions and beliefs held by members of the academic community revealed that there were striking differences between deans of students, on the one hand, and faculty and students, on the other, over the perception—or misperception—of the deans' assumptions and beliefs. For example, faculty members felt that deans were more supportive than they actually were of enforcing moral standards. The deans saw themselves as warm, friendly people, committed to student welfare, while the students viewed the deans as being less concerned with student welfare, more control oriented, and less willing to allow freedom for students to be self-determining (Dutton, Appleton, and Birch, 1970, pp. 21–22).

When the administrator's behavior generates negative or incorrect perceptions in others over an extended period, he or she faces the difficult challenge of deciding what to do. First one must assess how the problem is affecting job performance. One must also appraise value and ethical concerns and either try to adjust behavior or accept and live with the fact that a certain amount of negative perception or misperception is inevitable.

In the day-to-day rush to keep up and to respond to crises, little or no time is left to reflect on the diverse motivations of one's behavior. Research has shown that the work of top managers is characterized by discontinuity, brevity, and variety, with little time for general planning and reflection (Mintzberg, 1975, pp. 32–33). The demands on executives in higher education are increasing; the workload is rising so high that managers are overburdened with obligations and expectations from superiors, staff, and people outside of the institutions. Managers should delegate more authority, but this is not easy in the era of accountability. In the face of unrelenting pressures, the manager tends "to be superficial in his actions, to overload himself with work, encourage interruption, respond quickly to every stimulus, seek the tangible and avoid the abstract, make decisions in small increments, and do everything abrupt-ly" (Mintzberg, 1975, p. 66). To reduce this tendency, it is important to step back periodically and ask, "What am I doing and for what reasons? What is my behavior? What is stimulating it, and how does it relate to my beliefs and values?" Although managers must be prepared to re-spond to crises and problems, they must also have time to retreat from the detail and pressures of the day-to-day routine to think creatively about goals and the means of achieving them. This approach requires courage, because risks are involved, such as the pain of facing the reality of one's actions or needing to change one's style.

In coming to grips with one's work, it is important to identify carefully the roles one performs, to order them in terms of their impor-tance, and then to control the use of one's time so that high-priority roles are played. Ultimately, one's role is determined by what one does and how one's time is used. The administrator must control the use of his or her time, limit the impact of events, and limit expectations and influences of others on his or her performance. How does one find the time to plan and think in the rush of activity and constant pressures to do more in less time? One approach is to periodically select blocks of time away from the office for reading, reflection, and research. Another way to ensure time for planning and thought is to organize informal sessions away from the office with staff, students, or faculty on important issues. Again, "plan-ning" time should be scheduled, and although time is taken away from other administrative tasks the positive results of such activity justify the time spent.

If the administrator has a good understanding of what the job involves and what is expected, he or she will more likely use available time for the most critical aspects of the job and will build an overall organization to accomplish expectations. The chief student services administrator cannot do everything; critical functions must be identi-fied and allocated to other people. As the head of the organization, the chief executive must retain responsibility for overall leadership, coordi-nation, planning, decision making, communication, budget develop-ment, liaison with other campus leaders, organizational development, and evaluation. Operational authority must be delegated to line manag-ers, and mechanisms must be created to ensure that essential staff work is done in the areas of planning, policy making, and action.

The most difficult problem the administrator faces is designing and implementing a system that maximizes its members' contribution to established goals. This problem is particularly challenging in large, complex organizations, with their inherent tendencies toward deper-sonalization and alienation of staff. But the problems must be addressed if organizations are to succeed. People make organizations work, and they also make them fail. To maximize the effectiveness of the human resource, the prime consideration in all activity must be the worth, dignity, and involvement of the individual. Such a focus does not just happen; it must be accepted by administrators at all levels and must be woven into the fabric of the organization. The primary responsibility for ensuring that this commitment is developed and maintained rests with the top administrators.

References

Ardrey, R. *The Social Contract.* New York: Dell, 1970.

Carnegie Commission on Higher Education. *Priorities for Action: Final Report of the Carnegie Commission on Higher Education.* New York: McGraw-Hill, 1973.

Churchman, C. W., Ackoff, R. L., and Arnoff, L. E. *Introduction to Operations Research.* New York: Wiley, 1957.

Dutton, T. B., Appleton, J. R., and Birch, E. E. *Assumptions and Beliefs of Selected Members of the Academic Community.* Portland, Oreg.: National Association of Student Personnel Administrators, 1970.

Fuller B. "A Framework for Academic Planning." *Journal of Higher Education,* 1976, *47,* 65–77.

Huse, E. F., and Bowditch, J. L. *Behavior in Organizations.* Reading, Mass.: Addison-Wesley, 1973.

Kast, F., and Rosenzweig, J. E. *Contingency View of Organization and Management.* Palo Alto, Calif.: Science Research Associates, 1973.

Koontz, H., and O'Donnel, C. *Principles of Management: An Analysis of Managerial Functions.* New York: McGraw-Hill, 1972.

Likert, R., and Likert, J. G. *New Ways of Managing Conflict.* New York: McGraw-Hill, 1976.

May, R. *The Courage to Create.* New York: Norton, 1975.

Meyer, J. H. "The Matrix Concept as a Principle for Organizing a University Campus." Unpublished paper, Office of the Chancellor, University of California, Davis, 1977.

Mintzberg, H. "The Manager's Job: Folklore and Fact." *Harvard Business Review,* 1975, *53* (4), 49–61.

Regan, M. "Student Participation in Governance of a Complex Multi-Campus System." Unpublished paper, Department of Applied Behavioral Science, University of California, Davis, 1978.

Richman, B. M., and Farmer, R. N. *Leadership, Goals, and Power in Higher Education: A Contingency and Open-Systems Approach To Effective Management.* San Francisco: Jossey-Bass, 1974.

Steiner, G. A. *Comprehensive Managerial Planning.* Oxford, Ohio: Planning Executives Institute, 1972.

Cynthia S. Johnson
Cecelia H. Foxley

18

Devising Tools for Middle Managers

The responsibilities of middle managers in student services—supervisory staff members who are below the chief personnel officer but above the entry-level professional—are increasing both in volume and importance. The problems they face with accountability demands, declining budgets, and new personnel policies are compounded by the fact that new research on how students learn and grow is providing them with a theoretical base of concepts and tools that must be incorporated into existing programs. Steady-state budgets may not enable them to hire new people with up-to-date skills and current knowledge to round out their programs. This dilemma requires that they focus more clearly and imaginatively on management and on the acquisition of new management techniques, tools, and skills. Only in this way can middle managers and their units effect change and implement new programs and concepts without additional institutional resources.

According to Merton's 1969 study of the administrative skills of university leaders, those administrators who articulated goals well and are well organized are most effective and successful, as are those who respect the members of their groups, demonstrate their own competence, listen to others, expect negative as well as positive feedback, maintain contact with their groups, and use their power and authority as sparingly as possible. According to Merton, these leaders also communicate well, and ensure that their staff have the resources to comply with directives, that their directives are consistent with the values of people who receive them, and that their directives harmonize with the ends, purposes, and values of the organization.

These characteristics indicate specific tools that can be acquired and honed by the student services middle manager to enhance leadership skills. The two basic tools examined in this chapter are goal setting and management information systems. Suggestions are made for more effectively using present resources and for developing new ones in terms of staff, funds, and technology. Time management as a crucial tool for the middle manager is also discussed.

Goal Setting

A goal is a desired future state. Its time frame is long range, and it may be expressed quantitatively or qualitatively. Goals simply state where an individual, unit, or division wants to go. A goal is more specific than a mission statement, which focuses on the broad-based purpose of a college, university, or division. Objectives flow from goals and should be measurable and achievable within a specified time frame. Clearly stated goals, an overall mission statement, and measurable objectives tied to human and fiscal resources allow a manager to be focused and creative.

Much has been written about goal setting in a variety of environments. Hanson (1977) identifies goal-setting competencies and the ability to write behavioral goals and objectives as an important skill for implementing student development. McDaniel (1975) suggests three organizational levels for goal setting: organizational purpose, policy formulation, and procedure development. The middle manager has the most opportunity to influence the last level and to initiate activities through setting goals in his or her area of responsibility. Formulating policy with one's lateral group of managers also allows interventions.

There are a number of advantages for the middle manager in developing and implementing a goal-setting process, including opportunity for change, articulation, institutional support, performance evaluation, workload control, and staff development.

Goal setting offers an important opportunity for middle management (and below) to influence organizational change. Pockets of student development programming within a traditional student services unit can work from the bottom up rather than from the top down. For example, the goal of one residence hall might be an experiment in intentional moral development. Or, a career center might decide to set goals and objectives that structure service and program delivery on a developmental model.

Today, space and money are limited, and students and legislators are questioning institutional functions. Therefore, middle managers must be able to clearly and concisely state what they are about. Units that are not clearly understood are cut out of budgets. Proper goal setting allows student services to communicate goals to the faculty and to justify space and dollar requests to budget committees in precise and quantifiable terms.

Middle management must meet the expectations of both superiors and subordinates. Clearly stated, measurable goals and objectives help gain support for proposals from above as well as below. Specific plans and direct answers are vital. Only after the chief student services officer, the president, and the staff members of the unit concur can the manager feel free to move ahead with programs.

Group and individual goals should be tied to job descriptions and reviewed by middle managers with each staff member. This gives the manager agreed-on, measurable objectives by which to evaluate performance, and employees can get on with the job assured that they are acting in consort with their supervisors. For example, the residence hall staff members should not have to guess what they should be doing or spend precious energy trying to please everyone. Goals, objectives, and preplanned evaluation systems allow staff to proceed with only periodic progress reviews.

Deans of students, student governments, and others do not always define specifically what they are doing. Programs and functions remain poorly defined. Staff are often spread too thin, and job satisfaction and quality are sometimes sacrificed. Clear goals and objectives enable middle managers to define relevant functions and areas in their educational purview, and thus avoid duplication of work. They also give the manager a broader context within which to make program decisions and establish priorities.

By setting goals, staff members can acquire a skill essential in implementing student development, because they learn how to help students establish their own goals and growth plans. Setting achievable goals and objectives also enables the manager to have the satisfaction of seeing those ends reached. And it focuses energy allocation and decision making.

A number of goal-setting processes can be used. Most follow the management by objectives (MBO) concept originated by Drucker (1954) and popularized by Odiorne (1965). There are many variations of the MBO model, all based on the writing of specific measurable performance objectives by staff members and on evaluating achievement of these objectives. Goal-setting processes deal with development and evaluation of unit, as well as individual, goals and objectives.

Sequential Goal Setting Plan. The following step-by-step model has been used successfully at the University of California at Irvine. Experience indicates that Steps 1 through 9 require approximately twelve hours of total staff time annually.

Step	*Activities*
1	Identify and agree on mission statement.
2	Develop group and individual goals.
3	Define measurable objectives and methods of evaluation.
4	Set priorities on objectives.
5	Share plans with power structure and obtain input.
6	Finalize plan with staff.
7	Allocate resources—tie to job description and determine annual calendar.
8	Meet with individual staff members on individual goals and link to job description.
9	Distribute final plan for the semester, term, or quarter and tentative plan for the academic year.
10	Reevaluate every three months to determine if the plan was realistic and what changes need to be made.

The first step in this goal-setting process is stating a unit mission related to the university or college mission. If a mission statement already exists, it should be reviewed each year to obtain staff concurrence. Developing a mission statement can help integrate new staff and uncover philosophical differences. Care should be taken, however, that the process is not used for lengthy philosophical debates and that staff members do not feel threatened by the process. To prevent this, a subcommittee might be asked to develop a preliminary draft and then solicit input from all staff to reach final consensus. The open-system plan of determining overall function is useful if the staff is large and diverse or if achieving concurrence is difficult. Using this system, the manager requests staff to idealize a future program or unit. This frees participants of current restraints and issues and establishes a creative climate in which to realize an idealized future.

The second step is to develop group and individual goals. Group goals provide direction and cohesion, and individual goals allow staff to state what they want to accomplish in the coming academic year. A group goal, for example, may be to provide leadership training for all student organization presidents. An individual goal might be to acquire budget experience or to learn how to operate video equipment.

Measurable objectives should be developed for each goal. The difference between a goal and an objective is vitally important. A goal should be general; an objective is specific and limited. For example, in the goal "to provide leadership training for all student organization presidents," an objective might be to hold five minicourses per quarter to teach time management, group skills, fiscal management, publicity, and motivation skills to student organization presidents.

It is essential to determine an effective, efficient way to measure accomplishment of each proposed objective. Simple accounting procedures may suffice for some. However, objectives that require evaluating service quality or of behavior changes require more sophisticated strategies (see Oscar Lenning's chapter on evaluation).

Once the idea flow begins to wane, it is time for the manager to carefully review the goals and objectives and to ask and answer such questions as "Are all appropriate student groups being served? What about faculty resources? Have any data about student needs been used to identify objectives and goals?"

Next, managers must consider what is achievable. Currently available resources in terms of person hours and budget monies determine priorities for goals and objectives. What is most important? Priorities can be set by ballot, with staff ranking order of preference. Then the manager is ready to share mission, goal, and objective statements with all appropriate people, including the chief student services officer. If they concur, planning proceeds. If not, redevelopment and restructuring must be done.

A staff meeting to finalize the goals and objectives should then be held. At this time, resources, individual staff responsibility, and a general time frame must be set. Managers must also consider the budget. If sufficient resources are not available, then priorities must be adjusted or additional resources sought. The final draft should again be shared with the middle manager's supervisor.

A final step is developing a specific year-long calendar and linking group and individual goals to the job description for each staff member. A regular review of job descriptions in relation to actual goals and objectives can result in changes in the job description if appropriate. The manager must be supportive and encouraging during this process and must not inhibit ideas and contributions. The first steps in the process should take place in interruption-free sessions of about four hours—off campus, if possible. Paraprofessional, clerical, and student workers should be included if feasible.

Management Information System

One valuable tool that can be used by middle managers to plan and more effectively use existing resources is a management information system (MIS). Very simply, an MIS provides information that is used to manage. It can be a large system that requires a computer, or it can be a very simple procedure. Many data collection and record-keeping systems used by colleges and universities are a form of MIS. For example, placement office staff register senior students and place their names on file. After the student graduates, the office can conduct a follow-up survey determining each student's employment status. Later the placement office distributes a report that summarizes the office's success. In this case, the MIS functions basically to store information and to generate a report. The MIS stores the student's name, address, academic major, and date of graduation; later, job information is added. The MIS compiles and summarizes the information in report form. Similar forms of MIS are common in admissions, financial aids, personnel, and business offices.

Use of an MIS can provide a number of benefits to the manager:

1. *Planning.* Organization changes forecast future needs, but often so much change occurs that many important changes are not noticed or addressed. An MIS highlights important changes, thus facilitating comprehensive planning.
2. *Program evaluation.* Evaluation assesses the impact of new or existing programs. Unfortunately, managers too often neglect evaluation, partly because of its complexity and their own lack of organization. An MIS can organize the evaluation process.
3. *Budgeting and budgetary control.* Administrators spend large amounts of time on budgetary matters. An MIS can help them plan control budgets.
4. *Organizing and storing large amounts of information.* A properly running MIS enables staff to locate information quickly and to convert it to an easily understood form.
5. *Providing up-to-date information on the condition of the organization.* Like a fever thermometer, an MIS can provide information about the immediate health of the organization, supplying instant warnings of changing conditions.
6. *Modeling and simulating the operations of organizations.* An MIS

can model and simulate new programs and conditions within an organization, forecasting the effects of change before incurring the expense of full implementation.

Developing the System. Although not conceptually difficult, developing a successful MIS takes considerable time and effort. Precautions must be taken to educate and involve appropriate individuals throughout the entire process. The steps necessary to successfully implement an MIS are listed as follows. The reader will note that MIS and the goal-setting process are not only compatible management tools, but are also interdependent.

1. Determine the organization's goals.
2. Determine the tasks needed to achieve these goals in the areas of
   a. Programming
   b. Budgeting
   c. Planning
   d. Projecting
   e. Evaluating
3. Identify the information needed to complete the tasks:
   a. What type and amount is needed?
   b. What sources are to be used?
   c. How available is it?
   d. What is the cost of obtaining it?
4. Design and implement the system.
5. Evaluate the system and make modifications.

If the manager has done a solid job of goal setting and follow-through, Steps 1, 2, and part of step 3 are already accomplished. Steps 4 and 5 can logically follow without extensive time and effort. There are, however, a number of pitfalls in Steps 4 and 5, and managers are urged to seek consultation in setting up the system. Davis (1974) and Racippo and Foxley (1980) are helpful resources.

Deciding whether or not to computerize an MIS is often difficult. Many small MIS programs require only paper, pencil, and perhaps a calculator. The following guidelines should be helpful to the manager who is considering use of computers.

1. Computers are designed to handle quantitative data. If the specific MIS deals primarily with qualitative data, the fit will probably not be good.
2. Computers handle large amounts of information efficiently. Any information-handling task that requires more than one work day per

week to perform could more efficiently be handled by a computer. Computers are generally not necessary for smaller amounts of information.
3. Computers provide information very quickly. If time is an important factor in retrieving information, the manager should consider using a computer.
4. Computers are complex and do not handle all problems equally well. Computers are most effective in handling repetitive operations. Unique problems require new programming, and may also require different computers with varying capabilities.
5. Computers are expensive in terms of time and money needed to set up the system. The manager should be reasonably sure that the information will be productively used before making a commitment to use a computer.

Managers should certainly consider an MIS as a tool. It is not necessarily complex nor expensive and difficult to implement, and can result in more effective planning and use of resources. However, sloppy planning, hasty implemention, or inadequate technology can doom this approach. Therefore, managers are advised to work first on Steps 1–3 and proceed cautiously and with consultation as they work with Step 4—actual design of the system.

Resource Management and Development

Once a plan using goal-setting techniques has been developed and adopted, it is time to take a creative look at the management of available resources and possible development of additional ones. How can existing people be used more efficiently? How can additional money be obtained to help implement student development? Are there new resources on the horizon?

Human Resources. The hours of staff time allocated to an office represent the largest institutional investment in that function. The manager must make sure that staff time, skills, and talents are being used effectively. For example, the staff of a counseling center discovered that by teaching a class in personal growth they could have contact with 250 students for up to 30 hours each or a total of 6,000 contact hours. Using the same staff resources to see students individually would have resulted in far fewer students receiving services. Staff may at first resist conducting programs as opposed to using one-to-one counseling or advising techniques. Those trained in early Rogerian techniques may have an especially hard time letting go of such methods. But, with declining resources and increasing student interest in many services and programs, the middle manager must ensure the most effective and efficient use of staff time. Analyzing tasks is essential. Are staff doing work appropriate to their level? Can their tasks be done by students or by others? Staff are more productive if they are fully using their expertise and if they can learn the art of delegating tasks. Too often top-level managers underestimate the clerical help essential to free professionals to work in their field of expertise. In addition to clerical support, staff can be supplemented and helped in a variety of ways, such as by interns, paid student help, volunteers, and consultants.

One way to work effectively with staff is for the middle manager to switch from the role of supervisor to the role of teacher. This switch often produces behavioral changes and makes roles more enjoyable. Human development principles are more easily applied, skills and abilities can be better assessed, and ways to help staff stretch and grow can be identified. Young professionals encountering the political reality of academe can be taught to avoid cynicism or "burnout." Another suggestion is to work with staff members to identify the best and the worst characteristics of those people to whom you reported in the past. This can result in a list of expectations for a superior that can be helpful in discussing professional relationships with staff members. It might include such items as

- Someone you can respect
- Someone you can learn from
- Someone who has "feet on the desk" time to look down the road and see the bigger picture
- Someone you can trust
- Someone who lets you know where you stand—states clear expectations and gives feedback

Positive reinforcement and communication form the foundation of good manager–staff relationships. The student services professional is a seed planter and must work through others. Students may take years to realize and reinforce a person's contribution to their growth. Internal reinforcement is, of course, ideal; sometimes, however, workers need a project they can call their own and can point to with pride. Managers can reward staff by allowing growth opportunities. If travel or training budgets are limited, perhaps a staff member could be offered a choice between a management training program and a visit to a professional meeting and mandated to bring back a skill that can be used and taught to others. Staff exchanges and increased visibility and responsibility can also be used as rewards.

Fiscal Resources. Next to managing people, managing money might seem easy, but obtaining and allocating fiscal resources have become exceedingly complex and require new skills and techniques. Financing student services programs can be discouraging and difficult. The middle manager must find money, manage it, and know how to account for it in quantifiable, understandable terms.

Other than from traditional sources within the institution, where can one find money? As resources decline, more and more student services operations are charging fees for services. Student health costs have become a major item in the budget. Health fees can be charged, with special allowances made for low-income or disadvantaged students. Charges for vocational testing can help fund career planning and placement centers. And other resource dollars may be available within the institution, such as affirmative action funds to implement Title IX programs and funds for housing and student government.

Extramural funds may also be needed. Middle managers must develop skills in writing grant proposals and must take time to locate funding from both private and public sources. Campus libraries can help identify funding opportunities in private foundations and public agencies. Recently, one campus won a minigrant from the Exxon Foundation to computerize student interest files and to match them with campus organizations. Many grants are awarded to advance career education and other student services projects. However, competition is getting tougher, and efforts to secure extramural dollars require grant-engineering skills. Before entering the grant game, managers should ask themselves some basic questions: "How many hours am I willing to invest to acquire the grant dollar? Does the grant match our goals and objectives and allow permanent additions to our unit, or will it mean that we will need institutional money to support the program once the soft money is gone?"

Technology. Once staff have been made more effective and efficient and available fiscal resources have been tapped, what can a manager do if the need and/or demand for services and programs still exceed resources? As we move into the 1980s, the student services professional must consider the future integration of technology. There are many examples: videotapes in assertion training and other counseling skills; audiotapes to provide students overview information or to repeat missed programs; twenty-four-hour phone lines to provide calendar and/or job information; and, finally, computers. Computer technology is currently being used throughout the United States in student services in a variety of ways. As has already been discussed, computers can be useful in implementing MIS dealing with student data. One of the most obvious uses is in the registration process. On one campus, computers are used at orientation; parents are given a questionnaire to enable them to ask specific questions, via a computer terminal, about the campus. Orientation planners are thus able to quickly collect data about the areas of most concern to parents. The confidentiality of the response is preserved. Computer technology is also used to assist instruction, especially in areas of career guidance. Programs such as the System of Interactive Guidance and Information (SIGI) and the Discover Program provide self-paced, individualized career decision-making opportunities for students. Computer technology can also give managers relatively immediate information about their clients.

Time Management

Let us imagine that goals and objectives have been set. An action plan has been adopted. Individual and group goals have been integrated into job descriptions and a year-long calendar. Appropriate resources have been accumulated and integrated with the plan. A management information system is in place. Available technology has freed staff to use their professional expertise. But how do managers find enough time to manage staff, work with supervisors, develop lateral support within the institution, and also save time for personal growth and development?

The biggest time waster in higher education is committee meeting time. Are all those meetings necessary? It is estimated that 75 percent of a middle manager's time is spent going to meetings, leaving only 25 percent for planning and implementation. Often the work of those meetings could be accomplished through memos or telephone discussions. Meetings can also be held less frequently and for shorter periods of time. One good way to reduce meeting time is to hold meetings immediately before lunch or before the close of the day. Also, have a prepared agenda, do immediate follow-up, and delegate effectively within the meeting. Phone messages can all be collected by the receptionist and returned within a thirty- or forty-five-minute time period by the middle manager. Managers should constantly analyze their time to make sure they are in control and meeting their priorities. The most efficient way to handle paperwork is to deal with a simple "in" basket item immediately and in less than five minutes. The worth of one piece of paper should be judged carefully. If it can be picked up, looked at, and disposed of quickly, it should be. Dictating equipment and efficient clerical support can also be tremendous time savers.

A manager often goes home at the end of the day not feeling satisfied. Establishing priorities and planning for ten to fifteen minutes at the beginning of the day alleviates this problem. Successful managers list the three most important things to accomplish and do not leave until they are completed. Then, even if the time is chipped away by a hundred other interruptions, a sense of accomplishment remains. Controlling time is essential to success.

Summary

Many other tools, models, methods, and examples could be identified and cited. Attention to goal setting and management information systems are basic tools for the middle manager. Increasing attention and skills in human and fiscal resource management and using technology to offer services enhance the basic tools and improve effectiveness. And, to accomplish all this and achieve job and life satisfaction, the student services manager must manage his or her time carefully and intentionally.

References

Davis, G. B. *Management Information Systems: Conceptual Foundations, Structure, and Development.* New York: McGraw-Hill, 1974.

Drucker, P. F. *The Practice of Management.* New York: Harper & Row, 1954.

Hanson, G. "Tentative Taxonomy of Student Development, Staff Skills and Competencies: Stop the Bandwagon, ACPA Wants to Get On." Unpublished paper, 1977.

McDaniel, R. R. "Goal Setting for Student Personnel." Unpublished paper 75-33, Division of Student Affairs, University of Texas at Austin, 1975.

Merton, A. K. "The Social Nature of Leadership." *American Journal of Nursing,* 1969, *69,* 2614-2616.

Odiorne, G. A. *Management by Objectives.* New York: Pittman, 1965.

Racippo, V. C., and Foxley, C. H. "MIS: A Tool for Planning and Evaluation." In C. H. Foxley (Ed.), *New Directions for Student Services: Applying Management Techniques,* no. 9. San Francisco: Jossey-Bass, 1980.

Robert A. Kerr   19

Evaluating the Services

As Oscar Lenning's chapter earlier in this volume illustrates, evaluation or assessment occurs continually in student services: We appraise our own performance every day, we weigh the effectiveness of our colleagues consciously as well as unconsciously, and we judge the impact of our programs from a variety of clues, incidents, and trends. Student service administrators and staff are currently devoting significantly more time to *systematic* evaluation than ever before. In this chapter, we shall explore (1) some of the reasons behind this development, (2) some factors that influence evaluation, (3) the components of systematic evaluation, and (4) examples of systematic approaches both at the unit level within student services and at the campus-wide level. Student services, as one of the major organizational components of the university, cannot afford to ignore either the reasons for this increased attention to systematic evaluation or a commitment to this effort.

Reasons for Systematic Evaluation

Why should the student services staff use a systematic evaluation process? Perhaps the most pressing reason is the increased demand for accountability being placed on higher education institutions. Colleges and universities in both the public and private sectors have always felt accountable to a number of publics: students, parents, alumni, state and federal governments, churches, individual benefactors, and others. But, when campuses were experiencing substantial annual increases in enrollments and funding, creating new programs and hiring more staff took precedence over the thorough review of existing programs to determine if they were meeting their objectives or serving students' needs. Now, however, in the wake of reduced financial resources and declining enrollments, institutions in general and student services units in particular are being asked to account for their resources. A systematic approach to evaluation allows student services administrators and staff to develop evidence of effectiveness and to demonstrate a commitment to self-assessment in anticipation of external pressure rather than merely to react to each criticism, question, or cutback as it occurs. If a department fails to initiate its own comprehensive evaluation program, someone from outside the unit will probably do it for them. Budget officers, presidents and vice presidents, trustees, and legislators will make their own assessments and determine their own priorities regarding student services with no input from student services professionals unless the staff conducts its own self-assessment of its services.

The second obvious, yet frequently overlooked, reason for systematic evaluation is simply to improve programs or increase effectiveness. A systematic evaluation process is basically good management. Data obtained through the process can be useful in planning, allocating resources, staffing, and updating programs to assure the greatest possible impact. For example, a service may be directed at the wrong student audience or be performed by inappropriate staff. Evaluation can help determine whether the right students have been selected or if staff have the necessary skills. For many staff members, however, improved service is probably the most misunderstood reason for assessment. Staff frequently view the evaluation as a threat to their own security or to the continuation of their programs. Evaluation must emphasize improvement rather than punishment, and staff members must become accustomed to systematic self-evaluation at the individual, unit, and campus level in order to create a climate of trust and respect within the institution as well as to develop expertise in all aspects of evaluation.

A third reason, increased staff morale, is related to the preceding one. A systematic approach to evaluation incorporates all staff members at the outset and maximizes their involvement in the process. This reduces staff anxiety and generates self-confidence rather than defensiveness among staff.

Cost and efficiency is a fourth reason for evaluation. A good evaluation system should improve efficiency and save money, although it requires an initial investment. Any careful evaluation costs money, staff time, instrument development, and data analysis. Staff usually resist unplanned and unscheduled evaluation because they drain time and money from existing programs and disrupt staff work schedules. But if evaluation is built into the schedule and the budget, it will be accepted as a high-priority, regular obligation and will save the institution and the unit both time and money.

Credibility is a fifth reason. Many faculty members and administrators, as well as student services staff members themselves, are skeptical of impressionistic or informal evidence that seems to involve more value judgments than actual data. A systematic approach to data gathering, analysis, and interpretation gives results much greater credibility both within and outside the department. A high degree of validity and reliability is essential for data used as a basis for making decisions, particularly in deciding on future programming and staffing. Student service staff should make decisions and develop plans on the basis of valid and reliable evidence.

Increased coordination and communication within student services and with other segments of the institution constitutes a sixth reason. Ad hoc and unplanned evaluation too often operates on the premise that each unit or program is totally independent. This is rarely true. Most services and functions in institutions affect many other departments, requiring an equally complex evaluation plan. And, because programs and departments are interdependent, it is advantageous not only to involve staff members from related departments in the evaluation of a unit but also to keep faculty members and students up to date on the workings of the unit and to gain their reactions to existing programs and plans.

Finally, Miller and Prince (1976) point to a seventh purpose for evaluation: to test theory. Student services programs are based on various student development theories, and evaluation can test the usefulness of these theories.

This list of reasons for evaluation is not meant to be all-inclusive. It does, however, allow us to better understand why administrators are directing more staff time and money to evaluation. And it demonstrates that valid professional reasons exist for increased attention to evaluation in addition to outside political pressure.

Influences on Evaluation

Among the wide variety of influences on evaluation that have been discussed in the literature and that can affect its success or failure, those that most frequently pose problems can be categorized into one or another of the following six issues: methodology, subjectivity, rationalization, cost, definition, and attitudes.

Methodology. The methods used in evaluation play a large role in determining its effect. Care must be taken to weigh the pros and cons of various methodologies and to select approaches that yield the needed information. Choices can be made, for example, between informal or formal methods, comparative or absolute approaches, and internal or external assessments (Brown, 1974). Informal evaluations are usually performed within a short, undefined time span, lack the specificity and detail of lengthy procedures, and usually result in a verbal rather than a written report. In some cases, such an approach may suffice, but often more formal methods are needed, in which the evaluation is conducted with an agreed-on beginning and ending date, focuses on a specific agenda such as the appraisal of particular objectives or services and their outcomes, and concludes with a written report that discusses the evaluation process, summarizes the data, and, frequently, offers conclusions and recommendations.

The evaluation process can also be comparative or absolute (Anderson and others, 1975). For example, a decision maker may want to compare present performance with the past or with findings from other institutions. An absolute approach is used when the evaluator merely wants to compare present results against predetermined program objectives.

Evaluations may be conducted by people either internal or external to the unit, department, or service being evaluated. Here, as with the previous choices, the decision between reliance on self-study or on outside review should be based on the primary audience and what method they will accept as being valid and reliable.

Hodgkinson, Hurst, and Levine (1975) recommend multiple evaluation measurements, as opposed to only one, in constructing their procedures and recommend both internal and external evaluation by people such as program staff, faculty members, students, and nonuniversity evaluators.

Subjectivity. Subjectivity poses a second problem. When people invest themselves heavily in a program, they find it difficult to be totally objective or nondefensive. Evaluations may then be structured to demonstrate only what the partisans desire. Several techniques identified by Anderson and others (1975) for distorting evaluations include selecting only successful parts of the program or searching only for the failures, prolonging evaluation so that results lose their timeliness or the initial interest in the results wanes, and focusing attention on successes and playing down failures.

Rationalization. Another influence on evaluation is rationalization. Anderson and others (1975) offer the following examples: The effectiveness of a program cannot be measured in the short term because the objectives must be developed over time, the effects are too complex to measure, and the programs touch on certain aspects of students' lives (for example, academic), but at the same time many other variables outside the control of the program (for example, social, political, and religious) may significantly affect the students. Even negative findings can be rationalized by showing that at least a few people profited from the program.

Cost. One influence that administrators must address is cost. Hodgkinson, Hurst, and Levine (1975) state that, if the personnel do not fully support evaluation or if budget is unreasonable, then staff morale can be undermined by the position of evaluation in the budget. Support for evaluation comes from potential cost savings realized by eliminating unsuccessful projects and from documentation that leads to improving a program without necessarily increasing the cost.

Definition. A vital influence is definition. Educational administrators have difficulty defining their product. This deflates the motivation for evaluation. Astin (1974) observes that, because outcomes are not easy to define or measure, a thorough, objective evaluation process becomes very time consuming. It usually means designing a new evaluative instrument because most educational outcomes of a program are unique and therefore require special measurement tools. Then follow the mechanics of collecting and analyzing the data and distributing the results. To many administrators, the resulting information does not justify the time, energy, and expense involved. In contrast, managers in the business sector know their product, and the profit potential is sufficient motivation for evaluation.

Staff Attitudes. A sixth influence on evaluation is staff opinion. Many staff view evaluation as an assessment of their competencies (Oetting and Hawkes, 1974). Furthermore, most administrators who entered the profession before the recent emphasis on strict accountability have not received formal training on the ways and means of evaluation. The attitude of the institution's top administrators toward evaluation has a particularly significant influence on the quantity and quality of evaluation conducted by the campus staff. A systematic evaluative approach can best be modeled by incorporating it into planning and organizing for programs. It should not be an afterthought or an addition made only if time and resources permit. Hungate (1964) suggested that one way to ensure that evaluation is incorporated into the planning and organizing stages is to actually develop a department policy stipulating the role of evaluation within the department and its programs. Unit personnel should know the place of evaluation and, whenever possible, they should be used in the process.

Components of Systematic Evaluation

Bowen (1974) has described evaluation as being difficult, expensive, subjective, and judgmental. A systematic approach to gathering and analyzing facts, however, makes results more credible, lowers costs, and incorporates staff fully into the design and implementation stages of evaluation.

The movement toward accountability could suggest that evaluative efforts should be directed solely toward obtaining objective, quantitative information. Quite the contrary is true. A systematic evaluation process should include a comprehensive portrayal of a program's purposes, plans, history, present conditions, recent activities, and outcomes, as well as judgments about the merits and shortcomings of both the means (processes) and the final product (outcomes). Conceivably, an objective could be achieved to the highest degree but the objective may be inappropriate or outdated. The evaluation process must also be flexible enough to recognize unplanned activities resulting from a program.

Sagen (1974) has identified six additional components of systematic evaluation:

1. *Validity and reliability.* These are especially important because educational institutions are accountable to students, parents, faculty, business staff, and other institutional administrators.
2. *Timeliness.* In all aspects of decision making, timing is an important ingredient. Astin (1974) has stated that a fundamental goal of evaluation is to produce information that can be used in decision making. Data that is gathered too late is of no value to the administrator, regardless of its critical message. Likewise, if the administrator delays a decision until the information is available, the impact of the decision may be lessened. If evaluation is to play an important role in decision making, then its timing must be systematically designed into the sequence of events.
3. *Relevance to the issues at hand.* Much evaluation being performed simply does not address real issues. This is likely to happen when evaluation processes are quickly devised by overworked administrators who are merely reacting to accountability demands. This is another reason why administrators should insist on systematic evaluations where the personnel are proactive, not reactive, in assessing relevant issues.
4. *Comparability.* Frequently, administrators have nothing to compare the results with or have no alternatives to select from. Evaluative information itself is not enough. The information should present meaningful alternatives to the administrator.

5. *Data capable of merging into aggregates.* The information elements should be capable of higher-order groupings. This is especially true because the information is frequently used at various organizational levels.

6. *Costs matching the benefits.* The costs must not outweigh advantages derived from the evaluation. The aftereffects of an evaluation are more extensive than the initial investment of time and money. They can include, among other things, changes in organizational structure and a redistribution of responsibility. These outcomes should be anticipated rather than wrestled with after the fact.

Examples of Systematic Evaluation at the Unit Level

Depending on the size and organizational structure of the institution, staff and program evaluations may be conducted primarily at the individual unit level (for example, in the counseling or the learning skills center), may be division-wide, or may be a combination of both. Regardless of its origin, a systematic evaluation process begins with the individual staff member in a unit.

A first step in developing systematic evaluation mechanisms is to develop long- and short-term goals for the staff members, the unit, and the division. Staff members can then write concise objectives for their job. Collectively, these objectives describe the services and programs that the unit staff provide. Johnson and Foxley address the process of goal setting for units and individual staff members.

The resulting evaluation instruments are useful for assessing the unit's staff, programs, and services. Establishing a systematic evaluation process within the unit benefits the staff in at least two ways. First, timely information derived from systematic evaluations can help the staff make knowlegeable decisions regarding personnel, programs, and services. Second, supportive data are frequently called for by someone outside the unit when its staff are requesting that a program be expanded or initiated or that a new staff pattern be approved that results in new positions. Similarly, the unit's staff may be asked to provide evaluative information for a variety of division-wide reviews, including those with budget or personnel ramifications. In each of these instances, existing systematic evaluation mechanisms reduce staff work.

There are numerous examples of systematic evaluation tools used primarily within one unit. Many of them can be labeled as "consumer feedback mechanisms." Characteristically, they are inexpensive, simple in design and statistical analysis, short in duration, and immediately useful for modifying programs or services.

One example of an informal consumer evaluation mechanism is provided by Harry Canon, vice president for student affairs at Northern Illinois University. For one week, every six weeks, a 3-x-5-inch card is offered to every person who uses a student service at NIU. The card asks the participants to (1) state how long they waited to receive the service, (2) rank the receptionist on a five-point courtesy scale, (3) rate the degree to which their needs were met, (4) rate the service provided by the professional staff member, (5) identify an employee who they wish to commend for good service, and (6) make any other appropriate comments. Canon feels this evaluation mechanism provides important feedback for staff.

Other examples of informal consumer evaluation mechanisms at Northern Illinois include client ratings of counselors and participant assessment of various student services workshops (such as counseling and placement). Sometimes NIU staff use postcards and telephone surveys, rather than the standard questionnaire format to solicit evaluations. These mechanisms have been used in areas such as campus recreation programs and the campus health delivery system.

Indiana University employs a variety of qualitative evaluation mechanisms within its housing program. John Schuh, director of the program, reports that residents evaluate their hall staff, hall staff evaluate their supervisors and vice versa, and central office staff evaluate supervisors and vice versa. In addition, the housing staff assess their various formal staff development activities throughout the year.

The approximately 12,500 residents of NIU halls also engage in evaluation exercises that alert staff to the effectiveness of a program, inform them of students' perceptions of what presently exists, or identify current needs of the residents for use in planning programming and other services.

Each year, new residents evaluate the hall orientation program in an effort to facilitate the transition from home to a high-density living environment. In addition, students and hall staff periodically assess hall judicial boards to ensure due process. A variety of questionnaire and interview techniques are used in these evaluative efforts. Some people believe that the environment shapes people; others believe people influence the environment. The residents at NIU also annually assess the interrelationship between the environment and people. Finally, to bridge the gap between the present and the future, the residents are given the opportunity to complete an interest survey. This instrument represents an attempt to determine direction for hall programs and services.

Most of these consumer evaluation mechanisms collect qualitative data about programs and services. Some systematic evaluations, however, gather only quantitative information. Quantitative devices may require staff to tally each phone or in-person contact, note the amount of time spent per contact, categorize the nature of the interaction, or engage in a combination of these items. In some cases, such information may be collected to demonstrate demand for a particular program or service. In other instances, these data project the staff workload. A quantitative evaluation process should not be the only mechanism used in a unit's systematic evaluation system, but it can contribute to the collective portrait of the unit.

Examples of Campus-Wide Evaluations

An operative systematic evaluation process at the unit level serves as a good foundation for more comprehensive evaluation. Examples from three campuses will be used to illustrate divisional and campuswide evaluation work.

The Los Rios Community College District in California, composed on three community colleges, provides an example of a systematic evaluation process of an even larger scale. The foundation for the evaluation process was the development of a master plan, a flexible blueprint for the district's future ("Research Report, . . . ," 1978).

The district observed that it had two options in response to increasing changes influencing the colleges. "First, it can decide to define its present practices and maintain the status quo. However, if it unequivocally resists change over a prolonged period of time, it may so reduce its usefulness to society that the society will discard it. The second option is to anticipate change, prepare for it, and respond to it" ("Research Report . . . ," 1978, p. 2).

The district then proposed development of a master plan to guide planning and evaluation efforts. A master plan, as defined by the district, "consists of the acquisition of a large amount of data about the institution and the community that it proposes to serve, followed by the formulation of a set of recommendations for how it might better serve that community. It should involve a steering committee that represents a cross section of the students, employees, and community members who . . . are attempting to exert more influence on the day-to-day management of educational activities" ("Research Report . . . ," 1978, p. 2).

The research project coordinated by the steering committee focused on (1) the community's educational needs and (2) the educational services being provided by the district. Twelve study areas were identified, resulting in 130 different topics. An advisory committee was formed for each of the twelve areas, to direct the research. Information on current educational services was accumulated from interviews, district publications, reports, and computer data. Students, employees of the college, and community members were surveyed to determine the educational needs of the community. The final stage in the district's systematic evaluation process was for the steering committee to make recommendations related to the district's educational programs, facilities, and other areas. The information collected from the research study, along with the results of public hearings and interviews with district employees, served as the basis for the recommendations presented to the board of trustees.

Some of the five campus-wide systematic evaluation examples that follow reflect the campus with which I am most familiar, the University of California at Davis. They involve (1) annual reviews, (2) annual reports, (3) unit advisory committees, (4) institution-wide advisory committees, and (5) management improvement programs.

Annual Reviews. Dutton and Rickard, in Chapter Eighteen of this book, say that "Management is a process created for only one purpose: to facilitate the achievement of institutional goals. It is a means, not an end; it is a vehicle that can only be justified or retain vitality as long as it serves the educational mission of the institution." An annual review provides each student service agency with an opportunity to articulate its role in the educational mission of the institution by providing the following information:

1. *Purpose and background of the department.* The agency should state when the service was first offered, what circumstances led to its formation, how it has developed during the years, who its audience is, and what its major function(s) within the institution is.
2. *Statement of goals.* A list of the unit's ongoing goals should be provided.
3. *Current operations.* The department's specific objectives for meeting the unit's goals should be listed, broken down by subunits within the department.
4. *Future plans.* The agency should describe specific short- and/or long-range goals in addition to the operations, projects, and programs that are standard each year.
5. *Organizational chart.* This chart should depict current staff patterns.

The entire document is reviewed and approved by the chief campus administrators. In this manner, the campus consciously determines on an annual basis what student services will be made available within the university community and what support they will receive. It also provides the department with guidelines and support for future planning.

Annual Reports. The second example of systematic evaluation is an annual report that is more detailed than the preceding document and contains a self-evaluation of planned and unplanned activities for the year. Sections of the report include

1. *Statement of purpose.* This is similar to the first item in the annual review.
2. *Description of current operations.* This is similar to the third item in the annual review.
3. *Planned objectives.* The agency describes its planned objectives for the year and discusses the degree to which they were achieved (broken down by subunits within the department). The description highlights who provided and who received the objective, the process used for advancing it, and the various programs and activities used. Finally, a self-assessment statement specifies the outcomes of the objective. What success resulted and why? What were the shortcomings and why?
4. *Unplanned activities report.* The department describes the unplanned activities (broken down by subunits) that arose during the year and their outcomes. Unanticipated events are an integral part of most student services units. This section is not to be viewed as a reward to those departments with the fewest unplanned activities, but rather as a recognition that when dealing with people one cannot always predict every need or response to a program. It is important, however, to be able to adjust direction or to reestablish priorities. This section addresses the major unplanned activities encountered by the department throughout the year, the causes, the steps taken, and the results. In some instances, unplanned activities can consume more time and resources than planned ones.
5. *Objectives to be undertaken in the next year.* Given the present circumstances, what will be the major focus for the next fiscal year? The objectives are merely listed, by department subunits, without explicit details. These planned objectives will be evaluated in the following year's annual report.
6. *Organizational Chart.* Current staff patterns are shown in chart form.

Besides offering a systematic self-evaluation procedure for administrative staff within the department, the annual report is reviewed by a group of administrators from outside the department. This group is charged with giving the department constructive comments on how well they have accounted for their services during the year. This systematic review process accomplishes two goals: (1) it provides each student service unit with an objective evaluation of their outcomes for the year, and (2) it provides comprehensive information to administrators in other student services. To enhance the frankness of the constructive criticism, the written review goes only to the department administrators, not to their supervisors. The intent of this written review is to assist, not punish, the administrators in their future efforts.

Unit Advisory Committees. A third systematic evaluation approach is an advisory committee system quite different from the advisory groups normally found in higher education institutions. Typically, those groups are composed of knowledgeable individuals in an area who have an established task. The groups may be long-standing, with a continual flow of related tasks referred to its members, or it may be an ad hoc committee in which a group of individuals is identified, given a specific task, and, once the task has been completed, disbanded. But typically these groups do not have decision-making responsibilities.

In contrast, student affairs departments can have a standing advisory committee composed of students, faculty, staff, and administrators who have an expressed interest, but not necessarily any skills, in a particular student service (such as financial aids, recreation, or the counseling and health center). Staff from the respective departments can serve as *ex officio* members. The advisory committees report to the chief campus administrator through unit and general student service channels.

Committee members can be selected by a nominating committee that includes faculty, students, and staff. This committee is responsible for nominating members and for identifying a chairperson to the chief administrator for each advisory committee. One goal of the nominating committee can be to present a slate of people that will result in a balanced committee, including one third to one half returning members, men and women, various ethnic groups, and a variety of academic disciplines. Usually each advisory committee is thus more representative of the institution's community than are the department staff members.

The purpose of such a committee is not only to provide advice to the department's staff, but also to conduct a yearly evaluation of the unit's success in meeting its goals and objectives. This function can be perceived to be both positive and negative by the unit's staff members. Seen positively, the committee is a group of people none of whom are employed by the department but who collectively represent all aspects of the institution's community; therefore, they are in a position to provide an objective assessment of the unit's outcomes. Seen negatively, the committee is a group of novices in the area under study and therefore their advice is poorly received by the campus professionals in the area.

Such advisory committees actually perform unique evaluative and advisory functions, because they provide campus-wide participation through their membership. In addition, the meetings are publicized through the student newspaper, and the sessions are open to the campus community and to the press. In their deliberations, it is important for the committee members to exercise initiative in soliciting information from the department and its users. The findings and conclusions of the administrative advisory committees are made available to the campus administrators, the department's staff, and other interested people within the institution.

Institutional Advisory Committees. The fourth systematic evaluation approach is an institution-wide advisory committee that does not focus on only one student services unit but reviews and makes recommendations on all student services.

At the University of California at Davis, for example, a portion of each student's registration fee goes to support various student services. This is the only financial support for many services. The executive vice chancellor is responsible for distributing the income to the student services units. The registration fee advisory committee is composed of students and faculty who make the recommendations to the executive vice chancellor on the allocation of funds. This evaluation approach is probably the most demanding on the department, for it requires strict accountability of past and future activities. Each student services unit submits its annual report, budget expenditures for the current year, and a proposed budget for the next academic year. The department also makes a verbal presentation to the committee, followed by a question-and-answer period.

It should be remembered that the pool of available money depends on the number of students registered. When enrollment was significantly increasing each year, there was usually money available for both expanding existing services and programs and creating entirely new services. For most institutions, those days are gone, yet maintenance costs increase each year. Salaries, benefits, supplies, and utilities, among other items, continue to rise. This challenges the advisory committee to thoroughly and objectively evaluate each student service and to recommend the level of support for the next academic year.

To meet this yearly challenge, the student services units must provide accurate records of past activities and objective assessments of future needs. However, needs are relative to the information and experience of the individuals who determine them. Staff affiliated with a particular student service are most knowledgeable and aware of the students' needs in that area but are not necessarily in a good position to compare the need for their service to that for other services.

Also, self-interest, at least subconsciously, plays a role in these deliberations. Staff members have a vested interest in their program's outcome. This can make it difficult to remain objective about the results.

At the same time, staff who believe strongly in the services being offered to students are usually anxious to expand or be innovative and to add new programs and personnel. In some cases, they may even be struggling just to retain the existing staff pattern. There is a natural tendency to protect what already exists and to resist cutting back or eliminating programs, staff, or services.

Everything is relative, however, and during times of dwindling or unchanging resources, someone must make the hard decisions about how resources will be allocated. The executive vice chancellor has the challenge of accomplishing this task at Davis. This person can see the entire campus and can balance diverse student needs. The registration fee committee has the responsibility to provide this administrator with timely, objective advice.

At Davis, the vice chancellor for student services is a key figure in these fiscal decisions. This influence is exercised in at least three ways: (1) All the unit advisory committees dealing with student services report through the vice chancellor to the chancellor; (2) administrators on the vice chancellor's staff serve on various campus committees and work groups that relate to fiscal allocations, plus they have other informal opportunities to champion their own causes; and (3) the budget officer for student services is an *ex officio* member of the registration fee advisory committee. The recommendations from this committee often differ from unit advisory committees' advice, which in turn may differ from the department administrators' position. This ambiguity must ultimately be negotiated.

The executive vice chancellor, however, has many other helpers in this process. There is a high correlation, according to Richman and Farmer (1974), between scarce financial resources and the number of administrators seeking influence and power by controlling the budget. As documented in Baldridge's studies (1971a, 1971b), groups with vested interests bargain and apply pressure wherever possible, which diminishes the influence of recognized authority. In the end, decisions may not be defensible from a pure objective stance but are negotiated compromises among competing groups and ideals (Baldridge, 1971a, 1971b).

Management Improvement Programs. The final systematic evaluation approach is a permanent, ongoing effort to assess the quality of management on the campus. The stated objectives of Davis' Management Improvement Program (Division of Student Affairs, 1977) include

1. To assure adequate, effective, and responsive administrative support for the campus . . . service activities
2. To maintain and assure a highly satisfactory level of quality in the management of these services

3. To maximize the effectiveness of available limited resources by assuring the cohesiveness of each administrative service on campus regardless of where the activity is performed
4. To develop awareness of organizational and operating deficiencies and institute early and effective action to correct them in a systematic manner
5. To examine adherence to established policies and procedures and to resolve conflicts, inconsistencies, and obscurities in policies and procedures
6. To reduce to a minimum the scope and frequency of internal and external audits by establishing maximum reliance on internal management systems and procedures

To accomplish these objectives, the Davis chancellor has appointed a Management Improvement Program work group. This group is composed of five university staff: the executive vice chancellor as chairperson, the vice chancellor for business and finance, the assistant vice chancellor for planning and analysis, the dean of a school or college (this is a rotating position), and the appointed director of the entire Management Improvement Program, who is a staff member for the chancellor and secretary for this work group.

The work group reports to the chancellor and maintains administrative responsibility for the following areas (Division of Student Affairs, 1977):

1. Developing, maintaining, and implementing the campus management improvement program
2. Identifying an evaluation schedule that states the order in which campus functions (such as counseling, financial aids, and admissions) will be evaluated
3. Selecting and appointing evaluation teams
4. Establishing guidelines, policies, and so on for the general operations of the evaluation teams, use of staff in the evaluation process, format for evaluation reports, and so forth
5. Coordinating the Management Improvement Program with the four systematic evaluation steps already discussed
6. Reviewing evaluation team reports and submitting where appropriate a summary report and recommendations to the chancellor and other appropriate administrative staff
7. Approving plans and timetables for corrective action and following through to assure its satisfactory completion

The last responsibility distinguishes this evaluative program from others. This step further illustrates the importance of positive rather than negative actions within a systematic evaluation approach. The intent is to make the function more responsive, more efficient, and so on, not to eliminate it.

The evaluation teams are composed of approximately five members selected by the work group. The members are university faculty and staff who have interest in evaluation and credibility within the institution. The work group also selects a chairperson for each evaluation team, and the director of the Management Improvement Program is a member of each team.

The evaluation team is not a permanent group. Its primary task is to thoroughly study a function and make recommendations. In coordination with appropriate administrative staff, the team is also responsible (Division of Student Affairs, 1977) for

1. Performing a comprehensive review of the department(s), including the organization, management styles, staff pattern, policies, procedures, systems, budgets, and interactions with other campus and noncampus agencies
2. Establishing a schedule for beginning and concluding the assessment process
3. Compiling written materials from the department(s) that are related to the evaluation process, including historical files, records, statistics, manuals, procedures, and policies, among other things
4. Conducting interviews with the staff members to obtain additional information about the department(s), program(s), and so on
5. Preparing a report that includes the team's findings and recommendations and that is shared with the appropriate administrative staff before submitting it to the work group

The review focuses on a function, not on a single department. Counseling and advising are functions performed by many departments at Davis. The statement on the scope of the study (Office of the Chancellor, 1976, p. 1) said,

> The study will emphasize examination of the purpose and nature of services provided, the organization, staffing, policy and procedure development and implementation, planning, resource allocation, the interrelationships between the units providing such services, student needs, and the general effectiveness of the counseling/advising services function. This function is considered to be primarily performed by the Counseling Center, Advising Services, Women's Resources and Research Center, the First Resort, the House, Peer Advising and Counseling, the Student Health Psychiatric Services, Career Planning and

Placement, Alternatives in Birth Control, Students Special Services, and the Learning Assistance Center.

The study will require that the team understand and review all those activities which provide a counseling/advising service designed to assist students in understanding and coping effectively with environmental and educational problems. To achieve this understanding and effectively perform the review, it will be necessary for the team to understand the nature of counseling and advising which are available in areas such as the Housing Office, the Financial Aid Office, Services for International Students and Scholars Office, and Admissions.

The evaluation team's primary responsibility will be to report on the findings, conclusions, and recommendations as they relate to the provision of counseling/advising services to students.

The Management Improvement Program is the most thorough systematic evaluation process and consequently pays the greatest dividends. With the evaluation team focusing on just one function at a time, it can devote full attention to the affected departments. Likewise, the team's members work hand in hand with the administrative staff, which increases the quality of information gathered, reduces the threat of evaluation, and increases the credibility of the results.

Summary

Most administrators would agree that the most expedient way to confront an evaluation problem or challenge is through a systematic approach. This approach begins with the unit staff developing measurable goals and objectives and consumer evaluation mechanisms. These unit-based evaluative processes can then be used in making personnel and program decisions and to provide information for campus-wide reviews. Budget reallocations, master plans, annual reviews, annual reports, unit advisory committees, institutional advisory committees, and management improvement programs are seven approaches that can help campus administrators meet the increasing demands for quality management.

References

Anderson, S. B., and others. *Encyclopedia of Educational Evaluation: Concepts and Techniques for Evaluating Education and Training Programs.* San Francisco: Jossey-Bass, 1975.

Astin, A. W. "Measuring the Outcomes of Higher Education." In H.

Bowen (Ed.), *New Directions for Institutional Research: Evaluating Institutions for Accountability*, no. 1. San Francisco: Jossey-Bass, 1974.

Baldridge, J. V. *Power and Conflict in the University*. New York: Wiley, 1971a.

Baldridge, J. V. *Academic Governance*. Berkeley, Calif.: McCutchan, 1971b.

Bowen, H. (Ed.). *New Directions for Institutional Research: Evaluating Institutions for Accountability*, no. 1. San Francisco: Jossey-Bass, 1974.

Brown, D. G. "Taking Advantage of External Evaluation." In H. Bowen (Ed.), *New Directions for Institutional Research: Evaluating Institutions for Accountability*, no. 1. San Francisco: Jossey-Bass, 1974.

Division of Student Affairs, "U.C.D. Management Improvement Program." Davis: University of California, 1977. (Unpublished report.)

Hodgkinson, H. L., Hurst, J., and Levine, H. *Improving and Assessing Performance: Evaluation in Higher Education*. Berkeley: Center for Research and Development in Higher Education, University of California, 1975.

Hungate, T. L. *Management in Higher Education*. New York: Bureau of Publications, Teachers College, Columbia University, 1964.

Miller, T. K., and Prince, J. S. *The Future of Student Affairs: A Guide to Student Development for Tomorrow's Higher Education*. San Francisco: Jossey-Bass, 1976.

Oetting, E. R., and Hawkes, F. J. "Training Professionals For Evaluative Research." *Personnel and Guidance Journal*, 1974, *52*(6), 434-438.

Office of the Chancellor. *Quality of Management Program Evaluation-Campus Counseling/Advising Services Function: Statement on the Scope of the Study*. Davis: University of California, 1976.

"Research Report of the Master Plan Steering Committee to the Los Rios Community College District Board of Trustees." Sacramento, Calif.: AIDES West, 1978.

Richman, B. M., and Farmer, R. N. *Leadership, Goals, and Power in Higher Education: A Contingency and Open-Systems Approach to Effective Management*. San Francisco: Jossey-Bass, 1974.

Sagen, H. B. "Evaluation of Performance Within Institutions." In H. Bowen (Ed.), *New Directions for Institutional Research: Evaluating Institutions for Accountability*, no. 1. San Francisco: Jossey-Bass, 1974.

Harry J. Canon

20

Developing Staff Potential

Student services staff have an obligation to themselves and to their clientele to refine their skills, develop new responses to changing circumstances, and otherwise actively engage in their own personal and professional growth. This obligation is wholly consistent with the oft-stated intent of our profession to contribute to the growth and development of our student clientele. Indeed, the continuing growth of student services professionals is a prerequisite for implementing a coherent and effective program of student development.

Rationale for Staff Development

Staff development programs in student services divisions have been generated and justified on a variety of premises. The three most common student services are (1) the remediation and rehabilitation of marginally trained or skilled professionals, (2) the enhancement of accountability to our institutions for what we do as professionals, and (3) the exercise of professional responsibility in the form of ensuring our own continuing professional growth.

Each of these premises represents an honorable commitment to students, colleagues, and parent institutions, but as stated purposes they will be either more or less acceptable to those who participate in staff development programs, as may be obvious by analyzing each of them in turn.

Remediation. Staff development can be viewed first as one tool for professional remediation and rehabilitation. Geographic isolation, drastically cut travel budgets, a period of stagnant leadership, the ennui resulting from a scarcity of new job opportunities, membership in a protected class, or simply an increasing number of years since graduate school can and do contribute to declining professional skills and the arrest of professional growth. There is nothing inherently wrong about finding oneself at such a point; the evil lies in remaining there.

Student services staff must also come to grips with the diversity of skills and conceptual orientations that both bless and curse the profession. Tripp (1977) mentions the dilemmas faced by those who prepare young professionals for student services careers. The philosophical bases of graduate programs in higher education vary from one institution to another. The quality of training received by students enrolled in the same program may also vary widely. The diversity of talents—and deficits—becomes more marked as one considers the staff who move into student services from secondary education, applied behavioral sciences, business, or simply because they were once identified as faculty members who seemed to get along well with students. Remediation may involve helping colleagues develop a "common ground" or shared conceptual view of their role and mission in their particular college or university.

Introducing staff development programs as remediation and rehabilitation, however valid its acknowledgement of existing deficits, is likely to be received coolly by the target population. No one likes to be identified as being less than competent. Although planners of such programs may legitimately conclude that competency deficiencies exist, they would do well to avoid nomenclature such as "in-service training" or "brush-up seminar" that suggests that fact. Persistent and effective staff development programs can and do move easily from rehabilitation to more palatable stages.

A gentle reminder may be in order when we are tempted to judge that our colleagues need rehabilitation: The diverse interests and educational backgrounds of student services professionals tend to create a kind of agency ethnocentricity that blinds us to the contributions and resources represented outside our own immediate sphere. I recall with some discomfort and embarrassment the arrogance with which I and some of my counseling center director colleagues once offered our panaceas for the ills experienced by deans and vice presidents.

In short, we all take pride in our professional training and competencies. We understandably resent those who would impose unwanted—and in our view, unneeded—retraining. Moreover, each of us has ingrained resistance to change. Professional growth and change is, after all, a high-risk activity. It is almost always accompanied by pain and the anguish of re-sorting priorities to which we have made strong commitments.

Enhanced Accountability. Professional development can also enhance our institutional accountability. It has become convenient to think of accountability as the provision of data reflecting the number of clients seen, the number of programs offered, papers published, and other variants of the traditional credit-hour production theme. Many of us who work as student services middle managers and administrators are understandably and appropriately nervous about validating our worth to our particular institution. Staff development programs offer a different perspective and alternative forms of accountability.

We are, of course, accountable to our student constituents, who are rapidly becoming sophisticated consumers of services and programs. They are knowledgeable about what is being offered on other campuses and may rightfully wonder why their particular student services staff are not offering workshops and seminars that contribute to student growth. As we engage in staff development programs that benefit our student constituency, students will support our efforts.

Faculty consumers of our services and programs tend to be discerning, critical, and skeptical. They are, nonetheless, our strongest potential base of support. Where student services staff have provided finely honed skills that undergird and strengthen academically based or related ventures (such as learning skills centers, living-learning residential units, centers for improving undergraduate instruction, and cooperative education programs), faculty support for our activities is reflected in decreased sniping at our budgets and increased advocacy of shared goals. For most of us, effective contributions to the academic mission of the college or university require skills that have only recently emerged in the profession. Without a sustained staff development effort, we stand little chance of achieving the complex skills that demonstrable contributions require.

Each of us is accountable to our student services colleagues. In all too many instances, we meet the enemy only to discover that they are us. Intradivisional squabbling and sniping are endemic in the profession and commonly undermine perceptions of our value by the upper level of institutional administration. As we share competencies with our colleagues and make the greater effort required in allowing them to teach us, shared purposes and futures emerge. This sense of mutuality offers personal as well as professional support, a commodity we each sorely need. And if we consistently honor accountability to students, faculty, and student services colleagues, fewer annual agency reports may be needed.

Student services professionals both shape and are shaped by the stated objectives of their colleges and universities. Whether as statements of purpose in a catalogue, or as institutional master plans, these documents should affect—in a significant degree—the goals of staff development programs. One suspects that we have, as a profession, exerted more energy to assure the inclusion of humanistic objectives in master plans and catalogue statements than to assure our responsiveness to dimensions that other elements of the college or university have asserted as being critical and important.

More specifically, we have not focused on staff development tasks related to intellectual inquiry and the expansion of knowledge. The potentially adverse effect of neglecting these institutional dimensions is underscored by the fact that these two specific objectives are very nearly universal in higher education. Our unique contribution as a profession may be an emphasis on a humanistic environment for higher education, but we also need to focus on and model intellectual inquiry in that humanistic context.

Staff development programs that provide for and encourage intellectually rigorous pursuit of concepts related to professional concerns and that employ assessment tools derived from our parent academic disciplines should be standard components of both planning and implementation. A sophisticated appreciation of theoretical constructs, a willingness to test those constructs in operational programs, and the expository skills to communicate those findings to other members of the college or university community are minimal requirements for effectively asserting other and more humanistic needs and objectives.

Professional Duty. Professional development is ultimately our exercise of professional responsibility. Establishing an intentional, participatory, and continuing program of personal and professional growth for all student services staff needs no justification or rationale beyond a commitment to enhancing the human resources represented in that staff. There is only one core assumption: Each of us is capable of and needful of continuing growth. A corollary assumption is that the general health, productiveness, and quality of contributions made to students are functions of growth experienced by individual staff members. A second corollary holds that each staff member has an obligation to contribute to the growth of colleagues. The assumption and its corollaries have the advantage of face validity and at the same time obviate the need to imply that any staff member is a "bad person" or is otherwise

professionally inadequate. We all start out by being OK and intend to
become even better.

Professionalism is a life-long commitment to refining one's skills
and professional attributes. That is essentially an individual commitment, but we are also accountable to our peers and constituents for
carrying it out. Our peers have a special responsibility to hold us
accountable, to call us into question if we fail to meet that obligation.
Thus the process is ultimately shared by a community of colleagues.
And that is where meaningful and effective programs for professional
development begin.

Beginnings

The early steps implementing a staff development program make
few assumptions about the sophistication represented within a student
services division and do not deal extensively with conceptual breadth..
For the most part, one begins with an emphasis on expanding or honing
skills related to a given agency's mission. To a limited extent, one
acknowledges that skills developed in one agency might be shared and
translated for use in another office. These are acceptable, honorable
roots. In general, they are consistent with goal criteria offered by Brown
(1977, p. 9):

1. Making a commitment to personal and professional growth
   within an evolutionary, optimistic, and risk-taking perspective
2. Knowing who we are as persons and what our responses are
   to basic issues confronting man
3. Knowing ourselves as professionals in terms of how our individual responses to the basic life issues relate to our professional activities
4. Knowing each other as persons and as professionals
5. Developing a commonality of purposes, both general and
   specific
6. Developing knowledge, insights, and skills which help assist
   ourselves and students to know themselves

Until rather recently (Meyerson, 1974), staff development programs designed to encompass the division-wide needs of student services
tended to be offered irregularly (Stamatakos and Oliaro, 1972; Passons
1969). With the initiation of in-service programs at the University of
Nebraska-Lincoln (Meyerson, Griego, and Breckenridge, 1974), Northern Illinois University (Wanzek and Canon, 1975), and Pennsylvania
State University (McCormick, 1978), such efforts became institutionalized and thus an expected part of staff activities.

It is instructive that the impetus for creating ongoing programs came from different sources at each of these institutions. Some were initiated by the senior executive officer in the division, others by agency heads, and still others by line staff. Attitudinal responses to the concept of continuing staff development programs ranged from rejecting to tolerant to actively supportive. In spite of uneven commitment at various organizational levels, each staff development program has enjoyed continuing success.

Essentially, programs work best when they command commitment from all levels of personnel, but failure to initiate in-service programs because "the vice president won't support them" may well be a copout. Let us review potential contributions at various staff levels as well as enabling and facilitating structures.

The Basics. Minimum requirements for initiating a staff development program include the time and thoughtful effort of two or three middle managers. It is very, very helpful if the program concept is endorsed by the senior administrator and is allocated a few dollars, but one can get by in acceptable fashion if the senior officer simply tolerates the staff being so engaged. A modest schedule of one-hour offerings over several months and the employment of local talent to present those offerings represent a laudable start. Issuing index cards with a request for feedback after each program meets evaluation requirements. The necessary and sufficient justification for offering the program to colleagues is that this is something we owe ourselves.

The degree of intentionality invested in staff development may be the most critical variable. Being intentional suggests that released time may take occasional precedence over a burgeoning workload. It means that annual performance evaluations include a review of the staff member's participation in workshops and seminars offered by the division of student services. Intentionality requires that the administration back its commitments to staff development with budget support—however modestly.

Staff members, at all levels, can make valid contributions to the content of programs in which they participate. It is simply sound strategy to allow participants the opportunity to buy into offerings by giving them a genuine role in determining the specific content. They know, with a certainty others cannot have, what their specific needs may be. Senior administrators can and should identify more general goals and objectives but how to achieve goals can be self-determined. Cascio (1978) notes and underscores the interaction of training outcomes with organizational subsystems. The training is planned by the organization to further the organization's goals.

Participation also involves the people who make our agencies work: the clerical staff. Not only do secretaries represent our most critical interface with students, but they are also a rich and underused resource. The importance of incorporating clerical personnel into inservice training programs has a strong industrial precedent. Such firms as Standard Pressed Steel have had training opportunities for production line personnel both in the plant and in the form of reimbursement for collegiate and certification programs (Moski, 1979).

It is important that staff development efforts be built into the system, that they become institutionalized. If continuity is essential to successful programming, as we suggest, it is partially assured by assigning someone to coordinate the program as a part of their job duties rather than as a volunteer job. Such an assignment also opens the door for accountability.

The Staff Committee. The ultimate success of staff development programs depends on a representative and active committee. That committee recommends action to the senior student services officer, transmits ideas and interest from other associates, and disseminates committee projects to office colleagues. If genuinely representative of the divisional resources and concerns, the committee is in a position to mount those programs most likely to reflect the needs of associates.

How individuals get on the committee probably does not matter much. Elections may be fine if that is the prevailing tradition, but appointment from a list of volunteers may allow a better balance of interests and a higher degree of sophistication. Terms of office should probably overlap, for purposes of continuity. Clerical staff can bring enthusiasm to committee functions along with a working knowledge of "what really happens."

There are compelling arguments for appointing a chairperson who has clout (Wanzek and Canon, 1975). More specifically, where chairing the committee is an assigned duty, not an elective or voluntary function, the position assumes added strength. Time is then provided within a normal working day to carry out the plans evolved or recommended by the committee. In essence, the chairperson can function as an administrator and implementer for the committee, freeing individual committee members to work only on programs in which they have a special interest. Using the chairperson as an implementer also provides the committee with a leader who knows how to cover trivia and otherwise bring the institutional bureaucracy to the service of the committee.

Where the chairperson's workload permits, he or she may also edit a periodic divisional communique or newsletter. Editorial duties, at least in the early stages, can be burdensome. People must be reminded of deadlines, and secretarial support is essential. Over time, the chairperson editor can identify reliable correspondents in each office, suggest issues and exchanges between staff that attract wide interest, and develop a predictable and self-generating schedule.

The committee can serve an additional useful role by making recommendations to the chief student services officer. If institutional policy provides for sabbatical leaves, the committee may function as a screening and recommending body to the chief officer. It may serve in a similar capacity for identifying special regional workshops and recommending specific personnel who should be encouraged to attend. Some professional growth committees serve as occasional publishers for regional associations. If the institution offers small venture grants, the committee can screen and advance worthy proposals. In general, the committee structure is strengthened and further institutionalized by any input and participation it is accorded in division programs.

The Senior Student Services Administrator. There are very real limits to what chief administrators can accomplish by mandate. Whether the issue deals with implementing staff development programs or with other goals, the senior officer's tools are limited to persuasion through articulating objectives, reinforcement through warm notes and kind words, judicious allocation of limited funds, and only very occasional admonition. Staff who wish to interest their dean or vice president in in-service training need to keep these limitations in mind.

The persuasive powers of the chief administrator are considerably enhanced when his or her behavior reflects an active personal commitment to growth and change (Canon, 1977). If staff are expected to buy into professional growth, the administrator must be out front, taking risks along with the troops. As suggested earlier, change is usually accompanied by considerable discomfort. If the target group—the staff—is aware that the leadership is actively risking and experiencing both pain and the rewards of new understandings, they can vicariously rehearse the task. It is worth noting that modeling professional change is a healthy experience for the leader: He or she becomes a bit more understanding of the resistance some staff will display and more appreciative of their reluctance to move out of safe, comfortable spaces.

Clearly, the chief administrator has an obligation to define the general goals of a student services division. That enunciation is frequently and appropriately offered in conceptual terms. He or she carries the primary burden of articulating divisional objectives for programming for students and, in turn, of establishing ties between those objectives and in-service programs for staff.

The essence of articulation may be persistence. Leaders who persist tend to prevail. Committees, being committees, tend to wander off in pursuit of some hot new topic or issue and need occasional gentle reminders of what they started out to accomplish. Persistence also includes continuing attention to committee activities and efforts. A changing committee constituency, although clearly desirable, also has the less desirable effect of constantly changing directions. Goals must be reexamined and altered in the light of practical experience, but the senior administrator can help assure that change results from thoughtful examination rather than capriciousness.

The senior administrator can help the committee produce a balanced program pattern that contributes to personal growth and recreation, as well as to the primary purpose of skill acquisition. If tasks undertaken by staff are intended to model objectives for students, that kind of balance is necessary. With surprising frequency, professional personnel are reluctant to give themselves permission to play; that permission can effectively be communicated by the chief officer.

Inevitably, fiscal provisions for staff development programs must be made by the senior administrator. A top-level commitment to programs should be accompanied by dollars. A caveat: Programs that are dollar based rather than staff based will evaporate in the next budget cut. Staff development does not need to cost much money. Continuity is more likely when the funding is modest. Finally, the dean or vice president is well advised to solicit a budget from the committee. The penalty for not doing so is a year-long series of encounters with a panhandling committee.

The Programs. Programs developed in the interests of professional staff development should reflect, both in balance and breadth, the basic objectives referred to earlier: general professional growth, refinement of existing skills, and acquisition of new skills to meet changing needs. Not all these objectives are approached at the start. Initial offerings may have a distinctly "safe" or pedestrian quality, because the committee members, along with their colleagues, are undertaking some risk.

Meyerson and his colleagues (1974) suggest a "cafeteria" approach to staff development that serves as a useful model for programs just getting underway. The cafeteria of offerings simply represents a variety of workshops, outings, seminars, and social activities that each of the committee members is willing to undertake and that others in the division can attend or not as they choose. (See Table 1).

A scheduled series of one-time offerings permit staff to pick and choose in accordance with taste and degree of risk and at the same time does not force more burdensome commitments to programs that require continuing attendance. The number of people who appear at certain programs is fair evidence of their interest in certain issues or topics. With cafeteria programming, the committee and the presenters should probably establish minimal expectations for attendance. In programming for staff, as for students, it is critical that success or utility not be judged solely on audience count. If the presenters begin with the expectation

Table 1. Staff Development "Cafeteria" Samples

Program Titles	Resources
Orientation for new staff	Agency directors
What we know about students and what we need to know	Analytical studies
The role of student services in the university	Provost
Dinner and theater trip	Staff development committee
How to publish an article	Director of counseling, vice president for student services
Overview of election year	Professor of political science
Affirmative action	Assistant to the president
Computers in plain English	Computer center director
Ombudsman's perspective of student services	Ombudsman
Presidential campaign, 1976	Professor of political science
Craft workshops (three craft areas)	Recreation staff
Effective business communication	Professor of business education
Decision-making workshop	Director of counseling
Over-the-counter drugs	Health service pharmacists
Higher education and the legislature	State representative
All you want to know about university insurance	Insurance officer
Nutrition and weight loss clinic	Director of nursing
The "how of publicity and promotion"	Office of university information
Ski trip	Office of campus recreation
Preparing your income tax	Accounting office
Vacation planning	Office of campus recreation
How to be a successful convention-person	Vice president for student services

that eight participants represent a useful program, disappointments will be fewer and the program base is more likely to be extended.

The encouragement of personal growth programs requires including activities that may raise the hackles of a few agency directors. Again, and in the service of balance, it is legitimate to include an assessment of the gubernatorial race by a political scientist, noon-time macrame, a presentation on tax-sheltered annuities, and an excursion to a dinner theater. Clerical staff should, by all means, be offered value clarification workshops and life-planning workshops, along with communications programs they may design for themselves. Secretaries undoubtedly provide more interpretative information for students than does any other class of personnel. A receptionist in another office who endorses a student-oriented program on the basis of his or her personal experience of that program is a powerful referral source.

As the committee experiences some success with its cafeteria offerings, it can begin a more thoughtful assessment of divisional needs that may require other approaches. A divisional newsletter may be valuable; it can provide creative programmers with an opportunity to show and share their views, can humanize by giving a modicum of flesh and blood to colleagues one sees only occasionally, and can voice concerns that individual staff members may feel are important but neglected.

Staff development committees can also generate programs aimed at special needs or classes of employees. If funding is available, they may recommend a mini grant program for senior staff who wish to update skills through several weeks of residence on another campus. Supervisors may encourage such staff to submit applications outlining resources available at the institution they propose to visit, skills they expect to acquire, and anticipated costs. Following approval by the supervisor, the committee can review and set priorities for applications according to their perceptions of divisional needs and potential contributions to the agency, division, and general programmatic objectives.

Some regional workshops may be particularly appropriate and appealing to emerging professionals. The committee can judge competing applications for a limited number of funded slots to determine maximum divisional benefit on an expanded and less idiosyncratic base. In consultation with the administration, one such committee (Wanzek and Canon, 1975) established an in-house administrative fellows program designed to professionally advance individuals from protected groups, such as ethnic minorities. The fellows, selected by the staff development committee, were assigned to agency heads who served as mentors and models and who encouraged their particular fellows to participate in budgetary planning, to develop a specific project or study needed by the agency, and to "shadow" agency heads as they went about their daily chores. A modest expenditure of funds for limited professional travel, a thoughtfully designed series of weekly seminars coordinated by a senior staff member and involving administrators from various areas of the university, and some eight hours each week of released time from their regular assignments gave the participants valuable administrative experience.

Pitfalls and Promises. The tactics and strategies for mounting and sustaining a staff development program need not be complex but do require thoughtful preparation. Committee members and the chairperson should be prepared to monitor staff reactions, perceived access to development programs at all staff levels, supervisors' acceptance of the intent and thrust of the various offerings, and the general scope of emerging programming.

The risk of high-budget programming has been noted. A committee operating under fairly stringent budget constraints is more likely to seek out local resources. Neglected and knowledgeable experts at one's own institution can be converted into supporters of the student services enterprise. Just as each of us frequently wishes that "they'd just ask me," so our academic colleagues respond favorably to our solicitations of their expertise.

Agency directors may rather strongly resist giving staff released time to attend in-service programs. That resistance can double if the staff member in question is a secretary (which says something about what staff category is most critical to the operation). Both the committee members and the senior student services officer must be alert and sensitive to the problem. It is absolutely necessary to insist gently but relentlessly on the primacy of staff development and on the dean or vice president's expectation that staff will be encouraged to participate.

A consistent evaluation—however brief or modest—of every program offering gives added credibility to the value placed on the activity by the committee and by the administrators. The evaluations should, of course, be shared with the presenter(s). Cumulatively, they provide some understanding of what does and what does not work, and why.

Beyond Beginnings

The goal criteria offered by Brown (1977, p. 9) and cited earlier, are particularly suggestive of an added and critical dimension—developing "a commonality of purposes." That commonality of purposes carries the potential obligations of student services staff well beyond maintaining and improving narrowly defined professional skills. It calls us to acknowledge and respond to roles our skills and programs assume in the larger missions of student services division and of the college or university itself. There is, indeed, an obligation for at least some of us to come to grips with the role and mission of higher education in our society. Carried to that extreme, the task and obligations assume intimidating and nearly overwhelming proportions.

Student services practitioners have frequently struggled to identify objectives on which the rather disparate agencies within a division can agree. Even in instances where agreement has been obtained, operational plans for achieving those goals have been difficult to implement. Unfortunately, a perception of the faculty as a common enemy and an "us" (student services) versus "them" (the faculty) model (Brown, 1977; Canon, 1976), are often the most effective forces for cohesion within a student services division. There are better places to begin.

Brown (1977, p. 8) suggests that we first need to "take an explicit and public stance" in confronting the basic issues of human existence. I suspect he is correct and am at the same time appalled at the immensity of the task. The questions he raises are indeed central to the quality of human existence. Knowing "how we [can] help students reconcile self-interest and altruism" suggests that student services staff themselves are engaged in exploring the issue. Attempting to "promote the right balance between a competitive spirit necessary for economic survival in this country and the need for cooperation, sacrifice, and team work for society to survive" assumes a similar commitment by professionals (Brown, 1977, p. 8).

The fact is that student services personnel rarely consider such issues in spite of the fact that they represent the ultimate ends of our endeavors. Managerial concerns too often evolve into managerial styles ("we've got to make things run smoothly" or "we have to be accountable"). Intellectual interests and styles—the absolute prerequisites to exploration of these core philosophical issues—are decried as being impractical and ivory towerish. Reawakening and renewing exploration of gut philsophical issues may be our professional salvation. More promising still, they may—paradoxically—turn out to be the most practical vehicle for establishing commonality of purpose and the strength that comes from shared and unified effort. Obviously staff seminars dealing with such basic philosphical values involve higher risk. Any meaningful participation calls for assessing personal values against transcendent benchmarks of corporate social good. And the modeling of such behavior for students can have markedly powerful effects.

Continuing in the same vein, Brown (1977, p. 9) urges the development of "skills and programs that promote integration of the academic and personal development of students." That is not a new notion for Brown (1972) or for the profession. Tactics and strategies for weaving student development programs into the academic fabric of higher education have been a major preoccupation of the profession for the last half dozen years. Miller and Prince (1976) illustrate in detail many token approaches to the task. Our accomplishments are indeed modest, suggesting that we have a very long way to go. It would be tragic, however, if the enormity of the task were to deter us. The history of the effort is incredibly brief when measured against the history of higher education in America.

Realizing the dream of integrating personal and academic development depends absolutely on successfully developing student services staff and academic faculty. As noted, our beginnings are modest. Our efforts have probably been unfocused and ineffective. But realizing the dream demands that we begin—that we reach the highest levels of sophistication in our particular skill areas, that we learn from each other, that we seek assistance and information from our academic colleagues (before offering our bits of wisdom to them), that we acknowledge our commitment to the centrality of the intellectual mission of higher education, and, most importantly, that we persist.

An Organizational Model of Staff Development

We have been viewing staff development largely from the perspective of the individual staff member and how his or her needs match those of the student services enterprise and of the college or university. Presidents and senior-level administrators for academic, business, and student services functions have another perspective that should appropriately be shared with (and perhaps, by) staff development committees and their colleagues. The troublesome tendency of student services agencies—no less than academic disciplines—to confine their horizons to the boundaries of their own offices is a constantly confounding and frustrating fact of academic life. If however, the student services professionals within a college or university can be offered a valid and useful paradigm of what might be, there is reason for confidence in their prospect or movement toward that goal.

One such model (Canon, 1976, p. 179) postulates three levels of development for student services staff. At the first level of organizational development, staff primarily identify with a professional specialty and with their own subunit, such as financial aids, counseling center, or activites. The effectiveness of student services staff who function at this level is not high. Staff may lack awareness of what other agencies are doing, duplicate efforts, show pronounced territoriality, uncritically identify with students and their causes, have authoritarian relationships with upper-level administration, compete with other agencies for budgets and attention, and feel quite unappreciated by colleagues in other offices.

At the second level, staff primarily identify with student services and are very comptetent in subspecialties. Organizations operating at the second level tend to enjoy a measure of collegiality in decision making, the senior administrator is allowed a consultative role and is seen as an advocate who is expected to "produce" for that division, and agencies cross office boundaries with some frequency to mount cooperative programs. Consultations occur across agency lines, expertise in one office is cheerfully acknowledged by another, and budgetary accommodations are made for the greater good of the division (vis a vis "academic cost centers"). "Us versus them" relationships generally obtain with the faculty. Academic rank may be forgone in favor of competency and contributions as measures of professional worth. On the second level, the division's effectiveness is approximately equal to the sum of its parts.

On the third level of functioning, the staff primarily focuses on the institutional mission as seen through a strong, sophisticated understanding of the purposes of higher education. At this level, programming for students is the product of joint planning and implementation by student services staff and their faculty colleagues, jargonistic pronouncements are replaced by basic English, and the senior student services administrator is expected to invest major blocks of time in cementing ties with key individuals in the academic sector. Issues are explored in terms of their conceptual and philosophical implications, academically based student subcultures are designed, and there is occasional but regular support from faculty for division of student services budgets and programs. On this third level, the effectiveness of the division is equal to something more than the sum of its parts.

Although the comfortably familiar, Gestalt-ish conclusions for the third level may be unwarranted, they may encourage some to try scaling those giddy heights. In any event, the model attends to an occasionally neglected focus on the effects of cooperative and coordinated approaches to institutional change. At its core, the model harks back to the essentials of empowerment: As we arrive at the common roots of our institutional mission and share resources with others, we are enabled and empowered to bring about change.

Prospects

Continuing education units (CEUs) are rapidly becoming commonplace in medicine, its allied professions, and other professional groups and in some fields constitute one basis for relicensing or recertification. The establishment of CEUs for professionals in student services may not be too distant and probably should become a matter of professional concern in the near future. It is possible to establish student services CEUs without first treating the complexities associated with licensure and certification. A priority item for the American College Personnel Association and a genuine service to the profession could be the establishment of a registering body for regional and national workshops. Registered workshops and seminars would offer participants a specified number of CEUs on successful completion of each program. Continuing assessment of skills that participants gain in the workshops (posttesting) and simple evaluation forms completed by participants could help maintain the quality and integrity of the CEUs.

Home-grown programs that are particularly effective should be shared with neighboring institutions. Our profession is particularly addicted to show-and-tell behavior, with greater emphasis on the telling and much less showing others how. Interinstitutional exchange is further complicated by rivalry (which may hint at the motivation for telling rather than showing). Nonetheless, we do have a professional obligation to share what we have learned and to share programs that work. It is more economically feasible to share with neighboring colleges and universities than it is to escalate all of our efforts to the national level. With a more humble stance (and most student services staff have many attributes about which they can be appropriately humble), interinstitutional training efforts could become more common.

Finally, Brown and Citrin (1977) have offered a student development transcript in several forms (transcript of experiences, portfolio, annotated credentials) that deserves examination as a medium for recording professional development achievements and experiences. The concept has particular merit in that it requires nothing more than (1) the systematic recording of professional development activities by the individual staff member and (2) a willingness to use the transcript to support applications for employment, retention, and/or promotion. The annotated resume is enjoying some popularity and represents a tentative step in that direction. Validating the acquisition of new skills and documenting personal growth and change would serve both the candidate and the hiring institution. The net gains for the profession would be significant.

Brown's concept of a development transcript and our suggestion that such could be instituted as a part of continuing education for professionals was partially anticipated by Uris (1970), who plotted out an "employee skills developer." It is essentially a checklist of skills to acquire and then have a supervisor or colleague record them.

Self-Development for Student Development

In summary, the basic assumption underlying staff development in student services is that the quality of our programming for students, the success of our efforts to facilitate their development, the impact of our efforts on our individual institutions, and the quality of our contributions to the educational mission of colleges and universities in general are direct functions of our own continuing growth and development. Insofar as we risk personal and individual change ourselves, to the extent that each of us remains professionally alive, and as we model for students and cohorts the principles of lifelong learning and change, so we enable ourselves to be instruments for change for others.

References

Brown, R. D. *Student Development in Tomorrow's Higher Education: A Return to the Academy*. Washington, D.C.: American College Personnel Association, 1972.

Brown, R. D. "Professional Development and Staff Development: The Search for a Metaphor." Staff Development Monograph 1. DeKalb: Northern Illinois University, 1977.

Brown, R. D., and Citrin, R. S. "A Student Development Transcript: Assumptions, Uses, and Formats." *Journal of College Student Personnel*, 1977, *18*, 163–168.

Canon, H. J. "A Developmental Model for Divisions of Student Affairs." *Journal of College Student Personnel*, 1976, *17*, 178–180.

Canon, H. J. "The Role of the Chief Administrator in Staff Development." Staff Development Monograph 1. DeKalb: Northern Illinois University, 1977.

Cascio, W. F. *Applied Psychology in Personnel Management*. Reston, Va.: Reston Publishing, 1978.

McCormick, J. E. "An Approach to Staff Professional Development." *Journal of College Student Personnel*, 1978, *19*, 183.

Meyerson, E. "Meeting the Challenge: Staff Development for Student Affairs." *Campus/Community Mental Health Services Newsletter*, Feb. 1974, pp. 1–2.

Meyerson, E., Griego, B., and Breckenridge, J. "The Mini University: A Cafeteria Approach to Staff Training." Unpublished manuscript, Division of Student Affairs, University of Nebraska-Lincoln, 1974.

Miller, T. K. and Prince, J. S. *The Future of Student Affairs: A Guide to Student Development for Tomorrow's Higher Education*. San Francisco: Jossey-Bass, 1976.

Moski, B. A. *The Human Side of Production Management*. Englewood Cliffs, N. J.: Prentice-Hall, 1979.

Passons, W. R. "In-Service Training for Student Personnel Staff: A Pilot Project." *Journal of the National Association of Women Deans and Counselors*, 1969, *33*, 34–38.

Stamatakos, L. C., and Oliaro, P. M. "In-Service Development: A Function of Student Personnel." *NASPA Journal*, 1972, *9*, 269–273.

Tripp, P. A. "Student Personnel Work—Whence It Came and Whither It May Be Going." Staff Development Monograph 1. DeKalb: Northern Illinois University, 1977.

Uris, A. *The Executive Deskbook*. New York: Van Nostrand Reinhold, 1970.

Wanzek, R. P., and Canon, H. J. "Professional Growth in Student Affairs." *Journal of College Student Personnel*, 1975, *16*, 418–421.

Val R. Christensen   21

Bringing About Change

Managing change to make things happen is the challenge to every college administrator. Administrators who successfully achieve this goal find a great deal of personal satisfaction in their work and a wide range of support from students and faculty. There are some basic steps and principles that can be implemented to facilitate constructive change (Lewin, 1958; Frank, 1963; Coch & French, 1968). These are not new to people who have been successfully implementing new and innovative programs. But, for those who have been having difficulty, and even for the successful change agents, a review of these steps and principles may be useful.

Administrators have an obligation to be alert to what changes need to be made in order to improve growth experiences for students. They cannot wait for fires to begin or for problems to arise. Rather, they must anticipate problems and be able to generate solutions before small problems become large ones. Administrators who wait for the crisis to begin before generating solutions are constantly under attack and generally have both staff and students in disarray waiting for one crisis to be over before another begins.

No matter what causes an organization to move in a new direction, it generally happens more successfully if there is an organized plan of attack. Once that plan is developed, using many or all of the techniques listed in this chapter allows the administrator to make change happen much more quickly and much more successfully.

Implementing change on a university campus can be both tedious and challenging. It is more often successfully accomplished if a careful problem-solving process is used to analyze and recommend change. The simple process described here is just one of many that might be used. The important point is to use some systematic method of looking at and addressing problems.

Problems and Possibilities

Today, we all need to step back for a good look at the programs and services we are providing the university community. As we step back for that look at ourselves, we all find that we have some predicaments in common. Do any of the following sound familiar?

1. The office of the dean of students is constantly being asked to take on new projects and cannot decide what to do. How do we choose among the opportunities?
2. The student orientation program does not provide students with the necessary information to make good decisions about their academic programs.
3. The financial aids office is bogged down in paperwork. Many of the students are complaining that awards are not given in time for them to make decisions.
4. The student activity program is beset with confusion and disagreement. Student government leaders command very little respect on the campus, and the student body itself seems very apathetic toward many of the student activities.
5. The counseling office seems bogged down in traditional ways of reaching students. There is a constant division between counselors who want to maintain traditional counseling methods and those who want to implement a new and more innovative approach to mental health.
6. The placement and career center is having trouble attracting enough recruiters to campus. Many companies have eliminated the campus from their visits, thus making it difficult for graduates to identify work opportunities.

What would happen a year from now if you employed a simple problem-solving process wherein you could look at the various problems faced by student services administrators? Change in student services is much more easily achieved if administrators can operate within a uniform framework of looking at their problems and moving toward defined goals and objectives. If this were implemented systematically, a year from now you might find that:

1. You are now beginning to feel well organized. There are many projects that have been assigned to your office, but you seem to have the time to organize and plan them well.
2. A new program for orienting students to the campus has just been implemented with considerable success. There seems to be a much more unifying spirit on the campus. First-year students particularly feel a sense of belonging.
3. There seems to be a new interest in student government and activities, as witnessed by the increase in students who voted in the most recent election. Student leaders are experiencing much more interest in their programs and activities.
4. The counseling center is innovating with some new programs. There is much more unity among the staff and more willingness to cooperate in serving student needs.
5. The placement center is enthusiastic about an increase in the number of employers who plan to visit the campus for interviews. A new program implemented recently in order to attract these employers to the campus is meeting with considerable success.

The Change Process

A great deal can be done and a great amount of change can take place if student services administrators simply organize and clearly identify what exactly they want to accomplish. The following process is one that can be used effectively in solving problems on campus.

1. *Identify the problem.* Problems are existing situations that need changing. Every school has dozens of them. A problem statement must clearly explain an unsatisfactory situation that your institution wishes to change. The more specific the statement is, the better it is.

2. *Quantify the problem (facts and figures).* Quantifying is an important step that is often overlooked in the problem-solving process. It is important to list the facts and figures of the problem. To state there is an advising problem on campus is not enough. It is more useful to state the number of students, faculty, and administrators who feel that a problem exists. This step takes research, but the effort pays dividends.

3. *Identify the causes of the problem.* It is not always possible to identify clearly what is causing the problem, but some effort should be

made to do so. Again, an attempt to be specific pays off. The lack of a good advising program may be explained by the fact that there is no signature control, no faculty incentive, or unclear general education requirements.

4. *List the alternative solutions (brainstorm).* Listing alternatives is the brainstorming step in the process. Make a list of as many alternative solutions as is possible. It is important that no criticism enter into the discussion. There should be a free flow of ideas, the wilder the better. All possible alternatives should be listed. Judgment should be suspended until all the ideas are out. Judging and creativity should not go on at the same time.

5. *Select the best potential solution (judge alternatives).* There may be more than one solution to the problem, but choose that one that appears to present the most promise. During this step, judge the alternative solutions. List the solutions in order of importance, and then work on the best one first.

6. *Test the selected solutions (ask the right questions).* Testing is another step that is often overlooked. It is important to ask whether or not the solution will be accepted by those who must support it. Will the solution actually solve the problem? There is no point in recommending a new advising program for the students if the new program is too expensive and will not be accepted by the students and faculty.

7. *Determine your project objective.* Determining an objective is one step in an attempt to solve a problem. It is stated in terms of what is realistically achievable in a given span of time. It is aimed at action that can be measured. When all objectives have been met, the problem has been solved. Whenever possible, objectives should tell exactly how much of the desired result must be achieved to consider the effort successful.

8. *Develop the project tasks.* The next step is to develop the tasks needed to achieve the objective. The tasks should contribute directly to the objective. They should be feasible and dated within a time frame shorter than the objective to which they contribute. Likewise, it is best to develop them in a way that allows them to be measured.

9. *Evaluate the project.* A final step in the process is to evaluate the success of the project. Evaluation takes place throughout the process. If the objectives of the project are feasible, dated, measurable, and indicate a level of achievement, nothing could be easier to evaluate. Either you did, or you did not. Of course there are other factors to consider in the evaluation, but this simple problem-solving method allows you to look at the project in a precise way.

Applying the Process

On a university campus, the vehicle often used to look at the problems in more detail is the university committee. Universities are generally run by committees or task forces, which provide a forum for issues to come to the front. They can also be used to bury an idea or place on the shelf some unpopular problem that no one really wants to face. A typical university committee might face the following problem: A campus was troubled with growing dissatisfaction among students, faculty, and the administration concerning the advising program. Over a number of years, not much attention had been given to this problem, and the situation had deteriorated to the point that a considerable amount of open opposition existed. In response to a recommendation by student leaders, the central administration formed a committee to evaluate the process. The committee was given these specific objectives:

1. Identify and catalogue problems relating to advising.
2. Prepare a statement outlining the university goals for advising.
3. Design an advising system consistent with the following constraints:
   a. Academic advising should be handled at the department level.
   b. Any recommendation for change should acknowledge a financial limitation. It should not recommend massive administrative changes that would burden financial commitments already placed on the university.

The committee began its process by making an effort to determine the attitudes of the students, faculty, and administrators regarding advising. Questionnaires were distributed to all three groups. As the committee moved toward a solution to the problem, it used the simple problem-solving process to focus on the various elements.

1. *Identify the problem.* When the committee evaluated the responses from the students, faculty, and administrators, it identified a number of problems. High on the lists was infrequent student contact with faculty advisers. There was inadequate information about academic requirements, and the advisers were generally uninformed about university policies and procedures. Obviously, the students were not motivated to seek advising help. One major problem that seemed to face many of the students was the process used to assign advisers. Likewise, there was a large discrepancy in the number of advisees assigned. Some advisers had 200 students and others only 5 to 6. And the faculty felt they were not adequately compensated for good advising. They did not seem motivated to serve as adequate advisers. Each department had its own way of implementing the advising task, and very little cooperation or coordination took place. As a result, students and faculty were very confused, and considerable resentment existed.

2. *Quantify the problem.* A survey made clear that over half of the students opposed the advising program and found the process difficult. Nearly 80 percent of the faculty expressed the same concern, as well as over 70 percent of the department heads. It became apparent to the committee that some recommendation for change would be appropriate.

3. *Identify the causes.* In this step, the committee made every effort to identify in specific terms what was causing the problem. There were many causes, of course, but some of the most glaring were:

a. Infrequent student contact with faculty advisers
b. Inadequate long-range academic planning with faculty advisers
c. Inadequate information about academic requirements
d. Advisers uninformed concerning university policies and procedures
e. Lack of student motivation to seek advising help
f. Difficulty in locating advisers when needed
g. Unclear procedures for assigning advisers
h. Poor incentives for faculty to perform useful advising
i. Inadequate processes for evaluating the advising program

4. *List alternative solutions.* The next step for the committee was to list alternative solutions to the problem. This brainstorming process allowed members of the committee to place on the table a large number of ideas. No judgment was made until all of the ideas were out. A few of the suggestions were

a. Create an academic advising center and bring on board a large number of professional advisers to take the load from the faculty and staff, thus freeing them for teaching and research.
b. Employ one individual at the university level to help coordinate the program, and then identify representatives and coordinators in each of the colleges who would be responsible to administer the program more effectively.
c. Develop a peer advising program. Students would move into the advising process and assist the faculty with the advising program.
d. Develop a list of class and course requirements. Keep them current and make them readily available. Then allow students to do their own advising.

5. *Select the best solution.* After these and other solutions were recommended, the committee moved to select the best potential one. It concluded that there might well be more than one solution to the problem, but the committee recommended that the university develop a

central academic service center staffed by a director. The center would be responsible for coordinating the work of college service offices. The college offices would be responsible for making contact with the faculty and students and correlating the program at the college level.

6. *Test the solutions.* The next step was to test the selected solution. It was important to touch base with the people who would need to implement the program, in order to determine whether or not they would give support. At this point, the students, faculty, and administration were notified concerning the preliminary recommendations of the committee. After their input, some alterations were made, and the committee moved to the final step in the process, determining the project objective.

7. *Stating the project objective.* An effort was made to state the objective in realistic terms under a given span of time. The objective was stated: "The university will establish an academic service center by January 1, with college academic service offices designated in the eight university colleges. An administrator will be appointed to oversee the work by February 1."

8. *Develop the project tasks.* After determining the project objective, these are a few of the tasks needed to implement the program:

a. Prepare the final report and recommendation
b. Distribute the report to the students, faculty, and administration making presentations to these same groups
c. Designate individuals within each college to coordinate at this level
d. Appoint a director for the University Academic Service Center

9. *Evaluation.* An evaluation of the new program was planned for a year after it had been implemented. This allowed sufficient time to determine if the students and faculty had improved in their attitudes toward the program.

Suggestions for Change

This simple problem-solving process allowed a difficult and complex problem to be divided into steps that helped make it much easier to solve. Through the entire process, however, a number of important guidelines were observed that allowed for the successful conclusion of this project. These principles help move the change process more quickly through the difficult maze of people and policies.

1. *Securing support.* Secure the support from top administrators for a study of the problem. Whenever a change is needed in the university structure, it is imperative that the people at the top understand clearly

the need for change. Usually they must support and give direction to any recommendation. Therefore, it is necessary to achieve the support of these administrators from the very beginning. Likewise, it is important that the university community as a whole become aware of the problem and the need for change. This allows individuals outside the appointed committee to give input and provide expertise as needed.

For example, one dean worked extensively over a period of a few months to develop a reorganization plan for his college. The plan had the support of the department heads, faculty members, and students within his organization. But when the dean took the recommendation forward to the administration it was turned down. The president of the university resented the fact that a study had been made without his authorization. The dean finally concluded that, had he secured the blessing of the president at the beginning of the study, the final recommendations would have been accepted.

2. *Involving concerned individuals.* Involve those people who are most concerned with the results of the study. People tend to support what they help create. It is most important to involve those people in the problem-solving process who have the most concern and who have the most to win or lose with a decision. Occasionally committees or task forces work at a problem and recommend excellent changes only to encounter resistance from many of the people who will be affected by the changes.

One department head recommended eliminating one of the academic majors within her department. The recommendation was made without consulting faculty, staff, and students who would be affected by the elimination of the program. Although there was excellent economic and educational justification for eliminating the program, faculty and students organized resistance. Had the department head made an effort to involve the students and faculty in a discussion of the problem from the very beginning, the recommendations may have been accepted with very little resistance.

3. *Participating effectively.* Secure appointment to the committee, take an active part, and attend all meetings to make your proposal. If your interest in a problem is high, then make every effort to be appointed to the task force. Once appointed, make every effort to hang on to the end. Others who do not have the same commitment will fall to the side, thus allowing the more committed to incorporate their concerns in a final recommendation.

4. *Improving acquaintances.* Develop a technique to acquaint members of the task force with each other on a one-to-one basis. When challenging assignments are given to a task force, often no effort is made to make people acquainted with each other. It is important to take time

at the beginning of a project to introduce people in more than a superficial way. Increasing the trust level, even if only slightly, aids the problem-solving process when key differences emerge.

5. *Focusing efforts.* Work only on those problems that you have the power and authority to change in the long run. It does not make much sense to attack a problem with a committee if there does not seem to be any long-run power or authority to make change. Unless there is a commitment at the very top and among those people most concerned with the issue, there is no justification for spending effort to solve the problem. Before a study is undertaken, it is important to obtain a clear understanding that something can happen if the effort is exerted.

6. *Thinking constructively.* It is important at the beginning of any study to display a positive attitude toward the assignment. The chairperson can set the direction of the committee and the eventual success of the project by generating a constructive attitude. A negative, critical attitude can dull the enthusiasm of task force members. A positive, constructive attitude may encourage and increase interest and effort.

7. *Understanding history.* Learn the history of the problem. Before beginning the study, gain a background and understanding of what changes need to be made. One campus successfully implemented a registration program for first-year students because the committee given responsibility to develop new guidelines took enough time to survey administrators, faculty, and students concerning their recommendations. A thorough review was made of all reports from previous committees who had studied the problem.

8. *Keeping records.* Control the memory of the organization. Volunteer to be the secretary. Keep careful notes and minutes. Sometimes you can suggest recommendations in this manner. It is important not to manipulate others by leaving out important information or by placing in the minutes your own personal bias if this was not a part of the discussion. An effective secretary, however, can assist a chairperson by organizing the thoughts and ideas so as to move discussion and decisions rapidly toward a successful conclusion.

9. *Identifying obstacles.* Identify early resistance or constraints, such as money, time, or space, and place them on a shelf. If there are constraints that cannot be resolved, then put on your creative hat and work around them. Occasionally, groups work toward change and provide excellent recommendations to university administrators only to find that it is impossible to implement the recommendations.

10. *Devising solutions.* Find your own solutions. Quite often, when a study is undertaken to solve a major campus problem elaborate schemes are developed to research what is being done on other campuses.

A considerable amount of money is spent in travel and correspondence in order to secure this information. This type of information can be very useful. But most campus problems can be solved by pulling together the creative thinking of the people most concerned. Likewise, it is very difficult to take a program that may be successful on one campus and fit it to the personalities, training, and expertise of the individuals who must implement it on another campus. The experience of other people is useful, but the solution to most campus problems rests in the creative ability of the faculty, administrators, and students most affected by the problem.

11. *Involving observers.* Ask an outside consultant or observer to be a part of important meetings. Committee members and administrators often behave better when an outsider is included in meetings. Most of us are aware of how much better behaved children are when a neighbor comes for dinner. Likewise, bringing into a meeting an outside consultant, such as a faculty member from another campus or a student leader, may cause balking members of a committee to cooperate.

One budget committee had as one of its key members an individual who often expressed aggressive and critical comments. It became so difficult to operate within the committee that for a time the chairperson considered abandoning its purposes. The chairperson, however, with skill and vision invited key student leaders to participate in the discussions. Having the students in the meetings tended to reduce the tensions and conflict. So long as the students were present, the balking member of the committee behaved rather well. As a result, the committee moved along with its goal to a successful conclusion.

12. *Working sequentially.* Place your efforts on one or two issues at a time. Working at too many issues at a time reduces your effectiveness. It is better to break a large problem down into smaller segments. If a committee lists a number of recommendations to improve the Greek system, it may be advisable to implement the suggestions one at a time. It is important, however, that someone be responsible for keeping all issues on the table until all recommendations are implemented.

13. *Avoiding Overload.* Do not try to anticipate everything. Sometimes we move into a problem-solving process in an effort to solve every problem faced by the university. Recommendations that are implemented quickly often have a narrow and specific scope. If during the discussions a task force identifies other avenues or problems, these should be placed on the shelf for consideration and development at a later time.

14. *Facing difficulties.* Quickly tackle difficult projects within the assignment instead of putting them off. During a study of a placement office, one of the difficult problems was to survey the students,

faculty, and administration concerning their attitudes toward the service. This task would take a considerable amount of time. However, the committee moved forward very rapidly, making assignments and delegating responsibility, and within a few weeks gathered information from nearly half the student body, over half the faculty, and all of the department heads. Collecting this information at the very beginning of the study aided considerably in developing final recommendations.

15. *Listing responsibilities.* Develop a clear and concise list of all the important tasks the task force needs to perform. These tasks are generated by the chairperson before the first meeting and then enlarged as the group reflects on whatever else needs to be done. The problem-solving process can move along very rapidly. In the case of the placement study mentioned earlier, a number of tasks needed to be accomplished, including the difficult responsibility of surveying the campus community. Likewise, there was some need to research what had already been accomplished in previous studies. And the central administration needed to state its concerns. All these tasks were listed for the first session, and volunteers were immediately committed to a review of the program. This process continued as the information was gathered. The more clearly you define your tasks, the better chance you have of having committee members participate actively in the change process.

16. *Remaining objective.* Make every effort to understand all sides of the issue, and stay neutral until all of the facts are out. It is important to gather as much information as possible before recommendations are made. If members of the task force have hidden agendas and personal commitments to a solution, many problems can develop. In this situation, it is likely that the task force will fail. Members with strong feelings may be asked to subdue them for a while until all the facts are out.

17. *Improving communication.* Communicate with all concerned. Make sure that no one feels you are pulling a fast one, especially the students and the faculty. Occasionally changes are developed behind closed doors. The students, particularly, resent unilateral change made without their first being given the chance to give input.

Some years ago, the students on one campus returned after summer vacation only to find that a large number of parking stalls had been allocated to faculty and visitors. The decision caused such a turmoil that the administration finally altered its recommendation. The students were finally satisfied with the decision, but the administration spent many valuable hours trying to negotiate a settlement. The administration finally concluded that, had it kept the students informed, the confrontation would have never occurred.

18. *Avoiding bluffing.* Do not bluff your way through when you really do not know the facts. When you do not understand the problem completely, it is important to do adequate research to document the actual facts. Nothing can kill a recommendation more quickly than an accusation of not doing enough homework. Much effort and support disappears when recommendations are based on inadequate information.

19. *Informing administrators.* Keep the administration informed through the use of minutes or reports during the entire problem-solving process. Occasionally, the administration assigns a committee the responsibility for recommending changes in programs or services. The committee works feverishly for a long period of time and finally puts together its recommendation, only to learn that the administration considers the entire recommendation unfeasible. A task force chairperson will find it useful to keep the administration informed as recommendations are developed. This allows administrators to give input throughout the process so that at the end they are fully aware of what changes need to be made.

20. *Remaining realistic.* When considering change, do not expect everything to happen at once. Patience is a virtue when changes are being considered in the university setting. A university is often a slow-moving organization. It may take months and even years for changes to be implemented. Students find this process very perplexing and can occasionally move things forward rapidly with protests and threats. The radical years of the 1960s brought about rapid change at all levels of the campus. In retrospect, some of this change was counterproductive and caused more harm than good. Although it may take a considerable amount of time and energy, change that comes after careful consideration and planning often proves to be more beneficial. People recommending changes must maintain considerable patience.

21. *Avoiding proselytizing.* Do not force your opinions on others and then condemn them if they do not accept your recommendations. When recommendations for change are presented to those who are responsible for implementing them, they may not initially be considered favorable. It is important not to overreact to delay but to continue to work for implementation. Keep the project on the burner until it comes to a satisfactory conclusion. Above all, do not make your criticism public, but try to understand the delay and accept suggestions that might improve the recommendations.

22. *Planning a strategy.* Know when to fight and when to rest. Another important method for creating change on campus is knowing when to fight and when to rest. Only rarely will you find a considerable

number of people interested in any one issue. Because of this, you may very well get your way if you persist with an issue long enough.

A building administrator wanted to have the maintenance staff put under his control. There was justification for assuming this supervisory role but also a tremendous amount of resistance from the director of the physical plant, who wanted a consolidated maintenance force. The administrator realized that it was not a time to fight for a final conclusion. By resting for a period of time, these people resisting the recommendation softened, and the building director's recommendations were finally approved.

Student leaders have found this technique most helpful. A good example is the resistance many students received when they first asked for permission to sit on administrative boards and councils. Student leaders persisted with their requests, fighting and resting as needed. Now on many campuses the first person to be appointed to any important committee may be a student body president.

23. *Keeping calm.* While the process of recommendation is underway, stay calm and adult in your behavior. Listen.When someone objects to a recommendation, hear that person out rather than offer an immediate rebuttal. Occasionally, committee chairpersons themselves become defensive whenever someone challenges one of their premises or recommendations. It is well to listen carefully to any objection and help the individual clarify the disagreement. People who express strong opposition can often be mollified if someone listens. If you are patient, the opposition will either go away and stop objecting entirely or have enough freedom to change opinion as more information comes to light.

24. *Maintaining momentum.* Keep the process going long enough so that dissenters fall away. Sometimes people object to change just because they feel it is their duty to do so. Some people dissent without much thought or foundation. Of course, there are always legitimate, constructive, and worthwhile objections. What is important to consider is the individual who dissents just because she or he feels it a responsibility always to challenge. Generally, if you are patient with that individual and keep the process going long enough, she or he will fall by the wayside.

25. *Incorporating concerns.* Take everyone's suggestions seriously and try to alter the report to reflect these concerns. There is a tendency to turn off individuals who are very strong in their opinons. In order to move forward, it is important to clarify everyone's suggestions in as much detail as necessary and to reflect those suggestions in the final report as much as possible. This may allow individuals who initially oppose recommendation for change to actually accept the final draft.

26. *Avoiding delay.* Don't drag your feet. Move as rapidly as possible to bring forward ideas and recommendations. Occasionally, problems become worse or so complicated that they cannot be solved because committees take so long in suggesting changes. On one campus, a task force studied for a considerable amount of time the problem of first-year English requirements. They spent such a long time in making their recommendations that their ideas were outdated and totally unacceptable by the time the work was completed. It is not wise to move too rapidly, but it is important to keep the process moving rapidly enough so that you are not outdated before the recommendation comes to the front.

27. *Deliberating carefully.* Do not make snap decisions. It is important to move the change process along at a reasonable rate, but it is also wise to wait for everyone's input before a decision is made. All the ideas should be on the table. A decision made in this way has a much better chance for success.

28. *Remaining optimistic.* Do not become discouraged easily and begin to show it. It is not unusual for the change process to take so long that people become discouraged. Change in a university setting often comes very slowly. Patience is an absolute necessity as efforts are made to implement change. Even though it is important to move plans along as rapidly as possible the chairperson should not express an alarming amount of discouragement if projects do not develop as rapidly as they should.

Occasionally, a chairperson can work to reduce discouragement by redoubling his or her own effort. Refocusing on the problem or making contact with key administrators or committee members may jar the process into movement. Setting deadlines for projects or new program implementation may motivate movement. Encourage those who may be negatively affected by the delay to ask administrators to move toward change. It may be necessary to undertake a special analysis of the reason for delay and then to plan a whole new strategy to move into action.

29. *Retaining flexibility.* While gaining support for the recommendations, reflect the final report as preliminary. When moving forward recommendations to those who must implement them, it is important to reflect the report as being flexible until all parties have had a chance to review it and offer their own recommendations. Sometimes needed changes are shelved because someone's ego gets in the way or because all people who should provide input have not responded. The report occasionally runs into a person who feels she or he has been overlooked or ignored. Describing the report as preliminary will com-

municate to all concerned that there is still a chance for input, thus reducing resistance before all parties have a chance to give their opinion.

30. *Proposing options.* In recommending changes, offer a number of alternatives or models for the administration to consider. During a study of the registration process on one campus, the task force favored one direction above all others. But, in the final draft forwarded to the president, the committee suggested three alternate ways through which the new program might move. This allowed the president some opportunity to alter the final recommendation before it was actually implemented.

31. *Maximizing potential.* Keep it simple. Recommendations should be phrased simply. Occasionally, reports are so long and tedious that busy administrators do not have time enough to read all of the background material. Likewise, the recommendation for change should reflect simplicity. Complicated models and schemes that involve totally reorganizing large segments of the campus tend to be rejected. If the entire campus needs to be reorganized, it is more practical to begin at some small point and move on from there. Grandiose efforts receive predictable resistance almost every time.

32. *Accepting criticism.* Do not be oversensitive to honest criticism. On most campuses, a number of individuals will emerge as critics of the plan. Instead of becoming defensive and resentful of those critics, ask them for direct input, again making every effort to listen and to reflect these ideas in the recommendation. Occasionally, the criticism arises because of misunderstanding, not because the individual desires to destroy the work of the committee. Sometimes the critics need nothing more than to be heard and understood.

33. *Emphasizing ends, not means.* Do not act and talk as though the only right way to do a thing is the way your committee would like it to be done. Even after a report is designated as final, it is still important to reflect that there may be an even better way to accomplish the task. Make every effort to receive input from individuals who continue to offer suggestions. It is important to develop a campus atmosphere that allows for input to come even though it be critical. Administrators, faculty members, and students who close their minds to additional input inhibit the change process.

34. *Starting small.* While implementing the recommendations, start small and silent. We occasionally begin new programs in grandiose ways, without first conducting a pilot study or slowly moving on board with the new ideas. Of course, some programs need publicity, but most changes on university campuses can be initiated rather quietly and with very little fanfare. As the program develops and takes on responsibility

and stature, then it is appropriate to give it the publicity it needs for complete success.

35. *Following through.* Keep working at the problem. Follow through on decisions. Set deadlines and reward people so that they understand there is a payoff for doing good work and implementing good ideas. Sometimes recommendations are made, only to be placed on the shelf. The committee chairperson should carry on with the responsibility to see that the changes are implemented. If there are parts of the recommendations that are not acceptable to the administration or others who have the responsibility for implementation, then the committee chairperson should continue to work on the problem until the recommendations are satisfactory.

36. *Using the system.* Use a formal system. If you can get what you need from an administrator, do not use the task force approach. By directing your inquiry or your suggestion for change to an appropriate administrator, he or she may have the insight and resources necessary to move forward with the recommendation immediately. It is important, however, when this approach is taken, that all concerned with the change be notified completely. When you go directly to the top with a request for change, someone below may resist its implementation.

37. *Sharing praise.* Do not feel sore if you are not openly given credit for everything you do. In the change process, one should feel satisfied if change comes about, even if the process does not give credit to those individuals who may have made the greatest effort. A chairperson should pass on to the individual committee members or administrators recognition for making and implementing the change.

38. *Thanking participants.* Thank everyone who renders a service. Acknowledge outstanding contribution and timely input. Individuals who perform in outstanding ways should be acknowledged publicly and privately for their excellent service. Timely letters of appreciation to individual committee members, with copies to supervisors or deans, can maintain much support. Any acknowledgment of service should refer to the specific contribution made by the committee member. Likewise, praising for better-than-expected performance is always effective in assuring the good feeling of contributors. Commending those who are required to implement the recommended change also may provide good dividends. Reach out to as many people as possible with an acknowledgment of their fine work, and you will assure their continued support for future projects.

The Challenge

It is a challenge for the student services administrator to function as an agent of change on the campus. This person must have the ability to present ideas, projects and programs to the administration, faculty, and students. Making an effort to do this without an organized plan may contribute to failure. If the administrator knows how to plan for change and can develop an organized method of presenting recommendations, the chances for success increase measurably.

A great amount of satisfaction is derived from working with a plan to move a project from its beginning to a successful conclusion. Individuals who use a systematic way of solving problems find considerable success in achieving their goals. Staff members are much more enthusiastic about their job assignments. The entire student services division is considered innovative and creative in its approach to solving problems. The student leadership is supportive of the administration and works with greater effort to provide solutions to problems. There is a much more unifying spirit on the campus, and students feel they belong to a progressive and innovative organization. The staff begins to work harder and more enthusiastically and develops a better sense of cooperation and communication. When this begins, people at all levels within the university structure begin to listen more to the chief student services administrator, and this person finds that it is much easier to implement ideas and change among the students, faculty, and staff.

References

Coch, L., and French, R. P., Jr. "Overcoming Resistance to Change." *Human Relations*, 1968, *1* (4), 512.

Lewin, K. "Group Decision and Social Change." In T. M. Newcomb and E. L. Hartley (Eds.), *Readings in Social Psychology*. New York: Holt, Rinehart and Winston, 1958.

Frank, J. *Persuasion and Healing*. New York: Schocken Books, 1963.

Ursula Delworth
Gary R. Hanson

Conclusion: Structure of the Profession and Recommended Curriculum

The chapters in this book represent an implicit statement concerning who we are. It is time to make this statement more explicit. We are a profession committed to, and having expertise in, the integrated development of college students. We view student development as the product of person-environment interaction (Layton, Sandeen, and Baker, 1971) and are thus concerned with the nature and effectiveness of institutions of higher education as they affect and are affected by students. Singly or in combination, we are service providers, administrators, teachers, and researchers. Each of us may choose to play out only one or two of these roles during our professional lifetime, yet our professional training (both as graduate students and thereafter) must prepare us to understand, communicate, and to some extent participate in all these functions.

What, then, constitutes a profession? The dictionary states it is "an occupation requiring . . . advanced study in a specialized field." It is this "specialized" that matters. To call ourselves a profession, we must make explicit what our "specialty" is.

Some definitions of our profession assume a body of theory, knowledge, and practice that is uniquely ours, and some of our colleagues assert we possess these unique characteristics. We do not. We view our theory as coming mainly from the core behavioral and social science disciplines of psychology and sociology and the emerging field of organizational development. Our practice knowledge is shared as well with psychologists, organizational consultants, social workers, management specialists, and others.

If, then, our theory and practice are not unique, can we be a profession? We believe the answer is yes but that such a self-definition requires us to articulate and adhere to a viable definition of our specialty.

In this chapter, we outline and discuss what we see as the core components that define the structure of the student services profession. We describe in depth each major component and then discuss its implications for the student services profession. In particular, we consider the curriculum implications and present a model curriculum incorporating and integrating these essential components.

Structure of the Profession

We believe that five major, interrelated components define the structure of the student services profession. As shown in Figure 1, the components are (1) history and philosophy, (2) relevant theories, (3) models of practice, (4) professional competencies, and (5) management and organizational competencies.

It is no accident that these components form the first five sections of this book. We view these as fixed, essential, core components in the profession. However, we also believe that the *content* of each component will and should change over time. For example, being able to train paraprofessionals may be less important by the 1990s. External developments and an evolving consensus within the profession dictate core philosophy, theory, models, and so on at any given point in time. The components are generic and form the rationale and basis; the models change as needed.

The earlier sections of this book have, we believe, demonstrated the existence and relevance of each of these five components. The com-

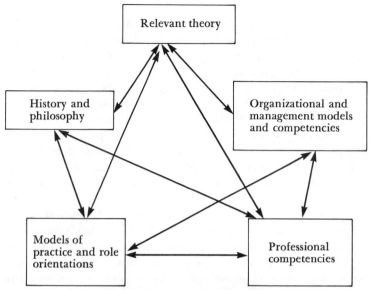

Figure 1. Structure of the Profession

pelling rationale to consider each of them essential is found in their interrelationship and in the gap left by omitting any. As Figure 1 demonstrates, each feeds into the next, with theories set somewhat out of sequence to show that much of our theory has been borrowed from core behavioral science disciplines such as psychology and sociology. The dotted lines indicate a constant interaction among all components of the model. That is, just as models of practice necessarily feed into professional competencies, so too competencies feed back into clearer definitions of practice models or even into the evolution of new models.

We can apply this basic idea to a more detailed discussion of the components. The material in Part One amply demonstrates that our profession does indeed have a history, one that includes both thought and action. On a day-to-day basis, our ideas and attitudes have evolved out of our history and philosophy. In building or choosing theories to use, we rely on ideas and concepts provided by our philosophy. As we develop or borrow and adapt theories, we can use them to develop role orientations or models; that is, we can better describe and define roles, functions, and ways of operating in our day-to-day practice. Successfully implementing these roles or models requires particular competencies. Naturally, different roles demand different combinations of competencies. Thus, there is a direct link between the role orientations we assume and the skills we employ. The way we use our competencies in our professional activities leads to a particular style or mode of operating we refer to as the "management" or "administration" of the profession. Embedded in the concept of management and administration is the value of self-assessment and self-evaluation. Administration and management of our services is one example of the loop back to the competency component. These five major building blocks of our profession, then, form a template to guide the future direction of student services. In the next section, we elaborate on these five components, and in doing so rely heavily on the insight and creativity of our contributing authors.

The History and Philosophy of Student Services. To fully appreciate the future potential of the student services profession, we must understand the present in terms of the events and ideas that have shaped us. We have tried to provide that perspective in the first three chapters of this book, which deal with historical roots and current trends.

As a profession, we have emerged and evolved by default. We have picked up activities that academic faculty and other administrators discarded as uninteresting or unimportant. Someone must admit, house, feed, and occasionally discipline students; all these functions are indispensable but by current standards certainly not within the realm of "academic" activity. In trying to understand how our profession has arrived and continues to stay at the periphery, Fenske has identified three major historical forces: a shift from a religious to a secular influence; an expansion in the size and complexity of colleges and universities; and a change from faculty focus on moral and character development of students to an emphasis on intellectual and academic interests. If we want to integrate student services into a more central position within the academic community, we must carefully analyze these historical forces and consider the continuing impact they have on the future of the profession.

Theories of the Profession. As shown earlier, the historical events and the philosophical beliefs that have guided the development of our profession led to particular ways of thinking, to borrowing and applying theories from various disciplines, and to developing our own conceptual approaches.

Theoretical statements have been and are currently being made and/or adopted in two major areas within the student services profession: (1) individual growth and development during the college years and (2) college students and their environments and the impact they have on each other. These two theoretical areas constitute the primary ways in which our professional ideas can influence our professional practice. We must know how students develop in order to provide services that facilitate their growth, and we must know and understand what characteristics of the college environment influence students in which directions. Nor can we simply focus only on individuals or only on the college environments, because students act on their environments just as the environments act on the students. We believe that to provide effective service to students we must understand the interaction of students with their environment. Thus it is helpful to examine theories of person-environment interaction as well.

Theories of Individual Development. A concern for the full development of individuals has always been central to student services, but only in the last two decades have theories emerged to explain how students grow and change as a result of attending college. As Knefelkamp, Widick, and Parker (1978) point out, if educators are to encourage human development we must know what development is, how and when it happens, and what factors facilitate and hinder student change. We must ask, "What developmental changes occur in individuals and what do they look like? How does the process of human development occur? Do college environments influence students? And, perhaps most importantly, toward what ends should development in college be directed?" Seeking answers to these questions, Kneffelkamp, Widick, and Parker abandon any hope of finding or creating THE theory of human development. Rather, they conclude that different theorists used different language to describe different aspects of development.

We agree with Kneffelkamp and her colleagues that no single theory is most useful but that student services workers must be familiar with several theories of development. For each theory, we can ask different questions, make different assumptions, and use different constructs to communicate our ideas about college student development. We do believe, however, that theories of individual development must be integrated with theories that deal with person-environment interaction to form a more complete picture of what actually occurs with college students and thus to guide our interventions.

Theories of Person-Environment Interaction. The need for theories of person-environment interaction arose out of the observation that personality characteristics and background variables only explain a relatively small proportion of student behavior on campus. It is not enough to study individuals or environments, we must also know how people and environments interact. We felt that it was important to introduce the theoretical concepts of person-environment interaction and that the most sensible approach to understanding such complex phenomenon was through a review of five models or theories of person-environment interaction and an analysis, which helps explain the "how" or process of that interaction.

In her chapter, Huebner identifies four critical assumptions regarding the person-environment interaction. Understanding these assumptions has important implications for day-to-day student services practice. For example, college student behavior is a continuous process of interaction between the person and the situation; the individual is an intentional, active agent in the interaction; cognitive factors are important; and the psychological meaning of the situation to the individual is an essential determinant of the person's behavior.

Both chapters on theory provide a conceptual base for organizing data about our profession, explaining our profession to others, guiding our day-to-day decisions, and building the future. The theories also lay the foundation for developing our models of practice.

Models of Practice or Role Orientations. Models of practice serve much the same purpose foundations serve for buildings—they shape the structure. Although they refer to the imprecise blueprints known as theories or theoretical approaches, they mandate, explicitly or implicitly, how the rest of the building will look. We therefore advocate full attention to choosing models of practice, or role orientations for professionals, as we look at the profession. Currently we see four predominant models, only two of which are widely translated into organizational practice. The newer models, those of educator and environmental manager, are outlined, advocated, and widely discussed. There are, however, few examples of either model providing a firm foundation on which a student services organization is built and operates. Perhaps this will come to be; perhaps these models or core roles will serve us best when they are integrated with each other or with the model of administrator or counselor. In the evolution of the profession, some integration of models seems the norm. This makes sense to us, but we see a danger when the models with which we operate are not made explicit. The danger is that we will thoughtlessly move from model to model and thus build a shaky foundation that will not support a solid superstructure of competencies and organization. Nor will such a foundation help us further develop our philosophy and theory.

Professional Competencies. Our day-to-day activities require certain professional competencies to successfully implement our models of practice. Even though different models may require different combinations of competencies, a common core of competencies must be mastered. Each chapter in Part Four of this book identifies a major set of competencies. Assessment and evaluation, consultation, counseling, and instruction are all currently essential and, we believe, are likely to remain so. The three more complex competencies that we identified (program development, environmental assessment and redesign, and training of paraprofessionals) are currently widely advocated and often practiced. This group of competencies is likely to increase in importance over the next decade. Also, the competencies we now identify as predominant may become less so by the end of the decade. Much depends on the models of practice that dominate the field, on developments in higher education, and on evolution in philosophy and theory. The projected steady state, or even decline, in students through the rest of this century, however, suggests that each of these three models will continue to be important and several may well increase their power in our profession over the next ten to twenty years.

Management and Organizational Competencies. The models and competencies necessary to organize and administer student services are drawn from history and philosophy, theory, practice models, and professional competencies. This component, perhaps more than any other except history and philosophy, intersects and depends on both the history and current development of higher education. As Dutton and Rickard stress in their chapter in Part Five, the structures, policies, and procedures of student services organizations depend heavily on the mission and organization of their parent institutions. The competencies needed to set up and effectively manage student services will clearly change as parent institutions and higher education change. We believe, however, that the basic guidelines articulated by Dutton and Rickard and by Johnson and Foxley are here to stay. The evaluation competencies presented by Kerr and the staff development programs discussed and advocated by Canon are very likely to increase in importance during the next decade, as demands for accountability at all levels proliferate. And Christensen's rules for change could well become required competencies for all administrators. The next decade will highlight competencies in this component. Trends in higher education seem to mandate this, and developments in our own profession seem to support it. This, in turn, may well lead to the predominance and further identification of those organizational theories most relevant to student services.

Curriculum for the Profession

In the previous section, we described the elements that define the structure of student services. Each component is important in its own right; taken together, they provide a useful way to look at our profession as it exists today. But our own history shows that professions—like people—grow, develop, and change. In the past, much of our growth evolved by default and was influenced by events beyond our control. By presenting a model curriculum, we can influence the future of our profession. We can take control. We can determine our destiny. And we can promote professional development through a viable curriculum, because we are what we teach.

Goals of the Curriculum. Before describing the nature of a model curriculum for student services, it is important to review our purposes. A curriculum plan can be used to (1) set professional standards, (2) assess current status and facilitate intentional change in the profession, (3) select and manage staff, and (4) establish our academic legitimacy. A brief explanation of each aspect shows why we must develop a curriculum that can be used for these purposes.

Setting Standards. Standards of excellence are important to a profession because they allow us to state our ideals, hopes, and goals. By building a strong curriculum at the graduate level, we can introduce ideas of excellence early and implant expectations of how we ought to think and act as professionals. The day-to-day delivery of student services are guided by standards introduced through the curriculum.

Assessing the Status of Our Profession. In planning a curriculum, we cannot avoid assessing who we are and dreaming about whom we might become. Teaching others what we do demands that we carefully examine our practice to become more aware of what we do well and what we do poorly. Planning a curriculum allows us to define our role. To become a "specialized" profession, we need to plan for the future by carefully developing the graduate curriculum. As we plan, we can anticipate both the direction and the role of our professional growth. A good curriculum allows us to introduce new ideas, concepts, and models of practice. Then we can evolve with a sense of purpose and direction, not by default.

Selecting and Managing Staff. The curriculum of a graduate program in student services can also be used to guide staff selection and management. As new staff join us, we can review job descriptions in light of the curriculum each new professional has experienced. We believe the curriculum presented in the next section will result in professionals well prepared to deal with the demands facing student services not only today but also in the future. As new staff join us, we must compare them with exisiting staff in terms of the knowledge, competencies, and attitudes the new staff bring with them from their respective graduate programs. The curriculum we propose not only serves to guide preservice education but can also be used for staff development training to build new strengths in existing staff.

Establishing Academic Legitimacy. A solid curriculum is essential to any profession. Like it or not, as professionals our right to exist depends to a certain degree on how legitimate, rigorous, and substantial our thinking is. When we compete for dollars to implement our practice, we state that what we have to offer is valuable. We are judged against others. If we can establish that our profession has academic legitimacy, we will be able to convince decision makers in higher education that what we do is based on good thinking, rigorous evaluation, and careful management. The foundation for these activities is a comprehensive curriculum.

In summary, all these purposes serve a common goal—to perpetuate and enhance our profession. We can achieve this goal only through clearly delineating appropriate curriculum. As they examine our proposed curriculum, we ask readers to keep in mind both current professional practice as well as ideas and visions for the next decade and beyond.

The Core Program. The model curriculum we present is a core model, designed for education of master's, or entry-level, student services practitioners. Adaptations and additions for doctoral education and in-service training programs are addressed later. We believe that the eight curriculum areas listed here are essential components of effective training programs. However, just as specific models and competencies change in the field, so they need to change in the curriculum. Thus, we see the curriculum areas as generic, the models and competencies as changing. Specific theories, models, and competencies suggested here represent our best thinking regarding what is relevant today and likely to remain so in the next few years.

Basic Components. These curriculum components follow our outline of components of the profession, but we have added several additions:

1. *History and Philosophy.* A minimum of one course in history, organization, and philosophy of higher education and student services is recommended.
2. *Theory.* We advise a minimum of two courses in this area. The most relevant current theories are (1) theories of human development and (2) theories of person-environment interaction.
3. *Models of practice and role orientations.* One course is recommended. It should examine relevant role orientations and discuss patterns of organization and specific agencies in student services in light of these models and roles. Professional ethics can also be introduced in this course.
4. *Core competencies.* A minimum of four courses, each dealing with one specific competency, is advised. At the present time, those should include assessment and evaluation, consultation, instruction, and counseling. Each course should include relevant theory and models and both a didactic and experiential skills component. The counseling course should include basic group skills unless a separate core course is offered in group work.
5. *Specialized Competencies.* At least one course in this area should be offered. Ideally, two to three should be available, and students should have choices. We see program development, environmental assessment and redesign, and paraprofessional training as the key

current specialized competencies, probably with program development as the priority course for most preparation programs.

6. *Administration and management.* At least one basic course should be offered. This should include some theory, but should focus on specific management tools needed by the professional in entry-level or intermediate positions.

7. *Practicum or field work.* A minimum of one year practicum is recommended, in at least two selected student services agencies. Students, faculty, and on-site supervisors should determine a training plan that ensures experience and supervision in at least two core competencies in each placement. In addition, at least one practicum should include experience in a specialized competency area, and at least one should involve some basic management tasks. A weekly seminar with a faculty member, required of all students enrolled in practicum should focus on integrating practical experience with previous and concurrent coursework.

8. *Additional theory and tool courses.* Each student should select a minimum of one additional theory course and one course that will provide additional tools or skills. A requirement of two courses in each of these areas would be *highly desirable*. These courses may be offered through the student services program but are more likely to be offered in behavioral science or business departments. Theory courses might include organizational or social learning theory or be focused on a specific population such as adult learners or women. Skill courses include elementary statistics, testing, business law, and computer technology.

Organizational Considerations. The organization and sequencing of the model curriculum depends, of course, on such factors as the subdivision of the academic year (such as semesters or quarters); the philosophy, competencies, and size of the faculty; and specialized goals of the preparation program. The basic curriculum components, as presented, could be arranged in a pattern of forty–forty-five semester hours, or three–four semesters of graduate work. However, other patterns may be preferable. Both core and specialized competencies lend themselves well to an intensive workshop format. The material on models of practice could be combined with the history and philosophy of student services. A number of topics could be dealt with in a seminar format, especially models of practice and history and philosophy. Self-paced modules using written, audio, and audiovisual materials might be especially useful in presenting at least some aspects of the theory component as well as portions of the core and specialized competencies. Preparation programs that emphasize a competency-based approach could combine formal class work with a variety of more individualized approaches.

Whatever organizational pattern is adopted, we believe that it is essential to include some experiential work near the beginning of the program and to schedule the first formal practicum or field experience during the first year.

Professional identity is a nebulous component that we believe is nevertheless essential in any viable preparation program. In developing a professional identity, students must address issues of ethics, professional behavior and expectations, and professional organizations as well as the material identified as core curriculum. How the knowledge, attitudes, and skills that comprise professional identity are integrated into the program is best left to each group of faculty and students. Some programs may find it useful to schedule a "pro-seminar" during the whole or part of a student's first term in order to introduce these issues. Others may design a seminar late in the program, and still others may decide to integrate this material into several courses and practicum experiences. Our recommendation is simply to take this area seriously and to design its inclusion with care and commitment.

Doctoral Programs. We believe that all doctoral students should complete the equivalent of our entry-level professional curriculum, either before or early in their doctoral program. The core of doctoral training in the profession should be

1. Demonstrated competence in both understanding and production of relevant research
2. Demonstrated mastery of core and specialized competencies that are essential for leadership in at least one of the role orientations or models of practice. Mastery of two models would be more desirable, but one could be set as a minimum

Research competence certainly involves coursework in statistics and design, as well as a dissertation. Beyond these basics, however, real comfort with and appreciation of research is accomplished only through systematic involvement in relevant research projects over a period of time. We recommend early and continued involvement of doctoral students in research projects being conducted by faculty, researchers in student services, or other appropriate persons and groups. This apprentice approach is the most effective way to facilitate both skills and commitment to research in doctoral students.

The apprentice model is also highly relevant in the area of core and specialized competencies. Advanced coursework lays a solid foundation, but mastery depends on opportunity to work closely and over an extended time period with one or more experts in the specific competency.

Doctoral training is training for leadership in the profession. Students should have the opportunity to experience themselves as emerging leaders by participating in professional organizations and meetings, publications, consultation with entry-level professionals, exchanges with other programs, and whatever additional methods are feasible.

In-Service Programs. Strong, effective in-service programs are essential, because staff turnover is declining. As Canon noted, such programs are only what we owe ourselves and our institutions. We predict a tremendous increase in well-conceptualized and organized staff development programs during the next decade. We recommend that such programs

1. Assess needs in terms of the core training components presented earlier
2. Set priorities on those areas that (a) develop competencies immediately needed in student services or the institution and (b) contribute most clearly to the mission and goals of the student services division and specific agencies within it
3. Use such resources as (a) faculty from student services and higher education preparation programs and behavioral science departments; (b) literature, especially monographs and sourcebooks that can be read quickly; (c) experts in the community or at nearby institutions
4. Facilitate and reward participation by staff members

The rationale and guidelines offered by Harry Canon in Chapter Twenty should be helpful to those who are just beginning in-service programs, as well as to those who are further along. We urge chief student services officers to set staff development as a priority and to commit the human and fiscal resources necessary to develop and implement an effective program. Staff development is probably the most powerful tool the chief officer has to build and maintain a division staffed with competent, invested professionals.

Summary

We are a profession. By whatever name we call ourselves— *student services, student development, student affairs*—we possess the understanding of theory, the philosophy, models, and competencies to designate ourselves a viable profession. What has been needed is a description and explanation of the components of our profession and a commitment to follow through on these in our professional activities, preparation programs, and in-service training. We and the authors of this book have presented and discussed the relevant components and the guidelines for ensuring that they will be effectively integrated in our work. Only you, as readers, can decide if our model for the profession is legitimate and, if so, make it "real" in the lives of students, staff members, and the entire campus community.

References

Knefelkamp, L., Widick, C., and Parker, C. A. (Eds.). *New Directions for Student Services: Applying New Developmental Findings*, no. 4. San Francisco: Jossey-Bass, 1978.

Layton, W. L., Sandeen, C. A., Baker, R. D. "Student Development and Counseling." In *Annual Review of Psychology*. Vol. 22. Palo Alto, Calif.: Annual Reviews, 1971.

Name Index

Subject Index